T0392656

Psychoeducational Assessment of Preschool Children

Psychoeducational Assessment of Preschool Children, Fifth Edition, provides academics and school-based practitioners such as psychologists, speech-language pathologists, and social workers with an up-to-date guide to the assessment of young children. Long recognized as the standard text and reference in its field, this comprehensive, skill-building overview is organized into four sections: foundations, ecological assessment, assessment of developmental domains, and special considerations. Chapters written by recognized scholars in the field cover theory, research, and application. This thoroughly revised new edition addresses current developments in preschool assessment, new policies and legislation, and student/family population demographics.

Vincent C. Alfonso, Ph.D., is former Dean of the School of Education at Gonzaga University, USA, Interim Dean of Ferkauf Graduate School of Psychology at Yeshiva University, USA, and past president of Division 16 (School Psychology) of the American Psychological Association.

Bruce A. Bracken, Ph.D., is Professor of Education at the College of William & Mary, USA, co-founder of the *Journal of Psychoeducational Assessment*, past president of the International Test Commission, and author of early childhood tests and curricula.

Richard J. Nagle, Ph.D., is a Distinguished Professor Emeritus and Louise Fry Scudder Professor of Psychology at the University of South Carolina, USA.

Psychoeducational Assessment of Preschool Children

Fifth Edition

Edited by Vincent C. Alfonso, Bruce A. Bracken, and Richard J. Nagle

Routledge
Taylor & Francis Group

NEW YORK AND LONDON

Fifth edition published 2020
by Routledge
52 Vanderbilt Avenue, New York, NY 10017

and by Routledge
2 Park Square, Milton Park, Abingdon, Oxon, OX14 4RN

Routledge is an imprint of the Taylor & Francis Group, an informa business

© 2020 Taylor & Francis

The right of Vincent C. Alfonso, Bruce A. Bracken, and Richard J. Nagle to be identified as the authors of the editorial material, and of the authors for their individual chapters, has been asserted in accordance with sections 77 and 78 of the Copyright, Designs and Patents Act 1988.

First edition published by Lawrence Erlbaum Associates 1983

Fourth edition published by Routledge 2007

Library of Congress Cataloging-in-Publication Data
Names: Alfonso, Vincent C., editor. | Bracken, Bruce A., editor. | Nagle, Richard J. (Richard Jude), 1946-
Title: Psychoeducational assessment of preschool children / Edited by Vincent C. Alfonso, Bruce A. Bracken, and Richard J. Nagle.
Description: Fifth edition. | New York, NY : Routledge, 2020. | Includes bibliographical references and index.
Identifiers: LCCN 2020000013 (print) | LCCN 2020000014 (ebook) | ISBN 9780367149512 (hardback) | ISBN 9780367149529 (paperback) | ISBN 9780429054099 (ebook)
Subjects: LCSH: Child development—Evaluation. | Ability—Testing. | Readiness for school.
Classification: LCC LB1115 .P963 2020 (print) | LCC LB1115 (ebook) | DDC 305.231—dc23
LC record available at https://lccn.loc.gov/2020000013
LC ebook record available at https://lccn.loc.gov/2020000014

ISBN: 978-0-367-14951-2 (hbk)
ISBN: 978-0-367-14952-9 (pbk)
ISBN: 978-0-429-05409-9 (ebk)

Typeset in Minion
by Swales & Willis, Exeter, Devon, UK

To all the young children in our world who are the greatest teachers we have, and to those who learn from, assess, and intervene with them, I dedicate this volume. Also, to my parents who supported me in my professional trajectory with love, freedom, and pride.

V. C. A.

With love to Mary Jo, Bruce Jr., Schnitzie, and Cali

B. A. B.

In the enduring spirit of brotherly love, I dedicate this book to my brother Maurice and late brother Garrett. They were my guardian angels during my preschool years and thereafter. Their guidance and "all for one and one for all" attitude toward family is something I will cherish forever.

R. J. N.

Contents

Notes on the Authors

Vincent C. Alfonso, Ph.D., is Interim Dean of the Ferkauf Graduate School of Psychology at Yeshiva University. Prior to this position, he was Professor in and Dean of the School of Education at Gonzaga University in Spokane, Washington, and Professor in and Associate Dean of the Graduate School of Education, Fordham University, New York City. He is Past President of Division 16 (School Psychology) of the American Psychological Association (APA), and Fellow of Divisions 16, 5, and 43 of the APA. He is also Fellow of the Association for Psychological Science. In February 2014 he received the *Outstanding Contributions to Training* award from the Trainers of School Psychologists, and in August 2017 he received the *Jack Bardon Distinguished Service Award* from Division 16 of the APA. He is co-author of *Essentials of WISC-V Assessment, Essentials of Cross-Battery Assessment (3rd Edition)* and co-editor of *Essentials of Specific Learning Disability Identification (2nd Edition)* and *Essentials of Planning, Selecting, and Tailoring Interventions for the Unique Learner,* all published by Wiley. In addition, he is co-editor of *Healthy Development in Young Children: Evidence-based Interventions for Early Education,* published by the APA, and *Psychoeducational Assessment of Preschool Children (5th Edition),* published by Routledge.

Bruce A. Bracken, Ph.D., is a Professor at the College of William & Mary. He obtained a B.S. from the College of Charleston, and an M.A. and Ph.D. from the University of Georgia. He has published scores of books, psychological tests, and professional materials, co-founded the *Journal of Psychoeducational Assessment,* is past president of the International Test Commission, chaired the American Psychological Association (APA) Committee on Psychological Tests and Assessment, and served on a panel for the National Research Council of the National Academies of Science. He is a Fellow in two divisions of the APA, a Charter Fellow of the American Educational Research Association, and is a Diplomate and Fellow in the American Board of Assessment Psychology. Bruce received a *Senior Scientist* award from the APA, a *Lifetime Achievement Award* from the University of

Georgia, and was the Featured Presenter for the *National Association of School Psychologists Legends in School Psychology* series.

Ali Brian, Ph.D., CAPE, is an Associate Professor in the Department of Physical Education at the University of South Carolina. Dr. Brian holds a Ph.D. in Kinesiology from The Ohio State University, with cognates in motor development and adapted physical education. Dr. Brian is a member of the Executive Committee of the International Motor Development Research Consortium, Sport Health and Physical Education America's Research Council, Secretary for the National Consortium for Physical Education for Individuals with Disabilities, and Director of Research for the Institute of Movement Studies for Individuals with Visual Impairments. Dr. Brian serves as an Associate Editor for *Research Quarterly for Exercise and Sport* and is on the Editorial Board for *Physical Education and Sports Pedagogy*. Dr. Brian presently has 66 peer-reviewed publications and 160 presentations on topics including motor development, adapted physical activity/education, and physical education.

Lena G. Caesar, Ph.D., is an Associate Professor in the Department of Speech-Language-Hearing Sciences at Loyola University Maryland. She received a B.S. in Communication Disorders from Andrews University in Michigan, an M.S. in Speech-Language Pathology from the University of Wisconsin-Madison, and two doctoral degrees from Western Michigan University. Caesar's research on bilingual and bi-dialectical assessment has been published nationally and internationally. She is the recipient of several research grants and awards, including a recent American Speech-Language-Hearing Association Foundation Clinical Research Grant that is funding her current research on the non-biased assessment of school-age Creole-speaking children in Guyana. Caesar's prior clinical, teaching, and administrative experience includes almost 5 years of university teaching and administration in Mexico, and 15 years as a Professor and Chair at Andrews University in Michigan.

Yin Cai is a School Psychology doctoral candidate at Lehigh University. Her research interests are parenting practices, infants and toddlers, and integrated care. Yin is working on several studies related to school readiness, early literacy, integrated care for young children, and parental play beliefs. She has given numerous presentations at national conferences. She also has two years of experience in conducting cognitive and achievement assessments for school-age children.

Joseph R. Engler, Ph.D., is an Associate Professor and Director of School Psychology at Gonzaga University. Dr. Engler received his B.A. from Minot State University and his Ph.D. from the University of South Dakota. Dr. Engler has served the field of school psychology in various roles. He has experience working as a school psychologist in the PreK-12 educational system as well as experience in multiple institutions of higher education. In addition to his professional responsibilities, Dr. Engler has served in state and national capacities. His scholarly pursuits involve preschool assessment, application of the Cattell-Horn-Carroll theory to test design and development, and studying the role of parent involvement in education.

Joseph Filachek is in his first year as a Nationally Certified School Psychologist within a full-day public preschool in Cape May, New Jersey. Joseph earned his Master's in School Psychology and his Educational Specialist Degree at the Philadelphia College of Osteopathic Medicine. Joseph's interests include applied behavior analysis and its implementation within preschool settings.

Sandra Glover Gagnon, Ph.D., is an Associate Professor in the Department of Psychology at Appalachian State University in Boone, North Carolina. Sandra earned her Ed.S. in School Psychology from The Citadel and her Ph.D. in School Psychology from the University of South Carolina. She worked in public schools for 12 years before joining the faculty at Appalachian State, where she has served as a School Psychology graduate trainer since 2002. In collaboration with Pam Kidder-Ashley, she studies preschool child temperament and various social-ecological correlates, including peer interactions, parent- and teacher-child relationships, and parenting- and teaching-stress. Her most recent project involves the implementation of a temperament-based intervention with young children and their parents and teachers, with a focus on examining the program's cultural relevance in rural schools. She also has written chapters about intervention fidelity and needs assessment.

Yael Gross completed her Master of Arts in Psychology at Rutgers University—Camden and is currently a doctoral student in School Psychology at Lehigh University. Her research interests focus on evaluating the collaboration between the family, school, and health systems for children with chronic health conditions.

Patti L. Harrison, Ph.D., is Professor Emeritus of the University of Alabama, where she served as a faculty member in the School Psychology program from 1985 to 2017. Her research and scholarship relate to professional issues in school psychology and assessment methods for children. She is co-author of the *Adaptive Behavior Assessment System*, now in its 3rd edition. She also is co-editor of *Best Practices in School Psychology* (6th ed.); *Contemporary Intellectual Assessment: Theories, Tests, and Issues* (1st, 2nd, & 3rd eds.); and *ABAS-II: Clinical Use and Interpretation*. Dr. Harrison is a Past President of the National Association of School Psychologists (NASP) and holds Fellow status in the American Psychological Association (APA) and American Educational Research Association. She received the *Jack Bardon Distinguished Service Award* from APA's Division of School Psychology and the *Lifetime Achievement Award* from NASP.

Kimberly J. Hills, Ph.D., is a licensed psychologist and Clinical Professor in School Psychology at the University of South Carolina. She has spent over a decade cultivating clinical expertise in evidence-based assessment for children with neurodevelopmental disorders, and her current work focuses on the early identification and differential diagnosis of autism spectrum disorder across the developmental continuum.

Abigail L. Hogan, Ph.D., is a Research Assistant Professor in the Psychology Department at the University of South Carolina. Her work focuses on characterizing early biobehavioral risk markers for autism spectrum disorder and anxiety disorders in siblings of children with autism spectrum disorder.

Robin Hojnoski, Ph.D., is an Associate Professor and Program Director in the School Psychology program at Lehigh University. Her research focuses broadly on school readiness and effective assessment practices and cross setting interventions in early learning and social behavior. She is particularly interested in early mathematical development and working with classroom teachers and families to support children's development in this area. Her current work uses shared book reading as a mechanism for developing children's mathematical vocabulary, concepts, and skills with diverse populations. Dr. Hojnoski publishes in the areas of early childhood, early childhood special education, and school psychology, and she serves on editorial boards in these disciplines.

Jeffrey Kelly, Psy.D., has been a practicing school psychologist for 22 years in southern New Jersey, currently serving the Lower Township Elementary School District. His interests include assessment and intervention practices of executive functions and the utilization of mindfulness-based approaches at the elementary school level. Jeffrey's dissertation, *Mindfulness-Based and Cognitive-Behavior Therapy for Anger-Management: An Integrated Approach*, received meritorious distinction from the Philadelphia College of Osteopathic Medicine in 2007.

Lisa Kelly-Vance, Ph.D., is a Professor of School Psychology at the University of Nebraska Omaha and serves as the Program Director. She received her Bachelor's degree from Purdue University and her Master's and Ph.D. from Indiana University. She began her career as a school psychologist in Council Bluffs, Iowa, serving children aged from birth through 21 years old. Her research and applied interests are assessment and interventions with preschool children in the context of play, mental health in early childhood, school-based academic and social interventions, prevention, and self-care. She is a Past President of the National Association of School Psychologists as well as the Iowa School Psychology Association and the Nebraska School Psychology Association.

Jessica M. Kemp is a doctoral candidate in School Psychology at the University of Massachusetts Amherst. Her clinical and research interests involve early prevention, as well as integrating trauma-informed care within positive behavioral interventions and supports throughout PreK-12 school settings. She has experience working in early childhood school settings facilitating systems-level consultation and intervention related to social-emotional and behavioral health. She also is experienced as an in-home behavioral therapist with an early childhood population in which she has assessed, monitored, and enhanced skills related to school readiness, including effective communication, pre-academics, and prosocial behaviors. Jessica's dissertation data were collected in a Head Start setting and focused on aligning a prominent social-emotional learning curriculum with daily classroom management strategies to support the generalization of social-emotional competencies.

Pamela Kidder-Ashley, Ph.D., is a Professor in the Department of Psychology at Appalachian State University in Boone, North Carolina. After earning her Ph.D. in School Psychology from the University of Minnesota and working for 13 years as a school psychologist in Charlotte, NC, she joined the faculty at Appalachian State in 1993, serving as director of the graduate program in School Psychology there from 2006 to 2018. She collaborates with co-author Sandra Gagnon on projects examining early childhood temperament and social competence, parenting and teaching stress, and parent- and teacher-child relationship quality. Other research interests include bullying and school crisis intervention, and she regularly presents her research at national and international conventions. She has served as an ad hoc reviewer for *Psychology in the Schools* and numerous psychology textbooks.

Doré R. LaForett, Ph.D., is a Senior Research Scientist at Child Trends, and an Advanced Research Scientist at the Frank Porter Graham Child Development Institute, University of North Carolina at Chapel Hill. Her areas of expertise include early childhood mental health, social-emotional and behavioral interventions, school readiness, and parent-child interactions. Her research has largely focused on low-income and ethnic minority families, including work with children who are learning more than one language at home and/or in their education settings. Dr. LaForett's Ph.D. is in Clinical Psychology, and in addition to being a researcher she is a licensed psychologist in North Carolina. As a practitioner, she has provided mental health consultation in early childhood classrooms and has conducted training for teachers on classroom management and promotion of children's social and emotional development.

Milim Lee received a Master of Education degree in Counseling and Human Services in 2015 from Lehigh University, where she is currently pursuing a doctoral degree in School Psychology. Milim's current research interests include early intervention for young children from low-socioeconomic-status families and integrated services of care for young children and their families to improve family capacity building.

Dominique Levert earned a Master of Science degree in Psychology from the University of North Florida. She is currently enrolled in Lehigh University's School Psychology doctoral program and is a part of the sub-specialization in pediatric school psychology. She is also working on obtaining her Board Certified Behavior Analyst certification. Dominique's current research interests include promoting early childhood mental health, coordination of services for low-resourced and disadvantaged families, and behavioral health.

Patricia H. Manz, Ph.D., Professor of School Psychology, earned her Ph.D. from the Graduate School of Education at the University of Pennsylvania. She has extensive research experience in aiming to advance family-centered, early intervention, and prevention for young children who experience socioeconomic disadvantage. Her research addresses integration of child development service systems to promote health among low-income infants and toddlers. Additionally, she has developed the *Little Talks* program, a comprehensive, culturally responsive approach to fostering language-rich parent interactions with infants and toddlers. Designed for use in home visiting, Little Talks also includes implementation supports for home visitors. Dr. Manz has led several federally and foundation-funded research projects in addition to authoring numerous publications that are focused on early intervention for low-income children.

George McCloskey, Ph.D., is a Professor and Director of School Psychology Research in the School of Professional and Applied Psychology of the Philadelphia College of Osteopathic Medicine and holds Diplomate status with the American Academy of Pediatric Neuropsychology. Dr. McCloskey has amassed 35 years of experience in test development, teaching, research, and assessment and intervention work with a wide range of clients and has developed a comprehensive model of executive capacities that can be used to assess strengths and deficits and guide efforts to foster growth and intervene with difficulties. Dr. McCloskey is the lead author of the books *Assessment and Intervention for Executive Function Difficulties* and *Essentials of Executive Functions Assessment*, and his most recent writing on interventions for executive function and executive skills difficulties appears in Chapter 10 of the book *Essentials of Planning, Selecting, and Tailoring Interventions for Unique Learners*. He also is the author of the *McCloskey Executive Functions Scales*, which have been standardized and published with Schoolhouse Educational Services. Dr. McCloskey is co-author, with his wife, Laurie McCloskey, of the children's book *The Day Frankie Left His Frontal Lobes at Home*.

Leslie McIntosh, Psy.D., is a national and New Jersey-certified school psychologist living and practicing in Jersey City, NJ, where he specializes in the early childhood age range (3–5 years). He is presently completing a doctoral fellowship with the National Center for Pyramid Model Innovations, where he is creating products and resources to support the executive skill development of all young children. His current professional interests include managing systemic change using implementation science, supporting the successful transition of students from pre-K to kindergarten, and the creation of learning environments that nurture the executive functions of every young learner.

R. A. McWilliam, Ph.D., is a Professor of Early Childhood Special Education at the University of Alabama, where he founded and directs the Evidence-based International Early Intervention Office, in the Department of Special Education and Multiple Abilities. With colleagues, he created the *Routines-Based Model for Early Intervention* (Birth to Five; RBM), a comprehensive system for supporting caregivers of young children with disabilities. This model is implemented in ten countries. It includes practices for assessing needs and developing functional and family goals, using a primary service provider, consulting collaboratively with caregivers to build their capacity, and measuring progress on goals, child functioning, and family quality of life. Dr. McWilliam has written over 80 peer-reviewed articles and eight books and has presented in over 20 countries. He is a Visiting Professor at the University of Silesia in Poland, where he has an implementation site.

Sally Taunton Miedema, Ph.D., CAPE, is a Postdoctoral Research Fellow in the Department of Physical Education at the University of South Carolina. Dr. Miedema holds a Ph.D. in Physical Education with an emphasis in Motor Behavior and Adapted Physical Education from the University of South Carolina. Her research interest includes examining the effects of integrated motor skill intervention programs on young children with and without disabilities as it relates to whole child development. Dr. Miedema currently has 24 peer-reviewed publications, 4 book chapters, and 52 national and international presentations related to children's motor skill development, physical activity, and social-emotional development during early childhood.

Kristen Missall, Ph.D., is an Associate Professor in the School Psychology program at the University of Washington. She specializes in studying school readiness, early school adjustment, and academic and social-emotional assessment and intervention for children aged 3 to 10. Her research appears in journals across the fields of school psychology, special education, and early intervention. She has received and managed external research funds from state and federal agencies, including the National Science Foundation and the Institute for Education Sciences, totaling over 4.4 million dollars. Missall currently serves as Associate Editor for the *Journal of Early Intervention*.

Eva V. Monsma, Ph.D., CMT, holds a Ph.D. in Kinesiology with an emphasis in sport psychology from Michigan State University, with cognates in motor development and developmental psychology. She is a Professor of Developmental Sport Psychology in the Department of Physical Education at the University of South Carolina, where she has taught motor behavior courses for over 20 years. She is also an Associate Editor of *The Sport Psychologist* and is on the editorial boards of the *Women in Sport and Physical Activity Journal* and the *Journal of Imagery Research in Sport and Physical Activity*. Her research interests include growth and maturation factors involved in athlete selection and maladaptive behaviors, cognitive factors involved in motor development and self-regulation, and mental training in sport, performance, and rehabilitation.

Catalina Patricia Morales-Murillo, Ph.D., is an Assistant Professor at the Valencia Catholic University San Vicente Mártir, in Spain. Her research focuses on the engagement of children in daily routines and the quality of early childhood education contexts. Dr. Morales-Murillo has several publications on these topics. She is a member of the Evidence-Based International Early Intervention Office of the University of Alabama, the RAM Group, the Council for Exceptional Children of the Division of Early Childhood, and Campus Capacitas-UCV. She collaborates with the implementation of the *Routines-Based Model* and its components, such as the *Engagement Classroom Model* (by R. A. McWilliam), in countries such as Spain, Paraguay, and Ecuador.

Richard J. Nagle, Ph.D., is a Distinguished Professor Emeritus in the Department of Psychology at the University of South Carolina. He was named the Louise Fry Scudder Professor of Psychology, which is the highest faculty award of the College of Liberal Arts, in recognition of his sustained record of excellence in research, teaching, mentoring, service, and contributions beyond the university. He was also an Adjunct Professor in the Department of Pediatrics at the University of South Carolina School of Medicine. Dr. Nagle served as the Kulynich/Cline Distinguished Visiting Professor in the Psychology Department at Appalachian State University. He is a Fellow in the American Psychological Association (Division 16). Dr. Nagle has an extensive publication record in preschool assessment and has served on the editorial boards of major journals in school psychology and related disciplines.

Samuel O. Ortiz, Ph.D., is Professor of Psychology at St. John's University. His Ph.D. is from the University of Southern California, and he has a credential in school psychology and postdoctoral training in bilingual school psychology from San Diego State University. He has served as a member and Chair of the American Psychological Association (APA)

Committee on Psychological Tests and Assessment, member of the Coalition for Psychology in Schools and Education, and member of the APA Presidential Task Force on Educational Disparities. He is an internationally recognized expert on issues involving assessment of English learners, Cross-Battery Assessment, and specific learning disabilities. He is author of the *Ortiz Picture Vocabulary Acquisition Test*, *Cross-Battery Assessment System Software v2.3*, and the *Culture-Language Interpretive Matrix*. His books include *Assessing Culturally and Linguistically Diverse Students*, currently under revision, and *Essentials of Cross-Battery Assessment, 3rd Edition*.

Sharlene Wilson Ottley, Ph.D., is the Director of Early Childhood Research and Practice at The River School. There, she oversees the research efforts and coordinates community-based programs for underserved populations. Dr. Ottley completed graduate studies in Speech-Language Pathology at Gallaudet University with an emphasis in Pediatric Aural Rehabilitation. Dr. Ottley then spent time in Mexico teaching English courses and completing intensive coursework in Spanish. She has worked in early intervention, school-based, and outpatient settings providing services to children from diverse backgrounds. She completed her Ph.D. in Communication Sciences and Disorders, focusing on children with cochlear implants from Spanish-/English-speaking homes. Dr. Ottley's research focuses on improving vocabulary and literacy outcomes for children with hearing loss, particularly those from socioeconomically disadvantaged and diverse backgrounds.

Bradley Petry is a school psychologist in Baltimore City Public Schools. He currently co-leads a team of related service providers in expanding roles of providers to focus on prevention and early intervention. His professional interests include systems change, peer and professional supervision, education reform, school safety and threat assessment, neuropsychological assessment practices, and professional presentation. He is the current President of the Maryland School Psychologists' Association (MSPA) and the 2012 MSPA *Outstanding Practitioner of the Year*. Brad lives in Laurel, Maryland, with his wife and two children.

Jane E. Roberts, Ph.D., is a Professor in School Psychology and Chair of the Psychology Department at the University of South Carolina. She has spent nearly 20 years cultivating expertise in developmental trajectories in children with neurodevelopmental disorders like autism spectrum disorder and fragile X syndrome (FXS), and she is one of the country's foremost researchers on early development in FXS. Her work has continuously been funded by the National Institutes of Health and private organizations.

Brigette Oliver Ryalls, Ph.D., is an Associate Professor and Chairperson of the Psychology Department at the University of Nebraska Omaha. She received her Bachelor's degree from Murray State University in Murray, Kentucky, in 1988 and her Ph.D. from Indiana University in 1994. Dr. Ryalls is broadly interested in the development of cognition and language in early childhood. In addition to her longstanding collaboration with Dr. Lisa Kelly-Vance studying play assessment and intervention, Dr. Ryalls has published work primarily on the acquisition and understanding of dimensional adjectives in children and adults.

Julia Mendez Smith, Ph.D., is a Professor of Psychology at the University of North Carolina, Greensboro. Her research involves the study of risk and protective factors for low-income and ethnic minority children and their families. She is specifically interested in children's school readiness, parent engagement in education, and the social and emotional adjustment of children across the early childhood and elementary school years. She is actively involved in the translation of scientific findings into strategies for promoting positive adjustment and school success for low-income children, including community initiatives such as Guilford Parent Academy and collaborative intervention studies with Head Start programs. Since 2013, Dr. Mendez Smith has been a co-investigator for the federally funded National Research Center on Hispanic Children and Families, which conducts research on poverty and early care and education opportunities for low-income Hispanic children in the United States. The Center is intentionally focused on understanding how ECE programs and child care policies support Latinx child development and learning opportunities in the family, school, and community settings. Dr. Mendez has training in school, community, and clinical psychology, and as a licensed clinical psychologist she has expertise in understanding the mental health and wellbeing of young children. She enjoys mentoring graduate and undergraduate students interested in research and clinical work promoting resilience among low-income and ethnic minority populations.

Marisa Solé completed her undergraduate degree at the University of California, Santa Barbara, with a B.A. in Psychology and Spanish with minors in Applied Psychology and Educational Studies and is currently a doctoral student at Lehigh University in the School Psychology program. Her research interests include ethnic-racial socialization in native-born African American and foreign-born Latinx families. As a bilingual-bicultural scholar, Marisa has assisted in qualitative and quantitative research connected to themes of social inequities, supporting disadvantaged children and families, and identifying areas of improvement to impact the ways larger systems deliver educational, psychological, and health services to underserved communities.

Cami Stevenson, M.A., is an administrator in the Multnomah Early Childhood Program, an early intervention program for children aged from birth to five years of age, in Portland, Oregon. She is the Associate

Director of the Routines-Based Model (RBM) Enterprise, which runs various training, material-development, and consultation activities to promote children's engagement and family empowerment. She works in partnership with Robin McWilliam to advance the RBM, with specific responsibility for logistics and management of the many materials associated with the model. Ms. Stevenson has a Master's degree in Early Childhood Special Education from the University of Oregon and an educational-administration certificate from Portland State University. She has been an Adjunct Assistant Professor at Portland State University.

Lea A. Theodore, Ph.D., Professor and licensed psychologist, is a member of the School Psychology Program at Adelphi University. Dr. Theodore received her Ph.D. from the University of Connecticut in 2002 and was awarded their *Early Career Alumni Award* in 2009, due in part to her ranking among the top 20 most productive authors in school psychology; she earned a similar ranking in 2016. Dr. Theodore received the College of William & Mary *Plumeri Award for Faculty Excellence* in 2013 and the *Jean Baker APA Division 16 Service award* in 2019. Dr. Theodore has consulted with the Virginia General District Court and Virginia Supreme Court, and with public and private schools, hospitals, publishing companies, and behavioral health centers. She edited the *Handbook of Evidence-Based Interventions for Children and Adolescents* and served as Associate Editor for *School Psychology Quarterly*, Division 16 Vice-President of Professional Affairs, Vice-President of Membership, and Division President. The American Psychological Association Board of Directors appointed Lea to serve on the Committee on Division/APA Relations and she was elected as a Division 16 Council Representative.

Carla A. Wall, M.S., is a doctoral student in School Psychology at the University of South Carolina. Her graduate and pre-doctoral work has focused on the early characterization and treatment of autism spectrum disorders with and without genetic syndromes.

Sara A. Whitcomb, Ph.D., is an Associate Professor and Training Director of the doctoral program in School Psychology at the University of Massachusetts Amherst. She received her doctoral degree from the University of Oregon in 2009. Her research and clinical interests are in behavioral assessment and intervention, school-based mental health, positive behavioral support systems, and behavioral and organizational consultation. Dr. Whitcomb teaches courses in social-emotional and behavioral assessment and consultation, and she coordinates an advanced practicum experience in organizational consultation. She has authored over 25 publications, including a text, *Behavioral, Social, and Emotional Assessment of Children and Adolescents,* and a social-emotional learning curriculum for young children, *Merrell's Strong Start Pre-K.*

Elizabeth A. Will, Ph.D., BCBA, is a Board Certified Behavior Analyst and postdoctoral fellow at the University of South Carolina. Dr. Will has over ten years' experience in research and treatment of autism and neurodevelopmental disorders. As a developmental scientist, her current research is focused on identifying profiles and early indicators of comorbid autism in young children with neurogenetic conditions such as Down syndrome.

Harriet G. Williams, Ph.D., is Distinguished Professor Emeritus in the Department of Exercise Science, School of Public Health, University of South Carolina. She holds a Ph.D. in Motor Development-Control from the University of Wisconsin-Madison and is recognized as one of the nation's foremost authorities in the perceptual-motor development of young children. She is the Founder and Past Director of the Perceptual-Motor Development Laboratory and the Functional Health Behaviors Assessment Laboratory, University of South Carolina. Through National Institutes of Health funded research with colleagues, she has developed a field-based protocol for assessing gross motor skills in preschool children and a published activity-based program on fall prevention for older adults, *Stay In Balance*. Dr. Williams has published widely in developmental and aging research (150+ publications and presentations) and currently serves as peer reviewer for a number of science-based journals. Her professional career includes invited visiting professorships at the University of California—Los Angeles, University of Texas at Austin, University of Oregon, and University of Western Australia.

Jane Y. T. Wong, M.A., is currently pursuing a doctoral degree in School Psychology (Bilingual Track) at St. John's University in New York. She holds a Master of Arts degree in Social/Personality Psychology from York University, Toronto. She was a Research Scientist for Multi-Health Systems (MHS), and a test publisher in Toronto from 2009 to 2018. During her tenure at MHS, she led the development of a number of psychoeducational as well as speech/language assessments, including the *Ortiz Picture Vocabulary Acquisition Test*. She oversaw the entire test development cycle, which includes conceptualization, literature review, item and test application development, data collection, norming, report development, and manual writing.

Acknowledgments

In academia, it is common for scholars to write or edit books. It is relatively uncommon, however, for those books to be accepted by professionals to the point of being taken into multiple editions. The *Psychoeducational Assessment of Preschool Children* was originally published in 1983. It is only through the superlative contributions of dedicated chapter authors, the careful editing of the co-editors to achieve a "single voice" throughout the volume, and the diligent care of the publisher from start to finish that this book has been rendered worthy of five editions. As such, the co-editors would like to acknowledge the expertise and committed contributions of our authors and the support and guidance we have received from our publisher, Taylor & Francis. From contract renewal to final edits and publication, Taylor & Francis professionals have made this project a pleasant and rewarding experience. Special appreciation goes to our Editor, Mr. Daniel Schwartz, for initiating and shepherding the book as it progressed from its initial outline to publication. Sincere thanks also to Ms. Ellie Jarvis, Production Editor, and Ms. Maya Berger, Copy Editor, for ensuring uniformity of style and format across the chapters and paying careful attention to every printed word.

Vincent C. Alfonso, Ph.D.
Bruce A. Bracken, Ph.D.
Richard J. Nagle, Ph.D.

Part I

Foundations

Chapter 1

Issues in Preschool Assessment

Richard J. Nagle, Sandra Glover Gagnon, and Pamela Kidder-Ashley

Historical Context of Preschool Assessment

The landscape of preschool assessment has changed significantly, albeit grad-ually, since the 1986 amendments (Public Law [P.L.] 99-457) to the *Education for All Handicapped Children Act* (P.L. 94-142) required that states provide a free and appropriate public education to children with disabilities aged 3 years to 5 years, and Part H of Section 619 established incentives for states to develop services for infants and toddlers with special needs. The ensuing regu-lation changes mandated that assessment practices stipulated for school-age children also be applied to the assessment of preschool children. Subsequent amendments were made in 1990 (P.L. 101-476), when the original act was renamed the *Individuals with Disabilities Education Act*, and in 1991 (P.L. 102-119), adding the category of *developmentally delayed* as an option for disabled children between the ages of 3 and 5 years. P.L. 102-119 also specified that developmental delay could be manifested in one or more of the following areas: physical, cognitive, communication, social or emotional, or adaptive. The 1997 reauthorization (P.L. 105-17) extended *developmental delay* to the age of 9 years, at the discretion of state and local education agencies. The act also stipulated that early intervention services should be delivered within natural environments and that states require local school district personnel to partici-pate in transition planning conferences for toddlers with disabilities who are about to enter preschool (Knoblauch & McLane, 1999).

The most recent reauthorization of the law occurred in 2004 (P.L. 108-446), when it was renamed the Individuals with Disabilities Education Improvement Act (although it continues to be referred to in most contexts as IDEA), but no further changes were made to provisions directly related to assessment and eligibility for preschool children. However, the 2004 amendments contained a provision that indirectly affected preschool assess-ment policy and procedures. That provision was the result of efforts, which began earlier in the mid-1990s, from a number of leading researchers in the field of learning disabilities (e.g., Fuchs, 1995; Gresham, 2002; Marston, 2001), to change the approach to identifying children with Specific Learning Disabilities (SLDs) under IDEA. They proposed that a systematic evaluation of a child's response to intervention (RTI) would be more valid than the traditional IQ-achievement discrepancy approach that had prevailed since P.L. 94-142 was passed in 1975. As a result of these efforts, the 2004 IDEA amendments allowed local education agencies to use "a process that determines if the child responds to scientific, research-based intervention as a part of the evaluation procedures" (IDEA—20 U.S.C. § 1414(b)(6)) when determining a child's eligibility for special education under the category of SLD.

This RTI process was the precursor to what is now referred to as *multi-tiered systems of support* (MTSS), a framework that is increasingly applied within early childhood programs. MTSS is a preventive *general education* framework that employs data-based problem solving in a tiered continuum of evidence-based instructional practices intended to improve academic, behavioral, and social-emotional outcomes for all students (Colorado Department of Education, 2015). Although MTSS is not a legislated initiative, the Every Student Succeeds Act (ESSA; P.L. 114-95), passed in 2015 to replace the No Child Left Behind Act, references tiered systems of support seven times and specifically endorses the use of a "schoolwide tiered model" to prevent and address students' educational needs. It also stipulates that ESSA grant funds may be applied to providing multi-tiered systems of support for literacy services (ESSA—20 U.S.C. § 2224(e)(4)). Furthermore, the law outlines the options for using Title I funding, the purpose of which is to improve the academic achievement of economically disadvantaged students, and expressly indicates that funds may be used for delivering early childhood educational programs. The law further stipulates that all Title I schools must develop a comprehensive plan that includes, among other things, a description of "strategies for assisting preschool children in the transition from early childhood education programs to local elementary school programs" (ESSA—20 U.S.C. § 6314 (b), (7), (A), (iii), (V)). In 2016, the United States Department of Education (USDOE) published a document entitled *Early Learning in the Every Student Succeeds Act: Expanding Opportunities to Support our Youngest Learners*, which highlighted key benefits of high-quality early childhood educational programs and explained in detail how local education agencies could apply ESSA provisions and funding to support them. Furthermore, a 2016 memorandum issued by the USDOE's Office of Special Education (OSEP, 2016) specified that local education agencies cannot *require* an "RTI process" and thereby delay IDEA eligibility evaluations of preschoolers who have been referred by individuals or agencies in the community.

Such legislative and policy support for early childhood services has developed in tandem with political and social justice efforts to address the achievement gap between white and minority students in public schools (Bohrnstedt, Kitmitto, Ogut, Sherman, & Chan, 2015; Hemphill & Vanneman, 2011) and, more broadly, to address the problems of poverty and inequality in the United States. Federal funding for preschool services began when Head Start was established in 1965 as part of President Lyndon Johnson's "war on poverty" and has continued to the present. In more recent decades, there has been increasing pressure from various sectors (e.g., business, law enforcement, military, education, and faith-based groups) to ensure that all children are adequately prepared—academically and socially—to start school at the age of 5 years. In 2015, the USDOE published *A Matter of Equity: Preschool in America*, documenting the benefits of high-quality preschool and early childhood educational programs and outlining the then-current state of public funding for such programs. The document reported that, from 2003 to 2015, states increased funding for preschool programs and services by more than 200%. However, the focus of such promotional efforts seems to be shifting from advocating for preschool programs that serve children from age 3 to 5 to a narrower focus on *pre-kindergarten* programs that specifically target 4-year-olds. In fact, a number of recent gubernatorial candidates have included the provision of universal pre-kindergarten (pre-K) in their political platforms (Wong, 2014). Although few states have funded mandated universal pre-K (indeed, some still do not mandate kindergarten enrollment), a recent report by the National Institute for Early Education Research (Friedman-Krauss et al., 2019) revealed that, since publishing their annual report in 2002, states have added funding for nearly 900,000 preschoolers, mostly 4-year-olds. The report, which did not distinguish between preschool and pre-K programs, indicated that during the 2017–2018 school year, approximately one-third of all 4-year-olds in the United States were enrolled in state-funded preschool programs; 44% when federally funded and mandated programs were counted.

The recent proliferation of preschool programs and pre-K programs for 4-year-olds has affected the practice of preschool assessment in a number of ways, most notably by increasing the number of 4-year-olds who are served by public schools and who, therefore, may be referred for evaluation by school personnel. Consequently, the proliferation also has increased the necessity of ensuring that school-based personnel are prepared to provide appropriate assessment services to this growing population.

Purposes of Preschool Assessment

Although there are various ways to categorize the purposes and types of assessments carried out within educational settings, there is broad agreement that the overarching purpose is to enhance student learning (National Association for the Education of Young Children [NAEYC], 2009). Through the process of assessment, educational professionals gather information to make well-informed decisions that promote student success. In its most recent publication outlining recommended practices for early intervention and early childhood special education services, the Division for Early Childhood (DEC, 2014) of the Council for Exceptional Children (CEC) listed the following purposes of assessment: "screening, determining eligibility for services, individualized planning, monitoring child progress, and measuring child outcomes" (p. 8). Others have included diagnosis (Nagle, 2007) and program evaluation for accountability (Bagnato, Goins, Pretti-Frontczak, & Neisworth, 2014) as additional critical purposes.

For individual children, assessment can be conceptualized as the first step in the intervention process. A clear and direct link between assessment and intervention is critical at every developmental level and is considered essential during early childhood (Bagnato, Neisworth, & Pretti-Frontczak, 2010). In recent decades, early childhood professionals and scholars have increasingly called for the use of assessment practices that are developmentally appropriate, conducted in natural contexts, and directly applicable to planning and evaluating children's learning experiences (Bagnato et al., 2010; DEC, 2014; Losardo & Syverson, 2011; NAEYC, 2009).

Screening

Screening typically involves the administration of brief, low-cost assessment procedures to large numbers of children or individual children to determine if further, more in-depth evaluation is warranted. Screening measures are frequently administered by paraprofessionals and given to the entire student population in an educational setting or, if conducted within a community or medical setting, to as many children as possible. Because screening measures are often used with large groups of children, they must be easy and inexpensive to use, while at the same time being sufficiently reliable and valid to ensure that they facilitate sound decision-making (Emmons & Alfonso, 2005).

Broadly speaking, there are two main types of screening—*developmental* and *universal*—employed with young children (DEC/CEC, NAEYC, & National Head Start Association, 2013). *Developmental screening* is used in educational, clinical, and medical settings and involves comparing a child's performance to that of a normative sample. Developmental screening is used to help determine if the child is developing as expected or appears to be at risk of having or developing a disabling condition, in which case follow-up diagnostic evaluation is warranted. As such, developmental screening often serves as a component of a school district's Child Find efforts, which are mandated under IDEA (20 U.S.C. § 1412(a)(3)).

Universal screening is used in educational settings and helps determine if a child is making expected progress with respect to the program's learning objectives and, if not, what types of targeted support or interventions might be put in place to facilitate the child's progress. Here, comparison is made with an instructional objective or criterion, often referred to as a *benchmark* (DEC/CEC, NAEYC, & National Head Start Association, 2013). Thus, screening is not intended to be diagnostic; rather, it should assist professionals in determining which children might need more in-depth evaluation to diagnose a disability or qualify the child for specialized services, or which children might need additional support or intervention.

Developmental screeners are routinely used in pediatric and family medical practices, and disorder-specific screenings are sometimes conducted as well. In fact, the *Recommendations for Preventive Pediatric Health Care* of the American Academy of Pediatrics (AAP, 2019) suggest that children be screened for general developmental issues and for autism, using validated tools, at specified ages. Although the AAP does not endorse specific screening tools, it does make available an extensive list of potential measures (American Academy of Pediatrics, 2017), which includes basic information about each tool's validity (specifically, its sensitivity and specificity, which are discussed below) as well as practical features such as completion-time estimates and cost. Developmental screeners are also commonly used in early childhood education settings, often in response to a concern voiced by a parent or educator that a child may have a disability. Many of the same screeners used by healthcare providers are also used in preschool settings.

Developmental screening tools must meet established reliability and validity criteria to ensure that errors are minimized. Potential screening errors include *false positives*—identifying a child as requiring follow-up when no true problem exists—and *false negatives*—failing to identify a child who actually has a disabling condition. To maximize their accuracy and usefulness, developmental screening measures should be used only if they meet established standards with respect to their *sensitivity* and *specificity*. *Positive predictive value* (PPV) and *negative predictive value* (NPV) are also important features to evaluate. Sensitivity and specificity are characteristics of the measure, whereas PPV and NPV are affected by the prevalence of the risk or disability in the screened population. Sensitivity refers to the proportion of children actually requiring follow-up evaluation who are accurately identified as such (i.e., the screener's accuracy in identifying *true positives*); measures with high sensitivity also tend to produce high *false positive* rates. In contrast, a screener's specificity is defined as the proportion of children who truly are not at risk or in need of follow-up evaluation who are correctly classified as such (i.e., the screener's accuracy in identifying *true negatives*); measures with higher specificity also identify more *false negatives* (Kilpatrick, 2015; Vitrikas, Grant, Savard, & Bucaj, 2017). (A full discussion of PPV and NPV is beyond the scope of this chapter; the reader may wish to consult Emmons & Alfonso, 2005, or Trevethan, 2017, for additional information.)

In general, an acceptable sensitivity for a screening measure is 70% to 80%, whereas a screener's specificity should be at least 80% (Mackrides & Ryherd, 2011); however, analysis of these qualities of screening tools is a highly complex matter, and the results are often not easily interpreted (Trevethan, 2017). The impact of screening errors on children and their families should be a major concern for professionals. The occurrence of false positives may cost families substantial, unnecessary worry and may precipitate the needless pursuit of costly follow-up diagnostic evaluations. Perhaps even more troubling, false negative conclusions from screeners may result in missed opportunities for children and their families to access needed early intervention services, causing the challenges they face to become even more serious and harder to remediate, possibly leading to ever-growing frustration and a sense of failure for the child (Tzivinikou, 2018).

Universal screening is typically conducted in early childhood education settings where MTSS is established. Universal screeners are chosen or developed so that they are closely aligned with a program's overall goals and its specific learning objectives. This systematic alignment increases the likelihood that professionals who are working with a child identified by the screener as needing extra support will perceive that finding as appropriate. Much of the early focus in MTSS implementation has been on language and literacy, with consequent development of universal screeners in those domains. Over time, literacy screeners have been developed specifically for preschoolers, including *Get Ready to Read! Revised* (Lonigan & Wilson, 2008), and the *EARLI* literacy probes (Reid, DiPerna, Morgan, & Lei, 2009). There also are options for screening preschoolers in early numeracy (e.g., Lei, Wu, DiPerna, & Morgan, 2009; Polignano & Hojnoski, 2012; Purpura & Lonigan, 2015), and there are several options for screening across multiple domains (e.g., the *Individual Growth and Development Indicators* and the *Profile of Preschool Learning and Development Readiness* developed by Hojnoski & Floyd, 2004; McConnell, Bradfield, Wackerle-Hollman, & Rodriguez, 2012; Missall & Roberts, 2014; as well as the *Ages & Stages Questionnaires, 3rd edition*, AEQ-3, by Squires & Bricker, 2009).

Diagnosis and Eligibility Determination

Assessment for the purpose of diagnosis or determining a child's eligibility for special services often follows a screening that suggests a child has a disabling condition or is at risk for developing one. These assessments, referred to as *evaluations* under Part C of IDEA, are conducted by highly trained professionals who use a broad array of specialized measures that tap data from multiple sources and settings (Losardo & Syverson, 2011). The measures typically tap multiple domains of functioning and often include norm-referenced, standardized measures. However, as discussed more fully later in this chapter, there is strong advocacy among many early childhood professionals for the use of more authentic, child- and family-centered approaches (Bagnato et al., 2010; DEC, 2014; Losardo & Syverson, 2011). As with screening tools, measures employed for diagnosis and eligibility determination are expected to meet or exceed established standards for reliability and validity and other psychometric features (American Educational Research Association, American Psychological Association, National Council on Measurement in Education, & Joint Committee on Standards for Educational and Psychological Testing, 2014).

Particularly in early childhood contexts, professionals conducting diagnostic and eligibility evaluations typically aim not only to verify that a disability is present or to qualify a child for special services, but also to identify the specific strengths and needs of the child and the strengths, goals, and preferences of the family (NAEYC, 2009; National Association of School Psychologists [NASP], 2015). A careful and comprehensive evaluation, as described below, facilitates sound intervention planning for the child and family, particularly when it is conducted within the context of an MTSS (NASP, 2015). Periodic reevaluation, which is required triennially under IDEA to verify continued eligibility for special education services, may occur more frequently during early childhood, due to the rapid developmental changes shown by young children. Such reevaluations may include measures that are different from those used in the initial evaluation, depending on the child's progress and evolving needs.

Individual Program Planning and Monitoring

As noted above, the comprehensive diagnostic/eligibility evaluation, when conducted according to best practice guidelines (NAEYC, 2009; NASP, 2015), should lead to well-informed individualized program planning, particularly in the initial stages when decisions are made regarding the overall scope of the child's strengths and needs and the best settings for delivering intervention and treatment. Such evaluations can guide the selection of evidence-based interventions that specifically address the child's needs (or "*next steps*") and capitalize on the child's strengths. Once the child is receiving services, curriculum-based measurement is particularly useful for systematically monitoring the child's attainment of individual and curricular goals and generating data that can further inform decisions regarding when to continue, modify, or discontinue an intervention or treatment protocol.

Most of the measures mentioned under the section above on universal screening (e.g., the *Individual Growth and Development Indicators*, the *Profile of Preschool Learning and Development Readiness*, and the AEQ-3) are commonly used for progress monitoring, as is the *Assessment, Evaluation, and Programming System for Infants and Children* (Bricker, Capt, &, Pretti-Frontczak, 2002). When progress data from multiple children enrolled in a particular program are aggregated, they provide evidence of the program's effectiveness.

Program Evaluation

Although there are many ways to conceptualize program evaluation, Newcomer, Hatry and Wholey (2015) describe it as "the application of systematic methods to address questions about program operations and results. It may include ongoing monitoring of a program as well as one-shot studies of program processes or program impact" (p. 7).

In their joint position statement on early childhood curriculum, assessment, and program evaluation, the NAEYC and the National Association of

Early Childhood Specialists in State Departments of Education (2003) spelled out a number of key indicators of effective program evaluation. In particular, they recommended that program evaluations be conducted by appropriately trained, unbiased assessors who use scientifically valid designs that are guided by the program's comprehensive goals and that tap multiple sources of program data, focusing on the appropriateness of the program's practices as well as indices of children's progress. They included specific cautions about limiting the use of individually administered, norm-referenced assessments and, if such tests are used, choosing them carefully to ensure their psychometric adequacy; relevance to identified program outcomes; and cultural, linguistic, and developmental appropriateness for the children in the program.

Another source of information about factors to be examined in evaluating preschool programs comes from the National Institute for Early Education Research (NIEER; Friedman-Krauss et al., 2019), which conducts annual state-by-state evaluations of policies for state-funded preschool programs. NIEER applies ten criteria in evaluating policies, some of which could be employed in evaluating individual programs as well. For example, NIEER sets criteria for preschool teacher and assistant degree levels and professional development, class size and staff-to-child ratio, support for curriculum implementation, and child screenings and referrals. The position statement of the NAEYC (2009) on developmentally appropriate practice (DAP) also provides standards that could be applied to the evaluation of preschool program policies and processes.

In addition to guidelines for program evaluation, there also are many tools available for evaluating preschool programs. One that examines program processes is the *Classroom Assessment Scoring System* (CLASS; Pianta, La Paro, & Hamre, 2008), which includes a version for pre-K classrooms and yields composite scores for three major dimensions of instruction (i.e., emotional support, classroom organization, and instructional support) as well as multiple subscales, all of which were developed to tap instructional behaviors that are linked in the empirical literature to student learning gains. Another available tool is *A Developmentally Appropriate Practices Template* (ADAPT; Lee Van Horn & Ramey, 2004), which is based on the 1987 version of the NAEYC's DAPs (Bredekamp, 1987) and is designed to assess everyday practices in a preschool classroom. The measure contains one global rating of DAP and 18 other items grouped conceptually into three subscales—Curriculum and Instruction, Classroom Management, and Interaction. A validation study by Lee Van Horn and Ramey (2004) found ADAPT to be an adequate measure of the 1997 NAEYC guidelines (Bredekamp & Copple, 1997).

Because program evaluation can have huge implications for a program's viability, and because choices about what aspects of a program should be evaluated and how to interpret the data obtained can become politicized, the National Forum on Early Childhood Program Evaluation (2007) developed a guide aimed at helping decision-makers become knowledgeable consumers of program evaluation information. The guide presents critical questions that should be asked in reviewing evaluation data and offers suggestions regarding what evidence to consider in answering each one. The questions shed light on the complexities of program evaluations and the decisions that may result from them, but the one most pertinent to a chapter on assessment is "How much impact did the program have?"

Guiding Principles for Preschool Assessment

There are several key principles that typically guide the efforts of those who aim to conduct high-quality preschool assessments. Among these guiding principles is the importance of ensuring that preschool assessments target the five domains of school readiness identified by the USDOE (2011): language and literacy development, cognition and general knowledge (including early mathematics and early scientific development), approaches toward learning, physical well-being and motor development, and social and emotional development. English Language Proficiency is an important domain to assess when working with children who are English Learners (United States Department of Health and Human Services & USDOE, 2016a). Assessments that consider all relevant domains of development are likely to provide the most comprehensive picture of a child's functioning. Although assessments generally aim to understand a child's needs or challenges, as mentioned previously, it is equally important to identify child and family strengths, as they can be used to facilitate progress and responses to interventions or treatments (NAEYC, 2009; NASP, 2015). Additionally, systematic data gathering in the natural environment, including parent/family and cultural variables and opportunities for learning (Bandel, Atkins-Burnett, Castro, Wulsin, & Putman, 2012), is a critical component of the assessment and intervention process.

Another guiding principle, advocated by multiple early childhood associations, is that preschool assessments should be conducted via an ecological approach that is aligned with early childhood standards, curricula, and instruction (United States Department of Education, Office of Elementary and Secondary Education, 2016) and incorporates multiple sources of information, using multiple methods (NAEYC, 2009) at multiple points in time. The most recent position statement of the NASP (2015) on early childhood services endorses the use of an MTSS framework for assessment and intervention that ensures formative assessment and data-based decision-making. The critical importance of using formative approaches to assessment, which typically involve the frequent use of low-stakes measures of a child's progress in attaining the skills they are being taught, warrants elaboration here. The rapid pace of development (Kelley & Melton, 1993), and the spurts and plateaus that occur during the first 5 years (Culbertson & Willis, 1993), necessitate repeated assessments to ensure that programming is appropriate for the child's unique developmental profile (Nagle, 2007).

Although data from formative assessments may be used as one source of information in a comprehensive diagnostic or eligibility evaluation, the primary purpose of formative assessment is to guide instruction and gauge children's responsiveness to interventions and progress toward goals (Race to the Top, 2011). As increasing numbers of schools adopt MTSS, there will likely be a shift away from diagnostic approaches toward greater reliance on formative processes. NASP also emphasizes the importance of ongoing collaboration among school- and community-based professionals and actively engaging family members to ensure that assessment and intervention are culturally and linguistically appropriate and sensitive to individual child and family needs. Like the NAEYC, NASP also encourages the use of multiple assessment methods that tap multiple informants and that include observations within the child's natural environments to ensure that assessment data are appropriately contextualized (NASP, 2015).

The necessities of ensuring that assessment processes actively engage the child's family and are culturally and linguistically appropriate are deeply intertwined. Although parent support and involvement in children's education and cultural and linguistic considerations are addressed more fully in subsequent chapters of this volume (by Manz et al. and by Ortiz, respectively), their central importance to preschool assessment and intervention justifies some additional attention here. Children develop within the context of their families, communities, and cultures, so assessment and intervention, if they are to be effective, must be sensitive and responsive to children's unique backgrounds and contexts, and family members must have opportunities to contribute meaningfully (NASP, 2015). The optimal assessment and intervention process would facilitate active parent engagement from the initial assessment planning stages through intervention selection, implementation, monitoring of progress, and follow-up.

Prior to conducting a formal diagnostic or eligibility assessment, it is important for the team to understand the family members' concerns about the child, their priorities for improvement, and existing resources and supports within the family and community (Benner & Grim, 2013). The first contact by a member of the team is often made by someone familiar to the family, such as a preschool teacher or another member of the child's early intervention team. That individual should explain in "real-world" language what will happen during and following the formal assessment (Geva & Wiener, 2015) and elicit the family's perspectives on the child's strengths and needs (Praetor & McAllister, 1995). This initial interaction can promote the family's trust and comfort surrounding the assessment process, which can enhance their commitment to the process and help ensure their meaningful involvement in subsequently implementing recommended interventions (Geva & Wiener, 2015). Prior to the first meeting, team members are advised to learn as much as they can about the family's unique characteristics, circumstances, and acculturation experiences.

In addition to establishing trust and eliciting the family's observations about the child's behaviors, the first contact provides an opportunity for the team member to explain the family's right to participate in the assessment and intervention procedures (Linder, 1993). The contacting team member also should seek to empower the family by emphasizing the importance of their input in helping the team understand the child's and family's strengths and needs and to select or develop appropriate and acceptable interventions (Nagle, 2007).

The initial contact also provides families the opportunity to express concerns not noted by the individual(s) making the referral, who may be unaware that additional problems exist (Nagle, 2007). Teachers and parents often perceive children's behaviors differently (Gagnon, Nagle, & Nickerson, 2007), and it is possible that behaviors of concern in the preschool setting do not occur with the same regularity in the home (Nagle, 2007).

Prior to the formal assessment session(s), evaluators should identify each team member, explain their roles, and describe the skills and abilities of the child that will be evaluated (Nagle, 2007). Doing so helps ensure that parents feel less overwhelmed and are more likely to suggest ways to engage the child and to identify activities or stimuli that might upset the child and disrupt the assessment.

At the completion of the assessment session, it is advisable for one or more members of the team to debrief the family member(s), providing an opportunity for them to ask questions and offer observations and insights regarding the assessment. When the team has compiled and integrated the results, they typically provide the family with an overview of their findings during a subsequent feedback meeting; using language that is easy for family members to understand is especially important at this stage. It is rare that parents understand the technical jargon and acronyms that are used in education—particularly special education—so it is critical for members of the team to avoid their use, as doing so may have a negative effect on parents' participation and relationship with the team (Weaver & Ouye, 2015).

The feedback meeting may be the first time the family has received a diagnosis or an explicit description of the child's challenges or prognosis, so the team should convey all information with sensitivity and compassion (Nagle, 2007) and remain responsive to the family's emotional reactions (Weaver & Ouye, 2015). Although sensitivity is important, it is equally important for team members to be straightforward and use accurate terminology regarding applicable diagnoses or IDEA disability categories, as this practice can help families accept a child's disability and allow them to participate fully in selecting or designing interventions (Nagle, 2007). Wright, Gronroos, Burkhartsmeyer and Johnson (2008) provide an excellent resource for teams to use as they prepare and deliver difficult feedback. Although the outdated term "mental retardation" should no longer be used when discussing an intellectual disability, the authors nonetheless provide valuable and practical information about key concepts and cultural considerations, as well as sample scripts for conducting difficult feedback meetings. Weaver and Ouye (2015) provide an additional resource in which they describe research on common meeting-related challenges and offer practical suggestions for improving meetings.

Although some professionals consider the feedback meeting to be the last step in the assessment process, it actually serves as a starting point for developing recommendations and identifying and selecting intervention strategies. The team should facilitate the family's understanding of the next steps in the process, which likely involve intervention planning, progress monitoring, and follow-up (Nagle, 2007). Teams must acknowledge that a family's unique characteristics and resources (e.g., income, time, education level, support, and primary language) influence each family member's ability to actively participate in assessment procedures and implement interventions or recommendations at home. Teams must carefully tailor recommendations that will fit with the child's and family's unique characteristics and circumstances. Incorporating the recommendations described here will enhance the likelihood that each family will feel like an integral part of the team and will remain effectively engaged throughout the assessment and intervention process.

A final guiding principle is that preschool assessments should be conducted by teams of professionals who work together to identify each child's and family's strengths, needs, and priorities. Young children with vulnerabilities and disabilities face a multitude of problems and often require a diverse range of services to meet their needs, necessitating a team-based approach to assessment and intervention. Such team-based approaches typically involve professionals from different disciplines (e.g., education, nursing, psychology, physical therapy, occupational therapy, speech-language pathology, audiology, social work, and nutrition) who have experience with or could provide support to the child as needed (Bondurant-Utz, 1994; Nagle, 2007). The early intervention literature has identified three models of team functioning that differ considerably in terms of the extent of interaction among the disciplines: multidisciplinary, interdisciplinary, and transdisciplinary.

Multidisciplinary Teams

The multidisciplinary approach is consistent with the medical model, in which professionals from each discipline carry out independent assessments of the child focused on their areas of expertise (Benner & Grim, 2013), with little interaction among team members (Nagle, 2007). Assessment results typically are shared with the family by each team member individually, necessitating numerous, time-consuming meetings in which results and recommendations may be redundant, confusing, or conflicting, and families are left to integrate the results and recommendations on their own. Another variant of the multidisciplinary approach calls for one professional to integrate all of the specialists' results, formulate recommendations, and share those with the family during one meeting. In that situation, that professional's individual perspectives or biases may alter the information that is shared (Benner & Grim, 2013). Neither of these approaches is optimal, as both lack essential collaboration among professionals. It is important to note that although the term "multidisciplinary" is commonly used to describe early childhood assessments, it actually only applies to the approach described above.

Interdisciplinary Teams

The interdisciplinary approach is more integrated and unified than the multidisciplinary approach, as there is a strong emphasis on communication and consultation among team members (Guralnick, 2000) as well as group decision-making and goal setting. Although professionals conduct discipline-specific assessments independently, intervention plans with common goals across disciplines are collaboratively developed, parents are part of the team, and the results are formally shared with the family (Nagle, 2007), resulting in a more consolidated view of the child's and family's strengths and needs. The interdisciplinary model represents a truly interactive team approach (Guralnick, 2000), but communication difficulties can arise if team members lack familiarity with terminology used by professionals from other disciplines (Benner & Grim, 2013), and disagreement about intervention priorities may emerge (Nagle, 2007).

Transdisciplinary Teams

Transdisciplinary teams also consist of individual specialists, but the majority of the assessment is conducted in a team format (Benner & Grim, 2013), thereby maximizing communication and collaboration among the various disciplines (King, Tucker, Desserud, & Shillington, 2009). Teams using this model often engage in *arena* assessments, in which one or two team members, which may include parents, interact with the child in a naturalistic manner while the other team members observe the child's behavior and interactions and record their findings across all developmental areas designated in the assessment plan (Nagle, 2007). Rather than having each professional conduct an assessment independently, they may take turns engaging the child in tasks relevant to their respective domains or simply observe while one team member interacts with the child and attempts to elicit behaviors and actions that shed light on important aspects of the child's functioning. One advantage of this approach is that a child's initiation of or response to a single activity may provide information of interest to more than one specialist. For example, when a child plays with blocks, the occupational therapist observes the child's fine motor skills, the physical therapist observes torso control, and the speech therapist observes the child's babbling or communication with the examiner/facilitator (Nagle, 2007). Another advantage of this approach is that the parents can suggest ways to help the child engage more effectively and can offer insight about how typical the observed behaviors are for the child, thereby enhancing the accuracy of the data gathered by team members.

Although this approach can be time-consuming for the team, completing the assessment in one session saves time for the family and reduces stress for the child. Advocates of play-based assessment (e.g., Kelly-Vance & Ryalls, 2014, this volume) argue that, because play comes naturally to most young children, it is a more developmentally appropriate and authentic context than conventional, standardized tests for assessing a young child's functioning. They also argue that play-based assessment is likely to be more palatable and more readily understood by parents and teachers, which may enhance their adherence to the interventions and treatments that are derived from assessment results.

Assessment Methods and Procedures

School-based practitioners who engage in team-based problem-solving activities, such as RTI and MTSS, may be familiar with the RIOT/ICEL matrix, which serves as an organizing framework for designing assessments in which data are collected from multiple sources regarding a range of factors that influence student learning (Christ, 2008; Christ & Arañas, 2014; Wright, 2010). Evaluators who do not work in the schools would benefit from knowledge of this system, as their assessment results are likely to be used by school-based teams who work within the problem-solving context. RIOT is an acronym for *Review, Interview, Observe,* and *Test*, which are the multiple methods that are typically used in assessments (Christ, 2008). One important reason to use multiple methods is that it minimizes bias from any particular source (Wright, 2010). ICEL stands for *Instruction, Curriculum, Environment,* and *Learner*, which serve as sources of assessment information (Christ, 2008; Christ & Arañas, 2014). Teams can use one or more of the RIOT methods to assess multiple ICEL factors that are relevant to the child's context.

The comprehensive nature of the RIOT/ICEL matrix provides a useful framework that promotes a multi-method, multi-informant, ecologically based approach to assessment and intervention, and we encourage assessment teams to use it as a guide for selecting assessment methods and sources of information to create a comprehensive evaluation. The ICEL factors, in particular, can remind teams to consider environmental variables that exist *outside* the child (instruction, curriculum, environment), instead of making the child (i.e., learner) the focal point of the assessment. Evaluators are encouraged to keep in mind that the ICE factors can be modified to promote children's learning, whereas the L reflects traits and characteristics *within* the child that are more fixed and typically only modifiable through medical means (Christ, 2008). Christ reminds us that "the only way to change the learner is to change the task and setting demands" (p. 168).

Instead of asking the question, "What is wrong with this child?" evaluators are encouraged to focus on, "What can we change in this child's environment to optimize their development and promote their success?"

To elucidate the use of the RIOT/ICEL framework in early childhood assessment, we offer Table 1.1, which provides an example of what the RIOT/ICEL matrix might include when a team is assessing a preschooler. As the table illustrates, each ICEL factor may be evaluated by one or more of the RIOT methods. Teams should consider all of the ICEL factors and, for each one, decide which source of RIOT information is available and relevant to the child's characteristics and circumstances. The idea is not to use all RIOT methods for each ICEL factor but to be as thorough as possible in planning and conducting the assessment. Teams also may assign members to focus on specific elements of the matrix. Although the complete matrix will not apply to all young children, it is a valuable "hands-on" tool that can help teams collect the most relevant and ecologically valid information about a child. An in-depth discussion of the assessment methods used in the RIOT/ICEL framework is beyond the scope of this chapter; interested readers are encouraged to consult the following and other resources for additional information: Christ (2008), Christ and Arañas (2014), and Wright (2010). One element of the model that does warrant elaboration here, however, is the *Test* category.

Numerous types of tests are used in preschool assessments, including standardized, norm-referenced measures of cognitive abilities, language skills, and pre-academic or school readiness skills, as well as curriculum-based measures and rating scales. Norm-referenced tests and curriculum-based measures are administered *directly* to a child, using standardized procedures. Rating scales are completed by individuals familiar with the child (e.g., caregivers, teachers) and provide *indirect* measures of individual traits (e.g., temperament) and developmental competencies or skills (e.g., social competence, adaptive behaviors). Some interview measures provide norm-referenced scores as well, but we will not discuss those here.

Rating Scales

Rating scales are indirect measures of children's skills, characteristics, and behaviors (e.g., temperament, adaptive skills, social competence), in which individuals familiar with the child provide ratings on a scale (e.g., *Always; Sometimes*) about the child's behavior over a specified period of time (Campbell & Hammond, 2014). They provide important sources of data and are frequently used in school and clinical settings; they may be administered as part of initial screening to identify concerns and help determine whether further assessment is needed, or they may be one component of a comprehensive evaluation. Rating scales are useful for understanding a child's strengths and weaknesses, identifying targets for interventions, and monitoring progress, and the use of familiar respondents helps illustrate the child's behaviors as they occur in their natural environment (Campbell &

Table 1.1 RIOT/ICEL Matrix Applied to Preschool Assessment

<table>
<tr><td rowspan="2"></td><td rowspan="2"></td><td colspan="4" align="center">ASSESSMENT METHODS</td></tr>
<tr><td>Review</td><td>Interview</td><td>Observe</td><td>Test</td></tr>
<tr>
<td rowspan="3">SOURCES OF INFOR-MATION</td>
<td>Instruction</td>
<td>• Developmental appropriateness of lesson plans, if enrolled in an instructional setting
• Temporal (time-of-day, length) appropriateness of lesson plans, if enrolled in an instructional setting</td>
<td>• Family members/teachers/caregivers regarding type, timing, and pace of typical teaching/learning experiences and opportunities to respond</td>
<td>• In home, school, and care settings to witness typical teaching/learning experiences, opportunities to respond</td>
<td>• Systematic manipulation of type/pace/length/timing of teaching/learning experiences, opportunities to respond and practice</td>
</tr>
<tr>
<td>Curriculum</td>
<td>• Scope, sequence, developmental, and sensory appropriateness of instructional materials, if enrolled in an instructional setting</td>
<td>• Family members/teachers/caregivers regarding developmental and sensory appropriateness of content and organization of teaching/learning experiences</td>
<td>• In home, school, and care settings to ascertain developmental and sensory appropriateness of the content and organization of teaching/learning experiences</td>
<td>• Systematic manipulation of developmental level and sensory aspects of the content and organization of teaching/learning experiences</td>
</tr>
</table>

Environment	• Dimensions and layout of caregiving/instructional space • Formal policies regarding behavior guidelines/rules, consequences for desired behaviors and infractions	• Family members/teachers/caregivers regarding physical setting and emotional climate, informal policies regarding behavior guidelines/rules, consequences for desired behaviors and infractions, criteria for success	• Size and arrangement of space relative to number and mobility/sensory needs of enrolled children • Appropriateness of furniture, work/play materials (e.g., scissors, crayons, puzzles) • Timing and nature of antecedents and consequences of behaviors of concern	• Systematic manipulation of arrangement of space • Systematic manipulation of timing and nature of antecedents and consequences of behaviors of concern, criteria for success
Learner	• Medical and educational records • Reports of prior evaluations • Work samples	• Family members/teachers/caregivers regarding their observations of the child's behavior, characteristics, strengths, and needs	• The child's behavior and characteristics to ascertain strengths and needs, responses to consequences and success/failure	• Using formal and informal measures to establish strengths and needs across relevant areas of development

Adapted from Christ, T. J., & Arañas, Y. A. (2014). Best practices in problem analysis. In P. L. Harrison & A. Thomas (Eds.) *Best Practices in School Psychology: Data-Based and Collaborative Decision Making*. (pp. 87–98). Bethesda, MD: NASP. Copyright 2014 by the National Association of School Psychologists, Bethesda, MD. Adapted with permission of the publisher. www.nasponline.org

Hammond, 2014). When they are norm-referenced, rating scales indicate how a child's behaviors compare to age-level expectations. It is common to find differences between the ratings provided by different respondents (Gagnon et al., 2007), and examiners should give equal consideration to the results from each respondent. Rater differences can help contextualize the child's behaviors, as some problems may occur more at home than at school, or vice versa. For comprehensive information about behavior rating scales, we refer the reader to Campbell and Hammond (2014).

Curriculum-based Measures

For young children enrolled in formal educational programs, curriculum-based measures (CBMs) are often used to inform academic interventions and track student progress toward academic goals. CBMs are relatively inexpensive, quick to administer, and sensitive to small changes in skills, and in some cases they allow for normative comparisons of a child's performance. CBM data can be presented in graphic form, which may be more easily understood by parents and teachers than standardized scores (McLane, n. d.). Because CBMs are unlikely to be appropriate or available for young children not enrolled in formal educational programs, standardized, norm-referenced tests may represent a more viable option, and they can provide useful data about a child's developmental level.

Standardized, Norm-Referenced Tests

Although current trends have seen decreases in their use, early childhood assessments commonly include standardized, norm-referenced tests (Benner & Grim, 2013), and they likely will continue to be used (Ortiz, 2014). These tests are administered directly to a child by an examiner in a one-on-one setting, using procedures and scoring methods that are standardized (i.e., the same for every child who takes the test). Scores on these tests compare a child's performance to that of other same-age children who make up the norm group.

Controversy exists over the appropriateness of individually administered, standardized, norm-referenced testing with preschool children. Bagnato et al. (2010) describe these *conventional* tests as highly structured, scripted procedures that are administered in a contrived situation in order to obtain normative scores for diagnosis. They contend that these procedures are "wasteful in time, effort, and usefulness" (p. 4), rely on standardized procedures that may interfere with rapport (National Research Council, 2008), may be ill-suited for young children's limited attention spans and activity levels, and may fail to reflect the rapid development that characterizes early childhood (Nagle, 2007).

As described below, the psychometric qualities of some tests are less than desirable for use with preschoolers, and they can be quite expensive and lengthy to administer and require extensive examiner training. McBride, Dumont, and Willis (n.d.) provide an informative, comprehensive overview of issues involved in preschool assessment, including a "Top 10 Problems with Normed Achievement Tests for Young Children" that evaluators are encouraged to consider. Using conventional tests with English Language Learners and other children from non-dominant cultures may compound these issues. We encourage the reader to consult the chapter by Ortiz in this volume for a comprehensive examination of issues related to the assessment of culturally and linguistically diverse populations.

When selecting and using any type of measure in preschool assessment, but particularly where tests are concerned, the examiner is accountable for ensuring that the measure chosen is *psychometrically sound*, which refers to how reliably and accurately the tool measures what it is purported to measure (Cohen & Swerdlik, 2018). All aspects of psychometric quality, including reliability, adequacy of the norm sample (if norm-referenced), and validity for the intended uses of the measure, are applicable to every type of preschool measure (e.g., interviews; observational tools; standardized, norm-referenced tests; and rating scales). Comprehensive discussions of these psychometric features can be found in any textbook on psychological tests and measurement (e.g., Cohen & Swerdlik, 2018; Salkind, 2018), and a discussion on the application of these features is found in this volume (Engler & Alfonso). Two psychometric features of standardized, norm-referenced tests, however, deserve particular attention in any discussion of preschool measures: *test floors* and *item gradients*. In simple terms, the concept of a *test floor* refers to the degree to which a measure has enough easy items to yield meaningful scores at the lower extreme. If a child were to complete just one item on a test (or subtest) correctly, that child's performance ought to yield a very low standard score. In more technical terms, a test (or subtest) can be judged to have an adequate floor if a summation of all raw scores of 1 (across all of the contributing subtests) yields a standard score that is at least two standard deviations below the mean for each composite standard score and for the test's total standard score (Bracken, 1987). The need for adequate test floors can be illustrated easily within the domain of cognitive ability assessment; a test used with young children must yield scores that meaningfully distinguish between the performance of typically developing children and those with intellectual disabilities (Nagle, 2007), as defined by IDEA and the American Association on Intellectual and Developmental Disabilities (Schalock et al., 2010). When a test has a poor floor, it is likely to yield inflated scores, which may lead to erroneous decisions (Bracken & Walker, 1997). In preschool assessment, where the objective is often to determine whether or not a child is experiencing a cognitive or general developmental delay, such errors are especially likely to be of the *false negative* variety. The evaluator might fail to identify a child's developmental delay, resulting in denial of access to needed services. *Item gradient* refers to how much a child's standard score changes as a function of the child's success or failure on just one item of the test (Bracken, 1987). If a child's performance on a single item results in a substantial change in the child's standard score, then the test (or subtest) has an inadequate item gradient. Such a measure may not be sufficiently sensitive to subtle differences in children's skills or abilities assessed by the measure. As the number of non-redundant items within a test (or subtest) increases, so does its item gradient and its resulting sensitivity to differences in children's performance (Williams, Sando, & Soles, 2014). We must evaluate test floors and item gradients in concert with each other and in relation to the mean of the test. For a subtest with a mean of ten and a standard deviation of three, the number of items between the test floor and the mean should be at least six for each age or grade level for which standard scores are produced. In other words, there must be at least three raw score points within each standard deviation of change in standard score between the floor and the mean. Likewise, for a test with a mean of 100 and a standard deviation of 15, the number of items between the test floor and the mean should be at least ten for each age or grade level (i.e., at least five raw score points within each standard deviation) (Bracken, 1987; Flanagan & Alfonso, 1995; Rathvon, 2004).

In part because of these psychometric issues, many experts and scholars in early childhood assessment eschew the use of conventional tests and advocate for the use of *authentic* assessment with young children (Bagnato et al., 2010; Bagnato & Yeh Ho, 2006; Neisworth & Bagnato, 2004). They contend that conventional testing is detrimental to young children, as it may lead to undesirable outcomes, such as premature assignment of disability labels or inappropriate placements in special education programs. They consider conventional tests invalid for use with young children and misaligned with the purposes of early childhood assessment and intervention. Critics also state that these tests assess discrete behaviors that do not promote future learning and performance (e.g., completing timed puzzles) and are not contextualized in children's real-world environments (e.g., home, classroom). Preschool children, they argue, are more likely to demonstrate their abilities through play activities than by performing scripted tasks in contrived, one-on-one testing situations involving what critics contend are antiquated methods.

Authentic assessment is an ongoing, systematic process of collecting data about children's learning and development through direct observations and ratings of their daily activities and functional behaviors in their natural environments (Bagnato et al., 2010; Bagnato & Yeh Ho, 2006; LeeKeenan & Chin Ponte, 2018), and it is considered a preferable alternative to conventional testing. Proponents consider this type of assessment to be developmentally appropriate, in part because individuals with whom the child is familiar and comfortable conduct it and it occurs within a child's natural environment, which is the actual context for their learning and development. Authentic assessment provides information about behaviors that are important for both current and future learning and development, and, because it is ongoing, it ensures formative monitoring of the child's developing skills and competencies. The reader is referred to an article by Bagnato and Yeh Ho (2006), which contains a table outlining operational features of conventional and authentic testing.

Supporters of standardized tests contend that when administered as one part of a comprehensive assessment and not considered the primary source of information about a child, they may provide valuable information (National Research Council, 2008) that can be used to help tailor interventions to children's unique characteristics (Mascolo, Alfonso, & Flanagan, 2014). Bracken (1994) has advised that instead of viewing conventional and alternative procedures as mutually exclusive, practitioners would benefit from viewing these methods as complementary. When used in conjunction with data from record reviews, observations, and interviews, *conventional* tests may help capture the multifaceted nature of young children's development and contribute to a holistic view of a child's strengths and needs. Teams should be flexible and creative when designing assessments to ensure that they capture the best representation of the child's functioning. Evaluators and teams should ask themselves the question, "Which methods will help us understand this child and know how to promote the best outcomes for them?" When designing assessments, preschool teams should keep in mind the eight standards for developmentally appropriate assessment outlined by Bagnato and colleagues (2010): *acceptability, authenticity, collaboration, evidence, multifactors, sensitivity, universality,* and *utility.* Details regarding what each standard entails can be found in the referenced article.

Professional Training in Preschool Assessment

Preschool assessment is a complex, multifaceted, and often challenging process requiring a broad range of examiner skills to meet the purposes of screening, diagnosis, monitoring child progress, intervention selection and design, and program evaluation (Paget & Nagle, 1986). Meisels and Provence (1989) posited that assessors of very young children require extensive and comprehensive training. Because psychologists and other evaluators involved in preschool assessment have numerous responsibilities, such as interpreting universal screening data; consulting with teachers, families, and service providers in the community; and using progress monitoring data to inform intervention effectiveness (NASP, 2015), a broad range of content and training experiences is recommended (Nagle, 2007). In order to meet the challenges of preschool service delivery, professionals need specialized training that goes beyond the usual preparation for assessment of school-age children. Thus, it is incumbent upon training programs to provide the requisite coursework and field experiences, such that their graduates can demonstrate mastery of the knowledge and skills needed to plan and complete comprehensive evaluations that accurately identify the strengths and needs of children and families.

Preschool psychologists should be able to evaluate the psychometric properties of assessment tools (Bracken, 1987; Engler & Alfonso, this volume; Flanagan & Alfonso, 1995) and be especially aware of the issues and potential problems associated with their use with preschoolers and children from diverse cultural or linguistic backgrounds (Benner & Grim, 2013). Evaluators should be familiar with the many tests and methods that are available and be able to select appropriate measures, plan and carry out assessments, integrate and interpret the results, and use the findings to guide intervention efforts. It is important that training programs prepare future practitioners to make well-informed, ethical choices about their use of tests, including knowledge of when and how to utilize testing accommodations, including testing-the-limits (Benner & Grim, 2013).

In terms of content, training should include a special focus on typical and atypical development, with emphasis on infancy through early childhood, developmental disabilities, biological and ecological correlates of risk and resilience, preschool service delivery models for typically developing children and children with disabilities and developmental delays, and appropriate curricula for preschoolers with disabling conditions. Given the central importance of the family in preschool programming, family systems theory, family life cycles, child-family interactions, and family structure also are critical curricular components (Meisels & Provence, 1989). Within this area, it is essential that psychologists develop the skills to build successful relationships with families throughout the assessment and intervention planning process. It is likewise important that psychologists working in preschool settings develop a firm understanding of the contributions of other disciplines within early childhood settings. In order to cultivate the knowledge and skills required for future collaboration and inter- or trans-disciplinary functioning, training should include deliberate and extensive exposure to the discipline-specific skills of other professionals involved in early intervention programs (Klein & Campbell, 1990; Mowder, 1996). Furthermore, it is also imperative that training programs foster development of the requisite skills for establishing collaborative relationships with community-based professionals and agencies and for enlisting their support for children and families.

Another essential goal of training is the development of cultural competence. In order to engage in best practice with children and families from various cultures, members of assessment teams should be knowledgeable about the processes of acculturation, language development, and second language acquisition (United States Department of Health and Human Services & USDOE, 2016b) and the ways in which these factors influence performance on conventional, standardized tests (NASP, 2015). When interpreters are involved, evaluators must become knowledgeable about how and when it is appropriate to engage them.

Since the primary focus of preschool assessment is to inform and guide intervention efforts, training in evidence-based interventions is critical. Team members should know how to access and evaluate interventions and tailor them to individual children, using existing child, family, school, and community resources to the maximum extent possible. Evaluators who do not work in the schools would benefit from training in MTSS, including universal screening and progress monitoring, as well as state and federal legislation that informs assessment procedures and eligibility decisions. To enhance their collaboration with community-based professionals, school-based practitioners should be familiar with diagnostic systems, such as the *Diagnostic and Statistical Manual of Mental Disorders, Fifth Edition* (DSM-5; American Psychiatric Association, 2013), that are used in non-educational contexts.

A final area of training, and one that may be lacking in many non-doctoral training programs, is program evaluation. Psychologists involved in evaluating the impact of preschool programs must be familiar with the methods for doing so, and training in strategic planning, systems-level consultation, organizational psychology, and applied research methods would provide good preparation for program evaluators. As described previously, the ten criteria recommended by the NIEER (Friedman-Krauss et al., 2019) may provide useful guidelines for content that should be included in program evaluation courses or professional development programs.

Conclusion

In this introductory chapter, we endeavored to provide the reader with an overview of the historical context of preschool psychoeducational assessment, including pertinent legislation, regulations, and political influences that have affected both the demand for preschool assessment and the various ways in which it has been conceptualized and conducted. We also have introduced the reader to the key purposes of assessment—screening, diagnosis and eligibility, individual planning and monitoring, and program evaluation—and to several principles that, taken together, form a guiding framework for preschool assessment. Proponents of these principles advocate for team-based assessments conducted from an ecological perspective, employing multiple methods, tapping multiple sources, and engaging the child and the child's family in meaningful ways. We have concluded the chapter with an overview of assessment methods and procedures that introduces the "RIOT/ICEL matrix," a framework for psychoeducational assessment that prescribes the use of multiple assessment strategies (i.e., *R*eview, *I*nterview, *O*bservation, *T*esting) to examine multiple factors that may be affecting a child's progress and performance (i.e., *I*nstruction, *C*urriculum, *E*nvironment, and *L*earner). Due to its particular centrality to this volume, we have further explicated the **Testing** component of the matrix, including a review of key psychometric considerations and a discussion of the relative merits and usefulness of conventional, norm-referenced tests versus more authentic methods of assessment. Much of what follows in this volume will serve to elaborate and clarify what we have introduced here.

References

American Academy of Pediatrics. (2017). *Screening tool finder.* Retrieved from https://screeningtime.org/star-center/#/screening-tools#top

American Academy of Pediatrics. (2019). *Recommendations for preventive pediatric health care.* Retrieved from www.aap.org/en-us/documents/periodicity_schedule.pdf

American Educational Research Association, American Psychological Association, National Council on Measurement in Education, & Joint Committee on Standards for Educational and Psychological Testing (U.S.). (2014). Standards for educational and psychological testing.

American Psychiatric Association. (2013). *Diagnostic and statistical manual of mental disorders* (5th ed.). Washington, DC: Author.

Bagnato, S. J., Goins, D. D., Pretti-Frontczak, K., & Neisworth, J. T. (2014). Authentic assessment as "best practice" for early childhood intervention: National consumer social validity research. *Topics in Early Childhood Special Education, 34,* 116–127. doi:10.1177/0271121414523652

Bagnato, S. J., Neisworth, J. T., & Pretti-Frontczak, K. (2010). *LINKing authentic assessment and early childhood intervention: Best measures for best practices* (2nd ed.). Baltimore, MD: Paul H. Brookes.

Bagnato, S. J. & Yeh Ho, H. (2006). High-stakes testing with preschool children: Violation of professional standards for evidence-based practice in early childhood intervention. *KEDI Journal of Educational Policy, 3,* 23–43. Retrieved from http://eds.b.ebscohost.com.proxy006.nclive.org/eds/pdfviewer/pdfviewer?vid=2&sid=33c1c1a7-ba89-48d9-b498-2cb9baa25e9c%40sessionmgr101

Bandel, E., Atkins-Burnett, S., Castro, D. C., Wulsin, C. S., & Putman, M. (2012). *Examining the use of language and literacy assessments with young dual language learners. Research report #1. Center for Early Care and Education Research-Dual Language Learners (CECER-DLL).* Chapel Hill, NC: The University of North Carolina, Frank Porter Graham Child Development Institute. Retrieved from www.researchgate.net/publication/260163604_Examining_the_Use_of_Language_and_Literacy_Assessments_with_Young_Dual_Language_Learners

Benner, S. M. & Grim, J. C. (2013). *Assessment of young children with special needs: A context-based approach,* 2nd ed.. New York, NY: Routledge.

Bohrnstedt, G., Kitmitto, S., Ogut, B., Sherman, D., & Chan, D. (2015). School composition and the black–white achievement gap (NCES 2015-018). U.S. Department of Education, Washington, DC: National Center for Education Statistics. Retrieved [date] from http://nces.ed.gov/pubsearch

Bondurant-Utz, J. A. (1994). The team process. In J. A. Bondurant-Utz & L. B. Luciano (Eds.), *A practical guide to infant and preschool assessment in special education* (pp. 59–71). Needham Heights: Allyn & Bacon.

Bracken, B. A. (1987). Limitations of preschool instruments and standards for minimal levels of technical adequacy. *Journal of Psychoeducational Assessment, 4,* 313–326. doi:10.1177/073428298700500402

Bracken, B. A. (1994). Advocating for effective preschool assessment practices. A comment on Bagnato and Neisworth. *School Psychology Quarterly, 9,* 103–108.

Bracken, B. A. & Walker, K. C. (1997). The utility of intelligence tests for preschool children. In D. P. Flanagan, J. L. Genshaft, & P. C. Harrison (Eds.), *Contemporary intellectual assessment: Theories, tests, and issues* (pp. 484–502). New York, NY: Guilford.

Bredekamp, S. (1987). *Developmentally appropriate practice in early childhood programs serving children from birth through age 8 (expanded edition)*. Washington, DC: National Association for the Education of Young Children.

Bredekamp, S. & Copple, C. (Eds.). (1997). *Developmentally appropriate practice in early childhood programs (revised edition)*. Washington, DC: National Association for the Education of Young Children.

Bricker, D., Capt, B., & Pretti-Frontczak, K. (2002). *Assessment, Evaluation, and Programming System for Infants and Children* (2nd ed.). Baltimore, MD: Brookes Publishing.

Campbell, J. M. & Hammond, R. K. (2014). Best practices in rating scale assessment of children's behavior. In P. L. Harrison & A. Thomas (Eds.), *Best practices in school psychology: Data-based and collaborative decision making* (pp. 287–304). Bethesda, MD: National Association of School Psychologists.

Christ, T. (2008). Best practices in problem analysis. In A. Thomas & J. Grimes (Eds.), *Best practices in school psychology V, Volume 2: Data-based decision making and accountability* (pp. 159–176). Bethesda, MD: National Association of School Psychologists.

Christ, T. J. & Arañas, Y. A. (2014). Best practices in problem analysis. In P. L. Harrison & A. Thomas (Eds.), *Best practices in school psychology: Data-based and collaborative decision making* (pp. 87–98). Bethesda, MD: NASP.

Cohen, R. J. & Swerdlik, M. E. (2018). *Psychological testing and assessment: An introduction to tests and measurement* (9th ed.). New York, NY: McGraw-Hill Education.

Colorado Department of Education. (2015). What is MTSS? Retrieved from www.cde.state.co.us/mtss/whatismtss

Culbertson, J. L. & Willis, D. J. (1993). Introduction to testing young children. In J. L. Culbertson & D. J. Willis (Eds.), *Testing young children: A reference guide for developmental, psychoeducational, and psychosocial assessments* (pp. 1–10). Austin, TX: Pro-Ed.

Division for Early Childhood of the Council for Exceptional Children, National Association for the Education of Young Children, & National Head Start Association. (2013). *Frameworks for response to intervention in early childhood: Description and implications*. Missoula, MT, Washington, DC and Alexandria, VA: Author.

Division for Early Childhood. (2014). DEC recommended practices in early intervention/early childhood special education 2014. Retrieved from www.dec-sped.org/recommendedpractices

Emmons, M. R. & Alfonso, V. C. (2005). A critical review of the technical characteristics of current preschool screening batteries. *Journal of Psychoeducational Assessment, 23*, 111–127.

Flanagan, D. P. & Alfonso, V. C. (1995). A critical review of the technical characteristics of new and recently revised intelligence tests for preschool children. *Journal of Psychoeducational Assessment, 13*, 66–90.

Friedman-Krauss, A. H., Barnett, W. S., Garver, K. A., Hodges, K. S., Weisenfeld, G. G., & DiCrecchio, N. (2019). The state of preschool 2018: State preschool yearbook. National Institute for Early Education Research. Rutgers, the State University of New Jersey. Retrieved from http://nieer.org/wp-content/uploads/2019/04/YB2018_Full-ReportR2.pdf

Fuchs, L. S. (1995). Incorporating curriculum-based measurement into the eligibility decision-making process: A focus on treatment validity and student growth. *Paper presented for the National Academy of Sciences Workshop on Alternatives to IQ Testing*. Washington, DC.

Gagnon, S. G., Nagle, R. J., & Nickerson, A. B. (2007). Parent and teacher ratings of peer interactive play and social emotional development of preschool children at risk. *Journal of Early Intervention, 29*, 228–242. Retrieved from http://eds.b.ebsco host.com.proxy006.nclive.org/eds/pdfviewer/pdfviewer?vid=0&sid=5273e9ee-b4e9-4682-91a5-d2d11d2d56ff%40pdc-v-sessmgr03

Geva, E., & Wiener, J. (2015). *Psychological Assessment of Culturally and Linguistically Diverse Children and Adolescents: A Practitioner's Guide*, pp. 61-84. New York: NY: Springer Publishing.

Gresham, F. M. (2002). Responsiveness to intervention: An alternative approach to the identification of learning disabilities. In R. Bradley, L. Danielson, & D. Hallahan (Eds.), *Identification of learning disabilities: Research to practice* (pp. 467–519). Mahwah, NJ: Lawrence Erlbaum.

Guralnick, M. J. (2000). Interdisciplinary team assessment for young children: Purposes and processes. In M. J. Guralnick (Ed.), *Interdisciplinary clinical assessment of young children with developmental disabilities* (pp. 3–15). Baltimore, MD: Paul H. Brookes.

Hemphill, F. C. & Vanneman, A. (2011). Achievement Gaps: How Hispanic and White Students in Public Schools Perform in Mathematics and Reading on the National Assessment of Educational Progress (NCES 2011-459). National Center for Education Statistics, Institute of Education Sciences, U.S. Department of Education. Washington, DC. Retrieved from http://nces.ed.gov/pubsearch

Hojnoski, R. & Floyd, R. (2004). *Individual growth and development indicators of early numeracy*. St. Paul, MN: Early Learning Labs, Inc.

Kelley, M. P. & Melton, G. B. (1993). Ethical and legal issues. In J. L. Culbertson & D. J. Willis (Eds.), *Testing young children: A reference guide for developmental, psychoeducational, and psychosocial assessments* (pp. 408–426). Austin, TX: Pro-Ed.

Kelly-Vance, L. & Ryalls, B. O. (2014). Best practices in play assessment and intervention. In P. L. Harrison & A. Thomas (Eds.), *Best practices in school psychology: Data-based and collaborative decision making* (pp. 261–272). Bethesda, MD: NASP.

Kilpatrick, D. (2015). *Essentials of assessing, preventing, and overcoming reading difficulties*. Hoboken, NJ: Wiley.

King, G., Tucker, M., Desserud, S., & Shillington, M. (2009). The application of a transdisciplinary model for early intervention services. *Infants & Young Children, 22*(3), 211–223.

Klein, N. K., & Campbell, P. (1990). Preparing personnel to serve at-risk and disabled infants, toddlers, and preschoolers. In B. A. Bracken (Ed.), *Handbook of early childhood intervention* (pp. 679–699). New York, NY: Cambridge University Press.

Knoblauch, B. & McLane, K. (1999). An overview of the individuals with disabilities education act amendments of 1997 (P.L. 105-17): Update 1999. ERIC Digest E576. ERIC Identifier: ED433668. Retrieved from https://files.eric.ed.gov/fulltext/ED433668.pdf

LeeKeenan, D. & Chin Ponte, I. (2018). Meaningful assessment and documentation: How directors can support teaching and learning. *Young Children, 73*, 87–92.

Lee Van Horn, M., & Ramey, S. L. (2004). A new measure for assessing developmentally appropriate practices in early elementary school, a developmentally appropriate practice template. *Early Childhood Research Quarterly, 19*. DOI: 10.1016/j.ecresq.2004.10.002

Lei, P., Wu, Q., DiPerna, J. C., & Morgan, P. L. (2009). Developing short forms of the EARLI numeracy measures: Comparison of item selection methods. *Educational and Psychological Measurement, 69*(5), 825–842.

Linder, T. W. (1993). *Transdisciplinary play-based assessment: A functional approach to working with young children.* Baltimore, MD: Paul H. Brookes.

Lonigan, C. J. & Wilson, S. B. (2008). *Technical report on the Get Ready to Read! Revised screening tool: Psychometrics and normative information.* New York, NY: National Center for Learning Disabilities.

Losardo, A. & Syverson, A. N. (2011). *Alternative approaches to assessing young children* (2nd ed.). Baltimore, MD: Paul H. Brookes.

Mackrides, P. S. & Ryherd, S. J. (2011). Screening for developmental delay. *American Family Physician, 84*(5), 544–549. Retrieved from: www.aafp.org/afp/2011/0901/p544.pdf

Marston, D. (2001). A functional and intervention-based assessment approach to establishing discrepancy for students with learning disabilities. *Paper written for the Office of Special Education Programs, U.S. Department of Education and presented at the OSEP's LD Summit conference.* Washington, DC.

Mascolo, J. T., Alfonso, V. C., & Flanagan, D. P. (2014). *Essentials of planning, selecting, and tailoring interventions for unique learners.* Hoboken, NJ: John Wiley & Sons.

McBride, G., Dumont, R., & Willis, J. (n.d.). Preschool assessment: (3-5). My school psychologist: A site for school psychologists and special education professionals. Retrieved from www.myschoolpsychology.com/testing-information/preschool-assessment-3-to-5/#general-information

McConnell, S., Bradfield, T., Wackerle-Hollman, A., & Rodriguez, M. (2012). *Individual growth and development indicators of early literacy* (2nd ed.). St. Paul, MN: Early Learning Labs, Inc.

McLane, K. (n.d.). What is curriculum-based measurement and what does it mean for my child? National Center on Student Progress Monitoring. Retrieved from https://osepideasthatwork.org/sites/default/files/12%20-%20What%20is%20CBM%20and%20What%20Does%20it%20Mean%20to%20My%20Child.pdf

Meisels, S.J., & Provence, S. (1989). Screening and assessment: Guidelines for identifying young disabled and developmentally vulnerable children and their families. Washington, DC: National Center for Clinical Infant Programs.

Missall, K. & Roberts, D. (2014). *Profile of preschool learning and development readiness (Pro-LADR).* St. Paul, MN: Early Learning Labs, Inc. www.myigdis.com

Mowder, B. A. (1996). Preparing school psychologists. In D. Bricker & A. Widerstrom (Eds.), *Preparing personnel to work with infants and young children and their families: A team approach* (pp. 217–230). Baltimore, MD: Paul H. Brooks.

Nagle, R. J. (2007). Issues in preschool assessment. In B. A. Bracken & R. J. Nagle (Eds.), *Psychoeducational assessment of preschool children* (4th ed., pp. 29–48). Mahwah, NJ: Lawrence Erlbaum Associates.

National Association for the Education of Young Children. (2009). Developmentally appropriate practice in early childhood programs serving children from birth through age 8. Retrieved from www.naeyc.org/sites/default/files/globally-shared/downloads/PDFs/resources/position-statements/PSDAP.pdf

National Association for the Education of Young Children, & National Association of Early Childhood Specialists in State Departments of Education. (2003). Early childhood curriculum, assessment, and program evaluation: Building and effective, accountable system in programs for children birth through age 8. Authors. Retrieved from www.naeyc.org/resources/position-statements

National Association of School Psychologists. 2015. *Early childhood services: Promoting positive outcomes for young children.* Bethesda, MD: Author. Retrieved from www.nasponline.org/x32403.xml

National Forum on Early Childhood Program Evaluation. (2007). Early childhood program evaluations: A decision-maker's guide. Retrieved from www.developing child.harvard.edu

National Research Council. (2008). Early Childhood Assessment: Why, What, and How. Committee on Developmental Outcomes and Assessments for Young Children, C.E. Snow and S.B. Van Hemel, Editors. Board on Children, Youth, and Families, Board on Testing and Assessment, Division of Behavioral and Social Sciences and Education. Washington, DC: The National Academies Press.

Neisworth, J. T. & Bagnato, S. J. (2004). The mismeasure of young children: The authentic assessment alternative. *Infants and Young Children, 17,* 198–212. Retrieved from http://eds.b.ebscohost.com.proxy006.nclive.org/eds/pdfviewer/pdfviewer?vid=3&sid=198352d2-50c8-465f-a033-20090486e75d%40sessionmgr102

Newcomer, K. E., Hatry, H. P., & Wholey, J. S. (2015). Planning and designing useful evaluations. In K. E. Newcomer, H. P. Hatry, & J. S. Wholey (Eds.), *Handbook of practical program evaluation* (4th ed., pp. 7–35). Hoboken, NJ: John Wiley & Sons.

Ortiz, S. O. (2014). Best practices in nondiscrimatory assessment. In P. L. Harrison & A. Thomas (Eds.) *Best Practices in School Psychology: Foundations* (pp. 61–74). Bethesda, MD: NASP.

OSEP. (2016). OSEP memo 16-07—Response to intervention (RTI) and preschool services. (April 29) Retrieved from www2.ed.gov/policy/speced/guid/idea/mem osdcltrs/oseprtipreschoolmemo4-29-16.pdf

Paget, K. D., & Nagle, R. J. (1986). A conceptual model of preschool assessment. *School Psychology Review, 15,* 154–165.

Pianta, R. C., La Paro, K. M., & Hamre, B. K. (2008). *Classroom assessment scoring system (CLASS) manual, pre-K.* Baltimore, MD: Paul H. Brookes.

Polignano, J. C. & Hojnoski, R. L. (2012). Preliminary evidence of the technical adequacy of additional curriculum-based measures for preschool mathematics. *Assessment for Effective Education, 37*(2), 70–83.

Praetor, K. K. & McAllister, J. R. (1995). Assessing infants and toddlers. In A. Thomas & J. Grimes (Eds.), *Best practices in school Psychology-III* (pp. 775–788). Bethesda, MD: National Association of School Psychologists.

Purpura, D. J. & Lonigan, C. J. (2015). Early numeracy assessment: The development of the preschool numeracy scales. *Early Education and Development, 26*(2), 286–313. doi:10.1080/10409289.2015.991084 Retrieved from: www.ncbi.nlm.nih.gov/pmc/articles/PMC4335720/

Rathvon, N. (2004). *Early reading assessment: A practitioner's handbook.* New York, NY: The Guilford Press.

Reid, M. A., DiPerna, J. C., Morgan, P. L., & Lei, P. W. (2009). Reliability and validity evidence for the EARLI literacy probes. *Psychology in the Schools, 46*(10), 1023–1035.

Salkind, N. J. (2018). *Tests & measurement for people who (think they) hate tests & measurement* (2nd ed.). Los Angeles, CA: Sage Publications, Inc.

Schalock, R. L., Borthwick-Duffy, S. A., Bradley, V. J., Buntinx, W. H. E., Coulter, D. L., Craig, E. M., & Yeager, M. H. (2010). *Intellectual disability:*

Definition, classification, and systems of supports (11th ed.). Silver Spring, MD: American Association on Intellectual and Developmental Disabilities.

Squires, J. & Bricker, D. (2009). *Ages & stages questionnaires* (3rd ed.). Baltimore, MD: Brookes Publishing.

Trevethan, R. (2017). Sensitivity, specificity, and predictive values: Foundations, pliabilities, and pitfalls in research and practice. *Frontiers in Public Health, 5*, 307. doi:10.3389/fpubh.2017.00307

Tzivinikou, S. (2018). Screening young children at risk for reading failure. In D. Farland-Smith (Ed.), *Early childhood education*. IntechOpen. doi:10.5772/intechopen.82081Retrieved from www.intechopen.com/books/early-childhood-education/screening-young-children-at-risk-for-reading-failure

U.S. Department of Education. (2011). Race to the Top – Early Learning Challenge (RTT-ELC) executive summary. Retrieved from www.ed.gov/sites/default/files/rtt-elc-draft-execsumm-070111.pdf

U.S. Department of Education, Office of Elementary and Secondary Education. (2016). *Non-Regulatory Guidance Early Learning in the Every Student Succeeds Act: Expanding Opportunities to Support our Youngest Learners*, Washington, DC, Retrieved from www2.ed.gov/policy/elsec/leg/essa/essaelguidance10202016.pdf

U.S. Department of Health and Human Services, & Department of Education. (2016a). *Policy statement on supporting the development of children who are dual language learners in early childhood programs*. Retrieved from (EDED566723). ERIC. https://files.eric.ed.gov/fulltext/ED566723.pdf.

U.S. Department of Health and Human Services, & Department of Education. (2016b). *Policy statement on family engagement from the early years to the early grades*. Retrieved from www2.ed.gov/about/inits/ed/earlylearning/files/policy-statement-on-family-engagement.pdf

Vitrikas, K., Grant, D., Savard, D., & Bucaj, M. (2017). Developmental delay: When and how to screen. *American Family Physician, 96*(1), 36–43. Retrieved from: www.aafp.org/afp/2017/0701/p36.html

Weaver, A. D. & Ouye, J. C. (2015). A practical and research-based guide for improving IEP team meetings. *NASP Communique, 44*(3). Retrieved from www.nasponline.org/publications/periodicals/communique/issues/volume-44-issue-3

Williams, M. E., Sando, L., & Soles, T. (2014). Cognitive tests in early childhood: Psychometric and cultural considerations. *Journal of Psychoeducational Assessment, 32*, 455–476.

Wong, A. (2014, November 19). The politics of 'pre-k': Preschool and prekindergarten are the same thing—aren't they? *The Atlantic*. Retrieved from www.theatlantic.com/

Wright, D. B., Gronroos, N., Burkhartsmeyer, J., & Johnson, D. (2008). *Delivering the hard news well: Your child has mental retardation*. Los Angeles, CA: Diagnostic Center, Southern California. Retrieved from www.pent.ca.gov/beh/dis/deliverhardnewswell08.pdf

Wright, J. (2010). The RIOT/ICEL matrix: Organizing data to answer questions about student academic performance and behavior. *Intervention Central*. Retrieved from www.interventioncentral.org/sites/default/files/rti_riot_icel_data_collection.pdf

Chapter 2

Observation of Preschool Children's Assessment-Related Behaviors

Bruce A. Bracken and Lea A. Theodore

Introduction

The broad practice of preschool evaluation includes standardized tests, as well as formal and informal clinical methods designed to assess children's cognitive, academic, behavior, social-emotional, neurological, and personality functioning. Testing is a process of administering formal tests such as intelligence or achievement tests, as well informal scales and third-party questionnaires or checklists. Tests are typically "standardized," meaning that the procedures for administering them are uniform or standard and test-takers are evaluated in a nearly identical manner, no matter where they live or who administers the test (Lezak, Howieson, Bigler, & Tranel, 2012).

Most high-stakes tests are also norm-referenced. Norm-referenced refers to testing wherein examiners convert obtained raw scores into standard scores based on a comparison of an examinee's performance on the test with the assessment outcomes of a comparable normative sample. A norm-referenced test of a child's reading abilities, for example, may rank that child's ability compared to other children of similar age or grade level; the child's comparative ranking is then converted into a standard score that comports to the characteristics of the normal curve. Norm-referenced tests are effective for measuring a multitude of constructs, traits, behaviors, or conditions (Gregory, 2016). A full psychological assessment is a multifaceted process that includes a combination of formal and informal tests and procedures, rating scales and surveys, grades, class tests and work products, clinical interviews, observational data, reviews of school and/or medical records, and a developmental history (Gregory, 2016).

The focus of this chapter is on the importance and use of clinical observations during the assessment of preschool children. Behavior observations gathered during a clinical, developmental, or educational assessment are especially useful for supporting, explaining, or refuting test scores. Clinical observations focus on the child's overt behavior rather than the latent traits or characteristics assumed to be measured by tests.

A Note on Clinical Observations

Psychological tests, as norm-referenced, objective, and standardized samples of behavior, have many assets. Typically, tests provide the examiner with several convenient bits of diagnostic information, including discernable profiles of performance, standard scores, percentile ranks, and age and grade equivalents. Because of the important implications associated with a child's test performance, professionals expect tests to meet minimal levels of technical adequacy (AERA, APA, NCME, 2014; Bracken, 1987; Wasserman & Bracken, 2003). Clinical observations and judgments, while focusing on overt behaviors rather than assumed latent traits, are often less objective than standardized tests, rendering them more situational, equivocal, and open to speculation and debate. Clinical observations generally lack norms, standard scores, percentile ranks, or age and grade equivalents. The absence of such critical data calls the reliability, validity, and interpretations of assessment observations and interpretations into question (Anderson & Sullivan, 2018).

Ironically, because observations are less objective it is easier for an examiner to defend decisions made based on objective test data than to defend judgments made on authentic behavior observed and interpreted in a more subjective, clinical fashion (Grove, Zald, Lebow, Snitz, & Nelson, 2000). On the other hand, some concerns with psychoeducational assessment seem to have stemmed from the practice of blindly using test scores for making placement decisions about children without the full use of clinical observations, judgments, and common sense (Faust, 2013). Therefore, it would make sense to use both objective and subjective data in the assessment and interpretation of young children's behavior. Clinical observations of authentic behavior represent a critical aspect of the assessment process that enriches the examiner's understanding of the child and the child's test performance (Leech & Onwuegbuzie, 2007).

Given the unique contributions of clinical observations, it is important that examiners use children's behavior to describe, explain, and triangulate their test and non-test performance. Moreover, clinical observations should be used to support the validity or invalidity of test scores, at least partially explain children's variable test performance, lend support for diagnoses and remediation strategies made on the basis of standardized test results, and provide the examiner with information needed to develop specific hypotheses concerning a child's individual strengths and weaknesses (Karg, Wiens, & Bkazei, 2013; Leech & Onwuegbuzie, 2007).

This focus on clinical observations and judgment does not imply that examiners should ignore issues related to subjectivity, reliability, and validity associated with observations; rather, examiners must develop objective, reliable, and valid observational skills. Clinical skill must complement the use of standardized tests if diagnosticians are to make accurate diagnoses, prognoses, and recommendations for the remediation of young children's deficiencies (Mazza, 2014).

Preschool Behavior Factors

For examiners to understand typical preschool behavior, it is essential that they know the range of normal and exceptional behaviors in all areas of child development. When parents or teachers describe a child as noncompliant, distractible, impulsive, easily frustrated, and emotionally labile, examiners frequently consider such tentative diagnostic hypotheses as Attention Deficit Hyperactivity Disorder (ADHD), Autism Spectrum Disorder (ASD), Post-Traumatic Stress Disorder (PTSD), Emotional Disturbance (ED), Learning Disabilities (LD), Oppositional Defiant Disorder (ODD), Anxiety Disorders or similar conditions. Although examiners often cite behavioral descriptors of these sorts as areas of concern among older children, the same behaviors often characterize many normal children between two and six years of age. For example, not every child who displays inattention or high activity levels has ADHD. Most young children impulsively utter things they did not mean to say, jump from one activity to another, make careless mistakes, or become forgetful and disorganized. These behaviors are considered typical behavior for a child of preschool age and do not necessarily mean the child has a disorder. Illnesses, accidents, middle ear infections (otitis media), and chronic abuse or stressful life events (e.g., moving, divorce, and death) can cause mimicked symptoms of ADHD, anxiety, and ODD (Ortiz, 2014). A normally agreeable preschooler who becomes inattentive or argumentative after their parents' separation, for example, is likely experiencing an adjustment reaction, not ADHD.

Developmental normalcy is especially difficult to define among young children. Frequently, even cohabiting biological parents differ in their perceptions of their children's behavior (e.g., Bracken, Keith, & Walker, 1998). Newer-generation behavior rating scales with stronger psychometric qualities (e.g., inter-rater reliability), such as the *Clinical Assessment of Behavior* (CAB; Bracken, 2005) and the *Behavior Assessment System for Children— Third Edition* (BASC-3; Reynolds & Kamphaus, 2015), have been developed to ameliorate some of these respondent differences by better objectifying behavior reporting.

During the preschool years, social, physical, communication, adaptive, and cognitive development occur at a rapid rate, and the range of development among normal preschool children is great. As children increase in age, their rate of development decreases and the range of behaviors among normal children likewise becomes narrower. It is sometimes difficult to differentiate preschool children with a disability from normal preschoolers due to variable rates of development (hence the preference for such descriptors as developmental delay rather than a diagnosed disability), whereas older children with mild disorders are more easily identified and stand apart from their typically developing peers. Preschool children, for example, usually exhibit higher energy levels, less self-control, and much more physical activity than socialized school-aged children do. At what point then, does the examiner cease considering an energetic and active preschooler as normal and begin to view them as atypical? Because there are no norms that provide a clear indication of normal energy levels for children of various ages, the question is impossible to answer; clinical experience and "internalized" norms guide most experienced diagnosticians in the determination of whether the child's behavior is exhibited with more intensity or frequency, or in longer duration, than is typical.

Environmental Effects

Professionals often incorrectly assume that a child's behavior exhibited during an evaluation is similar to the child's home, classroom, or recreational behaviors. Examiners should never unconditionally consider test behaviors as being representative of a child's typical behavior in other settings. The dynamics of an evaluation are very different from the contexts of a typical preschool, day care, kindergarten, or home environment. Even with older children, examiners should not assume that assessment behavior is typical behavior; but preschool children often have had little contact with schools, teachers, authority figures other than parents, or the extensive probing, questioning, and formality that is part of a psychoeducational evaluation. Thus, the preschool child's assessment-related behaviors may often be specific to the evaluation context and generalize poorly to non-assessment situations (Gregory, 2016).

When teachers or parents hear an examiner's description of their child's behavior during an evaluation, they sometimes express concern that the examiner must not have seen the child's true behavior. The evaluation setting provides enough structure and personal attention to keep many children eagerly on task, while other youngsters resist the structure and formality and refuse to participate in the assessment process, or they participate only half-heartedly. The unfamiliar adult-child interactions, materials, and settings that are part of psychoeducational evaluations may frighten or intimidate some children, whereas other youngsters may respond positively to the novel situation and personal attention.

Psychoeducational evaluations are extremely structured events. Examiners expect children to attempt all presented test items, whether enjoyable or not, and abide by the abundance of test rules and directions presented. Although examiners sometimes present psychoeducational assessments to examinees as "fun games" they will play together, it becomes readily apparent to most preschool children that the examiner is more interested in the child's performance than "having fun." There are very few occasions in a preschooler's life when time and behavior are as structured and controlled as during psychoeducational evaluations. Because children's atypical behavior may be common during an evaluation, examiners should note and interpret an examinee's test behaviors cautiously so that inappropriate generalizations are not made about the child's typical behavior. Although there has been a great deal of debate regarding how to present the evaluation to the child (e.g., as fun games or a more serious structured activity), a complete discussion of the controversy surrounding these issues is beyond the scope of this chapter. Readers are referred to other sources to familiarize themselves with this issue.

Situational structure and interpersonal interactions are but two possible environmental influences on a child's evaluation behavior. The examiner also needs to be cognizant of a wide variety of environmental influences on the child's performance. To develop a better understanding of the child's typical behavior, the examiner should observe the child in a variety of environments and contrast the child's non-evaluation behavior with behavior observed during testing. The examiner should observe the child in the preschool classroom during structured and unstructured activities, including quiet listening, active and passive individual and group participation, learning activities, cooperation, sharing, transitioning from one activity to another, and interactions with peers and adults. Examiners should also observe the examinee while the child is involved in free play on the playground for a more holistic, authentic view of the child's typical behavior. If examiners conduct observations in a variety of settings, the examiner can more reliably make diagnostic inferences based on the child's behavior (Ortiz, 2014).

Specific Behaviors and Behavioral Trends

Effective evaluation of children's behavior requires that the examiner be aware of the child's full range of specific behaviors and integrate them meaningfully into behavioral trends. Because the length of the typical preschool evaluation provides a relatively small sample of behavior, the observer must look carefully for noteworthy behaviors that trend across contexts, subtests, or events. Frequently, examiners come away from an evaluation with a "feeling" about the child because of observing specific behaviors that together formed an undefined behavioral trend. Undocumented feelings about a child's behavior, however, are not enough. It is the task of the examiner to observe, note, and integrate assessment and non-assessment behaviors to reveal behavioral trends that can be supported with specific observed behaviors. For example, rather than merely reporting that a child was "fearful" (i.e., a behavioral trend) during an evaluation, the examiner should support this claim with instances of when the child exhibited specific "fearful" behaviors. If the child withdrew from the examiner's touch, began to weep silently during an attempt to build rapport, spoke hesitantly in a shaky and quiet voice, was startled when the examiner placed test materials on the table, and avoided direct eye contact with the examiner, the examiner could unequivocally document and support an interpretation of fearfulness.

It is also important to document support of behavioral trends for later reference. If someone questions an examiner about their behavioral interpretations and judgments, it would be easier to support the existence of behavioral trends if the examiner observed and noted specific behaviors during the evaluation. Likewise, when examiners re-evaluate children after the initial evaluation, it is helpful to contrast the child's specific behaviors across the time interval. Moreover, examiners can use behavioral data to triangulate or contrast assessment-related behaviors and behavioral trends with the perceptions of parents and teachers and with actual classroom/playground behavior.

Examiners should examine specific actions carefully to identify behaviors that are also *inconsistent* with general behavioral trends. Inconsistent specific behaviors often form subtrends that reveal less obvious, yet important, strengths, weaknesses, fears, likes, dislikes, and so on. A child who smiles frequently, converses freely, jokes and teases with the examiner, readily complies with the examiner's requests, and spontaneously laughs and sings during an evaluation, likely would be identified as a friendly and cooperative examinee. The same child, however, may at times exhibit mild resistance, express a desire to terminate the evaluation, and require occasional redirection and encouragement. If examiners scrutinize the antecedent conditions for these incongruent specific behaviors, a diagnostically important behavioral subtrend may emerge. For instance, the child might find the verbal exchange with the examiner enjoyable but may have an aversion to tasks that require visual-motor integration. If examiners consider the pattern of incongruent resistant behaviors in the context of the tasks the child is performing, the examiner should see that this typically friendly preschooler becomes resistant only when faced with activities requiring visual-motor integration. Observations of this sort, combined with test data, may provide concomitant evidence for a diagnostic claim of a relative weakness in that area of functioning.

Can't Do vs. Won't Do

One distinction that examiners should make with behavioral observations is whether a child responded incorrectly to individual test items due to an inability to complete the task successfully or due to an unwillingness to attempt the task. It is common for shy preschoolers to refuse to attempt some assessment tasks, especially motor activities that require active physical participation and verbal tasks that require extensive vocalization. In such cases, a diminished subtest score also lowers the standard score associated with the scale to which the subtest belongs, as well as the total test score. For example, in addition to noting the detrimental effects of the child's limited vocalization on expressive language tests, the examiner should triangulate that deficit with observations in other contexts and the administration of instruments that require only receptive verbal abilities or nonverbal abilities. Examiners may also wish to "test the child's limits" to gain additional information regarding a child's optimal abilities and skills. Testing the limits involves the re-administration of incorrectly responded-to test items upon completion of the test. By giving the child more time to complete certain items, by providing extra cues, additional demonstrations or concrete examples, or by using an amalgamation of these tactics, the examiner may determine whether the child has the ability to solve the problem and, if necessary, the extent and type of assistance that the child needs to be successful (Gresham, 2014). It is imperative that the examiner be more than a test giver. If examiners use behavioral observations properly to distinguish between a child's inability and unwillingness (i.e., can't do vs. won't do) to perform tasks, the examiner will avoid making foolish or embarrassing statements about the child's relative weaknesses and the need for remediation.

Clinical Observation Best Practices

Detailed Descriptions of the Child's Behavior

Examiners frequently view the purpose of an evaluation as the identification of a child's difficulties or weaknesses so that a school or agency can properly service the child. In many instances, this problem identification function is the role of examiners since parents or preschool teachers often cite vague or undocumented concerns about the child's development or adjustment. However, such a deficit model of evaluation often results in a biased assessment orientation that is not balanced or totally objective.

Frequently, due to a deficit evaluation approach, many examiners look for or observe and report on the "absence" of problematic behaviors; they may note, for example, that the child was "neither overly active nor impulsive during the assessment process." To say that a child was "neither overly active nor impulsive" provides the parent or teacher with little useful information, and it may incorrectly highlight areas of parental concern. It is usually inferred from statements such as these that no problems were noted in the areas of concern; however, when it is reported that a specific behavior was not observed, the reader is left to imagine where on a continuum of behavior the child actually performed. If a child is "not overly active," the reader of a report cannot safely infer that the child was moderately active or even appropriately active during the evaluation. Without an accurate description of the child's actual behavior, one cannot safely infer anything except that the child was not overly active.

Preferably, the examiner should note exactly what the child does, and then describe and interpret the behavior in accurate and descriptive terms. Rather than describing a child as neither overly active nor impulsive, a clearer picture of the child is communicated when the examiner notes that the child eagerly performed all tasks presented, yet waited patiently for instructions to be read, materials to be readied, and the examiner's direction to begin. In this instance the examiner could have characterized the child as interested and patient (or used similar descriptors) and then provided sufficient support for the positively stated clinical judgment.

Supporting Behavioral Inferences

Too often, psychoeducational reports contain behavioral observations that are little more than a running chronology of behavior that fails to draw any meaningful inferences. Merely reporting what a child did during an evaluation without also providing an interpretation of that behavior in the context of the evaluation environment is severely inadequate. It is sometimes tempting to cite only what was actually observed during an evaluation rather than interpret the behavior because interpretations and inferences are much more subject to professional disagreement than are behavioral citations; but the temptation to avoid integration and interpretation should be resisted. The value of behavioral interpretations by far outweighs any difficulties that arise from professional disagreement.

Eye contact, for instance, is a behavior that examiners seem fond of reporting but frequently do not interpret. It is common for examiners to state in a psychoeducational report that the child made, or failed to make, eye contact throughout the evaluation. What is the significance of this observation? Alone, it is meaningless; yet, when coupled with an inferential interpretation this observation provides relevant and meaningful information. The possible explanations for a child's continued (or absence of) eye contact are numerous, and selecting the appropriate interpretation is important. Did the child make eye contact in an effort to secure assurance from the examiner that the child's test performance was acceptable? Was the eye contact hostile in nature and used as a nonverbal, passive-aggressive message of resistance? Did the child make eye contact with teary eyes, suggesting fear and an unspoken desire to terminate the evaluation session? Did the child make eye contact with eyes that expressed a lack of understanding and a need for a slower pace and greater explanation? Alternatively, did the child's continued anticipatory eye contact inform the examiner that the youngster viewed the evaluation with interest and excitement?

Meaningful Communication of Behavioral Observations

The ability to communicate the meaning of a child's behavior to parents, teachers, and others is an important and necessary assessment skill. To do this, examiners must expand their repertoire of behavioral descriptors and describe children's behavior in terms that reflect accurately not only the frequency, intensity, and duration of the child's behavior, but also the spirit with which the child exhibited the behavior.

To report that a child walked around the room during the rapport-building phase of the evaluation only minimally describes the child's behavior and leaves many interpretations available for consideration. The reason for the child's ambulation or the intensity of the child's walking behavior are unclear. Was the child interested in exploring the new environment? Were they afraid and unready to sit? Were they being resistant? Were they angry and walking off their anger? It is unclear what the walking child's intentions were without more information. There are also hosts of terms that refer to the nuances in the energy expended while walking that give a richer indication of the child's state of being at the time. If an examiner reported that the child *darted* around the examining room, there is a suggestion that the child exerted more energy than if the examiner described the child as having *sauntered* around the room. Likewise, *skipping* suggests a lighter mood than *trudging*, *pacing* connotes a higher level of anxiety than *strolling*, and *stomping* alludes to a greater degree of emotion than *tiptoeing*.

Although there is a greater likelihood of disagreement among professionals over whether a child was sauntering or strolling, marching or stomping, examiners should not hesitate to describe the behavior in terms they believe accurately connote the nuance of emotion and energy underlying the child's behavior. As mentioned previously, examiners can easily defend test results, but clinical observations are truly essential for making sense of the test results and providing a clearer understanding of the child.

When to Observe Behavior

Behavior is a continuous attribute that flows unendingly. Literally, every moment during an evaluation the child is doing something that is worth noting. To make sense of the child's continuous behavior flow, it is necessary to study the child's behavior temporally, in an ongoing manner, and within context.

Because much of the child's behavior is a reaction to the examiner or the examining situation, the child's responses to various situations should be studied meticulously to determine possible relationships between the task the child is asked to perform and the child's resulting behavior. Identification of relationships between tasks and resulting behaviors may lead to meaningful hypotheses about the child's abilities (Gregory, 2016). Why might a child kneel and lean forward in anticipation when presented with a verbal memory subtest, yet recoil and become anxious when asked to repeat numbers on a numerical memory task? The child's differential response to the two similar memory subtests may suggest a tentative hypothesis about the child's relative comfort with verbal as opposed to numerical information. Hence, the hypothesized function of the behavior is important to address.

The examiner should investigate hypotheses to determine whether the child made similar responses to other verbal and numerical subtests. If the child responds consistently, and verbal items are continually responded to more favorably than numerical items, then information is gained that can be used, along with obtained test scores, to explain the differences in the child's verbal and numerical abilities.

Examiners should also consider large and small contiguous temporal units when analyzing trends in a child's behavior. The examiner should compare the child's behavior at the beginning of the evaluation with that near the end of the evaluation. Did the child begin eagerly, but finish frustrated? Did the child separate from their parents with difficulty but gradually warm in mood so that by the end of the evaluation the examiner and child were mutually comfortable? Does the child work well once they start, but become anxious or frightened when required to cease one activity and initiate another? How does the child respond when a task is challenging or a question is difficult? Do they give up easily, fall to the floor, tantrum, or try diligently to solve the problem? Does the child respond to prompts or praising of effort? The examiner should also note the child's reaction to transitions in tasks, subtests, tests, and other activities and settings. By considering temporal units of behavior, whether large or small, the examiner can obtain information that will not only help explain the child's test performance but will provide parents and teachers insight into the child's variable behavior at home and in school.

What to Observe

Although it would be impossible to list all behaviors that are worthy of notice during a psychological evaluation, especially noteworthy behaviors are discussed below. The chapter authors hope that the reader will become more aware of preschool behavior, expand these suggestions as necessary, and learn to attend selectively to childhood behaviors that provide diagnostically useful information.

Appearance

During the course of an evaluation, the examiner should note, with photographic clarity, the child's physical appearance. This carefully recorded description will prove a useful recall aid later, when the details of the evaluation are no longer vivid. A description of this sort is also useful for professionals who will be working with the child in the future because it provides a concrete referent. Photographic descriptions of children also humanize the assessment report and make it clear to the reader that the report concerns an actual child. It is important that future teachers, counselors, and other school personnel see the preschooler as a living, breathing, red haired, freckle-faced youngster, for example, rather than merely a name–IQ paired association.

Height and Weight

A physical description of a child should include notes about weight and height, especially relative to the child's peers and normative expectations.

Developmental height and weight charts are usually available from pediatricians but are also frequently available in books on child development. As with most traits and characteristics, variance for normal height and weight is great during the preschool years. The examiner should note the interaction between the child's size and performance during the assessment. It is more meaningful, for instance, to describe a child as being seriously overweight and then discuss the ways in which the child's excess weight interfered with fine and gross motor tasks than to cite only that the child's weight is at the 99th percentile when compared to same-age peers. The examiner should also be aware that deviance in a child's physical development may have implications for the emotional, social, and educational well-being of the child and should be considered within the context of the psychoeducational evaluation.

Health

In addition to ascertaining a complete developmental history from the child's primary caretaker(s), it is important for the examiner to note the child's overall health during the evaluation. Children who reveal symptoms of the common cold (e.g., sniffling, sneezing) or allergies, or who appear tired and/or have somatic complaints, may not put forth their best efforts because they lack the mental acuity, concentration, and energy necessary to perform at their best. As such, test findings may not accurately represent the child's true abilities and skills. We, therefore, recommend that the examiner wait until problematic symptoms abate before administering any assessment (Gregory, 2016).

Physical Abnormalities

The examiner should be watchful for physical characteristics that are unusual and/or indicative of insufficient or inappropriate diet, physical or emotional abuse, lack of proper medical or dental attention, improper sleep or rest patterns, and physiological, psychological, or educational disorders. Awareness of physical abnormalities should be considered in light of possible physical abuse or neglect (Gregory, 2016).

Examiners should carefully survey the child for obvious sensory and motor abnormalities. Children typically evidence symmetrical motor development and functioning. While a young child's movements are typically not as smooth as an older child's movement, their movements should be neither jerky nor spasmodic. The examiner should observe the child for and note any tics, tremors, excessive clumsiness, and uncontrolled body movements.

The examiner should also be observant for signs of visual and/or auditory impairments. Visually, the examiner should look for obvious physical signs, such as red, swollen eyelids, crusty drainage around the eyes, eyes that neither track nor align properly, squinting, excessive blinking, grimacing, or evidence of impaired perception of orientation in space, size, body image, and judgment of distance. The examiner should also watch for physical signs of auditory impairment such as drainage from the ears, complaints of earaches or itchy ears, repeated requests for restated questions, tilting of the head for better reception, and so on. The child's speech may also provide indications of auditory dysfunction, such as frequent auditory discrimination errors, expressed confusion when there is auditory confusion or commotion, and inappropriate responses to questions, directions, or requests (Gregory, 2016).

Grooming and Dress

Observations of the child's grooming frequently provide the examiner with an indication of the care afforded the child at home. If the child's hands and face are dirty and their clothing bears traces of compounded soil, then examiners might safely infer that someone has not addressed the child's hygiene. An examiner should be careful, however, to discern whether the child is temporarily disheveled and dirty because of recent play or if the dirt is a more permanent and global indication of possible neglect.

The intent of considering a preschooler's clothing is not to attend to whether the child is stylishly dressed, but rather to infer the amount and quality of supervision given to the child's daily routines and care. As with grooming, a child's dress reflects the attention and care given to the child at home. It would be foolish to infer that a child in old clothes does not necessarily have their physical needs met; however, a young boy who comes to an evaluation with his shirt buttons and buttonholes misaligned, wearing socks of different colors, and has shoes on the wrong feet obviously had little attention paid to his dress that day. The examiner should follow up on this observation by asking the parents and preschool teacher about the child's usual dress and dressing routine. It is possible that this situation was unique due to a rushed schedule the day of the evaluation or possibly that the parents are attempting to teach the child through natural consequences to become more independent in and attentive to his daily functioning. Examiners should also include statements regarding a child's clothing, disheveled appearance, or torn or dirty clothes in the report to the extent to which they relate to referral concern(s) or support a hypothesis, such as parental neglect. Otherwise, examiners should not "judge" a child's dress and appearance, as the child's clothing may be hand-me-downs from an older sibling and is the best that parents can provide their child, and do not relate to testing or parental neglect.

Children's dress can also be a valuable source of information about their level of dependence on adults. If a child's shoes become untied during the evaluation, does the child ask the examiner to tie them or do they attempt to tie the shoes themselves? Does the child attempt to tuck in a shirt when it becomes untucked or do they obliviously leave it untucked? Does the child attempt to button buttons or snap snaps that have come undone or ask to have them done by an adult? The essence of the observation is whether the child evidences an attempt at age-appropriate independent functioning or is content and used to having others do for them. Obviously, the average 2-year-old would be expected to be primarily dependent on adults for dressing assistance, but 3- and 4-year-olds should be evidencing attempts at independent functioning even if these attempts prove unsuccessful; 5- and 6-year-olds should be quite independent in much of their normal daily functioning, requiring assistance much less frequently than their younger peers.

Speech

A preschooler's speech yields a great deal of information about not only the quality of the child's language skills but also the child's overall cognitive ability and level of social-emotional development. Gard, Gilman and Gorman (1993) provided a useful guide that describes qualitative characteristics of speech in children up to 36 months of age. In addition, the speech and language assessment chapter of this book addresses language development and basic concept attainment for preschool children. However, it is important for examiners to attend to a child's speech for insights into the child's thought patterns, problem-solving style, tolerance to frustration, awareness and understanding of the examining situation, and ability to communicate needs and follow directions.

Although stuttering, stammering, and mild lisps caused by the loss of baby teeth and imperfect enunciation are common among young children (especially among first graders), the examiner should note the child's speech difficulties and be particularly sensitive to whether the child evidences discomfort over speech production. If the examiner noted that the child's speech was unintelligible or marked by severe stuttering or stammering, or caused concern to the child or parents, then the examiner should make a referral for a language assessment and attempt to determine in what ways and to what degree the child's imperfect speech interfered with the overall evaluation (Bray, Kehle, & Theodore, 2014). In situations where a child's poor expressive speech results in lowered test scores, the examiner should assess the youngster's receptive vocabulary and nonverbal reasoning skills with instruments such as the *Bracken Basic Concept Scale – III* (Bracken, 2006) or the UNIT-2 (Bracken & McCallum, 2016), both of which require no verbal expression and are appropriate for early childhood assessments.

Many preschoolers express their thoughts verbally while attempting to solve problems, which provides the examiner with insights into the processes used in obtaining a solution. Although intelligence tests have been criticized historically for measuring intellectual product but not process, the astute examiner can infer aspects of the child's cognitive processing from the resultant product and the child's steps taken while working toward producing that product.

During test administration, when items become increasingly difficult, the examiner should note the child's response to the increasingly difficult tasks and more frequent item failures. Frequently young children remain on task as long as the task is within their ability. When the tasks become taxing, many young children focus only on particular words within the test questions and respond verbally in an elusive or tangential manner. For example, the examiner who asks a young child to complete the following sentence, "This pencil is made of *wood*, this window is made of ..." (Bracken, 2006), might get a response such as, "I want to look out the window." Many preschoolers use manipulative ploys in an attempt to avoid failure, while others use verbal redirection to avoid participating in the evaluation once they discover that the examiner's "games" are not as much fun as they first seemed. A clinician's reported observations about a child's redirecting attempts infrequently astonish parents who have been manipulated successfully by their children, though some parents may be unaware that their child has redirected them so effectively. An awareness of this sort is all some parents need to begin setting consistent limits and better managing their young children.

A child's level of verbal spontaneity often can be an indication of the child's level of comfort in the examining situation. A verbally expressive youngster who chatters happily throughout the evaluation is visibly more comfortable than a reticent child who speaks quietly, haltingly, and only when questioned. The examiner should question the validity of evaluation results when they deem that the child was overly inhibited during the assessment process. Further, it would be beneficial to contrast the child's performance on subtests that require verbal expression with tasks that require little or none for a better determination of the extent to which the child's shyness affected the test results. If the child scored consistently lower on verbal expressive measures than on verbal receptive items, the examiner should further determine whether the child is reticent due to a verbal deficiency or whether the observed verbal deficiency was a result of reticence. If the child is verbally fluent and spontaneous in non-test situations, an examiner might hypothesize that the child's shyness may have been the cause of the poor verbal test performance; in such a case, examiners might suggest interventions of an entirely different sort.

The examiner should attend to the preschooler's speech for insights into the child's overall affect. Does the child tease, joke, or attempt to be humorous verbally? Does the child use baby talk or regressive language at times of stress or frustration? When tasks become difficult, does the child utter silly nonsense phrases or respond seriously with a relevant response, whether correct or not? Youngsters sometimes become verbally aggressive when facing failure and petulantly inform the examiner, "I don't like you. I want to go home!"

The examiner should be watchful for how the child responds verbally as well as nonverbally to the multitude of situations that arise during an evaluation. It is helpful, for example, if an examiner notes that a particular child, like many preschoolers, becomes silent when faced with failure, disappointment, embarrassment, or frustration. Many parents react to a young child's silent dejection with over-stimulating attention; the examiner should advise that increased attention frequently exacerbates the problem and a more relaxed, soothing, and accepting approach may be most helpful in reopening the temporarily closed lines of communication (Bray et al., 2014).

Examiners should carefully consider the content of a child's verbalizations, not only to determine the relative maturity of the child's speech but also to detect emotional projections the child is making while performing tasks during the evaluation. The examiner should listen intently to the young child's interpretations of test pictures, test items, and spontaneous comments. With a verbally expressive preschooler, the examiner frequently has a great store of additional psychological information available; preschoolers typically have not acquired the sophistication to mask their feelings and have not yet developed strong defense mechanisms. An examiner who observes as well as tests can readily detect emotional issues and problems.

It is important to recognize the value of a child's speech and language, as language is the backbone of reading. Therefore, examiners should pay careful attention to a child's speech (e.g., articulation, voice) and language (e.g., expressive, receptive, or combination of both). In particular, with respect to speech, it is important to note misarticulation of sounds, syllables, or words, as well as substitutions, omissions, deletions, or additions of sounds. Red flags for expressive and receptive language include deficits in grammar, phonology, morphology, syntax, semantics, and pragmatics. For example, children with Autism Spectrum Disorder (ASD) often have difficulty with the use of social language. As mentioned previously, it is important to triangulate data obtained from testing, including observations such as lack of or minimal eye contact and preferring to play alone, not consistently linking facial expressions or gestures to verbal communication, difficulty communicating understanding of their own experience of several emotions, lack of insight into typical social relationships, and pragmatic language difficulties; all of which would indicate concerns related to ASD (Bray et al., 2014).

Fine and Gross Motor Skills

Since many early school experiences are motoric in nature, the examiner should attend closely to the child's motor development. Older-generation tests such as the *McCarthy Scales of Children's Abilities* McCarthy Scales of Children's Abilities (McCarthy, 1972) had direct measures of gross and fine motor ability, while most other preschool tests indirectly measure motor skills. Newer narrow band tests, such as the *Test of Gross Motor Development* (Ulrich, 2000), specifically assess motor functioning. The *Wechsler Preschool and Primary Scale of Intelligence, Fourth Edition* (Wechsler, 2012) is heavily weighted in fine motor and perceptual speed tasks, and although the *Stanford-Binet Intelligence Scale, Fifth Edition* (Roid, 2003) contains fewer motor tasks than previous editions, it still includes some useful motor activities. However, the Bayley scales of infant development (BSID) has a motor component that currently addresses issues up to 42 months of age, but a fourth edition of the test was released in September of 2019 (see Chapter 10, this volume, for additional information on these and other cognitive ability tests for preschoolers).

Examiners should always supplement formal motor assessments with direct behavioral observations. The examiner can easily identify the child who performs poorly on formal motor measures for reasons other than poor motor coordination. Children may score low on scales of motor development because of shyness, an unwillingness to attempt the task, fear of failure, embarrassment, or because motor tasks may lack the necessary structure for some children. In addition, one must question whether the child understood the test directions for motor tasks; even subtests that are motoric in nature frequently have long and complex verbal directions. Reviews of preschool and early childhood tests have shown that test directions are often replete with basic language concepts that children in large percentages do not understand (Bracken, 1986; Cummings & Nelson, 1980; Flanagan, Kaminer, Alfonso, & Raderc, 1995; Kaufman, 1978).

Informally, examiners should watch children to note how well they perform non-test motor tasks as well as formal motor tasks. Children who are lacking in educational experiences may look clumsy when drawing, coloring, or cutting with scissors, yet are able to button buttons, zip zippers, and manipulate small objects with obvious facility. The nature of the remediation for a child of this sort should be to engage the child primarily in educationally relevant motor activities because their adaptive behavior type motor skills are developmentally appropriate.

When assessing preschoolers, the examiner should observe the child's gross motor abilities, including the ability to climb stairs, walk, run, jump, skip, hop, balance on one foot, walk backwards, throw, and catch. Additionally, signs of gross asymmetrical development should be noted as possible indicators of neurological impairment, and the examiner should refer for a neuropsychological evaluation if warranted. As with fine motor development, the examiner should discern whether the child's gross motor difficulty is due to a lack of meaningful experiences or is due to a physical, visual, or perceptual limitation. While visual acuity and perceptual difficulties may be the cause of poor coordination in the truly awkward and clumsy child, and may require educational, optical, or physical intervention, the child lacking in experience may need only additional experience to develop better motor skills.

Activity Level

How active a child is during an evaluation has direct implications for the validity of the test results. It is likely that a child who is either lethargic or extremely active is not participating to an optimum degree, thus reducing the test's over-all validity. A child who must be motivated extrinsically to attempt tasks, encouraged to continue the assessment, and prodded to complete test items is problematic. The examiner should qualify a description of the child's poor per-formance with a note about the child's diminished activity level and reluctance to participate. The examiner should contrast the child's test and non-test behaviors, search for relevant behavioral trends, and watch for instances in which the child displays isolated bursts of interest and energy before making inappropriate diagnoses based on the affected test scores. If a child actively par-ticipates in tasks of a particular nature and remains listless for others, the resultant test profile and the examiner's behavioral notes, when coupled, should lead to diagnostically useful information.

The examiner should be aware of whether a child is currently medicated and any effect such medication might have on the child's activity level. Evaluations should be postponed and rescheduled when an examinee is taking medication that has a depressant effect until the youngster is health-ier and better able to give maximum effort. In instances of prolonged med-ical treatment, the examiner should acknowledge that it is likely that the test scores are depressed due to medication, and they should caution the user of the results to consider judiciously the effects of the child's physical condition on the test results. As mentioned previously, ill health may itself adversely affect the child's energy level and subsequent test performance. The examiner should note symptoms that indicate the onset of an illness and decide whether the evaluation should continue or be rescheduled.

Similarly, fatigue and drowsiness, common among preschoolers in the early afternoon, should be an indication to the examiner that optimal results on cognitive and achievement measures will not be obtained; upon observ-ing the child's fatigue, sleepiness, or irritability, the examiner should cease testing for the time being. Fatigue frequently accentuates soft signs of neurological impairment in children, and the examiner should be watchful for those signs. Testing preschool children as early in the day as possible is ideal for them giving their best effort, as they tend to wear themselves out by the afternoon.

Attention

Artifacts in test results caused by a child's inattentiveness may bring about inappropriate remediation recommendations unless examiners explain test results with the support of behavioral observations. For example, if a child obtains a relatively weak score on the Memory Scale of the UNIT-2 (Bracken & McCallum, 2016), an examiner might incorrectly conclude that the child's short-term memory is deficient. However, the examiner should explain this weakness as an attention issue rather than a memory issue if the child did not attend fully to the directions or the stimuli on short-term memory items. Because examiners cannot re-administer memory items, as they can most other test items, the child may consistently miss the crucial elements of test items due to inattentiveness rather than poor memory. The logical recommendation based on this observation would be to ensure that the child is attending carefully before teachers or parents present information they expect the child to recall.

Distractibility

Some children, although attentive during much of the evaluation, miss crucial information because they are easily distracted. These children may be attending appropriately but shortly discontinue attending to the task and shift their attention to inappropriate stimuli. Distractibility interferes with successful completion of many test activities, but it is particularly harmful on memory tests and timed tasks. The examiner should differentiate a child's failure due to inability and failure due to inconsistent attention. If the examiner properly explains the child's low scores, the subsequent recommendations should be more pertinent to the child's actual area of difficulty.

Impulsivity

Like inattentiveness and distractibility, impulsivity can severely limit the child's success on cognitive and achievement tests. If a child impulsively blurts out a response before the examiner completes the test question, initiates a task before the directions are finished, or says, "I know how to do it—let me try," as the examiner readies the test materials, the child is likely to fail many times and perform poorly on the test overall.

Examiners need to be aware that typical preschoolers are at times inattentive, distractible, and impulsive. However, the purpose of the examiner's observations should be to determine the degree to which the child's test performance was affected adversely by extreme behaviors and then judge the usefulness of the test scores. Although the examiner may believe that the test results are seriously deflated due to the child's test behavior and may be able to support this belief with a raft of behavioral notes, they should be careful when making optimistic claims about the child's likelihood of success in the classroom. If the child's behavior has interfered with their performance on the test, it may also interfere with their performance in the classroom and indeed may have been the reason for the initial referral.

Affect

Emotional lability is a common characteristic among preschool children. The examiner should become aware of the ways in which a child responds differentially to various situations. It is common for a young child to be exhilarated by success at one moment and demoralized by failure the next. Unfamiliar tasks may arouse fear and anxiety in a child who had previously completed familiar tasks calmly and confidently. An otherwise compliant and cooperative child may become "testy" and difficult during the unstructured interim between tests in a battery. A youngster who enters the examining room clinging to doors and furniture in fear may leave the room striding and exuding confidence.

The examiner should attend carefully to shifts in a child's affect related to changes in the environment and seek answers to the following types of questions: How does the child respond to structured versus unstructured activities? What is the child's reaction to praise, rebuke, failure, success, redirection, encouragement, etc.? What causes the child to become silent, to start crying, to withdraw, to jump up in excitement, to sing out with pleasure, or to strike out in anger? To what test activity is the child most attentive and which activities arouse the least interest? How does the child react to test materials, the examiner, the examining room, the parents, verbal interaction, and nonverbal, performance-related activities, and to being timed?

Although the examiner may see many mild or even dramatic shifts in the child's mood during an evaluation, the examiner should note the child's general mood as well. Overall, did the youngster seem happy? Fearful? Sullen? Confident? Examiners should cull all of the child's affective behaviors diagnostically and make inferences about the child's overall mood, level of adjustment, areas of concern, and areas of strength.

Anxiety

Closely associated with affect is the child's level of anxiety. The examiner should note what precipitates the child to become anxious and how the child displays signs of anxiety (Gregory, 2016). When asked several difficult questions near the ceiling of a test, the examiner should note extreme behaviors, such as whether the youngster begins to suck their thumb while tears well in their eyes. Does the child stare at the floor in silence while sitting on their hands? Does the child giggle nervously, cry, constantly clear their throat, bite their nails, urinate, blush, block while talking, breathe unevenly, or hyperventilate?

Although a psychoeducational evaluation frequently arouses anxiety in preschoolers, some children are more affected than others. Some youngsters are aroused to an optimal level during an evaluation, whereas other children may be debilitated by the stress. Some children are anxious throughout the evaluation, while others become anxious only in reaction to specific events or situations. By noting the child's behavior in several settings, the examiner is better able to determine whether the child's anxiety was specific to the evaluation or more general in nature, and the degree to which the child's anxiety interfered with the evaluation.

Comprehension and Problem Solving

The examiner should attend to the problem-solving approach used while the child seeks solutions to puzzles, mazes, block designs, and similar problems. Such observations yield clues about the child's comprehension of the task demands and solution. Does the youngster draw directly through a maze without regard for walls? Do they remain between the walls yet continually enter blind alleys? Alternatively, do they remain within the walls and attempt to avoid blind alleys but proceed too slowly and still fail the task? In each instance, each child's earned raw score would be zero, but the child's level of comprehension differs dramatically across examples. It is quite likely that the first child did not understand the nature of the task. The second child may have understood the nature of the task but did not fully understand that blind alleys were to be avoided. The third child fully understood the task but was unable to complete the item successfully because of the speeded nature of the task.

The child's reaction to test materials at times provides the examiner with surprising insight into the child's level of understanding. It is common for low-functioning young children to sniff or suck test materials as if they were edibles. Similarly, the brightly colored chips that are part of many preschool tests are sometimes mistaken for candy. Observations of this sort, when added to other behavioral notes, yield valuable information about the child's maturity, level of comprehension, and level of intellectual functioning.

The examiner should be watchful for the following: Does the child attempt to solve problems in a trial-and-error fashion or appear to have a strategy? If an attempt is unsuccessful, does the child continue to try the same approach or try other approaches? When solving a puzzle and puzzle pieces do not fit, does the child try a second piece or try to force the first piece into place? Does the child understand that puzzle pieces must be right side up in order to fit properly in the puzzle? On simple two- or three-piece puzzles, does the child impulsively shove adjacent pieces together without regard for the total picture? Observations of these sorts add a qualitative nature to the quantitative test scores. Although any two children may obtain the same scores on a given subtest, no two children will exhibit exactly the same behaviors while attempting the subtest items. The differences in children's behaviors help examiners understand the difference in their scores (Schrank, Decker, & Garruto, 2016).

Reactions to Other People and Situations

The examiner should note the preschool child's interactions with their parent(s), grandparent(s), primary caretaker(s), etc., together and apart, as well as the manner in which the child interacts with siblings, teachers, classmates, and strangers. Examiners should observe whether the child interacts with others by moving forward confidently or timidly holding back. Is the youngster aggressive with classmates in the classroom or playground, or is the child bullied? Does the child seek independence from the teacher or frequently ask for help, reassurance, and support? Does the child obey one parent's commands but ignore the other parent's directions? Does the child prefer the company of adults more so than the company of their peers? How well does the child accept redirection? What is the child's response to limits imposed by adults? When playing with other children and there is a disagreement, how does the child respond? Examiners should consider the child's interactions with the examiner as a person in authority. Overall, is the child compliant, manipulative, fearful, confident, respectful, flippant, etc.?

In many instances, children who have difficulty adjusting to assessment or classroom situations come from home or school environments that contribute to their problems. Although teachers and parents mean well and attempt to act in ways they believe are in the child's best interest, they at times fail to comprehend their role in their child's lack of adjustment. Consider, for example, the father who drops his daughter off at the nursery school. The moment the father attempts to leave his daughter in her class, she may begin to cry. As the daughter cries, her father attempts to console her, yet every time he begins to leave, she becomes more upset. This cycle repeats itself daily until the child begins crying before ever leaving her home, and school becomes a negative experience to which she reacts strongly. As any experienced preschool teacher knows, most young children stop crying almost immediately after their parents leave, and the best way to avoid unpleasant separations is to make departures warm yet brief.

Summary

Though the administration of psychoeducational tests to preschool children alone requires a great deal of training, skill, concentration, and coordination, an effective examiner must also have the clinical astuteness to observe, record, and interpret simultaneously the preschool child's assessment-related behavior. With a carefully collected sample of authentic behaviors, the examiner can support or refute specific test findings, explain a child's variable test performance, and attest to the validity or invalidity of the overall test results. The examiner should note the child's appearance and determine whether signs or symptoms of physical, emotional, or educational difficulties are present, and consider the effects of these symptoms on the child's performance. Behaviors that indicate a child's preferred cognitive style, language abilities, problem-solving approach, level of understanding, and reasons for individual item and subtest performance must likewise be observed and interpreted. These behaviors, along with observations of the child's affect, distractibility, dependence, reactions to others, fears, likes, etc., need to be integrated with obtained test data and triangulated with third-person reports to formulate accurate diagnoses, prognoses, and remedial recommendations.

References

American Educational Research Association, American Psychological Association, and National Council on Measurement in Education. (2014). *Standards for educational and psychological testing*. Washington, DC: American Psychological Association.

Anderson, D. & Sullivan, K. A. (2018). Cognitive assessment. In N. J. Pelling & L. J. Burton (Eds.), *The elements of psychological case report writing in Australia* (pp. 52–59). New York: Routledge/Taylor & Francis Group.

Bracken, B. A. (1986). Incidence of basic concepts in the directions of five commonly used American tests of intelligence. *School Psychology International, 7*, 1–10.

Bracken, B. A. (1987). Limitations of preschool instruments and standards for minimal levels of technical adequacy. *Journal of Psychoeducational Assessment, 4*, 313–326.

Bracken, B. A. (2005). *Clinical assessment of behavior*. Lutz, FL: Psychological Assessment of Behavior.

Bracken, B. A. (2006). *Bracken basic concept scale – III*. San Antonio, TX: Harcourt Assessments.

Bracken, B. A., Keith, L. K., & Walker, K. C. (1998). Assessment of preschool behavior and social-emotional functioning: A review of thirteen third-party instruments. *Journal of Psychoeducational Assessment. Reprinted from Assessment in Rehabilitation and Exceptionality, 1*, 331–346.

Bracken, B. A. & McCallum, R. S. (2016). *Universal nonverbal intelligence test – Second edition*. Itasca, IL: Riverside.

Bray, M. A., Kehle, T. J., & Theodore, L. A. (2014). Best practices in the assessment and remediation of communication disorders. In P. L. Harrison & A. Thomas (Eds.), *Best practices in school psychology VI* (Data-Based and Collaborative Decision Making) (pp. 355–365). Best Practices VI. Silver Springs, MD: National Association of School Psychologists.

Cummings, J. A. & Nelson, R. B. (1980). Basic concepts in oral directions of group achievement tests. *Journal of Educational Research, 73*, 259–261.

Faust, D. (2013). Increasing the accuracy of clinical judgement (and thereby improving patient care). In G. P. Koocher, J. C. Norcross, & B. A. Greene (Eds.), *Psychologists' desk reference* (3rd ed., pp. 26–31). New York: Oxford University Press.

Flanagan, D. P., Kaminer, T., Alfonso, V. C., & Raderc, D. E. (1995). Incidence of basic concepts in the directions of new and recently revised American intelligence tests for preschool children. *School Psychology International, 16*(4), 345–364.

Gard, A., Gilman, L., & Gorman, J. (1993). *Speech and language development chart* (2nd ed.). Austin, TX: Pro-Ed.

Gregory, R. J. (2016). *Psychological testing: History, principles, and applications* (7th ed.). New York: Pearson.

Gresham, F. M. (2014). Best practices in diagnosis of mental health and academic difficulties in a multitier problem-solving approach. In P. L. Harrison & A. Thomas (Eds.), *Best practices in school psychology VI* (Data-Based and Collaborative Decision Making) (pp. 147–158). Best Practices VI. Silver Springs, MD: National Association of School Psychologists.

Grove, W. M., Zald, D. H., Lebow, B. S., Snitz, B. E., & Nelson, C. (2000). Clinical vs. mechanical prediction: A meta-analysis. *Psychological Assessment, 12*, 19–30.

Karg, R. S., Wiens, A. N., & Bkazei, R. W. (2013). Improving diagnostic and clinical interviewing. In G. P. Koocher, J. C. Norcross, & B. A. Greene (Eds.), *Psychologists' desk reference* (3rd ed., pp. 22–26). New York: Oxford University Press.

Kaufman, A. S. (1978). The importance of basic concepts in individual assessment of preschool children. *Journal of School Psychology, 16*, 207–211.

Leech, N. L. & Onwuegbuzie, A. J. (2007). An array of qualitative data analysis tools: A call for data analysis triangulation. *School Psychology Quarterly, 22*, 557–584.

Lezak, M., Howieson, D., Bigler, E., & Tranel, D. (2012). *Neuropsychological assessment* (5th ed.). New York: Oxford University Press.

Mazza, J. J. (2014). Best practices in clinical interviewing parents, teachers, and students. In P. L. Harrison & A. Thomas (Eds.), *Best practices in school psychology VI* (Data-Based and Collaborative Decision Making) (pp. 317–3330). Best Practices VI. Silver Springs, MD: National Association of School Psychologists.

McCarthy, D. P. (1972). *McCarthy Scales of Children's Abilities.* San Antonio, TX: Pearson.

Ortiz, S. O. (2014). Best practices in nondiscriminatory assessment. In P. L. Harrison & A. Thomas (Eds.), *Best practices in school psychology VI* (Data-Based and Collaborative Decision Making) (pp. 61–74). Best Practices VI. Silver Springs, MD: National Association of School Psychologists.

Reynolds, C. R. & Kamphaus, R. W. (2015). *Behavior assessment system for children – Third edition.* Minnesota: Pearson.

Roid, G. (2003). *Stanford-Binet intelligence scales, fifth edition.* Itasca, IL: Riverside Publishing.

Schrank, F. A., Decker, S. A., & Garruto, J. M. (2016). *Essentials of WJ IV cognitive abilities assessment.* Hoboken, NJ: John Wiley & Sons, Inc.

Ulrich, D. A. (2000). *Test of gross motor development.* Austin, TX: Pro-Ed.

Wasserman, J. D. & Bracken, B. A. (2003). Psychometric considerations of assessment procedures. In J. Graham & J. Naglieri (Eds.), *Handbook of assessment psychology* (pp. 43–66). New York: Wiley.

Wechsler, D. (2012). *Wechsler preschool and primary scale of intelligence scale – Fourth edition* (4th ed.). San Antonio, TX: Harcourt Assessment.

Chapter 3

Creating the Optimal Preschool Testing Situation

Bruce A. Bracken and Lea A. Theodore

Introduction

The purpose of conducting a psychoeducational assessment is to gain information about a child's current overall level of functioning, as well as the child's functioning within any of several important domains (e.g., cognitive, motor, language, personality, academic). Gathering such global and specific information enables examiners to accurately describe and classify children's abilities overall and within and across the various domains. Importantly, information gleaned from psychoeducational assessments is then used to predict future outcomes with and without intervention to guide decisions about the need for and types of interventions that should be implemented to alter the predicted future outcomes.

One assumption made about the assessment process is that examiners have made every effort to eliminate all identifiable construct-irrelevant influences on the child's performance and the resultant test scores. That is, the goal is to ensure that assessment as much as possible focuses solely on construct-relevant attributes of interest (e.g., intelligence), while limiting the influences of construct-irrelevant sources of variation (e.g., fatigue, lack of cooperation, emotional lability). Before psychologists can make meaningful decisions about a child's future educational plans, possible treatments, or medications, examiners must have confidence in the validity of the assessment results. Only when all possible sources of construct-irrelevant variation have been eliminated or optimally controlled can an examiner attest to the validity and utility of assessment results.

This chapter identifies common sources of construct-irrelevant influences on young children's assessment performance and suggests means by which examiners can moderate these unwanted sources of variation by establishing and better controlling aspects of the examining situation. Psychologists can moderate most sources of construct-irrelevant variance through careful attention to common threats to validity (e.g., nonstandard administration); however, examiners can never fully control all of these unwanted influences. Examining children's assessment performance in light of these influences can help explain young children's variable performance on tests and contribute to a fuller understanding of the child's true skills and abilities.

When conducting assessments in a standardized fashion, astute clinical skill and wise selection of instruments go a long way toward reducing major sources of construct-irrelevant variability in children's test performance. This chapter addresses the issue of construct relevance and irrelevance and suggests means by which examiners can maximize the assessment of the desired construct while controlling potential threats to validity. That is, this chapter describes the means by which careful attention to the examining situation can facilitate the examiner's valid assessment of preschool children.

Construct-Relevant versus Construct-Irrelevant Influences on Young Children's Test Performance

Examiners should be aware that some influences on a child's test performance might be considered construct-relevant, while in other instances the same source of variation may be considered construct-irrelevant. The examiner must decide when such variation is useful to understanding the child's performance and when it inhibits a clear understanding of the child's abilities under various conditions. For example, a teacher might consider a bilingual child's English language proficiency as construct-relevant for classroom instruction; however, if the intent of the assessment is to measure the child's general intelligence, use of a test heavily laden with verbal directions could produce considerable construct-irrelevant variance related to English facility and comprehension (Bracken & McCallum, 2016). To control for the construct-irrelevant variance associated with limited English proficiency, the examiner might replace the language-loaded measure with a test that can be administered in Spanish or that requires no language reception or production (e.g., *Universal Nonverbal Intelligence Test—Second Edition*; Bracken & McCallum, 2016).

To conduct fair assessments, examiners must decide which constructs to target and must identify and moderate the possible variables that threaten the validity of the assessment. In the previous example, use of a nonverbal test of ability could reduce the language-related threat to validity and allow for a "purer" measure of the construct (i.e., general intelligence) without the confounding influence of English language proficiency. In a similar fashion, bi-cultural children's level of assimilation into the dominant society may constitute a construct-irrelevant influence on their test performance when instruments are heavily loaded with cultural content (Bracken & McCallum, 2016; Ortiz, Piazza, Ochoa, & Dynda, 2018), even when the test is administered without verbal directions.

In addition to linguistic proficiency and enculturation, other variables that can be either construct-relevant *or* construct-irrelevant, depending on the context and targeted construct, include prior educational and life experiences, exposure to various media, physical and sensory abilities, family socioeconomic status, and many other such non-test influences. When an examiner identifies an influencing variable as irrelevant to the assessed construct, that variable serves as a source of test bias that should be eliminated or moderated to as great an extent as possible. For example, when assessing a visually impaired child's school readiness skills, the examiner should strive to reduce the effects of the visual disability on the child's ability to demonstrate their overall readiness skills. Moderating the effects of the visual impairment might include arranging seating and lighting to facilitate the child's view of test stimuli (e.g., reducing glare, emphasizing the contrast between light and dark), ensuring that the child wears or uses prescribed corrective devices, and modifying the test stimuli when necessary (e.g., using larger than standard print or stimulus matter).

Although psychologists cannot change a child's limited range of life experiences, knowledge of such limitations might temper the examiner's interpretation of the child's test results. A child who has had limited previous experience with puzzles, blocks, and paper and pencil may perform poorly on similar experiential tasks typically found on early childhood intelligence tests. The child's poor academic motor skill, related at least in part to a lack of previous educational experiences, would negatively influence the child's test performance and lower the child's overall intelligence quotient. Given typical preschool and primary grade curricular experiences, the assessed experiential weakness may be "remediated" once the child is exposed to these activities in a systematic fashion. Examiners would err when placing too much emphasis on the child's artificially lowered estimate of overall intelligence, especially on tests that weight educationally related motor skills heavily, when the diminished test performance was due largely to a lack of previous educational opportunity or experience.

Moderating Construct-Irrelevant Influences on Students' Test Performance

There are four principal sources of construct-irrelevant influences on children's psychoeducational assessment results: 1) the examinee; 2) the examiner; 3) the environment; and 4) the instruments used. The remainder of this chapter addresses each of these four primary influences and suggests means by which examiners can moderate these unwanted influences by creating an examining situation that facilitates testing and reduces known threats to validity.

The Examinee

It may seem odd that a child would be considered a possible source of construct-irrelevant influence on their own test performance. However, personal variables and behaviors, within and outside the child's sphere of control, influence the child's day-to-day abilities in ways that can be observed and moderated. To whatever extent possible, these variables should be recognized and controlled during assessments, or at least considered when examiners evaluate the validity of children's assessment results.

Health

In addition to standard examiner inquiries regarding the examinee's health history, examiners should be observant of children's current health prior to initiating an assessment. Children who show symptoms of an illness, even an illness as mild as the common cold, may experience sluggish mental processing, slower speed of response, diminished ability to "find" the right word or produce a definition, lessened motivation, and/or decreased energy, concentration, or interest. Children who are ill or who are becoming ill often lack the physical and mental stamina and acuity to perform optimally during an evaluation. Examiners should seriously consider and address such health-related threats to assessment validity (Bracken & Theodore, this volume).

Young children quickly develop physical symptoms of illness and, fortunately, their health often improves just as quickly. When children complain about signs or symptoms of an on-coming illness (e.g., sniffles, fatigue, pains, upset stomach), examiners should consider whether these complaints are anxiety-based psychosomatic manifestations (e.g., internalizing behaviors, Bracken & Keith, 2004) or whether the child is truly becoming ill and it would be wise to postpone the evaluation until the child is free of such symptoms.

If an otherwise healthy child becomes ill within days after an assessment has been conducted, the examiner should consider whether the child's assessment-related behavior was representative of their typical behavior. If the child's assessment behavior was atypical, the examiner should reconsider the validity of the assessment results.

Importantly, examiners should evaluate children's physical symptoms associated with anxiety (e.g., stomachache, nausea) when considering whether an assessment should be postponed for days or merely delayed briefly until better rapport and overall comfort is established (Gregory, 2016). Children often report somatic complaints when they are fearful or anxious, and examiners should strive to reduce those complaints by working to alleviate the child's fears and anxieties. In such instances, postponement would not be appropriate, but the examiner's expenditure of a little more effort and time to establish a better rapport would be warranted. Use of behavior rating scales to gain parents' or teachers' perceptions of the typicality of such behaviors may also be useful prior to conducting the assessment with the child. The *Clinical Assessment of Behavior* (Bracken & Keith, 2004) assesses a full range of behavioral disorders and exceptionalities in children as young as two years of age.

Fatigue/Restfulness

Related to overall health considerations is the child's state of restfulness (Gregory, 2016). With preschool children, it is generally a good idea to conduct assessments as early in the day as possible, within reason. Because young children typically nap (or need naps) after lunch and then wear themselves out again by late afternoon, assessments are often more easily conducted and more valid during the morning hours when children are alert and fresh.

Young children who are tired often become "cranky," which can negatively affect their cooperation, motivation, and subsequent test performance. Therefore, examiners should be sensitive to signs of fatigue and postpone assessments or offer children breaks in an effort to keep their energy levels and participation at optimal levels. From a purely behavioral management standpoint, it behooves examiners to assess children who are alert and well rested—or the examiner should be prepared to struggle with the child's misbehavior and diminished effort throughout the assessment.

Fear/Anxiety

Because young children typically are not experienced with the formal nature of psychoeducational evaluations, fear and anxiety are common initial reactions among examinees. An optimal level of examinee arousal is highly desired to ensure that the child is sufficiently motivated to perform tasks with their best effort. However, the assessment should not start or continue when the child's arousal and anxiety are at a level that impairs the child's spontaneity, concentration, or active participation. The examiner should allay children's fears and anxiety by establishing a comfortable, safe, and engaging environment before initiating testing.

The manner by which examiners greet preschool children can do much to initiate a good testing situation. Examiners should meet preschool children by stooping or squatting down to the children's height and offer a warm, friendly, low-keyed greeting. If the child is reticent and not easily approached, the examiner might stand and shift their attention to the parent or guardian who accompanied the child to the evaluation. By addressing the parent, the examiner will allow the child an opportunity to become more familiar with the setting and the examiner, while learning a bit about the examiner through the parent-examiner interactions. Gradually the child will find the interaction between the adults boring and become more open to direct interactions with the examiner.

When the child shows interest in the examiner or the assessment environment, the examiner can re-engage the child by offering to show the child around a bit. Once the child's fears and anxieties have subsided, the examiner should gently "shepherd" the child to the examining room to begin the assessment. Shepherding is a process by which the examiner guides the child to the examining room by allowing the child to walk in the lead. To shepherd a child effectively, the examiner should place a hand between the child's shoulder blades and gently "steer" the child with slight hand pressure to the desired location. Because children lead the way when shepherded in this fashion, they typically do not feel forced or coerced as when examiners lead the child by the hand to the testing location.

Motivation

Some children are not motivated to demonstrate their potential during psy-choeducational assessments for a variety of reasons (Gregory, 2016). Pre-school children's limited motivation can be due to insufficient awareness or appreciation of the importance of test results. Sometimes children do not find test materials or activities very interesting or engaging, and, on occasion, the examiner or the child's parents have not sufficiently "prepared" the child for the types of tasks the child will be asked to complete. In addition, some children become less motivated as the assessment progresses, and they are faced with tasks that are difficult or particularly challenging or that are not as fun as the child had expected (Gregory, 2016).

To overcome initial instances of limited motivation among preschool examinees, the examiner must develop an introduction to the assessment process that prepares the child for what will occur (Gregory, 2016). The examiner's introduction to the assessment process should be honest and, 1) describe the types of tasks with which the child will be presented; 2) challenge the child to do their best on every task; 3) emphasize the importance of effort, persistence, and thoughtful responses; and 4) acknowledge that some of the activities may be difficult and beyond the current abilities of the child. The introduction should not suggest that the examiner and child will be playing games, because it quickly becomes apparent that the examiner is taking the game playing very seriously and that the "games" are not all that much fun. It is fair, however, to tell the child that much of what the child will do will in fact be fun. A sample introduction follows:

> Today we are going to do many interesting and exciting things together. We will work with blocks and puzzles; we'll be looking at some pictures; I'm going to ask you to draw some pictures for me; and, I'll ask you to answer some questions. We'll have a good time together. I won't expect you to be able to do everything I ask you to do, because some of the things we will do are meant for older children. It's okay if you can't do some of the things I ask you to do, but I want you to try your very best anyway. Let's get going and try some of the fun things I have for you.

During the assessment, if the child's motivation begins to wane, the examiner should remind the child of the salient aspects of the previous paragraph (e.g., "Remember, I told you some of these things would be hard to do;" "That was a tough puzzle wasn't it? I like how well you worked on it even though it was hard for you."). Reinforcing the child's effort is another means of motivating the child to concentrate and continue to give full effort. It is important that the examiner reinforce the child's effort rather than their successes, otherwise the reinforcement will abruptly end and become painfully absent when the child begins to fail items. It is also wise to remind the child that some of the items were intended for older children (in reality, for children who are more able, whether due to age or ability), and that the child is not expected to be successful on every task or item attempted.

Preparing the child for the assessment process in such a fashion before the child begins to experience frequent failure is more appropriate and helpful than after the child has already failed a succession of items. Warning the child before failure can forestall frustration by challenging the child to attempt the predicted tough problems; reminding the child after failure is often seen as pardoning the child's failures, which can increase the child's frustration and sense of failure.

Temperament

Examiners can facilitate the assessment of preschool children if they accommodate the temperament styles of their examinees. By considering each of the nine temperament characteristics identified by Thomas and Chess (1977), the examiner might better schedule the assessment, approach the examinee, address the child's needs, guide the assessment, and even select the instruments appropriate for administration. In short, the examiner should seek to create the "best fit" between the child and the assessment situation (Carey & McDevitt, 1995; Chess & Thomas, 1992).

Examiners can expect each child to demonstrate to some greater or lesser degree a *level of activity* that is different from other children the examiner has evaluated in the past. Expecting all young children to sit cooperatively in a chair for an hour or longer and participate actively in an assessment is unrealistic. If the examiner knows before the assessment, either through parent report or observation, that the child is generally very active, the examiner can plan ahead to accommodate the child's desire or need to move about. Understanding and accommodating the needs of children by differentially allowing them to stand, move about, handle test materials, assist with the test administration, and take breaks can go a long way toward maintaining rapport once it has been established. To be effective, the examiner must note, be sensitive to, and plan for the active child.

Selecting an appropriate time to begin an assessment and being sensitive to children's biological needs should be based on the child's *rhythmicity*—that is, the predictability of a child's bodily and somatic functions (e.g., times when the child is most alert, responsivity after lunch, how the child interacts after a nap). The examiner should select a window of opportunity for assessment in which the child is predictably in their best form.

In addition to children's differential responses to routines, children do not all respond in the same manner when approached by others. Some children respond in kind, while others withdraw. The child's *approach or withdrawal* tendency should be considered when planning how to meet and greet the child in the best fashion. If the child typically responds positively to a forward, gregarious introduction and approach, then the examiner should exude enthusiasm and excitement, and boldly introduce themselves. However, if the child is more reticent and timid, and typically withdraws from strangers, the examiner should proceed slowly and elicit the child's participation through subtle and indirect engagement. Again, parent or teacher reports, or behavioral observations in a classroom, can provide information about the child's typical response when approached by others.

Although some children are very flexible and respond favorably and without comment to unanticipated changes in routines or schedules, some children are hypersensitive to even minor changes in routine or schedule, anticipated or not. Advanced knowledge about the *adaptability* of children to changes in routine will forewarn the examiner about how the child will likely respond when removed from routine activities to participate in the assessment. The examiner may identify classroom routines or activities that child views less favorably than others and plan the assessment at a time when the child will be "excused" from participating in the less desirable activity, and thereby lessen the intensity of the child's response to an unpredicted change in routine.

By observing a child in the classroom, examiners can consider the child's unique level of *intensity of reaction* in various situations. Once this information is known, examiners can better anticipate the child's needs and provide as much emotional support, structure, or patience as necessary when they begin to experience frustration and failure. Similarly, examiners should note the child's *threshold of responsiveness* to stimuli during classroom observations; that is, how much stimulation does it take to evoke a response from the child? The examiner might arrange the instruments and activities in an assessment to accommodate the child as necessary. For example, if the child is slow to warm up and does not respond initially to tasks that require active participation and verbal exchange, the examiner might begin with high interest, less-demanding tasks (e.g., having the child draw pictures as an ice-breaking activity). Once the child becomes more comfortable, the examiner can introduce tasks that are more demanding and require more active participation and social interaction.

The examiner should consider the nature and quality of the child's typical *mood* prior to an evaluation. That is, what sort of mood characteristically defines the child—one of sadness, anxiety, anger, apathy, happiness, and so on? Anticipating the child's typical mood should help the examiner prepare strategies for working with children who are difficult, as opposed to those who are typically positive and cooperative.

Although many preschool children are by nature *distractible* and have short *attention spans* and limited *persistence*, examiners should be prepared to present the assessment according to the pace of the child. By keeping the assessment sufficiently quick-paced, examiners can generally minimize the effects of a child's short attention span and limited persistence. By organizing and arranging the examining room in a manner to minimize visual and auditory distractions, the examiner also can better limit the distractibility of young examinees.

The Examiner

Examiners can directly and indirectly influence the examining situation through their appearance, dress, and the manner in which they interact with the child. This section of the chapter addresses examiner characteristics that enhance the examining situation and reduce the potential threats to validity related to examiner characteristics (Gregory, 2016).

Approachability/Affect

The examiner must create just the right impression for the child to perceive them as approachable. This impression is a tightrope walk that requires a balance between being formal and business-like on one hand and being fun, interesting, and humorous on the other hand. Young children often "read" examiners and respond according to the behavioral messages communicated. When an examiner presents themselves in a formal manner, children may perceive the examiner as relatively cold, harsh, or unaccepting—but, importantly, as someone who cannot be easily manipulated. If the examiner comes across as lively and entertaining, the child may perceive the examiner as someone with whom it will be enjoyable to interact, but the child also may view such an examiner as a playmate with whom roles can be negotiated, requests can be refused, and who is not necessarily to be taken seriously.

It is important that the examiner balance approachability with an air of one who is "in charge." The examiner can maintain this delicate balance by pleasantly, but clearly, establishing expectations and firm limits. Examiners can communicate clear expectations in part by stating directives, rather making requests. Requests are polite forms of communication we tend to use with other adults, but requests imply that the other person has the right to refuse. In a testing situation, examiners should not give the impression of choice, unless choice is truly intended. For example, examiners should say to examinees, "I want you to sit here" rather than "Would you like to sit here?" The former statement is a clear directive and implies no option, whereas the latter question permits the child to say, "No" or "I want to sit over there." The rule of thumb is that examiners should propose questions or choices *only* when they are willing to go along with any answer or choice made by the examinee. If the examiner intends no choice, they should simply state an unambiguous directive, with a warm, engaging smile.

Physical Presence

The examiner should maintain a physical appearance that is conducive to assessing young children. Because many infant and preschool tests require active motor participation on behalf of the examiner, examiners should wear comfortable shoes and clothing that allow for easy performance of motor activities such as skipping, jumping, balancing on one foot, and so on. Because young children sometimes attempt to slide under the examining table to "escape" and avoid participation, examiners' should dress so they can readily crawl, kneel, or sit on the floor.

Examiners should also limit the amount of jewelry they wear during assessments so they do not create unintended visual or auditory distractions. For example, when performing the Hand Movements subtest of the *Kaufman Assessment Battery for Children*, Second Edition, Normative Update (K-ABC-II; Kaufman & Kaufman, 2018), examiners should avoid the distracting "clinking" sounds that are made when rings, watches, or bracelets come in contact with the table top. Similarly, bright, stimulating earrings, pins, broaches, necklaces, and neckties can create attractive but unwanted visual distractions for young children who would be better served focusing on test materials than the examiner's apparel.

Rapport

Establishing rapport with young children can be challenging for many reasons, but with some flexibility examiners can easily establish rapport. To establish rapport, examiners must overcome children's fears, trepidations, shyness, reticence, and reluctance. To overcome these negative affective conditions, it is imperative that the children quickly develop a sense of physical and emotional safety and comfort. Examiners can foster such conditions by displaying a personal attitude that is engaging and sensitive (Gregory, 2016).

To facilitate the maintenance of rapport, examiners should ensure that the testing environment is prepared for a variety of potentially disruptive situations. Examiners should ensure that someone is available to assist young examinees use the bathroom when necessary. They should have tissues at hand to dab crying eyes and wipe ubiquitous running noses. Play materials should be available to develop children's interest or to motivate children when their interests have waned. In addition, examiners should ensure that drawing paper and pencils or coloring materials are available for informal assessment activities, as well as to create a "gift" the child can proudly hand parents when the assessment is complete. Hand puppets, stuffed animals, or other such engaging materials are useful for establishing rapport or comforting younger children because these objects allow examinees and the examiner to talk indirectly through the safer medium. Examiners should anticipate possible situations that could jeopardize rapport and be prepared to deal with these situations proactively and constructively.

Behavior Management

To conduct psychoeducational evaluations with young children, examiners need proficient behavior management skills. Examiners must know when and how to question, direct, cajole, tease, laugh, act silly, be stern, reinforce, admonish, talk, be quiet, pat the child's head or hand affectionately, slow down or speed up the administration pace, show genuine empathy, and perform a variety of related behaviors with perfect timing and sufficient sincerity to maintain the child's motivation, cooperation, and participation.

Preschool children frequently cry when frustrated or when they wish to avoid an activity, and novice examiners often are fearful of young crying children. Knowing that a child's crying typically becomes exacerbated when one actively tries to stop the crying, it is usually better to sit back and let the child cry until they are ready to stop on their own. With tissue in hand, the examiner should wait until the child stops crying, and then tenderly dab the child's final tears soothingly, and immediately redirect the child to the next assessment task without comment. Mentioning the child's crying frequently results in the child's tears flowing again.

Given the labile emotions, variable activity level, and typical distractibility of preschool children, examiners need well developed and practiced behavior management skills. Examiners also need to recognize which examinee behaviors forewarn the examiner of potential problems, and, based on that information, the examiner should proactively and subtly change the course of the situation before the child's behavior requires direct intervention. It is always better to maintain rapport than to try to re-establish it once it has been lost.

Psychometric Skill

Proper and well-paced administration of tests during an assessment is essential for maintaining rapport and managing young children's behavior. Whereas adolescents may sit patiently (or sullenly) and wait for the examiner to fumble through the administration of a new instrument, preschool children do not have such patience. Idle hands do in fact make the devil's work when young children sit for even brief periods unattended while the examiner readies materials, rereads directions, reviews scoring criteria, or searches for needed stimuli. Therefore, examiners should keep the child actively engaged in appropriately paced assessment activities.

To facilitate test administration, examiners should be very familiar with the tests they select to administer. Examiners also should prepare the assessment room prior to the child's arrival and have test kits set up for immediate use. Pacing the assessment to match the characteristics and needs of the examinee is conducive to a successful testing session. A controlled pace occurs only when the examiner has mastered the test administration demands and is very familiar with the test's item content and stimulus materials (Gregory, 2016).

Experience with Preschool Children

Examiners who assess preschool children should be familiar with the developmental characteristics of this age group. Examiners who attribute adult or adolescent motivations to preschool children simply do not understand how young children operate. If the examiner is to reduce construct-irrelevant variance in preschool assessments, they must be comfortable and experienced working with young children and must understand typical and atypical preschool behavior. That is, examiners cannot downward extend their knowledge of older children and adolescents to preschoolers, as the preschool developmental stages and sequence can be quite different from that of older children (Alfonso, Ruby, Wissel, & Davari, 2020).

The Environment

A comfortable testing environment sets the stage for a successful assessment, especially for young children (Gregory, 2016). The effective assessment environment should be cheerful, convey safety, capitalize on the child's curiosity, and stimulate the child's participation. For a testing environment to do these things, it must be child-centered and friendly, and accommodate the needs of young children.

Furniture

Examining rooms intended for preschool children should include appropriately sized furniture. Chairs should allow children's feet to reach the floor, tabletops should be easily reached without straining, and bookshelves should be sufficiently low that children can readily obtain the books, puzzles, or other objects that may be handled before or after the evaluation. Examining rooms should be furnished appropriately for preschool children, rather than forcing preschool children to accommodate to adult-sized furniture and an adult-oriented environment.

Using child-sized furniture is not just a thoughtful consideration; it is an important safety factor. If examinees' feet do not touch the floor while sitting, circulation to their legs is reduced, as is the sense of feeling in their legs. Such loss of feeling and the subsequent "pins and needles" that accompanies restored circulation can cause children to wriggle about and increase the risk of their falling off or out of their chairs, also resulting in distractibility during the evaluation. Some young children opt to kneel or squat when tested in adult-sized chairs so they can better reach the materials on the tabletop. Squatting and kneeling, while a suitable alternative when necessary, can also lead to a loss of balance and falls, if the examiner fails to watch the child closely. Examiners should also consider that oversized chairs allow more than ample room for the child to escape the assessment by squirming between the chair and table and onto the floor.

Decorations

Examining rooms should be cheery, inviting places, with interesting and color-ful materials and decorations. However, examining rooms should not be so stimulating that the décor distracts examinees. Clean, nicely painted, appropri-ately furnished and modestly decorated rooms will provide the desired envir-onment for successful evaluations. When examining rooms include distracting decorations or window scenes, the examiner should arrange the seating to face the child away from the visual distractions. Importantly, examiners should ensure that the most stimulating aspects of the examining room are the exam-iner and the test materials.

Distractions

In addition to limiting visual distractions associated with decorations (e.g., win-dows, pictures, posters), the examiner should ensure that other distractions are similarly subdued. For example, telephones should be set so they do not ring; a "Do Not Disturb" sign should be placed on the examining room door; noise from hallways or adjacent rooms should be controlled; and every effort should be made to ensure that the assessment would be conducted in a room that is conducive to concentration and active participation. Visual, auditory, or per-sonal distractions affect children's test performance, and those children who wish to avoid participating require little distraction to direct their attention away from the evaluation.

Climate Control

Examining rooms should be maintained with temperatures that are sufficiently warm that the children do not sit in a hypothermic stupor, and the rooms should be sufficiently cool that the children are not lulled into a drowsy semi-hypnotic state. Often, examiners are required to use rooms (e.g., cloakrooms, closets) that were not designed for educational or psychological activities, and such examining rooms are not equipped for adequate or easily moderated cli-mate control. When locating a more suitable room is not possible, the exam-iner should open windows or keep doors ajar to allow fresh cool (or warm) air to circulate.

Table/Chair Arrangement

Examiners can do much to maximize behavior management through the arrangement of office furniture. When examining young squirmy children, the examiner can maximize control by providing subtle artificial boundaries and structure. To control an active child, especially one who would choose to leave their seat on a whim, the examiner should place the back legs of the child's chair against a wall—thereby disallowing the child to move their chair backward. The table can then be slid gently against the child's abdomen and thus be used as a "friendly" barrier to keep the child from getting up or sliding down at unwanted times.

When examiners configure the room in such a manner that the child's chair cannot be placed against a wall, the examiner should sit across an adjacent corner of the table from the child. This position allows the examiner to sit in close proximity to the child and thereby respond easily and quickly to the child's needs or actions. Such a position also permits the examiner to reposition or reinforce the child when necessary. For example, a friendly tussle of the child's hair or a tender pat on the shoulder, when done at just the right time can subtly keep the child from rising in their chair. A gentle pat on the back can bring the child closer to the tabletop and work area. Similarly, by placing one foot behind the front leg of the child's chair, the examiner can maintain the position of a squirmy child's chair so it remains in close proximity to the table, the workspace, and the examiner.

However the examiner chooses to situate the examining room, the examiner should ensure that the child is positioned farther from the door than is the examiner. By carefully modifying the seating arrangement, the examiner can forestall the child's efforts to separate from the testing materials and be in a better position to disallow the child to leave the room. By positioning themselves closer to the door, the examiner can cut off any attempts by the child to exit the room.

Psychometric Considerations

Although examiners can moderate many of the previously mentioned threats to validity by employing clinical judgment and skill, examiners have no means to control or alter the foibles associated with the various instruments they have available for use. Examiners can and should select instruments for use only after carefully considering each instrument's psychometric properties and unique characteristics (Alfonso, Shanock, Muldoon, Benway, & Oades-Sese, 2018, May) (see Chapter 10, this volume, for a review of several cognitive ability tests for young children).

Bracken (1988) identified ten common psychometric reasons why similar tests produce dissimilar results. The intent of that article was to reveal common psychometric threats to validity, which may or may not be obvious upon casual viewing of test manuals and materials. In an error-free world, multiple tests that purport to assess the same construct (e.g., intelligence) should produce identical results when administered to the same child. Sometimes, however, tests that purport to measure the same construct produce results that are significantly discrepant from each other, and the reasons for such discrepancies often are related to construct-irrelevant psychometric limitations of the instruments (Bracken, 1987; Wasserman & Bracken, 2002, 2003). The remainder of this section addresses these construct-irrelevant conditions and recommends possible solutions to these common psychometric limitations.

Test Floors

The floor of a test is an indication of the extent to which an instrument provides meaningful scores at very low levels of individual functioning. Given that examiners sometimes conduct psychoeducational tests to diagnose delayed or retarded levels of functioning, it is important that examiners use tests that are capable of reliably and accurately assessing such low levels of cognitive functioning (Gregory, 2016). Examiners should ensure that they use tests that are in fact capable of producing suitably low scores for the delayed children they serve. Bracken (1987) recommended that a *minimal* standard for subtest, composite, and total test floors should equal or exceed minus two standard deviations (i.e., the minimal level traditionally required to diagnose retarded functioning).

To identify the floor of a subtest, the examiner should locate the lowest standard score that can possibly be obtained at every age level, if the examinee were to pass only one item on that subtest. For any age at which a subtest raw score of 1 fails to generate a standard score equal to or greater than minus two standard deviations, the subtest is insufficiently sensitive to identify seriously delayed functioning. To determine the floors of composite or total test scores, the examiner should identify the corresponding standard score associated with an earned raw score of 1 on each of the subtests that contribute to the composite or total test. If five subtests contribute to the composite, the examiner would identify the corresponding standard score associated with a raw score of 5. If the composite standard score is less than two standard deviations below the normative mean, the composite has an insufficient floor for identifying retarded level functioning at the age level considered.

Historically, tests have frequently had insufficient floors for children below age 4 (Bracken, 1987; Flanagan & Alfonso, 1995), which results in construct-irrelevant reasons for the resulting inflated scores. That is, the child's test score would be inaccurate and give an over-estimate of the child's true level of functioning due in part to the psychometric foibles of the instrument used. Examiners must be especially careful to examine floors when conducting assessments on low-functioning younger children, especially those younger than 4 years. When composite and total test scores are truncated due to the construct-irrelevant limitations of the instrument employed, that test should not be used to guide decisions about the child's diagnosis and placement. Such a test should be considered biased against children of that particular age and ability level.

Test Ceilings

Ceilings within tests refer to the extent to which subtest, composite, or total test scores accurately reflect upper extreme levels of functioning among examinees. Because gifted functioning is typically characterized as beginning two or more standard deviations above the normative mean, tests intended for gifted identification should provide accurate scores at and above this criterion level. Ceilings are not generally as relevant among preschool tests as are test floors. It is easier to create suitable items for assessing the upper limits of young children's abilities than it is to develop items that discriminate between the extreme lower limits of ability at this age level. Conversely, it is more difficult to create items that accurately assess the upper extreme abilities of older adolescents than it is to develop items that assess lower limits of abilities among this older population.

Although ceiling limitations are relatively rare in preschool tests, examiners should be watchful just the same. Some tests include subtests specifically designed for younger children, which are discontinued for slightly older children. Subtests typically are discontinued within a battery when the subtests have serious ceiling or floor problems and are no longer appropriate for children at that age level.

Item Gradients

Item gradients refer to how steeply graded standard scores are arranged in relation to their respective raw scores. Ideally, the incremental change in standard scores that results from one raw score unit to the next (e.g., a raw score of 5 versus 6) should produce a comparably small standard score increase. Unfortunately, preschool tests are notorious for having steep item gradients, with correspondingly large standard score manifestations associated with minor increases or decreases in raw scores. Whenever a test has steep item gradients, only a rough discrimination between ability levels results from that instrument. Such crude discrimination between levels of ability leads to construct-irrelevant variation in the assessed construct related to the instrument rather than true differences in children's individual abilities.

Examiners should carefully examine norm tables for all age levels and determine the ages at which the test or subtests have item gradients that are too steep for accurate and finely graded discrimination of abilities. Bracken (1988) recommended that an increase or decrease of a single raw score should not alter the corresponding standard score by more than one-third standard deviation. That is, a raw score of x (e.g., 25) on a given measure should not produce a standard score that is more than one-third standard deviation greater than that which would result from a raw score one integer less or greater (i.e., $x \pm 1$ or 24/26). Tests with item gradients that are steeper than these guidelines are too crude to accurately assess individual differences in students' abilities (see Chapter 10, this volume, for a review of item gradients of cognitive ability tests for preschoolers).

Reliability

Tests with low reliability produce proportionately large portions of subtest and composite variability related to measurement error rather than true differences in the construct. A test with an Alpha Coefficient of .80 will produce variance that is 80% reliable, while 20% of the variance is due to measurement error. Obviously, error is a source of construct-irrelevant variance, and examiners should selectively employ only tests that possess reasonable levels of internal consistency and stability. Bracken (1988) and Wasserman and Bracken (2002, 2003) suggested that .90 be set as an acceptable level of internal consistency and stability for total test scores. Subtest and composite reliabilities should approximate .80, with median subtest reliabilities equal to .80 or higher. These guidelines provide a reasonable "rule of thumb" when selecting tests for individual assessments.

Validity

The sine qua non of construct-relevant assessment is test validity. Because validity is such an important element in assessment, test manuals must provide thorough and convincing evidence of content, construct, and criterion-related validity (AERA, APA, NCME, 2014). Because validity is a continuous variable, rather than a dichotomous variable, and ranges from the total absence of validity to perfect validity (though both of these absolutes are rare), examiners must determine whether the documentation and level of demonstrated validity justifies use of the instrument for its intended purpose. Any time a test with poor validity is selected, used, and contributes to diagnostic decision-making, the examiner knowingly and willingly introduces variance into the decision-making equation that is to some large extent construct irrelevant. Examiners have an ethical, professional, and legal responsibility to use instruments of the highest quality, and validity should be the most important aspect of technical adequacy considered.

Norms Tables

Norm tables may be an inadvertent contributor to construct-irrelevant variability in test scores. The norm tables of some preschool tests include age ranges that are too broad to be sensitive to the rapid growth and development that occurs during the first six years of life (e.g., six-month or one-year age ranges). Norm tables for preschool tests should not exceed three-month intervals, and at the youngest age levels (i.e., birth to 2 years) norms should reflect intervals as small as one or two months.

The easiest way to evaluate the quality of a norm table is to examine the difference in standard scores associated with a given raw score as you progress from one table to the next. If the standard score increases by large amounts (e.g., ± one-third standard deviation), the test may provide too gross an estimate of ability to instill much confidence in the resultant scores. Consider the importance of norm table sensitivity for a child who is on the very upper cusp of one age level and who is about to "graduate" to the next age level. A good test should not produce a large difference in standard scores based solely on whether the child was tested yesterday, today, or tomorrow, especially when the raw score remains the same across these three days. If a test is sensitive to the construct assessed, the child's obtained raw score should yield nearly identical standard scores across this hypothetical three-day range. For example, consider a child who is 2 years, 7 months, and 15 days old when tested on the old *McCarthy Scales of Children's Abilities* (MSCA; McCarthy, 1972). If this child obtained a raw score of 37 across the MSCA five scales (see Bracken, 1988), their total test score (i.e., GCI) would have been 112. However, if the same child earned an identical score on the following day when they were 2 years, 7 months and 16 days old (i.e., just one day older), their subsequent GCI would be 101, a decrease in functioning by more than two-thirds standard deviation.

Examiners should strive to eliminate or reduce such construct-irrelevant influences in the assessment of preschool children by selecting tests with appropriately sensitive norm tables. Sensitivity is needed most at the youngest age levels when children's development occurs at the fastest pace.

Age of Norms

Examiners are ethically bound by a variety of organizations to use only the most recent editions of tests (e.g., National Association of School Psychologists, American Psychological Association Ethical Guidelines, Standards for Educational and Psychological Testing; NASP, APA). There are several reasons for using only the most recent editions of tests; these include the benefits of improved and updated stimulus materials, the inclusion of recent perspectives and theoretical advances in each test, and the application of recent normative samples. This latter reason has direct implications for accurate assessment and decision-making.

Flynn (1984, 1987, 1999) demonstrated that on an international level, the general intelligence of the world's population is increasing at a rate of about 3 IQ points per decade. This increase in population intelligence is related to a variety of hypothesized factors, including improved diet and health care, the positive influences of various media, and improved economic conditions among more individuals. Whatever the reason for this documented longitudinal improvement in intelligence, the implications for using outdated tests is clear. Outdated tests inflate the estimate of children's intelligence in direct proportion to the age of the "softened" norms.

Examiners who use tests that are one, two, or three decades old might expect test scores to be inflated by a magnitude of 3, 6, or 9 IQ points, respectively. The differential effects of test age on assessed intelligence is not related directly to the construct being assessed (i.e., intelligence); rather, it is related to the artifactual effects of the age of the test's norms. To avoid these artifactual effects, examiners should not only be ethically bound but also practically and professionally bound to use only the most recent editions of instruments. When a test has not been revised within the past decade and a half, examiners should question whether to continue using the instrument. The MSCA, for example, was published originally in 1972 and has not been revised since. Examiners would be hard pressed to defend using such an instrument with norms that are more than 40 years old, given the construct-irrelevant influences of the age of the norms on the child's estimated level of functioning. If this example seems extreme, consider that the first author of this chapter, as a discussant for a conference paper presentation, was critical of a psychologist's continued clinical use of the 1973 *Stanford-Binet Intelligence Scale, Form L-M* (Bracken, 2004). The first author of this chapter also served as a consultant on a legal case in which a psychologist was continuing his practice of using the Wechsler Intelligence Scale for Children–Revised (WISC-R; 1975) for Social Security Administration disability determination assessments.

Basic Concepts in Test Directions

Before examiners can effectively assess a child's abilities with standardized instruments, they have to ensure that the child fully understands the test's directions. If a child fails to understand what is required of them while taking a test, then the test may assess listening comprehension or receptive vocabulary rather than the intended construct (e.g., intelligence). Researchers have consistently shown that the past several generations of preschool instruments have test directions that are replete with basic concepts beyond the conceptual understanding of most young children (Bracken, 1986, 1988; Flanagan & Alfonso, 1995; Flanagan, Kaminer, Alfonso, & Raderc, 1995; Kaufman, 1978). When the wording and vocabulary in test directions are more complex than the required task, the test is more a measure of language proficiency than a measure of the intended construct.

The relevance of test direction complexity and basic concept inclusion is especially important when assessing children who speak English as a second language or who speak a nonstandard form of English. Children from these minority linguistic groups may be especially disadvantaged when administered tests with complex verbal directions, especially when the construct purportedly assessed by the instrument is not language facility, fluency, or comprehension. To avoid the construct-irrelevant influence of complex test directions, examiners should seek instruments that provide simple test directions, as well as demonstration and sample items that ensure that the child understands the nature of the task requirements before beginning the task for credit. In some situations where language comprehension is a central referral issue, nonverbal tests of ability may be warranted to provide a contrast between performance on language-related tests and nonverbal measures. Comprehensive nonverbal tests of intelligence, such as the *Universal Nonverbal Intelligence Test—Second Edition* (UNIT2; Bracken & McCallum, 2016) or the *Leiter International Performance Scale—Third Edition* (Roid, Miller, & Koch, 2013, were designed for use when the examinee's language skills represent a construct-irrelevant contributor to test variance.

Conclusion

The focus of this chapter has been on creating an examining situation that systematically reduces construct-irrelevant influences in the assessment process and maximizes the examiner's confidence in the accuracy and interpretability of the test results. Examiners should employ clinical skills to reduce threats to the validity of the assessment by creating a safe, secure, and engaging environment. Examiners should also consider the child's current physical condition and health when planning an assessment and decide whether a valid estimate of the child's true abilities can be obtained given the child's current physical state. Finally, examiners should carefully examine and consider the psychometric properties and foibles of the instruments in their psychoeducational batteries. When tests fail to meet psychometric standards that are commonly considered as essential for testing older children, adolescents and adults, these instruments should not be used for the assessment of preschool children either.

When examiners carefully consider and address these important intrapersonal, interpersonal, environmental, and psychometric issues, they systematically reduce the construct-irrelevant variability in examinees' test scores. By reducing the variability in test scores that is attributable to measurement error, examiners can have more confidence in the test results and thereby make more defensible decisions.

References

Alfonso, V. C., Shanock, A., Muldoon, D., Benway, N., & Oades-Sese, (2018, May). Psychometric integrity of preschool speech/language tests: Implications for diagnosis and progress monitoring of treatment. *Poster presented at the annual meeting of the association for psychological science*, San Francisco, CA.

Alfonso, V. C., Ruby, S., Wissel, A. M., & Davari, J. (2020). School psychologists in early childhood settings. In F. C. Worrell, T. L. Hughes, & D.D. Dixson (Eds.), *The Cambridge handbook of applied school psychology* (pp. 579–597). Cambridge: Cambridge University Press.

American Educational Research Association, American Psychological Association, National Council on Measurement in Education, Joint Committee on Standards for Educational and Psychological Testing (U.S.). (2014). *Standards for educational and psychological testing*. Washington, DC: AERA.

Bracken, B. A. (1986). Incidence of basic concepts in the directions of five commonly used American tests of intelligence. *School Psychology International, 7*, 1–10.

Bracken, B. A. (1987). Limitations of preschool instruments and standards for minimal levels of technical adequacy. *Journal of Psychoeducational Assessment, 4*, 313–326.

Bracken, B. A. (1988). Ten psychometric reasons why similar tests produce dissimilar results. *Journal of School Psychology, 26*, 155–166.

Bracken, B. A. (2004). Discussant. Symposium on intelligence testing. *Presented at the national association of gifted children's annual conference*. November, Salt Lake City, UT.

Bracken, B. A. & Keith, L. (2004). *Clinical assessment of behavior.* Lutz, FL: Psychological Assessment Resources.

Bracken, B. A. & McCallum, R. S. (2016). *Universal nonverbal intelligence test – Second edition.* Itasca, IL: Riverside.

Bracken, B. A. & Theodore, L. A. (in press). Clinical observation of preschool assessment behavior. In V. Alfonso, B. Bracken, & R. Nagle (Eds.), *Psychoeducational assessment of preschool children* (5th ed.). New York: Routledge, Taylor & Francis Group.

Carey, W. B. & McDevitt, S. C. (1995). *Coping with children's temperament.* New York: Basic Books.

Chess, S. & Thomas, A. (1992). Dynamics of individual behavioral development. In M. D. Levine, W. B. Carey, & A. C. Crocker (Eds.), *Developmental –behavioral pediatrics* (2nd ed., pp. 84-94). Philadelphia: Saunders.

Flanagan, D. P. & Alfonso, V. C. (1995). A critical review of the technical characteristics of new and recently revised intelligence tests for preschoolers. *Journal of Psychoeducational Assessment, 13,* 66–90.

Flanagan, D. P., Kaminer, T., Alfonso, V. C., & Raderc, D. E. (1995). Incidence of basic concepts in the directions of new and recently revised American intelligence tests for preschool children. *School Psychology International, 16*(4), 345-364.

Flynn, J. R. (1984). The mean IQ of Americans: Massive gains from 1932 to 1978. *Psychological Bulletin, 95,* 29–51.

Flynn, J. R. (1987). Massive IQ gains in 14 nations: What IQ tests really measure. *Psychological Bulletin, 95,* 29–51.

Flynn, J. R. (1999). Searching for justice: The discovery of IQ gains over time. *American Psychologist, 54,* 5–20.

Gregory, R. J. (2016). *Psychological testing: History, principles, and applications* (7th ed.). New York: Pearson.

Kaufman, A. S. (1978). The importance of basic concepts in individual assessment of preschool children. *Journal of School Psychology, 16,* 207–211.

Kaufman, A. S. & Kaufman, N. L. (2018). *Kaufman assessment battery for children - Second edition, normative update.* San Antonio, TX: Pearson.

McCarthy, D. (1972). *McCarthy scales of children's abilities.* San Antonio, TX: The Psychological Corporation.

Ortiz, S. O., Piazza, N., Ochoa, S. H., & Dynda, A. M. (2018). Testing with culturally and linguistically diverse populations: New directions in fairness and validity. In D. P. Flanagan & E. M. McDonough (Eds.), *Contemporary intellectual assessment: Theories, tests, and issues* (4th ed., pp. 684–712). New York, NY: Guilford Press.

Roid, G. H., Miller, L. G., & Koch, C. (2013). Leiter international performance scale – third edition. Stoelting Wood Dale, IL.

Thomas, A. & Chess, S. (1977). *Temperament and development.* New York: Brunner/ Mazel.

Wasserman, J. D. & Bracken, B. A. (2002). Selecting appropriate tests: Psychometric and pragmatic considerations. In J. F. Carlson & B. B. Waterman (Eds.), *Social and personal assessment of school-aged children: Developing interventions for educational and clinical settings* (pp. 18–43). Needham Heights, MA: Allyn & Bacon.

Wasserman, J. D. & Bracken, B. A. (2003). Psychometric considerations of assessment procedures. In J. Graham & J. Naglieri (Eds.), *Handbook of assessment psychology* (pp. 43–66). New York: Wiley.

Part II

Ecological Assessment

Chapter 4

School Readiness and Academic Functioning in Preschoolers

Robin L. Hojnoski and Kristen N. Missall

Introduction

School readiness is an enduring topic of interest for social science research, public policy design, and public opinion. In 1991, the National Educational Goals Panel adopted the goal that "by the year 2000, all children will enter school ready to learn" (High, 2008). Since that time, educational policy has continued to include a focus on early education. For example, Preschool for All established federal-state partnerships to provide high-quality preschool for all 4-year-olds from low- and moderate-income families (U.S. Department of Health and Human Services, Administration for Children and Families, www.acf.hhs.gov/ecd/preschool-for-all), the Race to the Top: Early Learning Challenge focused specifically on improving quality in early childhood systems (U.S. Department of Health and Human Services, Administration for Children and Families, www2.ed.gov/programs/racetothetop-earlylearningchallenge/index.html), and the nation's revised general education legislation, the Every Student Succeeds Act (U.S. Department of Education, https://www2.ed.gov/programs/racetothetop-earlylearningchallenge/index.html), includes preschool programming. This most recent iteration of the general education funding bill also for the first time includes an emphasis on coordinating early learning service in the community, aligning preschool with early elementary school, and strengthening the capacity of communities to provide the highest-quality early learning opportunities. These policy initiatives have resulted in an increase in publicly supported preschool programs, primarily targeting 4-year-old children in the year before kindergarten with a focus on preparing children for kindergarten.

In 2017–2018, 44 states and the District of Columbia offered some type of early education for 4-year-olds (Friedman-Krauss et al., 2019). These initiatives have led to an increasing emphasis on assessment of school readiness that supports children's development and subsequent achievement (Howard, 2011). The purpose of this chapter is to present critical definitional and practical issues related to the multi-dimensional construct of school readiness, to summarize research that supports the connections between early academic functioning and later school achievement, and to provide recommendations for assessing early academic functioning as an indicator of school readiness.

What Is School Readiness?

Effective assessment of school readiness necessarily raises questions of how best to conceptualize the process of readiness development and to define school readiness, itself. As to the development of school readiness, there are varying conceptions, each with a different emphasis on the factors that contribute to a child's readiness for school, or readiness for learning (Kagan, 1990). For example, the ideal or nativist conception emphasizes a "within-child" perspective of readiness that is largely dependent on an internal maturational process. As such, children will either "be ready" for school or they will need more time to develop, such that they are "not ready" for school. In contrast, the empiricist or environmental conception defines school readiness as something outside of the child, requiring skills and behaviors that the child can be taught. This conception places more emphasis, then, on the environment and what the environment provides for the child through a process of cultural transmission. Although cultural transmission is implicated in the environmental conception, it is really the social constructivist framework that situates school readiness within the child's social and cultural context and recognizes that this context determines what skills and behaviors constitute readiness. With increased emphasis on the role of context, the interactionist conception merges the child's readiness with the school's readiness; that is, children will come to school "ready" with a range of skills and knowledge, and schools must be "ready" to meet children's individual learning needs. This conception is characterized by bidirectionality, with dual focus on the child and the environment and the relationship between the two (Meisels, 1999). Finally, contemporary conceptions of school readiness recognize the importance of the school setting as well as the larger community context (e.g., socioeconomic status, neighborhood safety and well-being, access to services) in understanding children's development relative to school success (Lipscomb et al., 2019).

As to a unified definition of school readiness, there is little consensus about the specific skills that comprise the construct (Boivin & Bierman, 2014; Carlton & Winsler, 1999; Farran, 2011). Empirical literature suggests a range of child characteristics, skills, and behaviors that are related to school readiness, including executive functioning (e.g., Sasser, Bierman, & Heinrichs, 2015), working memory (e.g., Sabol & Pianta, 2012), social competence (e.g., Denham et al., 2013), peer relationships (e.g., Torres, Domitrovich, & Bierman, 2015), and early academic functioning (e.g., Duncan et al., 2007). At the most basic level, "school readiness refers to the state of child competencies at the time of school entry that are important for later success" (Snow, 2006, p. 9). Most would agree that school readiness is a multidimensional construct that encompasses cognitive, social-emotional, behavioral, and physical dimensions (Miller & Kehl, 2019).

The relative importance of the multiple dimensions comprising school readiness may vary as perceived by important stakeholders such as parents and teachers. For example, parents and teachers in a Midwestern sample ranked skills such as communication, enthusiasm, and following directions as most important for school readiness, whereas more traditional pre-academic skills (e.g., counting, letter knowledge) were ranked as less important (Miller & Kehl, 2019). Similar results related to pre-academic skills were obtained with a sample of parents and preschool and kindergarten teachers from diverse backgrounds in an urban setting, although parents tended to rate pre-academic skills as more necessary for kindergarten than teachers (Piotrkowski, Botsko, & Matthews, 2000). Finally, parents and teachers from nationally representative samples have also placed more importance on learning-related social skills (i.e., communication, following directions, independence) as compared to pre-academic skills (Kim, Murdock, & Choi, 2005; Lin, Lawrence, & Gorrell, 2003). Interestingly, learning-related social skills have also been identified as skills with which children entering kindergarten tend to struggle. Roughly 50% of teachers from a large national sample reported that "about half their class or more" entered kindergarten with "difficulty following directions." Additionally, though, about one-third of the sample indicated that "about half their class or more" entered kindergarten with a "lack of academic skills" (Rimm-Kaufman, Pianta, & Cox, 2000).

School Readiness and Achievement

Variability in school readiness skills among children as they enter kindergarten is further underscored by empirical evidence supporting different patterns of school readiness and their associations with school achievement. For example, distinct patterns of school readiness comprised of teacher-observed, teacher-rated, and directly assessed pre-academic skills and social behavior have been identified among children enrolled in Head Start (McWayne, Cheung, Wright, & Hahs-Vaughn, 2012). These beginning-of-the-year preschool patterns were strong predictors of kindergarten outcomes of phonemic awareness, general knowledge, applied problems, problem-solving, and social skills. Similar results were obtained over a shorter period of time using a brief teacher rating of readiness during kindergarten (Stormont, Herman, Reinke, King, & Owens, 2015). Specifically, teacher ratings of readiness at the beginning of kindergarten predicted outcomes at the end of kindergarten after controlling for student demographics. Further, teacher ratings of readiness at the beginning of kindergarten demonstrated adequate classification accuracy within domains (e.g., academic and behavioral). Of particular note, the measure of readiness included only three items (i.e., academic, behavioral, and overall readiness), which provided an efficient means of rating all kindergarteners as part of universal screening efforts. These studies suggest that development of school readiness skills during preschool and as children enter kindergarten creates a foundation for children's continued school experience academically and behaviorally.

School readiness at the beginning of kindergarten has also demonstrated associations with longer-term outcomes. For example, patterns of school readiness have been identified in a large sample of Latino children with these patterns predicting literacy trajectories from grade 2 through grade 5 (Quirk, Grimm, Furlong, Nylund-Gibson, & Swami, 2016). Global teacher ratings of kindergarten readiness (i.e., multiple domains summed to a single score) in the first month of kindergarten have also been associated with grade 3 achievement in reading, mathematics, and writing after taking into account student-level demographics (e.g., gender, minority status, disability status, free and reduced lunch) and school-level demographics (i.e., proportion of students receiving free and reduced lunch, proportion of students receiving special education services; Goldstein, McCoach, & Yu, 2017). Further, teacher-rated school readiness during the first month of kindergarten with a similar measure was associated with reading fluency and social-emotional well-being in grade 5. More specifically, social-emotional readiness in kindergarten predicted social competence in grade 5, whereas cognitive readiness did not add to this prediction beyond what was already accounted for by social-emotional readiness. Conversely, cognitive readiness in kindergarten predicted reading fluency in grade 5, with social-emotional readiness not significantly adding to the prediction (Quirk, Dowdy, Goldstein, & Carnazzo, 2017). Within-domain relations suggest the importance of including both academic and social-emotional skills in conceptions of school success.

Specific Early Academic Skills

In addition to understanding how broad measures of school readiness relate to later outcomes, there is an interest in understanding the role of specific skills comprising school readiness with implications for assessment and early education. For example, it is clear that once established, mathematical performance tends to be stable over time without intervention (Aunola, Leskinen, Lerkkanen, & Nurmi, 2004; Missall, Mercer, Martinez, & Casebeer, 2012). Similar relations between early skills and later outcomes have been documented for literacy. A seminal study by Juel (1988) documented a .88 probability of being a poor reader in grade 4 if a student was considered as a poor reader at grade 1. In an effort to consider several specific skills simultaneously, Duncan and colleagues (2007) examined the predictive validity of early language and literacy, mathematics, and attentional and social-emotional skills at kindergarten entry to long-term achievement using six longitudinal data sets. Analyses controlled for family and child characteristics, and when data were available, prior cognitive ability and concurrent reading ability were also controlled.

Early academic skills were strong predictors of later academic achievement; specifically, early literacy skills predicted later reading achievement and early mathematical skills predicted later mathematical achievement. Moderate predictive power was found for attentional skills, whereas social-emotional skills demonstrated few statistically significant relations. In a meta-analytic regression, however, early mathematics was the strongest predictor of reading and math achievement; behavior problems and social skills were not associated with later academic achievement. These findings were replicated (Pagani, Fitzpatrick, Archambault, & Janosz, 2010), with additional support for an association between early mathematical skills and social-emotional skills at grade 3 (Romano, Babchishin, Pagani, & Kohen, 2010). Further support has been provided for early mathematics as a strong predictor of adolescent mathematics achievement, after controlling for early reading, cognitive, family, and child characteristics (Watts, Duncan, Siegler, & Davis-Kean, 2014).

Approaches to Learning

Although analyses of longitudinal data indicated only moderate predictive power for attentional skills, other research has examined attention-related skills as part of a broader set of non-cognitive skills important for school readiness. These skills include listening and following directions, working independently, persistence, and organization, among others, and are collectively termed "learning-related social skills" (McClelland & Morrison, 2003; McClelland, Morrison, & Holmes, 2000) or "approaches to learning" (ATL; McWayne, Fantuzzo, & McDermott, 2004). ATL has been identified as a key set of school readiness indicators (Li-Grining, Votruba-Drzal, Maldonado-Carreño, & Haas, 2010); ATL may influence children's perceptions of school, with positive ATL potentially serving as a protective factor in the face of later school difficulties (Daniels, 2014; McWayne, Green, & Fantuzzo, 2009). Children enter kindergarten with varying levels of ATL, and research suggests that subsequently, these children follow different academic trajectories, with children with better ATL demonstrating greater growth in reading and mathematics through elementary school (e.g., Li-Grining et al., 2010; McClelland, Acock, & Morrison, 2006; Morgan, Farkas, & Wu, 2011). Teacher-rated ATL in preschool also uniquely predicted kindergarten and grade 1 outcomes, including reading and mathematics achievement, the need for special services, and grade retention (Hunter, Bierman, & Hall, 2018). Further, in a nationally representative sample, better ATL at kindergarten entry was moderately more beneficial for children with lower academic skills at entering kindergarten (Li-Grining et al., 2010), with these findings replicated with a sample of children predominantly from low-income backgrounds (Razza, Martin, & Brooks-Gunn, 2015). Finally, ATL has been demonstrated to predict growth proficiency in vocabulary, language, and science in grade 2, though the specific indicators of ATL change over the early elementary period (McDermott, Rikoon, & Fantuzzo, 2014).

Engagement

One potential explanation for the association between ATL, or learning-related social skills, and academic achievement is that these skills support children's engagement in learning and interpersonal interactions. Increased engagement, then, is likely to lead to greater skill development and thus could serve as a mediating variable. Indeed, research with kindergarteners suggests that engagement mediates the relation between classroom quality and reading achievement (Ponitz, Rimm-Kaufman, Grimm, & Curby, 2009), and engagement as time-on-task has been related to gains in reading skills (Ponitz & Rimm-Kaufman, 2011). Engagement can be defined as the child's interaction with teachers, peers, and tasks within the classroom environment (Williford, Maier, Downer, Pianta, & Howes, 2013). In addition, the valence (i.e., positive or negative) of engagement is often considered in relation to outcomes of interest. Limited research examining engagement has been conducted with preschoolers, however, and this work has been restricted to growth in school readiness skills across the preschool year, with no studies to date examining the relation of engagement in early education to later achievement or social-emotional outcomes. The research that does exist suggests dimensions of engagement differ in their associations with school readiness outcomes, such as language, literacy, and ATL. For example, in a sample of children from low-income, racially and ethnically diverse backgrounds, positive engagement with teachers was related to improved literacy skills, whereas children's positive engagement with peers was related to improved language. Children's negative engagement in the classroom was associated with lower language and literacy skills and lower ATL (Sabol, Bohlmann, & Downer, 2018). Additionally, profiles of children's individual classroom engagement in preschool created by using a "snapshot" method predicted math, language, and literacy skill gains over the preschool year even after controlling for observed global classroom quality (Chien et al., 2010).

A growing and diverse body of evidence suggests that early skills in a range of domains (e.g., mathematics, literacy, ATL, engagement) are predictive of short- and long-term achievement. Such learning trajectories emphasize the need for effective early assessment practices to inform early intervention. Research suggests school readiness interventions delivered in various formats (e.g., summer programming, supplementary programming) can be effective in promoting children's skill acquisition (e.g., Bierman et al., 2008; Pears, Kim, Fisher, & Yoerger, 2016). For example, children from low-income backgrounds who participated in a high-intensity (e.g., increased learning opportunities), short-term (e.g., 16-session) school readiness intervention during the summer demonstrated significant gains in early literacy skills as well as gains in self-regulation as compared to children in a services-as-usual condition (Pears et al., 2014). Thus, when children are identified early in their schooling experience, ideally prior to kindergarten, appropriate interventions can be provided to shift trajectories toward more positive outcomes.

Assessing School Readiness

As is clear from a brief synthesis of the literature, assessing school readiness is a complicated endeavor. The first issue to address is defining the construct to be measured. A basic tenet of measurement theory is that validity requires a clearly defined construct (Shadish, Cook, & Campbell, 2002), and yet there is no consensus as to what skills are most important to school success. There is empirical support for multiple indicators of school readiness across domains of pre-academic skills, ATL, and social-emotional competencies (addressed in Chapter 8, this volume). Further, skills associated with school readiness reflect within-child factors (e.g., working memory; Sabol & Pianta, 2012), sociodemographic factors (e.g., gender, socioeconomic status), and contextual factors (e.g., classroom quality; Chien et al., 2010). The multidimensionality of school readiness and a transactional perspective of the development of school readiness may lead to numerous approaches to measuring the construct that (1) support a readiness-for-school or readiness-for-learning paradigm (Kagan, 1990); (2) favor one dimension over another (e.g., social-emotional versus academic skills); and (3) reflect a within-child approach or emphasize context.

Given the challenges inherent in assessing school readiness, we propose an assessment approach that is sensitive to paradigms of "children ready for school" and "schools ready for children" evidenced in a transactional perspective. We advocate for an approach that centers on supporting the learning and development of all children in a strengths-based context situated within instructional and curricular expectations for full grade-level access to instruction. Assessment of school readiness should provide information about an individual child's growth and development as well as information about how the child is situated in the broader context of learning to make predictions about ongoing and successful access to general instruction with grade-level matriculation. We suggest that effective assessment of school readiness focus on measuring critical key skills known to promote access to instruction, ongoing engagement and learning, and short- and long-term school success. We propose the use of measurement approaches that are idiographic, or individually sensitive and appropriate to differences, along with measures that are nomothetic, or informative of a child's progress as it relates to other same-age peers and broader educational expectations (Brassard & Boehm, 2007; National Association of School Psychologists, 2015; National Research Council, 2008).

Purpose of Assessment

The first step in the assessment of school readiness is defining clearly the purpose of assessment. How we intend to use readiness assessments determines how we select assessment tools in terms of content, methods for gathering information, technical features, and implications of the use of scores (Graue, 2006; Kettler & Feeney-Kettler 2011). Readiness has been conceptualized as two separate concepts, *readiness for school* and *readiness to learn* (Kagan, 1990; Lewit & Baker, 1995). The first indicates that there is a fixed standard of cognitive and social development that a child must attain to meet school-specific expectations and requirements, and the purpose of assessment from this perspective is to evaluate whether children have met the standard. Although research suggests there are skill sets that are associated with children's short-and long-term success (e.g., early mathematical skills, positive ATL, social-emotional competence), attainment of a fixed standard should not be the criteria for kindergarten entry. Indeed, the classification accuracy of early academic assessment measures is limited (e.g., Laracy, Hojnoski, & Dever, 2016; Wilson & Lonigan, 2010), which suggests that the purpose of assessing school readiness skills should be to identify the levels of support a child may need to be successful in the short term, with implications for later academic achievement (Howard, 2011). Further, an emphasis on school readiness that only considers the skills of a child fails to acknowledge contextual factors that contribute to child development and minimizes economic, experiential, and cultural inequities that often lead to identifying certain groups of children as at-risk (Graue, 2006; High, 2008). Such within-child practices have been challenged by a transition-to-school framework whereby children's readiness is viewed within a broader contextual perspective that considers the values, expectations, and supports related to learning (LoCasale-Crouch, Mashburn, Downer, & Pianta, 2008).

Instead, a child's present level of skills within important school readiness domains should be viewed within the context of readiness to learn. Readiness to learn has been defined as the level of development at which an individual of any age is ready to undertake the learning of specific material (Farran, 2011; Kagan, 1990; Miller & Kehl, 2019), and in the absence of significant cognitive impairment, all children should be seen as ready to learn (Farran, 2011). Assessment of school readiness should provide some indication of a child's present level of skills within domains important to short-and long-term success to assist schools in supporting all children's readiness to learn. To facilitate assessment within the larger population to the extent possible given practical considerations, we advocate for universal screening prior to kindergarten entry, or soon after kindergarten entry. The purpose of screening is to determine the intensity of instruction and the level of support that may be needed for the child to be successful and to guide additional, more in-depth assessment. Several studies support the utility of brief screening assessments early in kindergarten (Quirk et al., 2017; Stormont et al., 2015). Moreover, universal screening has been incorporated into preschool response-to-intervention frameworks for language and early literacy (e.g., Carta, Greenwood, Atwater, McConnell, Goldstein, & Kaminski, 2014). In addition to identification purposes, assessment of present level of skills provides baseline data that can be used in formative assessment to ensure that all children are making adequate progress toward identified goals.

Children enter school with varying levels of skills across different developmental domains, given the varied experiences children have prior to kindergarten that influence their development. School readiness assessments conducted prior to kindergarten entry or shortly after kindergarten entry can be useful to schools in designing programming that will meet children's diverse needs as opposed to excluding those children who may be most in need of high-quality education (High, 2008). Understanding children's present levels of skill development can inform instruction and intervention to ensure that all children establish a strong foundation for continued learning. Given that school readiness is an interaction between the child's developmental level and elements of the environment (Snow, 2006), children must be ready for school and schools must be ready for all children (e.g., Carlton & Winsler, 1999; Hojnoski & Missall, 2006). Thus, the primary purpose of school readiness assessment is to better understand the child's strengths and needs in order to design effective instruction that will support the development of key skills and provide a foundation for school success.

Key Skills

Frameworks for school readiness generally vary across the United States based on different stakeholder perceptions about what skills are necessary for early school success. These frameworks are often informed by organizational assessments and values. For example, the Head Start network serves preschoolers across the country, and it is typical for all Head Start programs to follow the Head Start Early Learning Outcomes Framework (U.S. Department of Health and Human Services, Administration of Children and Families, Office of Head Start, 2015). These ongoing practices are likely to influence educator perspectives about what data (e.g., pre-academic, social-emotional, attendance) are important for making decisions for kindergarten readiness, and even for how data should be collected (e.g., teacher observation, direct child assessment, parent report).

Similarly, states adopt unique Early Learning Standards that influence and guide instruction to promote school readiness, and perhaps assessment approaches, if state-funded programs are required to collect certain types of information with specific tools, and even more so if programs are required to report those data to state agencies or school districts. For example, the Colorado State Board of Education specifies three approved school readiness assessment tools (https://www.cde.state.co.us/schoolreadiness/assessment): Desired Results Developmental Profile for Kindergarten (DRDP-K; California Department of Education; https://drdpk.org/), HighScope Child Observation Record (COR) for Kindergarten (https://highscope.org/cor-advantage-kinder garten/), and Teaching Strategies GOLD (https://teachingstrategies.com/).

Assessments that may be driven, in part, by accountability requirements are likely to be broader in scope and include multiple developmental domains. Indeed, a position statement from the Early Education State Collaborative on Assessment and Student Standards recommends that school readiness assessments align with early learning guidelines and common core standards and include multiple developmental domains (Howard, 2011). Although we often identify distinct domains of school readiness (e.g., language, early literacy, and social-emotional skills), in reality, school readiness is a compilation of a range of skills and dispositions that support learning. Further, from a social constructivist framework (Meisels, 1999), what constitutes school readiness may be determined largely by the contexts of development; thus, the focus of assessment may shift to be consistent with the values and priorities in specific situations.

As the focus of this chapter is on academic functioning, we emphasize the importance of including attention to early literacy and early mathematical skills in addition to other skills that may be of interest in the assessment of school readiness. Evidence supports the importance of a strong foundation in these domains in relation to short- and long-term school achievement (e.g., Duncan et al., 2007). These skills are often included in early learning standards and classroom curricula, and research supports these skills as malleable and responsive to high-quality strategic instruction in preschool (e.g., Kruse, Spencer, Olszewski, & Goldstein, 2015; Nelson & McMaster, 2018) and in kindergarten (e.g., Clarke et al., 2016). Further, consensus documents and professional organizations provide guidance on key skills within these domains that could be the focus of assessment and instruction (e.g., National Early Literacy Panel, 2008; National Mathematics Advisory Panel, 2008). Understanding key skills in early literacy and early mathematics is important in evaluating the extent to which a school readiness assessment is including appropriate content. Here we briefly delineate key skills in these domains with a focus on the skills young children develop prior to kindergarten entry.

Early Literacy

In their synthesis of all published research on the skills and abilities of young children birth to age 5 that predict later literacy (e.g., reading, writing, spelling) outcomes, the National Early Literacy Panel (NELP, 2008) identified five early literacy variables that specifically demonstrated medium to large predictive and enduring relationships with measures of reading over time. These variables were: (1) *alphabet knowledge*; (2) *phonological awareness*; (3) *rapid automatic naming* of letters, digits, or colors; (4) *writing* or name writing; and (5) *phonological memory*, or listening comprehension. Of these, phonological awareness and alphabet/print knowledge were the most robust in predicting later literacy achievement. Additionally, although there are different perspectives of the relations between oral language, phonological awareness, and early literacy, there is general agreement they *are* related to one another in complex ways (e.g., Dickinson, McCabe, Anastasopoulos, Peisner-Feinberg, & Poe, 2003; NICHD Early Child Care Research Network, 2005) and, thus, oral language is important to consider as part of a general assessment of early-literacy-related school readiness. As evidence of the relation among these skills, phonological awareness, word reading, and vocabulary skills in kindergarten emerged as the strongest predictors of grade 1 reading achievement in a sample of Latino/a, dual language learner students (Edyburn et al., 2017). Similar findings have been demonstrated with English monolingual students when examining preschool early literacy performance predicting grade 1 reading (e.g., Lonigan, Burgess, & Anthony, 2000; Missall et al., 2007). Further, one longitudinal study demonstrated links between vocabulary, early literacy skills, oral narrative, and reading comprehension from 19 months old through adolescence (Suggate, Schaughency, McAnally, & Reese, 2018).

Early Mathematics

Although there are multiple strands within mathematics (e.g., algebra, data analysis, probability), the National Research Council (2009) identified the core areas of number, relations and operations, geometry (i.e., shape and space), and measurement as central to early mathematical development. Among these, number, relations and operations is the most well-developed domain in early mathematics research, and skills in this domain provide a strong foundation for continued mathematical learning (Clements, 2004). For example, children who early-on develop knowledge of the cardinality principle (i.e., the knowledge that the last count indicates the number of objects) have a deeper understanding of the relationship between set sizes and number words, or how number words are assigned to sets (Slusser & Sarnecka, 2011), that is related to later mathematical competencies (e.g., Geary et al., 2018). An understanding of the relations between numbers is a central concept that includes changing, comparing, and ordering sets as well as composing and decomposing sets. At least one study indicates that symbolic (e.g., printed numerals, number words) and non-symbolic (e.g., collection of dots on page) comparison skills in kindergarten are related to calculation and number fact knowledge in grades 1 and 2 (Desoete, Ceulemans, De Weerdt, & Pieters, 2012). Finally, symbolic representations of quantity are important to the functional use of numerals, and research suggests a relation between knowledge of numerals and numerical estimation (Berteletti, Lucangeli, Piazza, Dehaene, & Zorzi, 2010). Moreover, speed and accuracy in number naming in kindergarten accounts for considerable variance in basic numerical skills and has an influence on mathematical achievement at the end of grade 4 (Krajewski & Schneider, 2009).

The degree to which an assessment provides meaningful information about a child's development of key early academic skills should be evaluated within the context of the purpose of the assessment. For example, for universal screening purposes, assessment may focus on school readiness broadly, asking teachers to rate a child's academic readiness without specifying specific areas of academic readiness (e.g., Stormont et al., 2015). While this approach increases the efficiency of the assessment process, information about specific skills (e.g., number concepts, verbal ability, phonological awareness) within the broad domain of academic readiness may be desirable (e.g., Quirk et al., 2017). For the purposes of formative assessment, direct measurement of a child's skills and knowledge in specific areas (e.g., concept knowledge, phonological awareness, number sense) may be useful in developing instruction and supports and may be more sensitive to change over time.

Methods of Assessment

Generally, assessment should be a process of gathering information from multiple sources (e.g., parents, teachers) using multiple methods (e.g., rating scales, observation, direct assessment). Indeed, some sources and some methods are better suited for capturing certain types of information. For example, in assessing social-emotional readiness, ratings from parents and teachers offer perspectives of the child in different settings, and direct observation provides more detailed information about a child's strengths and needs. With academic functioning in the areas of language, early literacy, and mathematics, direct assessment methods are likely to be a primary source of data.

Direct assessments historically have been developed to have either a nomothetic or idiographic purpose. Data from nomothetic assessments provide an interpretation of a child's performance relative to a normative group, and typically through the use of a published, norm-referenced, standardized assessment (e.g., Bracken Basic Concept Scale-Third Edition: Receptive; Bracken, 2006). Data from idiographic assessment tools are used to compare a child's performance at one point in time to their performance at another point in time, typically using discrete-skill measurement of key skills (e.g., Individual Growth and Development Indicators; Hojnoski & Floyd, 2004; McConnell, Bradfield, Wackerle-Hollman, & Rodriguez, 2013). Contemporary approaches to assessment maintain this distinction between nomothetic and idiographic data, and at the same time, some assessments provide both frames of reference. For example, some assessments provide a normative standard (e.g., benchmark, cut-score) facilitating evaluation of a child's performance compared to a designated peer group while also providing data that can be used for idiographic comparisons when collected over time (e.g., Acadience Reading, DIBELS 8th ed., FastBridge Learning, AIMSweb+, EasyCBM). Advances in assessment technology have led to other forms of assessment, including computer-adaptive approaches (e.g., STAR Early Literacy, Children's Progress of Academic Assessment).

We recommend that direct assessment of school readiness include both data that can be used to evaluate a child's performance relative to a designated peer group, to better understand individual child need relative to group performance, and data that can be used in formative assessment to ensure that a child is making adequate progress toward identified goals. Further, given the limitations of direct assessment for children from diverse backgrounds, in assessing school readiness, the social, cultural, and linguistic contexts in which children develop should be considered carefully and efforts to minimize bias in assessment must be made to ensure that any evaluation fully captures children's strengths. In all cases, direct assessments should be supplemented with information gathered from parents and teachers about the child's functional use of academic skills in applied settings. Parents and teachers can describe the extent to which the child engages in early academic activities independently. For example, a parent may indicate that "he loves to read with me," or a teacher may report "she is very interested in measuring things in our classroom." Similarly, parents and teachers can provide their perceptions of children's ATL with regard to academic learning activities. Direct observation of children in the natural setting can provide additional descriptive information about the child's level of engagement and task persistence as well as the type and frequency of opportunities to develop academic skills and the instructional support provided.

Conclusion

Research is clear that early academic functioning is related to—and often predictive of—later school achievement. As a result, assessment of early academic functioning is likely to continue. We see the future of assessment of school readiness as focused on universal screening and progress monitoring of key skills, rather than on broad tests focused on nomothetic scoring and interpretation. Assessment of early academic functioning should be contextual and meaningful for making instructional decisions. In considering the assessment of school readiness, what is most critical is the consequential validity of the assessment, or how the data are used. School readiness data should be used to better understand children's strengths and needs, to develop effective instruction for diverse learners, and to support the learning and development of all children (Howard, 2011).

Any approach to assessing school readiness should not be viewed as high-stakes assessment. Given the variability of skill development in young children and variability in the environments in which they develop, data collected for the purpose of assessing school readiness should be used to drive instruction and acquisition and learning of key skills, not to encourage promotion, retention, eligibility, or any other high-stakes decision (Graue, 2006). Assessment should provide evidence about key skill development that is meaningful for supporting instruction and learning. The assessment process should be contextually appropriate, feasible, and standardized—assessment data must be easy to collect, comparable across children, consistent and reliable across children, and have localized and meaningful context for the school district. Although standardized, norm-referenced tests for school readiness are available, we should not be making decisions about whether children are ready for school. On the contrary, we should be making recommendations about the instruction children need to experience success. We advocate shifting from a dichotomous model of "ready" versus "not ready" to a focus on how to support individual children functionally for school success.

References

Aunola, K., Leskinen, E., Lerkkanen, M., & Nurmi, J. (2004). Developmental dynamics of math performance from preschool to grade 2. *Journal of Educational Psychology*, *96*, 699–713.

Berteletti, I., Lucangeli, D., Piazza, M., Dehaene, S., & Zorzi, M. (2010). Numerical estimation in preschoolers. *Developmental Psychology*, *46*, 545–551.

Bierman, K. L., Domitrovich, C. E., Nix, R. L., Gest, S. D., Welsh, J. A., Greenberg, M. T., … Gill, S. (2008). Promoting academic and social-emotional school readiness: The Head Start REDI program. *Child Development*, *79*, 1802–1817.

Boivin, M. & Bierman, K. L. (2014). School readiness: Introduction to a multifaceted and Developmental construct. In M. Boivin & K. Bierman (Eds.), *Promoting school readiness and early learning: Implications of developmental research for practice* (pp. 3–14). New York: Guilford.

Brassard, M. R. & Boehm, A. E. (2007). *Preschool assessment: Principles and practices*. New York: Guilford.

Bracken, B. A. (2006). Bracken basic concept scale –third edition: Receptive. Pearson Publishing.

Carlton, M. P. & Winsler, A. (1999). School readiness: The need for a paradigm shift. *School Psychology Review*, *28*, 338–352.

Carta, J. J., Greenwood, C. R., Atwater, J., McConnell, S. R., Goldstein, H., & Kaminski, R. A. (2014). Identifying preschool children for higher tiers of language and early literacy instruction within a response to intervention framework. *Journal of Early Intervention*, *36*(4), 281–291.

Chien, N. C., Howes, C., Burchinal, M., Pianta, R. C., Ritchie, S., Bryant, D. M., … Barbarin, O. A. (2010). Children's classroom engagement and school readiness gains in prekindergarten. *Child Development*, *81*, 1534–1549.

Clarke, B., Doabler, C. T., Smolkowski, K., Baker, S. K., Fien, H., & Cary, M. S. (2016). Examining the efficacy of a Tier 2 kindergarten mathematics intervention. *Journal of Learning Disabilities*, *49*, 152–165.

Clements, D. H. (2004). Major themes and recommendations. In D. H. Clements, J. Sarama, & A. DiBiase (Eds.), *Engaging young children in mathematics: Standards for early childhood mathematics education* (pp. 7–76). Mahwah, NJ: Lawrence Erlbaum.

Daniels, D. H. (2014). Children's affective orientations in preschool and their initial adjustment to kindergarten. *Psychology in the Schools, 51*, 256–272.

Denham, S. A., Kalb, S., Way, E., Warren-Khot, H., Rhoades, B. L., & Bassett, H. H. (2013). Social and emotional information processing in preschoolers: Indicator of early school success? *Early Child Development and Care, 183*, 667–688.

Desoete, A., Ceulemans, A., De Weerdt, F., & Pieters, S. (2012). Can we predict mathematical learning disabilities from symbolic and non-symbolic comparison tasks in kindergarten? Findings from a longitudinal study. *British Journal of Educational Psychology, 82*, 64–81.

Dickinson, D. K., McCabe, A., Anastasopoulos, L., Peisner-Feinberg, E. S., & Poe, M. D. (2003). The comprehensive language approach to early literacy: The interrelationship among vocabulary, phonological sensitivity, and print knowledge among preschool-aged children. *Journal of Educational Psychology, 95*, 465–481.

Duncan, G. J., Dowsett, C. J., Claessens, A., Magnuson, K., Huston, A. C., Klebanov, P., & Japel, C. (2007). School readiness and later achievement. *Developmental Psychology, 43*, 1428–1446.

Edyburn, K. L., Quirk, M., Felix, E., Swami, S., Goldstein, A., Terzieva, A., & Scheller, J. (2017). Literacy screening among Latino/a and dual language learner kindergarteners: Predicting first grade reading achievement. *Literacy Research and Instruction, 56*, 250–267.

Farran, D. C. (2011). Rethinking school readiness. *Exceptionality Education International, 21*, 5–15.

Friedman-Krauss, A. H., Barnett, W. S., Garver, K. A., Hodges, K. S., Weisenfeld, G. G., & DiCrecchio, N. (2019). *The state of preschool 2018: State preschool yearbook*. New Jersey: National Institute for Early Education Research.

Geary, D. C., vanMarle, K., Chu, F. W., Rouder, J., Hoard, M. K., & Nugent, L. (2018). Early conceptual understanding of cardinality predicts superior school-entry number-system knowledge. *Psychological Science, 29*, 191–205.

Goldstein, J., McCoach, D. B., & Yu, H. (2017). The predictive validity of kindergarten readiness judgments: Lessons from one state. *The Journal of Educational Research, 110*, 50–60.

Graue, E. (2006). The answer is readiness-Now what is the question? *Early Education and Development, 17*, 43–56.

High, P. C. (2008). School readiness. *Pediatrics, 121*(4), e1008–e1015.

Hojnoski, R. L. & Missall, K. N. (2006). Addressing school readiness: Expanding school psychology in early education. *School Psychology Review, 35*, 602–614.

Hojnoski, R., & Floyd, R. (2004). Individual Growth and Development Indicators of Early Numeracy—(IGDIs-EN). St. Paul, MN: Early Learning Labs.

Howard, E. C. (2011). *Moving forward with kindergarten readiness assessment efforts: A position paper of the Early Childhood Education State Collaborative on Assessment and Student Standards*. Washington, DC: Council of Chief State School Officers.

Hunter, L. J., Bierman, K. L., & Hall, C. M. (2018). Assessing noncognitive aspects of school readiness: The predictive validity of brief teacher rating scales of social–emotional competence and approaches to learning. *Early Education and Development, 29*, 1081–1094.

Juel, C. (1988). Learning to read and write: A longitudinal study of 54 children from first through fourth grades. *Journal of Educational Psychology, 80*, 437–447.

Kagan, S. L. (1990). Readiness 2000: Rethinking rhetoric and responsibility. *The Phi Delta Kappan, 72,* 272–279.

Kettler, R. J. & Feeney-Kettler, K. A. (2011). Screening systems and decision making at the preschool level: Application of a comprehensive validity framework. *Psychology in the Schools, 48,* 430–441.

Kim, J., Murdock, T., & Choi, D. (2005). Investigation of parents' beliefs about readiness for kindergarten: An examination of national household education survey (NHES: 93). *Educational Research Quarterly, 29,* 3–17.

Krajewski, K. & Schneider, W. (2009). Early development of quantity to number-word linkage as a precursor of mathematical school achievement and mathematical difficulties: Findings from a four-year longitudinal study. *Learning and Instruction, 19,* 513–526.

Kruse, L. G., Spencer, T. D., Olszewski, A., & Goldstein, H. (2015). Small groups, big gains: Efficacy of a tier 2 phonological awareness intervention with preschoolers with early literacy deficits. *American Journal of Speech-Language Pathology, 24,* 189–205.

Laracy, S. D., Hojnoski, R. L., & Dever, B. V. (2016). Assessing the classification accuracy of early numeracy curriculum-based measures using receiver operating characteristic curve analysis. *Assessment for Effective Intervention, 41,* 172–183.

Lewit, E. M. & Baker, L. S. (1995). School readiness. *The Future of Children, 5,* 128–139.

Li-Grining, C. P., Votruba-Drzal, E., Maldonado-Carreño, C., & Haas, K. (2010). Children's early approaches to learning and academic trajectories through fifth grade. *Developmental Psychology, 46,* 1062.

Lin, H. L., Lawrence, F. R., & Gorrell, J. (2003). Kindergarten teachers' views of children's readiness for school. *Early Childhood Research Quarterly, 18,* 225–237.

Lipscomb, S. T., Miao, A. J., Finders, J. K., Hatfield, B., Kothari, B. H., & Pears, K. (2019). Community-level social determinants and children's school readiness. *Prevention Science, 20*(4), 468–477.

LoCasale-Crouch, J., Mashburn, A. J., Downer, J. T., & Pianta, R. C. (2008). Pre-kindergarten teachers' use of transition practices and children's adjustment to kindergarten. *Early Childhood Research Quarterly, 23,* 124–139.

Lonigan, C. J., Burgess, S. R., & Anthony, J. L. (2000). Development of emergent literacy and early reading skills in preschool children: Evidence from a latent-variable longitudinal study. *Developmental Psychology, 36,* 596–613.

McClelland, M. M., Acock, A. C., & Morrison, F. J. (2006). The impact of kindergarten learning-related skills on academic trajectories at the end of elementary school. *Early Childhood Research Quarterly, 21,* 471–490.

McClelland, M. M. & Morrison, F. J. (2003). The emergence of learning-related social skills in preschool children. *Early Childhood Research Quarterly, 18,* 206–224.

McClelland, M. M., Morrison, F. J., & Holmes, D. L. (2000). Children at risk for early academic problems: The role of learning-related social skills. *Early Childhood Research Quarterly, 15,* 307–329.

McConnell, S. R., Bradfield, T., Wackerle-Hollman, A., & Rodriguez, M. (2012). *Individual growth and development indicators of early literacy.* Saint Paul, MN: Early Learning Labs.

McDermott, P. A., Rikoon, S. H., & Fantuzzo, J. W. (2014). Tracing children's approaches to learning through Head Start, kindergarten, and first grade: Different pathways to different outcomes. *Journal of Educational Psychology, 106,* 200–213.

McWayne, C. M., Cheung, K., Wright, L. E. G., & Hahs-Vaughn, D. L. (2012). Patterns of school readiness among head start children: Meaningful within-group variability during the transition to kindergarten. *Journal of Educational Psychology, 104,* 862–878.

McWayne, C. M., Fantuzzo, J. W., & McDermott, P. A. (2004). Preschool competency in context: An investigation of the unique contribution of child competencies to early academic success. *Developmental Psychology, 40,* 633–645.

McWayne, C. M., Green, L. E., & Fantuzzo, J. W. (2009). A variable-and person-oriented investigation of preschool competencies and Head Start children's transition to kindergarten and first grade. *Applied Developmental Science, 13,* 1–15.

Meisels, S. J. (1999). Assessing readiness. In R. Pianta & M. Cox (Eds.), *The transition to kindergarten* (pp. 39–66). Baltimore, MD: Brookes.

Miller, M. M. & Kehl, L. M. (2019). Comparing parents' and teachers' rank-ordered importance of early school readiness characteristics. *Early Childhood Education Journal, 47,* 445–453.

Missall, K., Reschly, A., Betts, J., McConnell, S., Heistad, D., Pickart, M., … Marston, D. (2007). Examination of the predictive validity of preschool early literacy skills. *School Psychology Review, 36,* 433–452.

Missall, K. N., Mercer, S. H., Martinez, R. S., & Casebeer, D. (2012). Concurrent and longitudinal patterns and trends in performance on early numeracy curriculum-based measures in kindergarten through third grade. *Assessment for Effective Intervention, 27,* 95–106.

Morgan, P. L., Farkas, G., & Wu, Q. (2011). Kindergarten children's growth trajectories in reading and mathematics: Who falls increasingly behind?. *Journal of Learning Disabilities, 44,* 472–488.

National Association of School Psychologists. (2015). *Early childhood services: Promoting positive outcomes for young children.* (Position statement). Bethesda, MD: Author.

National Early Literacy Panel. (2008). *Developing early literacy: Report of the National Early Literacy Panel.* Washington, DC: National Institute for Literacy.

National Mathematics Advisory Panel. (2008). *Foundations for success: The final report of the National Mathematics Advisory Panel.* Washington, DC: U.S. Department of Education.

National Research Council. (2008). *Early childhood assessment: Why, what, and how.* Washington, DC: National Academies Press.

National Research Council. (2009). *Mathematics learning in early childhood: Paths toward excellence and equity.* Washington, DC: National Academies Press.

Nelson, G. & McMaster, K. L. (2018). The effects of early numeracy interventions for students in preschool and early elementary: A meta-analysis. *Journal of Educational Psychology.* Advance online publication. doi: 10.1037/edu0000334.

NICHD Early Child Care Research Network, National Institute of Child Health and Human Development (Eds.). (2005). *Child care and child development: Results from the NICHD study of early child care and youth development.* New York: Guilford Publications.

Pagani, L. S., Fitzpatrick, C., Archambault, I., & Janosz, M. (2010). School readiness and later achievement: A French Canadian replication and extension. *Developmental Psychology, 46,* 984–994.

Pears, K. C., Healey, C. V., Fisher, P. A., Braun, D., Gill, C., Conte, H. M., ... Ticer, S. (2014). Immediate effects of a program to promote school readiness in low-income children: Results of a pilot study. *Education & Treatment of Children, 37*, 431.

Pears, K. C., Kim, H. K., Fisher, P. A., & Yoerger, K. (2016). Increasing pre-kindergarten early literacy skills in children with developmental disabilities and delays. *Journal of School Psychology, 57*, 15–27.

Piotrkowski, C. S., Botsko, M., & Matthews, E. (2000). Parents' and teachers' beliefs about children's school readiness in a high-need community. *Early Childhood Research Quarterly, 15*, 537–558.

Ponitz, C. C. & Rimm-Kaufman, S. E. (2011). Contexts of reading instruction: Implications for literacy skills and kindergarteners' behavioral engagement. *Early Childhood Research Quarterly, 26*, 157–168.

Ponitz, C. C., Rimm-Kaufman, S. E., Grimm, K. J., & Curby, T. W. (2009). Kindergarten classroom quality, behavioral engagement, and reading achievement. *School Psychology Review, 38*, 102–120.

Quirk, M., Dowdy, E., Goldstein, A., & Carnazzo, K. (2017). School readiness as a longitudinal predictor of social-emotional and reading performance across the elementary grades. *Assessment for Effective Intervention, 42*, 248–253.

Quirk, M., Grimm, R., Furlong, M. J., Nylund-Gibson, K., & Swami, S. (2016). The association of Latino children's kindergarten school readiness profiles with Grade 2–5 literacy achievement trajectories. *Journal of Educational Psychology, 108*, 814–829.

Razza, R. A., Martin, A., & Brooks-Gunn, J. (2015). Are approaches to learning in kindergarten associated with academic and social competence similarly? *Child & Youth Care Forum, 44*, 757–776.

Rimm-Kaufman, S. E., Pianta, R. C., & Cox, M. J. (2000). Teachers' judgments of problems in the transition to kindergarten. *Early Childhood Research Quarterly, 15*, 147–166.

Romano, E., Babchishin, L., Pagani, L. S., & Kohen, D. (2010). School readiness and later achievement: Replication and extension using a nationwide Canadian survey. *Developmental Psychology, 46*, 995–1007.

Sabol, T. J., Bohlmann, N. L., & Downer, J. T. (2018). Low-income ethnically diverse children's engagement as a predictor of school readiness above preschool classroom quality. *Child Development, 89*, 556–576.

Sabol, T. J. & Pianta, R. C. (2012). Patterns of school readiness forecast achievement and socioemotional development at the end of elementary school. *Child Development, 83*, 282–299.

Sasser, T. R., Bierman, K. L., & Heinrichs, B. (2015). Executive functioning and school adjustment: The mediational role of pre-kindergarten learning-related behaviors. *Early Childhood Research Quarterly, 30*, 70–79.

Shadish, W. R., Cook, T. D., & Campbell, D. T. (2002). *Experimental and quasi-experimental designs for generalized causal inference.* Belmont, CA: Cengage Learning.

Slusser, E. B. & Sarnecka, B. W. (2011). Find the picture of eight turtles: A link between children's counting and their knowledge of number word semantics. *Journal of Experimental Child Psychology, 110*, 38–51.

Snow, K. L. (2006). Measuring school readiness: Conceptual and practical considerations. *Early Education and Development, 17*, 7–41.

Stormont, M., Herman, K. C., Reinke, W. M., King, K. R., & Owens, S. (2015). The Kindergarten academic and behavior readiness screener: The utility of single-item teacher ratings of kindergarten readiness. *School Psychology Quarterly*, *30*, 212–228.

Suggate, S., Schaughency, E., McAnally, H., & Reese, E. (2018). From infancy to adolescence: The longitudinal links between vocabulary, early literacy skills, oral narrative, and reading comprehension. *Cognitive Development*, *47*, 82–95.

Torres, M. M., Domitrovich, C. E., & Bierman, K. L. (2015). Preschool interpersonal relationships predict kindergarten achievement: Mediated by gains in emotion knowledge. *Journal of Applied Developmental Psychology*, *39*, 44–52.

U.S. Department of Health and Human Services, Administration of Children and Families, Office of Head Start. (2015). *Head start early learning outcomes framework: Birth to age 5*. Washington, DC.

Watts, T. W., Duncan, G. J., Siegler, R. S., & Davis-Kean, P. E. (2014). What's past is prologue: Relations between early mathematics knowledge and high school achievement. *Educational Researcher*, *43*, 352–360.

Williford, A. P., Maier, M. F., Downer, J. T., Pianta, R. C., & Howes, C. (2013). Understanding how children's engagement and teachers' interactions combine to predict school readiness. *Journal of Applied Developmental Psychology*, *34*, 299–309.

Wilson, S. B. & Lonigan, C. J. (2010). Identifying preschool children at risk of later reading difficulties: Evaluation of two emergent literacy screening tools. *Journal of Learning Disabilities*, *43*, 62–76.

Chapter 5

Assessment of Parents' Support of Young Children's Learning through a Sociocultural Lens

Patricia H. Manz, Dominique Levert, Milim Lee, Yin Cai, Marisa Solé, and Yael Gross

Development in the first five years is foundational for children's success in later-life experiences involving academic achievement and social competence (Shonkoff & Phillips, 2000). Trajectories for children's ongoing acquisition of cognitive, language, and academic skills are set before they cross the threshold to kindergarten. Hart and Risley's (1995) longitudinal study demonstrated that trends for children's acquisition of language competence were evident at 1 year of age. Sadly, developmental gaps related to socioeconomic status (SES) were present by the time children were 3 years of age. Development does not occur in a vacuum; rather, it entails a swirling of ongoing reciprocal processes, internal and external to the child, that are shaped by sociocultural contexts (i.e., cultural heritage, SES) (Bronfenbrenner, 2001). Although complex, there is a single truth: a proximal process—a secure, reliable, and ongoing relationship with a caregiving adult (i.e., henceforth referred to as "parent")—is the essential ingredient that steers children's development (Bronfenbrenner, 2001).

Recognizing the importance of parenting during the first five years of a child's life, this chapter presents an overview of the role parents play in children's development, highlighting three critical assessment foci: parent-child interaction, parent involvement in early learning, and the home environment. Within each of these areas, exemplary measures are identified with descriptions of their intended use, scale development process, and psychometric quality. Aligned with Messick's unified theory of construct validity (Messick, 1995, 2000), psychometric quality in this chapter is described in terms of available statistical evidence for reliability and validity, as well as the extent to which the measure yields meaningful information for children who vary by culture and SES.

Family Processes and Young Children's Development

For young children, families are the bridge to society and the world around them. Families prepare children to function in external contexts; they interpret and frame societal phenomena, and they protect children against risks

(Stevenson, Davis, & Abdul-Kabir, 2001). In response to cultural and techno-logical changes in our society, family structure and the resources families can afford to protect and socialize their children are changing in ways that widen socioeconomic divide (Furstenberg, 2014). Common to all SES levels, trends show increasing rates of cohabitation rather than marriage, with correspond-ing higher rates of children being born to unmarried parents. Recent demo-graphics show a decline in the proportion of children in two-parent families, although this family structure continues to be most prevalent (CDC, 2017). Increasingly children are residing in female-headed, single-parent homes, where mothers are unlikely to be married. This is in contrast to the small portion of fathers who are single parents and are most likely to be divorced. Although there is a rise in middle-class and affluent adults who opt not to have children, those who become parents are likely to have children later in life, following the attainment of advanced education and job security. Further, these parents are likely to experience marital stability.

In contrast, lower-SES families are more likely to have young parents who have limited education, and among those who marry, the risk of mari-tal instability continues. Additionally, about 140,000 children each year are adopted, typically by parents who are non-Hispanic White and economically advantaged (Adoption Network, 2019). About one quarter of the children who are adopted are international children, while the remainder is equally represented by children who come from foster care or private, domestic agencies (Vandivere, Malm, & Radel, 2009).

This changing and increasingly diverse demography of families challenges early childhood professionals to understand linkages between families' struc-ture and resources, on the one hand, and children's learning and develop-ment, on the other. The Family Stress Model, a framework for understanding how stressors impact children via family processes, reveals the importance of attending to parents' sociocultural contexts when sup-porting them to foster their children's development and learning (Linver, Brooks-Gunn, & Kohen, 2002; Masarik & Conger, 2017). Accordingly, the experience of stress constrains parents' resources and competencies, increas-ing the likelihood of psychological distress and strained inter-parental rela-tionships. Stress related to socioeconomic disadvantage has been consistently demonstrated to impact child development; in fact, it is con-sidered the most powerful predictor of child outcomes (Shonkoff & Phillips, 2000). However, other sources of stress, often related to SES, include par-ents' social networks and supports, life stress, mental health, and homeless-ness (Cairney, Boyle, Offord, & Racine, 2003; DiSanto, Timmons, & Pelletier, 2016; Kohl, Lengua, & McMahon, 2000). For instance, low-SES parents who are ethnic/racial minorities are highly likely to experience dis-criminatory stress, and to work long and nonstandard hours while strug-gling to make ends meet, tend to have lower education levels, and are more likely to be single parents than parents from middle SES (Knopf & Swick, 2008; Prickett, 2018; Shonkoff & Phillips, 2000). As a result, low-SES parents are at risk for experiencing psychological distress such as maternal depression and parenting stress in addition to having limited resources for providing educational resources to their children. Consequently, these risk factors have an adverse influence on children's development, which in turn negatively impacts school readiness (Leventhal & Brooks-Gunn, 2001).

Pathways from stressors to poor child outcomes are, however, not deterministic. The Family Stress Model acknowledges resilient and protective factors. Positive parent-child interactions and parent involvement in children's learning can overcome the negative impact of risk factors on children's development (Ferguson, Bovaird, & Mueller, 2007; Flouri & Buchanan, 2004; Shonkoff & Phillips, 2000). Moreover, early intervention such as home visiting as well as education and care programs for young children have been largely effective in promoting resilience and reducing poor parent and child outcomes (Love, Chazen-Cohen, Raikes, & Brooks-Gunn, 2013; USDHHS, 2010). For these reasons, assessing parenting supports (i.e., parent-child interaction, parent involvement, and physical surroundings) is crucial to inform preventative and early intervention practices for children. However, changing family demographics demand that early childhood education systems are prepared to examine parental supports for a wide range of families competently and with equity.

Contexts for Assessment of Parental Supports

Including an assessment of parental supports in an overall evaluation facilitates identification of young children who present with risks or are expressing a developmental delay (Guevara et al., 2013; Hix-Small, Marks, Squires, & Nickel, 2007; Schonwald, Huntington, Chan, Risko, & Bridgemohan, 2009; Van Agt et al., 2007). Further, assessing parental supports will gather information that comprehensively informs intervention services to ensure they are appropriately matched to families' and children's needs (Hussey-Gardner, McNinch, Anastasi, & Miller, 2002; Zero to Three, 2010). Assessments that connect young children to effective early intervention place the child on an adaptive developmental trajectory to overcome any deficits, preventing the advancement of learning, behavioral, and developmental disabilities (Greenspan & Wieder, 2003).

The varying education and care experiences among young children, especially those below the age of 3 years, challenge early detection of developmental risks. Relative to other age groups, infants and toddlers (i.e., under 3 years of age) have the most varied experiences, including those who remain in the care of a parent (22%), a relative other than a parent (33%), or education and care centers (26%) (Child Trends, 2014). In 2010, the Maternal Infant and Early Childhood Home Visiting Program was established to implement national home visiting services for low-income children. Since its inception, the number of children under the age of 2 years who receive enriching, developmental services has increased three-fold, with present estimates of over 150,000 infants and toddlers (MCHB/HRSA, n.d.).

In the face of highly variable infant/toddler experiences, a common route for assessment entails routine developmental screening during well-baby visits with pediatricians at 9, 18, 24, and 30 months (CDC, 2019). Though these well-baby visits do not provide diagnoses, the healthcare provider can monitor children's attainment of developmental milestones and refer to outside services if delays are suspected. Developmental assessments can also be conducted by early interventionists, home visitors, early childhood teachers, or other trained early childhood education and care providers. Additionally, as mandated by the *Individuals with Disabilities Education Improvement Act* (IDEIA, 2004), states and local educational agencies have the responsibility to locate, evaluate, and identify children 3 to 21 who have a legal right to access special education and additional services. The use of assessments has been recognized as an avenue for state and local agencies to identify young children who may have developmental deficits. Standards of practice have been established to endorse the use of assessments to identify students' learning objectives, monitor their ongoing progress, and use data-based decision making to inform present and future interventions (Erwin, 1991).

Assessments of parental supports is a critical element of eligibility determination for infants and toddlers' receipt of early intervention services through Part C of the IDEIA. Following documentation that an infant/toddler meets criteria for a developmental delay or is at-risk for a development delay, a comprehensive developmental assessment is conducted to devise the Individualized Family Service Plan (IFSP; ECTA, 2014). Unlike the IDEIA services for children preschool age and older, Part C operates through a two-generational orientation by engaging parents as active providers of early intervention for their young child. In fact, the grand majority (88.9%) of Part C early intervention services are provided in children's homes to ensure parents' involvement (USDHHS, 2017).

As children age into the preschool years, they are more likely to attend early childhood programs, expanding opportunities for early detection of developmental delays and challenges in learning and socioemotional functioning. However, variation in their early childhood education experiences continues, with low-SES children showing lower enrollment rates. On average, 61% of the preschool-aged population (i.e., 3–6 years) is enrolled in early childhood education programs. However, the percentages for preschoolers who live in poverty, are low-income status (i.e., between the poverty threshold and two-times the threshold), and are affluent are 46%, 52%, and 72%, respectively (NIEER, 2018). Hispanic children are most underrepresented, as compared to other ethnicities and races (NIEER, 2018). Parental education is most strongly associated with preschool enrollment, with greater enrollment rates noted for highly educated parents (NCES, 2019). Therefore, the expansion of children into early childhood education programs differentially increases an opportunity for early detection and intervention for preschoolers of varying SES. Routine pediatric care as well as community-based early intervention services continue to be important contexts for identifying preschool children who are at risk for developmental, learning, and behavioral difficulties.

Assessment Domains

Parent-Child Interaction

Parents engage with their children in a variety of ways, as shaped by their beliefs, cultural values, and traditions, as well as socioeconomic circumstances. Developmental parenting narrowly refers to parenting behaviors that promote children's learning and development, including affection, responsiveness, encouragement, and teaching (Roggman, Boyce, & Innocenti, 2008). These behaviors, especially affection, are essential ingredients for children's socioemotional development and acquisition of skills that lead to successful school performance. Although parenting is the cornerstone of young children's development, it is vulnerable to the socioeconomic conditions in which families reside. Numerous studies demonstrate that the quality of parent-child interactions buffers the risks that low SES poses to young children's development and school readiness. Using a large, national database with longitudinal data for low-income children from birth to 5 years, Chazen-Cohen et al. (2009) demonstrated significant, positive predictions of parenting quality when children were 14 months of age to their language and early literacy skills at 5 years of age. Similarly, parenting quality when children were toddlers positively predicted children's emotional regulation at kindergarten entry. This large-scale study demonstrated that parenting behaviors were fairly stable. However, changes in parenting during these formative years coincided with changes in children's outcomes; improvements in parent-child interactions during the preschool years led to improvements in children's literacy, language, and emotional regulation at school entry.

Expanding upon the seminal work of Chazen-Cohen and colleagues, Mathis and Bierman (2015) replicated the association of early supportive parenting with children's later socioemotional outcomes. Conversely, their work illuminated the negative, longitudinal impacts of highly directive and critical parenting as children's acquisition of poor emotional regulation and attentional control. A nuance of this study is its contribution to emerging evidence that parenting behaviors differentially impact children's development during the formative years. Mathis and Beirman showed that the association between parents' affection and children's emotional regulation and attention control was stronger during infancy (i.e., birth to 3 years) than it was during preschool years (i.e., 3–5). The researchers note that this trend corresponds with the natural development of these behaviors. Parents' behaviors may be more impactful when emotional regulation and attentional control are emerging than they are as children acquire independence.

Culture provides a crucial framework for understanding parent-child interactions and their relationship to child development. Although research in this area is in its infancy, cross-cultural comparisons demonstrate that parenting has varying pathways for fostering children's development. Dotterer, Iruka, and Pungello (2013) revealed cross-cultural differences in the mediating role parental behaviors play in the association of SES and child outcomes. Common to African American and European American mother-child dyads, decrease in SES was associated with an increase in mothers' critical and intrusive parenting, which led to lower cognitive skills in 36-month-old children. For both groups, maternal sensitivity was positively associated with children's cognitive abilities. An interesting difference was found in the mediating role of maternal warmth in the association of low SES and children's outcomes. Only for the European American mother-child dyads did maternal sensitivity mediate this association. Similarly, Palermo, Ispa, Carlo, and Streit (2018) showed that supportive parenting behaviors mediated the relationship between SES and children's cognitive skills in a Latinx sample. However, this mediating role did not emerge for the relationship between low SES and children's socioemotional functioning. Interestingly, supportive parenting buffered the negative impacts of maternal mental health on children's socioemotional outcomes in this study.

Findings from cross-cultural research are indicative of the need to conceptualize (and measure) effective parenting within cultural and historical contexts rather than assuming a deficit orientation. For instance, many African American parents strive to prepare their children to cope with racial stress and discrimination, a process referred to as racial socialization (Stevenson et al., 2001). In this reality, African American parenting emphasizes unconditional love of their children, coupled with close monitoring and directing their children for effective negotiation of their roles as racial minorities in the mainstream culture (Stevenson et al., 2001). Thus, for African American children, the way in which low SES affects their cognitive outcomes could be intertwined with experiences of racial stress and discrimination. Offsetting this toxic combination likely requires parenting behaviors that differ from those seen in the majority population.

Measuring parent-child interactions can inform prevention and intervention efforts with young children, as demonstrated through the critical and long-term effects of parenting behaviors. Although the research is consistent in demonstrating that parental responsiveness, affection, and teaching are critical ingredients for all children's health development and learning (Barrueco, López, & Miles, 2007), the manner in which parenting interfaces with children's sociocultural contexts may vary (Bradley & Corwyn, 2005). Therefore, measurement should occur in a collaborative context with parents so that they can affirm and interpret the findings (García Coll et al., 2002).

Parent Involvement

Parent involvement in education (referred to as "parent involvement") encompasses parents' active participation in educational activities as well as their creation and support of opportunities for children to acquire skills (Giallo, Treyvaud, Cooklin, & Wade, 2013; Jeynes, 2005). Fueled by Joyce Epstein's community-based research (Epstein, 1995), contemporary conceptualization of parent involvement is multi-dimensional. For preschool and older children, three dimensions of parent involvement have emerged repeatedly in research: home-based involvement, school-based involvement, and home-school communication (Fantuzzo, Tighe, & Childs, 2000; Manz, Fantuzzo, & Power, 2004). Home-based involvement includes parents' direct support of learning activities at home as well as in the community. Parents teach skills to children, intentionally take them to community places to learn, ensure children are nourished, rested, and have the necessary resources for learning; they also foster children's acquisition of behaviors that enable learning, such as social competence, attention, and task persistence. Parents' involvement in activities that occur in schools or directly support schools comprise school-based involvement. Expressions of school-based involvement include parents' participation in parent-teacher associations and fundraising efforts as well as their assistance with classroom activities and events. Home-school communication is categorized by method of communication (i.e., in-person or written) and content, including parents' inquiries about learning activities and reciprocal communication about children's progress, concerns, or events that may affect school performance.

Parents' involvement in their children's education is based upon their characteristics, circumstances, and perceptions of the school climate. Collectively, the manner in which parents are involved shapes their interactions with their children around education and contributes to children's educational outcomes. Walker, Wilkins, Dallaire, Sandler, and Hoover-Dempsey (2005) illustrated the foundational processes and outcomes of multiple dimensions of parent involvement. The basis for involvement in education consists of parents' beliefs about their role and efficacy with regard to their children's learning, school personnel's engagement of parents, and parents' personal circumstances and supports. Parents' beliefs about the extent and way in which they are involved in their children's education are culturally based. Latinx parents may construct their involvement in a dichotomous manner, where they are more actively involved with their children outside of school contexts and respect the teachers' role for formally educating their children (Reese & Gallimore, 2000). Their role construction emerges from their values that children have strong moral character, trusting relationships with family members, and are respectful in relating to others. In a study of Latinx parents with Latin American and Caribbean heritage, Zarate (2007) revealed that they endorsed responsibilities in direct support of their middle-school children's academic performance in addition to ensuring their children's strong moral base and connectedness to family.

Zarate referred to this latter form of involvement as "life participation," including parents' actions to form trusting relationships with their children and their teachers, to be aware of and monitor their children's social events, and to foster their children's moral development. In a large qualitative study with a diverse Latinx sample, McWayne, Melzi, Shick, Kennedy, and Mundt (2013) demonstrated the applicability of Zarate's life participation and academic involvement behaviors to parents of preschool children.

Coinciding with the life participation emphasis, Latinx parents tend to respect the delegation of responsibility for academic learning to teachers, given their specialized training and credentials (Reese & Gallimore, 2000). In such circumstances, parents' support of their children's education would not be visible in school settings unless they were invited by the teacher, as noted in Walker's model. Similarly, Korean American parents tend to show less school-based involvement out of reverence for teachers' roles in formally educating their children (Lim, 2012). Even when invited into the school setting, Korean American parents may be less likely to assume leadership or decision-making roles. Thus, even though they demonstrate school-based involvement, it may look differently than that of Caucasian, middle-class US parents who will more readily participate in leadership and decision-making roles in school settings. These consistent findings highlight the importance of assessing parent involvement from the parents' perspective, as school personnel may have restricted observations.

A strong positive association between parent involvement and SES has been consistently reported in research (Arnold, Zeljo, Doctoroff, & Ortiz, 2008; Fantuzzo et al., 2000). To date, research has illuminated the complex association between SES and parent involvement. Low-income families' heightened stress, coupled with limited resources (Linver et al., 2002), are theorized to constrain parents' capacity for supporting their children's learning at home and school (Lim, 2012). However, the interrelationship of SES to involvement is not clear-cut when various dimensions are explored. Studies reporting that low SES is associated with lower parent involvement often exclusively measured school-based involvement (i.e., Arnold et al., 2008; Kingston, Huang, Calzada, Dawson-McClure, & Botman, 2013). Moreover, studies often relied on teacher reports, which further constrained measurement of school-based behaviors to those that they were able to observe. In contrast, home-based involvement has not been shown to fluctuate significantly with SES (Fantuzzo et al., 2000; Hartas, 2017). Further, SES is often confounded with ethnic/racial minority status. Emerging research suggests that SES and culture have discrete influences on parent involvement. In a study of Chinese families who were low- or middle-SES, Yamamoto, Li, and Lu (2016) revealed that lower-SES families had higher involvement and a greater sense of directing their children than middle-SES families. They attributed these counterintuitive findings to lower-SES families' residence in enclaves, which maintained stronger associations to traditional Chinese values. There was one exception: middle-SES Chinese families were more highly involved in reading with their preschool children than their lower-SES counterparts.

In addition to being influenced by SES, parent involvement has been shown to buffer the adverse impact of low SES on young children's learning and socioemotional development. With measurement of family and neighborhood SES, Kingston and colleagues (Kingston et al., 2013) showed that higher levels of school-based involvement weakened the association of low SES with poor child outcomes.

In summary, parent involvement is a critical ingredient in young children's attainment of the cognitive, social, and behavioral competencies necessary for educational success. Assessment of parent involvement should be multi-dimensional and account for children's sociocultural contexts. Moreover, parents' perspectives on their involvement will fully reflect their involvement, and therefore they should be the source of information. Evaluating parent involvement only through the perspectives of educators or other professionals can overlook parents' values and comfort with expressed involvement in educational settings.

Home Environment

Home is a young child's immediate environment, where they spend most of their time until they go to school (Bronfenbrenner, 2001). Following the seminal work of Hart and Risley (1995), which demonstrated the strong and long-term impacts of the home environment on children's development, researchers have sought to discern its pathways. A critical force in children's development, the home environment is multifaceted, including the provision of educational materials and social relationships, as well as emotional support through caregiver relationships that are warm and vigilant, but not harsh and critical (Bradley, 2009). The home environment can provide safety and stability through reliable routines and relationships.

Enriching and secure home environments are essential to young children's development, learning, and success in school. Several studies have shown that the quality of the home environment in infancy has a long-lasting impact on children's socioemotional and academic outcomes. With a large nationally representative sample of low-income children, Chazen-Cohen et al. (2009) found observational measures of home environment quality. When children were 14 months of age, the high quality of the home environment positively predicted their vocabulary attainment and learning behaviors. Conversely, poor home environment quality negatively predicted problem behaviors when children were 5 years old. Given that the home environment is dynamic, changes in its quality throughout the preschool period were also examined. A positive change in home visiting quality was positively associated with children's language skills at the age of 5. Similarly, Anders and colleagues (2011) demonstrated that poor home environment quality during the preschool years was negatively associated with children's receipt of special education services at the age of 10 years. Of note, home environments maintain their influence on children's development regardless of family demographics; thus, a high-quality home environment can offset the negative impact of poverty on children's development (Chazen-Cohen et al., 2009).

Parents establish the home environment, and therefore it is an expression of their beliefs, values, and cultures within the parameters of their socioeconomic resources (Anders et al., 2011). Culture is a prevailing influence on the formation of the home environment. Melzi, Shick, and Bostwick (2013) distinguish home environments that are child-centered and situation-centered. In cultures that perceive children as partners with adults in learning (e.g., European American), the home environment is formulated to encourage children's active engagement in activities and conversations with parents. For example, parents will interrupt activities, like book sharing and mealtime conversation, to elicit children's contributions. Conversely, situation-centered home environments are those where children's learning is believed to occur through observations of adults. For example, children are expected to listen to adults when they are speaking or sharing books with them. Links between culture and home environments are not so straightforward. SES plays a strong role in shaping the home environment, as it is a determinant in the resources afforded to families as well as in the emotional capacity parents may have for their children (Linver et al., 2002). Increasing immigration introduces considerations about the impact of acculturation on home environments as parents balance allegiance to their native culture with adaptation to that of the United States (Bradley, Pennar, & Glick, 2014).

Reflecting the complexity of home environments, measurements are multi-faceted, including observations of the physical environment as well as the relational context. Home environments are a broad overarching construct that incorporates parent-child interaction, relationship quality, and parent involvement while incorporating accounts of routines, family composition, and learning opportunities through available materials and activities. Matching the breadth of this construct is the influence of sociocultural factors, such as culture, SES, and immigration experiences. Although complex, measurements of the home environment are beneficial in the immediate and long term. Assessments of the home environment can identify elements that may be readily changed to yield powerful benefits for young children. They can guide practitioner-parent collaboration to plan for enriching experiences that match families' cultural values with regard to parenting and their resources (Roggman et al., 2008).

Exemplary Measures

Parallel to the growing recognition of the importance of birth-to-5 development for children's learning and later school success, measurement of salient family processes and home ecology is evolving. In the following sections, exemplary measures of parent-child interaction, parent involvement, and home environment for use in psychoeducational evaluations are presented. Exemplary measures were selected for infants/toddlers (i.e., birth to 3 years) and preschool children (i.e., 3–5 years). These measures were identified through a literature search that included databases (e.g., PsycINFO, Google Scholar, ERIC, psychARTICLES), the Mental Measurements Yearbook (Carlson, Geisinger, & Jonson, 2017), and historical search of articles. Exemplar instruments met a set of minimal criteria: a) author-stated intent for use by practitioners, b) published through a peer-review process, and c) reliability information. When multiple measures met these criteria, those measures that provided validity and multiple psychometric studies were identified as exemplars. Table 5.1 presents an overview of the content, development, psychometric properties, and unique cultural considerations for the measures that were selected as exemplary and are discussed below.

Parent-Child Interaction

Parent-child interaction for infants, toddlers, and preschoolers can be measured through various techniques, such as interviews, observations, and rating scales. Measurements should focus on the needs of the family and the child while taking into consideration feasibility, cost, and relevancy. Being knowledgeable about the interactions between individuals can provide insights into overall family functioning that could contribute to other areas of wellness. Therefore, identifying instruments that provide highly reliable and valid interpretations of the parent-child interaction can offer child educators, psychologists, and other professionals working with these populations a deeper understanding. A literature search yielded 53 publications that identified assessments of the parent-child interaction for children from birth to 5 years of age. Three exemplar measures met the inclusion criteria: designed for clinical or programmatic applications, published through peer-review process, and demonstrated acceptable reliability.

The **Parenting Interactions with Children: Checklist of Observations Linked to Outcomes** (PICCOLO; Roggman, et al., 2013) measures 29 different parenting behaviors across four domains: Affection (i.e., expressing physical or verbal positive regard) Responsiveness (i.e., reacting positively), Encouragement (i.e., support), and Teaching (i.e., sharing and encouraging knowledge development). These domains were chosen based on early developmental theory that has been previously supported in the literature. The final item count for this measure was grounded in previous research on parent-child interaction measures, as well as through a partnership with a community Head Start, which provided qualitative feedback on each item's perceived importance to a child's development. The test developers conducted a confirmatory factor analysis to affirm that the items represented the four domains of parent-child

Table 5.1 Exemplar Measures of Parental Support by Domain

Measure	Constructs Measured	Assessment Method	Development Sample	Demonstrated Reliability	Demonstrated Validity	Attention to Cultural Diversity
Parent-Child Interaction						
PICCOLO (Roggman, Cook, Innocenti, Norman, & Christiansen, 2013)	Affection Responsiveness Encouragement Teaching	Observation	A large, diverse sample representing European, African, and Latinx American	Interrater reliability and internal consistency for total and construct scores consistency: averaged .78 in each domain	Convergent validity for constructs and total score Predictive validity for total score and constructs relationship to cognitive, language, and socioemotional outcomes when children were 2, 3, and 5 years of age	Interrater reliability for coders of varying ethnicities Convergent validity for European, African, and Latino American subsamples
DPICS-III (Eyberg, Nelson, Duke, & Boggs, 2009)	Parent and child behaviors in four categories: Verbalization Vocalization Response Physical	Observation in three structured conditions: Parent-Directed, Child-Directed, and Clean Up	22 mother-child pairs with a child between the ages of 2 and 10	Item reliability of live and videotaped coding were predominantly acceptable	Construct validity had significant differences between different composite categories	
PRQ-P (Kamphaus & Reynolds, 2006)	Attachment Disciplinary Practices Involvement Parent Confidence Relationship Frustration	Self-report English only	4130 cases from 41 states with a diverse population of race/ethnicity, geographic location, and mother's education level, with the exception of limited respondents from the Northeast region	Test-retest reliability	Inter-scale correlations	Reliability and validity determined for diverse populations

(Continued)

Table 5.1 (Cont.)

Measure	Constructs Measured	Assessment Method	Development Sample	Demonstrated Reliability	Demonstrated Validity	Attention to Cultural Diversity
PCRI (Gerard, 1994)	Parent Support Parent Satisfaction Involvement Communication Limit Setting Autonomy Role Orientation	Self-report English only		Test-retest Internal consistency		
Parent Involvement						
FIQ (Fantuzzo et al., 2000)	Home-Based Involvement School-Based Involvement Home-School Communication	Self-report English & Spanish	Urban, low-income parents with a child in preschool through first grade	Internal consistency	Construct and Concurrent validity	Community-based, mixed-methods scale development
PIEL (Manz, Gernhart, Bracaliello, Pressimone, & Eisenberg, 2014)	Global indicator of involvement	Self-report English & Spanish	Low-income, largely Latinx parents enrolled in home visiting	Internal consistency Item and person reliabilities	Construct validity	Community-based, mixed-methods scale development Independent psychometric study of English and Spanish versions

Home Environment

HOME (Caldwell, Heider, & Kaplan, 1966)	Global Score Parent-Child Interaction Parent Involvement Physical Environment	Observation Parent self-report Interview	Middle-class samples	Inter-observer agreement Internal consistency Test-retest reliability	Concurrent validity	Test equivalence demonstrated for African American and Caucasian families, but not for Hispanic families Adapted versions of the HOME for cross-cultural use are available

interaction. The PICCOLO can be scored during live in-person observations or via video recordings. The developers recommend the video recording option, given this allows repeated viewing for reliability testing.

The PICCOLO was developed using a diverse sample of American mothers from various cultural backgrounds, including 2,048 European (n = 798), African (n = 792), and Latina (n = 468) women. Each mother had a child between the ages of 10 months and 47 months. Assessment requires an observational period between 5 and 10 minutes (though 10 minutes is considered ideal), and parents are encouraged to participate with their child in a variety of activities, such as book sharing, playing with toys, and engaging in pretend play. For this normative sample, interrater reliability was in the moderate range (i.e., average r = .77), with a range of coefficients from .74 (Responsiveness) to .80 (Affection). Cross-ethnicity reliability was also assessed (mean r =.80 for total scale), with subscale correlations ranging from .66 (Encouragement) to .78 (Affection). Average interrater percent agreement across items in each subscale ranged from 69% (Teaching) to 80% (Affection).

In terms of concurrent validity, correlations for the total sample of mothers as well as the subgroups (European, African, and Latina) were statistically significant for all PICCOLO domains and for the total scale scores (Brady-Smith, Fauth, & Brooks-Gunn, 2005; Roggman et al., 2013). Finally, predictive validity showed that child cognitive, language, and socioemotional outcomes were significantly correlated at ages 2, 3, and 5 for total scale and domain subscale scores (Roggman et al., 2013).

Practitioners who work with ethnically diverse parents of infants and toddlers should be aware of the PICCOLO's strength and its ability to measure parenting interactions. Applications of the PICCOLO can be used to track behavioral outcomes in parents as well as children. Specifically, practitioners can use the PICCOLO to monitor parent-child progress and effectiveness within parenting interventions. The PICCOLO has also demonstrated versatility in being used in group-childcare settings (Norman & Christiansen, 2013), working with parents who have a child with a disability (Innocenti, Roggman, & Cook, 2013), and for early father-child interactions (Anderson, Roggman, Innocenti, & Cook, 2013). Though the training materials are easy to use and follow, there is a fee to access them, with some resources being free to download. The measure has shown to be practical, feasible, and psychometrically strong.

The **Dyadic Parent-Child Interaction Coding System, Third Edition** (DPICS; Eyberg et al., 2009) is a comprehensive behavioral observational coding system that assesses the quality of the social interactions between parent and child, as well as the key aspects that contribute to negative interactions. Observations are conducted in three different situations: Child-Directed Interaction (where free play occurs), Parent-Directed Interaction (where the parent directs the activity with the child), and Clean Up (where parent and child clean up the materials used in the activities). Across the three scenarios, observers record 24 parent and child behaviors based on four categories (i.e., Verbalization, Vocalization, Response, and Physical). These four categories employ specific coding guidelines to assess behaviors in the overall Parent Category and Child Category. The Parent Category focuses on assessing polar parenting behaviors (i.e. punitive vs supportive), whereas the Child Category assesses disruptive behaviors.

Behavioral coding can occur during live sessions or through recorded videos. These options have demonstrably good reliability and validity in the Parent and Child categories. According to Fleiss (1981), inter-rater kappa values .4 to .6 are considered *fair*, .6 to .75 are *good*, and above .75 are *excellent*; most values for items observed during the Parent-Directed and Child-Directed Interaction conditions were demonstrated to be within these thresholds. Inter-rater agreement for DPICS items, when coded live during the Parent- and Child-Directed Interaction conditions, was satisfactory, with kappas above .4 on all items except for behavioral description (.24) and labeled praise (.13) (Bessmer & Eyberg, 1993). The kappa coefficients for videotaped coding of DPICS categories during mother-child interactions, as well as during the father-child interactions, across all three conditions were all above .4, except negative touch (.33) and destructive (.09) (Bessmer, Brestan, & Eyberg, 2005; Brestan, Foote, & Eyberg, 2005). Discriminant validity was documented for clinically referred and non-referred families of mother-child as well as father-child dyads (Bessmer et al., 2005; Brestan et al., 2005). No significant differences were found on three of the composite scores for father-child dyads (i.e., Total Commands, child Inappropriate Behavior, or child Prosocial Behavior), whereas no differences were found on only the frequency of child Prosocial Behavior composite for the mother-child dyads.

Broadly, this measure enables practitioners to understand better parenting abilities, parent-child attachment, and social interactions that contribute to child development, as well as changes in parenting behaviors after an intervention. One major application of the DPICS is to track changes in treatment progress during Parent-Child Interaction Therapy. However, this measure is adaptable to accommodate other clinical programs that focus on assessing aspects of the parent-child interaction. DPICS enables practitioners to pinpoint small changes in parent-child interactions that contribute to negative exchanges based on the specific observable behaviors identified in the Verbalization, Vocalization, Response, and Physical categories. Overall, the DPICS manual and guide are easily accessible on the internet, but training is required to conduct observations. The DPICS is a brief measure, requiring 5 minutes of observation each for the Parent-Directed, Child-Directed, and Clean Up conditions. Additionally, administrators have adapted the measure for use in a variety of settings, such as the home, clinic, or classroom. Though the norming data are limited, the DPICS has been used with a variety of families, primarily to evaluate pre- and post-behaviors after parent training programs.

The ***Parenting Relationship Questionnaire*** (PRQ: Kamphaus & Reynolds, 2006) is a four-point (Never, Sometimes, Often, Almost Always) self-report scale completed by parents to reflect the nature of the parent-child relationship. There are two forms available: a 45-item Preschool scale (PRQ-P) and a 71-item Child and Adolescent scale (PRQ-CA). The PRQ-P requires approximately 10 to 15 minutes to complete and at least a third-grade reading level in English. Summative scores can be generated using software or by hand-scoring. The PRQ-P has five scaled scores that measure: attachment, discipline practices, involvement, parenting confidence, and relational frustration.

The PRQ standardization was conducted between 2003 and 2005 with 4,130 cases from 41 states (Kamphaus & Reynolds, 2006). Though norm groups were created by age groups, the female-rater sample ranged from 500 to 750 (total $n = 3,500$), and the male-rater sample ranged from 100 to 150 (total $n = 630$). The sample represented a fairly diverse population regarding race/ethnicity, geographic location, and mother's education level, with the exception of limited respondents from the Northeast region of the United States. The median coefficient alpha for each scale across age groups exceeds .80. The lowest coefficient alpha was found on the Relational Frustration scale on the PRQ-P for the 2–5 age range. Test-retest reliability analysis of 33 to 35 days had scale reliability coefficients from .75 to .89 for the PRQ-P. Inter-scale correlations for PRQ-P were found to be moderate and in the expected directions. The PRQ-P's psychometric properties reveal that this instrument has good reliability and validity evidence across a diverse population. It should be noted that the measure is not recommended as a means for diagnosis (Rubinic & Schwickrath, 2010); instead, it could be used as a valuable supplement (e.g., used with Behavior Assessment System for Children, Third Edition (BASC-3)) to clinical assessment of the parent-child relationship.

Administration and scoring of the PRQ-P is user-friendly, quick, and convenient (e.g., hand-scored, computer-entry, and scannable forms available for purchase and use). The authors recommend that examiners have formal training in assessment and follow the test manual instructions (Rubinic & Schwickrath, 2010). According to the instrument's publisher, Pearson Canada Assessment (2019), the qualifications to purchase PRQ-P include: 1) a master's degree in a field related to the intended use of PRQ; 2) certification or full active membership in relevant professional organizations; 3) a degree or license to practice in the healthcare or a related field; or 4) formal supervised training in assessing children and formal training in the ethical administration, scoring, and interpretation.

The *Parent-Child Relationship Inventory* (PCRI; Gerard, 1994) is a self-report questionnaire that assesses parents' attitudes toward their parenting abilities and how they feel about their child within seven content areas. The PCRI contains 78 items on a Likert-type, 4-point response option (i.e., Strongly Agree, Agree, Disagree, and Strongly Disagree). The PCRI can be administered to individuals or by group and requires approximately 15 to 20 minutes to complete, with 5 minutes to score. At least a fourth-grade reading level is necessary, and the measure is available in English and Spanish. Higher scores on the measure indicate healthy parenting skills and a positive parent-child relationship. The Parent Support scale examines the level of emotional and social support available to the parent. The Satisfaction with Parenting scale measures the number of gratifying emotions, such as pleasure and fulfillment, experienced as a parent. The Involvement scale examines the parent's engagement with and knowledge about their child. The Communication scale assesses the parent's perception of effective communication with their child. The Limit Setting scale examines parental disciplinary experience with a child. The Autonomy scale examines the parent's facilitation of their child's independence. The Role Orientation scale examines attitudes present in child rearing with regard to gender roles.

Development of the PCRI scales combined expert ratings and field testing with parents. A factor analysis of 106 preliminary items led to the final 78-item PCRI (Gerard, 1994). Standardization of the PCRI was based on a predominantly White (85.7%) sample of 668 mothers and 471 fathers with children aged 3 to 15 years, from a variety of different schools and center-based care settings in four geographical regions of the United States (Gerard, 1994). Statistical analyses on parental demographic factors revealed that Black parents scored significantly lower than Caucasian parents on the Satisfaction with Parenting scale and Autonomy scale. Furthermore, parents with college degrees or higher scored higher on the Parent Support scale, and parents with less than a high school level of education scored lower than parents with at least a college education on the Autonomy scale. Lastly, the youngest parents in the normative sample (i.e., ages 18–24 years) scored lower than all other parental groups on the Satisfaction with Parenting, Involvement, and Autonomy scales.

Gerard (1994) provides psychometric evaluations for reliability in a detailed table from the PCRI manual. Test-Retest reliability was viewed as acceptable: after one-week stability coefficients ranged from .68 (Communication scale) to .93 (Limit Setting Scale); after five months coefficients ranged from .44 (Autonomy scale) to .71 (Parental Support scale and Role Orientation scale). Across the seven scales, internal consistency was acceptable with Cronbach's alpha coefficients ranging from .70 (Parental Support scale) to .88 (Limit Setting scale), with a median alpha of .80. Raver (2003) further verified the internal consistency for this measure in a longitudinal study including a sample of 94 mothers recruited from Head Start programs, where the Limit Setting scale of the PCRI had an alpha of .80 at time one and .77 two years later at time two. Contrarily, Reitman, Rhode, Hupp, and Altobello (2002) reported that their sample, which included 171 mothers recruited from a Head Start orientation, revealed low alphas for the Involvement (.36) and Autonomy (.55) scales, moderate alphas for the Communication (.67) and Limit Setting (.75) scales, and a moderate alpha for the Social Desirability indicator used to identify invalid data (.74).

Parent Involvement

Several measures of parent involvement in children's education are available in the research literature, including the Parent/Family Involvement Index (Cone, Delawyer, & Wolfe, 1985), Parent-Teacher Involvement Question-naire (INVOLVE; Reid, Webster-Stratton, & Beauchaine, 2001; Webster-Stratton, 1998; Webster-Stratton, Reid, & Hammond, 2001), Parent Involvement 3in Children's Education Scale (PICES; Fantuzzo, Tighe, McWayne, Davis, & Childs, 2002), Parent Involvement Survey (PIS; Lau, 2013), and Even Start Family Literacy Parent Education Profile (PEP Scales; Dwyer, RMC Research Corporation, & New York State Department of Education, 2003). All measures evaluate dimensions of parent engagement in educational experiences with their child at home and in school, as well as parent-teacher communication. These foci correspond with Epstein's (1995) definition of parent involvement.

Although these instruments met several of the exemplary measure inclusion criteria, the **Family Involvement Questionnaire** (FIQ; Fantuzzo et al., 2000) underwent a rigorous development process, has sound psychometric properties, is a multi-dimensional measure of involvement, and is a widely used measure specifically for the evaluation of parents of young children. As such, the FIQ was chosen as an exemplary measure in evaluating parent involvement in preschoolers' education. The FIQ was developed to evaluate involvement of parents of children in preschool, kindergarten, and first grade. The measure gathers information on the domains of parent home- and school-based involvement, which includes parenting behaviors geared toward child education (e.g., "I take my child to the public library" or "I attend parent workshops or training offered by my child's school"). The third domain assessed is the frequency of home-school conferencing, which includes parent-school communication and parent engagement (e.g., "I talk to my child's teacher about my child's accomplishments").

The FIQ was developed through a collaborative partnership with diverse stakeholders, including parents, teachers, school administration, and research study investigators. Two of the stages of development included parent focus groups and consultation to evaluate and yield the final scale items. To validate the measure, data were collected from 641 caregivers of children in a low-income, urban area. The majority of participants were female (90%) and were African American (57%). Additional demographic information on the initial validation sample is published and available (Fantuzzo et al., 2000).

The field-tested version of the FIQ consisted of 42 items that are rated on a 4-point Likert scale from Rarely (1) to Always (4), with higher scores indicative of greater involvement (Fantuzzo et al., 2000). Items were retained and associated with dimensions if they met several retention criteria: a) individual factors accounted for a minimum of 5% of the variance, 2) individual factors demonstrated adequate internal consistency (i.e., $\alpha \geq .70$), c) the factor solution was supported by Cattell's (1966) scree plot and parallel analysis (Lautenschlager, Lance, & Flaherty, 1989, 4) the final factor solution minimized inter-factor correlation and assignment of items to multiple factors, and 5) the final factor solution was theoretically and conceptually justified. Of the 42 field-tested items, 35 were retained in a three-factor solution. The FIQ factors demonstrated strong reliability and stability and were aligned with Epstein's (1995) framework of parent involvement. School-based involvement yielded a Cronbach's alpha of .85, home-based involvement yielded an alpha of .85, and home-school conferencing yielded an alpha of .81. Further, the FIQ factor structure was confirmed with an independent sample of low-income parents of young children (Fantuzzo et al., 2000).

Since its initial field test, research has advanced the FIQ as a reliable and practical measure for ethnically diverse young children. The FIQ factor structure has been replicated for geographically diverse Latinx samples in both English and Spanish versions (McWayne, Manz, & Ginsburg-Block, 2015). Recently, the utility of the FIQ was enhanced by creating a 21-item short form (i.e., FIQ-SF; Fantuzzo et al., 2013). The FIQ-SF has been demonstrated to be reliable and valid for low-income families who are African American and Latinx (Bulotsky-Shearer, Bouza, Bichay, Fernandez, & Gaona Hernandez, 2016; Fantuzzo et al., 2013). The FIQ-SF offers an efficient and quick evaluation of parent involvement in early childhood education (Fantuzzo et al., 2013).

There is a significant relationship between parent involvement and child behavior in preschool (McWayne, Campos, & Owsianik, 2008), on the one hand, and academic achievement, on the other (Fan & Chen, 2001); thus, having a measure that can help assess this level of involvement can be beneficial. Though there are potential limitations for the FIQ to be used in geographical locations other than urban landscapes, it has provided sufficient reliable and valid evidence for its intended use as an assessment tool for level of family involvement within the early childhood educational setting. Future researchers may wish to continue investigating the generalizability of the FIQ and utility of the FIQ-SF. Through the FIQ, researchers can gather information about the diverse features of parent involvement in child education that can identify areas in which to support parents and teachers further and, ultimately, improve child outcomes.

The extension of the conceptualization of parent involvement into the learning experiences of children under the age of 3 is in its early stages, with only one measure identified. *The Parent Involvement in Early Learning* (PIEL; Manz et al., 2014) is a promising measure of English- and Spanish-speaking parents' support of their infants' and toddlers' learning. The PIEL was developed through a mixed-methods approach. First, the PIEL content was developed through a series of focus groups with staff and parents involved in a national home visiting program serving low-income, inner-city infants and toddlers. After field testing, the initial 25-item checklist was created. The PIEL was developed in English, and translated into Spanish, and through a home visiting program in a large metropolitan area, the English and Spanish versions were independently developed through a combined classical test theory and item response theory approach. Although the independent scale analyses produced a single dimension of parent involvement for both versions, the item content was slightly different. The English version of the PIEL retained 17 items from the field-test version, whereas the Spanish version retained 18 of the original items. The two language versions share 15 items that measure expressions of parent involvement in direct teaching (e.g., naming colors and shapes), play (e.g., join child in play), community activities (e.g., go to a park), social interactions (e.g., take child to play with other children), and structuring television viewing (e.g., watch TV and movies together). Unique to the Spanish PIEL are items pertaining to well-baby visits, openly praising the child, and limiting TV and video watching. Unique to the English version are items related to parent-child games (e.g., peek-a-boo) and involving the child in errands. Strong internal consistency has been demonstrated in the development study as well as in a replication study of the English and Spanish versions of the PIEL (Manz et al., 2014; Manz et al., 2018). Given the developmental salience of play to children's learning, a study demonstrating that English- and Spanish-speaking parents' report on the PIEL positively correlated with their endorsement of play as a valuable learning mechanism for infants and toddlers offers initial validity evidence (Manz & Bracaliello, 2016).

The PIEL was developed to guide early intervention service delivery for infants and toddlers. It can be used to monitor the program engagement of families and to inform effective strategies for fostering parents' involvement with their young children in early learning experiences. The PIEL yields a single score that sums parents' item responses based on a 4-point Likert scale that identifies the frequency of involvement behaviors (i.e., Rarely, Sometimes, Often, Always). Given that the PIEL is in its early stages of development, normative data are not available. Therefore, interpretation of PIEL scores is relative to the specific application, such as comparing pre-/post-treatment scores.

Home Environment

Three measures of the home environment were identified in the literature search (i.e., the Family Environment Scale, Moos & Moos, 1994; the Home Quality Rating Scale, Meyers, Mink, & Nihira, 1990; and the Home Observation for Measurement of the Environment (HOME), Caldwell et al., 1966). Among these measures, only the HOME met the exemplary measure inclusion criteria. The HOME consists of observational, parent-report, and interview items, which require about one hour to administer (Caldwell et al., 1966). The HOME is appropriate for four age groups: infancy/toddlerhood (IT-HOME; 45 items), preschool/early childhood (EC-HOME; 55 items), school-age/middle childhood (59 items), and early adolescence (60 items). It assesses the overall home environment, including parent-child interaction, parent involvement, and physical surroundings at home. Researchers and interventionists, including home visitors, may use the HOME to inform how best to support children and their families or to evaluate whether an intervention has produced desired outcomes (Totsika & Sylva, 2004).

Numerous studies in the United States have incorporated the HOME, and the scale has been adapted for use in different countries to evaluate the quantity and quality of stimulation and support available for children's development (Jones et al., 2017). Research has provided evidence of strong psychometric properties for the HOME (Totsika & Sylva, 2004). Inter-observer agreement has been reported above .80 for IT-HOME and .90 for EC-HOME. Internal consistency is high as well (i.e., $r = .80$ for IT-HOME and $r = .90$ for EC-HOME). Internal consistency of the IT-HOME subscales ranges from .30 to .80, and that of the EC-HOME subscales is between .53 and .83. Concurrent validity of IT-HOME was reported as small to moderate correlations between the HOME and family SES. Test-retest reliability at 18 months ranges from .05 to .70. Low stability was indicated only on one subscale, Physical Punishment. In addition, research has indicated that scores on the HOME are moderately correlated with children's cognitive outcomes (Blums, Belsky, Grimm, & Chen, 2017; Elardo, Bradley, & Caldwell, 1975). The HOME has been extensively studied with populations that vary in terms of ethnicity, race, SES, and other risk factors (e.g., children with disabilities), in the United States as well as internationally (Jones et al., 2017; Totsika & Sylva, 2004). Studies of the HOME's measurement equivalence across racial/ethnic groups has yielded mixed results. For instance, its equivalence was demonstrated for African American and Caucasian families but not for Hispanic families (Bingenheimer, Raudenbush, Leventhal, & Brooks-Gunn, 2005).

Overall, the HOME is useful for providing practitioners with a snapshot of children's developmental and environmental needs so practitioners can support children and their families in a meaningful way. Caution should be taken when the HOME is used with families from diverse racial/ethnic backgrounds; however, some studies have advocated that the HOME interview can be adapted to accommodate across diverse populations (Totsika & Sylva, 2004). In addition, some items are on a binary scale (i.e., yes or no), which does not provide in-depth information of level of functioning (Totsika & Sylva, 2004), and therefore utilizing additional sources of data can assist in conceptualizing the information gathered from the HOME.

Conclusion

The merits of incorporating assessment of parental supports when evaluating the developmental needs of children under the age of 5 years stand on a substantial body of consistent theory and evidence for the critical role of parenting in children's present and later-life acquisition of cognitive, language, and social competencies. Assessment of parental supports complements direct assessment of children's abilities. The information generated from this assessment illuminates foci for intervening to support children's development, especially those children who are indicating early developmental delays. Interventionists can incorporate this information into collaborative problem-solving approaches with parents to prioritize their goals and concerns for their child, develop intervention strategies, and evaluate their progress (Knoche, 2013; Sheridan & Kratochwill, 2008).

Utilizing parental assessment in intervention planning and progress monitoring aligns with the two-generational orientation of early intervention for young children seen in common services such as Part C early intervention, Head Start programs, and home visiting models. This orientation is based on well-established theory documenting that enhancement of parental competence is highly associated with children's development, in both the short term and long term (Raikes et al., 2014). Parental assessment is especially applicable to educational and intervention programming for infants and toddlers given that families are key participants. This is evident in Part C's mandate for early intervention to improve both child and family outcomes, as documented in the IFSP (US Department of Education, 2019). Therefore, assessment of parental supports when evaluating young children is not an "add-on" but a must.

In this chapter, three major domains of parental supports were identified: parent-child interaction, parent involvement in education, and home environment. Exemplar measures that met or exceeded basic criteria for psychometric quality were identified for these domains. The greatest number of measures was available for assessing parent-child interaction, with options for observation (PICCOLO and DPICS) and self-report (PRQ-P and PCRI). Although only one measure of the home environment (HOME) emerged, this multi-method measure has a strong research base and is widely used. Measures of parent involvement are promising, particularly for preschool-aged children (FIQ). One measure of parent involvement for infants and toddlers was identified (PIEL), although this measure is preliminary and in need of further psychometric study. For both age groups, standardized measurement of parental involvement is yet to be developed.

Evident in the research supporting the critical role of parenting in children's development is the strong influence of SES (Shonkoff & Phillips, 2000). Although research unequivocally shows the direct impact of parenting on children's development (Roggman et al., 2008), the mediating role of parenting supports in the face of stressors, such as socioeconomic hardship, is also demonstrated (Linver et al., 2002; Masarik & Conger, 2017; Palermo et al., 2018). In addition to SES, interesting research shows that culture dually affects parenting behaviors and children's development. Expressions of parenting involve universal elements (i.e., responsiveness, sensitivity) (Barrueco et al., 2007; Roggman et al., 2008). Moreover, there are culture-specific elements, such as racial socialization, that must be considered (Stevenson et al., 2001), and emerging research demonstrates that parenting may facilitate children's development differently within different cultural frameworks (Bradley & Corwyn, 2005; Palermo et al., 2018).

In contrast to this rich and strong body of evidence for the critical forces of SES and culture on child development, measurement of parental support is lacking in its intentional development of content and psychometric support for children of varying backgrounds. As reflected in the exemplars selected for this chapter, scale development often favors Caucasian and middle-class families, underrepresenting children who are ethnic, racial, and linguistic minorities. Deliberate, cultural-specific study of the psychometric quality has not risen to a point of standard practice in scale development. And, although scales are frequently translated into languages other than English, the processes transform content derived for native English speakers without sufficient attention paid to the representation of constructs for the populations for which it is being adapted (Messick, 2000; Nair, White, Knight, & Roosa, 2009). With advances in scale development methods (i.e., mixed-methods approaches; Hitchcock et al., 2005; McWayne & Melzi, 2014) and statistical analyses (i.e., Item Response Theory; Smith, Conrad, Chang, & Piazza, 2002), cultural-specificity, as well as scale equivalence for a full range of SES samples and various cultures, should direct future research. With these limitations in mind, practitioners should carefully incorporate assessment of parenting in psychoeducational evaluation and intervention planning for young children through collaboration with parents (García Coll et al., 2002).

References

Adoption Network (2019). Adoption statistics. Retrieved from https://adoptionnet work.com/adoption-statistics

Anders, Y., Sammons, P., Taggart, B., Sylva, K., Melhuish, E., & Siraj-Blatchford, I. (2011). The influence of child, family, home factors and pre-school education on the identification of special educational needs at age 10. *British Education Research Journal*, 37(3), 421–441.

Anderson, S., Roggman, L. A., Innocenti, M. S., & Cook, G. A. (2013). Dads' Parenting Interactions with Children: Checklist of Observations Linked to Outcomes (PIC-COLO-D). *Infant Mental Health Journal*, 34(4), 339–351. doi:10.1002/imhj.21390

Arnold, D. H., Zeljo, A., Doctoroff, G. L., & Ortiz, C. (2008). Parent involvement in preschool: Predictors and the relation to preliteracy development. *School Psychology Review*, 37(1), 74–90.

Barrueco, S., López, M., & Miles, J. C. (2007). Parenting during the first year of life: A national comparison of Latinos and other cultural communities. *Journal of Latinos and Education*, 6, 253–265.

Bessmer, J. L., Brestan, E. V., & Eyberg, S. M. (2005). *The dyadic parent-child interaction coding system II (DPICS II): Reliability and validity with mother-child dyads.* Manuscript in preparation.

Bessmer, J. L. & Eyberg, S. M. (1993, November). Dyadic Parent-Child Interaction Coding System–II (DPICS): Initial reliability and validity of the clinical version. *Paper presented at the AABT Preconference on Social Learning and the Family*, Atlanta, GA.

Bingenheimer, J. B., Raudenbush, S. W., Leventhal, T., & Brooks-Gunn, J. (2005). Measurement equivalence and differential item functioning in family psychology. *Journal of Family Psychology, 19*, 441–455. doi:10.1037/0893-3200.19.3.441

Blums, A., Belsky, J., Grimm, K., & Chen, Z. (2017). Building links between early socioeconomic status, cognitive ability, and math and science achievement. *Journal of Cognition and Development, 18*(1), 16–40. doi:10.1080/15248372.2016.1228652

Bradley, R. H. (2009). The home environment. In M. H. Bornstein (Ed.), *Handbook of cultural developmental science* (pp. 505–530). New York: Psychology Press.

Bradley, R. H. & Corwyn, R. F. (2005). Care for children around the world: A view from HOME. *International Journal of Behavioral Development, 29*(6), 468–478.

Bradley, R. H., Pennar, A., & Glick, J. (2014). Home environments of infants from immigrant families in the United States: Findings from the New Immigrant Survey. *Infant Mental Health Journal, 35*(6), 565–579.

Brady-Smith, C., Fauth, R., & Brooks-Gunn, J. (2005). *Early Head Start research and evaluation project: Background and psychometric infor-mation for the child–parent interaction rating scales for the three-bag assessment 14-, 24-, and 36-month waves.* New York: Columbia University.

Brestan, E. V., Foote, R. C., & Eyberg, S. M. (2005). *The dyadic parent-child interaction coding system II (DPICS II): Reliability and validity with father-child dyads.* Manuscript in preparation.

Bronfenbrenner, U. (2001). The bioecological theory of human development. In N. J. Smelser & P. B. Baltes (Eds.), *International encyclopedia of the social and behavioral sciences* (Vol. 10, pp. 6963–6970). Amsterdam: Elsevier.

Bulotsky-Shearer, R. J., Bouza, J., Bichay, K., Fernandez, V. A., & Gaona Hernandez, P. (2016). Extending the validity of the family involvement questionnaire- short form for culturally and linguistically diverse families from low-income backgrounds. *Psychology in the Schools, 53*(9), 911–925.

Cairney, J., Boyle, M., Offord, D. R., & Racine, Y. (2003). Stress, social support and depression in single and married mothers. *Social Psychiatry and Psychiatric Epidemiology,38*, 442–449. doi:10.1007/s00127-003-0661-0

Caldwell, B. M. & Bradley, R. H. (2001). *HOME inventory and administration manual* (3rd ed.). Little Rock, AR: University of Arkansas for Medical Sciences and University of Arkansas.

Caldwell, B. M., Heider, J., & Kaplan, B. (1966) The inventory of home stimulation. *Paper presented at the meeting of the American Psychological Association*, New York.

Carlson, J. F., Geisinger, K. F., & Jonson, J. L. (Eds.). (2017). *The nineteenth mental measurements yearbook.* Lincoln, NE: Buros Center for Testing.

Cattell, R. B. (1966). The scree test for the number of factors. *Multivariate behavioral research, 1*(2), 245–276.

Center for Disease Control and Prevention (CDC). (2017). *Marriage and divorce.* Retrieved from www.cdc.gov/nchs/fastats/marriage-divorce.htm

Center for Disease Control and Prevention (CDC). (2019) *Developmental monitoring.* Retrieved from www.cdc.gov/ncbddd/childdevelopment/screening.html

Chazen-Cohen, R., Riakes, H., Brooks-Gunn, J., Ayoub, C., Pan, B. A., Kisker, E. E., … Fuligni, A. S. (2009). Low-income children's school readiness: Parent contributions over the first five years. *Early Education and Development, 20*(6), 958–977.

Child Trends (2014). Early education enrollment. Retrieved from www.childtrends. org/indicators/early-childhood-program-enrollment

Child Trends (2016). *Child care.* Available at: www.childtrends.org/?indicators=child-care

Cone, J. D., Delawyer, D. D., & Wolfe, V. V. (1985). Assessing parent participation: The parent/family involvement index. *Exceptional Children, 51*(5), 417–424.

DiSanto, A., Timmons, K., & Pelletier, J. (2016). "Mommy that's the exit.": Empowering homeless mothers to support their children's daily literacy experiences. *Journal of Early Childhood Literacy, 16*(2), 145–170.

Dotterer, A. M., Iruka, I. U., & Pungello, E. (2013). Parenting, race, socioeconomic status: Links to school readiness. *Family Relations, 61,* 657–670.

Dwyer, C., RMC Research Corporation, & New York State Department of Education (2003, October). Even start family literacy parent education profile. Retrieved from https://rmcresearchcorporation.com/portsmouthnh/wp-content/uploads/sites/2/2013/06/PEP-2nd-Ed.pdf

Early Childhood Technical Assistance Center (ECTA) (2014). Integrating family and child outcomes into the Individualized Family Service Plan (IFSP) process. Retrieved from https://ectacenter.org/~pdfs/eco/IFSP-OutcomesFlowChart.pdf

Elardo, R., Bradley, R., & Caldwell, B. M. (1975). The relation of infants' home environments to mental test performance from six to thirty-six months: A longitudinal analysis. *Child development, 46*(1), 71–76.

Epstein, J. L. (1995). School/family/community partnerships: Caring for the children we share. *Phi Delta Kappan, 76,* 701–712.

Erwin, T. D. (1991). *Assessing student learning and development: A guide to the principles, goals, and methods of determining college outcomes.* Retrieved from http://search.ebscohost.com.ezproxy.lib.lehigh.edu/login.aspx?direct=true&db=eric&AN=ED330256&site=ehost-live

Eyberg, S. M., Nelson, M. M., Duke, M., & Boggs, S. R. (2009). *Manual for the Dyadic Parent-Child Interaction Coding System, Third Edition.* Retrieved from http://citeseerx.ist.psu.edu/viewdoc/download?doi=10.1.1.627.4254&rep=rep1&type=pdf

Fan, X. & Chen, M. (2001). Parental involvement and students' academic achievement: A meta-analysis. *Educational Psychology Review, 13*(1), 1–22.

Fantuzzo, J., Gadsden, V., Li, F., Sproul, F., McDermott, P., Hightower, D., & Minney, A. (2013). Multiple dimensions of family engagement in early childhood education: Evidence for a short form of the Family Involvement Questionnaire. *Early Childhood Research Quarterly, 28*(4), 734–742.

Fantuzzo, J., Tighe, E., & Childs, S. (2000). Family Involvement Questionnaire: A multivariate assessment of family participation in early childhood education. *Journal of Educational Psychology, 92*(2), 367.

Fantuzzo, J. W., Tighe, E., McWayne, C. M., Davis, G., & Childs, S. (2002). Parent involvement in early childhood education and children's peer play competencies: An examination of multivariate relationships. *NHSA Dialog: A ResearchTo-Practice Journal for the Early Intervention Field, 6,* 3–21.

Ferguson, H. B., Bovaird, S., & Mueller, M. P. (2007). The impact of poverty on educational outcomes for children. *Pediatric Child Health, 12*(8), 701–706. Retrieved from: www.ncbi.nlm.nih.gov/pmc/articles/PMC2528798/

Fleiss, J. L. (1981). *Statistical methods for rates and proportions.* New York: Wiley.

Flouri, E. & Buchanan, A. (2004). Early father's and mother's involvement and child's later educational outcomes. *British Journal of Educational Psychology, 74*, 141–153.

Furstenberg, F. F. (2014). Fifty years of family change: From consensus to complexity. *The ANNALS of the American Academy of Political and Social Science, 654*(1), 12–30.

García Coll, C., Akiba, D., Palacios, N., Bailey, B., Silver, R., DiMartino, L., Chin, C. (2002). Parental involvement in children's education: Lessons from three immigrant groups. *Parenting: Science and Practice, 2*(3), 303–324. https://doi-org.ezproxy.lib. lehigh.edu/10.1207/S15327922PAR0203_05

Gerard, A. B. (1994). *Parent-Child Relationship Inventory (PCRI): Manual*. Lost Angeles, CA: Western Psychological Services.

Giallo, R., Treyvaud, K., Cooklin, A., & Wade, C. (2013). Mothers' and fathers' involvement in home activities with their children: Psychosocial factors and parental self-efficacy. *Early Child Development and Care, 183*(3-4), 343–359.

Greenspan, S. I. & Wieder, S. (2003). Infant and early childhood mental health: A comprehensive developmental approach to assessment and intervention. *Zero to Three, 24*(1), 6–13.

Guevara, J. P., Gerdes, M., Localio, R., Huang, Y. V., Pinto-Martin, J., Minkovitz, C. S., … Pati, S. (2013). Effectiveness of developmental screening in an urban setting. *Pediatrics, 131*(1), 30–37. doi:10.1542/peds.2012-0765

Hart, B. & Risley, T. R. (1995). *Meaningful differences in the everyday experience of young American children*. Baltimore, MD: Paul H. Brookes Publishing.

Hartas, D. (2017). Families' social backgrounds matter: Socioeconomic factors, home learning, and young children's language, literacy, and social outcomes. *British Education Research Journal, 37*(6), 893–914.

Hitchcock, J. H., Natasi, B. K., Dai, D. Y., Newman, J., Jayasena, A., Bernstein-Moore, R., … Varjas, K. (2005). Illustrating a mixed-methods approach for validating culturally specific constructs. *Journal of School Psychology, 43*(3), 259–278.

Hix-Small, H., Marks, K., Squires, J., & Nickel, R. (2007). Impact of implementing developmental screening at 12 and 24 months in a pediatric practice. *Pediatrics, 120* (2), 381–389. doi:10.1542/peds.2006-3583

Hussey-Gardner, B., McNinch, A., Anastasi, J., & Miller, M. (2002). Early intervention best practice: Collaboration among an NICU, an early intervention program, and an NICU follow-up program. *Neonatal Network, 21*(3), 15–22.

Individuals with Disabilities Education Improvement Act. Pub. L. No. 108,446. (2004). https://ies.ed.gov/ncser/pdf/pl108-446.pdf

Innocenti, M. S., Roggman, L. A., & Cook, G. A. (2013). Using the PICCOLO with parents of children with a disability. *Infant Mental Health Journal, 34*(4), 307–318. https://doi-org.ezproxy.lib.lehigh.edu/10.1002/imhj.21394

Jeynes, W. (2005). A meta-analysis of the relation of parental involvement to urban elementary school student academic achievement. *Urban Education, 40*(237). doi:10.1177/0042085905274540

Jones, P. C., Pendergast, L. L., Schaefer, B. A., Rasheed, M., Svensen, E., Scharf, R., … Murray-Kolb, L. E. (2017). Measuring home environments across cultures: Invariance of the HOME scale across eight international sites from the MAL-ED study. *Journal of School Psychology, 64*, 109–127. https://doi-org.ezproxy.lib.lehigh.edu/ 10.1016/j.jsp.2017.06.001

Kamphaus, R. W. & Reynolds, C. R. (2006). *PRQ: Parenting relationship questionnaire manual*. Minneapolis, MN: NCS Pearson.

Kingston, S., Huang, K. Y., Calzada, E., Dawson-McClure, S., & Botman, L. (2013). Parent involvement in education as a moderator of family and neighborhood socioeconomic context on school readiness among young children. *Journal of Community Psychology, 41*(3), 265–276.

Knoche, L. L. (2013). Implementation of Getting Ready: A relationship-focused intervention to support parent engagement, birth to 5. In T. Halle, A. Metz, & I. Martinez-Beck (Eds.), *Applying implementation science in early childhood programs and systems* (pp. 117–137). Baltimore, MD: Paul H. Brookes Publishing Co.

Knopf, H. T. & Swick, K. J. (2008). Using our understanding of families to strengthen family involvement. *Early Childhood Education Journal, 35*, 419–427.

Kohl, G. W., Lengua, L. J., & McMahon, R. J. (2000). Parent involvement in school conceptualizing multiple dimensions and their relations with family demographic and risk factors. *Journal of School Psychology, 38*(6), 501–523.

Lau, W. F. K. (2013). Examining a brief measure of parent involvement in children's education. *Contemporary School Psychology: Formerly" The California School Psychologist", 17*(1), 11–21.

Lautenschlager, G. J., Lance, C. E., & Flaherty, V. L. (1989). Parallel analysis criteria: Revised equations for estimating the latent roots of random data correlation matrices. *Educational and Psychological Measurement, 49*(2), 339–345.

Leventhal, T. & Brooks-Gunn, J. (2001). Poverty and child development. In N. J. Smelser & P. B. Baltes (Eds.), *International encyclopedia of the social & behavioral sciences* (pp. 11889–11894). Amsterdam: Elsevier.

Lim, M. (2012). Unpacking parent involvement: Korean American parents' collective network. *School Community Journal, 22*(1), 89–110.

Linver, M. R., Brooks-Gunn, J., & Kohen, D. E. (2002). Family processes as pathways from income to young children's development. *Developmental Psychology, 38*(5), 719.

Love, J. M., Chazan-Cohen, R., Raikes, H. R., & Brooks-Gunn, J. (2013). What makes a difference? Early Head Start evaluation in a developmental context. *Monographs of the Society for Research in Child Development, 78*(1).

Manz, P. H. & Bracaliello, C. B. (2016). Expanding outcome measurement for child development-focused home visiting programs: Collaborative development of the Toddler & Play Scale. *Early Childhood Research Quarterly, 36*, 157–167.

Manz, P. H., Fantuzzo, J. W., & Power, T. J. (2004). Multidimensional assessment of family involvement among urban, elementary students. *Journal of School Psychology, 42*(6), 461–475.

Manz, P. H., Gernhart, A. C., Bracaliello, C. B., Pressimone, V. P., & Eisenberg, R. A. (2014). Preliminary development of the Parent Involvement in Early Learning scale for low-income families enrolled in a child development focused home visiting program. *Journal of Early Intervention, 36*(3), 171–191.

Manz, P. H., Rigdard, T., Faison, J., Whitenack, J., Ventresco, N., Carr, D., Sole, M., and Cai, Y. (2018). Little Talks: A modular treatment approach for promoting infant and toddler language acquisition through parents' preferences and competencies. In S. Sonnenschein & B. Sawyer (Eds.), *Building on Black and Latino Families' Strengths to Support the Early Academic Development of Their Children*. New York, NY: Springer International Publisher.

Marjoribanks, K. (2001). Environments for education. In *International encyclopedia of the social & behavioral science* (Vol. 7, pp. 4693–4697). Amsterdam: Elsevier 10.1016/B978-0-08-097086-8.92077-4

Masarik, A. S. & Conger, R. D. (2017). Stress and child development: A review of the Family Stress Model. *Current Opinion in Psychology*, *13*, 85–90. doi:10.1016/j.copsyc.2016.05.008

Maternal Child Health Bureau/Health Resource Service Administration. (n.d.). Home Visiting. Retrieved from https://mchb.hrsa.gov/maternal-child-health-initiatives/home-visiting-overview

Mathis, E. T. B. & Bierman, K. L. (2015). Dimensions of parenting associated with child prekindergarten emotional regulation and attentional control in low-income families. *Social Development*, *24*(3), 601–620.

McWayne, C., Campos, R., & Owsianik, M. (2008). A multidimensional, multilevel examination of mother and father involvement among culturally diverse Head Start families. *Journal of School Psychology*, *46*(5), 551–573.

McWayne, C. M., Manz, P. H., & Ginsburg-Block, M. D. (2015). Examination of the Family Involvement Questionnaire-Early Childhood (FIQ-EC) with low-income Latino families of young children. *International Journal of School & Educational Psychology*, *3*(2), 117–134.

McWayne, C. M. & Melzi, G. (2014). Validity of culture-contextualized measure of family engagement in early learning of low-income Latino children. *Journal of Family Psychology*, *28*(2), 260–266.

McWayne, C. M., Melzi, G., Shick, A. R., Kennedy, J. C., & Mundt, K. (2013). Defining family engagement among Latino Head Start parents: A mixed-methods measurement development study. *Early Childhood Research Quarterly*, *28*, 593–607.

Melzi, G., Shick, A. R., & Bostwick, E. (2013). Latino family narratives during the preschool years. In H. Kreider & M. Caspe (Eds.), *Promising practices for engaging families in literacy* (pp. 45–57). Charlotte, NC: Information Age Publishing.

Messick, S. (1995). Validity of psychological assessment: Validation of inferences from persons responses and performances as scientific inquiry into score meaning. *American Psychologist*, *50*(9), 741–749.

Messick, S. (2000). Consequences of test interpretation and use: The fusion of validity and values in psychological assessment. In R. D. Griffin & E. Helmes (Eds.), *Problems and solutions in human assessment: Honoring Douglas N. Jackson at seventy* (pp. 3–20). New York: Springer Publishing.

Meyers, C. E., Mink, I. T., & Nihira, K. (1990). *Home quality rating scale manual*. Los Angeles, CA: Neuropsychiatric Institute, University of California.

Moos, R. & Moos, B. (1994). *The family environment scale manual* (3rd ed.). Palo Alto, CA: Consulting Psychologist Press.

Nair, R. L., White, R. M. B., Knight, G. P., & Roosa, M. (2009). Cross-language measurement equivalence of parenting measures for Mexican American population. *Journal of Family Psychology*, *25*(5), 680–689.

National Center for Educational Statistics (NCES). (2019). *Preschool and kindergarten enrollment*. Retrieved from https://nces.ed.gov/programs/coe/indicator_cfa.asp

National Institute for Early Education Research (NIEER). (2018). *The state of preschool, 2018*. New Brunswick, NJ: Rutgers University.

Norman, V. J. & Christiansen, K. (2013). Validity of the PICCOLO tool in child care settings: Can it assess caregiver interaction behaviors? *Infant Mental Health Journal*, *34*(4), 319–329. doi:10.1002/imhj.21391

Palermo, F., Ispa, J. M., Carlo, G., & Streit, C. (2018). Economic hardship during infancy and US Latino preschoolers' sociobehavioral health and academic readiness. *Developmental Psychology*, *54*, 890–902.

Pearson Canada Assessment (2019). Retrieved from www.pearsonclinical.ca/en/prod ucts/product-master/item-44.html

Prickett, K. C. (2018). Nonstandard work schedule, family dynamics, and mother-child interactions during early childhood. *Journal of Family Issues*, *39*(4), 985–1007.

Raikes, H. H., Roggman, L. A., Peterson, C. A., Brooks-Gunn, J., Chazan-Cohen, R., Zhang, X., & Schiffman, R. F. (2014). Theories of change and outcomes in home-based Early Head Start programs.*Early Childhood Research Quarterly*, *29*(4), 574–585.

Raver, C. C. (2003). Does work pay psychologically as well as economically? The role of employment in predicting depressive symptoms and parenting among low-income families. *Child Development*, *74*(6), 1720–1736.

Reese, L. & Gallimore, R. (2000). Immigrant Latinos' cultural model of literacy development: An evolving perspective on home-school discontinuities. *American Journal of Education*, *108*(2), 103–134.

Reid, M. J., Webster-Stratton, C., & Beauchaine, T. P. (2001). Parent training in Head Start: A comparison of program response among African American, Asian American, Caucasian, and Hispanic mothers. *Prevention Science*, *2*(4), 209–227.

Reitman, D., Rhode, P. C., Hupp, S. D. A., & Altobello, C. (2002). Development and validation of the Parental Authority Questionnaire – Revised. *Journal of Psychopathology and Behavioral Assessment*, *24*(2), 119–127.

Roggman, L. A., Cook, G. A., Innocenti, M. S., Norman, V., & Christiansen, K. (2013). Parenting interactions with children: Checklist of observations linked to outcomes (PICCOLO) in diverse ethnic groups. *Infant Mental Health Journal*, *34*(4), 290–306.

Roggman, L. A., Boyce, L. K., & Innocenti, M. S. (2008). Developmental parenting: A guide for early childhood practitioners Baltimore: Paul H. Brookes Publishing.

Rubinic, D. & Schwickrath, H. (2010). Review of Parenting relationship questionnaire. *Journal of Psychoeducational Assessment*, *28*(3), 270–275. doi:10.1177/0734282909346718

Schonwald, A., Huntington, N., Chan, E., Risko, W., & Bridgemohan, C. (2009). Routine developmental screening implemented in urban primary care settings: More evidence of feasibility and effectiveness. *Pediatrics*, *123*(2), 660–668. doi:10.1542/peds.2007-2798

Sheridan, S. M. & Kratochwill, T. R. (2008). *Conjoint behavioral consultation: Promoting family-school connections and interventions* (2nd ed.). New York: Springer.

Shonkoff, J. P. & Phillips, D. A. (2000). *From neurons to neighborhoods: The science of early childhood development*. Washington, DC: National Academy Press.

Smith, E. V., Conrad, K. M., Chang, K., & Piazza, J. (2002). An introduction to Rasch measurement for scale development and person assessment. *Journal of Nursing Measurement*, *10*(3), 189–206.

Stevenson, H. C., Davis, G., & Abdul-Kabir, S. (2001). *Stickin' to, watching over, and gettin' with: An African American parents' guide to discipline*. San Francisco, CA: Jossey-Bass.

Totsika, V. & Sylva, K. (2004). The home observation for measurement of the environment revisited. *Child & Adolescent Mental Health*, *9*(1), 25–35. https://doi-org.ezproxy.lib.lehigh.edu/10.1046/j.1475-357X.2003.00073.x

U. S. Department of Health and Human Services. (2010). *Head start impact study. Final report*. Washington, DC: Author.

U.S. Department of Education and U.S. Department of Health and Human Services. (2017). Collaboration and coordination of the Maternal, Infant, and Early Childhood Home Visiting Program and the Individuals with Disabilities Education Act and Part C Programs. Retrieved from https://sites.ed.gov/idea/files/ed-hhs-miechv-partc-guidance.pdf

US Department of Education. (2019). Individuals with Disabilities Education Act, 20 U.S.C. § 1436. Retrieved from https://sites.ed.gov/idea/statute-chapter-33/sub chapter-iii/1436.

Van Agt, H. M. E., van der Stege, H. A., de Ridder-sluiter, H., Verhoeven, L. T. W., & de Koning, H. J. (2007). A cluster-randomized trial of screening for language delay in toddlers: Effects on school performance and language development at age 8. *Pediatrics, 120*(6), 1317–1325. doi:10.1542/peds.2006-3145

Vandivere, S., Malm, K., & Radel, L. (2009). *Adoption USA: A chartbook based on the 2007 National Survey of Adoptive Parents*. Washington, DC: US DHHS.

Walker, J. M. T., Wilkins, A. S., Dallaire, J. R., Sandler, H. M., & Hoover-Dempsey, K. V. (2005). Parental involvement: Model revision through scale development. The Elementary School Journal, 106(2), 85–104.

Webster-Stratton, C. (1998). Preventing conduct problems in Head Start children: Strengthening parenting competencies. *Journal of Consulting and Clinical Psychology, 66*(5), 715.

Webster-Stratton, C., Reid, M. J., & Hammond, M. (2001). Preventing conduct problems, promoting social competence: A parent and teacher training partnership in Head Start. *Journal of Clinical Child Psychology, 30*(3), 283–302.

Yamamoto, Y., Li, J., & Lu, J. L. (2016). Does socioeconomic status matter for Chinese immigrants' academic socialization? Family environment, parent engagement, and preschoolers outcomes. *Research in Human Development, 13*, 191–206.

Zarate, M. E. (2007). *Understanding parental involvement: Perceptions, expectations, and recommendations*. Los Angeles, CA: The Thomás Rivera Policy Institute.

Zero to Three. (2010) *Infant/toddler development, screening, and assessment*. Retrieved from www.zerotothree.org/resources/72-infant-and-toddler-development-screening-and-assessment

Chapter 6

Assessment of Early Childhood School and Classroom Environments

R. A. McWilliam, Catalina Patricia Morales-Murillo, and Cami M. Stevenson

Principles of Early Childhood Classrooms

Early childhood teachers should follow four principles in the development of their classrooms. First, their classrooms should be developmentally appropriate and encourage play, exploration, and social interaction (Van Horn, Karlin, Ramey, Aldridge, & Snyder, 2005). In such classrooms, children learn primarily through play, although the teacher's role can also involve instruction. Teachers' direct involvement is important despite educational trends toward extreme social-constructivist notions that children create their own learning (Murray, 2015). Recognizing the importance of teachers and their unique role in the classroom, one of the pioneers of developmentally appropriate practices, Vygotsky (1997), described suitable *teaching* as occurring within the zone of proximal development, wherein children's learning is promoted by facilitating educational environments that are interesting, fun, and appropriate for the ages of the children in the room.

A second early childhood classroom principle recommends that these environments should be responsive to children's behaviors. This implies that the environment should provide natural feedback as children behave within the classroom as active participants, rather than passive observers or listeners. Although some early childhood materials such as blocks, paints, and ramps foster creativity in children through pretend play, these materials are not responsive per se (i.e., they are acted upon by the child). Other materials, such as books, pictures, and videos, may foster reflection and introspection, but they are not truly responsive either because they do not react or respond to children's behaviors. Conversely, materials that respond with physical cause and effect teach young children how to control their environment. This is especially important for young children with disabilities. Such contingent materials include interactive toys that respond to the child's actions by popping up or making a sound when the child presses a lever or button. Having materials that are contingent on a child's behaviors (e.g., touching, speaking) are helpful for developing a sense of personal control because the toy responds directly to the child's behaviors.

In addition to physical responsiveness as described above, the classroom environment should be socially responsive (Dunst & Kassow, 2008). During children's early years, this social responsiveness requires teachers to respond often and positively to children's appropriate behaviors. As children develop, they become increasingly sensitive to the social responsivity of their peers.

A third early childhood classroom principle guiding the creation of young children's learning environments is that the classroom should be emotionally secure. This emotional security can come from predictable and positive adult interactions. In one study, for example, including 63 childcare teachers, four different yet homogenous teacher-student interaction clusters were observed (de Kruif, McWilliam, Ridley, & Wakely, 2000). One cluster included average-level teacher-student interactive behaviors (i.e., neither particularly high nor particularly low). A second cluster included high ratings on teachers' "elaborating" behaviors and low ratings on "inappropriate redirection," and a third cluster included teachers with high ratings on "inappropriate redirection" and low ratings on all other teaching behaviors. The fourth teacher-student interaction cluster included teachers characterized by high ratings on "non-elaborative behaviors." The teaching style depicted in the first cluster is probably adequate for an emotionally secure environment, but not as secure as the teaching style in the second environment because it included teachers who were "high elaborators." The teacher interactive style observed in the third cluster is one of concern because these teachers create a less emotionally secure environment by frequently interrupting children's engagement and using considerable adult-led interaction. These teachers are not highly socially responsive. The fourth teacher interactive style involves teachers who praise and talk to children but fail to scaffold the child's existing learning behaviors adequately.

Effective behavior management is another important characteristic of an emotionally secure early childhood classroom environment (Dunst & Kassow, 2008). For example, all children benefit from knowing the limits of acceptable and unacceptable behaviors. As such, they learn rules of appropriate and inappropriate behaviors only if adults teach and model acceptable behaviors in a consistent manner.

The fourth early childhood classroom principle posits that classrooms should be family centered. That is, teachers and administrators should create positive interactions with families, including being responsive to parents' concerns and needs, and interactions should be oriented toward everyone in the family, not just the child. Teacher-family interactions should be friendly, sensitive, encouraging, and positive (McWilliam, Tocci, & Harbin, 1998). Being "nice" to families, however, is not enough to create positive teacher-family interactions (Turnbull et al., 2007). Families should be given opportunities to provide input into their children's education and make meaningful decisions about how to achieve desired learning outcomes or to reach planned intervention goals (McWilliam, 2010b). To be truly family centered means to help meet families' needs, whether those needs are directly related to the child or not. This orientation can be especially challenging for classroom programs compared to home-based programs, but the importance of providing supports to families of young children cannot be overstated, particularly if the children or families are vulnerable because of any demographic, personal, or familial variables or situations (Shonkoff et al., 2012).

Current School and Classroom Environment Assessment Methods

With these four early childhood classroom principles in mind, we now explore methods of assessing school and classroom environments. These methods stem from the findings from a number of studies, a federal initiative to understand the quality of environments, and the importance of assessing the environment by observing children within that environment.

Literature on Early-Childhood Classroom Assessment

The quality of the early childhood classroom environment has long been studied. For example, one large-scale investigation involved nearly 2,500 children observed in 671 pre-K classrooms across 11 states (Mashburn et al., 2008). The quality of teachers' instructional interactions predicted academic and language skills, and teachers' positive emotional interactions predicted children's teacher-reported social skills.

For many years and across the world, the Early Childhood Environmental Rating Scale (ECERS; Bailey, Clifford, & Harms, 1982) has been the most popular instrument for measuring classroom quality. In a factor analysis of the third edition of the ECERS (Harms, Clifford, & Cryer, 1998), the authors identified four factors. The defining factors consisted of Learning Opportunities, Gross Motor, Teacher Interactions, and Math Activities (Early, Sideris, Neitzel, LaForett, & Nehler, 2018). Despite the early popularity of the ECERS, in recent years the Classroom Assessment Scoring System (CLASS; Pianta, Karen, Paro, & Hamre, 2008) has become ubiquitous. The ECERS-3 factor structure corresponds with the CLASS characteristics, with moderate correlations reported between (a) the ECERS-3 total score and the four factor scores and (b) the three domains of the CLASS Pre-K (Early et al., 2018).

The CLASS three-factor structure has been investigated many times and provides insight into core domains of classroom instructional quality (Hamre, Pianta, Mashburn, & Downer, 2007). The first factor is Emotional Support, which consists of positive climate, negative climate, sensitivity, and regard for the child's perspective. The second factor is Classroom Organization, consisting of behavior management, productivity, and instructional learning formats. The third factor is Instructional Support, consisting of concept development, quality of feedback, and language modeling. In two studies, early childhood education teachers scored higher on Emotional and Organizational Support and lower on Instructional Support (Cabell, DeCoster, LoCasale-Crouch, Hamre, & Pianta, 2013; LoCasale-Crouch et al., 2016).

Assessment Findings

Studies of school and classroom environments address predictors of the quality of the environment (e.g., teacher characteristics and program culture) and outcomes of the quality of the environment (e.g., engagement, social-emotional competence). We depict this sequence in Figure 6.1.

Although characteristics of teachers, such as their training, have been associated with overall classroom quality, a review of seven major studies of early childcare and education indicated that teachers' educational attainment and their university major did not predict classroom quality (Early et al., 2007). A meta-analysis of childcare quality using all versions of the ECERS has shown variable results for different countries. For example, Australia, New Zealand, and the United States were rated higher than 21 other countries on the total ECERS score (Vermeer, van IJzendoorn, Cárcamo, & Harrison, 2016). The authors of this study, like Early and colleagues, concluded that classroom quality was more related to proximal quality of care (i.e., interpersonal characteristics), such as caregiver sensitivity, than to structural variables such as the caregiver-child ratio. In an analysis of data from 11 states, using spline regression of analysis, the quality of caregiver-child interactions and intentional instruction predicted high social competence and low problem behavior (Burchinal, Vandergrift, Pianta, & Mashburn, 2010).

An outcome of childcare quality of some interest is child engagement (Morales-Murillo, McWilliam, Grau Sevilla & García-Grau, 2019). In a study published more than 20 years ago, children's active engagement with adults predicted a) low ratings of the physical environment (i.e., when children spend more time with adults, it might well be because the physical

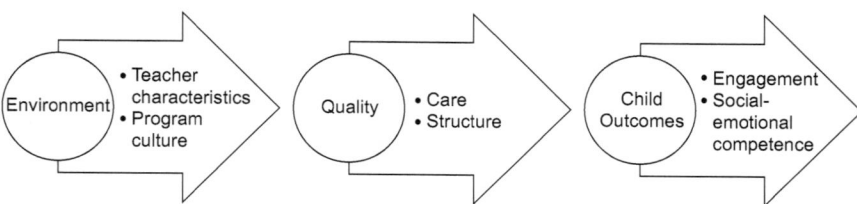

Figure 6.1 Predictors and Outcomes of the Quality of the Preschool or Early Childhood Classroom Environment

environment was so unstimulating); b) high ratings of the curriculum (i.e., the quality of classroom-based learning activities); c) fewer children in the classroom; and d) younger average student age (meaning a developmental component exists) (Dunst, McWilliam, & Holbert, 1986). In this study that included children with and without disabilities, the less severe the child's disability, the more active the engagement with peers. Active engagement with materials was predicted by staffing patterns and preparation (e.g., prepared for the next activity), scheduling, and fewer adults in the classroom. This was one of the first studies to measure types and levels of engagement and to show the impact of classroom organization, as well as child characteristics.

Recent research in preschools in Spain has provided insight into the links between classroom assessment and ratings of children's engagement. For example, indoor and outdoor free-play routines were related to higher sophistication levels of engagement (i.e., persistent, symbolic, encoded, and constructive behaviors), and more structured routines were associated with middle-range sophistication levels such as attending to the teacher or following instructions (Morales-Murillo, 2018). Children were more engaged with peers and materials during these routines and less during teacher-led activities. Not surprisingly, children's interactions with adults were more frequent during teacher-led activities. These results are consistent with those of other studies in the United States, demonstrating that different activities should be used to promote different types of engagement (Booren, Downer, & Vitiello, 2012). The Morales-Murillo study suggested structured activities, popular in preschools in Spain, are associated with ordinary engagement. Early childhood educators should reconsider how much time they spend in adult-led activities.

In this sense, the quality of the classroom environment and the quality of the teacher-child interaction were related to the amount of time allocated to free-play activities. In classrooms where children expended more time playing while following their interests, the ratings of the quality of the classroom environment and the quality of the teacher-child interaction were higher. Conversely, in those classrooms where children spent more time in teacher-led instruction, individualized worksheets, and little to no free play, the ratings of the quality of the classroom environment and teacher-child interaction were lower (Morales-Murillo, Grau Sevilla, McWilliam, & García-Grau, 2019). More research is needed to determine if the quality of the classrooms is perceived as higher because more time is allocated to free-play activities or if more time is allocated to free-play activities because the quality of the classroom environment is higher.

Quality Rating and Improvement System

In the United States, many states employ a quality rating and improvement system (QRIS) to "assess, improve, and communicate the level of quality in early and school-age care and education programs" (National Center on Early Childhood Quality Assurance, n.d.). Most states using a QRIS spend a portion of their Child Care and Development Fund (CCDF) from the federal Department of Health and Human Services to fund the development and implementation of the QRIS. Each QRIS has five common elements:

1.   Program standards: levels of standards beyond licensing requirements;
2.   Supports for programs and practitioners: Primarily in the form of training and technical assistance, states make resources available to programs to help them improve and sustain quality;
3.   Financial incentives: States have various mechanisms for financially rewarding programs that participate in QRIS;
4.   Quality assurance and monitoring: States have a mechanism for measuring quality, whether through direct observation, self-reporting, or using licensing information; and
5.   Consumer education: States provide information to families about how programs are rated, often using symbols such as stars to describe the differential quality of programs.

As an example from one state, Alabama, programs can qualify for one of five QRIS levels or stars. At the lowest level, a) all staff are enrolled in a professional development registry; b) the director completes a Program Administration Scale and basic training on the ECERS-R (Harms et al., 1998) and the Infant/Toddler Environment Rating Scale-Revised (ITERS-R) (Harms, Cryer, & Clifford, 1990); (c) teachers post developmentally appropriate daily schedules (including a minimum of 60 minutes of "vigorous active play"); (d) the director completes the Alabama Quality STARS Self-Assessment Checklist; and (e) the center informs families about child development and health, annually. To earn five stars, programs must meet all requirements for 1–4 stars and: a) staff at least 50% of classrooms with teachers with a child development short-term certificate or higher, b) have a high score on the Program Administration Scale, c) complete developmentally appropriate child assessments on each child three times a year, d) meet criteria for staff-child ratios and group sizes, e) have moderately high scores on the ECERS-R and ITERS-R, f) use results from an annual parent survey, and g) have a written parent engagement plan.

States select assessment instruments to determine how well their programs meet QRIS standards. For example, Maryland examined the data for their QRIS for 355 programs: 72% were center based, and 28% were family providers. They used four assessments, including the Scale for Teachers' Assessment of Routines Engagement (STARE; McWilliam, 2000). This instrument is completed by teachers or observers on one child per day, across at least six classroom routines. The rater scores the child's overall engagement, engagement with adults, engagement with peers, engagement with materials, and the complexity of the child's engagement. The first four ratings assess the time the child spends in each type of engagement, and the last rating is for the sophistication of the child's overall engagement, from non-engaged to sophisticated. The STARE did not indicate differences in Maryland's QRIS ratings for center-based programs, and neither did the CLASS (Swanson et al., 2017). In family childcare homes, however, students' overall-engagement score was aligned with the Engagement Check II (McWilliam, 1998), which reported the average percentage of children observed to be engaged during scans of the classroom. In these analyses, the STARE scores employed were overall engagement, complexity, and Engagement Check. Overall engagement was more often correlated with Maryland quality ratings than were the other two scores. Maryland chose the STARE as one measure in their QRIS because the instrument allows child engagement data to be collected easily compared to methods requiring video and micro-coding, such as those used in research (de Kruif & McWilliam, 1999; Ridley & McWilliam, 2000; Raspa, McWilliam, & Ridley, 2001). This research shows that direct observation by the teacher or another adult seems to be a necessary part of classroom assessment (Casey & McWilliam, 2007; Pohlman & McWilliam, 1999; Raspa, McWilliam, & Ridley, 2001; Ridley & McWilliam, 2000; Ridley, McWilliam, & Oates, 2000).

Observing Children to Assess the Environment

To assess the environment, perhaps no better measure exists than observing what children are doing within that environment. In this section, we argue that observation of child engagement should be the defining measure of the quality of a classroom.

Preschools and other early childhood environments are places to foster children's learning. Yet, for children, "school" is only one place where learning occurs. For children, learning occurs throughout the day, in the home, the school, and the community. This is especially true in the preschool years, before academic content predominates "education." How much the child learns depends in part on the level of their engagement (Ridley et al., 2000). Engagement is defined here as the amount of time a child interacts with adults, peers, or materials in a developmentally and contextually appropriate manner, at different levels of competence (McWilliam & Bailey, 1992; McWilliam & Casey, 2008). Other variables, such as age, race, SES, and IQ, might play a role in learning, but all are mediated by child engagement. If children are not engaged, they will not learn (McWilliam, Trivette, & Dunst, 1985). Learning is measured best when one considers children's pre-intervention and post-intervention scores. It is possible for the child not to do something or not to know something, receive intervention in the form of information or feedback, and then perform that skill or know that information. One cannot observe learning directly, but social constructivists argue that that the maturing individual will realize that they can or cannot do something or know something. Behaviorists argue that the likelihood of a behavior recurring is increased as a result of the application of one or more positive reinforcers.

When observing a classroom physical environment, we might make judgments based on the room arrangement, classroom decorations, and the organization of materials. We might also be influenced by how we endorse or rate items on an environment rating scale. Perhaps the true testament to the quality of a classroom is seen in the behavior of children. One teacher might have an interesting classroom, but children might not be engaged because adults in that classroom do not promote child participation within the interesting environment. Despite engaging materials, children might be exposed primarily to adult-led activities that follow the same routine across subsequent activities. In our experience, the more physically interesting a classroom is, the more likely teachers promote active child engagement.

The two extremes of classroom organization are the over-organized classroom and the chaotic classroom. In the former, even if the classroom is interesting, the children will not benefit greatly from that overly structured environment. In the latter classroom, children might benefit from the chaos because they can explore the classroom, and the classroom is considered the child's third teacher (Edwards, Gandini, & Forman, 1998).

Even in a boring classroom with a stilted physical arrangement, a child might still have high participation, as long as the adults or peers promote engagement. Adults can supersede the negative effects of unstimulating physical environments. In a qualitative study of over 90 activities, we discovered four contexts of teaching, as depicted in Figure 6.2 below (McWilliam, deKruif, & Zulli, 2002). These concentric contexts showed the interplay of the broad environment with interactions between teachers and children.

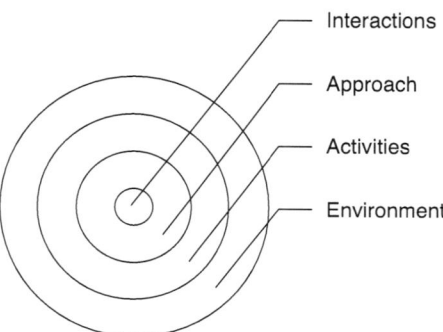

Figure 6.2 Four Contexts of Teaching in Preschool or Early Childhood Classrooms (McWilliam et al., 2002)

The distal effects of the classroom, the *environment* context, consisted of the program culture, the management (e.g., supervision), the model (e.g., developmentally appropriate, Montessori, Emerson Waldorf), and the physical environment. But, within the environment, the ecocultural niches or contexts were *activities* (Weisner, 2002). Within activities, teachers talked to certain children and encouraged or discouraged them from activity engagement. This *approach* context, which is often subconscious decisions teachers make as to whom to address and how to address them, has not been identified in other studies. Other studies have focused on teacher-child interactions, once they begin—not on what we labeled the approach. Finally, after the approach, the teacher engages in an interaction with the child. This *interaction* context can vary in how helpful it is for the child's engagement and, ultimately, learning. Studies have shown that following the child's lead with prompts for elaboration of what the child is doing is more effective than redirecting children's engagement from their own interests to those of the adult.

We have made the axiomatic point that meaningful participation in activities promotes learning. For many people, learning is the ultimate purpose of the classroom as a context, but we argue that a more basic purpose of the classroom context is for children to be safe and have fun. However, we assume they are having fun when we see them engaged. In our definition of "having fun," the child is doing something that they like doing. In classrooms where children are made to do things they do not like doing, such as completing worksheets or all coloring in the same seasonal picture, they might be engaged, but the sophistication of that engagement, according to McWilliam's (2008a) engagement levels, would be low.

When assessing the quality of classrooms, we observe how children spend their time. Do they spend enough time in interactions with adults, peers, or materials for the child's developmental age and the goals of the routine? Is that engagement simple and repetitive, or is it functional for the routine, or is it sophisticated? We have used the nine levels shown in Table 6.1 to code engagement in a number of studies (Casey, McWilliam, & Sims, 2012; de Kruif & McWilliam, 1999; Raspa et al., 2001).

Engagement varies by type of program and routine (Dunst et al., 1986; McWilliam et al., 1985). The more structure a program or activity has, the lower the engagement levels (Morales-Murillo, McWilliam, Grau Sevilla & García-Grau, 2018). Group engagement, as in the percentage of children engaged in activities, was found to be related to independent measures of program quality (i.e., ECERS and ITERS) (Ridley et al., 2000). Furthermore, group engagement differed as a function of the state's licensing level, which, in this case, consisted of two levels. Criteria included structural variables, such as teacher training, adult-child ratios, and square footage, as well as quality variables, such as ratings of the center's environment (Harms et al., 1998). Centers with the higher of the two levels had more engagement, suggesting the licensing criteria were appropriate.

Table 6.1 Child Engagement Sophistication Levels and Brief Definitions

Sophistication Level	Definition
Persistent	Makes two or more attempts to solve a challenging problem
Symbolic	Substitutes one object for another in pretend play or discusses something for which the referent is not present (i.e., past or future)
Encoded	Uses conventionalized language or follows rules in interactions with people
Constructive	Represents (i.e., makes) things in interactions with materials (e.g., draws things, builds things)
Attentionally focused	Maintains eye gaze on a person or object for 3 seconds or more
Differentiated	Does different things with people or objects to participate in the routine
Casually attentive	Looks or wanders around, not spending 3 seconds on anything
Undifferentiated	Makes repetitive actions or vocalizations
Nonengaged	Passive: "doing nothing," waiting, wandering. Active: crying, being aggressive or destructive, using inappropriate behavior.

Almost by definition, children with disabilities have lower engagement scores than do typically developing children (Dunst & McWilliam, 1988). Meaningful participation in routines is affected by a child's abilities and interests, in combination with the demands of the routine. This interaction or goodness of fit of the abilities and interests of the child with the demands of the routine, as shown in Figure 6.3, is central to the notion of meaningful participation and is central to the Routines-Based Model (RBM). The RBM is a comprehensive approach to early intervention for children with disabilities ages birth to 6 years and their families (McWilliam, 2016). The model focuses on naturalistic teaching, child functioning, and caregiver support. Naturalistic teaching is defined as children's caregivers using naturally occurring routines for teaching

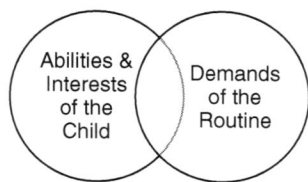

Figure 6.3 The Goodness of Fit Notion of Meaningful Participation

children (McWilliam, 2003). Child functioning is defined as children's engagement, independence, and social relationships when participating in routines (McWilliam & Casey, 2008). Caregiver support means providing emotional, material, and informational support to build caregivers' capacity to meet child and family needs and have high family quality of life (McWilliam et al., 1998). One component of the model is the Engagement Classroom Model; yes, a model within a model. The Engagement Classroom Model is described in a later section of this chapter.

When the abilities and interests of the child match the demands of the routine—that is, the child can do what is expected for their age in that routine and is interested in doing those things—successful functioning occurs. The child participates meaningfully. When the child has an impairment that prevents them from meeting the demands of the routine (e.g., cannot sit independently at circle time), functioning is compromised. If the child is not interested in circle time and resists, again functioning is compromised. Teachers, therefore, need to consider the demands of their routines as well as the characteristics of the child, if they are interested in functioning (i.e., engagement, participation). When the fit between the child's ability and interests and the activity is not optimal, we have at least three options: a) teach the child; b) change the routine; or c) change expectations (i.e., do not pick this battle).

Engagement is influenced by intra-individual characteristics such as a child's physical capabilities interests, activity level, and attention and environmental factors such as how stimulating the physical environment is, how responsive the caregiving environment is, how much fun other children are, and how novel or familiar the setting and materials are. In one study, poor-quality classrooms were consistently moderately associated with unsophisticated behavior; unsophisticated behavior was moderately positively associated with teacher sensitivity, teacher affect, and teachers' use of elaboratives; and higher child-teacher ratios were related to diminished differentiated engagement. That is, having more children in the classroom decreased children's general participation (Raspa et al., 2001).

The relationship between children's engagement and developmental level or age has varied in terms of percentage of time across studies, even within our own studies. Whereas in one study we showed a positive relationship between children's developmental level and high levels of engagement (de Kruif & McWilliam, 1999), in another study of 11 childcare teachers and 63 children, chronological age, developmental age, and ratings of persistence did *not* statistically significantly affect engagement (McWilliam, Scarborough & Kim, 2003). These studies have demonstrated the value of observing children to assess classrooms, rather than relying on general measures of the environment. We now turn to characteristics of classrooms that can influence engagement.

Physical Environment

Classroom assessment includes evaluation of the room arrangement and materials. As we discuss later, the delineation of the room into *zones* becomes important for transitions and ensuring engagement. Zones are clearly demarcated areas of the classroom, so each adult (and child) knows where one zone begins and another ends (Casey & McWilliam, 2011). Zones serve two purposes (Twardosz & Risley, 1982). First, they help children learn where activities take place. Second, they alert adults as to which children they are responsible for (i.e., zone defense).

In Cieszyn, Poland, we have an implementation site of the Engagement Classroom Model (Casey & McWilliam, 2011). To establish this site, we had the opportunity to design the environment to be consistent with the model. This alignment allowed us to make the following decisions:

1. The space was conceptually divided into zones. Because the model classroom was L shaped, this took some creativity and many changed minds.
2. An observation area was built to allow students and other observers to watch the classroom through so-called two-way mirrors. Furthermore, two cameras were installed, allowing researchers and supervisors to observe in real time from anywhere in the world.
3. All furnishings were made of natural, light-colored wood, following the precepts of Reggio Emilia.
4. All containers were basket or wood; no plastic.
5. A loft was built, with stairs, so children could learn stair climbing functionally. Underneath was a quiet, soft space.
6. The zone defense schedule was posted, so all adults could see their responsibilities for each time of the day (i.e., routine).

An anecdote from this center, Słoneczna Kraina (Sunnyland Preschool), involved another classroom arranged in typical Polish fashion, meaning no accessible toys and an open room with only a couple of tables with chairs. All toys were hidden in lockers. This room suffered from some aggressive behavior from three boys. During one outside break (Polish children go on walks instead of playing on playgrounds), we took in shelves and arranged the room in zones. We took doors off the lockers, so toys were visible. As soon as the children came back into the room, teachers and other observers noticed that engagement levels increased and child aggression decreased.

In addition to room arrangement, classroom materials are important. Materials need to be accessible to children. Again, following Reggio Emilia principles (as well as those of Emerson Waldorf), children should have easy access to materials to foster their creativity (Rinaldi, 2006; Steiner, 2003). The link between engagement and creativity has not been sufficiently explored, but, theoretically, it exists (McWilliam, 2008a). In Reggio Emilia and Montessori classrooms, natural-wood blocks and ramps are important for teaching children creativity, physics, and fun (Lillard, 2013).

The physical environment can make a difference to children's engagement, but it alone is not enough. Teachers' behavior is even more important.

Social Environment

When assessing the social environment of classrooms, we consider the types of children who are in the classroom and what the adults are doing. All children benefit from classrooms integrated with students with and without disabilities (McLeskey, 2007). The Division for Early Childhood of the Council for Exceptional Children and the National Association for Education of Young Children produced a joint statement on inclusion (mixing children with disabilities and children without disabilities) that emphasizes access, participation, and supports (Division for Early Childhood/National Association for the Education of Young Children, 2009). In high-quality inclusion, children have access to "a wide range of learning opportunities, activities, settings, and environments," compared to non-inclusive classrooms, where access might be restricted, participation might be lower, and supports might not be provided (p. 2).

For all children to have such broad access to participation, some classroom modifications or technology might be needed. Under the principle of universal design for learning, many methods for teaching and caring for young children with disabilities are also good for other children (Rose, 2000). We have already discussed the importance of children's participation in everyday routines. In inclusive settings, participation is especially important, so children are not simply placed with typically developing children: they need to be able to participate in the classroom life. This necessity to participate leads to the importance of supports; without supports, children are less likely to participate. Specialized supports can come from a variety of professionals: early childhood special educators, occupational therapists, physical therapists, speech-language pathologists, behavior specialists, psychologists, and so on. One method of service delivery that needs to receive more attention, because of the current inefficient and ineffective use of multidisciplinary services, is the primary service provider (PSP) (McWilliam, 2003a; Shelden & Rush, 2013), in which one professional, with the support of an interdisciplinary team, works consistently with the teacher. This method has the advantage of reducing the number of people coming into the classroom, allowing a strong relationship to build between the PSP and the teacher, and reducing the likelihood the teacher will receive conflicting suggestions. When different specialists work with the teacher and do not communicate with each other, the teacher is likely to get different recommendations. The PSP is like a funnel to the teacher, with the other disciplines providing whatever expertise is needed to supplement the PSP's expertise. Importantly, the PSP does not visit the classroom to work with the child. Rather, the PSP visits the classroom to build the capacity of the teaching staff, by enhancing the teachers' abilities to intervene with the child in regular routines, so teachers can support children throughout the week.

In addition to inclusion, another issue regarding the composition of children in the classroom is age grouping. In the United States, we have a strong tradition of grouping children by age, as in "the 2-year-old classroom." Some licensing regulations promote this type of grouping, especially for infants. But some research supports the idea of mixed-age grouping to promote developmental gain, language skills, and engagement (Bailey, Burchinal & McWilliam, 1993; McWilliam & Bailey, 1995; Roberts, Prizant & McWilliam, 1995). For children with disabilities and children under the age of 4 years, especially, mixed-age grouping is likely to be beneficial.

Adults

The mixture of children in a classroom is important, as is the influence of the adults in the room. We consider here the issue of adult-to-child ratios and teachers' behaviors.

Ratios

The ratio of adults to children is considered a structural variable having an impact on the quality of the early childhood environment (Pianta, Downer, & Hamre, 2016). The results of a meta-analysis on the effect of the adult-to-child ratio on children's developmental outcomes supported ratios of 1 adult for every 7.5 children as being associated with greater gains in cognitive and academic outcomes than were higher ratios (Bowne, Magnuson, Schindler, Duncan, & Yoshikawa, 2017). The results of other studies also demonstrated that smaller ratios promoted higher quality of teacher-child interactions (Vermeer, et al., 2016).

Adult Behaviors

As mentioned in the section on observing children to assess the environment, teaching occurs in four contexts: the environment, activities, approach, and interactions with children (McWilliam et al., 2002). The teacher approach and interactions are closely related to the behaviors of the adults in the classroom. Approach is the context no other study has isolated as a critical component of teaching. We saw that, within activities, teachers selected certain children to address and they were positive, neutral, or negative in their approach. Teachers, mostly, seem unaware of why they approach one child versus another; it appears to be an intuitive behavior for teachers. We can speculate that the attention-seeking children, the loud children, and the misbehaving children are likely to gain teachers' attention during activities. On the other hand, the low-maintenance child, the quiet child, or the child who has few abilities or little interest might be the child not approached. Teachers need to be vigilant about who they approach and what they do with that approach.

When teachers do interact with children, especially one-on-one, they have opportunities to use effective teaching strategies and to maintain positive affect with them. As described earlier, teachers can incorporate incidental teaching into their interaction, which allows for naturalistic teaching to occur, without disrupting the child's engagement—in fact, reinforcing it (Casey et al., 2012). The more positive affect teachers use, such as positive verbal comments and facial expressions, physical contact, and being responsive to children, the more engaged children will be (McWilliam et al., 2003).

Adult interactions and style are, therefore, critical to the contribution adults make to the social environment. In addition to the social environment, the organization of the classroom or school has an impact on children's learning—what McWilliam et al. (2002) called the environmental context of teaching.

Organization

The organization of a classroom program (e.g., a center with multiple classrooms) includes the pedagogical philosophy, the management style, the professional development of the teachers, and the overall school and classroom climate. Assessment of classrooms needs to include evaluation of these four dimensions.

Philosophy

A preschool's philosophy can broadly be described as occurring on a continuum from academic to play based. It can also range from an emphasis on prevention to an emphasis on intervention.

The preschool academic curriculum emphasizes children's acquisition of pre-academic or academic skills, particularly in the areas of literacy (e.g., reading, writing, language development) and numeracy (Early et al., 2007). An emphasis on pre-academics is often associated with much time devoted to teacher-led instruction, which is not considered appropriate for young children (O'Connor & Vadasy, 1996).

A multi-tiered system of supports has become a popular approach to inclusion, behavior management, and teaching in classrooms (Hemmeter, Ostrosky, & Fox, 2006). In this system (see Figure 6.4), all children receive classroom practices designed to prevent behavior problems, non-engagement, and learning failure. When those practices do not work, children receive individualized intervention. This intervention could consist of targeted incidental teaching, for example, especially focused on goals on the

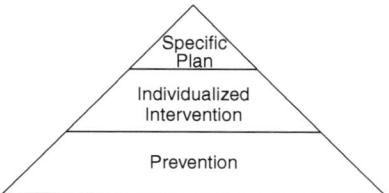

Figure 6.4 Multi-tiered System of Support for Preschoolers

child's individualized plan (Casey & McWilliam, 2008). If those naturalistic but individualized interventions fail, teachers—usually in concert with specialists—develop a specific plan to address the problem. These plans are usually quite structured and rely on evidence-based behavioral strategies (Gresham, 2007).

Management

The management of a classroom program can be assessed in terms of its technical and its supportive richness. These characteristics are considered important in the concept of *leadership* in implementation science (Halle, Metz & Martinez-Beck, 2013). Technical support from management (i.e., supervisors) consists of leaders seeking, developing, and implementing solutions. *Supportive* managers provide encouragement and focus on human relations. They value and promote their staff's ideas. Technical and supportive management styles are critical to the successful implementation of the organization's adoption of preferred practices.

Professional Development

Training to implement innovations needs to be of high quality. In a meta-analysis, three key features of professional development were identified (Dunst & Trivette, 2009). First, learners can gradually gather more and more information if a spiral teaching method is used (Reavis & Whittacre, 1969). Spiral teaching means learners do not need to master content before moving on to more detailed information about a practice. Second, learners need many opportunities to learn and implement the new knowledge and practice. Third, instructors must actually teach knowledge and skills and not simply wait for learners to "construct" their knowledge.

The most effective professional development is embedded in the job (Zepeda, 2014). When supervisors are also coaches, which is the ideal situation, to be effective, they engage in an interaction with staff that allows the staff to discuss what they have been doing. This reflective supervision is one of the hallmarks of effective professional development.

School and Classroom Climate

Together, many of these organizational features—the philosophy, the management, and the professional development—promote the school and classroom climate. This climate in turn influences teacher morale, which might be affected also by each teacher's meta-thinking about their autonomy. Meta-thinking occurs when a teacher reflects on how, why, and when they are independent. This reflection gives the teacher more awareness about how to be autonomous and when to be interdependent. When morale is good, teachers might appreciate being left alone. When they are stressed and not feeling good about their job, being left alone might feel like being abandoned. Unfortunately, more attention has been devoted to standards and accountability than to teachers' well-being, such as their morale, feelings of autonomy, and self-efficacy (Hall-Kenyon, Bullough, MacKay, & Marshall, 2014).

Engagement Classroom Model

Over the past 36 years, a method for organizing classrooms has been developed to promote children's engagement. This development occurred at (a) the Western Carolina Center (now the J. Iverson Riddle Developmental Center), (b) the Frank Porter Graham Child Development Center (now Institute) at the University of North Carolina at Chapel Hill, (c) through research at Vanderbilt University, (d) Siskin Children's Institute in Chattanooga, TN, and (e) the Słoneczna Kraina in Cieszyn, Poland. The Engagement Classroom Model has eight critical components that, together, promote the meaningful participation of children with disabilities in classrooms (McWilliam & Casey, 2008).

Participation with Families

Working hand-in-hand with families is manifest throughout the Routines-Based Model (McWilliam, 2016). In the Engagement Classroom Model (ECM), families choose goals when they complete the Routines-Based Interview (RBI; McWilliam, 2010a). Families discuss, in detail, their children's functioning in home routines, and teachers discuss children's functioning in classroom routines. Families use the information from both settings to decide on goals.

How can families, who have no training in our early intervention fields, decide on goals? When the emphasis is on functioning—that is, meaningful participation in everyday home and classroom routines—it takes familiarity and love to decide what the child needs to do, not a formal assessment of *cans* and *cannots*. Once families decide on what they want their children to be able to do, professionals help figure out why a child is not functioning well and the strategies that might help them be engaged.

In this process, caregivers report on child progress. Weekly, or whenever early interventionists check in, caregivers report on children's goal progress. In any one visit, one to four goals might be discussed, and caregivers (e.g., classroom teachers) discuss with the early interventionist how the child is doing. In addition, every six months, teachers complete the Classroom Measure of Engagement, Independence, and Social Relationships (ClaMEISR; McWilliam, 2014).

In the ECM, families are always welcome in the classroom. They do not need to make an appointment. Teachers help them feel a part of the classroom environment by pairing them with a member of the teaching staff, who follow a zone defense schedule (Casey & McWilliam, 2011). Families do not simply sit on the periphery, wondering what their role is. They become part of the fabric of the classroom.

Inclusion

As mentioned earlier, the classroom environment consists of the environment in which activities take place, in which teachers approach children, and in which interactions occur (McWilliam et al., 2002). In the RBM, inclusion incorporates ideas of horizontality (defined below), universal design for learning, and working with all types and levels of disability.

Placement of children with disabilities in settings where half or more of the children do not have disabilities is sometimes considered inclusion (Stowe & Turnbull, 2001). Some advocates use inclusion only to refer to proportional inclusion—the same percentage of children with disabilities as the percentage in the community. It is well-known that successful inclusion is best accomplished when the teaching staff have specialized support and when outcomes include the child's meaningful participation in activities, feeling like a member of the group, and developing friendships (Division for Early Childhood/National Association for the Education of Young Children, 2009; McLeskey, 2007; Peck, Staub, Gallucci & Schwartz, 2004).

Janson (2007) studied inclusion from a perspective of verticality and horizontality. Verticality occurs when adults manipulate situations to include the child with disabilities, whereas horizontality is peer driven. Janson has described three "demands" of horizontality (p. 410): a) it is peer directed, b) the child contributes to an activity rather than commands attention and assistance, and c) peers accept the contribution of the child. The goal of successful inclusion, therefore, is to promote maximal horizontality, which can require teachers to step back and create situations for children to have a role in the engagement of the child.

The specialized knowledge bases of early childhood special educators (ECSEs), occupational therapists, physical therapists, speech-language pathologists, behavior specialists, psychologists, and others are sometimes needed to help identify strategies to teach children with disabilities in inclusive settings. When specialists identify, in consultation with teachers, strategies good for all children, not only those with disabilities, teachers are more likely to use them, and the strategies do not isolate the child. This is the essence of universal design for learning (Courey, Tappe, Siker & LePage, 2013; Rose, 2000).

Too many parents have heard program directors tell them, "We can't meet your child's needs here." To parents' ears, this translates to, "Your child is too disabled to come here" and "We don't accept children with such severe disabilities." In the ECM, every classroom should be ready for every type of child. Children with severe intellectual disabilities, severe behavior challenges, and severe motor problems should all be accepted, welcomed, and engaged. Anything less amounts to discrimination. Inclusion in the ECM, therefore, means children are part of the fabric of the classroom, teachers use strategies beneficial to all children, and teachers figure out ways to promote the engagement of any child. From an ECSE perspective, this requires functional goals.

Functional Goals for Children

In almost all countries, children with disabilities have an intervention plan including goals. These goals traditionally were skills the child should acquire. They still are, but they should be functional and they should include goals for the family (Bailey, Winton, Rouse, & Turnbull, 1990). How do you determine what would be functional for the child and the family? The following paragraphs address this question.

Functional goals are those that identify skills the child would need to participate meaningfully in everyday routines. Routines are the everyday occurrences, times of the day, and activities the child goes through, at home, in the classroom, or in the community (McWilliam & Casey, 2008). Many skills on developmental checklists or discipline-specific assessments, therefore, would not be considered functional. For example, "maintain kneeling for 20 seconds." How is this functional? One could contrive scenarios where the skill would be functional, but the rationale is based on reverse logic— where we identify developmental steps and go looking for settings where one could say they were needed. A test item might be a good test item, but that does not make the skill functional.

Instead of developmental steps, in the ECM we look at the goodness of fit, as defined earlier and shown in Figure 6.3. As mentioned earlier, we ask three questions: a) what are the demands of the routine; b) what are the abilities and interests of the child (in this routine); and (c) how well do these match up? If the answer is *well*, we have goodness of fit (i.e., functioning). If the answer is *not well*, we have poor goodness of fit and we have to do something to address it.

How do we determine the child's functional goals and family goals? In the ECM, the answer is the RBI: a semi-structured interview of the family and the teacher. The family uses the information from the interview to decide on 10–12 functional child goals and family goals. In the United States, family goals and goals related to home routines, for the child, are uncommon on individual education programs (IEPs), but in the ECM they are considered necessary. The child still spends more time at home than in preschool, and families deserve support, despite family goals being absent on IEPs. Families are able to choose functional goals for the child because they know from their own experience and from the report from teachers how the child is engaged in different routines, how independent they are, and what their social relationships are like.

Integrated Specialized Services

In the ECM, specialized services such as those mentioned earlier (ECSE, therapies, etc.) are integrated into ongoing classroom routines. The classroom visitors providing these services use integrated therapy and collaborative consultation.

Children with disabilities who are taught by a general-education teacher usually have specialists involved on their individualized educational plans. One common model is a multidisciplinary service delivery model where different specialists see the child and might or might not communicate with each other (Boyer & Thompson, 2014). In a multidisciplinary approach, professionals address only their individual scope of practice. Another model—the one used in the ECM—is to use a PSP, where one person visits the classroom regularly and works with the teaching staff on goals in all areas of development (McWilliam, 2003; Shelden & Rush, 2013). This PSP is backed up by a team of professionals from other disciplines, who make joint visits, with the PSP, to the classroom to provide consultation. The benefits of the PSP approach are that the specialist deals with the whole child and family rather than just one aspect of the child, the teacher forms a strong relationship with the one specialist, and the teacher receives unified suggestions rather than conflicting ones (Shelden & Rush, 2010).

What do specialists do when they enter the room? If teaching staff are available for consultation, described in the next paragraph, the specialist consults with them. If not, the specialist joins the child in what the child is engaged in (i.e., part of the ongoing routine) and weaves intervention into that interaction. The purpose is to demonstrate the intervention for the teaching staff. This method of providing services is called *individualized within routines* (McWilliam, 1996). Individualized within routines involves the specialist's not removing the child from the ongoing routine, not working in isolation from the teaching staff, and not disrupting the ongoing routine. It involves specialists' strategically placing themselves to be visible to the teaching staff, using incidental teaching with the child, and communicating with the staff.

At some point during the visit to the classroom, the specialist talks to the teacher. This can occur while children are playing, in the middle of an activity, or on the side of the room, at any time in the visit. The specialist uses a "next-steps form" to review what teachers said they would do between the specialist's visits and what they wanted the focus of the next visit to be. An important principle of collaborative consultation to children's classrooms (CC2CC) is to provide the teacher with the opportunity to set the agenda. The visit to the classroom is therefore a mixture of conversation and demonstration. Some programs have the luxury of having sit-down meetings for specialists and teachers. These valuable meetings allow for conversations less distracting than those occurring in the classroom. On the other hand, meetings do not provide opportunity for practice, demonstration by the teacher, demonstration by the specialist, or observation of the child.

Incidental Teaching

One of the practices specialists demonstrate for the teachers is incidental teaching, as defined in this section (Hart & Risley, 1975). In the RBM, including the ECM, we have refined Hart and Risley's practice to cover all areas of development, in all routines, for all children. Incidental teaching has four steps. First, the adult ensures the child is engaged. Second, the adult follows the child's lead or interest. Third, the adult elicits a more sophisticated form of that behavior. This might mean the adult prompts the child to prolong their engagement, to use a more differentiated form of the behavior, or to perform a skill on the child's individualized plan (Casey et al., 2012). Fourth, the adult ensures the interaction was reinforcing for the child, which, by definition, increases the likelihood of the behavior being repeated (Premack, 1959).

For example, a teacher can have toys freely available during free play (the *engage* step). They observe Veronika in the dress-up zone, handling a fire fighter's hat. The teacher approaches her and says, "Do you think that hat will fit you?"

Veronika looks at the teacher but does nothing with the hat. The teacher says, "Try it on," and simultaneously uses hand-over-hand assistance to put the hat on Veronika's head (the *elicit* step). The teacher then says, "Let's look at you in the mirror" and points to the mirror. When Veronika looks at herself, the teacher says, "You look like a strong fire fighter. Do you have a fire engine?" (the *reinforce* step and another elicitation).

Veronika shakes her head. The teacher says, "Say, 'No, I don't'" (elicit).

Veronika says, "No."

The teacher says, "Good talking, Veronika! You said, 'No'" (reinforce).

The four steps of incidental teaching are versatile and easy to remember. The elicitation step is the most challenging one, because teachers need to use a variety of prompts, with careful timing (Reichow & Wolery, 2011).

Contingent Observation

An important subject to work with teachers on is behavior management, and, in the ECM, the default strategy is "sit and watch," formally "contingent observation" (Porterfield, Herbert-Jackson, & Risley, 1976; Tyroler & Lahey, 1980). We use this when all our attempts to prevent challenging behaviors by promoting engagement have failed, and the child is doing something they should not be doing.

The procedure, simply put, is as follows:

1. If the child is doing something not allowed, such as interfering with another child's play, the adult gives the child a direction (e.g., "Play with your own things, not Anthony's"). That's the first warning.
2. If the child does it again, the adult gives a second warning (e.g., "I told you to leave Anthony's things alone. Play with your own stuff."). Optionally, the adult could be explicit about this being the second warning (e.g., "This is Number 2. I told you to play with your own stuff.").
3. If the child does it again, the adult takes the child to the edge of the activity and tells them to sit down, saying, "I told you to leave Anthony's things alone. When you're ready to play nicely, you can come back and play." The adult says nothing more, to ensure their attention is not reinforcing.
4. The adult returns to the activity (perhaps joining Anthony) and makes it look as fun as possible. The adult does not interact with the child in sit and watch.
5. When the child returns to the activity, they are welcomed (e.g., "I'm happy you chose to play nicely. Do you want to continue playing with your things?").

The procedures include what to do when sit and watch does not work in this ideal manner, such as when a child repeats the disallowed behavior over and over, when a child has a tantrum in sit and watch, when a child stays in sit and watch, and so on. Fortunately, sit and watch is highly effective most of the time.

Zone Defense Schedule

One of the most helpful practices in the ECM is the use of the zone defense schedule, which addresses room arrangement, the organization of adults, and transitions between activities. Developed at the University of Kansas and refined at the University of Tennessee, this procedure came from the same group that began to emphasize engagement (Risley & Twardosz, 1976; Twardosz, Cataldo, & Risley, 1974; Twardosz & Risley, 1982).

The room is arranged in clear demarcated zones, so children know where different activities take place and where objects belong. Importantly, the middle of the classroom has shelving in it to create zones and avoid having a large open space (McWilliam & Casey, 2008). In *zone defense*, each adult is responsible for an assigned zone. As children move around the classroom, they might move from one adult's purview to another's.

Adults are organized with a schedule that has one column for each adult, with the rows indicating the time. One adult is always on *set up*, which means they set up the next activity, clean up the previous one, help with the existing one, and handle emergencies. One of the reasons for the set-up person is to protect the person in charge of the activity from being distracted. Table 6.2 shows an example of part of a day in a three-adult classroom. The person in charge has the activity in boldface. We found we can train teachers effectively to use the zone defense schedule, with the use of checklists (Casey & McWilliam, 2011).

At transitions between classroom activities, the teacher in charge of the main activity ensures the leader of the next activity is ready and gives children a 2-minute warning. The main activity leader announces to the children that they should clean up and go to the next planned activity (Risley & Cataldo, 1974). In the ECM, children are not required, however, to participate in most activities; they can choose free play, if that is available.

Table 6.2 Zone Defense Schedule

Beginning of Routine	A	B	C
7:00	Arrival	**Free Play**	Set Up
8:00	Set Up	Breakfast/Free Play	**Breakfast**
8:30	**Free Play/Centers**	Set Up	Bathroom
9:00	Outside	**Outside**	Set Up
9:45	Set Up	Music	**Music**
10:30	**Free Play**	Set Up	Free Play
11:00	Art	**Art**	Set Up
11:45	Set Up	Lunch	**Lunch**
12:15	**Nap**	Set Up	Teacher's Lunch
12:45	Teacher's Lunch	**Nap**	Set Up
1:15	Set Up	Teacher's Lunch	Free Play
2:00	**Story/Books**	Set Up	Story/Free Play
2:15	Snack/Free Play	**Snack**	Set Up
2:45	Set Up	Bathroom	**Free Play/Centers**
3:30	**Outside**	Set Up	Outside
4:15	Music	**Music**	Set Up
5:00	Departure	Set Up	**Free Play**

Children make their way at their own pace to the next activity. The previous set-up teacher is in place, ready to help children engage. The teacher of the previous activity stays until the last child has made the transition. This ensures the transition does not become a nonengaged time, which is common in classrooms, owing to a lack of organization of the adults (Wolery, Anthony, Caldwell, Snyder, & Morgante, 2002).

Reggio Emilia Inspiration

To make environments as engaging as possible and to capitalize on a philosophy of aesthetics, community, and respect for children, the ECM embraces many components of the Reggio Emilia approach (Edwards et al., 1998; Rinaldi, 2006). Rooms are decorated to be beautiful and comfortable for everyone in the room, including adults (New, 1990). These rooms have live plants, attractive wall decorations, natural materials, such as wooden toys and baskets, and neutral muted colors and a minimum of plastic. The philosophy is to have as much natural color and material as feasible.

When possible, natural light floods the classrooms. When electric light is needed, ECM classrooms use incandescent lighting and not fluorescent lighting. Apart from the preferred aesthetics of incandescent lighting, fluorescent lighting can cause headaches and be bothersome to some children with autism and other disabilities (Davidson & Henderson, 2016).

Somewhat independently of the Reggio Emilia approach, the project approach was born (Katz & Chard, 2000), but it is an integral part of Reggio Emilia. Katz and Chard have defined a project approach as an in-depth study of a topic by an individual child, a group of children, or the whole class. In the first stage, the teacher determines how much the children know about the topic, and teachers and children decide what they need to know more about. During the second, or developmental, stage, teachers provide children with experience with their topic. In the third or concluding stage, the children, potentially with adults such as their parents or teachers, present projects. We have included this approach as one of the components of the ECM. Children talk with adults about ideas that interest them to create a concept map or web, which captures ideas children bring up and connects them, when possible. Webbing helps children determine their project. Adults follow children's leads but also help them decide on projects that will be rich, engaging, and varied. Projects can vary enormously; for example, children might want to form a band, explore different types of wings, study frogs and the pond ....

A necessary component of a project approach, and one embraced by Reggio Emilia and the ECM, is documentation of children's activities and projects (Helm & Katz, 2016). This documentation usually includes photographs of children developing the project, which might go on for four or five months. It often includes quotations of children's commenting on the project. The documentation can end up in various places: the child's notebook, a website, e-mail messages to parents, and, commonly, on the hallway walls.

The ECM, therefore, pulls together many of the elements that should be assessed in classrooms: participation with families, inclusion, the functionality of goals, how specialized services are provided, the extent and quality of teaching, the behavior management procedure, the organization of space and adults, and the physical and social environment.

Conclusion

This chapter began with principles about preschool or early childhood classrooms and discussed current methods of assessing these classrooms and schools. We addressed the physical and social environment as well as the organization of classroom settings. Finally, we presented a model tying together many of the essential elements of high-quality classroom organization for inclusive classrooms.

Beyond a simple description of assessment of school and classroom environments, we have woven in three vital aspects of such assessment. First, we have made the point that assessment of classroom environments should emphasize what children are doing, not simply structural variables such as square footage, ratio of adults to children, or the curriculum. The dimension of child functioning we have elaborated on is child engagement—how the child spends time and at what level of sophistication. Second, we have discussed classrooms as inclusive settings, with the needs of children with disabilities as a major focus. Although usually reserved for special-education texts, we have made inclusion a theme to promote the importance of assessing the quality of classrooms for all children. Third, we have presented a model that works for all preschool children—one that promotes engagement, thus rounding out all three aspects of assessment of classroom environments: engagement, inclusion, and evidence-based practices.

References

Bailey, D. B., Burchinal, M. R., & McWilliam, R. A. (1993). Age of peers and early childhood development. *Child Development, 64*, 848–862.

Bailey, D. B., Clifford, R. M., & Harms, T. (1982). Comparison of preschool environments for handicapped and nonhandicapped children. *Topics in Early Childhood Special Education, 2*, 9–20.

Bailey, D. B., Winton, P. J., Rouse, L., & Turnbull, A. P. (1990). Family goals in infant intervention: Analysis and issues. *Journal of Early Intervention, 14*, 15–26.

Booren, L. M., Downer, J. T., & Vitiello, V. E. (2012). Observations of children's interactions with teachers, peers, and tasks across preschool classroom activity settings. *Early Education and Development, 23*, 517–538.

Boyer, V. E., & Thompson, S. D. (2014). Transdisciplinary model and early intervention: Building collaborative relationships. *Young Exceptional Children, 17*, 19–32.

Bowne, J. B., Magnuson, K. A., Schindler, H. S., Duncan, G. J., & Yoshikawa, H. (2017). A meta-analysis of class sizes and ratios in early childhood education programs: Are thresholds of quality associated with greater impacts on cognitive, achievement, and socioemotional outcomes? *Educational Evaluation and Policy Analysis, 39*, 407–428.

Burchinal, M., Vandergrift, N., Pianta, R., & Mashburn, A. (2010). Threshold analysis of association between child care quality and child outcomes for low-income children in pre-kindergarten programs. *Early Childhood Research Quarterly, 25*, 166–176.

Cabell, S. Q., DeCoster, J., LoCasale-Crouch, J., Hamre, B. K., & Pianta, R. C. (2013). Variation in the effectiveness of instructional interactions across preschool classroom settings and learning activities. *Early Childhood Research Quarterly, 28*, 820–830.

Casey, A. M., & McWilliam, R. A. (2007). The STARE: Data collection without the scare. *Young Exceptional Children, 11*, 2–15.

Casey, A. M., & McWilliam, R. A. (2008). Graphical feedback to increase teachers' use of incidental teaching. *Journal of Early Intervention, 30*, 251–268.

Casey, A. M., & McWilliam, R. A. (2011). The impact of checklist-based training on teachers' use of the zone defense schedule. *Journal of Applied Behavior Analysis, 44*, 397–401.

Casey, A. M., McWilliam, R. A., & Sims, J. (2012). Contributions of incidental teaching, developmental quotient, and peer interactions to child engagement. *Infants & Young Children, 25*, 122–135. doi:10.1097/IYC.0b013e31824cbac4

Courey, S. J., Tappe, P., Siker, J., & LePage, P. (2013). Improved lesson planning with universal design for learning (UDL). *Teacher Education and Special Education, 36*, 7–27.

Davidson, J., & Henderson, V. L. (2016). The sensory city: Autism, design and care. In C. Bates, R. Imrie, & K. Kullman (Eds.), *Care and design: Bodies, buildings, cities* (pp. 74–94). Hoboken, NJ: John Wiley & Sons.

de Kruif, R. E. L., & McWilliam, R. A. (1999). Multivariate relationships among developmental age, global engagement, and observed child engagement. *Early Childhood Research Quarterly, 14*, 515–536.

de Kruif, R. E. L., McWilliam, R. A., Ridley, S. M., & Wakely, M. B. (2000). Classification of teachers' interaction behaviors in early childhood classrooms. *Early Childhood Research Quarterly, 15*, 247–268.

Division for Early Childhood/National Association for the Education of Young Children. (2009). *Early childhood inclusion: A joint position statement of the Division for Early Childhood (DEC) and the National Association for the Education of Young Children (NAEYC).* Division for Early Childhood. The University of North Carolina, FPG Child Development Institute Chapel Hill.

Dunst, C. J., & Kassow, D. Z. (2008). Caregiver sensitivity, contingent social responsiveness, and secure infant attachment. *Journal of Early and Intensive Behavior Intervention, 5*, 40.

Dunst, C. J., & McWilliam, R. A. (1988). Cognitive assessment of multiply handicapped young children. In T. Wachs & R. Sheehan (Eds.), *Assessment of developmentally disabled children* (pp. 213–238). New York: Plenum Press.

Dunst, C. J., McWilliam, R. A., & Holbert, K. (1986). Assessment of preschool classroom environments. *Diagnostique, 11*, 212–232.

Dunst, C. J., & Trivette, C. M. (2009). Let's be PALS: An evidence-based approach to professional development. *Infants & Young Children, 22,* 164–176.

Early, D. M., Maxwell, K. L., Burchinal, M., Alva, S., Bender, R. H., Bryant, D., ... Griffin, J. A. (2007). Teachers' education, classroom quality, and young children's academic skills: Results from seven studies of preschool programs. *Child Development, 78,* 558–580.

Early, D. M., Sideris, J., Neitzel, J., LaForett, D. R., & Nehler, C. G. (2018). Factor structure and validity of the Early Childhood Environment Rating Scale–Third Edition (ECERS-3). *Early Childhood Research Quarterly, 44,* 242–256.

Edwards, C. P., Gandini, L., & Forman, G. E. (1998). *The hundred languages of children: The Reggio Emilia approach–advanced reflections.* Santa Barbara, CA: Greenwood Publishing Group.

Gresham, F. M. (2007). Response to intervention and emotional and behavioral disorders: Best practices in assessment for intervention. *Assessment for Effective Intervention, 32,* 214–222.

Halle, T., Metz, A., & Martinez-Beck, I. (2013). *Applying implementation science in early childhood programs and systems.* Baltimore, MD: Paul H. Brookes Publishing Company.

Hall-Kenyon, K. M., Bullough, R. V., MacKay, K. L., & Marshall, E. E. (2014). Preschool teacher well-being: A review of the literature. *Early Childhood Education Journal, 42,* 153–162.

Hamre, B. K., Pianta, R. C., Mashburn, A. J., & Downer, J. T. (2007). Building a science of classrooms: Application of the CLASS framework in over 4,000 U.S. early childhood and elementary classrooms. *Foundation for Childhood Development, 30,* 2008.

Harms, T., Clifford, R. M., & Cryer, D. (1998). *Early childhood environment rating scale-revised.* New York: Teachers College Press.

Harms, T., Cryer, D., & Clifford, R. M. (1990). *Infant-toddler environment rating scale.* New York: Teachers College Press.

Hart, B., & Risley, T. R. (1975). Incidental teaching of language in the preschool. *Journal of Applied Behavior Analysis, 8,* 411–420.

Helm, J. H., & Katz, L. G. (2016). *Young investigators: The project approach in the early years.* New York: Teachers College Press.

Hemmeter, M. L., Ostrosky, M., & Fox, L. (2006). Social and emotional foundations for early learning: A conceptual model for intervention. *School Psychology Review, 35,* 583–601.

Janson, U. (2007). Preschool cultures and the inclusion of children with disabilities. *The Japanese Journal of Special Education, 44,* 405–422.

Katz, L., & Chard, S. C. (2000). *Engaging children's minds: The project approach.* Stamford, CT: Ablex Publishing Corporation.

Lillard, A. S. (2013). Playful learning and montessori education. *NAMTA Journal, 38,* 137–174.

LoCasale-Crouch, J., Vitiello, G., Hasbrouck, S., Aguayo, Y. C., Schodt, S. C., Hamre, B., & Romo, F. (2016). Cómo medir lo que importa en las aulas de primera infancia: Un enfoque sobre las interacciones educadora-niño [How to measure what really matters in early childhood education classrooms: An approach to teacher-child interactions]. *Pensamiento Educativo. Revista De Investigación Educacional Latinoamericana, 53,* 1–14.

Mashburn, A. J., Pianta, R. C., Hamre, B. K., Downer, J. T., Barbarin, O. A., Bryant, D., … Howes, C. (2008). Measures of classroom quality in prekindergarten and children's development of academic, language, and social skills. *Child Development*, *79*, 732–749.

McLeskey, J. (2007). *Reflections on inclusion: Classic articles that shaped our thinking*. Arlington, VA: Council for Exceptional Children.

McWilliam, R. A. (Ed.). (1996). *Rethinking pull-out services in early intervention: A professional resource*. Baltimore, MD: Paul H. Brookes Publishing Co.

McWilliam, R. A. (1998). *Engagement Check II*. The University of North Carolina at Chapel Hill: Frank Porter Graham Child Development Center.

McWilliam, R. A. (2000). *Scale for Teachers' Assessment of Routines Engagement (STARE)*. Chapel Hill, NC: Frank Porter Graham Child Development Institute.

McWilliam, R. A. (2003). The primary-service-provider model for home- and community-based services. *Psicologia: Revista Da Associação Portuguesa Psicologia*, *17*, 115–135.

McWilliam, R. A. (2008a). Engagement as an outcome for young children with or without disabilities: Twenty-three years of inquiry. Paper presented at the 4th Global Conference on Creative Engagements Thinking with Children, Oxford University.

McWilliam, R. A. (2008b). *Practices for Instruction, Play, and Engagement Rating Scale (PIPERS)*. Chattanooga, TN: Siskin Children's Institute.

McWilliam, R. A. (2010a). Assessing families' needs with the routines-based interview. In R. A. McWilliam (Ed.), *Working with families of young children with special needs* (pp. 27–59). New York: Guilford.

McWilliam, R. A. (2010b). Introduction. In R. A. McWilliam (Ed.), *Working with families of young children with special needs* (pp. 1–7). New York: The Guilford Press.

McWilliam, R. A. (2014). *Classroom Measure of Engagement, Independence, and Social Relationships (ClaMEISR)*. Nashville, TN: The RAM Group.

McWilliam, R. A. (2016). The routines-based model for supporting speech and language. *Logopedia, Foniatría Y Audiología*, *36*, 178–184.

McWilliam, R. A., & Bailey, D. B. (1992). Promoting engagement and mastery. In D. B. Bailey & M. Wolery (Eds.), *Teaching infants and preschoolers with disabilities* (2nd ed., pp. 229–256). Columbus, OH: Merrill.

McWilliam, R. A., & Bailey, D. B. (1995). Effects of classroom social structure and disability on engagement. *Topics in Early Childhood Special Education*, *15*, 123.

McWilliam, R. A., & Casey, A. M. (2008). *Engagement of every child in the preschool classroom*. Baltimore, MD: Paul H. Brookes Co.

McWilliam, R. A., deKruif, R. E. L., & Zulli, R. A. (2002). The observed construction of teaching: Four contexts. *Journal of Research in Childhood Education*, *16*, 148–161.

McWilliam, R. A., Scarborough, A. A., & Kim, H. (2003). Adult interactions and child engagement. *Early Education and Development*, *14*, 7–27.

McWilliam, R. A., Tocci, L., & Harbin, G. L. (1998). Family-centered services: Service providers' discourse and behavior. *Topics in Early Childhood Special Education*, *18*, 206–221.

McWilliam, R. A., Trivette, C. M., & Dunst, C. J. (1985). Behavior engagement as a measure of the efficacy of early intervention. *Analysis and Intervention in Developmental Disabilities*, *5*, 59–71.

Morales-Murillo, C. P., McWilliam, R. A., Grau Sevilla, M. D., & García-Grau, P. (2018). Internal consistency and factor structure of the 3M Preschool Routines Functioning Scale. *Infants & Young Children, 31*, 246–257.

Morales-Murillo, C. P. (2018). *Estudio del engagement en el contexto educativo y su influencia en el desarrollo del niño de educación infantil (4 a 6 años). [Study of engagement in the educational context and its influence in the development of children in early childhood (4–6 years)]* (Unpublished doctoral dissertation). Catholic University of Valencia San Vicente Mártir, Valencia.

Morales-Murillo, C. P., Grau Sevilla, M. D., McWilliam, R. A., & García-Grau, P. (2019). Calidad del entorno y de las interacciones en educación infantil y su relación con el tiempo dedicado al juego libre [Quality of the environment and interactions in early childhood education and its relation to time allocated to free play]. *Infancia y Aprendizaje.*

Morales-Murillo, C. P., McWilliam, R. A., Grau Sevilla, M. D., & García-Grau, P. (2019). Evolución del estudio de la implicación desde tres enfoques [Evolution of the study of engagement from three approaches]. *Revista Internacional De Educación Y Aprendizaje, 6*, 245–258.

Murray, J. (2015). Early childhood pedagogies: Spaces for young children to flourish. *Early Child Development and Care, 185*, 1715–1732.

National Center on Early Childhood Quality Assurance. (n.d.). What is QRIS? Retrieved from https://ecquality.acf.hhs.gov/about-qris

New, R. S. (1990). *Projects and provocations: Preschool curriculum ideas from Reggio Emilia, Italy.* Syracuse, NY: Syracuse University.

O'Connor, R. E. N.-S. A., & Vadasy, P. F. (1996). Ladders to literacy: The effects of teacher-led phonological activities for kindergarten children with and without disabilities. *Exceptional Children, 63*, 117–130.

Peck, C. A., Staub, D., Gallucci, C., & Schwartz, I. (2004). Parent perception of the impacts of inclusion on their nondisabled child. *Research and Practice for Persons with Severe Disabilities: Research and Practice for Persons with Severe Disabilities, 29*, 135–143.

Pianta, R. C., Karen, M., Paro, L., & Hamre, B. K. (2008). *Classroom Assessment Scoring System (CLASS) manual, pre-k.* Baltimore, MD: Paul H. Brookes Publishing Company.

Pianta, R., Downer, J., & Hamre, B. (2016). Quality in early education classrooms: Definitions, gaps, and systems. *The Future of Children, 26*, 119–137.

Pohlman, C., & McWilliam, R. A. (1999). Paper lion in a preschool classroom: Promoting social competence. *Early Childhood Education Journal, 27*, 87–94.

Porterfield, J. K., Herbert-Jackson, E., & Risley, T. R. (1976). Contingent observation: An effective and acceptable procedure for reducing disruptive behavior of young children in a group setting. *Journal of Applied Behavior Analysis, 9*, 55–64.

Premack, D. (1959). Toward empirical behavior laws: I. Positive reinforcement. *Psychological Review, 66*, 219–233.

Raspa, M. J., McWilliam, R. A., & Ridley, S. M. (2001). Child care quality and children's engagement. *Early Education and Development, 12*, 209–224.

Reavis, C. A., & Whittacre, F. R. (1969). Professional education of teachers: A spiral approach. *Peabody Journal of Education, 46*, 259–264.

Reichow, B., & Wolery, M. (2011). Comparison of progressive prompt delay with and without instructive feedback. *Journal of Applied Behavior Analysis, 44*, 327–340.

Ridley, S. M., & McWilliam, R. A. (2000). Observing children at play: Using engagement to evaluate activities and the classroom environment. *Children and Families*, *14*, 36–38.

Ridley, S. M., McWilliam, R. A., & Oates, C. S. (2000). Observed engagement as an indicator of child care program quality. *Early Education and Development*, *11*, 133–146.

Rinaldi, C. (2006). *In dialogue with Reggio Emilia: Listening, researching and learning*. East Sussex: Psychology Press.

Risley, T. R., & Cataldo, M. F. (1974). *Evaluation of planned activities: The Pla-Check Measure of Classroom Participation*. Lawrence, KS: *Center for Applied Behavior Analysis*.

Risley, T. R., & Twardosz, S. (1976). The preschool as a setting for behavioral intervention. In H. Leitenberg (Ed.),*Handbook of behavior modification and behavior therapy*. (pp. 1–16)Englewood Cliffs, NJ: Prentice-Hall.

Roberts, J., Prizant, B., & McWilliam, R. A. (1995). Out-of-class vs in-class service delivery in language intervention: Effects on communicative interactions with young children. *American Journal of Speech-Language Pathology*, *4*, 87–93.

Rose, D. (2000). Universal design for learning. *Journal of Special Education Technology*, *15*, 45–49.

Shelden, M. L., & Rush, D. D. (2010). A primary-coach approach to teaming and supports in early childhood intervention. In R. A. McWilliam (Ed.), *Working with families of young children with special needs* (pp. 175–202). New York: Guilford Press.

Shelden, M. L., & Rush, D. D. (2013). *The early intervention teaming handbook: The primary service provider approach*. Baltimore, MD: Paul H. Brookes.

Shonkoff, J. P., Garner, A. S., Siegel, B. S., Dobbins, M. I., Earls, M. F., McGuinn, L., … Wood, D. L. (2012). The lifelong effects of early childhood adversity and toxic stress. *Pediatrics*, *129*, e232–e246.

Steiner, R. (2003). *What is Waldorf education?: Three lectures*. Hudson, NY: SteinerBooks.

Stowe, M. J., & Turnbull, H. R. (2001). Legal consideration of inclusion for infants and toddlers and preschool age children. In M. J. Guralnick (Ed.), *Early childhood inclusion: Focus on change* (pp. 69–100). Baltimore, MD: Paul H. Brookes Publishing Co.

Swanson, C., Carran, D., Guttman, A., Wright, T., Murray, M., Alexander, C., & Nunn, J. (2017). *Maryland Excels validation study*. Baltimore, MD: Johns Hopkins University.

Turnbull, A. P., Summers, J., Turnbull, R., Brotherson, M. J., Winton, P., Roberts, R., … Stroup Rentier, V. (2007). Family supports and services in early intervention: A bold vision. *Journal of Early Intervention*, *29*, 187–206.

Twardosz, S., Cataldo, M. F., & Risley, T. R. (1974). Open environment design for infant and toddler day care. *Journal of Applied Behavior Analysis*, *7*, 529–546.

Twardosz, S., & Risley, T. (1982). Behavioral-ecological consultation to day care centers. In A. M. Jeger & R. S. Slotnick (Eds.), *Community mental health and behavioral-ecology* (pp. 147–159). Boston, MA: Springer.

Tyroler, M. J., & Lahey, B. B. (1980). Effects of contingent observation on the disruptive behavior of a toddler in a group setting. *Child and Youth Care Forum*, *9*, 265–274.

Van Horn, M. L., Karlin, E. O., Ramey, S. L., Aldridge, J., & Snyder, S. W. (2005). Effects of developmentally appropriate practices on children's development:

A review of research and discussion of methodological and analytic issues. *Elementary School Journal: Elementary School Journal, 105*, 325.

Vermeer, H. J., van IJzendoorn, M. H., Cárcamo, R. A., & Harrison, L. J. (2016). Quality of child care using the environment rating scales: A meta-analysis of international studies. *International Journal of Early Childhood, 48*, 33–60.

Vygotsky, L. S. (1997). *The collected works of L. S. Vygotsky: Problems of the theory and history of psychology* (Vol. 3). Berlin, Germany: Springer Science & Business Media.

Weisner, T. S. (2002). Ecocultural understanding of children's developmental pathways. *Human Development, 45*, 275–281.

Wolery, M., Anthony, L., Caldwell, N. K., Snyder, E. D., & Morgante, J. D. (2002). Embedding and distributing constant time delay in circle time and transitions. *Topics in Early Childhood Special Education, 22*, 14–25.

Zepeda, S. J. (2014). *Job-embedded professional development: Support, collaboration, and learning in schools*. Abingdon, UK: Routledge.

Chapter 7

Play-Based Approaches to Preschool Assessment

Lisa Kelly-Vance and Brigette O. Ryalls

Introduction

Play is a natural activity engaged in by humans and non-human animals. For human children, play is a natural, joyful, self-directed activity that allows them to learn about their world, experience fun activities, and practice a variety of cognitive, social, and physical skills. Given that play is a ubiquitous behavior in children beginning in early infancy, it is not surprising that professionals interested in the assessment of children have used play as a window from which to examine children's current level of development, as well as a context for furthering development. This chapter begins with a brief discussion of classic research on children's play and then considers factors that affect children's play. We then describe and review several play-based approaches to preschool assessment. Benefits and cautions in using play assessment are also discussed.

Play assessment is a dynamic approach to learning about young children's developing skills. It became popular in the early 1990s as an alternative to traditional standardized tests and was viewed as a more child-friendly and parent/caregiver friendly approach (Myers, McBride, & Peterson, 1996). The history of play assessment has roots in play therapy, wherein children's social-emotional skills were addressed through the medium of play (Kelly-Vance & Ryalls, 2014). While play assessment and play therapy have the common element of using play as an approach to learn about children, they are distinguished from each other in how the information from children's play is utilized. In play therapy, children's inner worlds are viewed and interpreted through their overt play, and then play is viewed as the catalyst for helping children learn how to address their identified emotional issues. Play assessment, as discussed in this chapter, focuses on developmental skills and abilities seen in early childhood that relate to later school success. One of the advantages of play assessment is that all areas of child developmental can be observed and· evaluated, including cognition, socialization, and communication skills (Bergen, 2002). Moreover, emotion regulation, behavior, and motor skills and interventions are easily assessed, developed, and implemented through play-based assessments (Kelly-Vance & Ryalls,

2008, 2014). Further support for using the context of play for assessing young children comes from the universal cross-cultural nature of play (Meisels & Atkins-Burnett, 2000).

To illuminate the relevance of play assessment, it is imperative to understand the important role of play during the preschool years (Fisher, 1992). Studies show that play enhances children's competencies in the developmental domains linked to later school success (Singer, Golinkoff, & Hirsh-Pasek, 2006). Play is positively correlated with success in reading, mathematical ability, communication and language (Bergen, 2002), problem solving, and perspective taking (Ashiabi, 2007). Intervening in play in the early years may benefit later development, which points to the necessity of assessing play during the preschool years (Kelly-Vance & Ryalls, 2014).

Before reviewing research on children's play and play-based approaches to assessment, we must first grapple with defining exactly what is meant by "play." Although we all seem to recognize play when we see it, providing an operational definition for play has proven to be a more complex task than one might first assume (Pelegrini, 2009). In general, there is agreement that, across domains, play is an intrinsically motivated and pleasurable activity, that play is not a means to an end but an end in itself, and that play is engaged in by choice (Athanasiou, 2007; Garvey, 1990; Pelegrini, 2009; Thelen & Smith, 1994). When seeking to operationalize play, the exact characterization depends heavily on the domain(s) in question, including but not limited to those mentioned above, such as motor, cognitive, social, and emotional development. Finally, it is also recognized that the ways in which children play changes throughout childhood (Lyytinen, 1991); thus, any comprehensive description of play must also take into account such changes.

Research on Children's Play Behavior

In this chapter we focus primarily on the assessment of play within the cognitive domain and, to a lesser degree, the social domain. Both domains have long histories of study in the basic literature (e.g., Parten, 1932; Piaget, 1962; Smilansky, 1968; Vygotsky, 1967). Although it is impossible to disentangle different domains completely, various characterizations of play tend to focus more on certain domains than others, and many researchers have focused on the relationship between play and cognitive development. Piaget (1962) and Vygotsky (1967), two of the most influential developmental psychologists in history, wrote at length about the development of play and cognition. Their work continues to influence our current understanding of play and play assessment (Singer et al., 2006; Tamis-LeMonda & Bornstein, 1991). Piaget proposed four stages of cognitive development and noted that children's play changed in predictable ways as they progressed through these stages. Specifically, children move from exploratory play in infancy, to simple pretend play in early toddlerhood, to increasingly complex pretend play and play with rules through early childhood and into middle child-hood. Piaget's theory emphasized that children's cognition changes as a result of their interpersonal interactions within their natural environment. Because children spend so much time playing, the context of play was viewed as a major driver of cognitive development. In contrast to Piaget, Vygotsky (1967) emphasized sociocultural influences on children's cognitive development. That is, he emphasized the importance of interactions with older peers, parents, teachers, and others as a driving force in development. Thus, in Vygotsky's theory, play is perceived as being important to cognitive development because children interact regularly with older peers, parents, and teachers in this context.

In addition to cognitive development, other researchers have focused on the link between social development and play. One of the most famous theories in this domain is Parten's (1932). Parten proposed five stages of play, beginning in early infancy with the "onlooker" stage, and culminating in "cooperative" play in the preschool period (4–6 years). Like Piaget and Vygotsky, Parten recognized that in typically developing children the way that children play is highly related to their level of development.

Factors That Affect Children's Play

When assessing children in the context of play, it is important to be aware of factors that influence the ways in which children play. These factors include characteristics of the individual child, such as gender; characteristics of the child and their family, such as culture, ethnicity, and socioeconomic status; and the characteristics of the toys and other play materials available to the child. Each of these influences is considered in turn in relation to play-based assessment.

Gender

With regard to gender, researchers have shown that girls and boys show preferences for different toys from an early age (Todd et al., 2017; Trawick-Smith, Wolff, Koschel, & Vallarelli, 2014). Specifically, children tend to prefer toys stereotypically consistent with their gender, such as baby dolls for girls and trucks for boys. In addition, different toys can inspire different levels of play complexity for girls versus boys (Cherney, Kelly-Vance, Gill-Glover, Ruane, & Ryalls, 2003; Trawick-Smith et al., 2014). Thus, when conducting a play assessment, it is important to have a wide variety of toys attractive to girls and boys to ensure that children's optimal level of play can be elicited.

Culture, Ethnicity, and Socioeconomic Status

Play is inherently a cultural activity, influenced by beliefs and traditions (Farver, Kim, & Lee, 1995). For example, researchers have found that parents and teachers from different cultures may differ in their beliefs regarding the purpose of play (e.g., education vs. enjoyment), and these beliefs may influence the ways in which adults structure children's playtime and the materials they provide (Farver et al., 1995; Fasoli, 2014). Relatedly, Kenney (2012) found that children from different ethnic and economic backgrounds differed significantly in the amount of time they spent playing and the types of play activities in which they participated. Research has also shown that children from different cultures or from different SES levels do not necessarily play the same way with the same toys (Trawick-Smith et al., 2014). Thus, it is important that practitioners are aware of these potential influences and take them into consideration when conducting play assessments and interpreting the results of such assessments, taking care not to assume that differences in play are necessarily deficiencies (Farver et al., 1995).

Toys and Play Materials

Children's play can be influenced by the types of toys and play materials provided, with different toys eliciting different types of play. For example, some toys, such as dolls or train sets, are more likely to elicit pretend play, while other toys, such as blocks, may elicit a different type of play, such as construction or sorting (Cherney et al., 2003; Trawick-Smith et al., 2014). Additionally, toys can vary with regard to how closely they resemble real objects, which can influence how children play. Younger children play in more complex ways with highly realistic toys, while older children are able to engage in high levels of play with simpler objects, such as wooden shapes and cardboard tubes (Trawick-Smith et al., 2014). Thus, it is important that practitioners understand that the results of a play assessment are necessarily dependent on the nature of the toys and play materials used.

How Play Assessments Work

All play assessments employ observation of a child in the context of play to evaluate targeted skills. Common elements across all play assessments include an observation during free play with one or more adults observing the session. Parents/caregivers are typically present during the assessment, but their level of participation may vary depending on the assessment method used. Some methods include a standardized set of toys and instructions, while others are flexible with the toys and provide little or no guidance to the play session, wherein focus is on free, nondirected play. Still other approaches use a combination of nondirected and directed play.

The results of the assessment are typically expressed in terms of whether the child's skills are consistent with what is generally expected for the child's chronological age. Age-referenced guidelines are provided with all play assessment systems, and these guidelines are similar to developmental charts for physical and communication development in that age ranges rather than specific age equivalents are given. In addition, the observation allows for a description of the child's play, which can include toy selection, specific types of play observed, and interactions during play. Based on the assessment results, the evaluator determines if the child's play is age appropriate or in need of intervention. Information gained from play assessment can also be directly linked to interventions, which are also provided in the context of play. Many play assessment methods include intervention as part of their overall system.

Play assessments offer information that can supplement testing (Bagnato, 2007) and they differ from standardized tests in several ways. First and foremost, play assessments are not tests; they are observations. Therefore, the information obtained is part of a multimethod assessment and should not be used as the sole method of determining a child's eligibility or need for specialized services. Relatedly, no standard score is derived and age equivalents are the common metric. The level of structure provided during an assessment varies in that standardized tests require the examiner to adhere to a specified set of procedures and instructions whereas play assessments allow for flexibility in format. When used in eligibility decision-making, standardized tests provide standard scores that may be required by state guidelines. In contrast, play assessment results provide supportive information about development that is helpful when determining intervention needs. Finally, user qualifications vary for the two assessment approaches, with standardized testing requiring more credentials and play assessment allowing for a broad range of individuals to conduct them, including parents, paraprofessionals, and teachers.

Play Assessment Models

The increased popularity of play assessment has resulted in multiple models having been developed. Early versions of play assessment helped inform the development of more recent approaches. The most commonly used methods are described in the following sections.

The Play Assessment Scale (PAS)

Fewell (1992) provided an early version of play assessment that applies to children from 2 months to 3 years of age. To implement the PAS, play is observed under two conditions. The child is first allowed to play on their own in spontaneous play, which is observed by the examiner. Spontaneous play is followed by specific requests from the examiner that are intended to elicit different play behaviors. The PAS utilizes toy sets and a 45-item list of play skills that are developmentally sequenced. The PAS author describes this method of assessment as easy to administer and purports that early studies support its use (Fewell & Rich, 1987; Finn & Fewell, 1994).

Transdisciplinary Play Based Assessment (TPBA-2)

One of the most commonly used play assessment models used with children up to 72 months of age was developed by Toni Linder (Linder, 2008a). This comprehensive and collaborative approach uses an arena-style observation where multiple professionals observe the child in a free-play setting. The family is informed of the process prior to the session and provides the team with background information and estimations of the child's current functioning. Team members include the discipline-specific observers, the play facilitator and the family facilitator. A TPBA session lasts 60 to 90 minutes and consists of three phases, the first being solitary play where the child and play facilitator are in the play area but no facilitation occurs. Instead, play is entirely child directed.

In the second phase, the play facilitator encourages any play activities not seen during the first phase. Next, play partners, such as peers or parents/caregivers, are introduced. The third phase of the assessment provides a snack at the end of the second session, and parents/caregivers are given feedback.

The assessment process is fully described in Linder's series of books. Coding guidelines are used to interpret play and provide information about rates and sequences of cognitive, communicative, motor, and social-emotional development. The coding guidelines include detailed descriptions of subdomains within each area of development by which the evaluators compare the observational data and determine age equivalents for the child's skills. If skills are below the age-expected level, interventions are developed utilizing the accompanying intervention manual, which provides detailed suggestions for addressing students' needs (Linder, 2008b).

Research on TPBA is supportive but limited and only conducted on the original version, not the revised. Significant correlations were found between TPBA and the mental (MDI) and motor (PDI) subscales of the Bayley Scales of Infant Development-II (BSID-II) at $r = .75$ and .75, respectively (Kelly-Vance, Needelman, Troia, & Ryalls, 1999). As a measure of acceptability, parents and professionals were asked their preference for standardized measures, such as the BSID-II, or TPBA, and they rated TPBA higher on 13 out of 17 items (Myers et al., 1996), supporting its social validity.

The Learn to Play Assessment and Intervention System

Karen Stagnitti, an occupational therapist by training, has developed a system of play-assessment and intervention tools composed of three play assessment measures, the Symbolic and Imaginative Play Development Checklist (SIP-DC; Stagnitti, 1998), the Child-Initiated Pretend Play Assessment (ChIPPA; Stagnitti, 2007), and the Pretend Play Enjoyment Developmental Checklist (PPE-DC; Stagnitti, 2017b), and two intervention/training programs, the Learn to Play program (Stagnitti, 1998) and the Parent Learn to Play program (Stagnitti, 2017a). The three assessment measures are described in turn below.

The Symbolic and Imaginative Play Development Checklist (SIP-DC)

The SIP-DC was developed as part of the original Learn to Play intervention program (Stagnitti, 1998) as an observational assessment of play that includes play skills observed in typically developing children aged 1–5 years (Stagnitti, 2007). The checklist is divided into sections (called "charts") corresponding to the seven play skills covered in the Learn to Play intervention. The seven Learn to Play skills include: pre-imaginative play, play themes, sequence of imaginative play actions, object substitution, social interaction, independent role play, and doll/teddy bear play.

Administration of the SIP-DC requires a small, but specific, set of common toys (e.g., teddy bear, truck, spoon, container, doll house). In addition to observing the child play directly, parents and teachers can also be consulted regarding the child's typical level of play when completing this checklist. The SIP-DC was designed to be used prior to implementing the Learn to Play program to determine which activities to implement or as a progress monitoring tool during the course of the intervention, but it can be used independent of the Learn to Play program.

Child-Initiated Pretend Play Assessment (ChIPPA)

The ChIPPA is a standardized, norm-referenced assessment of children's ability to engage in spontaneous pretend play (as opposed to prompted or imitated pretend play). It is intended for use with children between 3 and 8 years of age. The assessment can be conducted in many different settings, by building a "cubby" or fort (e.g., placing a blanket over chairs) to eliminate distraction. This assessment takes 18–30 minutes, depending on the age of the child. The ChIPPA, which is purchased as a kit, comes with play materials designed to elicit conventional-imaginative play (with a set of common toys) as well as symbolic play (with more generic materials such as boxes, paper, blocks, and very simple cloth "dolls"). The play materials were specifically chosen to be developmentally appropriate and gender neutral. The ChIPPA measures three aspects of play: elaborateness of play, object substitutions (symbolic play), and reliance on a model (imitative play). Empirical investigations examining the ChIPPA have demonstrated satisfactory inter-rater reliability (k = .96–1.0), test-retest reliability (ICC = .73–.85 for pretend play actions), and construct validity (Stagnitti, 2007; Stagnitti & Unsworth, 2004; Stagnitti, Unsworth, & Rodger, 2000). Finally, the ChIPPA has been used effectively across multiple cultures and languages (Pfeifer, Queiroz Jair, Dos Santos, & Stagnitti, 2011; Stagnitti & Unsworth, 2004).

Pretend Play Enjoyment Developmental Checklist (PPE-DC)

The PPE-DC is the newest play-assessment tool developed by Stagnitti (2017b). The PPE-DC, like the SIP-DC, is an informal observational assessment. It is intended for use with children 1–6 years of age. The PPE-DC yields information about a child's engagement in pretend play across six of the seven areas included in Learn to Play and the SIP-DC cited previously. Pre-imaginative play is not assessed in the PPE-DC. In contrast to the SIP-DC, the PPE-DC also includes two scales, one for rating the child's enjoyment of play and one for rating the child's self-representation in relation to play. The play enjoyment scale is included because, as discussed earlier, one of the definitional components of play is that it is enjoyable. The self-representation scale is included as a means of examining the child's emerging sense of self (Harter, 2012), which develops in parallel with play abilities. Stagnitti's rationale for including information about self-representation is complex and includes the suggestion that this information may result in more effective intervention strategies (2017b).

The PPE-DC can be used to rate the child's performance when playing alone or in a group setting. No standardized toy set is required, although toys that encourage pretend play are necessary and there should be non-standard play materials available so that there are opportunities for behaviors such as object substitution to be observed. If the child is not actively playing, they can be invited to play and/or a play behavior may be modeled. The goal is to engage the child in play, if at all possible, without making demands on the child. The PPE-DC also includes a version that can be used by parents, based on their personal observations of their child's play behaviors.

The Revised Knox Preschool Play Scale (RKPPS)

The Revised Knox Preschool Play Scale (Knox, 1997) is a revision of a scale originally developed in 1968 by Susan Knox, an occupational therapist. The RKPPS is an observational measure designed to assess play in children from birth through age 6 years and includes information about motor, cognitive, and social aspects of play development. Specifically, the scale examines four major dimensions further subdivided into a total of 12 categories of play: (1) space management (gross motor and interest), (2) material management (manipulation, construction, purpose, and attention), (3) pretense/symbolic behavior (imitation and dramatization), and (4) participation (type, cooperation, humor, and language).

When using the RKPPS, children should ideally be observed at least twice for 30 minutes each time in a natural play setting, once indoors and once outdoors. These two observations in different settings should include a wide range of play materials, in order to observe both gross and fine motor movement. Children should also ideally be observed playing with peers to assess the participation dimension. Finally, given that true play is spontaneous and self-directed, children should be observed playing with as little instruction or direction from adults as possible. These guidelines can be adapted for use in a clinical setting, if necessary, as long as an attempt is made to maintain as many of these characteristics as possible.

When administering the assessment, the observer watches the child play, looking for specific behaviors listed on the scale. The scale provides descriptions of typical behaviors for each of the 12 categories, in increments of 6 months from birth to 3 years, then in 12-month increments from 3 to 6 years. For example, under the category "Humor" for a child aged 36 to 48 months is the behavior "laughs at nonsense words." The observer tracks the number of times each of the various behaviors occurs. Once the assessment is complete, the observer looks for the highest level of behavior to occur regularly and calculates an average play age for each dimension. These dimension averages can then be averaged for an overall play age.

The RKPPS has support in the empirical literature. For example, Jankovich, Mullen, Rinear, Tanta, and Deitz (2008) found high levels of interrater agreement, with independent raters' overall play scores falling within 6–8 months of age 87% of the time and within 4–6 months of age 74% of the time. Similarly, construct validity was supported by Jankovich and colleagues (2008) based on a close match between chronological age and their overall play score. The RKPPS has been used successfully to examine the behavior of children with learning disabilities in a preschool setting (Fallon & MacCobb, 2013) and to assess the effectiveness of a play-based therapy with children with Down's syndrome (Gokhale, Solanki, & Agarwal, 2014). The RKPPS was also recently adapted for use with Brazilian children (Sposito, Santos, & Pfeifer, 2019).

Play Assessment and Intervention System (PLAIS)

The PLAIS (pronounced "plays") (Kelly-Vance & Ryalls, 2014) has its roots in applied and basic research and includes a linked assessment and intervention system. The assessment system, the PIECES, is described in the following section. The PLAIS also includes intervention guidelines called the CLIPS (Children Learning in Play System), and the entire system is available for free on the PLAIS website (www.plaisuno.com).

Play in Early Childhood Evaluation System (PIECES)

The PIECES is the assessment component of the PLAIS and can be used with children ages 1 month to 5 years of age, or older if developmental delays are present. The focus of the system is primarily on cognitive development, but social skills and social communication can also be assessed.

The PIECES utilizes a free-play environment to assess cognitive development by observing a child's exploration of toys and pretend play. The authors report similar results across a variety of settings including home, childcare, preschool, laboratory setting, and play with peers or alone. The only requirement is a variety of appealing toys that elicit exploratory and pretend play. Suggested toys include kitchen set, dolls and accessories, blocks, tool set, phone, barn and farm animals, vehicles, shape sorter, stacking items, and stuffed animals. The assessment process consists of a 30-minute observation of a child in play, preferably with other children. Solitary play can also be observed and interpreted, but social skills cannot be evaluated in solitary play. Adults cannot guide or facilitate the play. The observer writes down every play behavior observed, which are called "play acts." Play acts are defined as anything a child does with a toy, and new play acts begin when a child changes the toy with which they are playing and/or the action engaged in with the toy. Observers also record the toys used, if others were present during the play act, and any interfering behaviors. The Play Assessment Recording and Coding Form (PARC) can be used to document the play and subsequently code the behaviors.

After the session, children's functioning is determined by comparing their play behaviors to a comprehensive developmental guideline of exploratory and pretend play called the Play Description and Codes (PDAC). The PDAC (see Table 7.1) begins with exploratory play behaviors, which the authors purport are early ways for children to learn about their environment, followed by simple and complex pretend play. Each individual play skill has a label, a rich description, and specific examples of play behavior. Anticipated typical age ranges are provided for each skill, generally expressed as, for example, "by 18 months." Each play act is first coded as either exploratory or pretend play. Then, the rater looks for themes, which are a combination of one or more play acts that can be labeled (e.g., naptime). These themes help determine the complexity of the play (Complex Pretend Play). Social interactions and interfering behaviors are summarized (Kelly-Vance & Ryalls, 2014).

The Play Summary and Progress (PSAP) form is used to document the results. Results are expressed in terms of highest level of play, variety of play types and toys used, and proportion of exploratory play, pretend play, and non-play behaviors. Multiple methods of interpretation can be used, with the most common being whether the play is age appropriate.

Reliability and validity data provide preliminary support for the PIECES. Interobserver reliability when coding the play of typically developing children was 90%, and it 100% for exceptional children. Test-retest reliability coefficients (three-week intervals) were reported for typically developing ($r = .48$) and exceptional children ($r = .58$); thus, they were moderately stable (Kelly-Vance & Ryalls, 2005). Because children's skills have the potential to change rapidly in younger years, the authors purport that these coefficients are reasonable for an observational method. Moreover, the developmental appropriateness of the categories of exploratory and pretend play have been validated (Kelly-Vance, Ryalls, & Gill-Glover, 2002). More independent research is needed on the PIECES due to the fact that available studies were conducted by the developers of the instrument.

A modification of the PIECES was used with children who were motorically challenged (Kokkoni et al., 2010; Ryalls et al., 2016). In addition, the

Table 7.1 Play Description and Codes Categories

Exploratory Play Skills	Basic Manipulation
	Single Functional Action
	Nonmatching Combination
	Similarity-based Combinations of Objects
	Functional Combinations of Objects
	Complex Exploration
	Approximate Pretend Play
Simple Pretend Play Skills	Self-Directed Play Act
	Object-Directed Play Act
	Other-Directed Play Act
	Repetitive Combinations
	Agentive Play Act
	Object Substitution Play Act
	Self Substitution Play Act
Complex Pretend Play Skills	2 Step Complex Pretend Play
	3 Step Complex Pretend Play
	4+ Step Complex Pretend Play
	Preplanned Complex Pretend Play
	Complex Pretend Play with Substitution
	Multi-theme Complex Pretend Play
Nonplay Behaviors	Unoccupied
	Transition
	Aggression
	Conversation
	Rough and Tumble
Social Skills	Play Initiation and Response
	Play Partners

PIECES includes a less formal approach to evaluating social skills that requires an observation of the child play with other children. A recent addition to the PLAIS is a social communication scale developed by speech language pathologists, and it is intended for use by any professional utilizing a play assessment format. Consistent with the coding guidelines for cognitive development, the social communication scale has rich descriptions of what is expected for developmental age ranges.

Along with determining intervention needs, the PIECES has been used as a classroom screening tool for determining which children have additional needs. Screening is briefer than a full play assessment. In the screening process, the observer watches one student at a time, and if age-appropriate play skills are seen the observer moves on to another child. The highest level of play observed for each child is documented and follow-up decisions are made about further assessment needs and interventions. If several students in one classroom show similar needs, a small group or classroom-level intervention can be implemented. The PIECES can also be used for program evaluation. Utilizing a pre/post-test methodology, educators can evaluate the impact of changing curricula, instructional strategies, and environment on play skill development.

Benefits and Application of Play Assessment

An obvious benefit of any method of play assessment is that it is an observation conducted in the children's natural environment, which is comfortable, non-invasive, and helpful in eliciting the demonstration of optimal skills. The results are easily understood by parents and caregivers (Myers et al., 1996) because they are provided in a similar format as physical and language development scales. Play assessment is inexpensive, especially when compared to the cost of standardized tests. Another advantage of play assessment is that it is relatively easy to learn. It is most commonly used by school psychologists, teachers, and speech language pathologists, but parents and paraprofessionals can also implement this assessment strategy, with training.

Play and Special Populations

The flexible format of play assessment allows examiners to adapt the assessment setting to the needs of the child. For example, the technique has been promoted for use with English Learners (Sempek, Kelly-Vance, & Ryalls, 2012). Because of its flexibility, observation of play in a natural context provides an additional or alternative means of assessing special populations who may be difficult to evaluate via standardized tests. For instance, play assessments have been used successfully with children who are deaf-blind (Finn & Fewell, 1994), children with Down syndrome (Fewell, Ogura, Notari-Syverson, & Wheeden, 1997), and children with multiple handicaps (Fewell & Rich, 1987). In all of these studies, significant correlations were found between play and various measures of cognition, language, and social skills. Ryalls et al. (2016) used a modification of the PIECES (described above) to evaluate the impact of a sitting intervention for preschool children with motor challenges and found that children's play increased in complexity as sitting improved. As a final example, Chang, Shih, Landa, Kaiser, and Kasari (2018) recently found that a play intervention improved not only the play skills of minimally verbal children with Autism Spectrum Disorder but also that improvements in play were associated with improved expressive language abilities.

One of the most powerful benefits of play assessment is that interventions are easily and directly derived from the results (Bagnato & Neisworth, 1996). These interventions may be important in helping children learn play skills that help them interact with others and practice what they see happening in their environment. Without adequate play skills, children will have difficulty socializing. During play, children learn how to negotiate, problem solve, share, and control their emotions. Most methods of play assessment have a companion intervention system, and these interventions have the advantage of being easy to understand and implement. Play assessment data can be used to examine intervention effectiveness in a pre/post-test design or with regular progress monitoring. Research shows that the interventions implemented in a play setting have a positive impact on improving play and social skills in a short time, making them less intense and more acceptable than interventions conducted in later years. Because pretend play is a demonstration of cognitive ability and is linked to later skills important in school, play interventions that target children's ability to pretend can be said to improve a child's cognitive skills (Malone & Langone, 1999).

For example, Mallory, Kelly-Vance, and Ryalls (2010) improved play skills in three at-risk 3- and 4-year-olds by implementing a divergent thinking approach. Similarly, Sualy, Yount, Kelly-Vance, and Ryalls (2011) improved play skills in preschoolers who had language delays. The intervention consisted of direct instruction of missing play skills and resulted in an increase in level of play and percent of time spent in pretend play. Conner, Kelly-Vance, Ryalls, and Friehe (2014) extended play interventions for use with children with language delays and found improvement in play and language skills in 2-year-olds. The Learn to Play program has been shown to be effective in improving children's level of play, language, and social skills (O'Connor & Stagnitti, 2011; Stagnitti, O'Connor, & Sheppard, 2012). Parents have been taught to increase their children's play levels successfully (Dempsey, Kelly-Vance, & Ryalls, 2013), suggesting that play interventions can be effectively implemented in the home. All of these interventions were eight weeks or less in duration.

Limitations of Play Assessments

Although play assessments are easily administered and yield rich information about children's current levels of functioning, many aspects of this approach lead to a series of limitations that must be considered when conducting play assessments. More research is needed before play assessments can be considered as standard practice in preschool assessments.

Because play assessments are observation-based, they are not commonly held to the same psychometric criteria as standardized tests, but they must be held to certain criteria nonetheless (Salvia, Ysseldyke, & Bolt, 2007). One major limitation of play assessment, in general, is the minimal amount of research conducted on the reliability and validity of such measures (Frahsek, Mack, Mack, Pfalz-Blezinger & Knopf, 2010; O'Grady & Dusing, 2015). Unfortunately, while there is some empirical support for some of the assessments reviewed in this chapter, much more empirical support is needed. Specifically, many more studies are needed to address the reliability of play across raters, settings, and time. The stability of the construct cannot be determined without this information. In addition, validity studies are critical and very few are in existence. Construct and criterion validity are essential to the assessment process and play assessment is found lacking in this area. More research is also needed on how play assessment might vary based on culture, race, disability, age, and gender.

A major purpose of play assessment is to determine intervention needs but there are limitations inherent in play interventions. Although play has long been assumed to be a major context of development and has been correlated with later skills important to school success, causation cannot be assumed. Improvements in play may benefit children in their later school success but more research is needed before this conclusion can be drawn definitively. Thus, the utility of play interventions may be questioned even though the impact on social skills appears intuitively promising.

Another purpose of early childhood assessment is to determine eligibility for specialized services. Play assessment has been utilized, with other measures, in eligibility decisions. However, this must be done with extreme caution due to the lack of reliability and validity studies. In no way should play assessment ever be the sole determinant of eligibility for early intervention services. Another purpose of assessment is to determine progress in a given intervention. Again, play assessments fall short here due to the lack of psychometric support.

Although a major advantage of play assessment is that little training is needed, it should be emphasized that a thorough understanding of human development and the basic principles of assessment are necessary. While most early childhood practitioners possess such knowledge, parents and other individuals may lack this understanding and thus require more training in order to effectively administer play assessments.

Conclusion

Play assessment is an inexpensive, developmentally appropriate means of assessing young children's developing play skills. It is easy to use and interpret and leads directly to intervention development. More research is needed to investigate the inter-rater reliability, stability, and criterion-related validity of play-based assessment approaches. Additional studies of how play assessment can be used with other measures to inform eligibility decisions for early intervention are also needed.

References

Ashiabi, G. (2007). Play in the preschool classroom: Its socioemotional significance and the Teachers role in play. *Early Childhood Education Journal*, 35, 199–207.

Athanasiou, M. S. (2007). Play-based approaches to preschool assessment. In B. A. Bracken & R. J. Nagle (Eds.), *The psychoeducational assessment of preschool children* (4th ed., pp. 219–238). NJ: LEA.

Bagnato, S. J. (2007). *Authentic assessment for early childhood intervention: Best practices*. New York: The Guildford Press.

Bagnato, S. J., & Neisworth, J. T. (1996). *Linking assessment and intervention: An authentic curriculum-based approach*. Baltimore, MD: Brookes.

Bergen, D. (2002). The role of pretend play in children's cognitive development. *Early Childhood Research & Practice, 4*, 1–12.

Chang, Y. C., Shih, W., Landa, R., Kaiser, A., & Kasari, C. (2018). Symbolic play in school-aged minimally verbal children with autism spectrum Disorder. *Journal of Autism and Developmental Disorders, 48*(5), 1436–1445.

Cherney, I. C., Kelly-Vance, L., Gill-Glover, K., Ruane, A., & Ryalls, B. O. (2003). The effects of stereotyped toys and gender on play assessment in 18–47-month-old children. *Educational Psychology, 22*, 95–106.

Conner, J., Kelly-Vance, L., Ryalls, B. O., & Friehe, M. (2014). A play and language intervention for two-year-old children: Implications for improving play skills and language. *Journal of Research in Childhood Education, 28*, 221–237.

Dempsey, J., Kelly-Vance, L., & Ryalls, B. (2013). The effect of a parent training program on children's play. *International Journal of Psychology: A Biopsychosocial Approach, 2013*(13), 117–138.

Fallon, J., & MacCobb, S. (2013). Free play time of children with learning disabilities in a noninclusive preschool setting: An analysis of play and nonplay behaviours. *British Journal of Learning Disabilities, 41*(3), 212–219.

Farver, J. A. M., Kim, Y. K., & Lee, Y. (1995). Cultural differences in Korean- and Anglo-American preschoolers' social interaction and play behaviors. *Child Development, 66*(4), 1088–1099. doi:10.2307/1131800

Fasoli, A. (2014). To play or not to play: Diverse motives for Latino and Euro-American parent-child play in a children's museum. *Infant & Child Development, 23*(6), 605–621. doi:10.1002/icd.1867

Fewell, R. R. (1992). *Play assessment scale* (5th rev.). Unpublished document. Miami, FL: University of Miami School of Medicine.

Fewell, R. R., Ogura, T., Notari-Syverson, A., & Wheeden, C. A. (1997). The relationship between play and communication in young children with Down syndrome. *Topics in Early Childhood Special Education, 17*(1), 103–118.

Fewell, R. R., & Rich, J. S. (1987). Play assessment as a procedure for examining cognitive, communication, and social skills in multihandicapped children. *Journal of Psychoeducational Assessment, 2*, 107–118.

Finn, D. M., & Fewell, R. R. (1994). The use of play assessment to examine the development of communication skills in children who are deaf-blind. *Journal of Visual Impairment & Blindness, 88*(4), 349–356.

Fisher, E. (1992). The impact of play on development: A meta-analysis. *Play & Culture, 5*, 159–181.

Frahsek, S., Mack, W., Mack, C., Pfalz-Blezinger, C., & Knopf, M. (2010). Assessing different aspects of pretend play within a play setting: Towards a standardized assessment of pretend play in young children. *British Journal of Developmental Psychology, 28*, 331–345. doi:10.1348/026151009X413666

Garvey, C. (1990). *Play*. Cambridge, MA: Harvard University Press.

Gokhale, P., Solanki, P., & Agarwal, P. (2014). To study the effectiveness of play based therapy on play behavior of children with Down's Syndrome. *The Indian Journal of Occupational Therapy, 46*(2), 41–48.

Harter, S. (2012). *The construction of the self. Developmental and sociocultural foundations* (2nd ed.). New York: The Guildford Press.

Jankovich, M., Mullen, J., Rinear, E., Tanta, K., & Deitz, J. (2008). Revised Knox Preschool Play Scale: Interrater agreement and construct validity. *American Journal of Occupational Therapy, 62*, 221–227.

Kelly-Vance, L., Needelman, H., Troia, K., & Ryalls, B. O. (1999). Early childhood assessment: A comparison of the Bayley Scales of Infant Development and a play-based technique in two-year old at-risk children. *Developmental Disabilities Bulletin, 27*(1), 1–15.

Kelly-Vance, L., & Ryalls, B. O. (2005). A systematic, reliable approach to play assessment in preschoolers. *School Psychology International, 26*(4), 398–412.

Kelly-Vance, L., & Ryalls, B. O. (2008). Best practices in play assessment and intervention. In J. Grimes & A. Thomas (Eds.), *Best practices in school psychology V* (Vol. 2, pp. 549–559). Bethesda, MD: National Association of School Psychologists.

Kelly-Vance, L., & Ryalls, B. O. (2014). Best practices in play assessment and intervention. In A. Thomas & J. Grimes (Eds.), *Best practices in school psychology* (6th ed., pp. 549–560). Bethesda, MD: National Association of School Psychologists.

Kelly-Vance, L., Ryalls, B. O., & Gill-Glover, K. (2002). The use of play assessment to evaluate the cognitive skills of two- and three-year old children. *School Psychology International, 23*, 169–185.

Kenney, M. (2012). Child, family, and neighborhood associations with parent and peer interactive play during early childhood. *Maternal Child Health Journal, 16*, S88–5101. doi:10.1007/s10995-012-0998-7

Knox, S. (1997). Development and current use of the Knox Preschool Play Scale. In L. D. Dans, Parham, & L. S. Fazio (Eds.), *Play in occupational therapy for children* (pp. 35–51). St. Louis, MO: Mosby.

Kokkoni, E., Dempsey, J., Harbourne, R. T., Kelly-Vance, L., Ryalls, B., & Stergiou, N. (2010). Developing sitting postural control and play in children with Cerebral Palsy. *Journal of Sports and Exercise Psychology, 32*, S43.

Linder, T. W. (2008a). *Transdisciplinary Play-Based Assessment-2*. Baltimore, MD: Brookes.

Linder, T. W. (2008b). *Transdisciplinary Play-Based Intervention-2*. Baltimore, MD: Brookes.

Lyytinen, P. (1991). Developmental trends in children's pretend play. *Child: Care, Health and Development, 17*, 9–25.

Mallory, J. M., Kelly-Vance, L., & Ryalls, B. O. (2010). Incorporating divergent thinking into play interventions for preschool children with developmental risk factors. *International Journal of Creativity and Problem Solving, 20*, 57–71.

Malone, D. M., & Langone, J. (1999). Teaching object-related play skills to preschool children with developmental concerns. *International Journal of Disability, Development and Education, 46*(3), 325–336. doi:10.1080/103491299100524

Meisels, S. J., & Atkins-Burnett, S. (2000). The elements of early childhood assessment. In J. P. Shonkoff & S. J. Meisels (Eds.), *Handbook of early childhood intervention* (pp. 231–257). New York: Cambridge University Press.

Myers, C. L., McBride, S. L., & Peterson, C. A. (1996). Transdisciplinary, play-based assessment in early childhood special education: An examination of social validity. *Topics in Early Childhood Special Education, 16*, 102–126.

O'Connor, C., & Stagnitti, K. (2011). Play, behaviour, language and social skills: The comparison of a play and a non-play intervention within a specialist school setting. *Research in Developmental Disabilities, 32*, 1205–1211.

O'Grady, M., & Dusing, S. (2015). Reliability and validity of play-based assessments of motor and cognitive skills for infants and young children: A systematic review. *Physical Therapy, 95*, 25–38.

Parten, M. (1932). Social participation among preschool children. *Journal of Abnormal and Social Psychology, 27*, 243–269. doi:10.1037/h0074524

Pelegrini, A. (2009). Research and policy on children's play. *Child Development Perspectives, 3;2*, 131–136.

Pfeifer, L., Queiroz Jair, M. A., Dos Santos, L., & Stagnitti, K. (2011). Cross-cultural adaptation and reliability of Child-Initiated Pretend Play Assessment (ChIPPA). *Canadian Journal of Occupational Therapy, 78*(3), 187–195.

Piaget, J. (1962). *Play, dreams, and imitation in childhood.* New York: Norton.

Ryalls, B. O., Harbourne, R., Kelly-Vance, L., Wickstrom, J., Stergiou, N., & Kyvelidou, A. (2016). A perceptual motor intervention improves play behavior in children with moderate to severe Cerebral Palsy. *Frontiers in Psychology, 7*, 643. doi:10.3389/fpsyg.2016.00643

Salvia, J., Ysseldyke, J. E., & Bolt, S. (2007). *Assessment in special and inclusive education* (10th ed.). Boston, MA: Houghton Mifflin.

Sempek, A., Kelly-Vance, L., & Ryalls, B. O. (2012). Cross cultural relations: Children's play, maternal acculturation, knowledge, and beliefs concerning play. *School Psychology: from Science to Practice, 5*, 12–22.

Singer, D., Golinkoff, R. M., & Hirsh-Pasek, K. (Eds.). (2006). *Play=learning: How play motivates and enhances children's cognitive and social-emotional growth.* New York: Oxford University Press.

Smilansky, S. (1968). *The effects of socio-dramatic play on disadvantaged preschool children.* New York: Wiley.

Sposito, A., Santos, J., & Pfeifer, L. (2019). Validation of the Revised Knox Preschool Play Scale for the Brazilian Population. *Occupational Therapy International, 2019*, 5. Article ID 6397425. doi:10.1155/2019/6397425

Stagnitti, K. (1998). *Learn to play: A practical program to develop a child's imaginative play skills.* Victoria, Australia: Co-ordinates Therapy Services.

Stagnitti, K. (2007). *The Child-Initiated Pretend Play Assessment manual and kit.* Melbourne, Australia: Co-Ordinates Therapy Services.

Stagnitti, K. (2017a). *Parent Learn to Play Facilitator Manual. Learn to Play.* West Brunswick, Victoria, Australia: Co-Ordinates Publications.

Stagnitti, K. (2017b). *Pretend play enjoyment developmental checklist. Learn to play.* West Brunswick, Victoria, Australia: Co-Ordinates Publications.

Stagnitti, K., O'Connor, C., & Sheppard, L. (2012). The impact of the Learn to Play program on play, social competence and language for children aged 5–8 years who attend a special school. *Australian Occupational Therapy Journal, 59*(4), 302–311.

Stagnitti, K., & Unsworth, C. (2004). The test-retest reliability of the Child-Initiated Pretend Play Assessment. *The American Journal of Occupational Therapy, 58*(1), 93–99.

Stagnitti, K., Unsworth, C., & Rodger, S. (2000). Development of an assessment to identify play behaviors that discriminate between the play of typical pre-schoolers and pre-schoolers with pre-academic problems. *Canadian Journal of Occupational Therapy, 67*(5), 291–303.

Sualy, A., Yount, S., Kelly-Vance, L., & Ryalls, B. O. (2011). Using a play intervention to improve the play skills of children with a language delay. *International Journal of Psychology: A Biopsychosocial Approach, 9*, 105–122.

Tamis-LeMonda, C. S., & Bornstein, M. (1991). Individual variation, correspondence, stability, and change in mother and toddler play. *Infant Behavior & Development*, *14*(2), 143–162.

Thelen, E., & Smith, L. B. (1994). *A dynamic systems approach to the development of cognition and action*. Cambridge, MA: MIT Press.

Todd, B., Fischer, R., Di Costa, S., Roestorf, A., Harbour, K., Hardiman, P., & Barry, J. (2017). Sex differences in children's toy preferences: A systematic review, meta-regression, and meta-analysis. *Infant and Child Development*, *27*(2). doi:10.1002/icd.2064

Trawick-Smith, J., Wolff, J., Koschel, M., & Vallarelli, J. (2014). Effects of toys on the play quality of preschool children: Influence of gender, ethnicity, and socioeconomic status. *Early Childhood Education Journal*, *43*(4), 249–256.

Vygotsky, L. (1967). Play and its role in the mental development of the child. *Soviet Psychology*, *12*, 62–76.

Part III

Assessment of Developmental Domains

Chapter 8

Behavior and Social-Emotional Skills Assessment of Preschool Children

Sara A. Whitcomb and Jessica M. Kemp

The healthy behavioral and social-emotional development of a preschool child can lay the groundwork for a lifetime of positive experiences, such as academic success, positive relationships, and overall wellbeing. Similarly, young children who develop maladaptive behavioral patterns early are more likely to experience negative outcomes, including mental health diagnoses, as adolescents and adults (Egeland, Pianta, & Ogawa, 1996). While children's behavior is influenced by their temperament, which is partially driven by biological makeup and heredity (Rothbart & Derryberry, 1981), it is also shaped by positive and negative learning experiences within their environment. Unfortunately, today, young children may be exposed to a multitude of negative experiences that influence their social-emotional and behavioral development. For example, 26% of children in the United States will either experience or witness trauma by the age of 4 years (National Center for Mental Health Promotion and Youth Violence Prevention, 2012). Additionally, data from the National Center for Mental Health Promotion and Youth Violence Prevention (2012) reveal that U.S. children are exposed to harsh preschool discipline practices that result in 250 preschool suspensions per day (Malik, 2017). Given these staggering statistics and the fact that early childhood is an especially vulnerable and rapid developmental period, caregivers, daycare providers, and preschool professionals are called to create environments in which children are exposed to healthy models of social-emotional behavior and in which they are explicitly and proactively taught critical social-emotional and behavioral skills. Further, to assess whether children's adjustment needs are being met and instruction and intervention is appropriately targeted, we must turn to effective assessment tools and practices.

The purpose of this chapter is to provide readers with resources and examples of a multi-method, multi-informant assessment framework. We begin with definitions of social-emotional and behavioral competency, define some of the challenges inherent in assessing young children in these domains, and then identify the purposes of assessing children's social-emotional and behavioral skills. We follow this with examples of assessment tools to be used with preschool-aged children, aged approximately 3 to 5 years.

Social-Emotional and Behavioral Competency

The Collaborative for Academic and Social Emotional Learning (CASEL, 2017) has identified five areas of social-emotional competence, distilled from years of research that is linked to positive academic and mental health outcomes for youth. These areas include: *self-awareness*, the ability to understand one's own emotions and behavior; *social awareness*, the ability to understand the emotions and behavior of others; *self-management*, the ability to manage emotions, behaviors, and impulses; *relationship skills*, the ability to develop and maintain positive connections with others; and *responsible decision making*, the ability to make helpful choices related to goal-directed behavior.

Developmentalists have further studied how these competencies develop and how they relate to one another. For example, Denham, Bassett, Zinsser, and Wyatt (2014) tested a model that depicts the relationships between overarching categories of social-emotional competency developed early in childhood, specific related skills or behaviors, and preschool and kindergarten readiness. Foundational competencies identified in this study included self-regulation and emotion knowledge. Behaviors related to self-regulation include inhibition of what might appear to be a more natural, but less acceptable, response (e.g., refrain from grabbing a preferred toy from another child), and emotion knowledge includes a child's recognition of a range of personal feelings in themselves and in others. Such foundational competencies, or lack thereof, can be linked to observable social behaviors. For example, a child who is developing self-regulation and emotion knowledge may be more likely to engage in prosocial behaviors such as listening, speaking quietly, sharing, and taking turns. Such behaviors are associated with positive classroom adjustment in early childhood settings, as rated by teachers (Denham et al., 2014). Children who are delayed or lagging in the development of these competencies may be more likely to develop behavioral patterns that reflect aggression or negative emotionality, such as crying, hitting, kicking, property destruction, and so on.

Young children do not develop skills related to self-regulation and emotion knowledge within a vacuum; rather, they constantly learn prosocial behaviors from their interactions with others in context (Bandura, 1986; Bronfenbrenner, & Morris, 1998, 2006). Caregivers and peers serve as models of social-emotional behaviors that children emulate. Further, children develop patterns of behavior as they learn the expectations of and reinforcing properties within an environment (O'Neill, Albin, Storey, Horner, & Sprague, 2015). A child raised in a family in which respectful, positive behaviors are expected and reinforced, in which emotions are named and validated, and in which healthy coping and emotion coaching are used, will more likely build the foundational competencies of self-regulation and emotion knowledge (Havighurst et al., 2013) than children exposed to harsh parenting, ambiguous expectations, and coercive behaviors (Smith et al., 2014).

Challenges in Early Childhood Assessment

While many prevention and intervention programs are available to teach young children critical skills related to social-emotional and behavioral competency, the assessment of such competencies and deficiencies or symptoms has lagged considerably. Whitcomb (2018) discussed a number of reasons why assessment of social-emotional competencies or skills in early childhood is challenging. First, there is a great deal of normative variation in the social and emotional behavior among young children, and behavior across contexts may be particularly inconsistent, making it difficult to accurately assess patterns of behavior and develop meaningful peer comparisons. Second, language development plays a role in the social-emotional behavior of young children. Specifically, deficits in language skills, such as those related to vocabulary development and expressive language, can predict problem behavior (Petersen et al., 2013); therefore, a focused assessment of social-emotional behavior may fail to identify the child's entire intervention needs. Third, there are fewer social-emotional measures overall that specifically target early childhood. Many assessments available are downward extensions of tools used with older populations, calling into question the sensitivity or appropriateness of items for preschool populations. Further, the technical adequacy of tools for early childhood populations is generally less strong than the technical adequacy of tests for older populations (Bracken, Keith, & Walker, 1998). Finally, some of the methods used to measure the social-emotional behavior of older populations may not be developmentally appropriate for young children (e.g., reliable self-reporting, interviewing).

Multi-method Approach to Early Childhood Assessment

The purpose of this chapter is to share effective methods for assessing social-emotional behaviors in young children across differing contexts. Our goal is to provide current resources for readers and illuminate the types of assessment questions that may be answered by certain kinds of assessments. The methods and tools presented here are not exhaustive; rather, they represent what is available in the field currently. We explore methods that identify strengths and competencies as well as symptoms and pathology, and we reflect on tools used most often in research versus practical settings and those that screen student behaviors and/or monitor developmental progress. Our perspective is that high-quality assessment practices are grounded in a multi-method, multi-source, multi-setting approach (Whitcomb, 2018). Multiple methods of assessment may include behavioral observation, interviews, and rating scales. Information from multiple sources, such as parents and teachers, can help to illuminate patterns of behaviors across multiple settings.

Behavioral Observation

Detailed information about observation of young children is provided else-where in this text (see Bracken and Theodore, this volume); however, it is worth noting here that behavioral observation of a child's social-emotional behavior is a powerful methodology as it allows for direct and authentic assessment of behavior within their ecology. Observers can objectively define and systematically observe particular target behaviors while also noting characteristics of the setting and the child's interactions with others (e.g., peers, teachers, parents). Observational data can provide an evaluator with important functional information that may include conditions under which certain behaviors are more likely to occur (O'Neill et al., 2015). For example, observers in a preschool setting may develop an understanding of how a student complies with expected classroom behaviors (e.g., sitting crisscross on the rug) as well as how a student regulates emotions and behaviors during difficult tasks (e.g., waiting for turn) and peer interactions (e.g., sharing, demonstrating empathy).

Early Screening Project

Behavioral observation can be used to validate other screening data, or it might be used to progress monitor students' development and use of par-ticular skills. Observations can be documented in a narrative format or they can be systematically coded. There are few commercially available social-emotional coding protocols for young children, but one option is from the Early Screening Project (ESP; Walker, Severson, & Feil, 1995). This tool is now embedded into the more widely recognized Systematic Screening of Behavior Disorders assessment system (Walker & Severson, 1992; Walker, Severson, & Feil, 2014) and is called the Social Behavior Observation (SBO). This direct observation protocol supports a systematic assessment that helps validate problematic social behaviors. The SBO enables observers to note student *antisocial behavior*, which includes negative social interactions or disobeying established behavioral expectations; *nonsocial behavior*, which might include tantrum behavior or children who play alone; and *prosocial behavior*, which is reflected in positive social interactions, parallel play, and following behavioral expectations. The duration of antisocial and nonsocial behaviors are recorded during 10-minute observations of free play or unstructured time during which the percentage of time engaged in problem-atic and prosocial behavior is calculated.

Minnesota Preschool Affect Checklist

Another observation tool is the Minnesota Preschool Affect Checklist (MPAC; Sroufe, Schork, Motti, Lawroski, & LaFreniere, 1984), which has been revised and shortened (MPAC-R/S; Denham et al., 2012b). The MPAC-R/S consists of 18 observation items related to preschoolers' emotional expression and regulation. Items reflect positive and negative emotions, positive and negative reactions to frustrating circumstances, prosocial behaviors, and productive involvement in the classroom. Observers are trained to identify these behaviors within 5-minute segments, and studies (Denham, Zahn-Waxler, Cummings, & Iannotti, 1991; Denham et al., 2012b) have supported the reliability and validity of this method of measuring young children's emotional skills.

With observational assessment approaches, it is helpful to gather peer comparison data to compare a target child's behavior with the behavior of peers within the same context. Additionally, it is recommended that multiple observations be conducted to evaluate the reliability and validity of the observational data collected (Briesch, Chafouleas, & Riley-Tillman, 2010; Doll & Elliott, 1994).

Interviews/Knowledge Assessments

Interviewing young children can present unique challenges; namely, accurately and reliably identifying and verbalizing their own behavioral patterns or history. Several researchers have, however, engaged in an interview-like format with young children to gain a sense of their perceptions of themselves and knowledge of their emotions. Such interviews often rely on predictable question formats and props to keep children interested and attentive.

Berkeley Puppet Interview

The Berkeley Puppet Interview (BPI; Ablow & Measelle, 1993) is one such method to interview young children (ages 4–8 years) directly about their perceptions of themselves and their relationships with others. The BPI was originally developed in the 1990s and was used primarily for research. Developers continue to offer training to researchers and clinicians in the administration of and coding associated with this interview. The format of the interview consists of several questions posed by the interviewer, who also holds two puppets (for examples, see Ablow & Measelle, 1993). Each puppet makes a statement such as, "I have lots of friends," or "I don't have lots of friends." The interviewer then poses, "How about you?" Questions fall into four primary domains including BPI Family Environment Scales, BPI Academic Scales, BPI Social Scales, and BPI Symptomology Scales. Items have also been studied in relation to the *Big 5* personality factors of extraversion, agreeableness, conscientiousness, neuroticism, and openness (Measelle, Ablow, John, Cowan, & Cowan, 2005). Children's responses have been found to agree highly with those of adult informants and even higher than the agreement between two adults' ratings of child behavior (e.g., teachers and parents; Measelle, Ablow, Cowan, & Cowan, 1998). The BPI has also been used with a diverse population of children from several countries (e.g., Stone et al., 2014).

Affective Knowledge Test

There are additional interview-like measures that enable researchers and clinicians to better understand children's knowledge of emotion, including emotion labels and emotion recognition in context. One such test is the Affective Knowledge Test (AKT; Denham, 1986). Like the BPI, the AKT uses puppets to prompt children to label emotions verbally and nonverbally. The puppet also performs different scenarios and children are prompted to label which emotion might be felt in such scenarios. This measure takes about 20 minutes to administer and can be used with young children up to about 54 months. Though this measure is nearly 35 years old, it continues to be used in research and in practice (e.g., Denham et al., 2014). This measure regularly demonstrates acceptable levels of reliability and validity (Denham et al., 2003; Denham et al., 2014) and has been shown to predict social competence later in childhood (e.g., Cutting & Dunn, 2002; Denham et al., 2012). The AKT has also been used to demonstrate changes in emotion knowledge over time (Domitrovich, Cortes & Greenberg, 2007).

Behavior Rating Scales

While direct observation and interviews are two methods that provide useful information about the social-emotional and behavioral knowledge and skills of young children, behavior rating scales are perhaps used most often in the assessment of young children. Some scales are developed specifically for early childhood while others are simply downward extensions of commonly used instruments. Many measure areas of strength as well as areas of deficit or symptomology. The measures that we share here generally have been extensively studied and have well-established technical properties. Behavior rating scales are excellent for screening purposes and provide users with important clinical information. The potential challenge of rating scales is that they reflect the perceptions of informants, which may not always be the most accurate representations of a child's behavior. See Table 8.1 for a brief overview of the rating scales discussed, including a description with intended use, psychometric properties, and the direct availability for linking to intervention.

The Ages & Stages Questionnaires: Social-Emotional, Second Edition (ASQ:SE-2)

The Ages & Stages Questionnaires: Social-Emotional, Second Edition (ASQ:SE-2; Squires, Bricker, Twombly, Murphy, & Hoselton, 2015), was designed to be an innovative, low-cost, and simple-to-administer measure for children 1–72 months (up to 6 years). The ASQ:SE-2 is intended to screen for social-emotional concerns and behavioral difficulties and to discern whether further assessment is needed. While the ASQ:SE-2 can be used as a screener for social-emotional functioning, developers suggest that additional measures, such as the

Table 8.1 Preschool Assessments for Behavior and Social-Emotional Skills

Assessment	Description	Method	Psychometric Quality	Materials for Direct Link to Intervention Available?
The Ages & Stages Questionnaires: Social-Emotional, Second Edition (ASQ: SE-2)	Screens and monitors competencies related to self-regulation, compliance, adaptive functioning, autonomy, affect, social-communication, and interaction. Used to discern whether further assessment is needed.	Screening and Progress Monitoring. As the child's age increases, additional items tailored for each developmental age range are completed.	Strong	No
The Social Emotional Assessment Measure (SEAM)	Two-part, strengths-based assessment measuring empathy, self-image, adaptive skills, healthy interactions with others, and emotional responses (SEAM Tool), as well as parenting skills (SEAM Family Profile). Helpful follow-up measure to identified concerns on the ASQ:SE-2 screening tool.	Intake Assessment and Progress Monitoring. Parent completion of questions targeting 10 benchmarks for social-emotional functioning and four benchmarks related to parenting strengths.	Moderate to Strong	Yes
The Devereux Early Childhood Assessment Preschool Program, Second Edition (DECA-P2)	Brief, strengths-based assessment intended to evaluate and support child resiliency through three within-child protective factors: Initiative, Self-Control, and Attachment. Includes subscale measuring behavioral concerns.	Screening and Intake Assessment. Parent Rating (38 items) and Teacher Rating (38 items).	Strong to Very Strong	Yes

(Continued)

Table 8.1 (Cont).

Assessment	Description	Method	Psychometric Quality	Materials for Direct Link to Intervention Available?
The Behavior Assessment System for Children, Third Edition (BASC-3), Preschool Forms	Widely utilized broadband rating scale for assessing adaptive skills and problem behaviors. Assesses clinical problem ability, functional impairment, executive functioning, and problem solving, as well as attentional, behavioral, and emotional control.	Intake Assessment. Teacher Rating (105 items) and Parent Rating (139 items).	Moderate to Very Strong	Yes
The Behavioral and Emotional Screening System (BASC-3 BESS)	Systematically identifies emotional and behavioral strengths and weaknesses. Can be used at the school, classroom, or individual level to determine need for comprehensive evaluation and when to apply interventions more systemically.	Screening. Teacher Rating (25 items) and Parent Rating (25 items).	Very Strong	Yes
The Early Childhood Rating Forms of the Achenbach System of Empirically Based Assessment (ASEBA System – CBCL/1 1/2-5 – parent ratings) (C-TRF)	Evaluates for concerns of anxiety/depression, emotional reactivity, somatic complaints, withdrawn behaviors, attention problems, and aggressive behavior. Language development survey for children 18-35 months or those with delayed language to assess word combinations and vocabulary, as well as risk factors.	Intake Assessment. Teacher and Parent Form (Both 99 items with four supplemental questions assessing the nature of the problem behavior, disability, and strengths of the child).	Very Strong	No

Measure	Description	Use	Psychometric Strength	Freely Available
The Conners Early Childhood Behavior Forms and Global Index Forms	Assesses inattention and hyperactivity, social functioning/atypical behaviors, defiant/aggressive behaviors, anxiety, and physical symptoms, as well as mood and affect. Used to determine when early intervention services may be necessary. Global Index forms are used to evaluate for presence of general psychopathology.	Intake Assessment Progress Monitoring. Teacher Rating (116 items) (48 items – short form) (10 items – Global Index) and Parent Rating (115 items) (49 items – short form) (10 items – Global Index).	Strong	No
Preschool and Kindergarten Behavior Scales – Second Edition (PKBS-2)	Screens for strengths and challenges related to social skills, as well as internalizing and externalizing problem behaviors. Appropriate to use when assessing typical problem behaviors.	Screening. Parent Rating (76 items)* and Teacher Rating (76 items).* *Identical items	Very Strong	No
Social Skills Improvement System (SSIS)	Evaluates social skills, academic competence, and behavior problems (including motivation to learn). Allows for comparison against grade-level expectations. Individual rating scales available for those with elevated concerns.	Screening. Teacher Rating 30 minutes (Entire class). Individual parent and teacher forms also available.	Very Strong	Yes
Strengths and Difficulties Questionnaire (SDQ)	Assesses hyperactivity, conduct difficulties, emotional symptoms, peer challenges, and prosocial behavior. Freely available in 21 languages.	Screening and Progress Monitoring. Parent Rating (25 items) and Teacher Rating (25 items).	Strong	No

ASQ-3, be used in tandem to screen other relevant areas, including communication, cognition, and motor functioning. At the preschool level, the screener can be appropriately administered every 6 months. Of note, this screening tool is less useful for children who have previously been diagnosed with a disability.

The ASQ:SE-2 has a set of questions for each of the nine developmental levels (2, 6, 12, 18, 24, 30, 36, 48, and 60 months). As the child's age increases, additional items tailored for each developmental age range are completed. Domains assessed include *self-regulation, compliance, adaptive functioning, autonomy, affect, social-communication,* and *interaction.*

Parents can complete the measure in approximately 10–15 minutes, with scoring requiring just 2–3 minutes. No teacher rating scale is provided. A visual summary is then generated to display evaluated social-emotional development, parental concerns, and a note for whether follow-up is recommended. Example questions relate to such behaviors as the child's tendency to "Show concern for other people's feelings" and "Stay upset for more than an hour after you leave." Response options include "Often or Always," "Sometimes," or "Rarely or Never," with additional options to place a check mark if the behavior is of particular concern for the parent, and an option to expand with a qualitative response.

The ASQ:SE-2 is one of a few commercially available social-emotional measures designed specifically for screening and may be considered to be the most psychometrically sound of them. The norming sample was composed of more than 14,000 parent ratings of children with and without social-emotional difficulties across several states. The sample was also stratified by gender and ethnicity. Average internal consistency coefficients of the ASE:SE-2 forms by age range was moderately high at .84, with a test-retest coefficient of .89. Research suggests the measure further demonstrates acceptable convergent validity with other similar measures. The ASQ:SE-2 also identifies children with and without social and emotional disabilities with high sensitivity, which the authors suggest is more accurate than clinical judgement or more broadband tools alone (Jee et al., 2010). In addition, the measure identified individuals in the "at risk" range of autism in 83.5% of screenings. This measure has demonstrated moderate to strong convergent validity with other measures such as the Child Behavior Checklist (CBCL; Achenbach & Rescorla, 2000) and Devereux Early Childhood Assessment for Infants and Toddlers (DECA-IT; Powell, Mackrain, LeBuffe & Lewisville, 2007). The ASQ:SE-2 also includes a "monitoring zone" that identifies which children may be near the clinical cut score and should be closely observed and rescreened in the future. In sum, the ASQ:SE-2 is considered to be highly reliable and relatively easy to use.

The Social Emotional Assessment Measure (SEAM)

The Social Emotional Assessment Measure (SEAM; Squires & Bricker, 2007) is appropriate for use with children from 2 months to 66 months (5.5

years). The SEAM is a two-part assessment intended to measure children's social-emotional and behavioral functioning (SEAM Tool) and parenting skills (SEAM Family Profile). Designed by the same authors as the ASQ:SE-2, the SEAM can be a helpful follow-up for identified concerns on the ASQ: SE-2. Of note, the SEAM is a highly functional assessment that promotes a linkage between assessment and intervention. As such, the SEAM can be used for progress monitoring, rendering it as an ideal means to assess the extent to which a child or the family is responding to intervention, with reduced risk over time.

The SEAM provides an evaluation of the child's strengths and incorporates three age intervals for evaluation: infants (2–18 months), toddlers (18–36 months), and preschoolers (36–66 months). Each interval includes 10 benchmark behaviors deemed critical to social-emotional functioning, including empathy, healthy interactions and engagement with others, an ability to regulate activity levels, cooperating with daily routines, self-image, adaptive skills, independence, and tendency to demonstrate and control a range of emotional responses. Qualitative responses are collected from parent reports. The four response options for rating the child's behavior are: 1) very true (consistently or most of the time); 2) somewhat true (sometimes, though not consistently); 3) rarely true (only once in a while); and 4) not true (does not yet show skill). An alternate form of the SEAM is also available (SEAM with Ages) that provides parents with a list of ages of expected skill acquisition within each item and facilitates discussion about children's social-emotional development across a continuum (e.g., 60 months, Shows Empathy for Others: Gives a toy back when another child shows distress).

The SEAM Family Profile is the second piece of the SEAM; it incorporates similar infant, toddler, and preschool age levels with questions targeted at determining parenting social-emotional strengths, as well as identifying areas where additional supports would be beneficial. The four primary benchmarks incorporated within this portion of the assessment are: responding to needs, ensuring predictable routines and an appropriate environment, providing activities for play, and providing home safety. In addition to the quantitative rating response, parents are asked to provide examples of how they engage in a particular skill and can check the "focus area" triangle next to an item if they would like to be a particular target for intervention. Although some parents may feel more comfortable than others reporting their parenting skills, the SEAM measure emphasizes the importance of building positive relationships with families during this evaluation and encouraging the increase of positive parent-child interactions during those critical early years. Completion times of the measures are expected to be in the ranges of 15–30 minutes (SEAM/SEAM with Ages) and 10–15 minutes (Family Profile). Example items on the SEAM Family Profile include: "I know how to successfully redirect my child's behaviors" and "I understand why my child engages in inappropriate behaviors and know how to modify the environment."

Psychometric data for the SEAM are relatively strong. Pearson product-moment correlations between benchmarks and overall SEAM scores were high, ranging from .73 to .88 for children at the preschool interval. In addition, Cronbach's coefficient alphas were calculated within each interval, with the preschool portion evidencing robust internal consistency at .96. Test-retest reliability coefficients computed when caregivers were given a second copy of the form to complete immediately after filling out the first questionnaire indicated high levels of stability at .99. Correlations of mean scores with age were low (r = .12), suggesting that social-emotional functioning is not a developmental phenomenon; this may also have been due to the large variability in social-emotional skills across settings and experiences. Concurrent validity evidence has also been provided between the SEAM and related measures, such as the DECA-IT, ASQ: SE, and Infant-Toddler Social Emotional Assessment (ITSEA), with moderate to strong consistency (r = .26 to .81). Additional research is needed to explore the SEAM psychometric properties with a stratified randomized national sample.

All SEAM forms are available in Spanish. The SEAM is simple to administer even by responders with little or no training in behavior or mental health interventions. Accordingly, Squires and colleagues (2012) found that 92% percent of practitioners claimed the tool provided useful information on student behaviors, and 90% of parents believed that the measure asked appropriate questions related to social-emotional functioning and was relatively quick to complete.

The Devereux Early Childhood Assessment Preschool Program, Second Edition (DECA-P2)

Derived from the larger Devereux Center for Resilient Children, The Devereux Early Childhood Assessment (DECA; LeBuffe & Naglieri, 2012) Preschool Program offers a variety of resources designed to promote social-emotional competencies not only in children but in caregivers as well. The program includes a brief, strengths-based assessment intended to evaluate and support child resiliency through three within-child protective factors: *Initiative, Self-Control,* and *Attachment.* At the bottom of the record form there is also a subscale measuring behavioral concerns. Given the strengths-building nature of the measure, the DECA-P2 offers an early childhood professional guide as well as a parent guide for linking assessment to intervention, building adult resilience, and transforming challenging behavior. The measure is for children ages 3–5 years and can be completed by parents and teachers in 5–10 minutes with paper and online scoring formats. A Spanish version is also available.

The DECA-P2 includes 38-items related to the three-factor structure of Initiative, Self-Control, and Attachment and can be used for screening and general assessment purposes. Charts are available for interpretation of clinical significance pre- and post-intervention. For example, a change in the total protective factors (TPF) of seven (teacher) or eight (parent) would indicate a clinically significant change in overall child protective factors. Example questions regarding a child's initiative refer to the child's ability to do things for themselves and try new things. Questions related to self-control include the child's ability to show patience and control their anger, among other behaviors. Lastly, attachment is assessed through items assessing the child's tendency to respond positively to an adult comforting them when upset and seeking help from children/adults when necessary.

The DECA-P2 meets or exceeds benchmarks for high quality with a nationally standardized sample of 3,553 and strong reliability and validity. The measure has high reported levels of internal consistency, ranging from .79 to .95, and test-retest reliability from .78 to .95 over a 6-to-8-day interval. Furthermore, the DECA-P2 has demonstrated moderate to strong convergent validity with both Strength and Problem Behavior Indexes of the Conners Early Childhood scale (Conners EC; Conners, 2009). Results suggest that the DECA-P2 Behavioral Concerns scale correlated positively with the Conners EC Global Index for both parents (corrected $r = .59$) and teacher (corrected $r = .65$). Accordingly, the Total Protective Factors scale of the DECA-P2 negatively correlated with the Conners Global Index for both parent (corrected $r = - .37$) and teacher (corrected $r = - .42$) raters. Overall, the DECA-P2 is a highly useful tool for assessing and building on the strengths of children and their families.

The Behavior Assessment System for Children, Third Edition (BASC-3) (Preschool Forms – TRS/PRS)

The Behavior Assessment System for Children, Third Edition (BASC-3; Reynolds & Kamphaus, 2015), is a widely used broadband rating scale for assessing the adaptive skills and problem behaviors of children and adolescents 2:0–25 years. In particular, the BASC-3 preschool forms are intended for children ages 2–5. The BASC-3 includes several indexes related to areas of clinical probability, functional impairment, executive functioning, and problem solving, as well as attentional, behavioral, and emotional control. All items are considered observable behaviors.

A Teacher Rating Scale (TRS, 105 items) and a Parent Rating Scale (PRS, 139 items) are available to measure behaviors in the school, home, and community settings. Response choices are rated on a four-point scale from "Never" to "Almost Always." Completion of the scale requires approximately 10–20 minutes. Although the forms can be scored by hand, online scoring through the Q-global database is available and generally takes 5 minutes. Example questions include: "Acts as if run by motor," "Does not seem to listen when spoken to," and "Has insomnia or excessive sleep almost every day." Results are converted into T-Scores, allowing for interpretation of clinical risk with the following classifications: "Normal risk" (T = 20–60), "Elevated risk" (61–70), or "Extremely elevated risk" (T = 71 or higher).

The BASC-3 has strong psychometric properties and a robust theoretical background to facilitate scale interpretation. Coefficient alpha reliabilities for the preschool-aged teacher rating scales range from .77 to .97, while parent rating scales range from .76 to .96. Test-retest reliabilities range from .79 to .95 for teacher rating scales and .92 to .93 for parent rating scales. The BASC-3 has demonstrated high correlation with other instruments that measure similar constructs. The clinical norming sample included children 4 to 18 years old identified with a diagnosis or educational classification of one or more behavior problems. Children with a variety of social, emotional, and behavioral challenges were selected for participation.

Hundreds of studies have used these scales and Spanish rating scales are available at all age levels. The BASC-3 rating scale system also offers paid access to interpretative reports, largely enabling the development of targeted behaviors for functional behavior assessments (FBAs) and behavior intervention plans (BIPS).

The Behavioral and Emotional Screening System (BESS; Kamphaus & Reynolds, 2015) is a shorter form of the BASC-3. The BESS can be used at the school, classroom, or individual level to determine who needs a more comprehensive evaluation and when to apply interventions more systemically. The BASC also offers a Behavior and Emotional Skill Building Guide intended to guide the implementation of appropriate interventions (Vannest, Reynolds, & Kamphaus, 2015).

The BESS is intended for use in mental health clinics, pediatric clinics, and school settings. Additionally, a strength of the BESS is that it can be used longitudinally across developmental stages, from preschool through high school (ages 3:0–18:11). The BASC-3 BESS at the preschool level includes teacher and parent forms with between 25 and 30 items each. The scale provides an overall Behavioral and Emotional Risk Index as well as three sub-risk indexes related to externalizing behaviors, internalizing behaviors, and adaptive skills. Recently, the BASC-3 BESS was normed on a population reported to resemble closely that of the U.S. Census population. The overall Behavior and Emotional Index generated by the BESS is a reliable and valid indicator of mental health concerns, with elevated scores likely warranting further evaluation.

The Early Childhood Rating Forms of the Achenbach System of Empirically Based Assessment (ASEBA System – CBCL/1 1/2-5 – Parent Ratings) (C-TRF)

The Achenbach System of Empirically Based Assessment (ASEBA; Achenbach, 2001b) provides a multitude of rating scales targeted at the comprehensive evaluation of adaptive and maladaptive child behaviors across numerous developmental stages. Primary scales include anxiety/depression, emotionally reactive, somatic complaints, withdrawn behaviors, attention problems, and aggressive behavior. It has also been reported from several psychologists and psychiatrists cross-culturally that these ratings tend to align rather well with DSM-5 classification criteria.

The preschool forms have recently been revised to include children entering childcare at increasingly early stages and are intended for children ages 1.5 to 5 years. Forms include a parent (Child Behavior Checklist; CBCL 11/ 2-5; Achenbach & Rescorla, 2000) and teacher/childcare provider measure (C-TRF; Achenbach, 2001a). These scales include 99 items with four supplemental questions assessing the nature of the problem behavior, disability, and strengths of the child. On the parent form, there is also a newly included two-page language development survey (LDS) for children 18–35 months, assessing use of word combinations and vocabulary, as well as risk factors. The LDS can also be used for those with delayed language development with comparison to up to 35-month norms. Scoring is available online in addition to hand scoring.

Example items include "Afraid to try new things," "Can't stand waiting, wants everything now," and "Disturbed by change in new routine." Response options include "Not true," "Somewhat or sometimes true," and "Very true or often true."

Mixed gender norms for the CBCL 11/2-5 are based on a well-stratified national sample of 700 children from an initial norming sample of 1,728 child ratings. The sample is thoroughly representative of children from a variety of socioeconomic backgrounds, geographical regions, races/ethnicities, genders and urban/rural communities. Further detailed information regarding the generally high technical properties of the CBCL 11/2-5 is in the assessment manual. In addition, the multicultural supplement to the manual for CBCL 11/2-5 further illustrates the psychometric strengths of this parent measure across individuals from various cultural backgrounds. Reports on multi-cultural results regarding internal consistency, confirmatory factor analyses, and cross-informant correlations, as well as distributions of scale scores and a list of the 300 publications utilizing this measure, can be found in this supplement. The norming sample for the C-TRF is also diversely representative and includes 1,113 child ratings from teachers and caregivers. The strong psychometric properties and the large sample size associated with the preschool age range and the current research available suggests this tool can be reliably used with young children.

The Conners Early Childhood – Behavior Forms and Global Index Forms

The Conners Early Childhood Behavior forms are a subset of the larger Conners Rating System, particularly the Conners Early Childhood (CEC; Conners, 2008). The CEC is intended to assist in early identification of social-emotional and behavioral concerns, as well as developmental milestones. The Conners Early Childhood Behavior forms are designed for evaluating the behavior of preschool children ages 2 to 6 years. Use of the Early Childhood Behavior rating scale by itself is appropriate when the primary concern is focused on problem behaviors and the child is generally meeting developmental milestones. Conners Behavior scales can be used for intake assessments as well as progress monitoring and target several different areas related to inattention and hyperactivity, social functioning/atypical behaviors, defiant/aggressive behaviors, anxiety, physical symptoms, and mood and affect. This questionnaire can be completed by parents (EC BEH–P, 115 items) and teachers/childcare providers (EC BEH–T, 116 items). The forms include questions related to behavior, general psychopathology (Global Index), impairment, additional indicators of clinical significance, and additional questions. A validity index is also used to identify individuals who may be reporting in an overly positive or negative manner. While these forms can be used during an initial intake, they can further be used as a means to assess progress over time, during or after the course of intervention.

Shortened versions of the behavior rating scale are also available in parent [Conners EC BEH–P(S), 49 items] and teacher/childcare provider versions [Conners EC BEH–T(S), 48 items]. While the wording of the items on the short form is the same as on the longer behavior form, this method of assessment may be helpful when time does not permit an extensive assessment or when there may be several administrations over time. Global Index forms are available as stand-alone measures for general psychopathology through two 10-item indexes completed by parents or teachers/childcare providers. Administration can be completed quickly online or using pen-and-paper format: Conners EC Behavior, 15 minutes; Conners EC Behavior Short, 10 minutes; Conners EC Global Index, 5 minutes. Example items include "Doesn't follow directions," "Lacks good friendships," and "Easily frightened." Progress reports can be generated to compare student performance across time using two to four administrations of the measure.

The normative sample for the Conners Early Childhood scales included 800 parent and 800 teacher/childcare provider reports. In addition, high levels of internal consistency (Cronbach's alpha) have been documented for the behavior forms with parents (M = .86) and teachers (.89). Convergent validity with moderate correlations has also been demonstrated with the Conners EC Global Index and the Attention Deficit Hyperactivity Index of the K-SADS-PL (.55–.73) and the CBCL (r = .60–.76) with a Spanish population (Morales-Hidalgo, Hernández-Martínez, Vera, Voltas, & Canals, 2017). Furthermore, test-retest data have been calculated over a 2- to 4-week interval and are to have excellent temporal stability (median r = .92).

Reported strengths of this measure include respectable validity and reliability, simple graphic representation of comparison across multiple raters, and the availability of the forms in Spanish. This measure has also been indicated as acceptable for screening, progress monitoring, and research purposes. In addition, the Conners assessments system as a whole has been noted to provide critical information around the potential classification of a student for special education or related services, according to the U.S. federal statute, Individuals with Disabilities Education Improvement Act (IDEIA, 2004).

The Preschool and Kindergarten Behavior Scales, Second Edition (PKBS-2)

The Preschool and Kindergarten Behavior Scales, Second Edition (PKBS-2; Merrell, 2002), assesses positive and negative social skills and behaviors of children aged 3 to 6 years. The measure is available in parent and teacher forms and is composed of 76 items identical on both forms, facilitating the comparative abilities of the multiple raters. The PKBS-2 has two primary subscales: Social Skills and Problem Behaviors. The Social Skills scale includes three subscales: Social Cooperation, Social Interactions, and Social Independence. The Problem Behavior scale is further divided into four subscales: Self-Centered/Explosive, Attention Problems, Overactive, and Antisocial/Aggressive behaviors. There are also two items associated with internalizing problem behaviors: Social Withdrawal and Anxiety/Somatic Problems.

Administration of the rating scale takes approximately 12 minutes. Example questions from the Social Skills scale include: "Works or plays independently" and "Is cooperative." Items from the Problem Behaviors scale include: "Acts impulsively without thinking" and "Becomes sick when upset or afraid." The manual includes numerous studies confirming the strong psychometric properties of the PKBS-2, including informant agreement as well as convergent, divergent, and construct validity demonstrated through comparison of the PKBS-2 with four other preschool rating scales. Internal consistency is very high and ranged from .96 to .97 for the two larger scales and from .81 to .95 for the smaller subscales. Test-retest reliability ranges from .69 to .78, given a three-month interval. The PKBS-2 was derived from a national normative sample of 3,317 children generally representative of the U.S. population.

PKBS-2 forms are also available in Portuguese and Spanish. Another particular strength of this measure is the content validation procedures used regarding early childhood development, specifically. Instead of extending this measure downward from a larger system of measurement instruments, such as with the BASC-3 or the ASEBA, this measure was designed for students in the preschool age range. These scales are appropriate to use when assessing typical problem behaviors; however, for more severe, low-frequency behavioral concerns, the CBCL 11/2-5 from the Achenbach rating system may be more appropriate.

The Social Skills Improvement System (SSIS)

The Social Skills Improvement System (SSIS; Gresham & Elliott, 2008) was developed by Gresham and Elliott in 2008 with the intention of replacing the previous Social Skills Rating System (SSRS; Gresham & Elliott, 1990). The SSIS is designed to evaluate the development of social skills, academic competence, and behavior problems. Teachers can use the Performance Screening Guide associated with the SSIS to screen their classes in approximately 30 minutes and measure student performance against grade-level expectations. In addition, individual rating scales are also available for those students who display more indicated concerns. The current scales have been revised and demonstrate several updates from the previous SSRS, such as enhanced psychometric properties, diversified norms, and additional sub-scales. Social skills assessed include assertion, communication, cooperation, empathy, engagement, responsibility, and self-control. Competing problem behaviors are evaluated through items related to bullying, hyperactivity and inattention, externalizing, internalizing, and autism spectrum behaviors. On the teacher form only, academic competence is assessed through math achievement, reading achievement, and motivation to learn.

Like the majority of the other rating scales, parent and teacher/child-care provider forms are available. Although the items are similar across the forms, wording of the items tends to differ moderately with reference to the context of the behavior. Although the larger SSIS rating scales assess children from ages 3–18, the preschool forms are intended for use with children 3–5 years old. These scales were created as extensions to the larger SSIS, rather than individually constructed for early childhood. Administration time is approximately 10–20 minutes per student, and example items include: "Has difficulty waiting for turn," "Keeps others out of social circles," and "Tolerates peer when they are annoying" (social strength).

In evaluating the factor structure of the measure, ratings were only based on 200 teacher reports and 400 parent reports. However, the sample is closely representative of the U.S. population (in 2006). Coefficient alpha reliabilities related to the subscales of this behavior form range from the lower .70 to upper .90 levels. In addition, total social skills score reliabilities are in the high .90 range with problem behavior score reliabilities in the mid-.90 range, for teacher and parent forms. Convergent validity has been established with moderate to high correlations with both the BASC-2 and larger SSRS measure. Regarding test-retest reliability, teacher and parent coefficient ratings range from .72 to .93. Evidence of cross-cultural validity has been reported by several studies using the previous preschool SSIS forms (Elliott, Barnard, & Gresham, 1989; Powless & Elliott, 1993). Supplemental research has also deemed the SSIS advantageous in identifying students at risk in Head Start classrooms (Fagan & Iglesias, 2000). A Spanish version of this measure is also available.

Of note, the SSIS provides a direct link to intervention, offering an aligned SSIS Social Emotional Learning (SEL) Edition for children 4–14 years old. Considering the difficulties in accurately measuring the outcomes of an SEL curriculum, the SSIS SEL Edition provides a class-wide evidence-based means to teach and assess skills related to academic competency and the five SEL competencies (CASEL, 2017). The SSIS also includes an intervention guide to aid further in the development of targeted social, academic, and behavioral supports for individual students based on rating scale results.

Strengths and Difficulties Questionnaire (SDQ)

The Strengths and Difficulties Questionnaire (SDQ) was developed by Robert Goodman in 1997. The SDQ is one of the most widely used brief screening tools for identifying prosocial behaviors and potential psychopathology intended for use with children 3–16 years old. The measure is freely available online and has been translated into 60 different languages. Pre-school-aged forms are available in parent (P2-4 years, P4-17) and teacher versions (T2-4, T4-17) and consist of 25 items each. While the SDQ is used in both clinical and school or community settings, the purposes of the assessment may be slightly different. For instance, Stone, Otten, Engels, Vermulst, & Janssens, (2010) posit that in a clinical setting, psychopathology may be assumed and this tool helps to provide information on the type and severity. On the other hand, in a school or community setting, psychopathology is not assumed for all individuals, rendering this measure important in assessing the developing presence of concerns that may later evolve into psychopathology. The SDQ has also been shown to be sensitive to treatment effects, suggesting its use as a pre- and post-intervention measure following parenting groups or social-emotional learning curriculums in a classroom. Results may be most accurate when aggregating scores across multiple raters. The SDQ also has an "added value" index that can be used to assess for changes not simply attributed to regression to the mean or spontaneous improvements over time.

The response options for the majority of items are: "Not True," "Somewhat True," and "Certainly True"; however, the last page of the measure includes an impact supplement. In this section, caregivers and teachers can also indicate perceived difficulties in the child's behavior, how long the difficulties have been occurring, their beliefs about distress felt by the child themselves, and the daily activities of the child, as well as the family/classroom. Administration takes approximately 5 minutes and scoring can be completed by hand or online. Example items include: "Considerate of other people's feelings", "Nervous or clingy in new situation, easily loses confidence," and "Constantly fidgeting or squirming."

Research investigating the psychometric properties of the SDQ is strong, particularly for the teacher measure. The SDQ has been utilized in 4,699 publications from 100 different countries. In a review of 48 studies (N = 131,223) of children 4–12 years, Stone et al. (2010) provided a general overview of the strong reliability and validity of the parent and teacher measures. Results also suggested high internal consistency, inter-rater agreement, and test-retest reliability. Of the 18 studies evaluating the five-factor structure of the scale, (emotional, inattention-hyperactivity, peer problems, conduct problems, prosocial behavior), 15 of them resulted in similar confirmation. Normative data have been collected in 10 countries, including the United States, Germany, Japan, and Spain. A recent study incorporated 16,659 families in evaluating the preschool-adapted SDQ measure specifically. Results suggested varied psychometric properties. Although the five-factor structure was confirmed, subscale reliability ranged from a low of .66 (peer problems) to a high of .83 (hyperactivity). In addition, strong correlations suggested a positive relationship between the ages 3 and 5 SDQ scores. This study also concluded that conduct and hyperactivity subscales each demonstrated predictive validity of later developmental and clinical trajectories two years after the initial assessment (Croft, Stride, Maughan, & Rowe, 2015). The SDQ is widely used in school and clinical settings for treatment outcome and research purposes.

Conclusion

The purpose of this chapter was to provide readers with foundational and practical knowledge about the assessment of social-emotional and behavioral skills of young children. Measuring such skills and competencies in everyday contexts is challenging as children are rapidly developing as they are exposed to more varied environments (e.g., school, playgroups). Though challenging, assessment can serve as a cornerstone during this period of tremendous growth and support caregivers and teachers as they work to target and teach specific skills, intervene with emerging maladaptive behaviors, and set children up to experience positive outcomes.

References

Ablow, J. C., & Measelle, J. R. (1993). *Berkeley puppet interview: Administration and scoring systems manuals.* Berkeley, CA: University of California.

Achenbach, T. M. (2001a). *Child behavior checklist for ages 6–18.* Burlington, VT: Research Center for Children, Youth, and Families.

Achenbach, T. M. (2001b). *Manual for the ASEBA school-age forms and profiles.* Burlington, VT: Research Center for Children, Youth, and Families.

Achenbach, T. M., & Rescorla, L. A. (2000). *Child behavior checklist for ages 1½–5.* Burlington, VT: Research Center for Children, Youth, and Families.

Bandura, A. (1986). *Social foundations of thought and action: A social cognitive theory.* Englewood Cliffs, NJ: Prentice-Hall.

Bracken, B. A., Keith, L. K., & Walker, K. C. (1998). Assessment of preschool behavior and social-emotional functioning: A review of thirteen third-party instruments. *Journal of Psychoeducational Assessment, 16*, 153–169.

Briesch, A., Chafouleas, S., & Riley-Tillman, T. (2010). Generalizability and dependability of behavior assessment methods to estimate academic engagement: A comparison of systematic direct observation and direct behavior rating. *School Psychology Review, 39*(3), 408–421.

Bronfenbrenner, U., & Morris, P. A. (1998). Theoretical models of human development. *Handbook of Child Psychology, 1*, 993–1028. Damon. W., & Lerner, RM (Eds.).

Bronfenbrenner, U., & Morris, P. A. (2006). The bioecological model of human development. In R. M. Lerner & W. Damon (Eds.), *Handbook of child psychology: Theoretical models of human development* (pp. 793–828). Hoboken, NJ: John Wiley & Sons Inc.

Collaborative for Academic and Social Emotional Learning. (2017). *Social and emotional learning competencies.* Retrieved from www.casel.org

Conners, C. K. (2008). *Conners 3: Conners Third Edition.* Toronto: Multi-Health Systems.

Conners, C. K. (2009). *Conners early childhood.* Toronto, Ontario, Canada: Multi-Health Systems.

Croft, S., Stride, C., Maughan, B., & Rowe, R. (2015). Validity of the strengths and difficulties questionnaire in preschool-aged children. *Pediatrics, 135*, 1210–1219.

Cutting, A. L., & Dunn, J. (2002). The cost of understanding other people: Social cognition predicts young children's sensitivity to criticism. *Journal of Child Psychology and Psychiatry, 43*(7), 849–860.

Denham, S. A. (1986). Social cognition, social behavior, and emotion in preschoolers: Contextual validation. *Child Development, 57*, 194–201.

Denham, S. A., Bassett, H. H., Way, E., Mincic, M., Zinsser, K., & Graling, K. (2012). Preschoolers' emotion knowledge: Self-regulatory foundations, and predictions of early school success. *Cognition and Emotion, 26*(4), 667–679. https://doi.org/10.1080/02699931.2011.602049

Denham, S. A., Bassett, H. H., Thayer, S. K., Mincic, M., Sirotkin, Y. S., & Zinsser, K. (2012b). Observing preschoolers' social-emotional behavior: Structure, foundations, and prediction of early school success. *Journal of Genetic Psychology, 173*, 246–278.

Denham, S. A., Bassett, H. H., Zinsser, K., & Wyatt, T. M. (2014). How preschoolers' social-emotional learning predicts their early school success: Developing theory-promoting, competency-based assessments. *Infant and Child Development, 23*, 426–454.

Denham, S. A., Blair, K. A., DeMulder, E., Levitas, J., Sawyer, K., Auerbach-Major, S., & Queenan, P. (2003). Preschool emotional competence: Pathway to social competence? *Child Development, 74*, 238–256.

Denham, S. A., Zahn-Waxler, C., Cummings, E. M., & Iannotti, R. J. (1991). Social competence in young children's peer relations: Patterns of development and change. *Child Psychiatry and Human Development, 22*, 29–44. doi:10.1007/BF00706057

Doll, B., & Elliott, S. N. (1994). Representativeness of observed preschool social behaviors: How many data are enough? *Journal of Early Intervention, 18*, 227–238.

Domitrovich, C., Cortes, R., & Greenberg, M. (2007). Improving young children's social and emotional competence: A randomized trial of the preschool "PATHS" curriculum. *Journal of Primary Prevention, 28*(2), 67–91.

Egeland, B., Pianta, R., & Ogawa, J. (1996). Early behavior problems: Pathways to mental disorders in adolescence. *Development and Psychopathology, 8*(4), 735–749. doi:10.1017/S0954579400007392

Elliott, S. N., Barnard, J., & Gresham, F. M. (1989). Preschoolers social behavior: Teachers' and parents' assessments. *Journal of Psychoeducational Assessment, 7,* 223–234.

Fagan, J., & Iglesias, A. (2000). The relationship between fathers' and children's communication skills and children's behavior problems: A study of Head Start children. *Early Education & Development, 11,* 307–320.

Gresham, F. M., & Elliott, S. N. (1990). *The social skills rating system.* Circle Pines, MN: American Guidance.

Gresham, F. M., & Elliott, S. N. (2008). *The Social Skills Improvement System (SSIS): Performance screening guide.* Minneapolis, MN: Pearson.

Havighurst, S. S., Wilson, K. R., Harley, A. E., Kehoe, C., Efron, D., & Prior, M. R. (2013). "Tuning into kids": Reducing young children's behavior problems using an emotion coaching parenting program. *Child Psychiatry and Human Development, 44,* 247–264.

Individuals with Disabilities Education Act of (2004), 20 U.S.C. § 1400. (2004). Individuals with Disabilities Education Improvement Act of 2004. *[Bethesda, MD :ProQuest].*

Jee, S., Conn, A., Szilagyi, P., Blumkin, A., Baldwin, C., & Szilagy, M. (2010). Identification of social-emotional problems among young children in foster care. *Journal of Child Psychology and Psychiatry, 51*(12), 1351–1358.

Kamphaus, R. W., & Reynolds, C. R. (2015). *Behavior Assessment System for Children – Third Edition (BASC-3): Behavioral and Emotional Screening System (BESS).* Bloomington, MN: Pearson.

LeBuffe, P. A., & Naglieri, J. A. (2012). *The devereux early assessment for preschoolers* (2nd ed.). Lewisville, NC: Kaplan. Users Guide and Technical Manual.

Malik, R. (2017). New data reveal 250 preschoolers are suspended or expelled every day. Retrieved from www.americanprogress.org/issues/early-childhood.

Measelle, J. R., Ablow, J. C., John, O. P., Cowan, P. A., & Cowan, C. P. (2005). Can children provide coherent, stable, and valid self-reports on the big five dimensions? A longitudinal study from ages 5 to 7. *Journal of Personality and Social Psychology, 89,* 90–106.

Measelle, J. R., Ablow, J. C., Cowan, P. A., & Cowan, C. P. (1998). Assessing young children's views of their academic, social, and emotional lives: An evaluation of the self-perception scales of the Berkeley puppet interview. *Child Development, 1998,* 1556–1576.

Merrell, K. W. (2002). *Preschool and Kindergarten Behavior Scales* (2nd ed.). Austin, TX: PRO-ED.

Morales-Hidalgo, P., Hernández-Martínez, C., Vera, M., Voltas, N., & Canals, J. (2017). Psychometric properties of the Conners-3 and Conners Early Childhood Indexes in a Spanish school population. *International Journal of Clinical and Health Psychology, 17*(1), 85–96.

National Center for Mental Health Promotion and Youth Violence Prevention (2012). *Childhood trauma and its effect on healthy development.* Washington, DC: American Institute for Research.

O'Neill, R. E., Albin, R. W., Storey, K., Horner, R. H., & Sprague, J. R. (2015). *Functional assessment and program development.* Stamford, CT: Cengage.

Petersen, I. T., Bates, J. E., D'Onofrio, B. M., Coyne, C. A., Lansford, J. E., Dodge, K. A., ... Van Hulle, C. A. (2013). Language ability predicts the development of behavior problems in children. *Journal of Abnormal Psychology, 122,* 542–557.

Powless, D. L., & Elliott, S. N. (1993). Assessment of social skills of Native American preschoolers: Teacher and parent ratings. *Journal of School Psychology, 31,* 293–307.

Powell, G., Mackrain, M., LeBuffe, P., & Lewisville, N. C. (2007). *Devereux early childhood assessment for infants and toddlers technical manual.* Lewisville, NC: Kaplan Early Learning Corporation.

Reynolds, C. R., & Kamphaus, R. W. (2015). *Behavior assessment system for children* (3rd ed.). Bloomington, MN: Pearson.

Rothbart, M. K., & Derryberry, D. (1981). Development of individual differences in temperament. In M. E. Lamb & A. L. Brown (Eds.), *Advances in developmental psychology* (Vol. 1, pp. 37–86). Hillsdale, NJ: Erlbaum.

Smith, J. D., Dishion, T. J., Shaw, D. S., Wilson, M. N., Winter, C. C., & Patterson, G. R. (2014). Coercive family process and early-onset conduct problems from age 2 to school entry. *Developmental Psychopathology, 26,* 917–932.

Squires, J., & Bricker, D. (2007). *An activity-based approach to developing young children's social and emotional competence.* Baltimore, MD: Paul Brookes Publishing.

Squires, J., Bricker, D., Twombly, E., Murphy, K., & Hoselton, R. (2015). *ASQ:SE-2 technical report.* Baltimore, MD: Brookes Publishing.

Squires, J. K., Waddell, M. L., Clifford, J. R., Funk, K., Hoselton, R. M., & Chen, C. I. (2012). A psychometric study of the infant and toddler intervals of the social emotional assessment measure. *Topics in Early Childhood Special Education, 33*(2), 78.

Sroufe, L. A., Schork, E., Motti, F., Lawroski, N., & LaFreniere, P. (1984). The role of affect in social competence. In C. E. Izard, J. Kagan, & R. B. Zajonc (Eds.), *Emotions, cognition, & behavior* (pp. 289–319). Cambridge: Cambridge University Press.

Stone, L. L., Otten, R., Engels, R. C., Vermulst, A. A., & Janssens, J. M. (2010). Psychometric properties of the parent and teacher versions of the strengths and difficulties questionnaire for 4-to 12-year-olds: A review. *Clinical Child and Family Psychology Review, 13*(3), 254–274.

Stone, L. L., van Daal, C., van der Maten, M., Engels, R. C. M. E., Janssens, J. M. A. M., & Otten, R. (2014). The Berkeley puppet interview: A screening instrument for measuring psychopathology in young children. *Child & Youth Care Forum, 43,* 211–225.

Vannest, K., Reynolds, C. R., & Kamphaus, R. (2015). *BASC-3 intervention guide & materials.* Bloomington, MN: Pearson.

Walker, H. M., & Severson, H. (1992). *Systematic screening for behavior disorders.* Longmont, CO: Sopris West.

Walker, H. M., Severson, H. H., & Feil, E. G. (1995). *The early screening project: A proven child find process.* Longmont, CO: Sopris West.

Walker, H. M., Severson, H. H., & Feil, E. G. (2014). *Systematic screening for behavior disorders* (2nd ed.). Eugene, OR: Pacific Northwest Publishing.

Whitcomb, S. A. (2018). *Behavioral, social, and emotional assessment of children and adolescents* (5th ed.). New York: Routledge.

Chapter 9

Adaptive Behavior Assessment of Preschool Children

Patti L. Harrison[1]

Adaptive behavior, or people's ability to take care of themselves and get along with others, is a significant focus for multi-dimensional assessment and intervention for preschool children. This chapter explores characteristics of adaptive behavior and relevance of adaptive behavior assessment for preschool children. Recommendations for preschool adaptive behavior assessment are described, including an overview of major standardized adaptive behavior rating scales and supplemental assessment techniques. The chapter emphasizes uses of adaptive behavior assessment for diagnosis and classification of preschoolers' possible disabilities and developmental problems and for planning effective intervention programs.

Foundations of Adaptive Behavior

Adaptive behavior is everyday competence and comprises people's practical skills to meet daily environmental demands, including those necessary to take care of themselves effectively and independently and to interact with others. Traditionally, the concept of adaptive behavior has focused on personal independence and social responsibility (Horn & Fuchs, 1987). Examples are making a bed, brushing teeth, organizing school assignments, greeting family members, shopping, playing with others, counting items, and a host of other activities needed to function effectively at home and in school and community settings. The American Association on Intellectual and Developmental Disabilities (AAIDD, 2010), the authoritative resource for understanding and measuring the construct of adaptive behavior, provided the following definition: "Adaptive behavior is the collection of conceptual, social, and practical skills that have been learned and are performed by people in their everyday lives" (p. 43).

Adaptive behavior is related to life functioning of children, as well as adults (AAIDD, 2010; Harrison & Oakland, 2015). All people use adaptive skills to function in their everyday lives. People experiencing adaptive behavior deficits have resulting problems in meeting the demands of their environments and have difficulties with important life activities, including peer relationships, addressing personal needs, learning new skills, and other types of general functioning in home, school, and community settings. Importantly, adaptive behavior interventions and supports provided through education and community programs are effective and can improve people's skills to address life needs. This section of the chapter provides information about the construct of adaptive behavior and an overview of the history of adaptive behavior assessment in services for individuals with disabilities.

Primary Dimensions of Adaptive Behavior

Current definitions and measures of adaptive behavior, such as those found in the official manual of the AAIDD (2010) and *Diagnostic and Statistical Manual of Mental Disorders*, 5th edition (DSM-5; American Psychiatric Association [APA], 2013), typically designate three major domains of adaptive behavior: conceptual skills, social skills, and practical skills. Similar dimensions were supported by a number of factor analytic studies (e.g., Reschly, Myers, & Hartel, 2002; Tassé et al., 2012). While not specifically identified as an adaptive behavior domain by the AAIDD, motor skills also are emphasized as a component of adaptive behavior for young children.

Although current definitions emphasize three broad domains of adaptive behavior, previous definitions (e.g., American Association on Mental Retardation [AAMR], 1992, 2002; now AAIDD) also listed 10 more specific adaptive skill areas. The more specific adaptive skill areas listed below assist in understanding the framework for broader domains (Harrison & Oakland, 2003, 2015):

- *Adaptive skill areas in the conceptual domain*: communication (e.g., expressive and receptive language skills); functional academics (e.g., basic reading, writing, math needed for daily functioning); self-direction (e.g., using a schedule, managing time).
- *Adaptive skill areas in the social domain*: social skills (e.g., interacting with others, cooperating, playing); leisure (e.g., playing with toys or games, watching television and videos).
- *Adaptive skill areas in the practical domain*: self-care (e.g., eating, toileting, dressing, hygiene); home living (e.g., clothing care, food preparation, housekeeping); community use (e.g., traveling in the community, using the library); health and safety (e.g., eating only edibles, communicating sickness or injury, following safety rules); work (e.g., job-related skills for older adolescents and adults).

According to the AAIDD (2010), individuals may have coexisting strengths and limitations in adaptive behavior skills. For this reason, the selection of an adaptive behavior instrument, as well as other supplemental methods for assessing adaptive skills, should ensure a comprehensive assessment of each individual child's profile across a number of adaptive skills. Developing an understanding of children's adaptive behavior profiles is critical for determining needs and developing interventions to improve their daily functioning.

Developmental Nature of Adaptive Behavior

Definitions of adaptive behavior emphasize the developmental nature of the construct, and children's skills increase and become more complex as they grow older (Sparrow, Cicchetti, & Saulnier, 2016). The developmental relevance of adaptive skills is related to children's physical maturation and also to the demands and expectations that are encountered in new environments or situations experienced by children (AAIDD, 2010). Children continue to acquire new adaptive skills, or refine and expand existing skills, and their skills become more complex as their social and environmental demands broaden. Thus, adaptive behavior assessment instruments typically include items that address specific skills important across various developmental periods (e.g., preschool, school-age, adolescent, adulthood).

Social, Cultural, and Contextual Components of Adaptive Behavior

Determination of "appropriate" adaptive behavior is typically based on social and cultural expectations about how individuals of certain ages should behave and the types of skills they should demonstrate in a given situation or context (Demchak & Drinkwater, 1998). An emphasis on developing a contextual understanding of children's adaptive behavior provides information about their competence to meet environmental, social, and cultural demands, as well as information about possible support systems and resources within environments that can be utilized in planning and implementation of interventions (Tassé & Craig, 1999). Cultural standards about age-appropriate behavior influence parent and teacher expectations for children's adaptive skills. In addition, children's adaptive behavior is very much influenced by the demands and expectations of the settings (e.g., home, school) in which they are involved.

Performance and Ability

Adaptive behavior is defined as performance of daily activities required for personal and social competence. Although an implicit assumption is that children must have abilities to perform daily activities, assessment of adaptive behavior underscores *observable performance* of activities. The definition of adaptive behavior detailed by the AAIDD (2010) emphasized expression, or performance, of adaptive skills as opposed to acquisition of skills. Sparrow et al. (2016) noted the following: "Factors such as limitations imposed by others or lack of motivation on the part of the individual can result in adequate ability not translating into adequate performance" (p. 10). Harrison and Oakland (2015) distinguished between skill deficits and performance deficits to measure and understand children's adaptive behavior in the best way.

Intelligence and Adaptive Behavior

Research by Keith, Fehrmann, Harrison, and Pottebaum (1987) provided support for the conclusion that intelligence and adaptive behavior are two distinct but related constructs. Professional resources (AAIDD, 2010; American Psychiatric Association, 2013; Harrison, 1990) offered the following rationale: (1) intelligence is conceptualized as a thought process while adaptive behavior emphasizes everyday behavior, (2) intelligence scales measure maximum performance (potential) while adaptive behavior scales measure typical performance, and (3) intelligence scales assume a stability in scores while adaptive behavior scales assume that performance can be modified.

A number of studies have found moderate correlations between scores from intelligence tests and adaptive behavior scales. Manuals for recent adaptive behavior scales, such as the Adaptive Behavior Assessment System, 2nd edition (ABAS-II; Harrison & Oakland, 2003), Adaptive Behavior Assessment System, 3rd edition (ABAS-3; Harrison & Oakland, 2015), and Vineland Adaptive Behavior Scales, 2nd edition (VABS-II; Sparrow, Cicchetti, & Balla, 2005), reported generally moderate correlations between adaptive behavior scales and intelligence test scores. Murray, McKenzie, and Murray (2014) found moderate correlations between intelligence and ABAS-II scores for a sample of referred children, with almost half of the children referred for possible intellectual disability.

Kanne et al. (2011) found that VABS-II scores for children with autism demonstrated moderate correlations with intelligence test scores. However, research suggested that the relationship between adaptive behavior and intelligence is different for children with high-functioning autism, compared to children with low-functioning autism (e.g., Lopata et al., 2013; McDonald et al., 2016). Lower correlations between adaptive behavior and intelligence were found for children with high-functioning autism, suggesting that adaptive behavior is lower than would be predicted for these children with higher intelligence. Lopata and colleagues (2012) found that autism symptoms were better predictors of ABAS-II scores for children with high-functioning autism, compared to using intelligence scores as predictors. Lopata et al. (2012) specifically found that total autism symptoms had significant inverse correlations with total ABAS-II scores and that autism symptoms of restricted and repetitive behaviors had significant inverse correlations with the social and practical composites of the ABAS-II.

Historical Importance in Services for Intellectual and Other Disabilities

Adaptive behavior assessment has its roots in services for individuals with intellectual disabilities. In the 1930s, Dr. Edgar Doll stressed that the primary component of diagnosis and interventions for people with intellectual disabilities should be their social competence, or their ability to take care of themselves and get along with others (Sparrow et al., 2016). Dr. Doll's pioneering work was overshadowed by the development and wide-spread use of intelligence tests, and measured intelligence became almost the sole criterion for diagnosis of intellectual disabilities. However, the American Association on Mental Deficiency (AAMD), which became the AAMR and now is the AAIDD, provided the first recognition of impairments in adaptive behavior, in addition to measured intelligence, for diagnosis of intellectual disability (Heber, 1959). The 11 subsequent editions of the AAMD/AAMR/AAIDD classification manuals, including the latest in 2010, each demonstrated increasing emphasis on adaptive behavior in official definitions of intellectual disabilities.

Legislation and litigation over the last 60 years continued to place importance on adaptive behavior assessment in diagnosis, classification, and interventions for individuals with intellectual disabilities (AAIDD, 2010; Reschly et al., 2002). One reason for the inclusion of adaptive behavior assessment when diagnosing intellectual disabilities in school settings was to ensure that assessments and placements decisions are nonbiased and comprehensive. Several lawsuits beginning in the 1970s and continuing through the 2000s (e.g., Larry P., PASE, Marshall, Lee v. Macon) focused on the use of intelligence test scores as the sole or primary criterion for placing children into special education programs for intellectual disabilities and an inadequate consideration of adaptive behavior assessment results when making classification and placement decisions.

Special education legislation also recognized the importance of adaptive behavior assessment in classification of disabilities and planning interventions. The most recent Individuals with Disabilities Education Improvement Act (IDEIA; 2004) mandated the importance of reducing disproportionate placement and overrepresentation of minority children in special education programs, along with a significant emphasis on implementing early intervention programs for all children, including those in groups that may be overrepresented in disability groups. In addition to requirements that adaptive behavior must be assessed for a classification of intellectual disability, special education legislation confirmed requirements for appropriate assessment practices for all children, with many applicable to adaptive behavior assessment. These assessment practices outlined in IDEIA included using multiple tools and strategies to gather information, obtaining information from parents, integrating tools that assess specific areas of educational need (not only intelligence tests), and using no single procedure as the only criterion for determining that a child has a disability. For preschoolers, special education legislation over the years has recognized adaptive behavior as an integral part of young children's development and indicated that remediation of deficits in adaptive behavior represents an important goal for early intervention programs. Later sections of this chapter outline specific types of disabilities and developmental problems (e.g., intellectual disability, developmental delay, autism) preschool children may have and the role of adaptive behavior assessment in diagnosis and interventions for these children.

Adaptive Behavior Assessment: Techniques for Preschool Assessment

Many assessment instruments and techniques are used to measure preschool children's adaptive behavior strengths and challenges. In this section of the chapter, general recommendations for adaptive behavior assessment are described. Summaries of several comprehensive adaptive behavior scales for use with preschool children are followed by a discussion of supplemental assessment techniques.

General Recommendations for Adaptive Behavior Assessment

Adaptive behavior assessment should be included as an essential component of data-based decision-making within a model of multi-tiered services for preschool children. Characteristics of this model include assessment of multiple domains, assessment from multiple sources, involvement of parents and teachers in the assessment, ecologically valid assessment, and assessment that leads to early intervention (see National Association of School Psychologists [NASP], 2015, for a comprehensive description of a multi-tiered services model for early childhood).

Comprehensive Assessment

Adaptive behavior assessment should be approached using principals of flexible, comprehensive assessment for preschool children (Harrison & Oakland, 2015). Assessment depends on information from multiple sources and settings and consideration of the validity and importance of each type of information. Effective assessment merges multiple assessments across major areas of functioning (e.g., cognitive, academic, behavior, language) and uses multiple assessment methods (e.g., standardized assessments, observations, interviews). Above all, effective assessment avoids relying solely on one test or rating scale alone for decision-making.

Multiple Respondents

Preschool assessment must be ecologically valid, or sample behavior appropriate to various environments (e.g., home, school, community) in which preschool children must function. Third-party adaptive behavior assessment is based on informants' observations of children's activities in their "real world," rather than being based on observations of children in artificial, structured testing situations. Harrison and Oakland (2015) recommended that adaptive behavior assessment should include data from two or more respondents when possible. Use of multiple respondents across multiple environments allows triangulation of information across settings, understanding of children's responses to different environmental demands and expectations, analysis of children's generalization of skills across environments, and consideration of unique perspectives of different respondents.

Parents and teachers are valuable informants to be used in adaptive behavior assessment and should be routinely included in the assessment process for preschool children. Research suggests that correlations between parent and teacher measures of adaptive behavior tend to be moderate to moderately high. Manuals for major adaptive behavior rating scales (e.g., Harrison & Oakland, 2015; Sparrow et al., 2016) reported correlations between parent and teacher scales that fell generally in the .50s and .60s. However, research with samples of children with autism suggested that there may be variation in patterns of teachers' scores being higher than parents' scores, or vice versa. For, example Dickson, Suhrheinrich, Rieth, and Stahmer (2018) found parent scores consistently higher than teacher scores on the VABS-II for children with autism. Jordan et al. (2019) found that teachers' scores were higher than parents' scores on the ABAS-3 General Adaptive Composite and Practical domain for children with autism.

When considering information from parents and teachers on adaptive behavior scales, professionals should carefully evaluate reasons for similarities and differences between parent and teacher ratings and consider multiple factors that may impact ratings, including differences in a child's behavior in response to different contexts, environments, and adult expectations across settings. Informal interviews with significant people in children's environments, including parents and teachers, and direct observations of children, may provide additional information about children and their environments and assist in exploring similarities and differences between informants' ratings on adaptive behavior scales.

Strengths and Limitations of Rating Scales

Standardized, norm-referenced, rating scales are a necessary component of adaptive behavior assessment of young children (Sparrow et al., 2016; Steiner, Goldsmith, Snow, & Chawarska, 2012). They provide age-based comparisons and resulting norm-referenced scores, as required in diagnostic criteria and professional standards. They measure major factors of adaptive behavior (conceptual, social, and practical) found in professional guidelines. They identify target skills for important adaptive skills interventions needed for daily functioning. However, third-party rating scales measuring any type of behavior, performance, or ability, including adaptive behavior, have advantages and limitations that must be understood and addressed during the assessment process.

Among the numerous advantages of rating scales are that they allow for a comprehensive, yet efficient, assessment of a large number of skills and behaviors, in comparison to direct testing or a professional's direct observation of the same skills and behaviors across multiple time periods. Rating scales involve important informants, such as parents and teachers, in the assessment process, and allow them to rate behaviors occurring in natural settings. They provide information from multiple perspectives and multiple sources. Of fundamental importance when assessing adaptive behavior, third-party informant rating scales provide information about what children actually do on a daily basis and how often they do it when needed at home, school, and community settings. Overall, third-party rating scales are considered to be the most valid and practical technique for assessing children's adaptive skills. As noted by the AAIDD (2010), "…significant limitations in adaptive behavior should be established through the use of standardized measures normed on the general population…" (p. 43).

There also are limitations inherent in any type of third-party behavior rating scale, including those measuring adaptive behavior. Although behavior rating scales have limitations, these limitations do not necessarily invalidate results as long as professionals understand the limitations and take them into account when interpreting and using assessments in decision-making. Thus, professionals should consider the following when interpreting behavior rating scales (AAIDD, 2010; Harrison & Oakland, 2015): (a) ratings for individual items reflect a summary of the relative frequency, rather than exact frequency, of children's behaviors; (b) ratings reflect respondents' standards and expectations for behavior, which may differ from respondent to respondent and setting to setting; (c) use of multiple respondents assists in providing information from different perspectives; (d) ratings reflect respondents' perceptions and honesty in communicating these perceptions; and (e) respondents' ratings may be influenced by child characteristics (e.g., appearance, cognitive ability, background) or factors related to respondents themselves, rather than the construct being assessed.

Norm-Referenced Adaptive Behavior Rating Scales

Adaptive Behavior Assessment System, 3rd Edition (ABAS-3)

The ABAS-3 (Harrison & Oakland, 2015) is a comprehensive, norm-referenced measure that retains major features of the ABAS-II (Harrison & Oakland, 2003), with about 78–88% of ABAS-II items updated or retained for the new edition. The ABAS-3 was standardized with large, nationally representative samples. The ABAS-3 consists of five rating forms completed by respondents familiar with individuals' daily functioning and adaptive skills in relevant settings: Parent/Primary Caregiver Form (ages 0–5), Teacher/Daycare Provider Form (ages 2–5), Parent Form (ages 5–21), Teacher Form (ages 5–21), and Adult Form (ages 16–89).

The ABAS-3 provides norm-referenced scores for a General Adaptive Composite and the three domains specified by the AAIDD (2010). In addition, the ABAS-3 provides scores for 10 specific adaptive skill areas within the domains. The three domains and each domain's adaptive skill areas are as follows: *conceptual* domain, with communication, functional academics, and self-direction adaptive skill areas; *social* domain, with leisure and social adaptive skill areas; *practical* domain, with community use, home living, health and safety, self-care, and work (only for older adolescents and adults) adaptive skill areas. In addition, a motor adaptive skill area is included for young children. Items of the ABAS-3 are organized within the adaptive skill areas and domains.

Each item of the ABAS-3 describes an important activity related to adaptive behavior. Respondents are instructed to use a rating of 0 for an item if the child *is not able* to perform the behavior, if the child cannot perform the behavior because they do not have the ability. If the child *is able* to perform the behavior, respondents are instructed to rate the item 1 if the child never (or almost never) performs the behavior when needed; 2 if the child sometimes performs the behavior when needed, or 3 if the child always (or almost always) performs the behavior when needed. Thus, the ABAS-3 item rating system provides a method of identifying skill and performance deficits with its rating system: if the child is not able to perform the activity (rating of 0) and, if the child is able, how often the child does so (ratings of 1, 2, or 3). Respondents also may check a box for "Check only if you guessed" if they estimated an item rating due to lack of knowledge about the child's behavior in the specific area or lack of opportunity to observe performance.

Age-based normative scores for the ABAS-3 General Adaptive Composite and domains include standard scores ($M = 100$, $SD = 15$) with confidence intervals and percentile ranks. Normative scores for adaptive skill areas are scaled scores ($M = 10$, $SD = 3$) and optional test-age equivalents. In addition to norm-referenced scores comparing an individual child's ABAS-3 performance to standardization samples for the same age, the ABAS-3 provides a number of ipsative analyses to compare across a child's own scores and identify a child's relative strengths, weaknesses, patterns, etc. Ipsative comparisons are useful for generating hypotheses, targeting priority intervention goals, and integrating adaptive behavior assessment results with other types of assessment. Two types of ipsative analyses are possible: *statistical significance* of differences between the child's scores in different areas and *base rates* that denote clinical or practical significance, using unusual or rare differences occurring in standardization samples. The ABAS-3 ipsative comparisons include adaptive domain comparisons, scatter in adaptive skill area scaled scores (range between high and low), strengths and weaknesses in adaptive skill areas, and comparisons between parent and teacher rating forms.

Several additional resources are available for the ABAS-3 to enhance its clinical utility. The ABAS-3 Intervention Planner (available in print format or online) details intervention suggestions for individual items. Additional tools include online administration and scoring of rating forms, interpretive reports, parent and teacher reports, and progress monitoring reports.

Vineland Adaptive Behavior Scales, 3rd Edition (VABS-3)

The VABS-3 (Sparrow et al., 2016) is a comprehensive, norm-referenced measure and retains major features of previous VABS editions, with updated items. The VABS-3 was standardized with large, nationally representative samples. The VABS-3 consists of three forms completed by respondents familiar with the individual's functioning and adaptive skills in relevant settings: Interview Form (Ages 0–90); Parent/Caregiver Form (Ages 0–90); and Teacher Form (Ages 3–21). Each of the three forms includes a longer version (Comprehensive) or briefer version (Domain-Level). The Interview Form uses a semi-structured, clinical interview format, and the Parent and Teacher Forms are rating forms.

The VABS-3 provides norm-referenced scores for an Adaptive Behavior Composite and three domains. In addition, it provides scores for three specific subdomains within each domain. The three domains and each one's subdomains are as follows: *communication* domain, with receptive, expressive, and written subdomains; *daily living skills* domain, with personal, domestic/numeric, and community/school community subdomains; and *socialization* domain, with interpersonal relationships, play and leisure, and coping subdomains. In addition, the VABS-3 includes two optional domains: *motor skills* domain (ages 0–9 years, with gross motor and fine motor subdomains) and *maladaptive behavior* domain (ages 3 and older, with internalizing, externalizing, and critical items subdomains). The VABS-3 items are organized within the domains and sub-domains.

Each item of the VABS-3 describes an important activity related to children's typical performance of adaptive behavior activities. Respondents are instructed to rate each item based on how often the child performs the activity as needed: Rating of 2 = Usually; Rating of 1 = Sometimes; or Rating of 0 = Never. Respondents also may check if they estimated an item rating due to lack of knowledge about the child's behavior in the specific area or lack of opportunity to observe performance.

Age-based normative scores for the VABS-3 Adaptive Behavior Composite and domains include standard scores ($M = 100$, $SD = 15$) with confidence intervals and percentile ranks. Normative scores for subdomains are v-scale scores ($M = 15$, $SD = 3$) and age equivalents/Growth Scale Values. Similar to the ABAS-3, the VABS-3 provides a number of ipsative analyses to compare across the child's own scores, identify relative strengths, weaknesses, and patterns; generate hypotheses; and target intervention goals. Two types of ipsative analyses, statistical significance and base rates, are included. The VABS-3 ipsative comparisons include strengths and weaknesses in domains, domain pair-wise comparisons, strengths and weaknesses in subdomains, and subdomain pair-wise comparisons.

The additional VABS-3 tools are online administration and scoring of rating forms, interpretive reports, multi-rater reports, and item-level information for comparisons between raters and for progress monitoring.

Other Adaptive Behavior Scales

A number of other adaptive behavior scales are available for use for preschool assessment. For example, the Scales of Independent Behavior—Revised (SIB-R; Bruininks, Woodcock, Weatherman, & Hill, 1996), for individuals ranging in age from infants through 80 years of age, consists of four adaptive behavior skill clusters (motor skills, social interaction and communication skills, personal living skills, and community living skills) and several subscales within these clusters. The Adaptive Behavior Diagnostic Scale (ABDS; Pearson, Patton, & Mruzek, 2016), for individuals 2 through 21 years of age, consists of three adaptive behavior domains (conceptual, social, and practical) and adaptive skill areas within the domains. The Adaptive Behavior Evaluation Scale, 3rd ed. (ABES-3; McCarney & House, 2017), for children 4 through 12 years of age, consists of three adaptive behavior domains (conceptual, social, and practical) and several adaptive skill areas within these domains. The Diagnostic Adaptive Behavior Scale (DABS; Tassé et al., 2017) is published by the AAIDD and is used for individuals ages 4–31 years; it measures the three domains of conceptual, social, and practical adaptive behavior and also includes items measuring naiveté, gullibility, and technology-based skills. See Floyd et al. (2015) for an excellent review and comprehensive evaluation of psychometric properties for 14 informant-based adaptive behavior scales used with preschool, school-age, and adolescent children.

Supplemental Techniques for Adaptive Behavior Assessment

As noted above, adaptive behavior assessment should include a comprehensive, norm-referenced measure of adaptive behavior. Additional observations, interviewing, and other techniques can supplement and expand the information obtained from standardized adaptive behavior scales (Harrison & Oakland, 2015; see also chapters in Oakland & Harrison, 2008). Supplemental methods of assessing adaptive behavior of preschool children can contribute to an understanding of respondents' ratings on standardized instruments, analyze children's specific adaptive skill strengths and limitations, and assist in decision-making and planning interventions.

Direct, naturalistic observations of children's adaptive behavior present opportunities for assessing behaviors in a variety of settings and situations. Although direct observations will not be possible for the wide range and large number of adaptive skills measured with third-party rating scales, they will allow professionals to investigate specific skills, including those identified as areas of difficulty on a rating scale. Direct observations allow professionals to see, firsthand, children's responses to the situational demands in their environments.

Interviews with respondents also present a means of informal discussion of issues related to adaptive behavior. Parent and teacher interviews may suggest possible areas of strength and limitation in children's adaptive behavior profiles that should be thoroughly investigated. Interviews may also provide some insight into environmental factors or parenting and teaching styles and expectations that may impact adaptive behavior.

Supplements to standardized adaptive behavior rating scales may include specific assessments of other types of related behaviors (e.g., social skills, internalizing/externalizing behavior, occupational behavior). These assessments assist professionals with exploring hypotheses, identifying impacts of adaptive skill deficits on related areas of behavior, and integrating adaptive behavior assessment results with assessments of other developmental areas. However, these other types of behavioral measures must not be used as substitutes for a comprehensive standardized adaptive behavior assessment because they generally do not measure the construct and domains of adaptive behavior (e.g., conceptual, social, practical) defined by widely-accepted professional standards (e.g., AAIDD, 2010; American Psychiatric Association, 2013). Frick, Barry, and Kamphaus (2010) emphasized, "Therefore, the assessment of adaptive behavior offered on scales such as the BASC-2 or Achenbach cannot be considered substitutes for more detailed evaluations such as through the Vineland-2 or ABAS-II" (p. 335).

Uses of Adaptive Behavior Assessment

Information obtained from adaptive behavior assessment is used for diagnosis and classification, placement decisions in special education programs and other agencies, intervention planning, and determining needed supports in the environment. For preschool children, a major function of adaptive behavior assessment is to provide information that leads to decisions about the nature, diagnosis, and classification of disabilities. A second and equally important use of adaptive behavior assessment is to acquire information that will assist in the determination of needed supports and development of appropriate interventions for young children with disabilities and other problems. Diagnosis and interventions are the focus of the following sections of the chapter; research to support these uses is summarized.

Diagnosis/Classification

Historically, as well as in current guidelines, adaptive behavior assessment has been used to diagnose and classify individuals with intellectual disabilities. Adaptive behavior assessment also has become a standard component of assessment and diagnosis for developmental delay and autism, two disabilities of particular importance in the early childhood period. In addition, adaptive skills are vital for all children, and comprehensive assessment of adaptive behavior is recommended for many types of disabilities and developmental problems that young children can experience.

The importance of adaptive behavior assessment for preschool children was confirmed in a large, extensive national study by Markowitz et al. (2006). The researchers investigated a number of developmental skills of 2,000 preschool and kindergarten students with disabilities, including self-care and self-direction adaptive skills as rated by teachers on the ABAS-II. For self-care adaptive skills, the studies found that young children with orthopedic impairments and autism demonstrated deficits greater than one standard deviation below the mean. Children with developmental delays and low incidence disabilities scored almost one standard deviation below the mean, on average, and children with autism scored significantly lower than children with developmental delays. Teacher ratings of the self-direction adaptive skill area on the ABAS-II rated children with autism at one standard deviation below the mean on average, and significantly lower than children in other disability groups.

Intellectual Disability

Adaptive behavior assessment is a required component of classification of intellectual disability in three separate systems in the United States: AAIDD (2010), DSM-5 (APA, 2013), and IDEIA (2004). IDEIA also impacts state education agency standards for special education. According to AAIDD (2010): "Intellectual disability is characterized by significant limitations in intellectual functioning and in adaptive behavior as expressed in conceptual, social, and practical adaptive skills. This disability originates before age 18" (p. 1). A comparable definition of intellectual disability is found in DSM-5 (APA, 2013). The IDEIA (2004) definition requires deficits in intelligence and adaptive behavior for a classification of intellectual disability, although it does not specify the conceptual, social, and practical domains of adaptive behavior. Thus, adaptive behavior assessment is a required component for diagnosis of intellectual disability across numerous professional and legal definitions.

The AAIDD (2010) provided specific criteria for a deficit in adaptive behavior: "…approximately two standard deviations below the mean of either (a) one of the following three types of adaptive behavior: conceptual, social, or practical or (b) an overall score on a standardized measure of conceptual, social, and practical skills" (p. 27). The DSM-5 (APA, 2013) does not include a specific score cut-off; the criterion is

...when at least one domain of adaptive functioning—conceptual, social, or practical—is sufficiently impaired that ongoing support is needed in order for the person to perform adequately in one or more life settings at school, at work, at home, or in the community.

(p. 38)

The DSM-5 (APA, 2013) also defines severity levels of intellectual disability in terms of adaptive behavior: "The various levels of severity are defined on the basis of adaptive functioning, and not IQ scores, because it is adaptive functioning that determines the level of supports required" (p. 33).

Federal regulations for IDEIA (2004) do not provide specific criteria for adaptive behavior deficits to be used in diagnosis of intellectual disability. A number of state special education regulations are more specific, but there is a great deal of variation from state to state. McNicholas et al. (2018) reviewed state special education regulations for a classification of intellectual disability. They found that 65% of states had no adaptive behavior score cut-off and 51% had no reference to a specific type of score.

Research supports that individuals with intellectual disabilities demon-strate deficits in adaptive behavior. Manuals for major adaptive behavior scales (e.g., Harrison & Oakland, 2003, 2015; Sparrow et al., 2005, 2016) provided results for samples of individuals with intellectual disabilities and reported average adaptive behavior scores that were consistently lower than two standard deviations below the mean and that distinguished between individuals with different severity levels of intellectual disability. Papazoglou, Jacobson, and Zabel (2013) investigated ABAS-II scores for children referred for neuropsychological assessment; they found that low adaptive behavior was most evident for three of the four clinical clusters (Low IQ/ Executive Function, Borderline IQ/Executive Function/Externalizing, and Executive Function/Internalizing cluster), but not for the Within Normal Limits cluster.

Developmental Delay

Under the provisions of IDEIA (2004) Part C, states provide early interven-tion services for infants and toddlers experiencing developmental delays. States also have the option to provide special education services under IDEIA Part B for children ages 3–9 years with developmental delays. Although states define the criteria used to determine a developmental delay, IDEIA (2004) specified that a developmental delay is identified in one or more of the following areas: physical development, cognitive development, communication development, social or emotional development, or adaptive development. Thus, adaptive behavior is an area of development considered in the diagnosis of a developmental delay. Adaptive behavior assessment often provides information about physical, communication, and social or emotional development, as well.

Research supports the validity of adaptive behavior scales in identifying developmental delays. The ABAS-II manual (Harrison & Oakland, 2003) and VABS-3 manual (Sparrow et al., 2016) presented findings that samples of children with developmental delays had average adaptive behavior scores greater than one standard deviation below the mean but higher scores than samples with intellectual disabilities. Milne and McDonald (2015) investigated ABAS-II and VABS-II scores for preschoolers referred for developmental delay; although VABS-II scores were significantly higher than ABAS-II scores, 87% of the sample had scores of two standard deviations below the mean or more on one or more domains on either instrument.

Autism

Adaptive behavior assessment is increasingly considered to be a necessary component of assessment for children with autism. Results from adaptive behavior instruments are used for diagnosis, identification of strengths and weaknesses, and intervention planning for children with autism. Steiner et al. (2012) noted the following: "When evaluating children for ASD [autism], it is important to consider adaptive functioning, which reflects the child's capacity for personal and social self-sufficiency in real-life situations" (p. 1191).

Autism is defined in DSM-5 (APA, 2013) and IDEIA (2004). DSM-5's autism criteria included persistent deficits in social communication and social interaction across multiple contexts and restricted, repetitive patterns of behavior, interests, or activities that are present in early childhood and that limit and impair everyday functioning. IDEIA (2004) described autism as deficits in verbal and nonverbal communication and social interaction, with other associated characteristics including repetitive activities, stereotyped movements, resistance to change in environment or daily routines, and unusual responses to sensory experiences.

Research related to adaptive behavior of children with autism has become more extensive in recent years and supports the importance of assessing adaptive behavior. Manuals for adaptive behavior scales (e.g., Harrison & Oakland, 2003, 2015; Sparrow et al., 2005, 2016) presented research results with samples of children with autism; adaptive behavior deficits are apparent, with lowest scores typically in social and/or communication domains. Additional studies documented similar findings. For example, Kanne et al. (2011) reported deficits in VABS-II scores for children with autism, with lowest scores in socialization.

A number of studies reported low adaptive behavior scores for children with high-functioning and children with low-functioning autism. McDonald et al. (2016), found that both groups demonstrated deficits on the ABAS-II, although lower scores were found for children with low-functioning autism. For children with low-functioning autism, the lowest scores were in the ABAS-II *practical* domain, compared to lowest scores in the *social* domain for children with high-functioning autism. Lopata et al. (2012) found deficits in all ABAS-II scores for school-age children with high-functioning autism, with the greatest weaknesses in social, home living, and self-direction skill areas and strengths in academics and community use skills areas. Lopata et al. (2013) compared VABS-II and ABAS-II scores for school-age children with high-functioning autism; VABS-II scores were significantly higher than ABAS-II scores, except in social skills. As noted earlier in the chapter, adaptive behavior scores of children with high-functioning autism were generally found to be lower than would be predicted from the children's cognitive abilities (Lopata et al., 2012, 2013; McDonald et al., 2016).

Adaptive Behavior Assessment for Other Preschool Children

Adaptive behavior assessment should also be used for the identification of disabilities or problems other than intellectual disabilities, developmental delays, or autism because it is reasonable to expect that many disabilities and developmental problems will result in limitations in personal and social functioning. Adaptive behavior should be assessed routinely for preschool children who have challenges that may interfere with daily functioning, as part of comprehensive assessments for evaluating strengths and limitations, for diagnosis and classification, and/or for identifying needs for services and supports. Research reviewed by Harrison (1990) 30 years ago suggested that individuals with learning disabilities, emotional disturbances, and sensory impairments experience deficits in adaptive behavior areas. Furthermore, chapters in Oakland and Harrison (2008) continued to stress that children with any type of disability benefit from interventions in specific adaptive skill areas.

Although not as extensive as research investigating children with intellectual disabilities, developmental delay, or autism, a host of studies have supported the need for adaptive behavior assessment for children with other disabilities or challenges. Manuals for major assessment instruments (e.g., Harrison & Oakland, 2003, 2015; Sparrow et al., 2005, 2016) summarized validity studies for samples of individuals with attention deficits and reported lower scores than control groups in a number of adaptive skills areas, with lowest scores found in self-direction, communication, and social skills. Manuals also reported adaptive behavior deficits for samples of children with emotional or behavior disorders, with lowest scores in self-direction and socialization. Papazoglou et al. (2013) investigated ABAS-II scores of children referred for neuropsychological assessment and found that low adaptive behavior was evident for children with either externalizing or internalizing problem behaviors, as well as those with lower intelligence.

Manuals for the ABAS-II and VABS-II (e.g., Harrison & Oakland, 2003; Sparrow et al., 2005) reported that samples of children with learning disabilities had greatest deficits in adaptive skill areas for communication, functional academics, and self-direction.

Several studies investigated adaptive behavior of children with physical, health, and sensory disorders. Development of the VABS-II and VABS-3 (Sparrow et al., 2005, 2016) included studies of children with visual impairments and children with hearing impairments and found adaptive behavior deficits relevant for planning interventions for these children. Validity studies reported in the ABAS-II manual (Harrison & Oakland, 2003) reported adaptive behavior deficits for samples with children with biological risk factors (low birth weight, fetal alcohol syndrome, etc.) and motor and physical impairments.

Several studies have investigated adaptive behavior deficits associated with children's health problems. Abend et al. (2015) found that electrographic seizures and electrographic status epilepticus were associated with adaptive behavior (ABAS-II) deficits. Anderson et al. (2013) investigated children 6 months after a traumatic brain injury and found moderate-severe brain injuries were associated with ABAS-II deficits more so than mild brain injuries. Lo et al. (2014) found that a measure of neurological impairment after children experienced a stroke predicted lower outcomes in adaptive behavior on the ABAS-II.

Intervention Planning

Links between assessment, intervention, and supports are critical for effective services for preschool children with disabilities, developmental challenges, and other problems. The major objectives of assessment, intervention, and supports for young children are to identify strengths and weakness in functional daily living skills and implement interventions and supports for improvement. Adaptive behavior assessment can be directly integrated with interventions for preschool children, and interventions targeting specific areas can result in increases in adaptive behavior of children. AAIDD (2010) and DSM-5 (APA, 2013) stressed the importance of designing and implementing interventions for increasing adaptive skills and emphasize that adaptive functioning determines the level of supports needed during intervention. As noted by the NASP (2015), early childhood interventions should "incorporate appropriate learning goals for all children with a focus on functional skills that increase children's participation in their daily environments" (p. 3).

Ecological validity is a fundamental factor for effective interventions. Thus, interventions must focus on skills that young children need during daily routines that occur naturally in home, school, community, and other environments and that allow them to become increasingly independent in these environments. Effective interventions also include consideration of demands from children's current environments to assist with transition to new environments, including to different school settings or less restrictive or more inclusive environments, and prioritizing intervention targets (AAMR 2002). Thus, professionals should identify skills needed by children to function now, skills needed to function in the target environment, and skills preferred by the child. Higher-priority skills for interventions may include those critical in domestic, personal, leisure, community, and vocational domains; those critical to the child's health and safety; those highly preferred by children, parents, and teachers; those leading to increased independence; and those contributing to the child's satisfaction and acceptance by others.

Harrison and Oakland (2015) outlined general steps for planning adaptive behavior interventions: (1) identify skills that the child needs for the current environment or, as applicable, transition into a new environment; (2) identify the child's adaptive behavior strengths and weaknesses relative to environmental requirements; (3) identify and prioritize intervention objectives for the child; (4) implement interventions; and (5) monitor implementation and progress. Armstrong (2015) recommended that continuous assessment of progress be incorporated into interventions by systematically measuring progress for specific goals for the child, guided by the following key questions: Is the intervention working? Is the child gaining skills? Are additional or new interventions needed by the child? What skill should be the next target?

Studies have supported improvement in children's adaptive skills as a result of different types of systematic interventions. For example, Woodman, Demers, Crossman, Warfield, and Hauser-Cram (2018) completed a longitudinal study with children with Down syndrome, motor impairment, or developmental delay and found that more hours of early intervention services were associated with greater improvement in adaptive behavior. Ahn and Hwang (2018) conducted a meta-analysis of cognitive interventions for children with neurodevelopmental disorders (e.g., intellectual disability, autism, ADHD), and found significant, moderate effect sizes for improvements in adaptive behavior.

Much intervention research has focused on children with autism. A meta-analysis of early intensive behavioral interventions for children with autism by Reichow (2012) found that interventions were associated with adaptive behavior gains. Ventola et al. (2014) investigated outcomes of the technique of behavioral treatment of pivotal response for preschool children with autism and found substantial gains in adaptive behavior. However, interventions for children with autism may be more effective for some adaptive behavior skills than for others. Eldevik, Hastings, Jahr, and Hughes (2012) found that young children with autism who received early intensive behavioral intervention had significant communication and socialization adaptive behavior gains but not gains in daily living skills. Similarly, Makrygianni, Gena, Katoudi, and Galanis (2018) performed a meta-analysis of applied behavioral analytic interventions for children with autism and found that the interventions were moderately effective in improving socialization adaptive behavior but not daily living skills.

Conclusion

Adaptive behavior assessment is a key component of a comprehensive data-based decision-making framework for assessment of preschool children with many types of difficulties, disabilities, disorders, and challenges. Adaptive behavior assessment can provide valuable contributions to diagnoses for preschool children, including those with disabilities such as intellectual disabilities, developmental delay, and autism. Most importantly, adaptive behavior assessment is a foundation for interventions and services to promote daily living skills and improve life functioning for preschool children.

Note

1 Author Note: As required by professional ethics codes of the NASP and other organizations, Patti Harrison discloses that she has financial interests (royalties) for several publications that are referenced in the current chapter and that she coauthored or coedited, including editions of the *Adaptive Behavior Assessment System* (ABAS; Harrison & Oakland, 2003, 2015) and the text *ABAS-II: Clinical Use and Interpretation* (Oakland & Harrison, 2008).

References

Abend, N. S., Wagenman, K. L., Blake, T. P., Schultheis, M. T., Radcliffe, J., Berg, R. A., ... Dlugos, D. J. (2015). Electrographic status epilepticus and neurobehavioral outcomes in critically ill children. *Epilepsy & Behavior, 49,* 238–244. doi:10.1016/j.yebeh.2015.03.013

Ahn, S., & Hwang, S. (2018). Cognitive rehabilitation of adaptive behavior in children with neurodevelopmental disorders: A meta-analysis. *Occupational Therapy International, Article ID 5029571,* 7 pages. doi:10.1155/2018/5029571

American Association on Intellectual and Developmental Disabilities. (2010). *Intellectual disability definition, classification, and systems of supports* (11th ed.). Washington, DC: Author.

American Association on Mental Retardation. (1992). *Definitions, classifications, and systems of supports* (9th ed.). Washington, DC: Author.

American Association on Mental Retardation. (2002). *Mental retardation: Definition, classification, and systems of supports* (10th ed.). Washington, DC: Author.

American Psychiatric Association. (2013). *Diagnostic and statistical manual of mental disorders* (5th ed.). Washington, DC: Author.

Anderson, V., Beauchamp, M. H., Yeates, K. O., Crossley, L., Hearps, S. J. C., & Catroppa, C. (2013). Social competence at 6 months following childhood traumatic brain injury. *Journal of the International Neuropsychological Society, 19,* 539–550. doi:10.1017/S1355617712001543

Armstrong, K. A. (2015, February). The ABAS-3 and young children with developmental issues. In T. Oakland & P. Harrison (chairs), *Evidence-based ABAS-3 assessment for disabilities and developmental problems*. Symposium presented at the annual meeting of the National Association of School Psychologists, Orlando, FL.

Bruininks, R. H., Woodcock, R. W., Weatherman, R. F., & Hill, B. K. (1996). *Scales of independent behavior, revised*. Chicago, IL: Riverside.

Demchak, M. A., & Drinkwater, S. (1998). Assessing adaptive behavior. In B. Vance (Ed.), *Psychological assessment of children: Best practices for school and clinical settings* (2nd ed., pp. 297–319). New York: Wiley.

Dickson, K. S., Suhrheinrich, J., Rieth, S. R., & Stahmer, A. C. (2018). Parent and teacher concordance of child outcomes for youth with autism spectrum disorder. *Journal of Autism and Developmental Disorders, 48*, 1423–1435. doi:10.1007/s10803-017-3382-z

Eldevik, S., Hastings, R. P., Jahr, E., & Hughes, J. C. (2012). Outcomes of behavioral intervention for children with autism in mainstream pre-school settings. *Journal of Autism and Developmental Disorders, 42*, 210–220. doi:10.1007/s10803-011-1234-9

Floyd, R. G., Shands, E. I., Alfonso, V. C., Phillips, J., Autry, B. K., Mosteller, J. A., … Irby, S. M. (2015). A systematic review and psychometric evaluation of adaptive behavior scales and recommendations for practice. *Journal of Applied School Psychology, 31*, 83–113.

Frick, P. J., Barry, C. T., & Kamphaus, R. W. (2010). *Clinical assessment of child and adolescent personality and behavior* (3rd ed.). New York: Springer.

Harrison, P. L. (1990). Mental retardation, adaptive behavior assessment, and giftedness. In A. S. Kaufman (Ed.), *Assessing adolescent and adult intelligence* (pp. 533–585). Boston: Allyn & Bacon.

Harrison, P. L., & Oakland, T. (2003). *Adaptive behavior assessment system and manual* (2nd ed.). Torrance, CA: Western Psychological Services.

Harrison, P. L., & Oakland, T. (2015). *Adaptive behavior assessment system, manual, and intervention planner* (3rd ed.). Torrance, CA: Western Psychological Services.

Heber, R. F. (1959). A manual on terminology and classification in mental retardation. Monograph supplement. *American Journal of Mental Deficiency, 64*, 1–111.

Horn, E., & Fuchs, D. (1987). Using adaptive behavior assessment and intervention: An overview. *Journal of Special Education, 21*, 11–26.

Individuals with Disabilities Education Improvement Act of 2004, Pub. L. No. 108-446, § 2, 40 Stat. 118 (2004). Individuals with Disabilities Act of 2006, Final Regulations, 34 C.F.R. Pt. 300 and 301, Assistance to States for the Education of Children with Disabilities and Preschool Grants for Children with Disabilities. (Fed. Reg. 71, 2006).

Jordan, A. K., Thomeer, M. L., Lopata, C., Donnelly, J. P., Rodgers, J. D., & McDonald, C. A. (2019). Informant discrepancies in the assessment of adaptive behavior of children with autism spectrum disorder. *Journal of Autism and Developmental Disorders*, doi:10.1007/s10803-018-03876-z

Kanne, S. M., Gerber, A. J., Quirmbach, L. M., Sparrow, S. S., Cicchetti, D. V., & Saulnier, C. A. (2011). The role of adaptive behavior in autism spectrum disorders: Implications for functional outcome. *Journal of Autism and Developmental Disorders, 41*, 1007–1018. doi:10.1007/s10803-010-1126-4

Keith, T. Z., Fehrmann, P. G., Harrison, P. L., & Pottebaum, S. M. (1987). The relationship between adaptive behavior and intelligence: Testing alternative explanations. *Journal of School Psychology*, *25*, 31–43. doi:10.1016/0022-4405(87) 90058-6

Lo, W., Gordon, A. L., Hajek, C., Gomes, A., Greenham, M., Anderson, V., ... Mackay, M. T. (2014). Pediatric stroke outcome measure: Predictor of multiple impairments in childhood stroke. *Journal of Child Neurology*, *29*, 1524–1530. doi:10.1177/0883073813503186

Lopata, C. L., Fox, J. D., Thomeer, M. L., Smith, R. A., Volker, M. A., Kessel, C. M., ... Lee, G. K. (2012). ABAS-II ratings and correlates of adaptive behavior in children with HFASDs. *Journal of Developmental & Physical Disabilities*, *24*, 391–402. doi:10.1007/s10882-012-9277-1

Lopata, C. L., Smith, R. A., Volker, M. A., Thomeer, M. L., Lee, G. K., & McDonald, C. A. (2013). Comparison of adaptive behavior measures for children with HFASDs. *Autism Research and Treatment*, Article ID 415989, 10 pages. 10.1155/2013/415989

Makrygianni, M. K., Gena, A., Katoudi, S., & Galanis, P. (2018). The effectiveness of applied behavior analytic interventions for children with Autism Spectrum Disorder: A meta-analytic study. *Research in Autism Spectrum Disorders*, *51*, 18–31. doi:10.1016/j.rasd.2018.03.006

Markowitz, J., Carlson, E., Frey, W., Riley, J., Shimshak, A., Heinzen, H., ... Klein, S. (2006). *Preschoolers' characteristics, services, and results: Wave 1 overview report from the Pre-Elementary Education Longitudinal Study (PEELS)*. Rockville, MD: Westat.

McCarney, S. B., & House, S. N. (2017). *Adaptive behavior evaluation scale-third edition*. Columbia, MO: Hawthorne Educational Services.

McDonald, C. A., Lopata, C. L., Nasca, B. C., Donnelly, J. P., Thomeer, M. L., & Rodgers, J. D. (2016). ABAS-II adaptive profiles and correlates in samples of children with HFASD or LFASD. *Journal of Developmental & Physical Disabilities*, *28*, 769–783. doi:10.1007/s10882-016-9508-y

McNicholas, P. J., Floyd, R. J., Woods, I. L., Singh, L. J., Manguno, M. S., & Maki, K. E. (2018). State special education criteria for identifying intellectual disability: A review following revised diagnostic criteria and Rosa's law. *School Psychology Quarterly*, *33*, 75–82. doi:10.1037/spq0000208

Milne, S., & McDonald, J. (2015). Assessing adaptive functioning in preschoolers referred for diagnosis of developmental disabilities. *Infants & Young Children*, *28*, 248–261. doi:10.1097/IYC.0000000000000037

Murray, A., McKenzie, K., & Murray, G. (2014). To what extent does *g* impact on conceptual, practical and social adaptive functioning in clinically referred children?. *Journal of Intellectual Disability Research*, *58*, 777–785. doi:10.1111/jir.12092

National Association of School Psychologists. 2015. *Early childhood services: Promoting positive outcomes for young children*. Bethesda, MD: Author. Position statement www.nasponline.org/research-and-policy/professional-positions/position-statements

Oakland, T., & Harrison, P. (Eds.). (2008). *ABAS-II: Clinical use and interpretation*. San Diego, CA: Academic Press.

Papazoglou, A., Jacobson, L. A., & Zabel, T. A. (2013). More than intelligence: Distinct cognitive/behavioral clusters linked to adaptive dysfunction in children. *Journal of the International Neuropsychological Society*, *19*, 189–197. doi:10.1017/S1355617712001191

Pearson, N. A., Patton, J. R., & Mruzek, D. W. (2016). *Adaptive behavior diagnostic scale*. Austin, TX: Pro-Ed.

Reichow, B. (2012). overview of meta-analyses on early intensive behavioral intervention for young children with autism spectrum disorders. *Journal of Autism and Developmental Disorders, 42,* 512–520. doi:10.1007/s10803-011-1218-9

Reschly, D. J., Myers, T. G., & Hartel, C. R. (Eds.). (2002). *Disability determination for mental retardation*. Washington, DC: National Academy Press.

Sparrow, S. S., Cicchetti, D. V., & Balla, D. A. (2005). *Vineland adaptive behavior scales and manual* (2nd ed.). Bloomington, MN: Pearson.

Sparrow, S. S., Cicchetti, D. V., & Saulnier, C. A. (2016). *Vineland adaptive behavior scales and manual* (3rd ed.). Bloomington, MN: Pearson.

Steiner, A. M., Goldsmith, T. R., Snow, A. V., & Chawarska, K. (2012). Practitioner's guide to assessment of autism spectrum disorders in infants and toddlers. *Journal of Autism and Developmental Disorders, 42,* 1183–1196. doi:10.1007/s10803-011-1376-9

Tassé, M. J., & Craig, E. M. (1999). Critical issues in the cross-cultural assessment of adaptive behavior. In R. L. Schalock (Ed.), *Adaptive behavior and its measurement* (pp. 161–183). Washington, DC: American Association on Mental Retardation.

Tassé, M. J., Schalock, R. L., Balboni, G., Bersani, H., Borthwick-Duffy, S. A., Spreat, S., … Zhang, D. (2012). The construct of adaptive behavior: Its conceptualization, measurement, and use in the field of intellectual disability. *American Journal on Intellectual and Developmental Disabilities, 117,* 291–303. doi:10.1352/1944-7558-117.4.291

Tassé, M. J., Schalock, R. L., Balboni, G., Bersani, H., Borthwick-Duffy, S. A., Spreat, S., … Zhang, D. (2017). *Diagnostic adaptive behavior scale*. Silver Spring, MD: American Association on Intellectual and Developmental Disorders.

Ventola, P., Friedman, H. E., Anderson, L. C., Wolf, J. M., Oosting, D., Foss-Feig, J., … Pelphrey, K. A. (2014). Improvements in social and adaptive functioning following short-duration PRT program: A clinical replication. *Journal of Autism and Developmental Disorders, 44,* 2862–2870. doi:10.1007/s10803-014-2145-3

Woodman, A. C., Demers, L., Crossman, M. K., Warfield, M. E., & Hauser-Cram, P. (2018). Part C early intervention dosage and growth in adaptive skills from early childhood through adolescence. *Early Childhood Research Quarterly, 43,* 73–82. doi:10.1016/j.ecresq.2018.01.007

Chapter 10

Cognitive Assessment of Preschool Children

A Pragmatic Review of Theoretical, Quantitative, and Qualitative Characteristics

Joseph R. Engler and Vincent C. Alfonso

Introduction

The passage of the Individuals with Disabilities Education Improvement Act (IDEIA) of 2004 requires schools to provide a free and appropriate public education to individuals birth to 21 years. This law, paired with the increase in the prevalence of developmental disorders such as autism spectrum disorders (American Psychiatric Association, 2013), along with the growing importance of early intervention (see Ramey & Ramey, 2004), has placed a necessary emphasis on preschool assessment (Alfonso, Engler, & Lapore, 2020; Alfonso & Flanagan, 2009). Preschool assessment involves working with an age group (i.e., 2:6 to 5:6 years) that is developmentally different than those of school-aged children and adults and should be treated differently (Alfonso, Ruby, Wissel, & Davari, 2020). As such, the conceptual framework utilized for interpreting preschool cognitive tests may differ from those used for adolescents and adults (see Flanagan, Mascolo, & Genshaft, 2004). Within the framework, Flanagan and colleagues described the importance of having expertise regarding the theoretical underpinnings of a test as well as a thorough understanding of the quantitative and qualitative characteristics of the test. Taken together, these considerations may help practitioners be better suited to use preschool cognitive tests more intelligently (Alfonso & Flanagan, 1999, 2009; Bracken, 1994).

This chapter begins with a review of the Cattell-Horn-Carroll Theory of Cognitive Abilities (CHC Theory) as a model for preschool cognitive test development and interpretation (see Schneider & McGrew, 2018 for the most updated information on CHC Theory). Then we highlight some of the most salient quantitative and qualitative characteristics that are necessary to evaluate preschool cognitive tests comprehensively. Finally, we review the theoretical, quantitative, and qualitative characteristics of five commonly used cognitive tests for preschool-aged children. Those cognitive tests are: the *Woodcock-Johnson IV Tests of Cognitive Abilities* (WJ IV COG; Schrank, McGrew & Mather, 2014), the *Wechsler Preschool and Primary Scale of*

Intelligence – Fourth Edition (WPPSI-IV; Wechsler, 2012a), the *Differential Ability Scales – Second Edition* (DAS-II; Elliott, 2007a), the *Stanford-Binet Intelligence Scales – Fifth Edition* (SB5; Roid, 2003a), and the *Kaufman Assessment Battery for Children – Second Edition: Normative Update* (KABC-II:NU; Kaufman & Kaufman, 2018b). These cognitive tests were selected because they measure cognitive abilities of children ages 2:6 to 5:6 years. Due to space limitations, we do not provide a rationale for or explain every rating; rather, we provide our overall review of each test, a summary, and recommendations for the future of cognitive assessment of preschool children.

Theoretical Underpinnings

The CHC Theory is perhaps the most well-established and validated theory of cognitive abilities and processes to date (Schneider & McGrew, 2018). Moreover, Lockwood and Farmer (2020) found that approximately 93% of university faculty surveyed currently teach CHC as an interpretive framework in cognitive assessment courses. Therefore, practitioners are now entering the field with a deeper knowledge of CHC Theory. This theory is a three-stratum hierarchical model that includes g or general cognitive ability, broad abilities, and narrow abilities to describe cognitive functioning. Stratum one includes narrow abilities or abilities presumed to be measured by task-specific demands on individual subtests. Currently, there are 90+ narrow abilities that have been identified by theorists and researchers. Stratum two is comprised of broad abilities that represent a cognitive construct that is a result of highly correlated narrow abilities. There are approximately 17 broad abilities identified within CHC Theory. Stratum three is general intelligence or g. Moreover, stratum three represents an individual's overall cognitive capacity. For an in-depth discussion of CHC Theory, interested readers are encouraged to see Schneider and McGrew (2018) for more information.

As CHC Theory has evolved, test developers and publishers have systematically included it in the blueprint for and in the construction of cognitive tests. Even the venerable Wechsler Scales, largely a-theoretical, have been revised to include more CHC abilities and processes that can be used to aid with test interpretation and intervention planning (Flanagan & Alfonso, 2017; Mascolo, Alfonso, & Flanagan, 2014). Currently, Flanagan, Ortiz, and Alfonso (2017) have used CHC Theory to classify over 1000 subtests on tests measuring various domains of functioning. With the advancements in CHC Theory, however, less attention and empirical support has been given to its relevance for preschool children (Ford, Kozey, & Negreiros, 2012).

Quantitative Characteristics

In addition to understanding the theoretical composition of cognitive tests for preschool children, it is also incumbent upon examiners to review critically review the quantitative (i.e., psychometric) characteristics of each test (see Alfonso & Flanagan, 2009 for a comprehensive review). There are several challenges that impact the psychometric integrity of cognitive assessments for preschool children. First, young children experience developmental peaks and valleys. That is, one can expect changes in development to happen rapidly (see Bracken & Theodore, this volume). Consequently, examiners may see relatively large cognitive changes over a short period of time. Therefore, cognitive tests should be sensitive to these changes. Second, given that traditional tests may not have been designed with preschool children in mind, their suitability for them has been questioned (Alfonso & Flanagan, 2009). Third, there are criticisms applicable to poor psychometric rigor of tests for preschool children (Bracken & Walker, 1997; Nagle, 2007).

Fortunately, researchers and assessment experts alike have spent decades working to quantify and apply psychometric criteria towards the evaluation of preschool cognitive tests as well as other assessments (see Alfonso & Flanagan, 1999, 2009; Bracken, 1987; Flanagan & Alfonso, 1995). When selecting a cognitive test, examiners should ensure that the standardization sample of the instrument is representative of the population at-large and includes individuals in the normative group similar to those who are being assessed. This match is necessary for comparative purposes and allows the examiner or evaluator to identify where a child performs relative to their peers (Salvia, Ysseldyke, & Witmer, 2017).

Test floors, ceilings, and item gradients are also important considerations when assessing preschool children's cognitive abilities (see Bracken & Theodore, this volume). Having adequate test floors ensures that assessments do not overestimate a child's performance at the lower end of functioning. Sound floors are accomplished by ensuring there is a sufficient number of easy items to differentiate performance (Alfonso & Flanagan, 1999). Similarly, having appropriate test ceilings ensures that assessments can reflect the upper ends of functioning of preschool children (Bracken & Theodore, this volume). It is necessary to have adequate ceilings, particularly when assessing preschool children for gifted identification. Item gradients are also necessary to evaluate to ensure that a subtle change in raw scores corresponds with a subtle change in scaled/standard scores. Again, the purpose of having gradual item gradients is to assist in differentiating performance among examinees. Flanagan and Alfonso (1995) found test floors and item gradients to be rated less adequately when compared to other quantitative characteristics for preschool cognitive tests. Bracken and Theodore (this volume) have noted that preschool tests generally have adequate ceilings.

A final quantitative characteristic to take into consideration when evaluating a preschool test is the *g* loadings of its subtests or tests. As previously discussed, *g* typically represents an individual's overall cognitive capacity and is normally summarized using a global composite. *g* loadings represent the relationship between subtests or tests and the global *g* factor. Therefore, when a global composite is comprised of subtests or tests with high

g loadings, it is thought to provide a good estimate of overall cognitive ability. For the purpose of this chapter, the authors provide the name of each test's global composite (estimate of g), list the subtests or tests that comprise the composite, summarize the test's g loadings, and give an overall evaluation of each test's estimate of overall cognitive ability.

Qualitative Characteristics

Another necessary, yet often overlooked, area of cognitive tests for preschoolers to evaluate is their qualitative characteristics. As mentioned earlier, traditional cognitive tests may not have been designed specifically with preschoolers in mind. Consequently, the intuitive appeal for preschool children may be lacking. For example, preschool children may have different attentional, motivational, and linguistical capacities than that of school-aged children and adults (Bracken & Theodore, this volume). Therefore, the construction and administration of a cognitive test must reflect these differences (Alfonso & Flanagan, 1999). Alfonso and Flanagan suggested cognitive tests for preschoolers should have the following test construction components: 1) Attractive materials, 2) Efficient administration procedures, 3) Limited expressive language demands, and 4) Appropriate nonverbal scales. They also suggested that administration components have: 1) Limited receptive language requirements, 2) Easily understood directions, 3) Opportunities to teach the task, and 4) Alternative stopping rules. By adhering to these test construction and administration components, cognitive tests may be better equipped towards addressing the unique challenges of assessing preschool children.

Woodcock-Johnson IV Tests of Cognitive Abilities (WJ IV COG)

The WJ IV COG (Schrank et al., 2014) is a cognitive test for individuals ranging from age 2 to age 90. It is based on the CHC Theory. The WJ IV COG measures seven CHC broad abilities (see Table 10.1) and is one of the most comprehensive and theoretically driven cognitive tests for preschool children. The WJ IV COG measures multiple narrow abilities within Comprehension-Knowledge (Gc), Fluid Reasoning (Gf), Visual Processing (Gv), and Learning Efficiency (Gl). If, however, an examiner is attempting to measure Auditory Processing (Ga), Processing Speed (Gs), or Working Memory Capacity (Gwm) more broadly, it may be more appropriate to use an instrument that supplements the abilities measured or select a separate narrow band measure that includes at least two narrow abilities within the aforementioned broad abilities (Flanagan, Ortiz, & Alfonso, 2013).

From a psychometric or quantitative perspective, the WJ IV COG was evaluated using previously established criteria (see Tables 10.2 and 10.3). The WJ IV COG standardization sample included more than 7000 individuals, with more than 200 individuals per year aged 3 to 5 years. The

Table 10.1 CHC Broad and Narrow Abilities Measured by Major Preschool Cognitive Tests

Broad Abilities Measured/ (Narrow Abilities)	Cognitive Test				
	WJ IV COG	WPPSI- IV	DAS-II	SB5	KABC-II:NU
Comprehension-Knowledge (Gc)	Yes (K0, VL)	Yes (K0, VL)	Yes (LS, VL)	Yes (CM, K0, LS, VL)	Yes (K0, VL)
Fluid Reasoning (Gf)	Yes (I, RG, RQ)	Yes (I)	Yes (I, RQ)	Yes (I, RG, RQ)	Yes (I, RG)
Visual Processing (Gv)	Yes (MV, Vz)	Yes (CS, Vz)	Yes (MV, Vz)	Yes (Vz)	Yes (CS, MV, SS, Vz)
Auditory Processing (Ga)	Yes (PC)	No	Yes (PC)	No	No
Processing Speed (Gs)	Yes (P)	Yes (P)	Yes (P)	No	No
Working Memory Capacity (Gwm)	Yes (Wc)	Yes (Wv)	Yes (Wa, Wc)	Yes (Wa, Wc, Wv)	Yes (Wa, Wc, Wv)
Learning Efficiency (Gl)	Yes (MA, MM)	No	Yes (M6)	No	No

Note: Classifications are based on the authors' review of several sources, including Flanagan et al. (2017) and Schneider and McGrew (2018), rather than the classifications provided in the technical manuals of the cognitive tests. Classifications reflect updated classification of CHC Theory. Auditory processing (Ga): Phonetic coding (PC); Comprehension-knowledge (Gc); General information (K0); Lexical knowledge (VL); Listening ability (LS); Communication ability (CM); Fluid reasoning (Gf); Induction (I); General sequential reasoning (RG); Quantitative reasoning (RQ); Learning efficiency (Gl); Associative memory (MA); Meaningful memory (MM); Free recall memory (M6); Processing speed (Gs); Perceptual speed (P); Visual processing (Gv); Closure speed (CS); Visual memory (MV); Spatial scanning (SS); Visualization (Vz); Working memory capacity (Gwm); Auditory short-term storage (Wa); Working memory capacity (Wc); Visual-spatial short-term storage (Wv).

normative tables are created in 1-month intervals (M. Ledbetter, personal communication, September 6, 2019). Therefore, the overall rating for this characteristic was judged *Good*. Moreover, the WJ IV COG standardization sample adequately matched the United States population (see Table 10.3). The only measure of reliability found within the *WJ IV Technical Manual* (McGrew, LaForte, & Schrank, 2014) was subtest and cluster internal consistency. Internal consistency ranged from *Inadequate* to *Good*. This wide range was largely due to variation between subtest and composite reliabilities, wherein subtests generally yielded lower internal consistency

Table 10.2 Criteria for Evaluating the Adequacy of the Psychometric Characteristics of Preschool Cognitive Tests

Psychometric Characteristic	Criteria	Evaluative Classification
Standardization[a]		
Size of normative group and number of participants at each age/grade interval	200 persons per each 1-year interval and at least 2000 persons overall	Good
	100 persons per each 1-year interval and at least 1000 persons overall	Adequate
	Neither criterion above is met	Inadequate
Recency of normative data		
	Collected in 2009 or later	Good
	Collected between 1999 and 2008	Adequate
	Collected in 1998 or earlier	Inadequate
Age divisions of norm tables		
	One to two months	Good
	Three to four months	Adequate
	Greater than four months	Inadequate
Match of the demographic characteristics of the normative group to the U.S. population	Normative group represents the U.S. population on five or more important demographic variables (e.g., gender, race) with SES included	Good
	Normative group represents the U.S. population on three or four important demographic variables with SES included	Adequate
	Neither criterion is met	Inadequate
Reliability		
Internal consistency reliability coefficient (subtests and composites)	Greater than or equal to .90 ($\geq$.90)	Good
	.80 to .89	Adequate
	Less than .80 (<.80)	Inadequate
Test-retest reliability coefficient (composites only)	Greater than or equal to .90 ($\geq$.90)	Good
	.80 to .89	Adequate
	Less than .80 (<.80)	Inadequate
Test-retest reliability coefficient (subtests only)	Greater than or equal to .80 ($\geq$.80)	Adequate
	Less than .80 (<.80)	Inadequate

(Continued)

Table 10.2 (Cont).

Psychometric Characteristic	Criteria	Evaluative Classification
Test-retest sample		
Size and representativeness of test-retest sample	Sample contains at least 100 participants and represents the U.S. population on at least five or more demographic variables	Good
	Sample contains at least 50 participants and represents the U.S. population on three or four demographic variables	Adequate
	Neither criterion is met	Inadequate
Age range of the test-retest sample	Spans no more than a 1-year interval	Good
	Spans no more than 2 years	Adequate
	Spans more than 2 years or extends beyond the preschool age range (i.e., 2–5 years), regardless of interval size	Inadequate
Length of test-retest interval[b]		
	Interval $\leq$3 months	Good
	Interval >3 and $\leq$6 months	Adequate
	Interval >6 months	Inadequate
Floors		
Subtests[c]		
	Raw score of 1 is associated with a standard score greater than 2 standard deviations below the normative mean	Adequate
	Raw score of 1 is associated with a standard score less than or equal to 2 standard deviations below the normative mean	Inadequate
Composites[d]		
	Composite standard score greater than 2 standard deviations below the normative mean	Adequate
	Composite standard score less than or equal to 2 standard deviations below the normative mean	Inadequate

(Continued)

Table 10.2 (Cont).

Psychometric Characteristic	Criteria	Evaluative Classification
Ceilings		
Subtests[e]		
	Highest raw score obtained is associated with a standard score greater than 2 standard deviations above the normative mean	Adequate
	Highest raw score is associated with a standard score less than or equal to 2 standard deviations above the normative mean	Inadequate
Composites[f]		
	Composite standard score is greater than 2 standard deviations above the normative mean	Adequate
	Composite standard score is less than or equal to 2 standard deviations above the normative mean	Inadequate
Item gradients[g]		
Item gradient violations		
	No item gradient violations occur *or* all item gradient violations are between 2 and 3 standard deviations below the normative mean *or* the total number of violations is <5% across the age range of the test	Good
	All item gradient violations occur between 1 and 3 standard deviations below the normative mean *or* the total number of violations is $\geq$5% and $\leq$15% across the age range of the test	Adequate
	All or any portion of item gradient violations occur between the mean and 1 standard deviation below the normative mean *or* the total number of violations is >15% across the age range of the test	Inadequate

(Continued)

Table 10.2 (Cont).

Psychometric Characteristic	Criteria	Evaluative Classification
Validity[h]		
Presence and quality of specific forms of validity evidences	5 or 6 forms of validity evidence and the authors' evaluation of available data	Good
	4 forms of validity evidence and the authors' evaluation of available data	Adequate
	<4 forms of validity evidence and the authors' evaluation of available data	Inadequate

a An overall rating is obtained as follows: Good = All Goods; Adequate = Goods and Adequates; Inadequate = Goods and/or Adequates, and Inadequates.
b The criteria presented here regarding the length of the test-retest interval differ from traditional criteria used with school-age children because young children's abilities change rapidly.
c Assuming a scale having a mean of 100 and a standard deviation of 15, a raw score of 1 that is associated with a standard score of ≤69 would constitute an adequate floor.
d Floors are calculated based on the aggregate of the subtest raw scores that comprise the composites, where one item per subtest is scored correctly.
e Assuming a scale having a mean of 100 and a standard deviation of 15, the highest raw score possible is associated with a standard score ≥131 and would constitute an adequate ceiling.
f Ceilings are calculated based on the aggregate of the subtest raw scores that comprise the composites, where all items in a subtest are scored correctly.
g An item gradient is defined as the increase in standard score points associated with a one-point increase in raw score values. An item gradient violation occurs when a one-point increase in raw score points is associated with a standard score increase of greater than one third of a standard deviation (Bracken, 1987).
h The standards for validity in the 2014 publication *Standards for Educational and Psychological Testing* differ from those in the 1999 publication of the same name. Most notably, in the 2014 publication there is one overarching standard or guiding principle for validity with 25 standards subsumed under three clusters. The third cluster, namely Specific Forms of Validity Evidence, has 15 of the 25 standards subsumed under 6 forms of validity evidence. These 6 forms of validity evidence are akin to the 5 sources of validity evidence found in the 1999 publication and in earlier versions of this table. Ratings of *Good* or *Adequate* were made only when the available validity evidence was reviewed positively by the authors and corroborated by other reviews in the extant literature.

Source: From *Evidence-Based Practice in Infant and Early Childhood Psychology* (pp. 146–148), by B. A. Mowder, F. Rubinson, and A. E. Yasik (Eds.), 2009, Hoboken, NJ: John Wiley & Sons. Copyright 2009 by John Wiley & Sons. Adapted with permission.

coefficients than did composites/clusters. For example, the Phonological Processing subtest yielded an internal consistency coefficient of .77 at ages 3 and 4 years, which accounted for an *Inadequate* rating. Consequently, examiners are cautioned against using this subtest when making high-stakes decisions for children ages 3 and 4. Beyond this subtest and age level, however, the majority of subtest and cluster reliability coefficients for the WJ IV COG were considered *Adequate* to *Good*.

Table 10.3 Quantitative Review and Evaluation of Psychometric Characteristics of Major Preschool Cognitive Tests

	Cognitive Test				
	WJ IV COG	WPPSI-IV	DAS-II	SB5	KABC-II:NU
Standardization					
Normative Group	Good	Adequate	Good	Good	Good
Recency of Normative Data	Good	Good	Adequate	Adequate	Good*
Age Divisions of Norm Tables	Inadequate	Good	Good	Good	Good*
Match of Demographic Data to U.S. Population	Good	Good	Good	Good	Good
Reliability					
Internal Consistency	Inadequate to Good	Inadequate to Good	Inadequate to Good	Adequate to Good	Inadequate to Good*
Test-Retest Reliability (Composites)	Inadequate	Adequate to Good	Inadequate to Good	Adequate to Good	Inadequate to Good
Test-Retest Reliability (Subtests)	Inadequate	Inadequate to Adequate	Inadequate to Adequate	Adequate to Good	Inadequate to Adequate
Test-Retest Sample					
Size/ Representativeness Of Sample	Inadequate	Adequate	Inadequate	Inadequate	Good
Age Range of Sample	Inadequate	Adequate	Adequate	Inadequate	Adequate
Length of Interval	Inadequate	Good	Good	Good	Good
Floors					
Subtests	Inadequate	Adequate	Adequate	Adequate	Adequate*
Composites	Inadequate	Adequate	Adequate	Adequate	Adequate*
Ceilings					
Subtests	Inadequate	Adequate	Adequate	Adequate	Adequate*
Composites	Inadequate	Adequate	Adequate	Adequate	Adequate*
Item Gradients					
Violations	Inadequate	Good	Good	Adequate	Good*
Validity					
Presence and Quality of Evidence	Good	Good	Adequate	Adequate	Adequate

Note. Ratings are based upon the criteria set forth in Table 10.2. Review and evaluation include *core* and *supplementary* subtests and composites. * Decision was made using *KABC-II Normative Update* (Kaufman & Kaufman, 2018a) as well as *KABC-II: Manual Supplement* (Kaufman & Kaufman, 2018a).

The global composite for the WJ IV COG is called the General Intellectual Ability (GIA). The GIA is comprised of the Oral Vocabulary, Number Series, Verbal Attention, Letter-Pattern Matching, Phonological Processing, Story Recall, and Visualization tests. Based upon their *g* loadings, Oral Vocabulary was rated as a good measure of *g*, whereas Number Series, Verbal Attention, Letter-Pattern Matching, Phonological Processing, Story Recall, and Visualization were rated as fair measures of *g* (Sattler, Shaw, Schultz, D'Intino, Roger, Daou, & Cousineau-Pérusse, 2018). As such, the tests that make up the GIA can be described as a fair estimate of overall cognitive ability.

No information was found in the *WJ IV Technical Manual* (McGrew et al., 2014) regarding the test-retest stability coefficients or the adequacy of floors, ceilings, and item gradients. As a result of the missing data, these important technical characteristics were rendered *Inadequate*. In a previous review of the WJ IV COG, however, Floyd, Woods, Singh, and Hawkins (2016) questioned the appropriateness of the cluster floors prior to age 6:0. In regards to validity, the *WJ IV Technical Manual* (McGrew et al., 2014) provides ample evidence of construct validity. For example, the WJ IV COG was designed and developed with CHC Theory as a blueprint. McGrew and colleagues (2014) expanded the evidence for content-related validity by using multidimensional scaling in addition to expert consensus. The authors included exploratory and confirmatory factor analytic studies to support the internal structure of the test. This, in addition to several examples of construct and concurrent validation, has rendered an overall validity rating of *Good* (see Ding & Alfonso, 2016 for a comprehensive review of validity evidence).

Qualitatively, the WJ IV COG was rated much lower than all the other cognitive tests for preschoolers reviewed here due to several less-than-desirable qualitative characteristics (see Table 10.4). First, the lack of manipulatives and other attention-grabbing materials may make it difficult for the examiner to sustain the attention of a preschooler for a long enough duration to complete the test. Second, the administration of the subtests appears to be more appropriate for adolescents and adults due to their administration length and the complexity of basic concepts in test directions, especially for preschool children who are culturally and linguistically diverse. Third, the majority of subtests have an expressive language component. Although the expressive language demands typically require only a word or two, the inclusion of more subtests that rely on pointing or gesturing may be helpful for preschool children with limited language abilities. Further, eight of the 18 WJ IV COG subtests have a high degree of either linguistic demand or cultural loading (see Table 10.5), calling into question its overall utility for culturally and/or linguistically diverse preschool children.

In sum, the WJ IV COG is one of the most theoretically driven tests of cognitive abilities for preschool children. Theoretical foundation is a strength of the test, especially due to the breadth of CHC broad and narrow abilities that the WJ IV COG measures (see Schneider, 2016). Psychometrically, the characteristics that could be found within the *WJ IV Technical Manual* (McGrew et al., 2014)

Table 10.4 Qualitative Review and Evaluation of Major Preschool Cognitive Tests

Qualitative Characteristic	Cognitive Test				
	WJ IV COG	WPPS-I-IV	DAS-II	SB5	KABC-II:NU
Attractive Test Materials (e.g., manipulatives, colorful test materials)		✓	✓	✓	✓
Efficient Administration Procedures (e.g., alternates between verbal/nonverbal subtests, begins tasks with stimulating task)	✓	✓	✓		✓
Limited Expressive Language Requirement (e.g., majority of tasks require one- or two-word response, and/or gestures)	✓	✓	✓		✓
Incorporates Nonverbal Score(s)		✓	✓	✓	✓
Limited Receptive Language Requirements (e.g., all subtests have brief directions)		✓			✓
Directions are Suitable for Preschoolers		✓	✓		✓
Includes Opportunities to "Teach Task" (e.g., uses sample items, includes multiple trials, provides demonstrations)	✓	✓	✓		✓
Includes Alternative Stopping Rules	✓		✓		
Translation or Adaptation Available in Other Languages			✓		✓
Appropriate Degree of Language Demands and Cultural Loading	See Table 10.5 For Test-by-Test Breakdown				

Note: A checkmark indicates that the authors deemed this qualitative characteristic as being met. Certain qualitative characteristics are more subjective in nature than other characteristics reviewed in this chapter. Therefore, readers are encouraged to review cognitive tests independently using the above criteria.

were typically rated as *Adequate* or *Good*, which also represents a relative strength of the WJ IV COG. However, given that much of the psychometric information was unavailable to review, it is difficult to evaluate several characteristics such as floors, ceilings, and item gradients. Therefore, readers are encouraged to use this review, as well as other independent reviews (see Ding & Alfonso, 2016; Schneider, 2016), to gain a more comprehensive understanding of the strengths and weaknesses of the WJ IV COG. For future editions of the WJ COG, it would be helpful to have more information readily and easily available to enable examiners to evaluate the psychometric properties of the test.

Table 10.5 Number of Subtests with Corresponding Linguistic Demand and Cultural Loading Throughout the Test

Linguistic Demand/ Cultural Loading	Cognitive Test				
	WJ IV COG	WPPSI-IV	DAS-II	SB5	KABC-II:NU
Low/Low	4	2	6	I	6
Moderate/Low	2	2	2	I	4
High/Low	2	0	I	I	0
Low/Moderate	2	3	4	0	0
Moderate/ Moderate	2	0	3	I	2
High/Moderate	3	I	I	2	0
Low/High	0	2	0	0	I
Moderate/High	0	2	2	0	0
High/High	3	3	2	4	3

Note. Subtest linguistic demand and cultural loading were determined via the Culture-Language Interpretive Matrix (C-LIM) function of the Cross-Battery Assessment System Software (X-BASS; Flanagan et al., 2017).

One of the main weaknesses of the WJ IV COG is its lack of appeal to preschoolers. For example, the overall easel design and visual attractiveness of the materials could be made more contemporary. It appears as if the WJ IV COG is a downward extension of a cognitive test for school-aged children, adolescents, and adults rather than a test that incorporated manipulatives and tasks designed with a preschooler in mind.

Wechsler Preschool and Primary Scale of Intelligence – Fourth Edition (WPPSI-IV)

The WPPSI-IV (Wechsler, 2012a) is an individually administered test designed to assess cognitive abilities and problem-solving processes of children aged 2:6 to 7:7 years. From a CHC theoretical perspective, the WPPSI-IV measures five broad abilities (Table 10.1): Gc, Gf, Gv, Gs, and Gwm. Of those broad abilities, the WPPSI-IV measures only Gc and Gv sufficiently. That is, those are the only two broad abilities comprised of multiple narrow abilities. Therefore, if the examiner wants to measure Gf, Ga, Gs, Gwm, or Gl comprehensively, they may want to supplement the WPPSI-IV with a test that better measures the desired abilities.

Quantitatively, the standardization of the WPPSI-IV was rated as *Adequate* to *Good* across all characteristics. Generally, the reliability coefficients (e.g., internal consistency) for the subtests and composites across all ages were *Adequate* to

Good. The two exceptions were the Cancellation and Animal Coding subtests, which yielded the lowest coefficients, ranging from .71 to .74 at ages 4:0 to 5:5. The test-retest reliability coefficients for the composites ranged from .82 to .93, which is considered *Adequate* to *Good.* The characteristics related to the test-retest sample were also *Adequate* to *Good.* For example, there was a sufficient number of children included in the test-retest sample and the length of time between test administrations was appropriate. Additionally, the test-retest sample approximated the United States population on four demographic variables. Nearly all of the subtests met the floor criteria by age 3:6; however, examiners should review individual subtests to make sure that the child's ability is not over-estimated for those performing at the lower level of cognitive functioning. Regarding composite floors, all of the WPPSI-IV composite floors were rated as *Adequate.* The subtest and composite ceilings were rated as *Adequate.* There were fewer than 5% item gradient violations, which yielded a rating of *Good.*

The WPPSI-IV provided all six evidences for validity found in the *Standards for Educational and Psychological Testing* (American Educational Research Association, American Psychological Association, & National Council on Measurement in Education, 2014). For example, the *WPPSI-IV Technical and Interpretive Manual* (Wechsler, 2012b) describes the processes used to design and develop the content for the test using expert panels and literature reviews. In addition, factor analytic studies were provided to support the internal structure of the test for the 2:6 to 3:11 and 4:0 to 7:7 age ranges (see also, Niileksela & Reynolds, 2019). The publisher provides relationship data with several other measures of cognitive abilities, as well as clinical data to show evidence of concurrent and predictive validity. The culmination of support led to an overall validity rating of *Good.*

The global composite for the WPPSI-IV is called the Full Scale IQ (FSIQ). The FSIQ is comprised of the Receptive Vocabulary, Information, Block Design, Object Assembly, and Picture Memory subtests at ages 2:6 to 3:11. Based upon their g loadings, Receptive Vocabulary and Information were rated as good measures of g, whereas Block Design, Object Assembly, and Picture Memory were rated as fair measures of g (Sattler, Dumont, & Coalson, 2018). At ages 4:0 to 7:7, the FSIQ is comprised of Information, Similarities, Block Design, Matrix Reasoning, Picture Memory, and Bug Search. Information and Similarities were rated as good measures of g, whereas Block Design, Matrix Reasoning, Picture Memory, and Bug Search were rated as fair measures of g (Sattler, Dumont, & Coalson, 2018). Overall, the g loadings suggest that the subtests making up the FSIQ are a fair to good estimate of overall cognitive ability.

The qualitative characteristics of the WPPSI-IV revealed a particular strength of the test. It was clear that the WPPSI-IV utilizes attractive materials that are likely to gain and sustain the attention of preschoolers. The WPPSI-IV, however, could increase the number of manipulatives used in the test. In addition, the directions for each subtest include very short sentences using basic concepts that young children should easily understand. The receptive and expressive language requirements of the test appear to be minimal with the exception of the Vocabulary subtest, which requires multiple word responses. A weakness of the WPPSI-IV is the linguistic demand and cultural loading of its subtests. For example, eight of the 15 subtests have either high linguistic demand and/or cultural loading (see Table 10.5). This shortcoming suggests that the WPPSI-IV may not be an appropriate measure for culturally and/or linguistically diverse preschool children.

In sum, the WPPSI-IV measures five CHC broad abilities but only two sufficiently. Therefore, it is one of the weakest preschool cognitive tests in terms of its theoretical underpinnings. This is not surprising since the Wechsler Scales were designed from an a-theoretical perspective and it was not until more recently that CHC Theory was applied to the tests by others (e.g., Flanagan & Alfonso, 2017; Flanagan, McGrew, & Ortiz, 2000). The psychometric characteristics of the WPPSI-IV were *Adequate* to *Good* across nearly all criteria. This strength indicates a psychometrically sound cognitive test for preschoolers, particularly after age 3:6. The qualitative composition of the WPPSI-IV appeared to be a strength for use with preschool children. It was evident that the test was designed to capture preschoolers' attention through engaging and interactive subtests. In particular, the use of a dauber for Bug Search was an innovative and creative way of assessing processing speed. The main qualitative weakness of the WPPSI-IV was that more than 50% of the subtests had high linguistic demand and/or culture loading. As such, it may be difficult to determine the role that culture and/or language account for in the scores obtained by preschool children on the WPPSI-IV.

Differential Ability Scales – Second Edition (DAS-II)

The DAS-II is a comprehensive, individually administered test designed for assessing cognitive abilities. The test may be administered to children and adolescents ages 2:6 to 17:11 across a broad range of development levels. The DAS-II measures seven CHC broad abilities. Of those seven broad abilities, the DAS-II measures Gc, Gf, Gv, and Gwm comprehensively. Therefore, if an examiner wants to conduct a broad cognitive assessment of a preschooler, or if the referral question is related to crystallized knowledge, novel problem solving, visual processing, or working memory, the DAS-II is a logical choice. If the referral question is related to auditory processing, processing speed, or learning efficiency, an examiner or practitioner may want to supplement the DAS-II with another test that more comprehensively measures those abilities.

The standardization characteristics for the DAS-II were rated as *Adequate* to *Good*. The only standardization characteristic that could be improved upon was the recency of the normative data. The normative data are 12 years old, which suggests that they may need to be updated soon to reflect the current population. The internal consistency coefficients ranged from

.68 to .96 across subtests and composites. At the subtest level, the majority of the subtests were in the .80s to .90s, rendering internal consistency as *Adequate* to *Good*. Similarly, internal consistency coefficients for nearly all composites were in the upper .80s to mid .90s. Of all the preschool cognitive tests evaluated, the DAS-II has the fewest number of item gradient violations (< 1%). Moreover, the only subtest that included item gradient violations was the Recall of Objects – Delayed. This finding suggests that for this subtest, it may be difficult to detect subtle differences in performance. Otherwise, the DAS-II has a sufficient number of easy items to differentiate performance at the low range of performance. Subtest floors were *Adequate* from ages 2:6 to 5:5 with the exception of the Recall of Objects – Delayed subtest at ages 4:0 to 5:5, as well as a few of the subtests within the Diagnostic Battery. The subtest and composite ceilings were rated as *Adequate*, suggesting that the DAS-II may be appropriate for assessing giftedness in preschool children. The *DAS-II Introductory and Technical Handbook* (Elliott, 2007b) describes several sources of evidence to support the validity of the test. Expert consensus was used to develop the content of the test and the internal structure was determined using Confirmatory Factor Analysis (CFA). The author provides different CFA models for the 2:6 to 3:5 age group as compared to the 4:0 to 5:11 age group. In addition, Elliott (2007b) correlated the DAS-II with other measures of cognitive ability and academic achievement, supporting the test's relation to other commonly accepted tests. This, in addition to other information provided, yielded an *Adequate* rating for its validity.

The global composite for the DAS-II is called the General Conceptual Ability (GCA). The GCA is comprised of the Verbal Comprehension, Naming Vocabulary, Picture Similarities, and Pattern Construction subtests at ages 2:6 to 3:5. Naming Vocabulary and Pattern Construction were rated as good measures of *g*, whereas Verbal Comprehension and Picture Similarities were rated as fair measures of *g* (Sattler, Dumont, Willis, & Salerno, 2018). At ages 3:6 to 6:11, the GCA is comprised of the Verbal Comprehension, Naming Vocabulary, Picture Similarities, Matrices, Pattern Construction, and Copying subtests. Based on *g* loadings, Naming Vocabulary and Pattern Construction were rated as good measures of *g*, whereas Verbal Comprehension, Picture Similarities, Matrices, and Copying were rated as fair measures of *g* (Sattler, Dumont, Willis, et al., 2018). Overall, the *g* loadings suggest that the subtests making up the GCA are a fair to good estimate of overall cognitive ability.

Qualitatively, the DAS-II has a number of characteristics that make it particularly attractive for the preschool population. The DAS-II has a variety of subtests that utilize manipulatives and other attention-grabbing stimuli. In general, the DAS-II requires very little expressive language requirements of preschoolers. For example, the majority of subtests include only a one- or two-word response, or the preschooler can answer by pointing. The only characteristic rated for improvement was the receptive language requirements for the examinee. As the subtests increase in complexity, the directions become much longer and utilize concepts that may be difficult for a preschooler with limited English language. That said, a qualitative strength of the DAS-II is that fewer than 30% of the pre-school-aged subtests are rated as having high linguistic demands and/or high culture loadings, making the DAS-II one of the more logical choices when assessing preschoolers who are culturally and linguistically diverse.

Overall, the DAS-II measures a wide range of CHC broad abilities. Of the seven broad abilities included in CHC Theory, the DAS-II measures four of them comprehensively. Psychometrically, the DAS-II obtained *Adequate* to *Good* ratings across the majority of the characteristics evaluated. Given the test's publication date, it would be appropriate to update the test and its normative sample in the near future. One of the many strengths of the DAS-II is having adequate floors so that performance can be accurately assessed for those functioning at the lower limits of the test and ability levels. Qualitatively, the DAS-II was rated very highly compared to other major cognitive tests for preschool children. In particular, the DAS-II has a noticeable balance of subtests that measure specific cognitive abilities while minimizing the influence of language and culture on performance.

Stanford-Binet Intelligence Scales – Fifth Edition (SB5)

The SB5 is a comprehensive set of individually administered subtests and testlets that measure various aspects of cognitive ability for individuals ranging in age from 2 to 85 years. The test consists of two general domains: Verbal and Nonverbal. The SB5 measures four CHC broad abilities. Those broad abilities are Gc, Gf, Gv, and Gwm. Of the four broad abilities, the SB5 measures all but Gv comprehensively. Therefore, referral questions regarding a preschooler's ability to apply crystallized knowledge, novel problem solving, and working memory could likely be addressed using the SB5. It may be necessary to use a different cognitive test for referral type questions involving other cognitive abilities and processes.

The standardization characteristics of the SB5 were rated as *Adequate* to *Good*. The test is outdated in that it was published more than 15 years ago, warranting a normative update or revision of the entire test to represent better the current population. Subtest and composite internal consistency coefficients ranged from the .80s to .90s, which is higher than all other preschool tests included in this review. At the subtest level, approximately half of the subtests were rated as *Adequate* to *Good*, whereas all composite scores received such ratings. The characteristics of the test-retest sample represented a quantitative weakness of the test. Moreover, there was an inadequate number of children included in the sample and the age range was relatively large. By age 3:10, nearly all the floors were met at the subtest level and all were met at the composite level. At the upper level of functioning, the SB5 was rated as having *Adequate* subtest and composite ceilings. Of all the tests reviewed, the SB5 had the highest number of item gradient violations, suggesting that subtle differences in cognitive functioning may not be differentiated as well as by some of the other cognitive tests reviewed. The *SB5 Technical Manual* (Roid, 2003b) describes the evidence for SB5 validity. The test was designed using expert consensus and CHC Theory as a blueprint. Roid (2003b) provided factor analytic studies to support a five-factor model as the model of best fit. Additionally, there were correlational studies provided to support the predictive relationship between other measures of cognitive abilities and academic achievement. This, in addition to other information, led to a rating of *Adequate* for the validity of the SB5.

The global composite for the SB5 is called the Full Scale IQ (FSIQ). The FSIQ is comprised of the Verbal Quantitative Reasoning, Verbal Visual-Spatial Processing, Verbal Fluid Reasoning, Verbal Working Memory, Verbal Knowledge, Nonverbal Quantitative Reasoning, Nonverbal Knowledge, Nonverbal Visual-Spatial Processing, Nonverbal Working Memory, and Nonverbal Fluid Reasoning subtests. Based on their g loadings, all subtests were rated as good measures of g except Nonverbal Fluid Reasoning, which was rated as a fair measure of g (Sattler, Salerno, & Roberts-Pittman, 2018). As such, the subtests that make up the FSIQ can be described as good measures of its overall general factor.

The evaluation of the qualitative characteristics of the SB5 is found in Table 10.4. Qualitatively, the SB5 was rated lower than the other four cognitive tests. While the SB5 utilizes many manipulatives that may be attractive for preschoolers, the test has some significant limitations. For example, the SB5 was rated as not having efficient administration procedures. In addition, the SB5 directions and/or responses necessary to complete the test are language heavy. In particular, the verbal subtests appear to require a great deal of concept knowledge as well as highly developed expressive language abilities. This verbal overload was further substantiated by the number of subtests from the SB5 that involve either high linguistic demand or culture loading. Moreover, 70% of the subtests were rated high in one or both of those domains. These latter issues make the SB5 one of the least appropriate tests for preschool children who are culturally and/or linguistically diverse.

Overall, the SB5 measures four CHC broad abilities (three comprehensively). Quantitatively, the majority of ratings were *Adequate* or *Good*. More specifically, the overall reliability of the SB5 was found to be a strength as compared to other cognitive tests reviewed. This finding is consistent with other reviews of the SB5 (see Alfonso & Flanagan, 2005). A major quantitative weakness of the SB5 is that it was published nearly 16 years ago. The age of its norms raises concerns regarding the representativeness of the test to the current population. For example, preschoolers today are being compared to preschoolers from the early 2000s, which may not be appropriate. Qualitatively, the SB5 was rated as the weakest cognitive test for preschoolers. The SB5 relies heavily on language and/or culture, which may have a confounding influence on the overall results of the assessment. Consequently, the SB5 may not be an appropriate measure of cognitive abilities for those who are culturally and linguistically diverse.

Kaufman Assessment Battery for Children – Second Edition: Normative Update (KABC-II:NU)

The KABC-II:NU (Kaufman & Kaufman, 2018b) is an individually administered test of cognitive abilities for children and adolescents aged 3–18 years. The KABC-II:NU measures four CHC broad abilities. Those broad abilities are Gc, Gf, Gv, and Gwm, and the KABC-II:NU measures all four of these broad abilities comprehensively. Therefore, if an examiner or practitioner had a referral question regarding a preschooler's crystallized knowledge, novel problem solving, visual processing, and/or working memory, the KABC-II:NU would be a logical choice. If, however, the referral question involved auditory processing, processing speed, or learning efficiency, perhaps a different cognitive test battery should be administered to supplement the KABC-II:NU (see Flanagan et al., 2017).

The psychometric properties of the KABC-II:NU related to its standardization were all rated as *Good*, largely due to the normative update released in 2018. The internal consistency coefficients of the subtests and composites ranged from .74 to .99. Coefficients within this low to high range are similar to all other preschool cognitive tests reviewed. At the subtest level, Word Order and Gestalt Closure at age 3 had the lowest coefficients (.74 and .78, respectively) whereas all of other subtests fell within the .80s to .90s. At the composite level, internal consistency coefficients ranged from .91 to .98. The test-retest sample included more than 200 children and spanned two years. All children were retested within 12 to 45 days, with a mean of 24.2 days. In general, approximately half of the subtest floors were adequate by age 3:9 years, with nearly all adequate by 4:6. This floor effect suggests that children's cognitive functioning may be overestimated, especially prior to age 4:6. Similar to several of the other tests reviewed, the KABC-II:NU was rated as having *Adequate* ceilings at the subtest and composite level. There were fewer than 5% item gradient violations found; thus, this characteristic was rated as *Good*.

To assess the test's validity, we reviewed information from the *KABC-II Manual* (Kaufman & Kaufman, 2004b) as well as the *KABC-II: Manual Supplement* (Kaufman & Kaufman, 2018a), the latter of which was released as part of the normative update. Kaufman and Kaufman (2018a) support the internal structure of the test using intercorrelations. At the younger ages (i.e., 3–5 years old), subtest intercorrelations are modest. The authors also provide correlations between other measures of cognitive abilities and academic achievement to support the external validity of the test. In the original *KABC-II Manual* (Kaufman & Kaufman, 2004b), information was provided demonstrating different factor structures for the younger ages. This information, as well as other information, led to an *Adequate* rating for the validity evidence of the KABC-II:NU.

The global composite for the KABC-II:NU is the Mental Processing Index (MPI) or Fluid-Crystallized Index (FCI), depending on the examiner's theoretical foundation. The MPI/FCI is comprised of the Word Order, Conceptual Thinking, Face Recognition, Triangles, Atlantis, Expressive Vocabulary (FCI only), and

Riddles (FCI only) subtests for 3-year-olds. For children ages 4 to 5 years, the MPI/FCI is comprised of the Number Recall, Word Order, Conceptual Thinking, Face Recognition, Pattern Reasoning, Triangles, Atlantis, Rebus, Expressive Vocabulary (FCI only), and Riddles (FCI only) subtests. Based on their *g* loadings, Expressive Vocabulary and Riddles are rated as good measures of *g*, whereas Word Order, Conceptual Thinking, Triangles, Atlantis, Number Recall, and Pattern Reasoning are rated as fair measures of *g*. Facial Recognition and Rebus are rated as poor measures of *g*. Thus, the majority of subtests that compromise the MPI/FCI can be described as fair measures of the overall general factor.

Qualitatively, the KABC-II:NU is easy to administer and includes a number of manipulatives and colorful photos to attract and sustain the attention of preschoolers. In particular, the authors found the Rover subtest especially creative and innovative. The main criticism of the materials is that they are beginning to become dated. For example, there are several pictures that may not accurately represent objects that preschoolers have seen. In general, the KABC-II:NU requires very little expressive and receptive language abilities, suggesting that it minimizes the influence of language throughout the test. The directions are often brief and include simple sentence structures, making the directions easily understood by young children. Moreover, only 25% of the subtests have a high degree of linguistic demand and culture loading (Table 10.5), making it one of the most appropriate cognitive tests for preschoolers who are culturally and/or linguistically diverse.

In sum, the KABC-II:NU was designed and grounded in CHC Theory. The KABC-II:NU measures four CHC broad abilities well. Psychometrically, the test was rated as *Adequate* to *Good* across almost all characteristics. This finding is consistent with the other major cognitive tests for preschool children. Qualitatively, the test is easy to administer and has several characteristics that make it appealing for preschoolers. It uses several manipulatives which are likely to gain and sustain a child's attention. A weakness, however, is that the test materials (e.g., pictures) are becoming outdated given the test is approximately 16 years old. One of the most noticeable and commendable strengths of the KABC-II:NU is how well it minimizes the influence of language and culture on test performance. As a result, the KABC-II: NU is a logical choice when assessing students who are culturally and linguistically diverse.

Summary

In this chapter we reviewed and evaluated the theoretical, quantitative, and qualitative characteristics of five commonly used cognitive tests for preschoolers. Each major cognitive test had its relative strengths and weaknesses. For example, the WJ IV COG and DAS-II were the only two cognitive tests to measure seven CHC broad abilities. Thus, the WJ IV COG and DAS-II provided the most comprehensive assessment of cognitive abilities and processes. Although there were many similarities among the tests regarding quantitative characteristics, the WPPSI-IV, DAS-II, and KABC-II:NU were the highest rated given that the SB5 is very dated, and there was relatively little information provided in the *WJ IV Technical Manual* (McGrew et al., 2014) to address the evaluated characteristics. Qualitatively, the WPPSI-IV, DAS-II, and KABC-II:NU were rated higher than the WJ IV COG and SB5. It was more evident that the former tests were designed with preschool children in mind. Moreover, the WPPSI-IV, DAS-II, and KABC-II:NU are specifically designed to assess a smaller age range of examinees than the WJ IV COG and SB5, which likely accounts for the qualitative differences. Of the WPPSI-IV, DAS-II, and KABC-II:NU, the DAS-II and KABC-II:NU appear to be better cognitive tests for preschoolers who are linguistically and culturally diverse, as compared to the WPPSI-IV.

Based upon the collective information provided, it is the authors' opinion that the DAS-II and KABC-II are the two most well-rounded cognitive tests for preschoolers. This conclusion is based on their comprehensive coverage of CHC abilities, relatively strong psychometric properties, and qualitative appeal for young children. It is important to note that the other tests also have strengths that may be desirable for assessing preschool children. Thus, examiners should choose a test that best addresses the referral question and matches the characteristics of the child being assessed. As CHC Theory, psychometrics, and cognitive tests continue to evolve, it is recommended that test authors, publishers, and consumers alike balance these three areas to provide the most well-rounded and informative tests that measure cognitive performance of preschoolers. Additionally, the authors recommend that training programs prepare graduate students who can critically evaluate tests for their intended purposes and interpretive value. Doing so can aid in the evaluation, accurate diagnosis, and recommendation/intervention strategies for preschool children.

References

Alfonso, V. C., Engler, J. R., & Lapore, J. C. C. (2020). Assessing and evaluating young children: Developmental domains and methods. In V. C. Alfonso & G. J. DuPaul (Eds.), *Healthy development in young children: Evidence-based interventions for early education* (pp. 13–44). Washington, DC: American Psychological Association.

Alfonso, V. C., & Flanagan, D. P. (1999). Assessment of cognitive functioning in preschoolers. In E. V. Nuttall, I. Romero, & J. Kalesnik (Eds.), *Assessing and screening preschoolers* (2nd ed., pp. 186–217). New York: Allyn & Bacon.

Alfonso, V. C., & Flanagan, D. P. (2005). Best practices in the use of the Stanford-Binet Intelligence Scales, Fifth Edition (SB5) with preschoolers. In B. A. Bracken & R. Nagle (Eds.), *Psychoeducational assessment of preschool children* (4th ed., pp. 267–296). Mahwah, NJ: Lawrence Erlbaum Associates.

Alfonso, V. C., & Flanagan, D. P. (2009). Assessment of preschool children: A framework for evaluating the adequacy of the technical characteristics of norm-referenced instruments. In B. Mowder, F. Rubinson, & A. Yasik (Eds.), *Evidence based practice in infant and early childhood psychology* (pp. 129–166). New York, NY: John Wiley & Sons.

Alfonso, V. C., Ruby, S., Wissel, A. M., & Davari, J. (2020). School psychologists in early childhood settings. In F. C. Worrell, T. L. Hughes, & D.D. Dixson (Eds.), *The Cambridge handbook of applied school psychology* (pp. 579–597). Cambridge: Cambridge University Press.

American Educational Research Association, American Psychological Association, & National Council on Measurement in Education. (2014). *Standards for educational and psychological testing.* Washington, DC: American Educational Research Association.

American Psychiatric Association. (2013). *Diagnostic and statistical manual of mental disorders* (5th ed.). Washington, DC: Author.

Bracken, B. A. (1987). Limitations of preschool instruments and standards for minimal levels of technical adequacy. *Journal of Psychoeducational Assessment, 4,* 313–326.

Bracken, B. A. (1994). Advocating for effective preschool assessment practices: A comment on Bagnato and Neisworth. *School Psychology Quarterly, 9*(2), 103–108.

Bracken, B. A., & Theodore, L. A. (this volume). Creating the optimal preschool testing situation. In V. C. Alfonso, B. A. Bracken, & R. J. Nagle (Eds.), *Psychoeducational assessment of preschool children* (5th ed.). New York: Routledge.

Bracken, B. A., & Walker, K. C. (1997). The utility of intelligence tests for preschool children. In D. P. Flanagan, J. Genshaft, & P. Harrison, *Contemporary intellectual assessment: Theories, tests, and issues* (pp. 484–502). New York, NY: Guilford Press.

Ding, Y., & Alfonso, V. C. (2016). Overview of the Woodcock-Johnson IV: Organization, content, and psychometric properties. In D. P. Flanagan & V. C. Alfonso (Eds.), *WJ IV clinical use and interpretation: Scientist-practitioner perspectives* (pp. 1–30). Boston, MA: Elsevier.

Elliott, C. D. (2007a). *Differential Ability Scales-Second Edition.* San Antonio, TX: Harcourt Assessment.

Elliott, C. D. (2007b). *Differential Ability Scales-Second Edition introductory and technical handbook.* San Antonio, TX: Harcourt.

Flanagan, D. P., & Alfonso, V. C. (1995). A critical review of the technical characteristics of new and recently revised intelligence tests for preschool children. *Journal of Psychoeducational Assessment, 13,* 66–90.

Flanagan, D. P., & Alfonso, V. C. (2017). *Essentials of WISC-V assessment.* Hoboken, NJ: John Wiley & Sons.

Flanagan, D. P., Mascolo, J., & Genshaft, J. L. (2004). A conceptual framework for interpreting preschool intelligence tests. In B. A. Bracken (Ed.), *The psychoeducational assessment of preschool children* (3rd ed., pp. 428–473). Mahwah, NJ: Lawrence Erlbaum Associates Publishers.

Flanagan, D. P., McGrew, K. S., & Ortiz, S. O. (2000). *The Wechsler intelligence scales and Gf-Gc theory: A contemporary approach to interpretation.* Needham Heights, MA: Allyn & Bacon.

Flanagan, D. P., Ortiz, S. O., & Alfonso, V. C. (2013). *Essentials of cross-battery assessment* (3 rd ed.). Hoboken, NJ: John Wiley & Sons.

Flanagan, D. P., Ortiz, S. O., & Alfonso, V. C. (2017). *Cross-battery assessment software system (X-BASS).* (Version 2.0) [Computer software]. Hoboken, NJ: John Wiley & Sons.

Floyd, R. G., Woods, I. L., Singh, L. J., & Hawkins, H. K. (2016). Use of the Woodcock-Johnson IV in the diagnosis of intellectual disability. In D. P. Flanagan & V. C. Alfonso (Eds.), *WJ IV Clinical use and interpretation: Scientist-practitioner perspectives* (pp. 271–289). Boston, MA: Elsevier.

Ford, L., Kozey, M. L., & Negreiros, J. (2012). Cognitive assessment in early childhood: Theoretical and practice perspectives. In D. P. Flanagan & P. L. Harrison (Eds.),

Contemporary intellectual assessment: Theories, tests, and issues (3rd ed., pp. 585–622). New York, NY: The Guilford Press.

Kaufman, A. S., & Kaufman, N. L. (2004a). *Kaufman Assessment Battery for Children – Second Edition*. Bloomington, MN: Pearson.

Kaufman, A. S., & Kaufman, N. L. (2004b). *Kaufman Assessment Battery for Children – Second Edition manual*. Bloomington, MN: Pearson.

Kaufman, A. S., & Kaufman, N. L. (2018a). *Kaufman Assessment Battery for Children – Second Edition manual supplement*. Bloomington, MN: Pearson.

Kaufman, A. S., & Kaufman, N. L. (2018b). *Kaufman Assessment Battery for Children-Second Edition Normative Update*. Bloomington, MN: Pearson.

Lockwood, A. B., & Farmer, R. L. (2020). The cognitive assessment course: Two decades later. *Psychology in the Schools, 57*, 265–283. https://doi.org/10.1002/pits.22298.

Mascolo, J. T., Alfonso, V. C., & Flanagan, D. P. (Eds.). (2014). *Essentials of planning, selecting, and tailoring interventions for unique learners*. Hoboken, NJ: John Wiley & Sons.

McGrew, K. S., LaForte, E. M., & Schrank, F. A. (2014). *Technical manual*. Woodcock-Johnson IV. Rolling Meadows, IL: Riverside.

Mowder, B. A., Rubinson, F., & Yasik, A. E. (Eds.). (2009). *Evidence based practice in infant and early childhood psychology*. Hoboken, NJ: John Wiley & Sons.

Nagle, R. J. (2007). Issues in preschool assessment. In B. A. Bracken & R. J. Nagle (Eds.), *Psychoeducational assessment of preschool children* (4th ed., pp. 29–48). Mahwah, NJ: Erlbaum.

Niileksela, C. R., & Reynolds, M. R. (2019). Enduring the tests of age and time: Wechsler constructs across versions and revisions. *Intelligence, 77*, 1–15.

Ramey, C. T., & Ramey, S. L. (2004). Early learning and school readiness: Can early intervention make a difference?. *Merrill-Palmer Quarterly, 50*, 471–491. doi:10.1353/mpq.2004.0034

Roid, G. H. (2003a). *Stanford-Binet Intelligence Scales-Fifth Edition*. Torrance, CA: Western Psychological Services.

Roid, G. H. (2003b). *Stanford-Binet Intelligence Scales-Fifth Edition technical manual*. Torrance, CA: Western Psychological Services.

Salvia, J., Ysseldyke, J. E., & Witmer, S. (2017). *Assessment in special and inclusive education* (13th ed.). Boston, MA: Cengage.

Sattler, J. M., Dumont, R., & Coalson, D. L. (2018). Wechsler Preschool and Primary Scale of Intelligence – Fourth Edition. In J. M. Sattler (Eds.), *Assessment of children: Cognitive foundations and applications* (6th ed., pp. 439–527). La Mesa, CA: Jerome M. Sattler, Publisher, Inc.

Sattler, J. M., Dumont, R., Willis, J. O., & Salerno, J. D. (2018). Differential Ability Scales – Second Edition. In J. M. Sattler (Eds.), *Assessment of children: Cognitive foundations and applications* (6th ed., pp. 597–666). La Mesa, CA: Jerome M. Sattler, Publisher, Inc.

Sattler, J. M., Salerno, J. D., & Roberts-Pittman, B. (2018). Standford-Binet Intelligence Scales – Fifth Edition. In J. M. Sattler (Eds.), *Assessment of children: Cognitive foundations and applications* (6th ed., pp. 557–596). La Mesa, CA: Jerome M. Sattler, Publisher, Inc.

Sattler, J. M., Shaw, S. R., Schultz, E., D'Intino, J. S., Roger, K., Daou, A. Z., & Cousineau-Pérusse, M. (2018). Woodcock-Johnson IV Tests of Cognitive Abilities. In J. M. Sattler (Eds.), *Assessment of children: Cognitive foundations and applications* (6th ed., pp. 667–704). La Mesa, CA: Jerome M. Sattler, Publisher, Inc.

Schneider, W. J. (2016). Strengths and weaknesses of the Woodcock-Johnson IV tests of cognitive abilities: Best practice from a scientist-practitioner perspective. In D. P. Flanagan & V. C. Alfonso (Eds.), *WJ IV Clinical use and interpretation: Scientist-practitioner perspectives* (pp. 191–210). Boston, MA: Elsevier.

Schneider, W. J., & McGrew, K. S. (2018). The Cattell-Horn-Carroll theory of cognitive abilities. In D. P. Flanagan & E. M. McDonough (Eds.), *Contemporary intellectual assessment: Theories, tests, and issues* (4th ed., pp. 73–163). New York, NY: The Guilford Press.

Schrank, F. A., McGrew, K. S., & Mather, N. (2014). *Woodcock-Johnson IV Tests of Cognitive Abilities.* Itasca, IL: Riverside.

Wechsler, D. (2012a). *Wechsler Preschool and Primary Scale of Intelligence – Fourth Edition.* Bloomington, MN: Pearson.

Wechsler, D. (2012b). *Wechsler Preschool and Primary Scale of Intelligence – Fourth Edition technical and interpretive manual.* Bloomington, MN: Pearson.

Chapter 11

Assessing Communication, Language, and Speech in Preschool Children

Lena G. Caesar and Sharlene Wilson Ottley

Introduction: Born to Communicate

The ability to communicate using appropriate speech and language modes represents a significant developmental achievement for young children. For most typically developing children, speech and language acquisition occurs naturally. In fact, only rarely does a "reasonably normal infant ... fail to learn a natural language" (Perkins & Kent, 1986, p. 1). At birth, the human infant is already equipped with most of the anatomical structures and perceptual abilities that are necessary for developing communication skills. For example, the human newborn is equipped with fully functional vocal folds (as demonstrated by the initial birth cry and other cries produced thereafter), as well as a fairly mature auditory system that will permit the child to hear and be responsive to human and environmental sounds. Most children will continue to develop and refine these skills with only minimal intentional adult input.

Sometimes, however, something either goes wrong or works differently in this otherwise natural and spontaneous process. Although the exact reasons for a specific child's communication delay or disorder cannot always be ascertained, we do know that a delay or disorder may occur in conjunction with several factors, including (a) injuries to the brain occurring before or after birth (e.g. tumors, infections, trauma), (b) cognitive delays or intellectual disabilities, or (c) simply a delay in the timing of an otherwise typical progression. Perceptual deficits such as hearing loss or blindness may also disrupt normal speech and language acquisition. However, as many as 7% of children experience a specific language impairment (SLI) without a co-existing condition or diagnosis (Bishop, 2006; Tomblin et al., 1997). Regardless of the cause, children whose communication development differs significantly from the typical processes of language acquisition experience significant setbacks. The earlier they can be identified and get back on track, the greater the chances of forestalling later academic, behavioral, and social problems (Guralnick, 2011).

This chapter will address issues surrounding the early and accurate assessment of communication, language, and speech in preschool-aged children. Guidelines regarding typical communication development will be provided as well as information regarding appropriate assessment tools specific to this population. Assessment considerations for specific populations with cultural and linguistic differences and/or perceptual deficits will also be described and discussed.

Defining the Terms: Communication, Language, and Speech

Communication, language, and speech are different but related terms. Communication is a broad term that refers to the sending and receiving of messages by a variety of means (including speech and language). Communication can be further defined as the means by which communication partners achieve mutual understanding through a process of encoding and decoding information. Language and speech refer to two interrelated modes of communication by which information can be shared. Whereas language refers to a symbolic, rule-governed system for sharing information, speech represents the verbal expression of the language mode. Reading, writing, and gestural systems such as American Sign Language (ASL) are other modes by which communication may be accomplished (Owens, 2017) (see Figure 11.1).

Language is a complex, coded system involving rules for the correct use of both spoken and written forms. Speakers and listeners must master these rules in order to become effective communicators. Language rules are not consistent across languages but differ among the more than 7,000 languages spoken around the world (Lyovin, Kessler, & Leben, 2017). Most languages have common elements involving specific linguistic subcomponents (or rule systems) that must be mastered in order to effectively encode and decode both spoken and written messages. The five subcomponents or rule systems found in many languages (including English) are as follows:

1. Phonology: Rules for ordering, sequencing, and distributing speech sounds
2. Morphology: Rules related to the use of the smallest meaningful units of language
3. Syntax: Rules related to the form and structure of a sentence
4. Semantics: Rules governing the meaning or content of words or word combinations
5. Pragmatics: Rules governing the appropriate socially acceptable use of language

Speech is the verbal component of language and involves the coordinated movement of muscles of the face and mouth, and muscles controlling the respiratory system and vocal tract. For speech to occur, there must be (a) a source of air (lungs), (b) structures that shape the airstream (articulators), and (c) membranes that are capable of a vibrating (vocal folds of larynx).

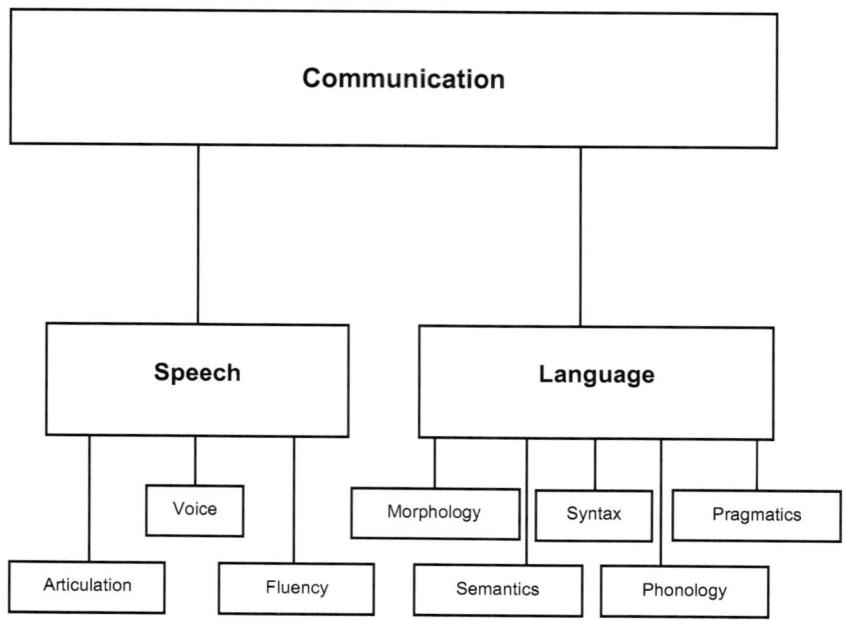

Figure 11.1 Components of Communication

All of these complex anatomical and physiological processes are directed by the brain (Weismer & Holt, 2016).

The complexity of the definitions of language and speech gives us some insight into the complexity of assessing language and speech disorders. As indicated above, language is multidimensional and involves the knowledge and interaction of several rule systems—any or all of which may be impaired in the developing child. On the other hand, although speech may appear to require fewer linguistic rules, several anatomical structures (lungs, larynx, head, and face structures) are involved in the production of spoken language (Owens, 2017).

Typical Speech and Language Development

In children, speech and language skills develop sequentially and systematic-ally. Although this development may vary from child to child, most children follow a predictable age-related schedule. Speech and language development usually progresses from simple to complex—beginning with the child pro-ducing and comprehending language at the one-word level and progressing steadily over time to express longer and more complex forms. The first three years of a child's life is a period of intensive speech and language development, which many scientists believe may be related to periods of excessive brain activity and synaptic growth. Language development in young children should therefore be assessed in a developmental context with the awareness that the child's occasional deviations from a typical developmental trajectory may or may not be indicative of a disorder.

The majority of typically developing children will virtually master the basic rule systems of the language used in their environment during the first few years of life. For example, by age 3 most children have mastered the speech sounds of their home language and are able to speak with sufficient meaningfulness and clarity for a stranger to understand them (Owens, 2017). According to the National Institute on Deafness and Other Communication Disorders (NIDCD, 2014), it is possible to predict the specific speech and language skills that children should demonstrate at different age ranges. Knowing which language skills should be demonstrated as the child grows, permits parents, medical professionals, and school personnel to determine whether a child may be typically developing or falling behind. Table 11.1 outlines the age-related speech and language milestones that typically developing children should be expected to achieve.

In addition to being predictable, speech and language development is also inter-related with other developmental areas such as cognition, perception, and social awareness. Research has shown that there are specific cognitive skills that children need to master in order to achieve communicative competence. For example, Piaget (1952) identified five early cognitive skills that typically developing children demonstrate during the sensorimotor stage of cognitive development. These cognitive pre-requisites for language acquisition include imitation, causality, means-end, object permanence, and symbolic play. Other developmental areas which parallel speech and language development include perceptual abilities (auditory and visual) and social awareness. In fact, according to Johnson (2010), appropriate language development is highly dependent on the coordinated functioning of other related domains such as biological, social, perceptual, and cognitive ones. For this reason, the assessment of young children (age 0–5) should incorporate not only a linguistic perspective but also a description of the child's cognitive, perceptual, social, and neurobiological functioning. The young child's eventual mastery of communication depends on (a) the availability of sensory information, (b) the ability to process that information, (c) the integrity of the organs and muscles that are necessary to produce speech, and (d) access to an appropriate socially stimulating environment (Singleton & Schulman, 2013).

Given the multiple domains involved with typical language acquisition and development, it is imperative that young children's communicative development be assessed by multidisciplinary teams representing a variety of related disciplines and professions. Communication does not occur in a vacuum and should always be described and assessed using a context-based approach that is both comprehensive and "intersystemic" (Nelson, 2010).

Table 11.1 Typical Speech and Language Milestones

Age Range	Receptive Milestones	Expressive Milestones
Birth–5 months	• Reacts to sounds • Turns head toward noise • Recognizes caregiver's voice • Stops/starts sucking in response to sounds	• Vocalizes pleasure and displeasure • Makes noise when talked to • Smiles when they see you
6–11 months	• Follows sound with eyes • Responds to change in tone of mother's voice • Understands "no-no" • Notices toys that make sounds • Pays attention to music	• Begins babbling/laughs • Makes sounds like/p, b, m/ • Makes gurgling sounds • Repeats sounds • Communicates using gestures
12–17 months	• Attends to a book or toy for ~2 minutes • Follows simple directions with gestures • Answers simple questions nonverbally • Points (objects, pictures, & people)	• Says two or three words to label a person or an object • Tries to imitate simple words • Has 1 or 2 words by their first birthday (e.g. "mama," "dada")
18–23 months	• Enjoys being read to • Points to pictures, when named, in books • Uses 1-to-2-word questions (e.g. "Go bye-bye?") • Follows simple commands without gestures • Points to simple body parts (e.g. ears) • Understands verbs like "eat" and "sleep"	• Says 8–10 words • Requests food items • Makes animals sounds • Begins to combine words (e.g. "more milk") • Correctly pronounces most vowels and/n, m, p, h/in syllables and speech sounds
2–3 years	• Knows about 50 words • Understands some spatial concepts • Knows pronouns like "you," "me," "his" • Answers simple questions • Uses descriptive adjectives (e.g. "pretty") • Uses/k, g, f, t, n/sounds	• Speaks in 2-to-3-word phrases • Says around 40 words • Uses inflection to ask questions (e.g. "My bottle?") • Begins using plural and past-tense words (e.g. socks, jumped)
4–5 years	• Says about 200–300 words • Understands complex questions	• Defines words • Uses irregular past verbs (e.g. "ran") • Answers "wh" questions

(Continued)

Table 11.1 (Cont.)

Age Range	Receptive Milestones	Expressive Milestones
	• Understands spatial concepts • Speech is intelligible • Pays attention to short stories and answers simple questions • Tells stories that stay on topic • Says most sounds correctly except/l, s, z, r, v, ch, sh, th/	• Describes how to do things • Lists items into categories
5 years	• Understands more than 2,000 words • Understands time sequences (first, then, finally) • Understands rhyming • Sentences can be 8 or more words in length	• Uses compound, complex sentences • Describes objects • Engages in conversation • Uses imagination to create stories

Source: Adapted from National Institute on Deafness and Other Communication Disorders (NIDCD), 2014.

Communication Disorders Defined

There are many perspectives on what actually constitutes a speech and/or language disorder. One of the earliest definitions came from Charles Van Riper, a pioneer in the field of communication disorders. He defined a communication disorder based on its functional impact on the individual by stating that "speech is defective when it calls attention to itself, interferes with communication, or causes its possessor to be maladjusted" (Van Riper, 1939). This functional definition has evolved over time to include much broader cognitive, linguistic, neurological, and physical perspectives. Also, whereas early definitions focused primarily on the output aspect of communication (speech production) and ignored the receptive (comprehension) aspect, current definitions are more comprehensive and encompass the entire communication process. Three of the most frequently used are outlined in Table 11.2.

A communication disorder may vary in terms of: (a) the *severity* of the disorder (ranging from mild to severe); (b) the *timing or onset* of the disorder—prenatal (occurring before birth), perinatal (occurring during the birth process or shortly after), or postnatal (diagnosed after a period of typical development); and/or (c) its *co-morbidity patterns*, which may range

Table 11.2 Definitions of Communication Disorders

Source/Year	Definition
The American Speech-Language Hearing Association (1993)	*"An impairment in the ability to receive, send, process, and comprehend concepts or verbal, nonverbal and graphic symbol systems. A communication disorder may be evident in the processes of hearing, language, and/or speech."*
The Individuals with Disabilities Education Improvement Act (IDEA, 2004)	*"A communication disorder is a disorder such as stuttering, impaired articulation, a language impairment, or a voice impairment that adversely affects a child's educational performance."*
The Diagnostic and Statistical Manual of Mental Disorders —Fifth Edition, (American Psychiatric Association, 2014)	Divides communication disorders into five categories: language disorder, speech sound disorder, childhood-onset fluency disorder, social (pragmatic) communication disorder, and unspecified communication disorder.
	• Language disorder: "Persistent difficulties in the acquisition and use of language across modalities (i.e. spoken, written, sign language, or other) due to deficits in comprehension or production" and language abilities that are "substantially and quantifiably" below age expectations.
	• Speech sound disorder: The key diagnostic criterion for speech sound disorder includes "persistent difficulty with speech sound production that interferes with speech intelligibility or prevents verbal communication of messages."

from occurring in isolation to co-occurring with other disabilities, such as hearing impairments, autism spectrum disorders, or intellectual disabilities.

In summary, communication disorders are usually divided into two main categories: language disorders and speech disorders. Whereas language disorders affect the comprehension and production of language, speech disorders impair the production of speech, the fluency of speech, and the quality of the voice.

Assessing Communication Disorders

The Purpose of Assessment

In the context of speech and language, assessment is the process used to: (a) determine whether or not a communication problem exists; (b) identify the nature of the communication problem; (c) indicate the severity of the communication problem; and (d) determine specific next steps or goals for ameliorating the communication problem (Haynes & Pindzola, 2012). In young children, a communication problem may manifest as either a speech or language delay or a speech or language disorder. A speech or language *delay* implies that although the child is following a typical, predictable sequence in the development of speech or language skills, the rate of acquisition may be slower than expected. On the other hand, a speech or language *disorder* refers to atypical and erroneous acquisition that may not follow a predictable sequence. One of the goals of assessing the speech and language of young children is to deferentially determine the presence of a delay versus a disorder (ASHA, 1993). In the context of the Individuals with Disabilities Education Improvement Act (IDEA, 2004), assessment also serves to identify early intervention (EI) services for which the child and family may qualify.

Assessment is, therefore, never an end in itself but a process that should always lead to a conclusion regarding the "next possible step" based on information obtained from the child and other persons (such as family members and professionals) who share the child's environment. Assessment can therefore be viewed as the "entryway" to appropriate and relevant service.

Accurate assessment should therefore be designed to answer the following questions:

- Is there a speech or language problem?
- Alternatively, is the child at risk for a speech or language problem?
- If so, what is the nature of the problem?
- How severe is the problem in terms of its limitations on communication?
- Given the impact of the problem on the child's communicative abilities, what types of intervention and treatment options should the child have access to?

The Process of Assessment

The assessment of a child's speech and language skills should follow an orderly sequence. Steps in the assessment process include referral, screening, test administration, diagnosis, prognosis, and intervention planning. Each of these terms are defined and discussed below.

Step 1: Referral. The assessment process for young children is usually initiated by a parent, pediatrician, or other professional who may be concerned about the child's speech and language development. The individual who initiates the process is known as the "referral source." A referral typically triggers the screening process.

Step 2: Screening. In the context of assessment, screening is the process of determining whether or not a problem exists and, if a problem does exist, determining the direction for further assessment (Crais, 2011). Children may also be identified as being "at risk" following screening programs conducted at physician's offices, or while attending school programs such as Head Start or pre-kindergarten. A determination of being "at risk" may trigger either further screening or a complete assessment.

Screenings can be accomplished in several different ways, including: (a) a speech-language pathologist (SLP) or other professional making direct contact with the child, (b) a parent providing verbal information, or (c) a parent or other caregiver completing a formal screening tool. In the context of young children, parents may be the most reliable and best-informed source of information regarding their child's speech and language skills (Fenson et al., 2006). The SLP's responsibility is to choose a screening instrument that is fair, efficient, and linguistically appropriate.

After screening is completed, a determination is made as to whether the child has "passed" or "failed" the screening process. If the child passes, the referent is informed and information regarding typical developmental milestones and language enhancement techniques may be discussed and shared. If the child does not pass, the SLP will discuss findings with the parents/caregivers and seek their permission to initiate the assessment process. Prior to initiating the assessment process, the SLP should always seek ways of ascertaining that cultural, communication, and language differences did not interfere with or influence the results of the screening. Table 11.3 provides a list of screening tools frequently used to determine typical speech and language development.

Step 3: Test Administration. If the screening process has determined that the child may not be developing speech and language skills in a typical manner, the child's communication skills are then subjected to a more in-depth evaluation. The assessment phase is both diagnostic and therapeutic in its focus since the two main purposes of assessment are to (a) determine the specific diagnostic category into which the disorder fits and (b) develop a plan for providing intervention services.

IDEA (2004) provides specific guidelines as to how the assessment should be undertaken. With regard to evaluation (assessment), the law specifies that:

- A variety of testing procedures, measures, and strategies should be used (including parent information and clinician opinion)
- Testing should evaluate all suspected areas of disability
- No single measure should be used as the sole basis for diagnosis and eligibility
- Only relevant tools that support decision-making should be employed
- Formal assessments should be technically sound and non-discriminatory

Table 11.3 Speech and Language Screening Tools for Infants and Toddlers

Screening Tool	Author(s)	Age Range	Test Focus
Ages and Stages Questionnaires: A Parent-Completed Child-Monitoring System—Third Edition (2009)	Squires, J., Bricker, D., Mounts, L., Twonbly, E., Nickel, R., Clifford, J., Murphy, K., Hoselton, R., Potter, L., & Farrell, J.	4–60 months	• Developmental questionnaire for parents of at-risk children
Assessing Linguistic Behavior (1987)	Olswang, L., Stoeol-Gammon, C., Coggins, T. E., & Carpenter, R. L.	0–24 months	• Assesses play, communicative intention, cognitive antecedents, language production, and comprehension
The Brigance Infant and Toddler Screen (2002)	Brigance A., & Glascoe, F.	0–23 months	• Screens communication and motor development, self-help, and social-emotional skills
Developmental Indicators for the Assessment of Learning—Fourth Edition (2011)	Mardell-Czudnowski, C. & Goldenberg, D. S.	2–6 years	• Screens motor abilities, concepts, and language development
Denver Developmental Screening—Second Edition (2002)	Frankenburg, W., Dodds, J., Archer, P., Bresnick, B., Maskchka, P., Edelman, M., & Shapiro, J.	0–6 years	• Identifies children with gross motor, language, fine motor, and personal-social developmental delays
Early Screening Profiles (1990)	Harrison, P. L., Kaufman, A. S., Kaufman, N. L., Bruininks, R. H., Ilmer, S., Rynders, J., Sparrow, S. S., & Cicchetti, D. A.	2–7 years	• Identifies at-risk or gifted children in areas of cognition, language, motor, and self-help skills
Fluharty Preschool Speech and Language Screening Test—Second Edition (2000)	Fluharty, N. B.	0–3 years; 6–11 years	• Identifies children in need of further speech and language testing
Hawaii Early Learning Profile (1992)	Parks, S.	0–3 years	• Criterion-referenced charts for cognitive, language, gross motor, fine motor, and self-help skills

(Continued)

Table 11.3 (Cont.)

Screening Tool	Author(s)	Age Range	Test Focus
Kaufman Survey of Early Academic and Language Skills (1993)	Kaufman, A. S. & Kaufman, N. L.	3–6 years	• Assesses expressive and receptive skills, pre-academic skills, and articulation
The Rossetti Infant-Toddler Language Scale (1990)	Rossetti, L.	0–3 years	• Uses parent interviews and questionnaires to gather early speech and language skills
Vineland Adaptive Behavior Scales—Third Edition (2016)	Sparrow S., Balla C., & Cicchetti, D.	0–90 years	• Uses parent questionnaire to assess expressive & receptive communication, socialization, daily living, and motor skills
Symbolic Play Scale Checklist (2000)	Westby, C.	0–5 years	• Describes symbolic play development through typical language development; checklist administered by SLPs and teachers

Step 4: Diagnosis. Information obtained from the tests and measures that describes the child's speech and language skills can be used to determine the child's diagnostic category and eligibility for services.

Step 5: Prognosis. A prognosis is a statement that predicts the child's chances of full recovery, the possible duration of the disorder, and responsiveness to intervention. Information obtained during the assessment process is usually the basis for the prediction.

Step 6: Intervention Planning. In recent years, there has been a specific effort to plan intervention within the functional contexts of the culture of the child and family. This may involve embedding intervention into everyday routines and activities as well as involving family members and professionals in planning for "next steps."

Speech and Language Assessment Techniques

Both IDEA (2004) and ASHA (2008) recommend using a range of assessment techniques for identifying speech and language disorders in preschool children. The advantages of using a variety of methods (instead of a single measure) include greater individualization, more possibilities for family involvement, and wider opportunities for assessing the child in functional and naturalistic contexts. Best practice in communication assessment recommends combining the two broad categories of assessment methods, namely, formal measures and informal measures.

Formal Assessment Procedures

Formal assessments are types of measures for which there are specified procedures for obtaining, scoring, and interpreting information. These types of assessments are designed to compare specific aspects of the child's performance with either a normative or a criterion-referenced population. Formal assessments are also referred to as standardized or norm-referenced tests. Formal measures have several limitations, including their static nature, their lack of relevance to real life, their ability to capture only a single point in time, and their propensity for being influenced by non-cognitive factors such as illness, fatigue, or reduced attention. Despite the limitations of formal measures, they do have advantages that may offset some of their negative characteristics. For example, formal assessments are efficient and easy to administer, yield quantifiable and objective results, allow children to be compared with age- and grade-matched peers, and generally yield quantifiable, objective results (Shipley & McAfee, 2016). However, professionals need to be careful about not using formal tests for purposes for which they were not intended. Inappropriate uses include using formal measures to test children who are not represented in the norming sample—such as bilingual or culturally and linguistically diverse (CLD) children—or using tests that do not measure the child's targeted skills or abilities. Table 11.4

Table 11.4 Formal Speech and Language Assessment Measures

Formal Measure	Author(s)	Age Range	Test Focus
Bankson Language Test—Third Edition (2016)	Bankson, N.	3–8 years	• Assesses semantic knowledge, morphological/syntactic rules, and pragmatics
Bankson-Bernthal Test of Phonology (1990)	Bankson, N. W. & Bernthal, J. E.	3–9 years	• Assesses articulation and phonological processes using: a whole word accuracy analysis, a traditional consonant articulation analysis, and a phonological process analysis
Battelle Developmental Inventory—Second Edition (2005, pp. 15–16)	Newborg, J.	0–8 years	• Assesses speech, language, social-emotional, cognitive, motoric, learning, and hearing skills
Boehm Test of Basic Concepts-3 Preschool—Third Edition (2001)		3–5 years	• Measures concepts relevant to preschool and early childhood curriculum, with each concept tested twice to assess understanding across contexts; Braille version available
Bracken Basic Concept Scale—Third Edition (2006)	Bracken, B.	2.6–8 years	• Assesses receptive knowledge of basic concepts; Spanish translation available
Clinical Assessment of Language Comprehension (1995)	Miller, J. F., & Paul, R.	8 mos–10 years	• Informal assessment for children who are very young or difficult to test and includes pointing, object manipulation, conversation, and behavioral compliance responses

Assessment	Author(s)	Age Range	Description
Clinical Evaluation of Language Fundamentals—Preschool—Third Edition (2013)	Wiig, E. H., Secord, W. A., & Semel, E.	3–6 years	• Assesses language abilities of pre-school-aged children who will be in academic-oriented settings
Communication and Symbolic Behavior Scales Developmental Profile (2002)	Wetherby, A. M., & Prizant, B. M.	9 mos–2 years	• Assesses language stage (prelinguistic, early one-word, late one-word, multiword) with caregiver form and play observations
Comprehensive Receptive and Expressive Vocabulary Test—Third Edition (2013)	Wallace, G., & Hammill, D. D.	4–18 years	• Assesses receptive and expressive oral vocabulary strengths and weaknesses
Diagnostic Evaluation of Language Variation (2005)	Seymour, H. N., Roeper, T., & de Villiers, J. G.	4–12 years	• Comprehensive speech and language test, which includes items specifically designed to neutralize the effect of variations from Mainstream American English (MAE) in order to assess true language abilities
Dynamic Assessment and Intervention: Improving Children's Narrative Abilities (2001)	Miller, L., Gillam, R. B., & Peña, E. D.	Preschool through elementary years	• Dynamic assessment that identifies storytelling ability in children
Early Language Milestone Scale—Second Edition (1993)	Coplan, J.	0–36 months	• Designed to assess auditory expressive, auditory receptive, and visual skills
Expressive One Word Picture Vocabulary Test—Fourth Edition	Gardner, M.	2–12 years	• Assesses expressive vocabulary in children
Functional Emotional Assessment Scale for Infancy and Early Childhood (2001)	Greenspan, S. I.	0–48 months	• Uses play to observe emotional development based on levels of communication

(Continued)

Table 11.4 (Cont.)

Formal Measure	Author(s)	Age Range	Test Focus
Goldman-Fristoe Test of Articulation—Third Edition (2015)	Goldman, R., & Fristoe, M.	2–16 years	• Measures articulation of sounds-in-words, sounds-in-sentences, and stimulability
Hodson Assessment of Phonological Patterns—Third Edition (2004)	Hodson, B.	3–8 years	• Designed for highly unintelligible children to assess major phonological patterns
MacArthur-Bates Communicative Development Inventories (2006)	Fenson, L., Marchman, V. A., Thal, D., Dale, P. S., Reznick, J. S., & Bates, E.	1–3 years	• Uses a parental checklist format to assess first signs of understanding, comprehension of early phrases, and talking; alternate languages available
Oral and Written Language Scales—Second Edition (2011)	Carrow-Woolfolk, E.	3–21 years	• Measures receptive and expressive language through comprehension examining semantics, syntax, pragmatics, and supralinguistics
Oral-Motor/Feeding Rating Scale (1990)	Jelm, J. M.	All ages	• Summarizes oral-motor and feeding functioning in eight areas: breast feeding, bottle feeding, spoon feeding, cup drinking, chewing, and straw drinking
Peabody Picture Vocabulary Test—Fourth Edition (2007)	Dunn, L. M., Dunn, L. M., & Williams, K. T.	2–90 years	• Uses a picture-pointing task to assess receptive vocabulary
Preschool Language Assessment Instrument—Second Edition (2003)	Blank, M., Rose, S., & Berlin, L.	3–5 years	• Assesses abilities needed to meet the demands of classroom discourse
Preschool Language Scale—Fifth Edition (2011)	Zimmerman, I. L., Steiner, V. G., & Pond, R. E.	0–6 years	• Assesses comprehensive language skills for comparison with norms for children birth through 6 years; Spanish version available

Test	Author(s)	Age	Description
Receptive-Expressive Emergent Language Scale—Third Edition (2003)	Bzoch, K., & League, R.	0–3 years	• Designed in the U.K. to help medical professionals identify children with developmental language delays or disorders
The Rossetti Infant-Toddler Language Scale (1990)	Rossetti, L.	0–3 years	• Observed, elicited, or reported behaviors organized by age; parent interview and questionnaire
Structured Photographic Expressive Language—3rd Edition (2005)	Werner, E., & Kresheck, J. D.	3–5 years	• Presents photographs and uses structured questions to elicit early developing morphological and syntactic forms
Test for Auditory Comprehension of Language—Fourth Edition (2014)	Carrow-Woolfolk, E.	3–10 years	• Uses picture pointing to assess comprehension of word classes and relations, grammatical morphemes, elaborated sentence constructions
Test of Early Language Development—Fourth Edition (2018)	Hresko, W. P., Reid, D. K., & Hammill, D. D.	2–8 years	• Measures receptive and expressive language form and content
Test of Early Reading Ability—Fourth Edition (2018)	Reid, D. K., Hresko, W. P., & Hammill, D. D.	3–8 years	• Measures emergent and early reading abilities: knowledge of contextual meaning, alphabet, and conventions
Test of Early Written Language—Third Edition (2012)	Hresko, W. P., Herron, S, Peak, P., & Hicks, D. L.	3–10 years	• Measures emergent written language
Transdisciplinary Play-Based Assessment—Second Edition (2008)	Linder, T. W.	6 mos–6 years	• Informal assessment for social-emotional, cognitive, language and communication, sensorimotor development
Vineland Adaptive Behavior Scales—Third Edition (2016)	Sparrow S., Balla C., & Cicchetti, D.	0–90 years	• Parent questionnaire that assesses expressive/receptive communication, socialization, daily living, and motor skills

contains a description of formal assessments measures frequently used with preschool populations.

Informal Assessment Procedures

Informal assessments, also known as authentic assessment approaches, employ observational and semi-structured techniques to determine the child's specific communicative strengths and weaknesses. Unlike most formal assessments, informal assessments generally take place in realistic, functional contexts, such as on the playground, during family activities, or as observations in the preschool context. Informal assessments of young children may occur in the context of conversations, shared book experiences, dramatic play, or even during non-verbal interactions. Informal assessments can therefore be used to document the presence of specific communicative behaviors, as well as document frequency of occurrence and the context in which they occur. Informal measures, however, rarely yield quantifiable results, can be time-consuming, are sometimes difficult to administer and interpret, and require higher levels of examiner competence (Shipley & McAfee, 2016).

In addition to formal and informal assessment measures for measuring speech, language, and communication, a speech-language pathologist (SLP) conducting an assessment session with a young child will utilize a range of tools and activities for gathering information, including: (a) a thorough case history; (b) interviews with family members, the child, and/or knowledgeable adults; and (c) screening of hearing, vision, motor, and cognitive abilities.

Types of Informal Assessment Procedures

Parental Tools and Measures

Parent reports and observations are essential components of the process of assessing young children. In fact, parents may be a more reliable source of information than any other formal or informal measure. Besides being valid and reliable, parental information may also be one of the most realistic and functionally useful sources of information available to the SLP (Crais, Douglas, & Campbell, 2004; Fenson et al., 2006). Parents tend to know their child better than any other person on the assessment team and are therefore capable of providing accurate, realistic descriptions of the child's speech and language performance. In addition, the parental advantage of being able to interact with the child in varied naturalistic contexts provides information that would otherwise be difficult to obtain (Dale, 1991). Unfortunately, many professionals do not consistently solicit parental involvement in the assessment process. Results of a study by Crais, Roy, and Free (2006) found that although parents were not frequently asked to be involved in their child's assessment, parents do feel that they should be involved and are typically willing to provide information.

Parental assessments are generally structured in the form of vocabulary checklists (for words produced or comprehended), parental reports of behaviors observed, or developmental inventories. All of these sources can provide a picture of the child's current developmental stage. Examples of norm-referenced parent report measures include instruments such as the MacArthur-Bates Communicative Development Inventories (CDI; Fenson et al., 2006), and the Bayley Scales of Infant Development, Third Edition (Bayley—III; Bayley, 2006).

Play-Based Assessments

Regardless of culture or language, it has been demonstrated that most children are born with an innate propensity toward play. Due to the interactive and communicative nature of a young child's play activities, play has the capacity to serve as an appropriate context for observing and documenting language. Assessments of young children during play activities may be done either during parent-child interactions or during professional-child interactions. In addition, the assessment may take place during both free play and structured play opportunities. Meyers, McBride, and Peterson (1996) reported several advantages of the use of play assessments as compared to traditional assessments. They found that compared to traditional assessments, play-based assessments are capable of yielding a greater quantity of information in significantly less time. In addition, information obtained during play assessments was found to be more useful than results obtained from formal assessment measures.

Although informal versions of play-based assessments can still be accessed in the literature (see McCune, 1995; Westby, 1998), other widely used semi-formal tools include the Transdisciplinary Play-Based Assessment tool (Linder, 2008) and the Communication and Symbolic Behaviors Scale Developmental Profile (CSBS DP; Wetherby & Prizant, 2002). Linder's criterion-referenced instrument involves play interactions between the child's parents and peers and assesses four domains related to communication: social-emotional, sensorimotor, cognitive, and language. The CSBS is a norm-referenced tool and uses both a caregiver questionnaire and direct observation of play behaviors to assess the child's communicative competence. The four areas of focus in the CSBS are: communicative function, communicative means, reciprocity, and social affective signaling. Other common informal instruments that can be administered in a play-based format are the Assessment, Evaluation and Programming System for Infants and Children (Bricker & Squires, 1999) and the Rossetti Infant-Toddler Language Scale (Rossetti, 1990).

Dynamic Assessment

Dynamic assessment (DA) refers to a non-static, interactive method of language assessment that is designed not only to assess *what* the child knows but *how* the child learns. Dynamic assessment utilizes a teaching process that allows the examiner to observe both the child's rate of learning and style of learning. This teaching process is referred to as a mediated learning experience (MLE) and consists of deliberate teaching by the examiner, careful observation of the child's response to the instruction, and an adjustment in teaching style based on the child's learning style (Feuerstein, 1979; Lidz, 1987). These learning experiences measure both what the child is able to do alone and how much the child is able to accomplish with the help of an adult or peer (facilitator). In contrast with static, standardized measures, information gleaned from DA can provide information that is pertinent to intervention planning for young children (Peña & Gillam, 2000).

Currently, there are no known published or structured DA measures that are designed to use with young children. However, most formal tests can be administered "dynamically" using a test-teach-retest approach. One example of a dynamic approach may be having the examiner administer and score a particular test item according to the test's instructions and then re-administer the identical item while providing the child with cues and prompts. Even though the child's performance on the second administration would not be reported as a "score," information obtained from the second attempt could provide the examiner with useful information with regard to the child's learning potential when provided with feedback (Haywood & Lidz, 2007).

Language Sampling

Language sampling is an assessment method used to capture a snapshot of a child's communication competence in real time. Language sampling typically occurs in naturalistic settings with the goal of collecting a representative sample of a child's day-to-day communication in a non-contrived situation. In other words, the language sample should be a true representation of the child's typical communicative performance. By providing an integrated picture of the child's speech, language, and social communication skills, language sampling is capable of providing information regarding both the content and context of language. Language sampling continues to be an assessment measure frequently used by speech-language pathologists in preschool settings. Results of a series of surveys (Arias & Friberg, 2017; Caesar & Kohler, 2009; Kemp & Klee, 1997) have consistently found language sample analysis to be the informal method of choice for the vast majority of SLPs (85–94%) who work with young children.

Language samples are usually elicited in one of two basic formats: conversational modes or narrative modes (Miller, 1981). Conversational samples are typically collected during casual conversational exchanges between the child and an adult, or between the child and an age-matched peer. These exchanges can be focused on either "here-and now" or "there-and-then" topics. In young children, age-appropriate play activities provide excellent contexts in which conversational interactions can occur. Narratives samples, on the other hand, are designed to assess the child's ability to produce connected discourse that is focused on a single theme as opposed to an interactive conversational style. Narratives can be elicited through the use of prompt questions involving television or storybook characters as well as by language elicitation through regular or wordless story books. Narratives samples can either be elicited as spontaneous stories (e.g. "tell me about your favorite TV show") or story retells ("I am going to tell you a story, and then you will tell it back to me") (Heilman, Miller, Nockerts, & Dunaway, 2010).

In order to obtain reliable, representative samples, professionals should follow some simple basic guidelines. These include: (a) asking broad questions in open-ended formats; (b) refraining from the use of yes/no questions; (c) collecting multiple samples in multiple contexts; (d) varying the conversational partners to capture audience-related variability; and (e) projecting a sense of calm and warmth throughout the interactions (Nelson, 2010; Shipley & McAfee, 2016). In addition, language samples should also be audio- or video-recorded for subsequent transcription and analysis.

Assessing Specific Areas of Children's Early Communication

Emotional & Social Development

Children come into the world with instinctive desires for forming attachments and communicating with their caregivers. In fact, Legerstee (2005) theorized that children may be born with pre-communicative abilities that not only allow them to be aware of their own mental states but also recognize the emotions of other persons in their environment. Legerstee proposed that these abilities may all be housed in a neuro-biological structure, which he refers to as the affect sharing device (AFS). He proposes that the AFS may be the driving force behind the infant's ability to match and mirror the emotions of others very shortly after birth. Examples of these early engagement abilities include: (a) the ability of an infant (younger than 1 week) to differentiate and imitate others' facial expressions, such happy, sad, or surprised ones; (b) the 6-week-old infant's ability to initiate social play by fixating on the mother's eyes; and (c) the ability of the infant (by the age of 12 months) to engage in social referencing. The latter is a term used to refer to the child's ability to gauge another person's affect (as in the case of fear) and respond appropriately (Singleton & Schulman, 2013).

There is a growing body of research that suggests that early social and emotional attachments are important precursors to later language development. For example, children who demonstrate significant delays in social and emotional development have been observed to exhibit greater communication delays. Important areas of emotional attachment that may warrant assessment include attention, self-regulation, mutual engagement and attachment abilities, and the early use of various means of communication such as gaze, vocalizations, and gestures (Crais, 2011). Examples of formal instruments for assessing infants' social-emotional behaviors include the Social Emotional Scale (Greenspan, 2006) and the Social Emotional Growth Chart (Greenspan, 2004).

Communication Intentions

As children's communicative abilities develop during their early years, they progress from being communicatively unintentional at birth to becoming fully intentional by the age of 13 to 18 months. The emergence of children's communication intentions has been described as occurring in three age-related stages: the perlocutionary or pre-intentional stage (0–8 months), the illocutionary or semi-intentional stage (8–12 months), and the locutionary or symbolic stage (12–18 months (Bates, 1976; Singleton & Schulman, 2013).

During the perlocutionary stage, children have no goal awareness and no communicative intentionality. However, caregivers infer intention from the infant's instinctive coos, smiles, and even cries. The illocutionary stage (8–12 months) marks the child's first attempt to intentionally gain the adult's attention through the use of conventional gestures and vocalizations. Some communicative gestures exhibited during this stage include pointing, showing self, raising arms to be picked up, and taking objects to the caregiver to signal help.

The child's production of the first meaningful word signals attainment of the locutionary or symbolic stage. The child is now fully aware of the functions of language and is consistently using words with or without gestures to achieve communicative intent. Examples of early intentions encoded during this stage include protesting, requesting an answer, labeling, answering, greeting, and calling (Owens, 2017).

The frequency with which the toddler uses specific communicative functions may serve as a prognostic indicator of later language skills. For example, typical 12-month-olds are expected to demonstrate communicative intentionality at least once per minute, 18-month-olds at least twice per minute, and 24-month-olds about five times per minute (Wetherby, Cain, Yonclas, & Walker, 1988). Thus, while higher rates of communicative intention are tied to advanced language outcomes, lower rates may be predictive of delayed language outcomes.

Assessment of the presence and frequency of these communication functions are typically done informally through: (a) descriptions of the child's communicative intentions over time; (b) counts of the frequency of the child's communicative attempts; and (c) observations of whether or not the child initiates interaction during play activities with peers, parents, or professionals.

Language Comprehension

Children's comprehension of spoken language typically precedes the production of their first words. Whereas first words are usually produced within 3 months of the child's first birthday, the child has been exhibiting word comprehension abilities from as early as 7 or 8 months. In fact, by the age of 8 months, an infant may be able to comprehend as many as 20 words (Fagan, 2009). Young children appear to use a variety of strategies to figure out what words mean. These strategies include the use of rhythmic or prosodic cues, such as pauses or pitch changes, to figure out communicative intent or associating predictable, familiar words with contextual cues or events (Owens, 2017). As children reach their preschool years, they continue to use a range of contextual and linguistic strategies to figure out the meaning of new words and complex multi-word structures.

Infants and toddlers who demonstrate difficulty in comprehending spoken language are at significant risk for later language delays. Many studies have demonstrated that early comprehension delays in toddlers may be predictive of a later diagnosis of chronic language disorders such as autism spectrum disorders (ASD) (Baranek, 1999; Paul, 2000; Wetherby et al., 2004). If comprehension difficulties extend into the preschool years, children may demonstrate difficulty understanding both verbal and nonverbal concepts—although by this stage many have developed compensatory strategies (e.g. word-order cues, visual cues, context) for dealing with their difficulty in processing verbal information.

Although only a few formal tests for assessing word comprehension in infants and toddlers are available, the most frequently used measures for this population include parent report measures such as the Infant/Toddler Checklist and the CDI-WG, and other examiner-administered tools such as the Preschool Language Scale, Fourth Edition: PLS-4 (Dunn, Dunn, & Williams, 2007), the Mullen Scales for Early Learning (Mullen, 1995), and the Vineland Adaptive Behavior Scales: Second Edition. Formal tests for assessing language comprehension in preschool-aged children include the Test of Auditory Comprehension of Language—Fourth edition (TACL-R; Carrow-Woolfolk, 2014) and the Structured Photographic Expressive Language Test—Third Edition (SPELT-3; Dawson, Stout, & Eyer, 2005). See the list of other formal assessment measures in Table 11.3.

Vocabulary Development

Compared to language comprehension, young children's language expression is relatively easy to assess. Most young children will produce their first word sometime around their first birthday and will continue to expand their vocabulary throughout the rest of their lives. Children's first words are usually restricted to people, activities, and events that are relevant to their own restricted worlds. First words tend to fit into one of four categories:

nominals (names of people, places, or things); actions (mostly verbs or words used in place of verbs); modifiers (adjectival or adverbial descriptors such as "nice" or "more"); and social terms ("hi," "bye," or "please"). Two-word utterances usually begin to emerge between the ages of 18 and 24 months, although the child continues to produce a significant amount of one-word utterances. The content of these multiword utterances are similar in both content and structure to the one-word utterances and fit into one of three categories: (a) word combinations that are equivalent (e.g. "mommy shoe"), (b) pivot schemas in which a key word is used to determine the intent (e.g. "more juice," "more cookie"), and (c) item-based constructions in which word combinations follow word-order rules (e.g. "baby eat," "daddy come") (Tomasello, 2006).

Children's expressive language continues to develop rapidly throughout the early preschool years. In fact, children between the ages of 18 months and 6 years may add as many as five words per day to their lexicon and demonstrate understanding of up to 4,000 more. The 3-year-old should be able to demonstrate the ability to relate past experiences, engage in pretend play, and manipulate language well enough to describe their needs and wants. By the age of 4½ years, the preschool child should be a fairly effective communicator and be able to efficiently apply the basic rules of language to everyday speech. As the child approaches the early school years, they will again experience another vocabulary surge due to the introduction of advanced vocabulary related to specific academic areas (Kaderavek, 2011). Vocabulary development, therefore, may be an important prognostic indicator not only of later communication development but also of academic success.

Common tools that can be used to assess vocabulary development in infants and toddlers include the McArthur-Bates Communicative Development Inventories (CDI; Fenson et al., 2003) as well as observational tools and parental checklists. In the case of preschoolers, language sampling may be the method of choice for obtaining functional information regarding the range and complexity of their vocabulary knowledge as well as their grammatical or syntactic mastery.

Assessing Speech and Language in Special Populations

Children with Hearing Loss

Children with hearing loss account for 2 to 3 out of every 1,000 children in the United States—with 90% of them being born to parents with typical hearing (NIDCD, 2016a, 2016b). Parents who elect to use spoken language as the primary mode of communication with their children need to not only consider the importance of appropriate amplification but also the significance of professional and family collaboration to the optimum development of spoken language skills. Even the mildest form of hearing loss can contribute to difficulties with sound discrimination or perception, especially in the presence of background noise (Anderson & Matkin, 1991). These difficulties can result in the young child missing out on some of the nuances of language and vocabulary, particularly during the critical period of language development. Additionally, difficulties with socialization may arise if children are unable to keep up with the fast-paced conversations of peers. These are all important aspects to consider when assessing children diagnosed with hearing loss. This section will primarily address assessment considerations related to children who use spoken language as their primary mode of communication. However, techniques can also apply to those who are using a manual form of communication.

Before conducting any formal speech and language assessment, a hearing screening should be done to rule out any difficulties with hearing. If further testing is warranted, a comprehensive hearing evaluation, done by an audiologist, the primary professional for diagnosing hearing, should be the first step for a child suspected of having hearing loss. Audiologists will provide type and degree of hearing loss, as well as offer recommendations regarding amplification and/or cochlear implantation, depending on the degree of loss and eligibility. Hearing loss can range from mild to profound and the type of loss may be conductive, sensorineural, or a combination of both, resulting in a mixed loss. A conductive hearing loss occurs when there is disruption to the outer or middle ear. A sensorineural hearing loss results when there is damage to the cochlea (the organ of hearing) or the auditory nerve. A mixed loss occurs when there is both a conductive and a sensorineural component.

Hearing aids may be provided depending on the degree of loss. Alternatively, a child may be recommended for cochlear implantation. A cochlear implant (CI) consists of an external and internal component, which is surgically implanted underneath the skin. While a hearing aid amplifies sound, the CI is designed to bypass the damaged inner ear structures to stimulate the auditory nerve. Additional testing may be needed to determine the cause of hearing loss, which may be due to genetic or non-genetic factors, or idiopathic in nature, or of an unknown cause or origin (Tye-Murray, 2014).

Assessment of children with hearing loss should utilize a dynamic approach and incorporate a variety of formal and informal measures. Although this section focuses primarily on the assessment of communication skills, cognitive, motor/balance, and academic skills should also be assessed by an interdisciplinary team of professionals. Such a comprehensive assessment will provide a holistic view of a child's development across several developmental domains. Auditory/listening skills along with communication skills are two important areas that should be assessed in a child with hearing loss, regardless of age. Specific measures used will be dependent both on the age and developmental level of the child being evaluated.

Auditory/Listening Skills

In order to assess functional listening skills, knowledge of the developmental progression of auditory skill development is essential. The hierarchy of auditory skill development developed by Norman Erber (detection, discrimination, identification, comprehension) (Tye-Murray, 2014) is critical when assessing functional auditory skills, and it helps the evaluator or clinician understand where a child may fall on the continuum. As a first step in the process, information should be obtained from an audiologist regarding the type and degree of hearing loss. This information will allow a professional to determine what sounds a child is able to access when provided with appropriate amplification. The hierarchy of auditory skill development framework can then be used to guide appropriate targets for intervention.

Another tool for assessing listening skills is the *Auditory Learning Guide*, developed by Walker (2009). This instrument provides a framework for understanding auditory skill development, as a child becomes able to (a) detect that a sound exists in their environment, (b) determine differences between sounds (discriminate), (c) attach meaning to a sound (i.e. identify exactly what a sound means), and (d) comprehend discourse.

For very young children, measures such as the *Infant-Toddler Meaningful Auditory Integration Scale* (Zimmerman-Phillips, Osberger, & Robbins, 2001) or the *LittlEars Auditory Questionnaire* (Coninx, Weichbold, & Tsiakpini, 2003) provide information on how a child responds to sounds in the environment and how a child may respond to amplification. As a child gets older, and listening skills become more sophisticated, more formalized measures, such as the *Test of Auditory Processing Skills—Fourth Edition* (Martin, Brownell, & Hamaguchi, 2018) examine how a child discriminates subtle sound differences, auditory memory, and phonological processing skills, and how well a child processes, understands, and is able to integrate auditory memory. The *Cottage Acquisition Scales for Listening, Language and Speech* (Wilkes, 1999) is another tool that can be used for both assessment and intervention as it provides not only speech and language milestones when assessing children with hearing loss, but also provides expected auditory skills across a developmental continuum.

Communication Skills

In addition to the typical areas assessed with children who do not have hearing loss (e.g., communicative functions, receptive and expressive language, vocabulary development), a specific focus should also be given to the emotional and social development of children with hearing loss. Many may have difficulties with socialization due to not possessing the language skills to navigate interactions with their peers with typical hearing (Sorkin, Gates-Ulanet, & Mellon, 2015). Observing the child as they interact with peers as well as using formal measures may provide useful information regarding the child's use and understanding of the social nuances of a language. Measures such as the *Test of Pragmatic*

Language—Second Edition (Phelps-Terasaki & Phelps-Gunn, 2007) or the *Social Language Development Test—Elementary: Normative Update* (Bowers, Huisingh, & LoGiudice, 2016) can be used to assess critical thinking and problem-solving skills in a social context.

Assessment of communication and listening skills in children with hearing loss should incorporate a dynamic approach, using both formal and informal measures. Collaboration between the speech and language professional, audiologist, family, and other members of an interdisciplinary team of professionals is critical for the development of children's spoken language skills.

Children from CLD Backgrounds

It is estimated that by 2025, 50% of the United States will be comprised of minority populations (Bagli, 2012). As a result, there continues to be an increasing number of children who speak a language or dialect that differs from Standard American English (SAE). When assessing children from culturally and linguistically diverse (CLD) backgrounds, particular caution should be taken when relying solely on standardized measures to determine speech and language skills. If standardized measures are used, they should be used in conjunction with a variety of informal assessment tools and strategies, as formal measures may be biased against children from diverse backgrounds (Roseberry-McKibbin, 2018).

A thorough case history with family, teachers, or those who interact with the child regularly, is critical to understanding what is considered typical within the environment and community in which the child lives and communicates (Wyatt, 2012). This should be the first step of a comprehensive communication assessment. For example, information regarding birth and developmental history, the communication environment, languages or dialects spoken in the home, and any communication difficulties that may exist in the context of the community, should be obtained.

Informal measures can serve as unbiased alternatives for assessing children from CLD backgrounds as they allow for more individualization and examination of a child's functioning in more naturalistic contexts (Caesar & Kohler, 2007). For example, the use of dynamic assessment, where a speech and language professional would examine the student's ability to learn over time when provided with instruction, is a method that has been successful for children who use a dialect or a language other than English (Peña & Gillam, 2000). Language sampling allows examination of the content, use, and form of language and can be used across languages and dialects. Assessment of a student's ability to create or retell a story can also be useful to evaluate language structures, topic maintenance, and a student's ability to organize and sequence their thoughts.

There are a number of informal measures that have proved successful in providing a more holistic view of the intricacies and complexities of children who use one or more dialect or language. For example, African American English (AAE) is a dialect that is used by some but not all members of the African American or Black community. It has its own rule-governed system and is represented across all domains of language (e.g. syntax, semantics, morphology, phonology, pragmatics). While some standardized speech and language assessments account for the use of dialect in their scoring procedures, relying solely on these measures may result in a misdiagnosis of language disorder versus a language difference.

Stockman (1996) and Stockman, Guillory, Seibert, & Boult (2013), proposed the use of a minimal competence core (MCC) for examining the oral language productions of African American children. The MCC involves a set of "fundamental competencies" that are shared among typical speakers of a language (although some variability among speakers and situations exist). Therefore, when assessing a child who is a speaker of AAE, a clinician could examine the use of these core competencies, as a means of differentiating between typical and atypical language development (Stockman et al., 2013). Additional tools, such as the Black English Scoring System (BESS) (Hyter, 1984) or using a list of features that have been documented as occurring regularly in the dialect (Craig, Thompson, Washington, & Potter, 2003) and comparing it to the productions obtained during language sampling, can provide a more comprehensive understanding of the language system of a child who uses AAE. Additionally, the Diagnostic Evaluation of Language Variation (DELV) is a norm-referenced assessment that has been widely used to assess the language of children who speak non-Mainstream English varieties (Seymour et al., 2013).

To summarize, children from CLD backgrounds represent an increasing population within our society. Assessment should not rely solely on standardized measures but should also incorporate informal measures which may provide a more comprehensive understanding of the language system of a child who speaks more than one language or dialect.

Conclusion

This chapter provided an overview of assessment processes as well as assessment products used to identify preschool children experiencing delays or disorders in their speech and language development. A detailed overview of typical development was provided as well as a rationale for using specific types of tools for obtaining the most accurate and relevant types of information. Types of assessment measures described included screening tools, parental checklists, and questionnaires, as well as formal and informal instruments. Given the significance of early intervention, this chapter makes it clear that assessment is not an endpoint in itself but rather an entryway that allows children access to the therapeutic or intervention space.

References

American Psychiatric Association. (2013). *Diagnostic and statistical manual of mental disorders* (5th ed.). Washington, DC: Author.

American Psychiatric Association. (2014). Social (Pragmatic) Communication Disorder. *In Diagnostic and Statistical Manual of Mental Disorders* (5th ed.). 47–49.

American Speech-Language-Hearing Association (ASHA). (1993). *Definitions of communication disorders and variations [Relevant Paper]*. Retrieved from www.asha.org/policy.

American Speech-Language-Hearing Association (ASHA). (2008). *Assessment and valuation of speech-language disorders in schools*. www.asha.org/SLP/Assessment-and-Evaluation-of-Speech-Language-Disorders-in-Schools/

Anderson, K. L., & Matkin, N. D. (1991). Relationship of degree of long-term hearing loss to psychosocial impact and educational needs. *Educational Audiology Association Newsletter, 8*, 17–18.

Arias, G., & Friberg, J. (2017). Bilingual language assessment: Contemporary versus recommended practice in American schools. *Language, Speech, and Hearing Services in Schools, 48*(1), 1–15. doi:10.1044/2016_LSHSS-15-0090

Bagli, Z. (2012). Multicultural aspects of hearing loss. In D. E. Battle (Ed.), *Communication disorders in multicultural and international populations* (pp. 208–242). St. Louis, MO: Elsevier Mosby.

Bankson, N. (2016). *Bankson language test—3ʳᵈ edition*. Baltimore, MD: University Park Press.

Bankson, N. W., & Bernthal, J. E. (1990). *Bankson-Bernthal test of phonology*. Austin, TX: Pro-Ed.

Baranek, G.T. (1999). Autism during infancy: A retrospective video analysis of sensory-motor and social behaviors at 9–12 months of age. *Journal of Autism and Developmental Disorders, 29*, 213–222.

Bates, E. (1976). *Language and context: The acquisition of pragmatics*. New York, NY: Academic Press.

Bayley, N. (2006). *Bayley Scales of Infant Development* (3rd ed.). San Antonio, TX: The Psychological Corporation.

Bishop, D. V. M. (2006). What causes specific language impairment in children? *Current Directions in Psychological Science, 15*(5): 217–221. doi:10.1111/j.1467-8721.2006.00439.x

Boehm, A. (2001). *Boehm test of basic concepts-3 preschool—3ʳᵈ edition*. San Antonio, TX: Pearson Education.

Bowers, L., Huisingh, R., & LoGiudice, C. (2016). *Social Language development test—Elementary: Normative update*. Austin, TX: Pro-Ed Inc.

Bracken, B. (2006). *Bracken Basic Concept scale—3ʳᵈ edition*. San Antonio, TX: Pearson Education.

Bricker, D., & Squires, J. (1999). *Ages and Stages Questionnaires (ASQ): A parent-completed child-monitoring system* (2nd ed.). Baltimore, MD: Brookes.

Bricker, D., Squires, J., Mounts, L., Potter, L., Nickel, R., & Farrell, J. (2009). *Ages and stages questionnaires: A parent-completed child-monitoring system—Third edition*. Baltimore, MD: Paul H. Brookes.

Brigance, A., & Glascoe, F. (2002). *The brigance infant and toddler screen*. North Bellerica, MA: Curriculum Associates.

Bzoch, K., & League, R. (2003). *Receptive-expressive emergent language scale—3ʳᵈ edition (REEL-3)*. Austin, TX: Pro Ed.

Caesar, L. G., & Kohler, P. (2007). The state of school-based bilingual assessment: Actual practice versus recommended guidelines. *Language, Speech and Hearing Services in Schools, 38*, 190–200.

Caesar, L. G., & Kohler, P. K. (2009). Tools clinicians use: A survey of language assessment procedures used by school-based speech-language pathologists. *Communication Disorders Quarterly, 30*, 226–236.

Carrow-Woolfolk, E. (2011). *Oral and written language scales—2nd edition (OWLS-II).* Austin, TX: Pearson Assessments.

Carrow-Woolfolk, E. (2014). *Test for auditory comprehension of language* (4th ed.) (TACL-4). Austin, TX: PRO-ED.

Coninx, F., Weichbold, V., & Tsiakpini, L. (2003). *LittlEARS Auditory Questionnaire.* MED-EL Corporation: Innsbruck, Austria.

Coplan, J. (1993). *Early language milestone scale—2nd edition (ELMS-2).* Austin, TX: Pro-Ed.

Craig, H. K., Thompson, C. A., Washington, J. A., & Potter, S. L. (2003). Phonological features of child African American English. *Journal of Speech, Language, and Hearing Research, 46,* 623–635. doi:10.1044/1092-4388(2003/049).

Crais, E. R. (2011). Testing and beyond: Strategies and tools for evaluating and assessing infants and toddlers. *Language, Speech and Hearing Services in Schools, 42,* 341–364.

Crais, E., Douglas, D., & Campbell, C. (2004). The intersection of the development of gestures and intentionality. *Journal of Speech, Language, and Hearing Research, 47,* 678–694.

Crais, E. R., Roy, V. P., & Free, K. (2006). Parents' and professionals' perceptions of the implementation of family-centered practices in child assessments. *American Journal of Speech Language Pathology, 15,* 365–377.

Dale, P. (1991). The validity of a parent report measure of vocabulary and syntax at 24 months. *Journal of Speech and Hearing Research, 34,* 565–571.

Dawson, J. I., Stout, C. E., & Eyer, J. A. (2005). *Structured photographic expressive language test.* (3rd ed.). DeKalb, IL: Janelle Publications.

Dunn, L. M., Dunn, L. M., & Williams, K. T. (2007). *Peabody picture vocabulary test—4th edition (PPVT-4).* San Antonio: TX: Pearson Assessments.

Fagan, M. K. (2009). Mean length of utterance before words and grammar: Longitudinal trends and developmental implications of infant vocalizations. *Journal of Child Language, 36,* 495–527.

Fenson, L., Marchman, V. A., Thal, D., Dale, P. S., Reznick, J. S., & Bates, E. (2006). *MacArthur-Bates Communicative Development Inventories* [Measurement instrument]. Baltimore, MD: Brookes. www.brookespublishing.com

Feuerstein, R.(1979). *Dynamic assessment of retarded performers.* Baltimore, MD: University Park Press.

Fluharty, N. B. (2000). *Fluharty preschool speech and language screening test—2nd edition.* Austin, TX: Pro-Ed.

Frankenburg, W., Dodds, J., Archer, P., Bresnick, B., Maskchka, P., Edelman, M., & Shapiro, J. (2002). *Denver developmental screening—2nd edition.* Denver, CO: Denver Developmental Materials.

Goldman, R., & Fristoe, M. (2015). *Goldman-Fristoe test of articulation—3rd edition (GFTA-3).* Circle Pines, MN: AGS Publications.

Greenspan, S. I. (2001). *Functional emotional assessment scale for infancy and early childhood.* Bethesda, MD: Interdisciplinary Council on Developmental and Learning Disorders.

Greenspan, S. I. (2004). *Social–Emotional growth chart.* San Antonio, TX: Harcourt Assessment, Inc.

Greenspan, S. I. (2006). *Social emotional scale of the Bayley Scales of Infant and Toddler development* (3rd ed.). San Antonio, TX: Harcourt Assessment.

Guralnick, M. J. (2011). Why early intervention works: A systems perspective. *Infants & Young Children, 24,* 6–28.

Hresko, W.P., Herron, S., Peak, P., & Hicks, D.L. (2012). *Test of Early Written Language* (3rd ed.). Austin, TX: Pro-Ed.

Harrison, P., Kaufman, A., Kaufman, N., Bruininks, R., Rynders, J., Ilmer, S., … Cicchetti, D. (1990). *Early screening profiles.* Circle Pines, MN: American Guidence Service, Inc.

Haywood, C. H., & Lidz, C. S. (2007). *Dynamic assessment in practice: Clinical and educational applications.* New York, NY: Cambridge University Press.

Haynes, W. O., & Pindzola, R. H. (2012). *Diagnosis and evaluation in speech pathology* (8th ed.). New Jersey: Pearson.

Heilmann J., Miller J. F., Nockerts A., & Dunaway C. (2010). Properties of the Narrative Scoring Scheme Using Narrative Retells in Young School-Age Children. *American Journal of Speech Language Pathology.* 19(2): 154–166. [PubMed: 20008470].

Hodson, B. (2004). *Hodson assessment of phonological patterns—3rd edition.* East Moline, IL: Linguisystems.

Hresko, W. P. (2012). *Test of early written language—3rd edition (TWEL-3).* San Antonio, TX: Pearson.

Hresko, W. P., Reid, D. K., & Hammill, D. D. (2018). *Test of early language development—4th edition (TELD-4).* Austin, TX: Pro Ed.

Hyter, Y. (1984). *Reliability and validity of the Black English sentence scoring system* (Unpublished master's thesis). Western Michigan University, Kalamazoo, MI.

Individuals with Disabilities Education Improvement Act of 2004, Pub. L. No. 108-446 §118 Stat. 2647 (2004).

Jelm, J.M. (1990). *Oral-motor/feeding rating scale.* Tucson: Therapy Skill Builders.

Johnson, J. (2010). Language development and literacy: Factors that influence language development. In *Encyclopedia of early development.* British Columbia, Canada, Montreal, QC: CEECD. http://www.child-encyclopedia.com/sites/default/files/textes-experts/en/622/factors-that-influence-language-development.pdf

Kaderavek, J. N. (2011). *Language disorders in children.* Upper Saddle River, NJ: Pearson Education.

Kaufman, A. S., & Kaufman, N. L. (1993). *Kaufman survey of early academic and language skills (K-SEALS).* San Antonio, TX: Pearson Education.

Kemp, K., & Klee, T. (1997). Clinical language sampling practices: Results of a survey of speech-language pathologists in the United States. *Child Language Teaching and Therapy, 13,* 161–176.

Legerstee, M. (2005). *Infants' sense of people: Precursors to a theory of mind.* London, England: Cambridge University Press.

Lidz, C. S. (Ed.). (1987). *Dynamic assessment: An interactional approach to evaluating learning potential.* New York: Guilford.

Linder, T. W. (2008). *Transdisciplinary play-based assessment—2nd edition.* Baltimore, MD: Paul H. Brookes.

Lyovin, A. V., Kessler, B., & Leben, W. R. (2017). *An introduction to languages of the world.* New York: Oxford University Press.

McCune, L. (1995). A normative study of representational play at the transition to language. *Developmental Psychology, 31,* 200–211.

Meyers, C. L., McBride, S. L., & Peterson, C. A. (1996).Transdisciplinary play-based assessment in early childhood special education: An examination of social validity. *Topics in Early Childhood Special Education, 16,* 102–126.

Mardell-Czudnowski, C., & Goldenberg, D. S. (2011). *Developmental indicators for the assessment of learning—4th edition*. San Antonio, TX: Pearson Education.

Martin, N., Brownell, R., & Hamaguchi, P. (2018). *Test of auditory processing skills—Fourth edition*. Novato, CA: Academic Therapy Publications.

Miller, J. F. (1981). *Assessing language production in children: Experimental procedures*. Austin, TX: PRO-ED.

Miller, J. F., & Paul, R. (1995). *Clinical assessment of language comprehension*. Baltimore, MD: Paul H. Brookes.

Miller, L., Gillam, R. B., & Peña, E. D. (2001). *Dynamic assessment and intervention: Improving children's narrative abilities*. Austin, TX: Pro-Ed.

Mullen, E. (1995). *Mullen Scales of Early Learning*. Circle Pines, MN: AGS.

National Institute on Deafness and Other Communication Disorders (NIDCD). (2014). *Speech and language developmental milestones*. www.nidcd.nih.gov/health/speech-and-language

National Institute on Deafness and Other Communication Disorders (2016a). Quick statistics about hearing. Retrieved from www.nidcd.nih.gov/health/statistics/quick-statistics-hearing#2

National Institute on Deafness and Other Communication Disorders (2016b). Speech and language developmental milestones. Retrieved from www.nidcd.nih.gov/health/speech-and-language

Nelson, N. W. (2010). *Language and literacy disorders: Infancy through adolescence*. Boston, MA: Allyn and Bacon.

Newborg, J., Stock, J., & Wnek, L. (2005). *Battelle developmental inventory—2nd edition* (pp. 15–16). Itasca, IL: Riverside Publishing.

Olswang, L., Stoeol-Gammon, C., Coggins, T. E., & Carpenter, R. L. (1987). *Assessing linguistic behaviors: Assessing prelinguistic and early linguistic behaviors in developmentally young children*. Seattle, WA: University of Washington Press.

Owens, R. E. (2017). *Language development: An introduction*. Upper Saddle River, NJ: Pearson Education.

Parks, S. (1992). *Hawaii early learning profile (HELP)*. Palo Alto, CA: VORT Corporation.

Paul, R. (2000).Predicting outcomes of early expressive language delay: Ethical implications. In D. V. M. Bishop & L. B. Leonard (Eds.), *Speech and language impairments in children: Causes, characteristics, intervention, and outcome* (pp. 195–209). Hove, UK: Psychology Press.

Paul, R., Norbury, C., & Gosse, C. (2018). *Language disorders from infancy through adolescence* (5th ed.). St. Louis, MO: Elsevier.

Peña, E. D., & Gillam, R. B. (2000). Dynamic assessment of children referred for speech and language evaluations. In C. Lidz & J. Elliott (Eds.), *Dynamic assessment: Prevailing models and applications* (Vol. 6, pp. 543–575). Oxford: Elsevier Science.

Perkins, W. H., & Kent, R. D. (1986). *Functional anatomy of speech, language and hearing: A primer*. Needham Heights, MA: Allyn & Bacon.

Phelps-Terasaki, D., & Phelps-Gunn, T. (2007). *Test of pragmatic language—Second edition manual*. Austin, TX: Pro-ed Inc.

Piaget, J. (1952). *The origins of intelligence in children*. New York: International University Press.

Reid, D. K., Hresko, W. P., & Hammill, D. D. (2018). *Test of early reading ability—4th edition (TERA-4)*. Austin, TX: Pro-ed.

Roseberry-McKibbin, C. (2018). *Multicultural students with special language needs: Practical strategies for assessment and intervention* (5th ed.). Oceanside, CA: Academic Communication Associates, Inc.

Rossetti, L. (1990). *The Rossetti infant-language scale.* East Moline, IL: Linguisystems.

Seymour, H. N., Roeper, T., & de Villiers, J. G. (2005). *Diagnostic evaluation of language variation.* San Antonio, TX: Harcourt Assessment.

Shipley, K. G. & McAfee, J. G. (2016). *Assessment in speech-language pathology: A resource manual* (4th ed.). Boston, MA: Cengage.

Shipley, K. G. & McAfee, J. G. (2016). *Assessment in speech language pathology: A resource manual* (5th ed.). Boston, MA: Cengage Learning.

Singleton, N. C., & Schulman, B. B. (2013). *Language development: Foundations, processes and clinical applications.* Burlington, MA: Jones & Bartlett.

Sorkin, D. L., Gates-Ulanet, P., & Mellon, N. K. (2015). Psychosocial aspects of hearing loss in children. *Otolaryngologic Clinics of North America, 48*(6), 1073–1080.

Sparrow, S., Balla, C., & Cicchetti, D. (2016). *Vineland adaptive behavior scales—3rd edition.* Bloomington, MN: Pearson Education.

Squires, J., Bricker, D., Mounts, L., Twombly, E., Nickel, R., Clifford, J., Murphy, K., Hoselton, R., Potter, L., & Farrell, J. (2009). *Ages and stages questionnaires: A parent-completed child-monitoring system* (3rd ed.) [Measurement instrument].

Stockman, I. J. (1996). The promises and pitfalls of language sample analysis as an assessment tool for linguistic minority children. *Language, Speech, and Hearing Services in Schools, 27*(4), 355–366.

Stockman, I. J., Guillory, B., Seibert, M., & Boult, J. (2013). Toward validation of a minimal competence core of morphosyntax for African American children. *American Journal of Speech-Language Pathology, 22,* 40–56.

Tomasello, M. (2006). Acquiring linguistic constructions. In W. Damon, R. M. Lerner, D. Kuhn, & R. Siegler (Eds.), *Handbook of child psychology, Vol.2: Cognitive perception and language* (pp. 235–298). Hoboken, NJ: Wiley.

Tomblin, J. B., Records, N. L., Buckwalter, P., Zhang, X., Smith, E., & O'Brien, M. (1997). Prevalence of specific language impairment in kindergarten children. *Journal of Speech and Hearing Research, 40,* 1245–1260.

Tye-Murray, N. (2014). *Foundations of aural rehabilitation: Children, adults, and their family members* (4th ed.). Clifton Park, NY: Delmar Cengage Learning.

Van Riper, C. (1939). *Speech correction: Principles and methods.* New York: Prentice-Hall Inc.

Walker, B. (2009). Auditory learning guide. Retrieved from www.psha.org/member-center/pdfs/auditory-learning-guide.pdf

Wallace, G., & Hammill, D. D. (2013). *Comprehensive receptive and expressive vocabulary test—3rd edition.* Austin, TX: Pro-Ed.

Weismer, G., & Holt, J. D. (2016). *Foundations of speech and hearing: Anatomy and physiology.* San Diego, CA: Plural Publishing.

Werner, E., & Kresheck, J. D. (2005). *Structured photographic expressive language—3rd edition (SPELT-3).* DeKalb, IL: Janelle Publications, Inc.

Westby, C. (2000). A scale for assessing development of children's play. In K. Gitllin-Weiner, A. Sandgrund, & C. E. Shafer (Eds.), *Play diagnosis and assessment* (2nd ed. ed., pp. 15–57). New York: Wiley.

Wetherby, A., Cain, D., Yonclas, D., & Walker, V. (1988). Analysis of intentional communication of normal children from the prelinguistic to the multiword stage. *Journal of Speech and Hearing Research, 31,* 240–252.

Wetherby, A., Woods, J., Allen, L., Cleary, J., Dickinson, H., & Lord, C. (2004). Early indicators of autism spectrum disorders in the second year of life. *Journal of Autism and Developmental Disorders, 34,* 473–493.

Westby, C. (1998). Social–emotional bases of communication development. In W. Haynes & B. Shulman (Eds.), *Communication development: Foundations, processes, and clinical applications* (2nd ed., pp. 165–204). Baltimore, MD: Williams & Wilkins.

Wetherby, A. M., & Prizant, B. M. (2002). *Communication and symbolic behavior scales developmental profile.* Baltimore, MD: Paul H. Brookes.

Wiig, E. H., Secord, W. A., & Semel, E. (2013). *Clinical evaluation of language fundamentals-preschool—5th edition.* San Antonio, TX: Pearson Education.

Wilkes, E. M. (1999). *Cottage acquisition scales for listening, language and speech user's guide.* San Antonio, TX: Sunshine Cottage School for Deaf Children.

Wyatt, T. (2012). Assessment of multicultural and international clients with communication disorders. In D. E. Battle (Ed.), *Communication disorders in multicultural and international populations* (pp. 243–274). St. Louis, MO: Elsevier Mosby.

Zimmerman-Phillips, S., Osberger, M. J., & Robbins, A. M. (2001). Infant-Toddler Meaningful Auditory Integration Scale. Sylmar, CA: Advanced Bionics Corporation.

Zimmerman, I. L., Steiner, V. G., & Pond, R. E. (2011). *Preschool language scale—5th edition.* San Antonio, TX: Harcourt Assessments.

Chapter 12

Assessment of Gross Motor Development in Preschool Children

Eva V. Monsma, Sally Taunton Miedema, Ali S. Brian, and Harriet G. Williams

I. Introduction

Gross Motor Development: What Is It?

Motor *development* generally refers to the changes in movement competence over time. *Gross* motor development is inferred from assessments measuring competence in specific motor skills involving the large and small muscle groups, which is categorically different from competence in skills involving fine motor skills (e.g., finger tapping). Historically, motor competence has been commonly referred to as motor coordination, motor ability, motor proficiency, motor performance, and most often involving fundamental movement/motor skills (FMS). Aligned with the recommendations of a systematic review of FMS terminology in the literature (Logan, Ross, Chee, Stodden, & Robinson, 2018), FMS are categorized into three groups: locomotor skills (i.e., the ability to move the body through space, such as when running), object control skills (i.e., the ability to move and control objects, such as when throwing), and stability skills (i.e., the ability to maintain postural control, such as when balancing on one foot) (Clark & Metcalfe, 2002; Haywood & Getchell, 2020). Not only are FMS such as jumping, running, and kicking seen as "building blocks" for more complex movement patterns necessary for participating in physical activities, games, and sports, they are seen as critical in the promotion and maintenance of healthy developmental trajectories (Logan et al., 2018; Stodden et al., 2008).

Where earlier conceptualizations of motor competence focused on maturation and movement outcomes, the contemporary approach to assessment of gross motor development is to characterize motor competence as qualitative changes of observable body movement patterns, associated quantitative outcomes, and mechanisms underlying those changes associated with aging, task demands, and environmental characteristics (Clark, 2017; Clark & Whitall, 1989; Newell, 1986). More specifically, the conceptualization of motor competence has evolved to include process and product observable outcomes (Clark, 2017; Clark & Whitall, 1989). The quality of movement processes or "process characteristics" of movement (i.e., mature patterns, biomechanical efficiency) underlies changes in product characteristics that are objectively measurable outcomes (e.g., speed, distance, force, hitting a target) (True, Brian, Goodway, & Stodden, 2017). Process characteristics and product outcomes are directed by a synchrony of underlying processes linked to: 1. growth and maturation of body systems (e.g., skeletal, muscular, nervous, adipose, endocrine); 2. perceptual, cognitive, and psychological development (e.g., motivation, mental rehearsal, self-perceptions); 3. the demands of the motor task (e.g., throwing for speed versus accuracy; long distance running versus sprinting); and 4. environmental influences (e.g., parental encouragement, coaching, built environment) (Clark & Whitall, 1989; Haywood & Getchell, 2020; Newell, 1986).

In many ways, motor development generally follows the same pattern of human growth; first cephalocaudal (i.e., head to toe – a baby learns how to lift the head and move arms before learning to walk) and proximal-distal (i.e., from the body outwards toward the limbs – an infant learns to move the arms and legs before manipulating objects with hands and fingers). Changes in gross motor development are known to be sequential, continuous, age-related processes whereby movement progresses from simple, unorganized, and unskilled, to highly organized, complex motor skills and finally to the adjustment of skills used in sport, exercise, and dance (Haywood & Getchell, 2020). These ideas evolved from four assumptions of stage theory: qualitative changes (i.e., observable changes over time); hierarchical incorporation (i.e., motor development builds upon previous motor skills sequentially); intransitive (i.e., everyone passes through each stage in the same order, and regression to previous stages does not happen without injury or aging of the body systems); and structural wholeness (i.e., change in one system involves change in the whole system) (Gallahue, Ozmun &, Goodway, 2013; Roberton, 1978).

Interacting Factors Underlying Gross Motor Development

What contributes to the marked age-variability of motor development? Dynamical Systems Theory (DST: Kugler, Kelso, & Turvey, 1980) offers a holistic explanation of behavioral emergence and is one of the most common explanations of motor development. Development is dynamic because a subsystem can be changing or static while other subsystems are changing; moreover, the pattern of change in a window of development can be linear, curvilinear, spiraling, or stepping. The underlying basis of DST is the interaction of three constraint categories, or subsystems: individual, task, and environmental constraints. These constraints interact with one another to self-organize and create spontaneous behavior, which is the foundation for subsequent purposeful, controlled movement.

Karl Newell's (1986) practical translation of DST, known as his Model of Developmental Constraints, explains changes in gross motor development. For example, in the development of throwing, a child's current size and strength (e.g., individual structural constraints) underlie how far and fast the ball will travel when throwing for distance (e.g., task constraint) as opposed to for accuracy. If that child is motivated to practice (i.e., individual functional constraint) outside of team practices, the interaction of structural and functional characteristics (i.e., size and motivation) with the task condition (e.g., throwing for distance) should lead to performance improvements in terms of distance thrown. Moreover, if practice is directed by a coach trained in providing developmentally appropriate opportunities and feedback (e.g., environmental constraints), and where a parent provides feedback cues representing proper biomechanical form, the interaction of constraints representing all three categories of subsystems enables the emergence of the most advanced motor performance in terms of process (e.g., biomechanical form) and product (e.g., distance) characteristics for that child. Assessment of motor skills such as throwing are thus highly variable because of the marked variability in physical size and psychological functioning that are age related, not age specific. Practitioners must consider these constraints as essential elements in the assessment process because they help to explain a child's limitations and represent target factors that can be manipulated to elicit improvement.

A systematic review of 59 studies focusing on developmental constraints conducted between 1994 and 2014 indicated that age shows the most consistent relationship (positive) with all aspects of motor competence, regardless of how competence is defined. Additionally, children scoring higher on global scores of motor competence tend to be more physically active and weigh less than those with lower scores. These relationships were not apparent when examining subscale scores, and there were very few studies that examined cognitive and psychological factors (functional constraints) or cultural and social factors (environmental constraints) (Barnett et al., 2016). Typically, when one modifies environmental constraints to support learning regardless of functional constraints, improvement can occur. However, when factors such as functional and/or environmental constraints fail to explain a child's struggles with motor competence and the child does not have some other developmental disorder (e.g., autism spectrum disorders, cerebral palsy) it possible that developmental coordination disorder may be present.

Developmental Coordination Disorder (DCD) and Developmental Delay (DD)

Childhood assessment of gross motor skills can be compared to sex- and age-based assessment norms to determine whether a child is behind, on track, or advanced for age. When the degree of delay reaches certain thresholds depending on the assessment used, a child may be diagnosed with developmental delay (DD) or, in extreme cases, developmental coordination disorder (DCD). The two most common assessments for diagnosing DD are the *Test of Gross Motor Development* (TGMD; Ulrich, 1985, 2000, 2019) and the *Bruininks-Oseretsky Test of Motor Proficiency* (BOT; Bruininks, 1978; Bruininks & Bruininks, 2005b). Scores on at least two motor skills of an assessment that are two standard deviations below respective norms constitute a DD diagnosis and can qualify the child for occupational or physical therapy to remediate delay.

In contrast, DCD is defined as impaired motor function in the absence of a neurological condition, interfering with activities of daily living and academic, vocational, and/or leisure activities (American Psychiatric Association, 2013). Clumsy child syndrome, Dyspraxia, sensory integration disorder, and developmental coordination disorder were once used to describe what is now known as DCD. The most common assessment for diagnosing DCD is the *Movement Assessment Battery for Children – Second Edition* (MABC-2; Henderson, Sugden, & Barnett, 2007) which is more sensitive than the other assessments. Scoring below the 5th percentile on the MABC-2 results in a DCD diagnosis, and scoring below the 15th percentile results in a DD diagnosis. Unlike DD, a DCD diagnosis implies dyspraxia or impaired learning of basic gross and fine motor skills. However, children with DCD often receive intervention services to improve basic gross and fine motor skills, which increases participation in activities that require basic motor skills, improving overall quality of life (Maiano, Hue, & April, 2019).

Motor Development Links to Early Learning, Physical Activity, Health, and Wellness in the Early Years

Early Learning Process

Motor development is known to be an important dimension of child development and is a universally recognized means for assessing the overall rate and level of development of the child during the early months and years after birth (Gesell, 1973; Haywood & Getchell, 2020) The years from 2 to 6 are considered the "golden years" of motor development (Williams, 1983). During this period, most children acquire a basic repertoire of manipulative and locomotor skills, develop goal-directed motor behaviors, and learn to coordinate two or three movement sequences to accomplish specific end goals. These behavioral achievements are contingent upon the child's acquisition of an adequate base of motor development. Motor development may in part determine the rate of development of a child's perceptual, cognitive, academic, and physical abilities.

Three things are clear from the past three decades of motor development research: 1. most children, with and without disabilities are delayed in developing their gross motor skills; 2. those skills can dramatically improve with just minimal intervention (Logan, Robinson, Wilson, & Lucas, 2012; Morgan et al., 2013; Taunton, Brian, & True, 2017); and 3. there is compelling evidence to support the idea that relationships among motor skills, perceived competence in those skills, physical fitness, and physical activity in childhood and adolescence also exist in early adulthood (Sackett & Edwards, 2019). The early years of motor development set the foundation for neuro-muscular coordination used by the individual throughout life to manage a multitude of mental, social, emotional, and recreational dimensions of living. A lag in early motor skill proficiency beyond the parameters of nat-ural age-related variability may initiate a patterned spiral of negative effects limiting health, wellness, and human development.

Cognitive Development

Accumulating evidence suggests that early motor and cognitive development are interrelated, stemming from infancy with evidence of lasting effects into adulthood (Murray, Jones, Kuh, & Richards, 2007). Neuroimaging studies show that motor and cognitive tasks elicit coactivation of similar brain areas (e.g., neocerebellum and dorsolateral prefrontal cortex), and abnor-malities in these brain areas result in cognitive and motor deficiencies (Dia-mond, 2000). Locomotor and object control skills have been shown to be associated with cognitive development in toddlers (Veldman, Santos, Jones, Sousa-Sá, & Okely, 2019). In a systematic review of 21 studies, examining categories of cognitive and motor development associations in children aged 4 to 16 years indicated weak to strong positive relationships. Stronger rela-tionships were found in pre-pubertal participants (< 13 years) than post-pubertal, and the strongest associations were with cognitive skills involving ball control and timed performance skills (van der Fels et al., 2015).

Cognitive development measures that target executive function include a set of control processes that help manage and direct attention, thoughts, and actions (Best & Miller, 2010). Examples of executive functions include working memory (e.g., remembering information and manipulating it), inhibition (e.g., staying focused by blocking attention to irrelevant environmental cues), and attention shifting (e.g., perspective taking – narrowing and expanding atten-tional focus) (Diamond, 2013). Early motor development is associated with executive function at several points in later life. For example, attaining motor skill milestones at earlier ages predicts processing speed and working memory later at ages 6 to 11 years (Piek, Dawson, Smith, & Gasson, 2008), education scores at 16 years (Jaakkola, Hillman, Kalaja, & Liukkonen, 2015), and intellec-tual performance at ages 8, 26, and 53 (Murray et al., 2007).

In fact, as children's motor skills increase often so does executive func-tion, a foundational component of school readiness in young children (Mulvey, Taunton, Pennell, & Brian, 2018). The Head, Toes, Knees, Shoul-ders (HTKS; McClelland et al., 2014) assessment is one example for assess-ing young children's executive function – specifically, working memory, cognitive flexibility, and inhibitory control. This measure involves gross motor movements in response to asking children to perform the opposite of what is stated to them. After training and practice items, the experimenter gives 10 commands (two for head, three for toes, two for shoulders, and three for knees; order: head, toes, knees, toes, shoulders, head, knees, knees, shoulders, toes). The child is asked to do the opposite (head = toes; toes = head; shoulders = knees; knees = shoulders).

The total assessment is scored out of 60 possible points. Children are rated on a 3-point scale, 0 for an incorrect response (i.e., prompted to touch shoulders and touched shoulders), 1 for a self-correct response (i.e., prompted to touch head, began to touch head but then corrected and touched toes), 2 for a correct response (e.g., prompted to touch head and touched toes). The HTKS is divided into three parts, with each part building on the previous one and increasing in difficulty. During the first part of the evaluation, children are asked to touch their head when prompted to touch their toes, they touch their toes when prompted to touch their head. If a child completes enough correct attempts (4 correct attempts) on part 1, they proceed to part 2. On part 2 of the evaluation, the child is asked to perform the opposite of the prompt, but now the prompts use only knees and shoulders. If a child performs enough correct attempts (4 correct attempts), they may then proceed to part 3. Part 3 is the highest level of difficulty in which part 1 (head and shoulders) and part 2 (knees and toes) are combined. Children must recall the appropriate opposite response for each of the four prompts: head, toes, knees, shoulders.

Educational Achievement

Motor development links to educational achievement during early childhood as evident from studies on executive function and reading and mathematical abilities. Longitudinal evidence indicates that children with learning difficulties develop locomotor and ball skills at least three years later than peers (Westendorp et al., 2014). Relationships between motor development and reading are highly variable; where some studies indicate comorbidity of low motor development and reading abilities (Bellocchi, Tobia, & Bonifacci, 2017), negative relationships between motor skill proficiency and reading, particularly among boys, and positive relationships between motor skill proficiency reading among pre-readers (Milne, Cacciotti, Davies, & Orr, 2018) have been shown. Motor-enriched learning activities have been shown to improve math performance among 7-year-old children where gross motor skill interventions showed significantly better improvements than fine motor skill interventions (Beck et al., 2016).

Accordingly, the *Head Start Early Learning Outcomes Framework: Birth to Five* recognizes the importance of gross and fine motor development, cognitive development, and social-emotional development as being interrelated and essential to learning and development in later life (Administration for Children and Families, 2015). This framework outlines age-related outcomes in four domains, including perceptual, motor, and physical development that can be cross-referenced to garner an understanding of how outcomes from other domains interrelate with those in the motor domain.

Physical Health

Motor skills, particularly fundamental motor skills, are critical for children's physical health throughout adolescence and adulthood (Robinson et al., 2015; Stodden et al., 2008). Seefeldt (1980) proposed a hypothetical "proficiency barrier" in which children must develop skills, such as reflexes, reactional skills, and fundamental movement skills (i.e., running, kicking, throwing), in order to overcome a hypothesized "proficiency barrier" to participate in more complex movement patterns required for sport and other activities required to be physically active. Developing fundamental motor skills during a critical time in early childhood (3 to 7 years old) is an essential component for overcoming the "proficiency barrier," a motor skill performance threshold required for successful integration of fundamental skills into more complex sport skills. Motor skills introduced, taught, and developed during this time period can place children on either a negative or positive spiraling trajectory of engagement linked to physical health throughout the lifespan (Robinson et al., 2015; Stodden et al., 2008). Children who develop basic fundamental movement skills tend to follow a positive spiraling path, demonstrating higher levels of physical activity, and are thus at lower risk for hypokinetic diseases (e.g., obesity, diabetes) later in adolescence and adulthood.

Recent findings indicate that 90% of 6- to 12-year-old children are below an established motor competence proficiency barrier and do not meet national guidelines of 60 minutes of moderate to vigorous physical activity (MVPA) per day (DeMeester et al., 2018). Additionally, youth sport athletes ages 11 to 18 years with dysfunctional movement as measured by the *Functional Movement Screen* (FMS™; Cook, Burton, Kiesel, Rose, & Bryant, 2010) were three times more likely to be injured than those above the proficiency threshold scores (i.e., $\leq$ 14 and $\leq$ 15) (Pfeifer et al., 2019). Although not developed for young children, the FMS™ is an assessment of motor competence employing seven tasks (i.e., overhead deep squat, hurdle step, inline lunge, shoulder mobility, active straight leg raise, trunk stability push-up, and rotary stability). Each task is rated on a 0- to 3-point scale, where 0 indicates pain with movement and 3 indicates optimal task functioning. Without the development of critical fundamental motor skills, children typically follow a negative spiral of disengagement at an early age, are at risk for lower levels of physical activity, and are at increased risk of disease. Therefore, early assessment of children's fundamental motor skills is essential for determining proficiency status and associated barriers. Assessments may provide practitioners, therapists, and other key stakeholders in children's life key with information needed to ensure children overcome the "proficiency barrier" and begin to follow a positive path of physical health throughout the lifespan.

Studies have shown the mere perception of movement skill inadequacies may be insufficient to inhibit the adoption of an active lifestyle, leading to decreased levels of health and fitness (Welk & Eklund, 2005). Another area of essential assessment during childhood is children's perception of motor skill competence relative to the child's actual level of motor skill competence. Childhood is marked by a common gap between children's perceptions of competence and actual motor competence (i.e., children perceive themselves as more competent in a skill than their actual performance of the skill reflects). However, as children develop more self-actualization during middle childhood (8–10 years old) the gap narrows between children's perceptual and actual motor competence (i.e., children are more accurate in perceptions of their actual skill competence). Assessment of motor skills perceptions is important as perceived motor competence is an underlying mechanism to the development of fundamental motor skills and one of the greatest predictors of physical inactivity and obesity (Babic et al., 2014; Robinson et al., 2015; Stodden et al., 2008).

Notably, children with intellectual disabilities (e.g., Fragile X syndrome, Down syndrome, Williams syndrome) are characterized by fundamental motor skill deficits greater than those without intellectual abilities. These deficits can affect their conceptual, social, and practical skills, as well as their ability and willingness to participate in physical activities. The greater a child's deficit, the less physically active the individual will be, which increases overweight and obesity risk (Maiano et al., 2019).

Psychological and Mental Health

Associations between motor skill proficiency and mental health (i.e., biological conditions associated with changes in the brain) and psychological health (i.e., the ability to think, express, and behave in relation to emotions) are intertwined, and they have become more prominent in the literature. While advanced motor development and physical activity are associated with one another and with positive psychological and mental health benefits, motor deficits are linked to negative consequences. For example, children with probable DCD are twice as likely to self-report depression, and their parents are four times more likely to report their child's mental health difficulties than parents of children without DCD, but these associations depend on the child's level of verbal intelligence, social communication, and self-esteem (Lingam et al., 2012). The Elaborated Environmental Stress Hypothesis (EESH; Cairney, Rigoli, & Piek, 2013) is a common conceptual framework for explaining the complex relationship of how poor motor skills (originally operationalized as DCD in childhood) contribute to greater internalization of problems, which is symptomatic of depression and anxiety (see Figure 12.1). According to the EESH, poor motor skills are proposed to be a primary source of stress, indirectly contributing to internalizing problems through secondary stressors, which include the lack of social (e.g., social support) and personal (e.g., self-esteem) resources, and more recently added factors of physical inactivity and obesity. Studies have shown the negative relationship between motor skills and internalizing problems exists in DCD and community-based samples (Mancini,

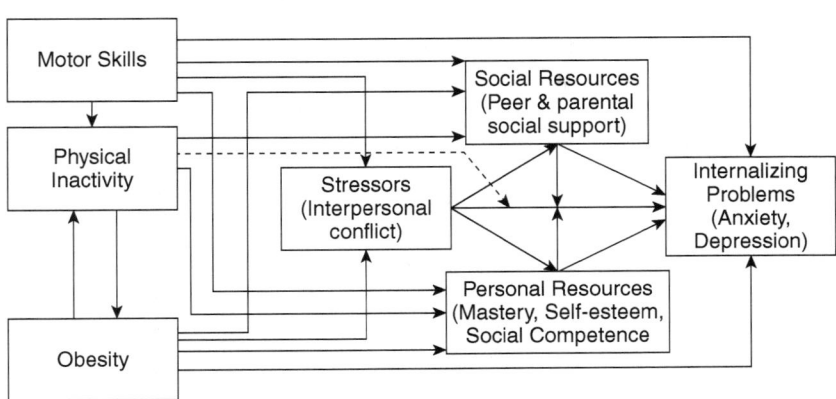

Figure 12.1 An Adapted Elaborated Environmental Stress Hypothesis (Mancini, Rigoli, Heritage, Roberts, & Piek, 2016).

Note: This adapted version examines motor skills across the full spectrum of ability; the original Elaborated Environmental Stress Hypothesis described by Cairney et al. (2013) specifically focused on children with developmental coordination disorder (DCD).

Rigoli, Roberts, Heritage, & Piek, 2018; Poole et al., 2015), highlighting the wider population benefits of universal motor skill intervention programs, particularly during childhood.

Motor difficulties are also common among children with ADHD, which is the most common neurobehavioral disorder during childhood, affecting approximately 5–6% of school-aged children in the United States (Danielson et al., 2018) and worldwide (Polanczyk, de Lima, Horta, Biederman, & Rohde, 2007). Symptoms of ADHD include high activity, impulsivity, and behavioral distractibility, and are more common among boys. A review of studies found that 30–50% of children with ADHD may also be affected by motor problems, but it is unclear whether ADHD and motor difficulties share common etiology or if they simply occur together (i.e., are co-morbid) (Goulardins, Marques, & De Oliveira, 2017). Medication and behavioral intervention are common ADHD treatments, but 53% of children aged 2 to 17 years receiving treatment do not receive behavioral therapies (Danielson et al., 2018). Motor skills are important for physical and psychological functioning. Although motor skills are used initially to explore the immediate environment in infancy, in childhood motor skills are often performed in a sociocultural context where parents, peers, and teachers provide feedback through encouragement, approval, play, and then sport participation opportunities. Motor delays can alter the timing, frequency, and type of feedback that are important for developing perceived competence, which is closely tied to self-esteem. Perceived competence in a variety of abilities, such as academic, social, and physical, are critical for the development and maintenance of self-esteem (Harter, 1990). The negative relationship between motor skill competence and self-esteem is well established with moderate to large effect sizes (Miyahara & Piek, 2006), and this relationship is apparent in children as young as four years of age (Lodal & Bond, 2016). The motor skills and self-esteem relationship is complex and, in addition to age, it depends on gender and other co-morbidities. Motor delays and low self-esteem extending into adolescence are associated with poor social outcomes and anxiety, especially among females (Lodal & Bond, 2016). Because self-esteem is important for maintaining psycho-social wellbeing, intervening on associated factors such as motor skills may be preventative of mental illness (Rigoli et al., 2017) or remediating of ADHD (Goulardins et al., 2017) and other DCD co-morbidities.

Why Should We Assess Gross Motor Development in Childhood?

Motor skills are no longer thought to be temporarily problematic or that children will grow out of their problems once in adolescence. Linkages between motor development and learning, physical activity, health, and wellness are well documented in the literature. Relationships are predicated on the measurement, which can serve several interrelated functions:

Diagnosis – Determining the extent to which a student's motor performance (i.e., competency) corresponds with criteria of an assessment tool. Through diagnosis, competency levels are established, and DCD and developmental delays are identified. Diagnostic results help to guide instructional programming, intervention, and direct Individual Education Plans (IEPs) and help to provide feedback to students and parents.

Placement – Scores of gross motor development assessments can be used to assign children into intervention groups or ability-based programming (e.g., IEPs, Head Start).

Evaluation of Achievement – The essence of development relies on documenting growth or change over time. Change from baseline to post-instruction, -intervention, or -programming involve administering the same assessment at least twice across time to document motor development changes (see Logan et al., 2012; Morgan et al., 2013; Taunton, Brian, & True, 2017).

Motivation – When assessment scores are shared with the learner, they serve as future performance targets. Associating instruction with being as good or better than the individual's last performance can enhance intrinsic motivation (i.e., engaging in an activity to learn, to improve, and for enjoyment), laying an important foundation for redefining success in a society where winning is highly valued.

Prediction – Motor skills are linked to physical activity, which is linked to weight status and cardio-metabolic health (Rodrigues, Stodden, & Lopes, 2015), learning mental health (Poole et al., 2015), self-esteem (Lodal & Bond, 2016), and ADHD (Goulardins et al., 2017).

Program Evaluation – the effectiveness of motor skill interventions is determined by evaluating the degree of change relative to intervention programs, including the curriculum, its duration, and instructor characteristics. For example, recent systematic reviews provide details about the effectiveness of several FMS intervention studies on typically developing children (Engel, Broderick, van Doorn, Hardy, & Parmenter, 2018; Logan et al., 2012; Morgan et al., 2013) and those with intellectual disabilities (Maiano et al., 2019).

In addition to physical activity and its related health benefits, early childhood professionals can be the first line of defense in early identification of motor delay using a variety of assessments to make appropriate referrals for remediation (i.e., IEP). Because motor skill development is a critical dimension of the overall development of the young child, it is important to have information about the child's present level of motor skill development to establish a baseline against which to monitor the growth and development of the child. In this respect, assessment of gross motor development is integral to screening identification of children who may not be developing or progressing as expected (i.e., motor delay, DCD).

In general, screening or preliminary assessment of gross motor development is necessary for identifying the following: 1. the nature and extent of children's needs, 2. determining if additional diagnostic testing is needed, 3. deciding if and what type of enrichment may be appropriate for promoting optimum development, and 4. predicting potential neurodevelopmental outcomes at a later age. In the school setting, outcomes of motor development assessment are especially important for planning and developing appropriate instructional strategies. It is also important to provide assessment information on the child's gross motor skills to parents and other concerned individuals, particularly those who are or may be involved in providing for follow-up support for the child with disabilities. Results or outcomes of any evaluation of gross motor development should identify strengths and weaknesses and highlight those skills that are lagging or deficient, along with the nature and extent of the deficiencies.

II. The Development of Gross Motor Skills

A simple description of some proposed steps in motor skill development can help us understand the complexity of the processes and factors involved in this aspect of the child's development. The following discussion describes some broad categories or steps involved in motor skill development (Burton & Miller, 1998). Generally, the child first develops or acquires the foundational processes necessary for the development of motor skills. The child then acquires the so-called motor development milestones, followed by the development of fundamental gross motor skills. Ultimately, these skills and/ or behaviors are manifested in a variety of specialized movement skills typical of the older child and young adult. Progressions are age-related but not age-specific (Roberton, 1978; Seefeldt, 1980).

Motor Skill Foundations. This aspect of motor skill development includes factors and processes important to the development and performance of all motor skills. These factors include, among others: gender, body size and composition, cardiovascular endurance, flexibility/range of motion, muscular strength, neurological integrity, adequate sensory system function, perception, and cognition. These underlying factors contribute to the pattern of gross motor development and play a critical role in what the nature of that pattern will be.

Early Motor Development. The term *milestone* is often used to describe early motor skill development and highlights the influence that motor skills acquisition has on the social, perceptual, and cognitive development of the infant and young child. These milestones include locomotor and object manipulation skills that appear before the child achieves an easy upright stance and locomotion, including rolling, crawling, creeping, sitting, standing, walking, object manipulation, and other skills. The onset of walking, which occurs on average around 12–13 months, is the last of the early motor development milestones. Lags or issues in the appearance of these milestones often signal potential difficulty in continued development and/or acquisition of subsequent fundamental motor skills.

Fundamental Motor Skills. These gross motor skills are universally observed in the young between 2 and 7 years of age. They appear in an orderly sequence during this developmental period and include the locomotor and object control skills described previously. Balance skills also undergo rapid development during this period.

Functional Motor Skills. Functional motor skills are performed in natural and/or meaningful contexts comprising daily activities, sport skills, and specialized movement behaviors. For example, supine to stand, running fast, getting into and out of a car, shooting a free throw, driving a car, fielding a ground ball, and specialized career-related behaviors (e.g., performing surgery or activities of first responders). Ultimately, many situations require automated motor skills and the pathway to automaticity is directed during the preschool period.

The Development of Fundamental Gross Motor Skills and Balance

For *fundamental* motor skills, in contrast to *functional* motor skills, development generally refers to sequential, age-related changes in locomotor and object control skills that occur concurrently with changes in balance skills. Although locomotor skills tend to develop slightly in advance of object control skills, there is considerable overlap in the development of these skills. Balance is an important element in the mastery of locomotor and ball handling skills (Williams, 1983). All fundamental motor skills develop during the preschool years and have many of the characteristics of mature patterns. Typically, balance progresses from balancing with the feet shoulder width apart to balancing with the feet together, with the feet in semi-tandem and tandem positions, and finally to balancing on one foot with the eyes open.

Balance with eyes closed develops later. Children typically run, jump, and gallop in that order; most children gallop by age 3 years. The hop and skip tend to be the last of the locomotor skills to appear. Most children skip by age 6 years. Although there is considerable overlap in the development of object control skills, the typical order of mastery is: 1. throw, 2. kick, 3. catch, 4. strike, and 5. ball bounce.

The preschool years are a period of rapid and important changes in the development of large muscle or gross motor coordination. Developmental sequence often referred to as steps or stages help identify the qualitative changes that occur as children acquire or master gross motor skills. General progressions or changes in and developmental characteristics of selected locomotor and object control skills are provided in Tables 12.1 and 12.2, respectively. The information in these tables provides a brief overview and succinct summary of recognized changes in the development of these skills, including balance. Selected aspects of developmental changes in the skills included in the tables are discussed below.

Balance

Early balance development is manifested in the child's ability to maintain equilibrium in a variety of positions (e.g., on all fours, on the knees, in a standing position). This equilibrium mastery is followed by attempts to stand, to walk, and to navigate around objects in the environment. Once some success is achieved in these behaviors, the child attempts to walk on narrow objects (e.g., balance beams, rails, lines) and shows some beginning ability to maintain balance on one foot. By 6 years of age, most children can balance for long periods of time on the preferred foot with the eyes open (Mean = 22 sec). Balancing on the non-preferred foot is more difficult (Mean = 14 sec) and balancing with the eyes closed is just beginning to be mastered (Mean = 7 sec). Most children, at this age, can walk a balance beam (4 feet long by 2½ inches wide) in a controlled heel-toe manner in 23 seconds.

It is important to note that although the early versus later changes described for each skill can be loosely associated with chronological age, the relationship between these changes and chronological age per se is at best a tenuous one. One of the most dramatic characteristics of gross motor development in the preschool child is its great variability (Keogh & Sudgen, 1990). Some children fall nicely into a rather traditional "change with age" association, but many do not. Thus, ages have been intentionally de-emphasized in the discussion of developmental changes in gross motor skills in this chapter. The reader also should be aware that the changes described for individual skills are not mutually exclusive; children typically display changes in more than one skill at any given time (Roberton & Langendorfer, 1980). To date, there is a consensus that motor skill interventions can improve balance among children with (Maiano et al., 2019) and without disabilities (Logan et al., 2012).

Table 12.1 General Developmental Characteristics and Progressions in Gross Motor Development: Locomotor and Body Projection Skills in the Preschool Years

Motor Skill	Initial	Mid	Later
Walking and Running Progressions: • Walking occurs before running. • Walk or run a straight path before a circular or curved one. • Walk or run a straight path before they walk or run around obstacles.	• The early run resembles a fast walk; it is a series of hurried steps with a wide base of support and no period of suspension. • Weight is received on a flat foot. • Children run with short strides (there is minimal flexion/extension of the legs); they also run at a slow pace. Arms are used minimally, if at all, and often are extended for balance; later arms move smoothly in opposition to the legs.	• Later the run involves a period of suspension; the base of support is narrower; the feet are placed one in front of the other. • Later, weight is received on the heel and shifted to the ball of the foot (slow pace). In a faster run, weight is often received on the ball of the foot. • Later, children run with longer strides (there is greater flexion/extension of the legs) and they run at a faster rate.	• With practice, running becomes more automatic; the child can start, stop, and turn easily. • Running is incorporated readily into games and other activities.
Jumping Progressions: • Children exhibit a series of "bunny hops" before they perform a true standing broad jump. • Children jump down from an object before they jump up onto or over an object.	• Jumps cover short distances (there is minimal flexion/ extension of the legs). • Arms are not used or are used awkwardly.	• Jumps cover increasingly longer distances (there is more complete flexion/extension of the legs). • Arms initiate the jumping action and are coordinated with the action of the legs. Initially balance is often lost upon landing.	• The child maintains balance on landing.

- Children execute jumps from lower heights before higher heights.
- When jumping down from obstacles, children progress from aided jumping to jumping alone with a one-foot step down to jumping alone with a simultaneous two-foot propulsion.
- Children pass through the same progression described above at each height from which a jump is attempted.

Galloping Progressions:
- Children gallop before they hop or skip.
- Children gallop with the preferred foot leading before they gallop with the opposite foot in the lead.
- Children usually gallop in rudimentary form by age 3.

Hopping Progressions:
- Children "hop" on both feet prior to developing a true hopping action on one foot.
- Children hop in place before they perform a moving hop.

- Children gallop with the body in a sideways position (a sliding action).
- Arms are not used.
- Early on, children execute 3–4 cycles of the gallop and then lose the pattern.

- Hopping development is erratic.
- Initially, there is minimal suspension in the hop (minimal flexion/extension of the legs). Weight is received on the whole/flat foot.

- Gallop through a 50' distance without losing the pattern.

- Children gallop with their body facing forward.
- Two arms are used together (bilaterally) to support the leg action.

- Hopping in a straight path.
- Good suspension in the hop (flexion/extension of the legs are more complete).

- Weight is received on the ball of the foot.
- Arms are used together in a bilateral action and are coordinated with the leg action.

(Continued)

Table 12.1 (Cont).

Motor Skill	Initial	Mid	Later
• Children hop first on the foot on the preferred side; later, they hop on the foot on the opposite side.	• Arms flail or are used awkwardly.		
Children usually hop by age 3–4 years and complete 3–5 hops on the preferred side.			
Skipping Progressions:	• 2–3 cycles of the skipping pattern are executed.	• Begin to gallop.	• Skipping action is maintained for 50+ feet without loss of the pattern.
• The last locomotor skill to appear. Children may not skip until 6 years or later.	• Arms are not used.		• Arms move in opposition to the legs.
• Consists of a step and a hop on alternating sides.			
• Progresses from a shuffle step to a skip on one side to a skip on alternating sides.			
Stair Climbing Progressions:	• Climbing a short flight of stairs or a ladder with rungs close together.	• Feet alternate to climb short flights of stairs but still mark time on longer flights of stairs.	• Proficiency in descending a longer flight of stairs or a ladder with rungs farther apart.
• Marking time (i.e., both feet placed on rung or step before next step is attempted) precedes alternation of feet in climbing.		• Use of alternating feet in descending stairs.	
• Use of alternating feet appears first in ascending steps.		• Proficiency in climbing a longer flight of stairs or a ladder with rungs farther apart.	
• Children typically ascend a set of stairs before they descend.			

Table 12.2 Some Developmental Changes in Gross Motor Development: Ball Handling and Object Control Skills in the Preschool Years

Motor Skill	Initial	Mid	Later
Throwing Progression: • Children throw a smaller ball farther than a large one. • They develop a better throwing pattern if they throw forcefully. • Throwing at a target develops later than throwing for distance. • Targets should be large and at a close distance, initially; later, they can be smaller and farther away. • Progression toward shorter periods of acceleration; that is, the necessary joint actions occur in shorter periods, thus creating increased force of the throw.	• The ball is held in the palm of the hand. • Action is largely arm action in the vertical plane. • No trunk rotation. • No shift of weight.	• The ball is held in the tips of the fingers. • The whole body is involved in initiating the throwing action. • There is block trunk rotation. • Weight is shifted onto the foot on the same side as the throwing arm.	• Arm action involves lateral and medial rotation of the shoulder and elbow extension. • Differentiated trunk rotation. • Weight is shifted onto the foot opposite the throwing arm.
Kicking Progressions: • Stationary balls are kicked successfully before rolling balls. • Large, light balls are contacted more easily than smaller, heavier balls. • Rolling balls are kicked with greater success if rolled slowly and directly toward the child. • Rolling balls to the right and left.	• Leg action stops at ball contact. • Leg is swung forward only. • Inconsistent ball contact with the toes, the top of the foot/leg, or with the side of the foot. • Arms are not involved in the kicking action.	• The child kicks through the ball. • The child swings the leg backward and then forward and through the ball.	• Contact is more consistent and appropriate for different types of kicks. • Arm opposite the kicking leg swings forward and upward as the ball is contacted.

(Continued)

Table 12.2 (Cont).

Motor Skill	Initial	Mid	Later
Catching Progressions:	• Hands/arms used as a single unit.	• Ball is trapped against the body.	• Ball is contacted and controlled with the hands/fingers.
• Children intercept (stop) a rolling ball before they catch or intercept a bounced or aerial ball.	• Ball contact is occasional.	• Ball is contacted but is immediately dropped.	• The child moves toward the ball and gets to the ball in time for making effective contact.
• Bounced balls are caught more easily than aerial balls.	• Children fixate on, and track, the oncoming ball minimally or with little consistency and do not judge the speed or direction of a moving ball accurately and consistently; they often do not get to the ball in time to intercept or catch it.	• Children revert to using hands and arms as a single unit when they initially attempt to intercept a small ball; at the same time, they easily coordinate the use of hands and fingers in catching a larger ball.	
• Balls bounced or tossed from shorter distances are easier to catch than balls bounced or tossed from greater distances.	• "Avoidance reaction" to the oncoming ball; eyes close and/ or head turns away as the ball approaches.	• Ball is tracked more effectively; speed and direction of moving ball judged more accurately and consistently. With increasing skill and confidence, avoidance disappears.	
• Large balls are intercepted before small balls.			
Striking Progression:	• The bat is held against the shoulder.	• Ball is held out away from the body.	• Weight shift onto the foot on the side opposite the preferred hand.
• Children initially use a one-arm striking pattern and gradually develop a two-arm striking pattern. Children are successful in hitting a stationary ball before hitting a moving ball.	• The child faces the oncoming ball.	• Children stand with the side of the body toward the ball.	• The weight shift initiates the striking action
	• Arm action is a vertical chopping action.	• Action is in the horizontal plane.	

- Children are more successful using a large, light bat/implement than a small, heavy bat/implement.

Bouncing Progressions
- Children attempt a two-hand bounce before a one-hand bounce.
- Children bounce a smaller ball (one that fits the hand) before a larger ball.
- Children perform a series of "bounces-and-catches" before they perform a continuous bounce.
- The ball is bounced in a stationary position before bouncing the ball while moving.

- Arm action stops at ball contact.
- No shift of weight.

- Ball is bounced with whole-body action.
- Children "slap" at the ball with a flat/whole hand.

- The implement is swung through the ball.
- Step is onto the foot on the same side as the preferred hand.

- Arm/hand is used independently of body action while stationary.

in a kind of step and swing pattern.

- Arm/hand is used independently of body action while continuously bouncing and moving.

Gender Differences

Figure 12.2 shows the age in months of the emergence of several gross motor skills and the approximate age at which 60% of boys and girls perform proficiently (Seefeldt & Haubenstricker, 1982). The numbers in the figure refer to the changes or *stages* that have identified characteristics and are part of the process of mastering or showing skill proficiency (1 = beginning or early characteristics of skill performance; 4 = proficiency and/or more mature characteristics). Observed gender differences indicate that boys acquire proficiency before girls in running, jumping, throwing, kicking, and striking. Gender differences in running and jumping are minimal (6–8 months); differences are

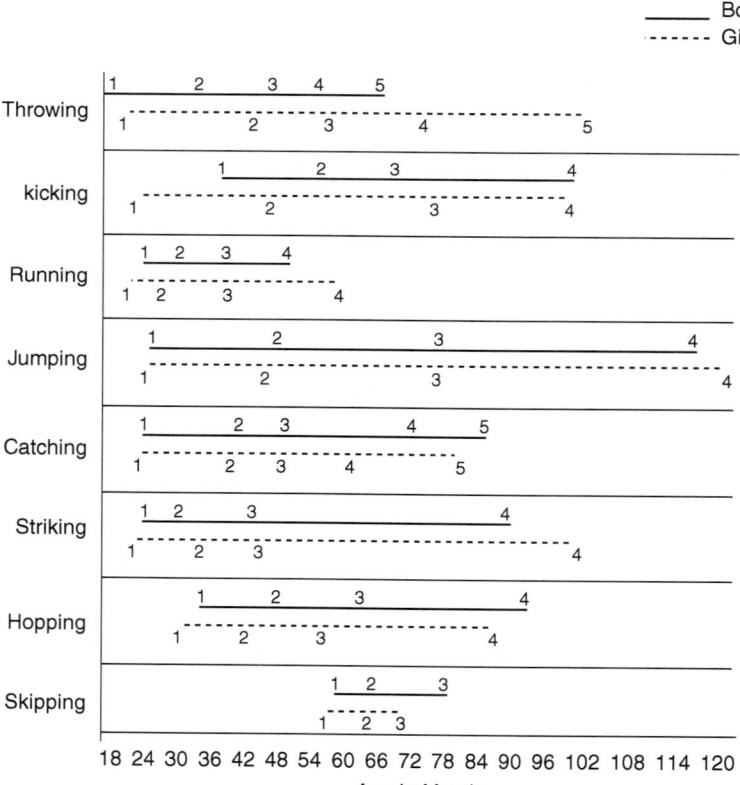

Figure 12.2 Age in Months at Which 60% of Boys and Girls Exhibit Selected Characteristics of Fundamental Motor Skills

Note: Adapted from Seefeldt and Haubenstricker (1982); numbers refer to the presence of selected characteristics in motor skill performances at different points in the developmental process.

greater for kicking and striking (12–16 months). Interestingly, differences are more evident in throwing; boys tend to demonstrate proficiency around 69 months, while girls show proficiency around 102 months, some 33 months later. In contrast, girls have an advantage over boys in hopping, skipping, and catching and demonstrate proficiency some 6–10 months before boys (Seefeldt & Haubenstricker, 1982). Garcia (1994) and Greendorfer and Ewing (1981) documented gender differences in the development of fundamental motor skills. It is important to note that in addition to gender differences, there is also considerable variability in the timing of the changes that occur in motor skill development for all children. For example, girls and boys show some arm-foot opposition and heel-toe contact in running at about 3 years of age (Stage 3). However, boys show full proficiency (Stage 4) in running just 10 months later, while girls do not exhibit proficiency until some 20 months later.

Although some developmentalists have attributed differences between boys and girls to physical differences, it is generally the case that boys and girls do not differ substantially in physical size or muscular strength prior to puberty. Thus, cultural differences associated with opportunities for practice and encouragement may play a greater role in skill development than once was thought to be the case. A review of 59 studies (Barnett et al., 2016) indicates that boys tend to be better at object control skills than are girls. This finding is important for practitioners for two reasons. First, object control skills are strong predictors of physical activity (Visser et al., 2019). Second, physical activity among girls declines significantly, especially with age, so if their motor coordination, as reflected in object control skills, is also low, they may be at risk for a negative spiral of engagement, which is a concern for maintaining a healthy weight status (Barnett & Goodway, 2018).

III. Assessment of Gross Motor Development

Competence and development of the gross motor skills and balance characteristics described thus far can be assessed using a variety of assessments depending on whether the goal involves product outcomes (e.g., speed, hitting a target, balancing time) or process qualities (e.g., quality of moving body segments). Product assessments measure quantifiable changes observed in some motor behavior processes across the lifespan (Haywood & Getchell, 2020) (e.g., how many times a target is hit, running speed, throwing distance). In order to capture the most comprehensive view of motor competence and developmental change, researchers recommend using both process and product measures (Logan et al., 2018). The following is a review of measures to consider, but it is by no means a comprehensive list because motor development research is currently burgeoning.

IV. Process Assessments

Test of Gross Motor Development, Second Edition (Ulrich, 2000) and Third Edition (Ulrich, 2019)

The Test of Gross Motor Development (TGMD; Ulrich, 2000) is one of the gross motor assessments most commonly used by practitioners to assess young children's gross motor development. The TGMD measures fundamental motor skills of children between the ages of 3 years and 10 years and 11 months. The TGMD-2 (Ulrich, 2000) is a validated product- and process-oriented assessment comprised of 12 fundamental motor skills representing two separate subscales, each comprised of six skills (2000). **Locomotor skills** include running, jumping, hopping, leaping, sliding, and leaping; **object control skills** include striking, kicking, throwing, catching, dribbling, and rolling. The general administrative protocol for each skill involves a demonstration of the skill followed by a non-scored practice trial. If the child performs the appropriate skill after the demonstration, the child then completes two scored practice trials. If the child does not perform the appropriate skill after the demonstration, the child receives another demonstration and practice trial before another two scored trials. Each skill includes three to five critical elements (e.g., arms extend above head when jumping). A child receives a 1 if the critical element is present during the scored trial and a score of 0 if the critical element is not present. Each of the critical elements is summed for each practice trial for an overall skill raw score that ranges from 6 to 10 points, depending on the skill. Scores for each skill within a scale are summed and the maximum score per scale is 48. Subscale raw scores are then transposed into normative measures based on the age in 6-month age bands and gender. Normative measures include a percentile rank that can be transposed into a gross motor quotient or an age equivalent.

In 2019, Ulrich released the TGMD third edition (TGMD-3; Ulrich, 2019). The TGMD-3 follows the same procedures as the TGMD-2, but it has a few minor changes, including: 1. TGMD-2 object control skills are referred to as ball skills; 2. leaping and rolling skills were removed; 3. skipping was added to the locomotor scale while one-hand striking and tossing were added to the ball skills scale; 4. changes were made in some critical elements within each subscale; 5. as a result of the subscale changes, a maximum of 46 points are attainable for the locomotor subscale and 54 points for the ball skills subscale.

The CHAMPS (Children's Activity and Movement in Preschool Study) Motor Skill Protocol (CMSP: Williams et al., 2009)

The CHAMPS CMSP is a tool for assessing motor skills of preschool children ages 3, 4, and 5 years in a field-based setting. It is comprised of six locomotor skills (i.e., run, broad jump, slide, gallop, leap, hop) and six object control skills (i.e., overarm throw, underhanded roll, kick, catch, stationary strike, stationary dribble), scored separately and summed to comprise a composite total score. The scoring criteria for each of the scales are presented in Tables 12.3 and 12.4. The CMSP battery was developed systematically based on a review of assessments existing at the time; it aimed to test the effectiveness of an intervention developed for a large-scale, epidemiological study. The CMSP is reliable, valid, and simple to use in live settings, requiring minimal space and no recording device. The CMSP was based on the TGMD-2, addressing clearer skill criteria, behavioral descriptions of criteria, and expanded scoring that includes a protocol for establishing handedness for improved sensitivity. For each skill, criteria are marked as present (1) or absent (0), except for the throw and strike, where hip/trunk rotation is scored as differentiated (2), block (1), or no rotation (0), and for the catch, where the ball is cleanly caught with finger tips (2) or trapped against the body (1). The total number of skill components checked as present over two trials are summed to give a composite score for each skill. Locomotor skill scores are summed separately from object control skills to comprise two subscale scores; subscale scores are summed for a total CMSP score. Concurrent validity coefficients between the TGMD-2 range from .94 to .98 and construct validity was evidenced by age differentiation where score means were significantly different between 3- and 4- and 5-year-olds (Williams et al., 2009). Sex differences in CMSP scores are also evident where boys tend to have better object-control skills than girls, with greater competence observed for kicking and overarm throw, while girls are more competent in running, hopping, and galloping (Foulkes et al., 2015).

Zurich Neuromotor Assessment – Quick Version (ZNA-Q; Kabekeeke et al., 2018)

The quick version of the ZNA is a truncated version that assesses static and dynamic balance in children between 3 and 6 years of age in less than 5 minutes (Kakebeeke et al., 2019). It includes several gross motor tasks, such as: standing on one leg, tandem stance, hopping on one leg, walking on a straight line, and jumping sideways. All tasks are measured on an ordinal scale. Although this version of the ZNA shows promise in terms of efficiency, preliminary results of test-retest reliability were low ($r = .17$ to $.7$, median $= .41$). The ZNA-Q is based on the ZNA-2 (Kabekeeke et al., 2018), which focuses on motor abilities of children 3 to 18 years of age. Motor ability is a concept that specifically reflects the child's neurological development. The five motor abilities measured by the ZNA-2 are fine motor tasks, pure motor tasks, dynamic balance, static balance, and movement quality (i.e., the intensity of Contralateral Associated Movements).

Table 12.3 Locomotor Subscale

Skill	Movement Characteristics
Run	1. Arms move in opposition to legs, elbows bent 2. Brief period of suspension (both feet off the ground) 3. Narrow foot placement; lands on heel or toe; not flat footed 4. Length of stride even; path of movement horizontal 5. Nonsupport leg flexed to approximately 90° 6. Eyes focused forward
Broad jump	1. Preparatory: flexion of both knees; arms behind body 2. Arms extend forcefully; forward and upward to full extension above the head 3. Take-off and landing on both feet simultaneously 4. Take-off on both feet simultaneously; landing non-simultaneous 5. Arms move downward during landing 6. Balance maintained on landing
Slide	1. Body turned sideways; shoulders aligned with line on floor to initiate 2. Steps sideways with lead foot; slides trail foot next to lead foot 3. Minimum of four continuous step-slide cycles to right 4. Minimum of four continuous step-slide cycles to left 5. Arms used to assist leg action 6. Body maintained in sideways position moving to right 7. Body maintained in sideways position moving to left
Gallop	1. Arms (elbows) flexed and at waist level at take-off 2. Step forward with lead foot; step with trail foot to a position adjacent to or behind lead foot 3. Heel–toe action of lead foot 4. Assumes initial position facing forward 5. Final position facing forward 6. Brief period of suspension; both feet off the floor 7. Maintains rhythmic pattern (four consecutive gallops)
Leap	1. Take off on one foot; land on opposite foot 2. Brief period of suspension (both feet off the ground) 3. Forward reach with arm opposite the lead foot
Hop	1. Nonsupport leg swings forward in pendular motion to assist force production 2. Foot of nonsupport leg remains behind body 3. Arms flexed; swing forward together to produce force 4. Weight received (lands) on ball of foot 5. Takes off and lands three consecutive times on preferred foot 6. Takes off and lands three consecutive times on nonpreferred foot

Table 12.4 Object Control Subscale

Skill		Movement Characteristics
Overarm throw	1.	Wind-up initiated by downward movement of hand/arm
	2.	Hip and shoulder rotated so that nonthrowing side faces target
	3.	Steps (weight transferred) onto foot opposite throwing arm
	4.	Differentiated trunk rotation (2)
	5.	Block trunk rotation (1)
	6.	Timing of release/flight of ball appropriate (late release = downward flight; early release = upward flight)
	7.	Arm follows through beyond release (down and across the body)
Underhand roll	1.	Ball arm/hand swings down/back of trunk; chest/head face forward
	2.	Arm action in vertical plane
	3.	Foot opposite ball hand strides forward toward cones
	4.	Bends knees; lowers body
	5.	Ball held in fingertips
	6.	Ball released close to floor; bounces less than 4 inches high
Kick	1.	Rapid and continuous approach to ball
	2.	Elongated stride or leap immediately prior to ball contact
	3.	Nonkicking foot placed even with or slightly in back of ball
	4.	Leg swing is full; full backswing and forward swing of leg
	5.	Backswing coordinated with forward action of nonkicking leg
	6.	Ball contacted with instep of kicking foot (shoelaces) or toe
	7.	Kicks through ball; leg action does not stop at ball contact
Catch	1.	Preparatory: hands in front of body; elbows flexed
	2.	Arms extend toward ball as it moves closer
	3.	Ball caught cleanly with hands/fingers (2)
	4.	Ball trapped against body/chest (1)
	5.	Ball tracked consistently and close to point of contact
	6.	Doesn't turn head/close eyes as ball approaches
Stationary strike	1.	Dominant hand grips bat just above nondominant hand
	2.	Nonpreferred side of body faces imaginary "pitcher"; feet parallel
	3.	Steps (transfers weight) onto foot opposite dominant hand to initiate strike
	4.	Differentiated trunk rotation (2)
	5.	Block trunk rotation (1)
	6.	Arm action/plane of bat movement horizontal
	7.	Ball contacts bat
	8.	Swings through ball (action does not stop at ball contact)
Stationary dribble	1.	Arm action independent of trunk
	2.	Ball contacted with one hand at about belt/waist height
	3.	Pushes ball with fingertips (does not slap at ball with flat hand)
	4.	Ball contacts surface in front of or to the outside of foot on preferred side
	5.	Controls ball for four consecutive bounces; feet not moved to retrieve ball

Product Assessment

Movement Assessment Battery for Children-2

The Movement Assessment Battery for Children (Movement ABC; Henderson, 1992) and its second version (Movement ABC-2; Henderson et al., 2007) have been the most comprehensive, and widely used test batteries for assessing motor development in children. This assessment was designed to provide process and product information about children's motor development. It consists of an objective *test*, which includes a product and process component, and a *checklist* (described earlier). The objective test is appropriate for use in arriving at a more detailed description of motor development needs. The test component of the Movement ABC is divided into different age bands; the youngest age band spans the years from 3 to 6. Each age band consists of eight tasks. Tasks in each age band are categorized as follows: manual dexterity (fine motor tasks), ball skills, and static and dynamic balance. The latter three categories assess gross motor development. For each task there is a quantitative or product score (e.g., time in balance, number of steps) and a series of process characteristics to be checked. The process characteristics listed below, for the most part, are paraphrased and do not represent the verbatim wording found in the battery. Demonstration of and practice on all tasks is required; after practice, children are given 1 or more trials, up to 10, to perform the task. Tasks in the age band for 4-, 5-, and 6-year-olds include:

1. putting coins through a slot in a box
2. threading beads
3. drawing a single continuous line within a boundary
4. catching a bean bag tossed from 6 feet away
5. rolling a ball into a goal 6 feet away
6. one-leg balance
7. jumping over a cord knee high
8. walking 15 steps on a line with the heels raised.

Directions for administering and scoring each item are provided in simple straightforward language. Means and standard deviations are given for total impairment scores by age and by gender. Cut scores for the 5th and 15th percentiles are provided. Scores below the 5th percentile are indicative of a definite motor development lag, while scores between the 5th and 15th percentiles suggest borderline motor development difficulties. Sample case studies are described in detail. Normative data for both the test and checklist components are based on 1,200 children from 4 to 12 years of age; the sample in the age range from 4 to 6 years was 493 children. Boys and girls of different ethnic origins and from diverse regions of the United States were included. The battery has been used throughout the world for assessing motor skill development in children. A second edition of the Movement ABC (MABC-2) was released in 2007 (Henderson et al., 2007). The updated edition features a larger age band (i.e., 3–16 years old for the objective test and 3–12 years old for the checklists), updated test items, instructions, and normative data to improve test clarity, stronger assessments items to indicate motor impairments or delays, and updated normative referencing for identification and placement into services (Brown & Lalor, 2009).

Peabody Developmental Motor Scales-II

A widely used tool for assessing motor development in young children is the *Peabody Developmental Motor Scales* (Folio & Fewell, 2000). The scales were designed to evaluate gross and fine motor skills in children with and without disabilities from birth to 6 years. The gross motor scale consists of 170 items, 10 items at each of 17 age levels. Items are grouped at 6-month intervals beginning at 2 years. The areas of gross motor development considered include reflexes (in children up to 1 year of age), balance/non-locomotor behaviors, locomotor skills, and object manipulation skills. The gross motor development scale requires approximately 30 minutes to administer and is straightforward in administration, scoring, and interpretation. All items are scored 0 (the child cannot or does not perform the task), 1, or 2 (the child performs the task according to the differential criteria listed). Basal and ceiling ages are determined, and raw scores can be converted into percentile ranks, standard scores, and a gross and fine motor quotient. Normative data on 2,003 children (85.1% Caucasian) from a wide variety of geographical locations (northeastern, northern, central, southern and western United States) are provided. Of the total number of children in the standardization sample, there were at least 92 2-year-olds, 103 3-year-olds, 50 4-year-olds, and 55 5-year-olds. The Peabody Motor Activities Program is available for use by teachers.

Bruininks-Oseretsky Test of Motor Proficiency

The Bruininks-Oseretsky Test (Bruininks, 1978) is designed for use with children 4½ through 14½ years of age. It consists of eight subtests (46 separate items) that provide a broad index of the child's proficiency in both gross and fine motor skills. A short form of the test (14 items) provides a brief overview of the child's general motor proficiency. Four of the subtests measure gross motor skills; these subtests include running speed and agility, balance, bilateral coordination, and upper limb coordination. Raw scores on gross motor items are converted to point scores that are then converted to standard scores. The standard scores are summed to give a gross motor composite; this is converted into a composite standard score. The standard score is used to determine a percentile rank for the individual child. Some age-equivalent data are provided, and norms are established at 6-month intervals. The standardization sample was based on 68 children for the 4-year, 6 month to 5-year, 5-month range and 82 children for the 5-year, 6-month to 6-year, 5-month range.

In 2005, the *Bruininks-Oseretsky Test of Motor Proficiency – Second Edition* (BOT-2; Bruininks & Bruininks, 2005a) was released to expand the age range to 4 to 21 years of age, providing up to date normative references of children's motor proficiency. Most notably, an "overhaul" of the assessment was conducted to strengthen the data for the lower ages (4–5 years), as well as provide an extension of fine and gross motor test items in tandem with strengthening the overall practicality of the assessment (Cools et al., 2009). The BOT-2 now includes 53 items across eight subtests. Furthermore, the BOT-2 provides sub-assessments such as a short form, fine motor form, and gross motor form as targeted options of motor proficiency. In 2010, Bruininks and Bruininks created the BOT-2 Brief Form (Bruininks & Bruininks, 2010), a 12-item assessment (i.e., selection of 1 item for each subtest of the BOT-2 Complete Form) to provide a quicker assessment of motor proficiency, with less equipment, and give one overall score of motor proficiency. The BOT-2 is primarily used by practitioners and researchers for evaluations and decisions regarding diagnosis and screening for motor impairments or disorders as well as placement into services to help remediate or improve motor impairments (Cools et al., 2009). Assessment time for the BOT-2 ranges from 45 to 60 minutes for the complete form, 25 to 30 minutes for a sub-test form (e.g., fine or gross), and 10 to 20 minutes for the Short or Brief Forms, providing practitioners and researchers with multiple assessment options based upon specific issues or research questions in regard to children's motor skills.

Gross Motor Function Measure (GMFM; Russell, Rosenbaum, Avery, & Lane, 2002)

The GMFM is a clinical assessment tool designed to evaluate change in gross motor function in children with cerebral palsy, but it can also be used to evaluate motor development in children with Down syndrome or with other children whose skills are at or below those typically observed in 5-year-olds. The original test consists of 88 items (GMFM-88); a more recent version consists of a subset of 66 items (GMFM-66). The tasks included span a range of skills from lying and rolling through walking, running, and jumping skills; the 88-item battery takes approximately 45–60 minutes to administer. Normative data are on children from 5 months to 16 years. A 4-point scale is used to score each item; detailed standards for scoring are provided. The GMFM-88 scores can be summed to determine raw scores and percentile ranks for the child's overall performance.

Multidomain Tests

Zittel (1994) and Maiano et al. (2019) review important considerations in selecting an instrument for assessing gross motor development for use in accessible movement contexts. Together with the review of Logan et al. (2018), these works provide excellent overviews of several test batteries that could be used with young children.

V. Use of Assessment Results

As we know that children who lag in motor development are more likely than their peers to display difficulties in adapting to school and play environments, information about the level and nature of motor skill development is of major importance to their parents, teachers, school psychologists, and family physicians. It may be easy to note that a child moves awkwardly; however, it is another matter to describe or determine precisely what was missing from or contributed to the lack of skillful performance. Poor or underdeveloped motor skills may be the product of a complex set of factors that include not only poor coordination and control but also lack of appropriate spatial/body awareness, underdeveloped sensory function, lack of self-confidence, fear of failure, or other factors. Thus, a scientifically sound and insightful description and diagnosis of gross motor development should be based on information from formal and informal product and process assessments of gross motor behaviors along with outcomes of a variety of other developmental measures.

Regarding using assessment results in the United States, if a child is ranked below a certain percentile on two validated motor assessments, the child can be placed on an Individual Education Plan (IEP) as early as age 3 years. Historically, if a child is ranked below the 25th percentile on a motor assessment the child could be identified as being at risk of developmental delay. If a child ranks between the 5th and 15th percentiles on two formal and validated motor assessments, the child could be diagnosed with a motor delay or impairment (e.g., DCD). Qualifications regarding the extent of formal diagnosis are different in each state. With an IEP, children may receive services such as adapted physical education or occupational or physical therapy to remediate delays and improve mobility and quality of life related to a child's overall motor development. Once the child is on an IEP plan, members of the child's IEP team (e.g., school psychologists, classroom teachers, occupational therapists, school administration, physical therapists, speech and language pathologists, physical education or adapted physical education teachers) will examine the child's formal motor assessment data and begin to set yearly motor goals for up to three years. Information from product- and process-oriented assessments will be used by the IEP team to create sub-goals based upon assessment results to help the child to make continual progress to achieve the overall IEP goals each year. From assessments and goals, teachers, therapists, and physical educators can write effective lesson plans or treatment plans to meet each sub-goal and major motor milestones within the child's IEP.

Formal measures of gross motor development support, clarify, and extend observations of motor behavior made with informal instruments. Formal product measures of motor development are valuable because they provide a frame of reference for interpreting the current status of the child's motor development. It is important to note, however, that it is imprudent and unfair to act as though figures or descriptions in a table or on a chart are an irrefutable indication of whether a child is normal or typical.

Process information is used to elaborate on the product outcome frame of references and is especially important because it considers directly how the body is moved and attempts to identify what is missing from or contributing to the child's lack of adequate motor control. Process assessment techniques are particularly important for gaining insight into how the child attempts to solve the problem of performing a motor task. This type of information is integral to an accurate description and/or ultimate diagnosis of the level of gross motor development because lags in motor development can be as much a function of the young child's understanding of the "what" and "how" of a task as they are of the child's ability to perform the task. The most significant, direct, and immediate uses that can be made of information from gross motor development screening and evaluation include the following:

1. *Planning and evaluating effective gross motor curricula for young children.* To individualize early sensory and motor learning experiences for young children, professionals need to be able to group or identify children according to levels of motor competence. When specific aspects of the gross motor behavior of the child are known, basic tasks can be modified in a variety of ways to encourage individual refinement of and success in motor skill performance at the child's present level of development, as well as to promote growth toward higher levels of skill mastery.

2. *Early identification of motor dysfunctions.* Motor dysfunctions can impede the child's physical, mental, social, and emotional development. Information about gross motor development can be valuable to the teacher of the young child for maximizing early learning potential and for educational counseling. Such information is vital when making decisions about whether the child possesses the basic skills needed to succeed in simple classroom activities. The child who devotes a major share of their energy to assuming and maintaining basic postures or to controlling movements of the body will have much less energy to devote to other important activities that are integral to optimal development. Data about the child's level of gross motor development are important in determining when and/or if a child should enter school,

or whether they should be placed in a developmental enrichment environment.

3. *Design of individual programs of enrichment activities.* Motor skill deficiencies often accompany and contribute to other learning, behavior, and attention problems the young child may experience. When this is the case, some attention almost always is required to improve the motor capacities of the child before other learning and behavior problems can be effectively addressed. If, on the other hand, the young child has learning, memory, and/or attentional problems but no accompanying motor development difficulties, gross motor activities may be used in creative ways to help stimulate improvement in other dimensions of development.

Results of gross motor skills screening and evaluation of preschool children are most useful as a part of a comprehensive, multidimensional assessment of the young child. At a minimum, information about the child's fine motor control or eye-hand coordination (e.g., cutting, peg manipulation, pencil or crayon usage), simple perceptual skills (e.g., identification of colors, color matching, visual, verbal, and tactile-kinesthetic discrimination of shapes and sizes, as well as figure-ground perception), and general characteristics of cognitive function ought to accompany the child's motor development record. It is only when information from gross motor development testing is used or viewed in conjunction with information about these other aspects of sensory and motor development that appropriate prognostic statements and remediation techniques for gross motor and other dimensions of development can be established or prescribed.

If the child has gross motor deficiencies only (e.g., no accompanying deficits in other sensory and motor behaviors), it is more likely that the motor development problems observed are temporary and simply reflect an uneven growth process that will self-correct with time. If, on the other hand, gross motor deficits are accompanied by fine motor and/or other sensory-perceptual or cognitive difficulties, there may be underlying neurological problems. In this case, referral to a pediatric neurologist and/or other appropriate medical personnel for further evaluation is appropriate. The motor system (including the control of eye muscles) is more likely than other systems to show deficits when something has gone awry with basic central and/or peripheral neurophysiological processes. At a behavioral level, information-gathering behaviors (e.g., the way children use their eyes to pick up information from the environment) and information-interpretation skills (e.g., figure-ground perception) can contribute significantly to the lack of refined fine and gross motor skills. Gross motor deficits are often, at least in part, a reflection of inadequate support skills in visual perception. Therefore, remediation and enrichment programs for children with both gross motor and simple perceptual deficits need to focus on improving support behaviors as well as the movement behaviors themselves.

Professionals working in educational settings with preschool children should use the following guide to gross motor development:

- Screen all children in gross motor development prior to or early in their entry into the preschool program. For initial screening, use a simple motor development screening tool such as the Denver Developmental Screening test or the Williams Preschool Checklist.
- Observe the children in naturalistic play settings.
- Use this information to determine which children need closer observation.
- Use a formal instrument to screen more carefully the children identified as potentially having gross motor process and product deficiencies.
- Examiners who must choose one measure over another should be sure to include some evaluation of the process characteristics of the child's motor skill performance.
- Children with questionable abilities should be referred to a motor development specialist, physical education teacher, or school psychologist for a more formal and comprehensive evaluation that includes a broad base of developmental information.
- Based on the total developmental profile, develop and implement appropriate instructional strategies and experiences to promote the motor development of the young child.
- When in doubt about the child's motor development difficulties, talk to or refer the child to the appropriate personnel within or outside the school setting.
- Remember that scores, percentiles, and other outcomes do not always tell the whole story about the child's overall motor development status and/or needs.
- Provide more out-of-school movement opportunities for children with DCD because of the clear connections between motor delays, low self-esteem, and mental illness.

References

Administration for Children and Families. (2015). *Head Start Early Learning Outcomes Framework. Ages Birth to Five.* Retrieved from https://eclkc.ohs.acf.hhs.gov/sites/default/files/pdf/ohs-framework.pdf

American Psychiatric Association. (2013). *Diagnostic and statistical manual of mental disorders* (5th ed.). Arlington, VA: American Psychiatric Publishing.

Babic, M. J., Morgan, P. J., Plotnikoff, R. C., Lonsdale, C., White, R. L., & Lubans, D. R. (2014). Physical activity and physical self-concept in youth: Systematic review and meta-analysis. *Sports Medicine, 44*(11), 1589–1601.

Barnett, L. M., Lai, S. K., Veldman, S. L. C., Hardy, L. L., Cliff, D., Morgan, P. J., … Okely, A. D. (2016). Correlates of gross motor competence in children and adolescents: A systematic review and meta-analysis. *Sports Medicine, 46*, 1663–1688. doi:10.1007/s40279-016-0495-z

Barnett, L., & Goodway, J. (2018). Perceptions of Movement Competence in Children and Adolescents from Different Cultures and Countries. *Journal of Motor Learning and Development, 6*, 1–6. doi:10.1123/jmld.2018-0024.

Beck, M. M., Lind, L. L., Geertsen, S. S., Ritz, C., Lundbye-Jensen, J., & Wienecke, J. (2016). Motor-enriched learning activities can improve mathematical performance in preadolescent children. *Frontiers in Human Neuroscience, 10*, 645. doi:10.3389/fnhum.2016.00645

Bellocchi, S., Tobia, V., & Bonifacci, P. (2017). Predictors of Reading and Comprehension Abilities in Bilingual and Monolingual Children: A Longitudinal Study on a Transparent Language. *Reading and Writing, 30*, 1311–1334. doi:10.1007/s11145-017-9725-5.

Best, J. R., & Miller, P. H. (2010). A developmental perspective on executive function. *Child Development, 81*, 1641–1660.

Brown, T., & Lalor, A. (2009). The Movement Assessment Battery for Children—Second Edition (MABC-2): A review and critique. *Physical & Occupational Therapy in Pediatrics, 29*(1), 86–103. doi:10.1080/01942630802574908

Bruininks, R. H. (1978). *Bruininks-oseretsky test of motor proficiency*. Circle, MN: AGS Publishing.

Bruininks, R. H., & Bruininks, B. D. (2005a). *Test of motor proficiency, 2nd edition manual*. Circle Pines, MN: AGS Publishing.

Bruininks, R. H., Bruininks, B. D. (2005b) *BOT2 :Bruininks-Oseretsky test of motor proficiency: manual*. Minneapolis, MN: Pearson Assessments.

Bruininks, R., & Bruininks, B. (2010). *Bruininks-Oseretsky Test of Motor Proficiency, Second Edition - Brief Form (BOT-2 Brief Form)*. Sydney, Australia: Pearson.

Burton, A., & Miller, D. (1998). *Movement skill assessment*. Champaign, IL: Human Kinetics.

Cairney, J., Rigoli, D., & Piek, J. (2013). Developmental coordination disorder and internalizing problems in children: The environmental stress hypothesis elaborated. *Developmental Review, 33*, 224–238. doi:10.1016/j.dr.2013.07.002

Clark, J. E. (2017). Pentimento: A 21st century view on the canvas of motor development. *Kinesiology Review, 6*(3), 232–239.

Clark, J. E., & Metcalfe, J. S. (2002). The mountain of motor development: A metaphor. *Motor Development: Research and Reviews, 2*(163–190), 183–202.

Clark, J. E., & Whitall, J. (1989). What is motor development? The lessons of history. *Quest, 41*(3), 183–202.

Cook, G., Burton, L., Kiesel, K., Rose, G., & Bryant, M. F. (2010). *Movement: Functional movement systems: Screening, assessment, corrective strategies*. Aptos, CA: On Target Publishing.

Cools, W., Martelaer, K. D., Samaey, C., & Andries, C. (2009). Movement skill assessment of typically developing preschool children: a review of seven movement skill assessment tools. *Journal of Sports Science & Medicine, 8*(2), 154–168.

Danielson, M. L., Bitsko, R. H., Ghandour, R. M., Holbrook, J. R., Kogan, M. D., & Blumberg, S. J. (2018). Prevalence of parent-reported ADHD diagnosis and associated treatment among U.S. children and adolescents. *Journal of Clinical Child & Adolescent Psychology, 47*(2), 199–212. doi:10.1080/15374416.2017.1417860

DeMeester, A., Stodden, D., Goodway, J., True, L., Brian, A., Ferkel, R., & Haerens, L. (2018). Identifying a motor proficiency barrier for meeting physical activity guidelines in children. *Journal of Science and Medicine in Sport, 21*, 58–62.

Diamond, A. (2000). Close interrelation of motor development and cognitive development and of the cerebellum and prefrontal cortex. *Child Development, 71*, 44–56.

Diamond, A. (2013). Executive functions. *Annual Review of Psychology, 64*, 135–168.

Engel, A. C., Broderick, C. R., van Doorn, N., Hardy, L. L., & Parmenter, B. J. (2018). Exploring the relationship between fundamental motor skill interventions and physical activity levels in children: A systematic review and meta-analysis. *Sports Medicine, 48*, 1845–1857.

Folio, M., & Fewell, R. (2000). *Peabody Developmental Motor Scales (PMDS-2)*. Austin, TX: PRO-ED.

Foulkes, J. D., Knonwles, Z., Fairclough, S. J., Stratton, G., O'Dwyer, M., Ridgers, N. D., & Foweather, L. (2015). Fundamental movement skills of preschool children in Northwest England. *Perceptual and Motor Skills, 121*, 260–283.

Gallahue, D. L., Ozmun, J., & Goodway, J. D. (2013). *Understanding Motor Development: Infants, Children, Adolescents, Adults* (7th ed.). Boston, MA: McGraw-Hill.

Garcia, C. (1994). Gender differences in young children's interactions when learning fundamental motor skills. *Research Quarterly for Exercise and Sport, 65*, 213–225.

Gesell, A. (1973). *The first five years of life: A guide to the study of the preschool child.* New York: Harper & Row.

Goulardins, J. B., Marques, J. C., & De Oliveira, J. A. (2017). Attention Deficit Hyperactivity Disorder and Motor Impairment. *Perceptual and Motor Skills, 124*(2), 425–440.

Greendorfer, S. L., & Ewing, M. E. (1981). Race and gender differences in children's socialization into sport. *Research Quarterly for Exercise and Sport, 52*, 301–310.

Harter, S. (1990). Developmental differences in the nature of self-representations: Implications for understanding, assessment and treatment of maladaptive behaviour. *Cognitive Therapy and Research, 14*, 113–142.

Haywood, K. M., & Getchell, N. (2020). *LifeSpan motor development* (7th ed.). Champaign, IL: Human Kinetics.

Henderson, S. E. (1992). Movement assessment battery for children. *The Psychological Corporation.*

Henderson, S. E., Sugden, D. A., & Barnett, A. L. (2007). *Movement assessment battery for children – 2 examiner's manual.* London: Harcourt Assessment.

Jaakkola, T., Hillman, C., Kalaja, S., & Liukkonen, J. (2015). The associations among fundamental movement skills, self-reported physical activity and academic performance during junior high school in Finland. *Journal of Sports Sciences, 33*(16), 1719–1729. doi:10.1080/02640414.2015.1004640

Kakebeeke, T. H., Knaier, E., Chaouch, A., Caflisch, J., Rousson, V., Largo, R. H., & Jenni, O. G. (2018). Neuromotor development in children. Part 4: new norms from 3 to 18 years. *Developmental Medicine & Child Neurology, 60*, 810–819. doi:10.1111/dmcn.13793

Kakebeeke, T. H., Chaouch, A., Knaier, E., Caflisch, J., Rousson, V., Largo, R. H., & Jenni, O. G. (2019). A quick and qualitative assessment of gross motor development in preschool children. *European Journal of Pediatrics, 178*, 565. doi:10.1007/s00431-019-03327-6

Keogh, J., & Sudgen, D. (1990). *Problems in movement skill development.* Columbia, SC: University of South Carolina Press.

Kugler, P. N., Kelso, J. A., & Turvey, M. T. (1980). On the concept of coordinative structure as dissipative structures: I. Theoretical lines of convergence. In G. E. Stelmach (Ed.), *Tutorials in motor behavior* (pp. 3–47). Amsterdam: North-Holland.

Lingam, R., Jongmans, M. J., Ellis, M., Hunt, L. P., Golding, J., & Emond, A. (2012). Mental health difficulties in children with developmental coordination disorder. *Pediatrics*, *129*(4), 882–891. doi:10.1542/peds.2011-1556

Lodal, K., & Bond, C. (2016). The relationship between motor skills difficulties and self-esteem in children and adolescents: A systematic literature review. *Educational Psychology in Practice*, *32*(4), 410–423. doi:10.1080/02667363.2016.1206847

Logan, S. W., Robinson, L. E., Wilson, A. E., & Lucas, W. A. (2012). Getting the fundamentals of movement: A meta-analysis of the effectiveness of motor skill interventions in children. *Child: Care, Health and Development*, *38*(3), 305–315.

Logan, S. W., Ross, S. M., Chee, K., Stodden, D. F., & Robinson, L. E. (2018). Fundamental motor skills: A systematic review of terminology. *Journal of Sports Sciences*, *36*, 781–796.

Maiano, C., Hue, O., & April, J. (2019). Effects of motor skill interventions on fundamental movement skills in children and adolescents with intellectual disabilities: A systematic review. *Journal of Intellectual Disability Research*, *63*, 1–17. doi:10.1111/jir.12618

Mancini, V. O., Rigoli, D., Heritage, B., Roberts, L. D., & Piek, J. P. (2016). The relationship between motor skills, perceived social support, and internalizing problems in a community adolescent sample. *Frontiers in Psychology*, *7*, 1–11. doi:10.3389/fpsyg.2016.00543

Mancini, V., Rigoli, D., Roberts, L., Heritage, B., & Piek, J. (2018). The relationship between motor skills, perceived self-competence, peer problems and internalizing problems in a community sample of children. *Infant and Child Development*, *27*, e2073. doi:10.1002/icd.2073

McClelland, M. M., Cameron, C. E., Duncan, R., Bowles, R. P., Acock, A. C., Miao, A., & Pratt, M. E. (2014). Predictors of early growth in academic achievement: The head-toes-knees-shoulders task. *Frontiers in Psychology*, *5*, 599.

Milne, N., Cacciotti, K., Davies, K., & Orr, R. (2018). The relationship between motor proficiency and reading ability in Year 1 children: A cross-sectional study. *BMC Pediatrics*, *18*(1), 294. doi:10.1186/s12887-018-1262-0

Miyahara, M., & Piek, J. (2006). Self-esteem of children and adolescents with physical disabilities: Quantitative evidence from meta-analysis. *Journal of Developmental and Physical Disabilities*, *18*(3), 219–234.

Morgan, P. J., Barnett, L. M., Cliff, D. P., Okely, A. D., Scott, H. A., Cohen, K. E., & Lubans, D. R. (2013). Fundamental movement skill interventions in youth: A systematic review and meta-analysis. *Pediatrics*, *132*(5), e1361–e1383.

Mulvey, K. L., Taunton, S., Pennell, A., & Brian, A. (2018). Head, toes, knees, SKIP! Improving preschool children's executive function through a motor competence intervention. *Journal of Sport and Exercise Psychology*, *40*(5), 233–239.

Murray, K. G., Jones, P. B., Kuh, D., & Richards, M. (2007). Infant developmental milestones and subsequent cognitive function. *Annals of Neurology*, *62*, 128–136.

Newell, K. (1986). Constraints on the development of coordination. In M. Wade & H. Whiting (Eds.), *Motor development in children: Aspects of coordination and control* (pp. 341–361). Amsterdam: Martin Nijhoff.

Pfeifer, C. E., Sacko, R. S., Ortaglia, A., Monsma, E. V., Beattie, P. F., Goins, J., & Stodden, D. F. (2019). Functional Movement Screen in youth sport participants: Evaluating the Proficiency Barrier for Injury. *International Journal of Sports Physical Therapy*, *14*(3), 436–444.

Piek, J. P., Dawson, L., Smith, L. M., & Gasson, N. (2008). The role of early fine and gross motor development on later motor and cognitive ability. *Human Movement Science, 27,* 668–681.

Polanczyk, G., de Lima, M. S., Horta, B. L., Biederman, J., & Rohde, L. A. (2007). The worldwide prevalence of ADHD: A systematic review and metaregression analysis. *The American Journal of Psychiatry, 164,* 942–948.

Poole, K. L., Schmidt, L. A., Missiuna, C., Saigal, S., Boyle, M. H., & Van Lieshout, R. J. (2015). Motor coordination and mental health in extremely low birth weight survivors during the first four decades of life. *Research Developmental Disabilities, 4,* 87–96. doi:10.1016/j.ridd.2015.06.004

Rigoli, D., Kane, R. T., Mancini, V., Thornton, A., Licari, M., Hands, B., & Piek, J. P. (2017). The relationship between motor proficiency and mental health outcomes in young adults: A test of the Environmental Stress Hypothesis. *Human Movement Science, 53,* 16–23. doi:10.1016/j.humov.2016.09.004

Roberton, M. A. (1978). Longitudinal evidence for developmental stages in the forceful overarm throw. *Journal of Human Movement Studies, 4,* 167–175.

Roberton, M., & Langendorfer, S. (1980). Testing motor development sequences across 9–14 years. In N. C. Nadeau, et al. (Eds.). *Psychology of motor behavior and sport* (pp. 269–279). Champaign, IL: Human Kinetic Press.

Robinson, L. E., Stodden, D. F., Barnett, L. M., Lopes, V. P., Logan, S. W., Rodrigues, L. P., & D'Hondt, E. (2015). Motor competence and its effect on positive developmental trajectories of health. *Sports Medicine, 45*(9), 1273–1284. doi:10.1007/s40279-015-0351-6

Rodrigues, L. P., Stodden, D. F., & Lopes, V. P. (2015). Developmental pathways of change in fitness and motor competence are related to overweight and obesity status at the end of primary school. *Journal of Science and Medicine in Sport.* doi:10.1016/j.jsams.2015.01.002

Russell, D. J., Rosenbaum, P. L., Avery, L. M., Lane, M. (2002). *Gross Motor Function Measure (GMFM-66 and GMFM-88) User's Manual.* London, UK: MacKeith Press.

Sackett, S. C., & Edwards, E. S. (2019). Relationships among motor skill, perceived self-competence, fitness, and physical activity in young adults. *Human Movement Science, 66,* 209–219.

Seefeldt, V. (1980). Developmental motor patterns: Implications for elementary school physical education. *Psychology of Motor Behavior and Sport, 36*(6), 314–323.

Seefeldt, V., & Haubenstricker, J. (1982). Patterns, phase, or stages: An analytical model for the study of developmental movement. In J. A. S. Kelso & J. E. Clark (Eds.), *The development of movement control and coordination* (pp. 309–318). New York: John Wiley & Sons, Ltd.

Stodden, D. F., Goodway, J. D., Langendorfer, S. J., Roberton, M. A., Rudisill, M. E., Garcia, C., & Garcia, L. E. (2008). A developmental perspective on the role of motor skill competence in physical activity: An emergent relationship. *Quest, 60*(2), 290–306.

Taunton, S. A., Brian, A., & True, L. (2017). Universally designed motor skill intervention for children with and without disabilities. *Journal of Developmental and Physical Disabilities, 29*(6), 941–954.

True, L., Brian, A., Goodway, J., & Stodden, D. (2017). Relationships between product- and process-oriented measures of motor competence and perceived competence. *Journal of Motor Learning and Development, 5*(2), 319–335.

Ulrich, D. A. (1985). *Test of Gross Motor Development.* Austin, TX: PRO-ED.

Ulrich, D. A. (2000). *Test of Gross Motor Development-Second Edition (TGMD-2)*. Austin, TX: PRO-ED.

Ulrich, D. A. (2019). *Test of Gross Motor Development-Third Edition (TGMD-3)*. Austin, TX: PRO-ED.

van der Fels, I. M., Te Wierike, S. C., Hartman, E., Elferink-Gemser, M. T., Smith, J., & Visscher, C. (2015). The relationship between motor skills and cognitive skills in 4–16 year old typically developing children: A systematic review. *Journal of Science and Medicine in Sport*, *18*(6), 697–703.

Veldman, S. L. C., Santos, R., Jones, R. A., Sousa-Sá, E., & Okely, A. O. (2019). Associations between gross motor skills and cognitive development in toddlers. *Early Human Development*, *132*, 39–44.

Visser, E., Mazzoli, E., Hinkley, T., Lander, N., Utesch, T., & Barnett, L. (2019). Are children with higher self-reported wellbeing and perceived motor competence more physically active? A longitudinal study. *Journal of Science and Medicine in Sport*, *23*, doi:10.1016/j.jsams.2019.09.005.

Welk, G. J., & Eklund, B. (2005). Validation of the children and youth physical self-perceptions profile for young children. *Psychology of Sport and Exercise*, *6*(1), 51–65. doi:10.1016/j.psychsport.2003.10.006

Westendorp, M., Hartman, E., Houwen, S., Huijgen, B. C. H., Smith, J., & Visscher, C. (2014). A longitudinal study on gross motor development in children with learning disorders. *Research in Developmental Disabilities*, *35*, 357–363.

Williams, H. (1983). *Perceptual and motor development in young children*. Englewood Cliffs, NJ: Prentice-Hall.

Williams, H. G., Pfeiffer, K. A., Dowda, M., Jeter, C., Jones, S., & Pate, R. R. (2009). A field-based testing protocol for assessing gross motor skills in preschool children: The Children's Activity and Movement in Preschool Study Motor Skills Protocol. *Physical Education and Exercise Science*, *13*(3), 1–35.

Zittel, L. (1994). Gross motor assessment of preschool children with special needs: Instrument selection considerations. *Adapted Physical Activity Quarterly*, *11*, 245–260.

Part IV

Special Considerations

Chapter 13

Screening and Diagnosis of Autism Spectrum Disorder in Preschool-Aged Children

Abigail L. Hogan, Kimberly J. Hills, Carla A. Wall, Elizabeth A. Will, and Jane Roberts

Autism spectrum disorder (ASD) is characterized by social communication impairments as well as repetitive or restricted interests and behaviors (American Psychiatric Association, 2013). ASD can be severely impairing and is highly prevalent, with approximately 1 in 59 children affected in the United States (Baio et al., 2018). The majority of ASD cases are of unknown etiology, in that there is no clear, identifiable reason a child developed ASD. However, several genetic and environmental factors have been identified that are known to place children at increased risk for ASD. For example, because of the moderate-to-strong heritability of ASD (Ronald & Hoekstra, 2011), having an older sibling with ASD places a child at a much higher risk (~20%) for being diagnosed with ASD themselves (Ozonoff et al., 2011). Furthermore, certain rare genetic and metabolic disorders appear to confer increased risk for ASD symptoms and diagnoses.

According to a recent meta-analysis, ASD rates are significantly elevated in tuberous sclerosis complex (~36%), fragile X syndrome (~30%), Cornelia de Lange syndrome (~43%), Rett syndrome (~61%), Angelman's syndrome, and Cohen's syndrome (~54%) (Richards, Jones, Groves, Moss, & Oliver, 2015). However, the role that environmental factors play in ASD risk cannot be ignored. For example, advanced parental age is known to increase ASD risk, as are extreme preterm birth and birth complications that are associated with trauma, ischemia, or hypoxia (Modabbernia, Velthorst, & Reichenberg, 2017). It is important to note that maternal smoking, vaccinations, and thimerosal exposure do not result in increased ASD risk (Modabbernia et al., 2017), despite persistent misinformation to the contrary in mass media and popular culture. Knowing which children are at highest risk for developing ASD enables appropriate developmental monitoring, screening, and early ASD diagnosis.

ASD in the First Two Years of Life: Screening for Early ASD Symptoms

In most children who are diagnosed with ASD, the earliest behavioral signs, or "red flags," of ASD emerge by about 12 months of age. The most commonly observed red flags in infancy include failure to respond when their name is called, reduced attention to the faces of others, and absence or reduced use of joint attention (e.g., showing, pointing to direct attention, following another's point) (Adrien et al., 1993; Baranek, 1999; Osterling & Dawson, 1994). Other salient signs of ASD in infancy include difficulty disengaging and shifting visual attention (Zwaigenbaum et al., 2005). For more details on the early behavioral signs of ASD and video examples of ASD "red flags" in toddlers, the website www.autism navigator.com is an excellent resource for professionals and parents alike.

The early behavioral signs of ASD usually increase in consistency and severity in the second year of life, and other symptoms, such as repetitive motor behaviors or sensory sensitivities, begin to emerge. By 24 months of age, ASD can be reliably diagnosed in many children (Kleinman et al., 2008); however, the median age of ASD diagnosis in the United States is 4.3 years (Baio et al., 2018). Evidence clearly indicates that participation in specialized behavioral intervention programs before the age of five can mitigate symptoms and optimize outcomes of children with ASD (Warren et al., 2011). Thus, many children in the United States who are diagnosed at 4 or 5 years (or older) miss out on critical early intervention years due to delays in formal diagnosis. This highlights the importance of early identification of ASD.

Effective screening in infants and toddlers, particularly those at increased risk for ASD, can reduce the age of diagnosis and thus facilitate delivery of specialized early intervention programs. The American Academy of Pediatrics (AAP) has recommended that health care professionals (e.g., pediatricians) conduct ASD-specific screening at the 18- and 24-month wellness visits and broad-based developmental screeners at 9-, 18-, 24-, or 30-month visits (Council on Children with Disabilities, 2006; Johnson & Myers, 2007). Pediatricians are advised to refer a child for an ASD diagnostic evaluation and/or early intervention when they screen positive on an ASD-specific or broad-based screener or when parent and/or physician concerns are present (even after a negative screen). However, studies have shown that pediatricians report significant barriers to screening for early ASD symptoms (e.g., limited time with patients, inadequate training on early ASD symptoms, limited resources for screening and referral, patient access to health care), and many children showing signs of early ASD and/or developmental delay are not referred for diagnostic evaluations and early intervention in a timely manner (Sheldrick, Merchant, & Perrin, 2011; Zuckerman, Lindly, & Sinche, 2015).

For example, one study revealed that only 60% of pediatricians conduct ASD-specific screening at 18 months, and 50% at 24 months (Arunyanart et al., 2012). Another study found that, on average, three years elapsed between parents first discussing their concerns with their child's pediatrician and their child's eventual ASD diagnosis (Warren, Stone, & Humberd, 2009). Nonetheless, specialized training in screening procedures has proven effective in increasing provider knowledge and compliance with screening procedures and results in more successful screening. For example, one study from the Netherlands (Oosterling et al., 2010) revealed that when health care providers in one region were trained in the use of a formal ASD screening tool, the mean age of diagnosis dropped from 82.9 months to 63.5 months, and children in that region were nine times more likely to be diagnosed before 36 months of age than children in surrounding regions.

Several screening measures have been developed to identify children who are showing signs of ASD and/or developmental delay. These measures differ from diagnostic measures in that they are designed only to identify symptoms consistent with ASD and/or developmental delay and do not provide a definitive diagnosis. They are also typically briefer than diagnostic measures and require less training and experience to administer. Therefore, screening tools are meant to serve on the "frontline" of a multi-step process that involves screening, referral for a comprehensive diagnostic evaluation, and, if warranted, referral to early intervention (Aylward, 1997). Screening measures can be categorized into Level 1 and Level 2 screeners.

Level 1 screeners are designed to identify children at risk for developmental disorders from the general population and are most often used in pediatric or primary healthcare settings, typically during routine wellness visits. They are administered to all children, regardless of parent or physician concern or evidence of developmental delay. Therefore, they need to be inexpensive, brief, and easy to administer, score, and interpret. The goal of Level 2 screening is to differentiate children at risk for ASD from children who are at risk for broader developmental or language delays. Level 2 screeners are commonly used in community-based settings such as early intervention programs and clinics by providers who serve young children with a broad range of developmental concerns (e.g., speech-language pathologists, occupational therapists). Specialists in these settings are often able to spend more time with children and can thus administer screening measures that involve more time, training, and experience. Importantly, the use of a Level 2 screening tool can provide important information on ASD risk as well as identify specific treatment goals that can be implemented immediately without waiting for a full diagnostic evaluation. Thus, Level 2 screening tools can facilitate access to early intervention in ways that a traditional diagnosis-intervention model, which requires full diagnosis before initiation of treatment, cannot (Ibanez, Stone, & Coonrod, 2014). This is particularly beneficial because many families that are referred for comprehensive diagnostic evaluation face long waitlists, thus delaying access to services further. A brief summary of screening measures is presented in Table 13.1. For a full review of Level 1 and Level 2 screeners, as well as a thorough discussion on best practices in ASD screening, see Ibanez et al. (2014).

Diagnosis of ASD in Preschool-Aged Children

Gold Standard Diagnostic Procedures

A diagnosis of ASD is based on behavioral observations and informant (e.g., parent, caregiver, teacher) reports, and the gold standard for ASD diagnosis continues to be "expert clinical opinion" (Chawarska, Klin, Paul, & Volkmar, 2007).

Generally, best practice in ASD diagnosis involves a comprehensive evaluation and ASD-specific testing by a multidisciplinary team of clinicians; this process has been shown to be more reliable in detecting ASD than community diagnoses (Hausman-Kedem et al., 2018) or clinician observation alone (Daniels & Mandell, 2013). The criteria used to diagnose ASD are outlined in the Diagnostic and Statistical Manual of Mental Disorders – Fifth Edition (DSM-5) (American Psychiatric Association, 2013). These criteria require individuals to exhibit persistent deficits in social communication, including deficits in social reciprocity, deficits in nonverbal communication, and deficits in developing, maintaining, and understanding friendships. Individuals must also exhibit at least two symptoms of restricted, repetitive patterns of behavior, interests, or activities (e.g., repetitive motor movements, insistences on sameness, restricted interests, hyper-/hyposensitivity to sensory stimuli). Symptoms must be present early in development, they must cause clinically significant impairment, and they cannot be better explained by intellectual disability or global developmental delay.

The DSM-5 also requires that clinicians specify overall levels of symptom severity levels in the social communication and restricted, repetitive interest and behavior (RRB) domains as part of the diagnostic process. Within both domains, severity levels comprise the following three qualitative categories: Level 1 = requiring support; Level 2 = requiring substantial support; and Level 3 = requiring very substantial support. Often these ratings are conceptualized as the number and type of environmental modifications that a child may need to function. For example, a child with Level 3 impairment in the RRB domain may exhibit marked and disruptive distress in transitions or changes in routine. It is worth noting, however, that there are no currently agreed-upon quantitative recommendations for distinguishing between these different ratings.

Because of the critical role clinical judgment plays during the diagnostic process, the importance of clinician expertise and experience cannot be understated. Furthermore, clinician proficiency must entail not only ASD symptoms and behaviors but a solid understanding of typical development as well, because a clinician's subjective understanding of what behaviors are developmentally appropriate compared with those that are clinically significant and impairing is implicit in the diagnostic process. Hence a critical factor in competent ASD assessment is knowledge of typical development for the age range of clients served. To help guide clinician training, the Centers for Disease Control and Prevention (CDC) developed the "Learn the Signs Act Early" campaign, including booklets listing normal child developmental milestones, which are available as a free download (www.cdc.gov/ncbddd/actearly/freematerials.html). The CDC also provides training video clips of the key early signs of ASD to assist clinicians in the diagnostic process (www.cdc.gov/NCBDDD/video/actearlycurriculum/index.html).

Throughout the diagnostic assessment, a holistic approach to data collection and observation increases the validity of the information collected. For

Table 13.1 Level 1 and Level 2 Screening Measures Commonly Used to Identify ASD Risk in Infants and Preschool-Aged Children

Measure Name	Type	Format	Age Range	Clinician Expertise Required	Clinician Time Required
Level 1					
Parents' Evaluation of Developmental Status (PEDS; Squires & Bricker, 2009)	Broad-based Development	Informant Questionnaire	1–95 months	Minimal	Minimal
Ages and Stages Questionnaire – Third Edition (ASQ-3; Squires & Bricker, 2009)	Broad-based Development	Informant Questionnaire	1–66 months	Minimal	Minimal
Infant/Toddler Checklist (ITC; Pierce et al., 2011)	Language/ Communication	Informant Questionnaire	<24 months	Minimal	Minimal
Modified Checklist for Autism in Toddlers (M-CHAT; Robins, Fein, Barton, & Green, 2001)	ASD-Specific	Informant Questionnaire + Interview	16–30 months	Moderate	Moderate
Early Screening of Autistic Traits Questionnaire (ESAT; Swinkels et al., 2006)	ASD-Specific	Informant Questionnaire	8–20 months	Minimal	Minimal
First Year Inventory (FYI; Watson et al., 2007)	ASD-Specific	Informant Questionnaire	12 months	Minimal	Minimal
Level 2					
Screening Tool for Autism in Toddlers (STAT; Stone, Coonrod, & Ousley, 2000)	ASD-Specific	Behavioral Observation	12–24 months	High	Moderate
Autism Observation Scale for Infants (AOSI; Bryson, Zwaigenbaum, McDermott, Rombough, & Brian, 2008)	ASD-Specific	Behavioral Observation	6–18 months	High	Moderate

(Continued)

Table 13.1 (Cont).

Measure Name	Type	Format	Age Range	Clinician Expertise Required	Clinician Time Required
Systematic Observations of Red Flags (SORF; Dow, Guthrie, Stronach, & Wetherby, 2017)	ASD-Specific	Behavioral Observation	16–24 months	High	Moderate

example, observing social interactions and play behaviors outside of the formal testing environment (e.g., in the waiting room, at the child's daycare) is critical to obtaining the most comprehensive picture of the child possible. Furthermore, restricted interests and repetitive behaviors may occur during times of transition and during unstructured time, as well as during the assessments designed to elicit such behaviors, so clinicians should be watching for these behaviors at all times. Because it can be difficult to discriminate well-rehearsed social behaviors displayed as part of familiar routines from spontaneous socially motivated overtures, observing across settings allows one to evaluate whether the child's social interaction behavior is scripted (i.e., using the exact same statements and sequence during a greeting) and routinized versus truly spontaneous. Clinicians must also remain vigilant of their own confirmation bias (i.e., tendency to search for and interpret information to confirm one's preexisting hypothesis), which can manifest as using the presence/absence of one behavior (e.g., eye contact, response to name) to confirm/disconfirm diagnosis. Some children with ASD may display "social strengths" (e.g., a skill not *typically* seen in ASD); however, that does not preclude them from a possible diagnosis if other deficits and impairments are present at diagnostic levels.

Measures that Support the Diagnostic Process

The exact components of a comprehensive ASD assessment vary slightly depending on the individual's age and developmental level as well as the presenting concerns, but all comprehensive ASD assessments should assess the core symptoms of ASD across contexts using a multi-method, multi-informant (when possible), multi-setting assessment battery. Additionally, because ASD symptoms often mask or co-occur with symptoms of other disorders (e.g., attention deficit/hyperactivity disorder [ADHD], anxiety, attachment disorder) and because many children with ASD also have global developmental delay and/or intellectual disability, it is critically important to assess for co-occurring or alternative diagnoses. At minimum, a diagnostic assessment for ASD should include: 1) developmental history; 2) clinical interviews with primary caregivers; 3) assessment of adaptive skills (i.e., real-world skills) and developmental functioning; and 4) at least *two* ASD-specific measures (which may include an ASD-specific clinical interview). An ASD-specific psychological evaluation also typically includes standardized cognitive (intelligence quotient [IQ]), academic, behavioral, and emotional assessments. The DSM-5 does not specify measures or personnel within the context of evaluation, but it does indicate that the evaluation should include direct assessment and comment on the presence of intellectual disability and/or language impairment (American Psychiatric Association, 2013).

Developmental History

A full history should be obtained, including the developmental course of the presenting concerns, history of the child's prenatal development and birth, medical history, and treatment/service history (i.e., previous assessments, intervention services received). When available, medical records, medication records, prior assessments, educational records, and/or service records (e.g., intervention progress reports, treatment summaries) should be reviewed. Because ASD is highly genetic and often runs in families, a family history of ASD or ASD-like symptoms should be obtained. All children should receive a hearing screening to rule out hearing loss as part of the effort to secure an accurate diagnosis because one of the most salient early indicators of ASD is a lack of orienting when one's name is called (Schaefer & Mendelsohn, 2013). Results of hearing, vision, and speech/language screenings should also be obtained prior to direct observation/testing.

ASD-specific Diagnostic Instruments

Most ASD-specific diagnostic measures are designed to elicit and assess behaviors consistent with ASD. ASD measures primarily reflect two categories of assessment: parent/caregiver report (e.g., interviews, rating scales) and direct observation measures. These measures usually provide valuable insight into past and current ASD symptoms but offer only limited information and guidance regarding prognosis and intervention planning. All ASD-specific diagnostic measures should be considered *tools* in the assessment process rather than definitive markers of diagnosis. The Autism Diagnostic Interview – Revised (ADI-R; Rutter, LeCouteur, & Lord, 2003) and Autism Diagnostic Observation Schedule – Second Edition (ADOS-2; Lord et al., 2012) are considered the "gold standard" measures for assessing ASD symptoms and diagnosing ASD. However, as explained earlier in this chapter, the "gold standard" assessment process includes a clinical assessment conducted by a multi-disciplinary team that concludes with a clinical judgment regarding diagnosis (Falkmer, Anderson, Falkmer, & Horlin, 2013). In other words, ASD-specific diagnostic measures should never be used in isolation or as the only source of information guiding diagnosis.

DIRECT OBSERVATION

The ADOS-2 is a well-established, standardized observation instrument that assesses social communication, social interaction, and restricted/repetitive behaviors and interests (Lord et al., 2012). It involves a series of standardized activities and takes 45–60 minutes to administer. The ADOS-2 consists of five modules that are administered based on the child's level of expressive language and chronological age. Each module provides different tasks, including activities (e.g., "Demonstration Task"), playful elements (e.g., "Birthday Party" with a baby doll), and verbal tasks (e.g., Conversation and Reporting). The ADOS-2 is designed such that each activity involves the examiner using a hierarchy of structured and unstructured social presses to elicit engagement with the least amount of scaffolding required. For each module, between 29 and 41 behavioral characteristics are coded and a selection of these codes form the algorithm that is used to determine the ADOS-2 score. The selected algorithm items for each module were chosen to maximize the sensitivity and specificity for ASD diagnoses.

Trained evaluators from any discipline, such as speech-language pathologists, psychologists, nurses, and educators, can administer the ADOS. However, given the complexity of the administration and coding, the ADOS-2 requires intensive training and supervision to ensure standardized administration and coding. The scoring guidelines for ADOS-2 items often include ambiguous specifications (e.g., "reduced," "sometimes," "most"), which leave room for subjective interpretation and inter-individual differences in ratings. Furthermore, inter-rater reliability and coding accuracy are influenced by a variety of factors, including an examiner's experience with the ADOS-2, characteristics of the case, and quality of the administration. Thus, adequate and continuous training is typically required to ensure valid administration and coding.

It is important to remember that ADOS-2 scores are based solely on a discrete assessment in a structured and standardized environment and may not offer a complete picture of a child's skills. Much of the research published utilizes the first version of the ADOS and/or is based on datasets that include the ADOS and ADOS-2. A recent meta-analysis (Randall et al., 2018) evaluating ASD diagnostic measures for preschool populations found that ADOS sensitivity ranged from 0.76 to 0.98 (summary 0.94; 95% confidence interval 0.89 to 0.97), and specificity ranged from 0.20 to 1.00 (summary 0.80; 95% confidence interval 0.68 to 0.88). Studies evaluating the inter-rater reliability of the ADOS-2 typically involve highly-trained research-based clinicians under optimal conditions, which may not reflect daily clinical practice (Kamp-Becker et al., 2018).

CLINICAL INTERVIEWS

A significant portion of the assessment process involves listening to and talking with families (and possibly other caregivers, teachers, and service providers) about the child in order to understand the child's developmental history, current behaviors, strengths, and weaknesses. A clinical interview for ASD should also collect information from parents reflecting the diagnostic symptom domains of ASD and common comorbidities.

The Autism Diagnostic Interview – Revised (ADI-R) is one of the most extensively studied and validated diagnostic measures (Rutter et al., 2003). The ADI-R requires extensive formal training and takes at least 90 minutes to administer. There are two cut-off points for the ADI-R, a clinical one and a research one. The clinical cut-off has higher sensitivity (i.e., the percentage of individuals correctly identified as having ASD) and lower specificity (i.e., the percentage of individuals correctly identified as not having ASD) compared to the research cut-off (Kim & Lord, 2012). Systematic review studies consistently demonstrate that the ADI-R and the ADOS have the largest evidence base and highest sensitivity and specificity, especially when used together (Falkmer et al., 2013). Research also indicates that the ADOS and ADI-R may not completely agree due to the fact that these measures assess different aspects of ASD, utilize different sources of information, and are collected in different contexts (Bishop & Norbury, 2002; Kim & Lord, 2012). Although the ADI-R provides significant information, it is also burdensome given that it can take up to three hours to complete.

The Criteria Diagnostic Interview (CRIDI-ASD/DSM-5) is a clinical assessment tool for the diagnosis of ASD in Spanish-speaking children and adolescents of Latin-American heritage, including those living in the United States. The CRIDI-ASD/DSM-5 is a semi-structured observational interview based on DSM-5 criteria. It consists of questions organized in the two dimensions: 1) deficits in social communication and interaction, and 2) restricted and stereotyped patterns of behavior and interests and unusual sensory reactivity. Recent work evaluating the reliability and validity of this measure when compared to other measures (e.g., ADI-R) in a sample of 88 children age 18 months to 18 years indicates strong inter-rater reliability ($M = 0.86$), sensitivity (92%), and specificity (95%) (Gallo et al., 2019).

CLINICIAN-RATED SCALES

The Childhood Autism Rating Scale – Second Edition, Standard Version (CARS-2; Schopler, Van Bourgondien, Wellman, & Love, 2010) consists of 15 items and can be used with children younger than 6 years. Scoring of the CARS-2 is based on a clinician's overall observations of ASD-related behaviors over the course of an assessment as well as information from caregiver reports. Although the CARS-2 takes about 10 minutes to complete, this does not reflect the time needed to collect the information and observations. Recent systematic reviews and meta-analyses (Moon et al., 2019; Randall et al., 2018) investigating the

CARS-2 indicate acceptable reliability and sensitivity. However, the level of specificity varied widely across studies, suggesting that CARS-2 should be used in conjunction with other diagnostic tools. Other systematic reviews demonstrate strong correct classification rates for the CARS (Falkmer et al., 2013) and strong correlation between the CARS-2 and the ADOS-2 (Park, Yi, Yoon, & Hong, 2018). Although the utility of the CARS in children under the age of 2 years has not been established, it has adequate sensitivity and specificity in preschool-aged children (Perry, Condillac, Freeman, Dunn-Geier, & Belair, 2005) and good agreement with clinical diagnosis in 2- and 3-year-olds (Coonrod et al., 2003). However, some studies suggest that it may overidentify ASD risk in 2-year-old children, particularly those with intellectual disability (Lord, 1995, 1997).

The Checklist for Autism Spectrum Disorder (CASD) is appropriate for children 1–16 years of age; the clinician or caregiver assesses the presence or absence of ASD symptoms (either currently or in the past) based on a semi-structured interview with the parent, information from the child's teacher or child care provider, observations of the child, and other available records. The CASD is for children 1–16 years of age and takes approximately 15 minutes to complete (which does not include the time required to gather the information needed to complete the checklist). Previous standardization work indicates that the clinician-completed CASD differentiated children with and without ASD with 99.5% accuracy (Mayes, 2012). Classification accuracy for the CASD completed independently by the parents was 98.1%. In another study (Mayes et al., 2009), the CASD differentiated children with ASD from children with ADHD with 99.5% accuracy and from typical children with 100% accuracy. The CASD also showed strong convergent validity with diagnostic agreement of 100% in a sample of children with ASD (Mayes et al., 2001), 98% between CASD and the CARS (Mayes, 2012), and 93% between the parent-completed CASD and the ADI-R (Murray, Mayes, & Smith, 2011).

DSM-5 CHECKLISTS

The use of a DSM-5 Checklist (a list of all of the ASD DSM-5 symptoms) is based on a clinician's overall observations of ASD-related behaviors over the course of an assessment as well as information from caregiver reports and the results of all additional assessment measures. The use of a DSM-5 Checklist can be helpful in obtaining a summary conclusion of the evidence for each symptom criteria.

INFORMANT-RATED SCALES

Informant-rated scales are an additional mechanism for obtaining information from parents, caregivers, and teachers and can be incredibly useful in collecting information across contexts. Parent/Caregiver rating scales are a complement to, rather than a substitute for, a diagnostic interview. Observations and input from preschool staff are extremely valuable when assessing for ASD (Nilsson Jobs, Bölte, & Falck-Ytter, 2019). It is important to be aware that it can be difficult for parents and other caregivers/reporters to answer questions about broad and narrow (item-level) conceptualizations of social communication, interaction, and behaviors (Charman et al., 1998). Some parents may have limited experience with other young children/peer norms and/or limited opportunity to observe their child in social contexts. Preschool teachers may evaluate individual children more accurately because they can compare the individual child with a range of peers (Reed & Osborne, 2013). Nonetheless, the research to date indicates that parents and preschool staff are accurate at differentiating children with ASD from their typically developing peers; however, teachers are better at discriminating children with ASD from children with other developmental delays (Aldridge, Gibbs, Schmidhofer, & Williams, 2012; Larsen, Aasland, & Diseth, 2018; Stickley et al., 2017).

The most commonly used informant-report measures are the Social Responsiveness Scale – Second Edition (SRS-2) (Constantino & Gruber, 2005) and the Social Communication Questionnaire (SCQ, Rutter, Bailey, & Lord, 2005). The SRS-2 is an ASD-specific questionnaire for individuals aged 3 to 99 that is widely used in research and clinical practice. The SRS-2 Preschool form is available for ages 2 years and 6 months to 4 years and 6 months. The SRS-2 consists of 65 items completed by a parent and/or teacher and can be completed in 15 minutes. It has been validated for use in the general population; however, it is more often applied as a screening instrument in high-risk populations. Several studies support the ability of parent-reported SRS-2 to discriminate between children with ASD and those with other psychiatric disorders (e.g., Kamio, Inada, & Koyama, 2013). Further, it shows adequate convergent validity with the ADOS (Duvekot, van der Ende, Verhulst, & Greaves-Lord, 2015). The SCQ (Rutter et al., 2005) is a 40-item informant-report questionnaire designed to screen for ASD symptoms in individuals aged 4 years or older with a mental age of at least 2 years. It is based upon the ADI-R and can be administered to assess symptoms in the past three months ("Current" version) or over the course of the individual's lifetime ("Lifetime" version). The SCQ has been shown to have high agreement with the ADI-R; however, it is more effective at screening for ASD in older children than in younger children, and it is not validated on children under the age of 4 years, so it should be used cautiously in preschool-aged children (Barnard-Brak, Brewer, Chesnut, Richman, & Schaeffer, 2016).

Along with the SRS-2 and SCQ, a variety of additional informant-rated scales exist, such as the Gilliam Autism Rating Scale (GARS) (Gilliam, 2014) and the Autism Spectrum Rating Scales (ASRS) (Goldstein & Naglieri, 2010). However, empirical work on these measures is limited or, in the case of the GARS, suggests that the measures are not appropriate for certain children (Lecavalier, 2005; South et al., 2002). It is strongly recommended that clinicians use measures that have been extensively validated across a variety of developmental periods, levels of functioning, and socioeconomic backgrounds.

The ASD Diagnostic Process: Important Considerations

Comprehensive evaluation and careful consideration of differential diagnosis is critical in the context of ASD due to the overlapping phenotypes of ASD with many other neurodevelopmental and psychiatric disorders. These include but are not limited to intellectual disability (ID), genetic syndromes, ADHD, anxiety disorders, and speech/language disorders. The most common and challenging differential diagnoses during the preschool developmental period include intellectual disability, comorbid psychiatric disorders, and sex differences in clinical presentation.

Intellectual Disability and Language Disorders

Current estimates suggest that approximately one-third of children with ASD have a comorbid intellectual disability (ID) diagnosis (Baio et al., 2018). Intellectual disability is characterized by significant deficits in intellectual and adaptive functioning (American Psychiatric Association, 2013). These deficits include impairments in cognitive abilities, such as reasoning, abstract thinking, and problem solving, as well as impairments in daily living skills, including functional communication, personal independence, and social skills. However, difficulties with abstract thinking, poorer social communication skills, and impairments in adaptive behaviors are characteristic of ASD as well, even when comorbid ID is absent. As a result, this phenotypic overlap between ASD and ID often leads to diagnostic overshadowing, or a focus on ID and lack of recognition of comorbid ASD, inaccurate diagnoses, and poor treatment (Hurley & Levitas, 2007).

Current diagnostic assessment instruments are most accurate in identifying ASD in the context of children with mild ID with some verbal skills (Lord, Corsello, & Grzadzinski, 2014) and, therefore, may be less accurate when assessing preschool children with more severe cognitive impairments (de Bildt et al., 2015; Oosterling et al., 2010). In addition, although ASD presents with its own unique communication deficits, it is worth noting that ASD and language disorders co-occur at above-chance levels (Loucas et al., 2008). Research suggests that children with ASD often present with a delay in receptive language relative to their expressive language, and this split may help distinguish ASD from other speech/language disorders (Loucas et al., 2008).

Comorbid Psychiatric Disorders

Children with ASD are more likely than not to exhibit one or more co-occurring psychiatric conditions such as ADHD and/or anxiety (Simonoff et al., 2008). Co-occurring conditions can exacerbate ASD symptom severity and make treatment more challenging. Hence, for ASD interventions to be maximally effective, common comorbid diagnoses need to be considered and targeted within treatment plans and routine progress monitoring (Antshel & Russo, 2019).

The comorbidity rate of ASD and ADHD is high, with approximately 30% of children with a diagnosis of ASD presenting symptoms of ADHD (Simonoff et al., 2008). ADHD and ASD have shared genetic heritability and the behavioral phenotype of ADHD overlaps with ASD, especially in children with ASD without intellectual disability (Mikami, Miller, & Lerner, 2019). Recent literature reviews suggest that displaying negative social behaviors and an absence of positive behaviors could be indicative of comorbid ADHD (in addition to meeting symptom criteria symptoms; Mikami et al., 2019).

The presence of one or more anxiety disorders in children with ASD is also common, with up to 65% meeting diagnostic criteria for a DSM-based anxiety disorder (van Steensel, Bögels, & Perrin, 2011). When present, anxiety disorders result in additional impairment and distress. Thus, awareness of the high comorbidity of anxiety with ASD is critical for two reasons. First, anxiety should be considered in the differential diagnostic procedure to determine that ASD features are independent of, or not better accounted for by, anxiety (e.g., social anxiety versus ASD). Second, the surveillance of anxiety disorders to monitor their emergence during preschool or later in development is critical to direct targeted treatment. The developmental trajectory of anxiety disorders suggests that symptoms may emerge and be reliably detected during preschool, but that the expression of symptoms warranting the diagnosis of anxiety typically does not happen until older childhood and adolescence for most anxiety disorders. In addition to consideration of the developmental expression of anxiety in young children with ASD, evidence suggests that anxiety in ASD may reflect symptoms and timing that differ from anxiety in non-ASD samples (Kerns & Kendall, 2012).

Sex Differences in ASD

There is a well-documented sex difference in ASD prevalence, with 26.6 per 1,000 males compared to 6.6 per 1,000 females diagnosed. Additionally, since the first documented cases of ASD, our understanding of the diagnosis of ASD has been predominately restricted to males (e.g., Kanner, 1943). Due to this history and the difference in prevalence, our understanding of ASD in females falls far behind that in males (Halladay et al., 2015). Although preliminary evidence indicates that females with ASD require a higher threshold of symptoms to receive a diagnosis, there is a concern among ASD researchers that less-impaired females are being mis- or under-identified (Dworzynski, Ronald, Bolton, & Happé, 2012; Halladay et al., 2015). For example, among females and males with similar ASD traits, females with more behavior problems or ID, or both, are more likely to be recognized and diagnosed than their male peers (Dworzynski et al., 2012; Frazier, Georgiades, Bishop, & Hardan, 2014). As such, higher-functioning females without ID may be missed by current diagnostic systems. Further, minority females may be especially vulnerable to missed or delayed diagnosis given racial and ethnic disparities in age of diagnosis (Mandell et al., 2009). These sex differences may largely be due to the fact that ASD diagnostic criteria and existing assessment tools historically come from research with majority male samples (Watkins, Zimmermann, & Poling, 2014). Some theories, however, suggest that there may be biological or genetic causes of this disparity (Ferri, Abel, & Brodkin, 2018).

Importantly, there is evidence to suggest differences in the presentation of ASD amongst males and females (Hiller, Young, & Weber, 2014). In the social communication domain, studies of attention to social information suggest that females across the spectrum tend to exhibit more typical social motivation and nonverbal communication compared males with ASD (Chawarska, Macari, Powell, DiNicola, & Shic, 2016; Whyte & Scherf, 2018). Further, girls with ASD experience similar value in friendship and similar friendship patterns compared to females with typical development but more significant social challenges (Sedgewick, Hill, & Pellicano, 2018; Vine Foggo & Webster, 2017). In the restricted and repetitive interests domain, there do not seem to be many sex differences, except that older females with ASD and those that have higher cognitive functioning may have fewer of these symptoms (Knutsen, Crossman, Perrin, Shui, & Kuhlthau, 2018). Notably, there do not seem to be major sex differences in sensory behaviors in ASD (Bitsika, Sharpley, & Mills, 2018). Importantly, subtle differences and relative strengths seen in females with ASD may cause them to intentionally mask or camouflage their social symptoms, leading to considerable effort and exhaustion (Bargiela, Steward, & Mandy, 2016).

Cultural and Socioeconomic Considerations

Although the overall rate of ASD in children is approximately 2%, there are a number of demographic considerations that contribute to our understanding of the prevalence of this disorder. Evidence points to diagnostic disparities among children with ASD due to race, ethnicity, and socioeconomic factors. For example, per the CDC (Baio et al., 2018), the estimated prevalence among White children (17.2 per 1,000) is 7% greater than that among Black children (16.0 per 1,000) and 22% greater than that among Hispanic children (14.0 per 1,000). Fortunately, recent reports suggest that these differences in diagnostic rates are attenuating due to increased outreach efforts in targeted communities (Baio et al., 2018).

Racial and ethnic disparities in diagnosis are exacerbated when taking socioeconomic status into account. For children on Medicaid, White children receive their first diagnosis at 6.3 years of age on average, African American children at 7.9 years, and Latinx children at 8.8 years (Mandell, Ittenbach, Levy, & Pinto-Martin, 2007). Children near poverty receive a diagnosis later than their peers, as do children with parents with less education (Goin-Kochel, Mackintosh, & Myers, 2006; Mandell, 2005). In addition, there are barriers to access to care at the systems level for these families. For example, although screening is federally mandated for Medicaid-enrolled children, pediatricians do not regularly screen for ASD in community practices (Radecki, Sand-Loud, O'Connor, Sharp, & Olson, 2011). Furthermore, among those children who do eventually receive an ASD diagnosis, Latinx children receive fewer services than their White peers and have more unmet service needs (Zuckerman et al., 2013). Early identification and targeted intervention are crucial to achieving optimal outcomes for children with ASD (Dawson et al., 2010). Hence, these early differences in identification and barriers to treatment may result in cascading effects on minority children's later development.

After the Diagnosis

Once the diagnosis of ASD is determined by a trained clinician, this information needs to be conveyed to the family. Given the complexity of deriving an ASD diagnosis and recognizing the individual differences that are part of the diagnosis (e.g., ID), care should be given to provide diagnostic feedback to family members in a clear and supportive manner. Specifically, families should be told the child's unique features that support the ASD diagnosis and any other comorbid conditions with cultural competence and sensitivity. Given that evidence suggests a familial component to ASD, clinicians should be aware that family members may also be affected by ASD-like characteristics and/or related psychiatric problems (e.g., anxiety disorders). Thus, there may be a need for follow-up to rule ASD out in other family members or to provide family support.

When communicating an ASD diagnosis to a family member, the level of functioning and recommendations for intervention need to be outlined and should include educational, community, and family supports. It is important to remember that the language and overall narrative a clinician provides can impact the narrative the parents create for themselves and their child, which affects the feelings and actions they take related to the diagnosis and their child. Hence it is critical to communicate an accurate and empowering narrative about the child while also holding space (e.g., allowing time) for the parents to share their thoughts, reactions, and concerns. Holding space gives the clinician the opportunity to tune in to the narrative the parents are constructing and provides an opportunity to offer revisions to that narrative in a way that will serve them and their child.

Timely and accurate diagnosis is critical in order to implement targeted and early intervention. There is wide consensus that early intervention, that is within the first five years of life, provides the greatest opportunity to alter developmental trajectories for children with ASD, behaviorally as well as neuro-biologically (Boyd, Odom, Humphreys, & Sam, 2010; Dawson et al., 2010; Rogers et al., 2012). Intervention approaches deemed most effective are those that employ tenants of applied behavior analysis (i.e., operant learning principles), focus on developmentally appropriate and child-directed learning targets, and are implemented in a naturalistic social context (Schreibman et al., 2015). While there are a variety of these types of behavioral interventions, sharing these common features establishes these approaches as Naturalistic Developmental Behavioral Interventions (NDBIs), which currently hold the strongest evidence base for increasing skills in young children with ASD. These comprehensive approaches can be used to target a range of skills, including verbal communication, social interaction, play, motor, and language skills (see Schreibman et al., 2015 for review). Some have also demonstrated efficacy when parent mediated (Boyd et al., 2010; Ingersoll & Wainer, 2013) and delivered via telehealth (Vismara, Young, & Rogers, 2012), which provides opportunity for those farther from a specialized clinic or treatment center to still access services. Additionally, given that challenging behaviors are common in children with ASD, parent consultation regarding the management of these challenges should be considered as part of the treatment plan. There are still many considerations for access to early intervention (Boyd et al., 2010), and families can explore the best options for them through consultation with local service providers and guidance from the diagnosing clinician. An additional resource that may be useful to parents is the 100 Day Kit provided by Autism Speaks (www.autismspeaks.org/tool-kit/100-day-kit-young-children). This resource provides a detailed overview of autism interventions and answers common questions that parents often have in the aftermath of their child's ASD diagnosis.

References

Adrien, J. L., Lenoir, P., Martineau, J., Perrot, A., Hameury, L., Larmande, C., & Sauvage, D. (1993). Blind ratings of early symptoms of autism based upon family home movies. *Journal of the American Academy of Child and Adolescent Psychiatry, 32,* 617–626.

Aldridge, F. J., Gibbs, V. M., Schmidhofer, K., & Williams, M. (2012). Investigating the clinical usefulness of the social responsiveness scale (SRS) in a tertiary level, autism spectrum disorder specific assessment clinic. *Journal of Autism and Developmental Disorders, 42,* 294–300.

Antshel, K. M., & Russo, N. (2019). Autism spectrum disorders and ADHD: Overlapping phenomenology, diagnostic issues, and treatment considerations. *Current Psychiatry Reports, 21,* 34.

Arunyanart, W., Fenick, A., Ukritchon, S., Imjaijitt, W., Northrup, V., & Weitzman, C. (2012). Developmental and autism screening. *Infants & Young Children, 25,* 175–187.

American Psychiatric Association. (2013). *The diagnostic and statistical manual of mental disorders.* Washington, DC: American Psychiatric Association.

Aylward, G. P. (1997). Conceptual issues in developmental screening and assessment. *Journal of Developmental and Behavioral Pediatrics, 18,* 340–349.

Baio, J., Wiggins, L., Christensen, D. L., Maenner, M. J., Daniels, J., Warren, Z., ... Dowling, N. F. (2018). Prevalence of autism spectrum disorder among children aged 8 years — Autism and developmental disabilities monitoring network, 11 sites, United States, 2014. *MMWR. Surveillance Summaries, 67,* 1–23.

Baranek, G. T. (1999). Autism during infancy: A retrospective video analysis of sensory-motor and social behaviors at 9–12 months of age. *Journal of Autism and Developmental Disorders, 29,* 213–224.

Bargiela, S., Steward, R., & Mandy, W. (2016). The experiences of late-diagnosed women with autism spectrum conditions: An investigation of the female autism phenotype. *Journal of Autism and Developmental Disorders, 46,* 3281–3294.

Barnard-Brak, L., Brewer, A., Chesnut, S., Richman, D., & Schaeffer, A. M. (2016). The sensitivity and specificity of the social communication questionnaire for autism spectrum with respect to age. *Autism Research, 9,* 838–845.

Bishop, D. V. M., & Norbury, C. F. (2002). Exploring the borderlands of autistic disorder and specific language impairment: A study using standardised diagnostic instruments. *Journal of Child Psychology and Psychiatry, and Allied Disciplines, 43,* 917–929.

Bitsika, V., Sharpley, C. F., & Mills, R. (2018). Sex differences in sensory features between boys and girls with autism spectrum disorder. *Research in Autism Spectrum Disorders, 51,* 49–55.

Boyd, B. A., Odom, S. L., Humphreys, B. P., & Sam, A. M. (2010). Infants and toddlers with autism spectrum disorder: Early identification and early intervention. *Journal of Early Intervention, 32,* 75–98.

Bryson, S. E., Zwaigenbaum, L., McDermott, C., Rombough, V., & Brian, J. (2008). The autism observation scale for infants: Scale development and reliability data. *Journal of Autism and Developmental Disorders, 38,* 731–738.

Charman, T., Swettenham, J., Baron-Cohen, S., Cox, A., Baird, G., & Drew, A. (1998). An experimental investigation of social-cognitive abilities in infants with autism: Clinical implications. *Infant Mental Health Journal, 19,* 260–275.

Chawarska, K., Klin, A., Paul, R., & Volkmar, F. (2007). Autism spectrum disorder in the second year: Stability and change in syndrome expression. *Journal of Child Psychology and Psychiatry and Allied Disciplines, 48,* 128–138.

Chawarska, K., Macari, S., Powell, K., DiNicola, L., & Shic, F. (2016). Enhanced social attention in female infant siblings at risk for autism. *Journal of the American Academy of Child and Adolescent Psychiatry, 55,* 188–195.

Constantino, J. N., & Gruber, C. P. (2005). *The social responsiveness scale (SRS).* Los Angeles, CA: Western Psychological Services.

Coonrod, E. E., Lee, E. B., Brissie, J., Weiss, B. H., Stone, W. L., Hepburn, S. L., & Ashford, L. (2003). Can autism be diagnosed accurately in children under 3 years? *Journal of Child Psychology and Psychiatry, 40,* 219–226.

Council on Children with Disabilities. (2006). Identifying infants and young children with developmental disorders in the medical home: An algorithm for developmental surveillance and screening. *Pediatrics, 118,* 405–420.

Daniels, A. M., & Mandell, D. S. (2013). Children's compliance with American Academy of Pediatrics' well-child care visit guidelines and the early detection of autism. *Journal of Autism and Developmental Disorders, 43,* 2844–2854.

Dawson, G., Rogers, S., Munson, J., Smith, M., Winter, J., Greenson, J., ... Varley, J. (2010). Randomized, controlled trial of an intervention for toddlers with autism: The Early Start Denver Model. *Pediatrics, 125,* e17–e23.

de Bildt, A., Sytema, S., Zander, E., Bölte, S., Sturm, H., Yirmiya, N., ... Oosterling, I. J. (2015). Autism Diagnostic Interview-Revised (ADI-R) algorithms for toddlers and young preschoolers: Application in a non-US sample of 1,104 children. *Journal of Autism and Developmental Disorders, 45,* 2076–2091.

Dow, D., Guthrie, W., Stronach, S. T., & Wetherby, A. M. (2017). Psychometric analysis of the systematic observation of red flags for autism spectrum disorder in toddlers. *Autism, 21,* 301–309.

Duvekot, J., van der Ende, J., Verhulst, F. C., & Greaves-Lord, K. (2015). The screening accuracy of the parent and teacher-reported social responsiveness scale (SRS): Comparison with the 3Di and ADOS. *Journal of Autism and Developmental Disorders, 45,* 1658–1672.

Dworzynski, K., Ronald, A., Bolton, P., & Happé, F. (2012). How different are girls and boys above and below the diagnostic threshold for autism spectrum disorders? *Journal of the American Academy of Child and Adolescent Psychiatry, 51,* 788–797.

Falkmer, T., Anderson, K., Falkmer, M., & Horlin, C. (2013). Diagnostic procedures in autism spectrum disorders: A systematic literature review. *European Child and Adolescent Psychiatry, 22,* 329–340.

Ferri, S. L., Abel, T., & Brodkin, E. S. (2018). Sex differences in autism spectrum disorder: A review. *Current Psychiatry Reports, 20,* 9.

Frazier, T. W., Georgiades, S., Bishop, S. L., & Hardan, A. Y. (2014). Behavioral and cognitive characteristics of females and males with autism in the simons simplex collection. *Journal of the American Academy of Child and Adolescent Psychiatry, 53*(3), 329–340.

Gallo, L. A., Escoto Lopez, J. J., Suarez, G. T., Ruiz, B. C., Solis Bravo, M. A., Tapia Guillen, L. G., ... Salazar, J. S. (2019). Validity of the diagnostic interview CRIDI - autism spectrum disorders as a gold standard for the assessment of autism in Latinos and Mexicans. *Neuropsychiatry, 9*(1), 2047–2055.

Gilliam, J. E. (2014). *Gilliam autism rating scale* (3rd ed.). Austin, TX: Pro-Ed.

Goin-Kochel, R. P., Mackintosh, V. H., & Myers, B. J. (2006). How many doctors does it take to make an autism spectrum diagnosis?. *Autism, 10,* 439–451.

Goldstein, S., & Naglieri, J. A. (2010). *Autism spectrum rating scales.* North Tonawanda, NY: Multi-Health Systems.

Halladay, A. K., Bishop, S., Constantino, J. N., Daniels, A. M., Koenig, K., Palmer, K., ... Szatmari, P. (2015). Sex and gender differences in autism spectrum disorder: Summarizing evidence gaps and identifying emerging areas of priority. *Molecular Autism, 6,* 1–5.

Hausman-Kedem, M., Kosofsky, B. E., Ross, G., Yohay, K., Forrest, E., Dennin, M. H., ... Holahan, J. P. (2018). Accuracy of reported community diagnosis of autism spectrum disorder. *Journal of Psychopathology and Behavioral Assessment, 40,* 367–375.

Hiller, R. M., Young, R. L., & Weber, N. (2014). Sex differences in autism spectrum disorder based on DSM-5 criteria: Evidence from clinician and teacher reporting. *Journal of Abnormal Child Psychology, 42,* 1381–1393.

Hurley, A. D., & Levitas, A. S. (2007). The importance of recognizing autism spectrum disorders in intellectual disability. *Mental Health Aspects of Developmental Disabilities, 10,* 157–161.

Ibanez, L. V., Stone, W. L., & Coonrod, E. E. (2014). Screening for autism in young children. In F. R. Volkmar, et al. *Handbook of autism and pervasive developmental disorders, assessment, interventions, policy, the future: assessment, interventions, and policy, fourth edition, volume 2.* Hoboken, NJ: John Wiley & Sons. pp. 585–608.

Ingersoll, B., & Wainer, A. (2013). Initial efficacy of project ImPACT: A parent-mediated social communication intervention for young children with ASD. *Journal of Autism and Developmental Disorders, 43,* 2943–2952.

Johnson, C. P., & Myers, S. M. (2007). Identification and evaluation of children with autism spectrum disorders. *Pediatrics, 120,* 1183–1215.

Kamio, Y., Inada, N., & Koyama, T. (2013). A nationwide survey on quality of life and associated factors of adults with high-functioning autism spectrum disorders. *Autism, 17,* 15–26.

Kamp-Becker, I., Albertowski, K., Becker, J., Ghahreman, M., Langmann, A., Mingebach, T., ... Stroth, S. (2018). Diagnostic accuracy of the ADOS and ADOS-2 in clinical practice. *European Child and Adolescent Psychiatry, 27,* 1193–1207.

Kanner, L. (1943). Autistic disturbances of affective Content. *Nervous Child, 2,* 217–250.

Kerns, C. M., & Kendall, P. C. (2012). The presentation and classification of anxiety in autism spectrum disorder. *Clinical Psychology: Science and Practice, 19,* 323–347.

Kim, S. H., & Lord, C. (2012). New autism diagnostic interview-revised algorithms for toddlers and young preschoolers from 12 to 47 months of age. *Journal of Autism and Developmental Disorders, 42,* 82–93.

Kleinman, J. M., Ventola, P. E., Pandey, J., Verbalis, A. D., Barton, M., Hodgson, S., ... Fein, D. (2008). Diagnostic stability in very young children with autism spectrum disorders. *Journal of Autism and Developmental Disorders, 38,* 606–615.

Knutsen, J., Crossman, M., Perrin, J., Shui, A., & Kuhlthau, K. (2018). Sex differences in restricted repetitive behaviors and interests in children with autism spectrum disorder: An Autism Treatment Network study. *Autism, 23*(4), 858–868.

Larsen, K., Aasland, A., & Diseth, T. H. (2018). Brief report: Agreement between parents and day-care professionals on early symptoms associated with autism spectrum disorders. *Journal of Autism and Developmental Disorders, 48,* 1063–1068.

Lecavalier, L. (2005). An evaluation of the Gilliam Autism Rating Scale. *Journal of Autism and Developmental Disorders, 35,* 795–805.

Lord, C. (1995). Follow-up of two-year-olds referred for possible autism. *Journal of Child Psychology and Psychiatry, 36,* 1365–1382.

Lord, C. (1997). Diagnostic instruments in autism spectrum disorders. In D. Cohen & F. R. Volkmar (Eds.), *Handbook of autism and pervasive developmental disorders.* New York, NY: John Wiley & Sons. pp. 730–771.

Lord, C., Corsello, C., & Grzadzinski, R. (2014). Diagnostic instruments in autistic spectrum disorders. In *Handbook of autism and pervasive developmental disorders* (4th ed., Hoboken and New Jersey: John Wiley & Sons, Inc. pp. 919–926).

Lord, C., Rutter, M., DiLavore, P., Risi, S., Gotham, K., & Bishop, S. L. (2012). *Autism diagnostic observation schedule-2nd edition (ADOS-2).* Los Angeles, CA: Western Psychological Corporation.

Loucas, T., Charman, T., Pickles, A., Simonoff, E., Chandler, S., Meldrum, D., & Baird, G. (2008). Autistic symptomatology and language ability in autism spectrum disorder and specific language impairment. *Journal of Child Psychology and Psychiatry, 49,* 1184–1192.

Mandell, D. S. (2005). Factors associated with age of diagnosis among children with autism spectrum disorders. *Pediatrics, 116*, 1480–1486.

Mandell, D. S., Ittenbach, R. F., Levy, S. E., & Pinto-Martin, J. A. (2007). Disparities in diagnoses received prior to a diagnosis of autism spectrum disorder. *Journal of Autism & Developmental Disorders, 37*, 1795–1802.

Mandell, D. S., Wiggins, L., Carpenter, L. A., Daniels, J., DiGuiseppi, C., Durkin, M. S., ... Kirby, R. S. (2009). Racial/ethnic disparities in the identification of children with autism spectrum disorders. *American Journal of Public Health, 99*, 493–498.

Mayes, S. D. (2012). *Checklist for autism spectrum disorder*. Chicago, IL: Stoelting.

Mayes, S. D., Calhoun, S. L., & Crites, D. L. (2001). Does DSM-IV Asperger's disorder exist? *Journal of Abnormal Child Psychology, 29*, 263–271.

Mayes, S. D., Calhoun, S. L., Murray, M. J., Morrow, J. D., Yurick, K. K. L., Mahr, F., ... Petersen, C. (2009). Comparison of scores on the checklist for autism spectrum disorder, childhood autism rating scale (CARS), and Gilliam Asperger's disorder scale (GADS) for children with low functioning autism, high functioning autism or Asperger's disorder, ADHD, and typical development. *Journal of Autism and Developmental Disorders, 39*, 1682–1693.

Mikami, A. Y., Miller, M., & Lerner, M. D. (2019). Social functioning in youth with attention-deficit/hyperactivity disorder and autism spectrum disorder: Transdiagnostic commonalities and differences. *Clinical Psychology Review*, doi:10.1016/j.cpr.2018.12.005

Modabbernia, A., Velthorst, E., & Reichenberg, A. (2017). Environmental risk factors for autism: An evidence-based review of systematic reviews and meta-analyses. *Molecular Autism, 8*, 13.

Moon, S. J., Hwang, J. S., Shin, A. L., Kim, J. Y., Bae, S. M., Sheehy-Knight, J., & Kim, J. W. (2019). Accuracy of the Childhood Autism Rating Scale: A systematic review and meta-analysis. *Developmental Medicine & Child Neurology, 61*(9), 1030–1038.

Murray, M. J., Mayes, S. D., & Smith, L. A. (2011). Brief report: excellent agreement between two brief autism scales (checklist for autism spectrum disorder and social responsiveness scale) completed independently by parents and the Autism Diagnostic Interview-Revised. *Journal of Autism and Developmental Disorders, 41*, 1586–1590.

Nilsson Jobs, E., Bölte, S., & Falck-Ytter, T. (2019). Spotting signs of autism in 3-year-olds: Comparing information from parents and preschool staff. *Journal of Autism and Developmental Disorders, 49*, 1232–1241.

Oosterling, I. J., Roos, S., De Bildt, A., Rommelse, N., De Jonge, M., Visser, J., ... Buitelaar, J. (2010). Improved diagnostic validity of the ADOS revised algorithms: A replication study in an independent sample. *Journal of Autism and Developmental Disorders, 40*, 689–703.

Oosterling, I. J., Wensing, M., Swinkels, S. H., Van Der Gaag, R. J., Visser, J. C., Woudenberg, T., ... Buitelaar, J. K. (2010). Advancing early detection of autism spectrum disorder by applying an integrated two-stage screening approach. *Journal of Child Psychology and Psychiatry and Allied Disciplines, 51*, 250–258.

Osterling, J., & Dawson, G. (1994). Early recognition of children with Autism: A study of first birthday home videotapes. *Journal of Autism & Developmental Disorders, 24*, 247–257.

Ozonoff, S., Young, G. S., Carter, A., Messinger, D., Yirmiya, N., Zwaigenbaum, L., ... Stone, W. L. (2011). Recurrence risk for autism spectrum disorders: A Baby Siblings Research Consortium study. *Pediatrics, 128*, e1–e8.

Park, H. S., Yi, S. Y., Yoon, S. A., & Hong, S.-B. (2018). Comparison of the Autism Diagnostic Observation Schedule and Childhood Autism Rating Scale in the diagnosis of autism spectrum disorder: A preliminary study. *Journal of the Korean Academy of Child and Adolescent Psychiatry, 29*, 172–177.

Perry, A., Condillac, R. A., Freeman, N. L., Dunn-Geier, J., & Belair, J. (2005). Multisite study of the Childhood Autism Rating Scale (CARS) in five clinical groups of young children. *Journal of Autism and Developmental Disorders, 35*, 625–634.

Pierce, K., Carter, C., Weinfeld, M., Desmond, J., Hazin, R., Bjork, R., & Gallagher, N. (2011). Detecting, studying, and treating autism early: The one-year well-baby check-up approach. *The Journal of Pediatrics, 159*(3), 458–465.

Radecki, L., Sand-Loud, N., O'Connor, K. G., Sharp, S., & Olson, L. M. (2011). Trends in the use of standardized tools for developmental screening in early childhood: 2002-2009. *Pediatrics, 128*, 14–19.

Randall, M., Egberts, K. J., Samtani, A., Scholten, R. J., Hooft, L., Livingstone, N., … Williams, K. (2018). Diagnostic tests for autism spectrum disorder (ASD) in preschool children. *Cochrane Database of Systematic Reviews, (7)*.

Reed, P., & Osborne, L. A. (2013). The role of parenting stress in discrepancies between parent and teacher ratings of behavior problems in young children with autism spectrum disorder. *Journal of Autism and Developmental Disorders, 43*, 471–477.

Richards, C., Jones, C., Groves, L., Moss, J., & Oliver, C. (2015). Prevalence of autism spectrum disorder phenomenology in genetic disorders: A systematic review and meta-analysis. *The Lancet Psychiatry, 2*, 909–916.

Robins, D. L., Fein, D., Barton, M. L., & Green, J. A. (2001). The Modified Checklist for Autism in Toddlers: An initial study investigating the early detection of autism and pervasive developmental disorders. *In Journal of Autism and Developmental Disorders, 31*(2), 131–144.

Rogers, S. J., Ph, D., Estes, A., Ph, D., Lord, C., Ph, D., … Ph, D. (2012). Effects of a brief early start denver model (ESDM) - Based parent intervention on toddlers at risk for autism spectrum disorders: A randomized controlled trial. *Journal of the American Academy of Child and Adolescent Psychiatry, 51*, 1052–1065.

Ronald, A., & Hoekstra, R. A. (2011). Autism spectrum disorders and autistic traits: A decade of new twin studies. *American Journal of Medical Genetics. Part B, Neuropsychiatric Genetics, 156*, 255–274.

Rutter, M., Bailey, A., & Lord, C. (2005). *SCQ: The social communication questionnaire manual.* Los Angeles: Western Psychological Services.

Rutter, M., LeCouteur, A., & Lord, C. (2003). *Autism diagnostic interview – revised (ADI–R) manual.* Los Angeles: Western Psychological Services.

Schaefer, G. B., & Mendelsohn, N. J. (2013). Clinical genetics evaluation in identifying the etiology of autism spectrum disorders: 2013 guideline revisions. *Genetics in Medicine, 15*, 399–407.

Schopler, E., Van Bourgondien, M., Wellman, J., & Love, S. (2010). *Childhood autism rating scale—Second edition (CARS-2).* Los Angeles, CA: Western Psychological Services.

Schreibman, L., Dawson, G., Stahmer, A. C., Landa, R., Rogers, S. J., McGee, G. G., … Halladay, A. (2015). Naturalistic developmental behavioral interventions: Empirically validated treatments for autism spectrum disorder. *Journal of Autism and Developmental Disorders, 45*, 2411–2428.

Sedgewick, F., Hill, V., & Pellicano, E. (2018). 'It's different for girls': Gender differences in the friendships and conflict of autistic and neurotypical adolescents. *Autism, 23*(5), 1119–1132.

Sheldrick, R. C., Merchant, S., & Perrin, E. C. (2011). Identification of developmental-behavioral problems in primary care: A systematic review. *Pediatrics, 128*, 356–363.

Simonoff, E., Pickles, A., Charman, T., Chandler, S., Loucas, T., & Baird, G. (2008). Psychiatric disorders in children with autism spectrum disorders: Prevalence, comorbidity, and associated factors in a population-derived sample. *Journal of the American Academy of Child & Adolescent Psychiatry, 47*, 921–929.

South, M., Williams, B. J., McMahon, W. M., Owley, T., Filipek, P. A., Shernoff, E., … Ozonoff, S. (2002). Utility of the Gilliam Autism Rating Scale in research and clinical populations. *Journal of Autism and Developmental Disorders, 32*, 593–599.

Squires, J., & Bricker, D. (2009). *Ages & stages questionnaires® (ASQ) A parent-completed, child-monitoring system* (3rd ed.). Baltimore, MD: Brookes.

Stickley, A., Tachibana, Y., Hashimoto, K., Haraguchi, H., Miyake, A., Morokuma, S., … Kamio, Y. (2017). Assessment of autistic traits in children aged 2 to 4½ years with the preschool version of the social responsiveness scale (SRS-P): Findings from Japan. *Autism Research, 10*, 852–865.

Stone, W. L., Coonrod, E. E., & Ousley, O. Y. (2000). Brief report: Screening tool for autism in two-year-olds (STAT): Development and preliminary data. *Journal of Autism and Developmental Disorders, 30*, 607–612.

Swinkels, S. H. N., Dietz, C., Van Daalen, E., Kerkhof, I. H. G. M., Van Engeland, H., & Buitelaar, J. K. (2006). Screening for autistic spectrum in children aged 14 to 15 months: The development of the Early Screening of Autistic Traits Questionnaire (ESAT). *Journal of Autism and Developmental Disorders, 36*, 723–732.

van Steensel, F. J. A., Bögels, S. M., & Perrin, S. (2011). Anxiety disorders in children and adolescents with autistic spectrum disorders: A meta-analysis. *Clinical Child and Family Psychology Review, 14*, 302–317.

Vine Foggo, R. S., & Webster, A. A. (2017). Understanding the social experiences of adolescent females on the autism spectrum. *Research in Autism Spectrum Disorders, 35*, 74–85.

Vismara, L. A., Young, G. S., & Rogers, S. J. (2012). Telehealth for expanding the reach of early autism training to parents. *Autism Research and Treatment, (2012,* 1–12.

Warren, Z., McPheeters, M. L., Sathe, N., Foss-Feig, J. H., Glasser, A., & Veenstra-VanderWeele, J. (2011). A systematic review of early intensive intervention for autism spectrum disorders. *Pediatrics, 127*, e1303–e1311.

Warren, Z., Stone, W., & Humberd, Q. (2009). A training model for the diagnosis of autism in community pediatric practice. *Journal of Developmental and Behavioral Pediatrics, 30*, 442–446.

Watkins, E. E., Zimmermann, Z. J., & Poling, A. (2014). The gender of participants in published research involving people with autism spectrum disorders. *Research in Autism Spectrum Disorders, 8*, 143–146.

Watson, L. R., Baranek, G. T., Crais, E. R., Steven Reznick, J., Dykstra, J., & Perryman, T. (2007). The first year inventory: Retrospective parent responses to a questionnaire designed to identify one-year-olds at risk for autism. *Journal of Autism and Developmental Disorders, 37*, 49–61.

Whyte, E. M., & Scherf, K. S. (2018). Gaze following is related to the broader autism phenotype in a sex-specific way: Building the case for distinct male and female autism phenotypes. *Clinical Psychological Science, 6,* 280–287.

Zuckerman, K. E., Lindly, O. J., & Sinche, B. K. (2015). Parental concerns, provider response, and timeliness of autism spectrum disorder diagnosis. *The Journal of Pediatrics, 166*(6), 1431–1439.

Zuckerman, K. E., Mattox, K., Donelan, K., Batbayara, O., Baghaee, A., & Bethell, C. (2013). Pediatrician identification of Latino children at risk for autism spectrum disorder. *Pediatrics, 132,* 445.

Zwaigenbaum, L., Bryson, S., Rogers, T., Roberts, W., Brian, J., & Szatmari, P. (2005). Behavioral manifestations of autism in the first year of life. *International Journal of Developmental Neuroscience, 23,* 143–152.

Chapter 14

Psychoeducational Assessment of Culturally and Linguistically Diverse Preschool Children

Samuel O. Ortiz and Jane Y. T. Wong

Introduction

Assessment of children from culturally and linguistically diverse (CLD) backgrounds is a unique aspect of preschool assessment. Moreover, preschool assessment is itself a unique activity encompassed within assessment at the broadest level. In this sense, readers can expect more complex differences in this chapter compared to other chapters in this volume, considering the appropriateness of various tests in relation to preschool children's developmental trajectory, or rather, their suitability for evaluating the cognitive or linguistic attainment in relation to developmental milestones of preschool children. The difference between this chapter and the other chapters rests primarily on the developmental course of CLD children, which varies greatly in relation to their mainstream peers, as well as among other CLD children.

That which makes preschool children from diverse backgrounds different from children within the core culture is not primarily contingent upon obvious cultural, ethnic, or racial characteristics per se. Yet, race and ethnicity are typically at the forefront of what many people consider as cultural diversity. Of course, language is also readily viewed as an important characteristic to consider (i.e., a CLD child not being a monolingual, native-English speaker). Other characteristics that make CLD children unique are often believed, erroneously, to be less relevant influences on assessment outcomes. Admittingly, socio-economic status and extreme poverty carry with them important and implicit "cultural" difference that must be considered when evaluating CLD children. Unfortunately, these characteristics are frequently neglected, despite their utmost importance in influencing children's performance in the various instruments upon which evaluators relied heavily in comprehensive preschool assessments. It is not merely that a child is poor, linguistically different, or of Hispanic or African American descent that influences how an evaluation should be approached. Rather, it is the knowledge and understanding of how these factors interrelate to influence developmental trajectories that may not be the same as, let alone comparable to, monolingual, native-English speaking children. Yet these monolingual, English-speaking children have been considered the yardstick against whom CLD children are compared. Without understanding cultural and linguistic influences on child development, there can be little-to-no hope of ensuring fairness and equity for children from diverse backgrounds.

Culture and Language

Children from culturally and linguistically diverse backgrounds are not different from monolingual, native-English speaking preschoolers simply because of skin color or native language. Given similar circumstances, opportunities, and environmental experiences, all 4-year-old children would be expected to be developmentally similar around the world. Physical, psychological, neurological, emotional, and behavioral growth and development do not vary significantly as a function of being raised in another country or speaking a different language. While there may be minor variations due to specific life conditions or language structure, the reality is that children of the same age are all very much alike regardless of where they were raised or live. Contrary to common beliefs, early childhood development is universal, and the nature and extent of that development and growth are predictable, irrespective of culture, race, ethnicity, or language.

What is it, then, that makes the assessment of CLD preschool children different than that which characterizes the assessment of monolingual, native-English speakers? In the simplest form, it is the recognition that some developmental processes are linked inextricably to content exposure, knowledge acquisition, and experiences and opportunities that are economic-, cultural-, and language-specific. When the measurement of a developmental process employs instruments that were developed for use on children from a particular culture or language, then those tools or instruments are influenced by construct irrelevant variance associated with cultural or linguistic differences. While any two preschool children of the same age may have the same linguistic capabilities regardless of the language they acquire, if they do not speak the same language they cannot be fairly compared in terms of their overall language development in another language (Rhodes, Ochoa, & Ortiz, 2005). And while much the same can be said of economic differences, particularly in light of the overrepresentation in the lower socio-economic strata of some cultural and linguistic subgroups in the United States (U.S. Census Bureau, 2014), the focus of the present chapter is primarily on the influence of cultural and linguistic factors on development and its measurement.

For monolingual, native-English speakers, language development and knowledge acquisition are closely tied to age. It is for this reason that age-based norms are ubiquitous in tests designed to evaluate virtually all abilities, including cognition, language development, and neuropsychological functioning. This practice holds true primarily because for monolingual, native-English speakers, there is only *one* language and *one* culture in the child's experience.[1] Therefore, age-based norms largely control for variation in the development among monolingual, native-English speakers, and they provide an appropriate basis for the relative comparison of performance, although subcultural and socio-economic differences still exist among native-English speakers to some degree. In contrast, consider that for CLD children living in the United States the assumption of an individual developing under one language and one culture only no longer holds. English learners (ELs) typically do not live in a home where the "mainstream" culture is transmitted by the parents, nor do they live in a home where there is only one language spoken, with that language being English.

While ELs may well experience a single language and culture at home, by definition their residency in the United States and subsequent formal education, which often begins in preschool, will invariably include instruction in English. Also, ELs face the expectation that they will accumulate requisite acculturative knowledge that reflects the culture within which they live. These expectations are evident in the assumptions made by the various types of tests and examinations used to evaluate preschool children. According to Wolfram, Adger, and Christian (1999), "the key consideration in distinguishing between a difference and a disorder is whether the child's performance differs significantly from peers with similar experiences" (p. 105). The fact that a child does not speak one language only (and that their native or heritage language [L1] is not English), along with the reality that a child is likely being raised by parents with little or no knowledge of the U.S. mainstream culture, makes that child significantly different in terms of their experiences. When tests are used to evaluate development predicated upon exposure to and experience with English and the mainstream U.S. knowledge, the child is at a significant disadvantage.

In summary, the acquisition of language and acculturative knowledge cannot be presumed to be comparable between any two individuals when one of those individual's experiences are characterized by more than one language and when experiences in the home are not based entirely on the U.S. mainstream culture. The violation of the assumption of comparability precludes the use of tests that do not account for developmental differences related to cultural or linguistic differences (i.e., construct irrelevant differences). As noted by Salvia and Ysseldyke (1991),

> when a child's general background experiences differ from those of the children on whom a test was standardized, then the use of the norms of that test as an index for evaluating that child's current performance or for predicting future performances may be inappropriate.
>
> (p. 18)

For this reason, it is necessary to understand that age will no longer be an accurate estimate of that child's expected level of performance when evaluating the language or cognitive development of preschool children from diverse backgrounds within the mainstream U.S. culture. Rather, their performances will be an interaction of their true developmental progress and their cultural and linguistic acculturation. That is, because acculturative knowledge acquisition is also a developmental process, performance on tasks that rely on or assess age- or grade-expected knowledge will also reflect the extent to which the child has had exposure to and experience with such culturally bound knowledge. Regardless of the extent of acculturation, the assessment of a CLD child's test performance will be lower than that of the child's true developmental progress. Misunderstanding or misinterpretation of the difference between a CLD child's hypothetically "true development" and assessed level of development may result in the failure to identify properly diverse children with advanced abilities because they appear to be merely "average" as compared to same-age, monolingual peers. Another possible scenario would involve the misidentification of diverse children as having a language or learning disorder because they appear to be below average as compared to same-age, monolingual English-speaking peers. In both cases, the performance differences/discrepancy in performance in relation to expectancy are potentially discriminatory, when it is quite possible that such differences are nothing more than a reflection of an experiential difference in relation to culture and language.

Developmental Language Proficiency

The key factor that influences equitable measurement of CLD preschool children is rooted in the difference between the rate of development that is typical for a monolingual, native-English speaker versus that achieved by an EL, who has only recently begun learning English. A growing body of research on bilingual children, including bilingual preschoolers, continues to point to the idea that bilinguals are not two monolinguals in one head (Grosjean, 1989; Grosjean & Li, 2013) and that the effects of exposure to two or more languages are significant and measurable even in early infancy (Bialystok, 2001). As children grow, what they are expected to be able to say and do with respect to language increases according to a well-known developmental pattern. This rate of growth is controlled in most psychometric tests via the stratification of age or grade in the normative sample. The problem, of course, is that a 4-year-old monolingual, native-English speaker has been learning English for four years, but a 4-year-old EL may have been learning English for only one year or less. To expect the EL to perform comparably to the native-English speaker simply because they are the same age is inequitable and discriminatory. According to Fisher and Frey (2012),

> It is unlikely that a second-grade English learner at the early intermediate phase of language development is going to have the same achievement profile as the native English-speaking classmate sitting next to her. The norms established to measure fluency, for instance, are not

able to account for the *language development differences* between the two girls. A second analysis of the student's progress compared to linguistically similar students is warranted.

(p. 40; emphasis added)

The specification regarding "language development differences" emphasizes that the assessment of preschool children who are culturally and linguistically diverse must account for the degree of development possessed by the child as assessed in the language in which the test is administered. This premise holds true even when evaluating children in their heritage or native language (L1). As noted, once a second language is introduced, a child can no longer be considered monolingual. Therefore, evaluation in the native language and subsequent comparison to norm samples comprised of monolingual speakers of that language may be no fairer than evaluating the child in English. With few exceptions (c.f., BESA; Peña, Gutiérrez-Clellen, Iglesias, Goldstein, & Bedore, 2018; Ortiz PVAT; Ortiz, 2018), even when bilinguals or ELs are included in a test's norm sample there is no attempt to control for the significant variability in language development that exists among individuals in the sample. Failure to do so is akin to creating a test for use with "children" without regard to any differences in age. Without proper attention to linguistic and cultural differences in the linguistic, cultural, and cognitive development among diverse children, the assumption of comparability that underlies testing is simply not met when working with ELs, regardless of the language of evaluation or their apparent representation in norm samples (Salvia & Ysseldyke, 1991).

Acculturative Knowledge Acquisition

This section discusses what is meant by cultural difference—a phrase that is all too often thought to refer simply to racial or ethnic characteristics or, alternatively, to acculturation and the process of assimilation. These misconceptions stem from older (i.e., not scientifically supported) notions that factors such as race, ethnicity, degree of acculturation, or cultural identity somehow interact with the structure of tests and testing. Valdés and Figueroa (1994) long ago pointed out that such factors do not affect the developmentally based scope and sequence that is inherent in developmental tests. That is, neither race, ethnicity, acculturation, nor identity induce individuals to respond in random or group-specific ways that depart from the normal sequence of development. In many ways, acculturative knowledge acquisition is similar to the developmental process of language. While there are always individual differences in learning, the general pattern of how much and what specific content knowledge should be possessed by a given age or grade is predictable and well known, as illustrated in particular by the structure and curricula of formal education.

It is also important to consider that acculturative knowledge acquisition and language acquisition may very well be two sides of the same coin. In much the same way that reading and writing are distinct, but highly correlated skills, so too are the acquisition of cultural knowledge and language (Schipolowski, Wilhelm, & Schroeders, 2014; Schneider & McGrew, 2018). The development of one influences the development of the other. For example, humor cannot be understood properly without the necessary cultural context and familiarity. Likewise, the use of idiomatic expressions and colloquially based language are learned against the backdrop of the culture in which the language is used. With limited exposure comes limited knowledge acquisition—every bit as much as limited language acquisition (Schipolowski et al., 2014). It is reasonable to consider and examine the impact of language difference on test performance, with an understanding that language acquisition is inherently tied to acculturative knowledge acquisition (Ortiz, 2019).

Practice Issues

Test Score Validity

The preceding section provided the foundation for understanding the fact that assessment of CLD children requires the comparison of measured performance against other individuals who are not merely of the same age but have also had the same degree of opportunity for them to develop and acquire the language abilities and acculturative knowledge being assessed on a given test. For monolingual, native-English speakers, such comparisons are rather easy, because age is generally sufficient to control for developmental differences for monolingual, English-speaking preschool children. For CLD children, however, the presence of two languages and cultures means that age, by itself, is insufficient for creating the necessary peer group that permits valid comparison for and interpretation of performance on cognitive/language tests.

There are two basic ways in which failure to provide "true peer" comparison on the basis of equivalent levels of language development affects the performance as well as the subsequent test score interpretation. The first relates to construct validity of scores obtained from tests. If a preschool child is given a test of visual processing in which the instructions are at an age-expected level that exceeds the English (L2) development of the child, then an inability to perform well can be attributed more to limited language development than to limited visual processing ability. Thus, a low score is no longer a valid estimate of the child's ability level in visual processing; instead, it is a reflection of the degree of comprehension of the instructions given in English. This is what might be encountered in the case of an EL who does not possess the same level of English language development as the children on whom the test was normed. Note that this does not happen in the case of a monolingual, native-English speaker where the instructions are presumed to be developmentally appropriate for a given age; in that case, poor performance can be rightly attributed to poor visual processing skills (or, alternatively, a receptive language disorder).

The second issue has to do with interpretation rather than test score invalidity. This issue occurs when the construct being measured is in fact intended to measure language ability or acculturative knowledge, rather than the construct itself. For example, if a preschool EL is given a test of listening comprehension in English and performs poorly, it may be fairly and validly concluded that the child's listening ability is poor *in English*. What cannot be stated accurately, however, is that the child's listening ability is poor in general. The validity of the original interpretation of a low test score can extend only insofar as English is concerned, and it is fair to indicate that the performance rightly implies that the child's listening comprehension skills are indeed limited in English. To state that the low test score is suggestive of poor listening comprehension skills without any consideration of the language the task was given in would indicate interpretive invalidity and is therefore indefensible. This is especially true in light of a lack of evidence of similar problems in the native language.

Intervention versus Diagnostic Questions

The difference between construct invalidity and interpretive invalidity may be best understood in light of how data are used to address various referral questions. In general, preschool evaluations typically examine two distinct issues: intervention and diagnosis. Intervention questions may center on what instructional modifications are needed to address academic difficulties or how far a particular child is behind grade-level standards. In this case, comparison to age- or grade-level standards would be appropriate, even if those standards are based primarily on monolingual, native-English speakers. There is never any good reason to lower expectations or standards of the performance for CLD students. Knowing their relative standing to their age- and grade-level peers is useful information in determining the degree of instructional needs and/or intensity of intervention that may be required to support them in an effort to reach such standards. In contrast, when the question pertains to diagnostic concerns (i.e., to find an explanation or reasons why a child's test performance is below or behind age- and grade-level peers), then comparison to true peers with matched levels of language development is required. Efforts to establish a diagnosis of any type of disorder can only be accomplished fairly and validly when individuals are compared to other individuals of the same age, who possess the same level of exposure, experience, and development in the language in which the evaluation was conducted.

This issue is also relevant in the evaluation of academic skills, where the lack of development in reading and writing in English, as evidenced by low test scores, can only be used to establish grade-level performance. This lack of expected academic achievement cannot be used to establish a CLD preschool child's disability status. Whether the data that are used for this purpose are collected via a Multi-tier System of Support (MTSS), via a Response-to-Intervention (RTI) approach, or through the use of standardized tests, the issue remains the same—such data are suitable for determining intervention and grade- or age-level standing, but they do not inform questions regarding possible disability or disorder. For such data to serve a diagnostic purpose it would need to compare a child's academic performance against standards based on true peers with matching levels of development in English. Such standards are not generally or readily available for MTSS, RTI, or standardized testing.

Attempts to Address Problems with Test Score Validity

Given the small extent to which the preceding issues have been understood or incorporated into any particular measurement paradigm, practitioners have had little choice but to proceed in conducting evaluations of ELs. For many practitioners, doing so is part and parcel of their daily responsibilities and there is not an option to do nothing. To that end, several methods are available. On the surface, these methods appear to be ways of addressing test score validity in order to permit defensible interpretation. However, even a cursory examination of these methods reveals that they all suffer from intrinsic flaws that mostly outweigh their advantages and ultimately leave the issue of test score validity unresolved. How such methods fail in this regard merits a brief discussion.

Modified Methods of Assessment and Evaluation

Initial recommendations for attempting to address test score validity are centered on modifications or alterations to the testing process as a way of working around the language issue. The most notable example of this method is the use of a translator/interpreter for test administration. While the use of a translator/interpreter can certainly help overcome the language barrier, it also represents a clear violation of standardization protocol of a test as much as any other such violation. There is a need in the field for the development of tests that are designed to be given by a translator/interpreter with the appropriate standardization and normalization methods. Only when test norms are created based on the administration of these tests to be given in the same language spoken by the examinee and the interpreter, along with adequate control for differences in language development among the individuals in the norm sample, will the use of translator/interpreters no longer be questionable. The use of currently available test norms when testing with a translator/interpreter will continue to undermine test score validity. However, this is not to say that the use of translators/

interpreters is not recommended. In fact, in some cases, there may be no other choice than to employ a translator/interpreter in an effort to communicate with the examinee. The main concern relates to the use of a translator/interpreter that is inadequate in ensuring the validity of any test results obtained. This is because the effect of the use of the translator/interpreter cannot be quantified. Even in cases where the translator/interpreter is highly trained or experienced, there is no manner in which one can determine to what degree their use has hindered or helped the examinee. Without an established normative sample and corresponding information on the psychometric properties for a test given by a translator/interpreter, we cannot interpret performance fairly. There is simply no guarantee that the parameters of the test's original normative sample would be exactly the same as those for individuals tested in a completely different manner.

Testing the Limits

Other similar attempts to address fairness involve efforts to help the examinee perform up to the best of their ability. Such attempts are frequently couched under the umbrella of "testing the limits." These testing practices may involve alterations or modifications of test items or content, mediation of task concepts to ensure comprehension prior to actual administration, a repetition of test instructions (despite not being permitted as per the instructions), scoring any response provided in a language that is not the target language of the test as correct as long as the response is conceptually similar to the target response, the extension or complete elimination of any specific time constraints for speeded or timed items, and so on and so forth. Such methods represent noble attempts to increase the "validity" of the results; nevertheless, they violate a test's standardization protocol. Thus, these attempts at testing the limits fail in providing results that can be considered valid, let alone interpretable. Even in cases where such procedures may be "permitted" by a test publisher, it is important to note that without actual norms based on the type of altered or modified administration used, the test's norms remain inappropriate for performance comparisons. In short, any alteration of the testing process that violates the standardized administration and scoring procedures undermines the psychometric properties of the test, effectively invalidating the scores, and, in so doing, it precludes the interpretation of or assignment of meaning to the test scores.

Much like with the use of a translator/interpreter, however, the existence of these issues does not mean that such procedures should be summarily dismissed. Testing the limits is often quite useful in deriving qualitative information and data that may well inform the purpose of and questions relevant to the assessment. Such qualitative information can be a valuable adjunct to other assessment results. Nevertheless, if the intent is to generate test scores to guide interpretation, assist in diagnosis, and inform the decision-making process, then those scores must be generated via standardized administration. Thus, the question is not *whether* such procedures should be used or not but, rather, *when* they should be used. Specifically, it would make the most sense to administer a test in a standardized manner first. This way, validity concerns can be subsequently addressed, thus allowing for interpretation. Follow-up evaluation of suspected areas of weakness could then be analyzed more carefully and informally through the use of any of the modifications or alterations. Such modifications in administration would serve to refute or add additional validity evidence to scores that were obtained properly. In essence, assessment cannot proceed initially via modification. On the other hand, the use of test modifications at a later stage can certainly add insightful and valuable information and assist in further examination to supplement test scores that are deemed to be valid, having drawn upon standardized administration/scoring procedures. For example, if a child completes items given extended time, then it would be clear that the child does not necessarily lack the ability being assessed; this result would make the argument against the child having an intrinsic deficit. Likewise, instructional expectations may then be adjusted to permit informal accommodations such as providing the child with extra time so as not to adversely affect educational performance arbitrarily on the basis of speed. Likewise, if a child's performance improves significantly following extended explanation of task instructions or mediation of the concept prior to item administration, this might point to a lack of procedural or factual knowledge but an otherwise adequate level of ability to learn. Classroom interventions can then be modified to focus on the provision of additional, detailed instructions regarding assignments and tasks to ensure full comprehension.

Nonverbal Methods of Assessment and Evaluation

Although the term "nonverbal testing" has become popular and is commonly used in testing practices, it is more accurate to refer to it as "language-reduced" testing. The implication has been that "nonverbal" equates to "no language." However, this is not strictly correct. It is impossible to administer any test of any kind without some form of communication occurring between the examiner and the examinee. There is no test that is simply placed in front of an examinee without the examiner having to express any type of instruction, whether by verbal or nonverbal means (e.g., gestures or pantomime). Nonverbal assessment does serve to reduce the reliance on language as a part of the testing process, but it cannot be said that avoiding or minimizing the use of language in the instructions eliminates all task requirements regarding language, let alone acculturative knowledge acquisition that is inherent in terms of task demands. Indeed, some nonverbal tests rely on tests that have cultural knowledge deeply embedded in them, such as when real objects that are relevant to specific cultures—often North American cultures—are used (e.g., pictures of toys, vehicles, people). Nonverbal tests may well reduce language demands on the part of the examinee, but they do not become cultural knowledge-free just because language ability is not required for responding to the items.

It is also important to consider the extent to which avoidance of language is an acceptable decision in the context of evaluation of various types of disorders. Two of the most common disability categories for which preschool children are likely to be referred for evaluation include language development that is related to crystalized intelligence and learning problems, particularly those related to pre-literacy skills involving phonological awareness. Because nonverbal tests are, by definition, not designed to measure language, their use in these contexts will not provide information that would be helpful in identifying possible disorders related to language or any of the preschool skills related to literacy.

Despite some disadvantages, nonverbal tests remain quite useful, especially when attempting to measure other abilities without the influence of language abilities. The issues are more centered on the fact that without language, there are limits as to what can be measured and in what way. The reduction of language in evaluation is quite helpful when working with CLD individuals, particularly preschool children whose language development is less than that of their older peers. Nonverbal testing may well provide better estimates of their true functioning in these nonverbal areas, but they should not be viewed as representing a whole or completely satisfactory solution with respect to test score validity, particularly because the impact of language and culture can never be completely removed. In addition, research that examines the fairness of nonverbal tests with subgroups of ELs to determine the extent to which developmental differences in language and acculturative knowledge acquisition affect performance is lacking in the literature.

Dominant Language Assessment and Evaluation

Another approach to establishing test score validity stems from the concept of first determining an individual's dominant language and then choosing to evaluate in that language. This is done often at the exclusion of the other, non-dominant language. This approach is particularly popular among bilingual practitioners because they possess the ability to evaluate in whichever language that is determined to be dominant. This is, of course, not an option for monolingual, English-speaking practitioners. This process, however, provides an illusion of legitimacy that is unwarranted. Dominance only implies that one language the child uses is better developed than the other language the child uses. Dominance does not imply that the child is as developmentally proficient in that language as same-age peers who are monolingual speakers of that language. An EL preschooler may well be "dominant" in English after having been exposed to English from age 3 upon entering kindergarten, as a function of receiving formal education and instruction in English, relative to not having received any formal instruction in the native language. Nonetheless, to consider the child as being as developmentally proficient as their same-age monolingual, English-speaking 5-year-old peers is erroneous, and the use of norms that are based on such monolingual English speakers remains discriminatory to the young EL. Moreover, the concept of dominance does not help inform instructional intervention, progress/growth, or expected test performance—it merely indicates that performance, in whatever way it is measured, will be better or higher in the dominant language. It does not mean that a CLD child's test performance will or should be "average" as compared to monolingual, English-speaking peers of the same age or same grade.

To complicate matters further, dominance is often affected by other factors, including the requirement that all ELs learn English, as well as personal preference, which is shaped markedly by social factors such as community structure, implicit messages of the lack of value or affirmation to ELs' heritage language and culture based on school programming, personal identity development, desire for acceptance, and sometimes even parental aspirations that are borne out of a natural desire to have their children succeed by learning English. In cases where dominance resides in the heritage or native language, direct evaluation in that language can be conducted only by a bilingual evaluator, and thus it remains an option not available to monolingual English-speaking practitioners. It should not even be presumed, however, that bilingual ability equates perfectly to competency in equitable assessment. According to Flanagan, McGrew, and Ortiz (2000), "mere possession of the capacity to communicate in an individual's native language does not ensure appropriate, non-discriminatory assessment of that individual ... Traditional assessment practices and their inherent biases can be easily replicated in any number of languages" (p. 291). In some cases, an EL may have even been formally designated as a "fluent English speaker" (FES) by virtue of having passed the state exam used to monitor English language acquisition. Such testing often serves to justify dominance and evaluation in English (L1), in an attempt to avoid the difficulties associated with evaluation in the now non-dominant, heritage language (L2).

Evaluation in the heritage language poses many of its own obstacles as well. For example, in contrast to assessment conducted in English (L2) with preschool EL children and other populations, evaluation in L1 (i.e., the heritage language) is a relatively new method of practice and sorely lacks any substantive empirical base with which to guide or support standards of practice. This has led to the increasing ambiguity of the meaning of what a "bilingual evaluation" involves. There is no consensus or current guidelines to make a determination of what a bilingual evaluation truly is, let alone whether or not such evaluation was conducted in a manner that would be considered appropriate or in line with any standards.

As a whole, evaluation in either L1 or L2, irrespective of dominance, does not avoid the problem that the normative samples of the tests used for the assessment would very likely fail to provide any control for variability in language and acculturative knowledge development between ELs and monolingual, native-English speakers, as well as among ELs relative to their own amount of exposure to English or their heritage language. Current methods for addressing test score validity remain largely inadequate, and they do not permit interpretation of test scores even when the ubiquitous cautionary statement is used—that is, "Because Rosita is an EL, these results may not be accurate estimates of her true ability and therefore should be interpreted with extreme caution." Such statements do nothing to bolster the validity of test scores, especially when subsequent interpretation that is offered is simply an interpretation with no evidence of any applied caution. In fact, there may be no way to interpret scores cautiously other than to not interpret them at all—something that practitioners rarely do, perhaps because of the need to justify the effort in generating the scores in the first place. Whatever the case, when scores are derived from modified/altered testing, or from evaluations done in the "dominant language" following efforts in establishing dominance, validity is not established. Any subsequent interpretation of the meaning of test scores would be specious and amount to nothing more than a guess.

Determining Test Score Validity

The preceding section outlined the most popular approaches designed to address test score validity. It also outlined the various problems inherent in their application. In general, such approaches do little to assist practitioners in their ability to work effectively with preschool CLD children. They do not generate results that are valid. Nor do they support subsequent diagnostic impressions and educational decisions. Despite the difficulties inherent in achieving the above goals, advances in recent years in both test development and the application of research findings to guide practice has resulted in options that are available to practitioners to ensure or assist in determining test score validity.

The Culture-Language Interpretive Matrix

The oldest of these developments is the Culture-Language Interpretive Matrix (C-LIM), originally developed in 1998 by Ortiz, McGrew, and Flanagan and evolving over time (Flanagan & Ortiz, 2001; Flanagan, Ortiz, & Alfonso, 2007, 2013; Ortiz, Melo, & Terzulli, 2017). The basic idea of the C-LIM was to bridge the gap created by the lack of any normative samples while controlling for language and acculturative differences between ELs and monolingual English speakers by using available research to quantify the difference in performance on intellectual, cognitive, and linguistic tasks and presenting it in a manner that would facilitate group comparisons. To accomplish this task, Ortiz and colleagues (1998), then Flanagan and Ortiz (2001), initially used subtest characteristics to classify tests on the basis of the degree to which they relied on language ability or acculturative knowledge. Because performance on tests of academic skill or domain-specific knowledge are subject to additional factors—notably, formal education—such tests are not included in the C-LIM. This method was later refined to classify tests based on the actual mean performance of ELs (Flanagan et al., 2007). This new method was adopted so that the classifications were driven strictly by empirical findings on how ELs performed relative to monolingual, native-English speakers. In this way, the C-LIM and its attendant graph provide what is essentially a research-based pattern of performance that represents "average" or typical functioning for ELs when evaluated on and compared to monolingual, English-speaking norms. Not surprisingly, research has indicated that, in general, as a subtest relies more on language and acculturative knowledge, the more the scores on that subtest are attenuated (Cormier, McGrew, & Ysseldyke, 2014). But perhaps the most important aspect of the C-LIM is that it also allows practitioners to consider the additional effect of comparing an EL's performance to that of other ELs.

The aggregation of data on ELs and their performance on tests is sufficient to establish a general level of expected performance as compared to monolingual, native-English speakers. However, ELs are not a monolithic group. Two ELs of the same age may not possess the same level of language development in either of the two languages they speak. Test performance also varies as a function of how much English language and acculturative knowledge development any given EL may have relative to other ELs (Dynda, 2008; Sotelo-Dynega, Ortiz, Flanagan, & Chaplin, 2013). By incorporating this additional research into its structure, the C-LIM allows practitioners to gauge more accurately the validity of their obtained test scores by ensuring greater precision in establishing a true peer comparison of performance. This comparison remains somewhat crude, given the limitations of sampling, but it does permit examination of three levels of language development and acculturative knowledge acquisition in ELs (slight, moderate, marked) relative to each other (Ortiz, 2019).

In the absence of test publisher norms that control for language and acculturative development differences, the C-LIM represents the only manner by which practitioners have been able to evaluate the extent to which their obtained test scores are likely to be valid (i.e., not systematically affected by the presence of differences in language and acculturative knowledge acquisition) or invalid (i.e., primarily affected by the presence of differences in language and acculturative knowledge). While some have claimed that the C-LIM does not demonstrate validity for its intended purpose (e.g., Styck & Watkins, 2013, 2014), their analyses failed to correctly identify the expected pattern of performance for their EL samples who possessed disabilities versus EL samples without disabilities. Thus, their conclusions were in error. The actual data contained within these studies reflect the very same patterns of EL performance seen historically and contemporaneously, and the data demonstrated that the C-LIM was consistent with at least 93% of the clinical decisions regarding disability that had been made in their sample. Despite some potential problems, taken together these findings provide considerable support for use of the C-LIM in establishing the validity of obtained test scores, including with preschool populations. A completely free version of the C-LIM v4.0, along with other supporting documentation, is available for download (Ortiz, 2020).

Advances in Tests for Preschool English Learners

Bilingual English-Spanish Assessment

The Bilingual English-Spanish Assessment (BESA; Peña et al., 2018) represents a major step forward in attempting to address test score validity by considering the amount of language exposure and development that bilingual children have in each language. The BESA was designed specifically to assist practitioners with the preschool transition period where young children are entering the formal academic environment for the first time. As such, it has a limited age range that encompasses ages 4:0 to 6:11 years, but it provides measurement of three key areas of language development: morphosyntax, semantics, and phonology.

The heart of the BESA is not that its three subtests can be given in Spanish and English, or that the Spanish versions are not simply direct translations of the English ones. Rather, it is that the normative samples were constructed in a manner that specifically attempts to control for the amount of language exposure in either language, which is determined primarily via the examiner's use of two semi-structured questionnaires (parents and teacher) regarding home- and preschool-based language use and frequency. In this way, a 5-year-old EL who has limited exposure to one of the languages (English or Spanish) is not directly compared to other 5-year-old ELs who may have been learning that language for two years or more. The purpose of the BESA is to provide a much broader and far more accurate view of language development of bilingual children by considering growth and development in each language across the three different domains and to also permit progress monitoring (Peña et al., 2018).

Not surprisingly, the BESA was developed by speech-language pathologists (SLPs) based on their long history and experience in bilingual issues. Because language is at the center of the field of speech and language, considerations regarding language development and differential language exposure in bilingual children are part and parcel of the BESA. It is natural for SLPs to recognize and consider how to operationalize the theoretical concepts necessary for engaging in fair and equitable evaluation of ELs. In this effort, the authors of the BESA have succeeded in ways that effectively resolve the type of issues, concerns, and obstacles discussed in prior sections. Nevertheless, there are some limitations to the use of BESA. For example, it is applicable only to ELs whose heritage language is Spanish.

While Spanish speakers represent the vast majority of the entire EL population in the United States (estimates range up to 62%; Ryan, 2013), Spanish is not the only language spoken by children in U.S. public schools. According to the last American Community Survey conducted in 2015, there are at least 350 different languages spoken in the United States. In addition, the BESA is designed specifically for preschool transition, so it does not have norms or utility for younger preschool ELs or older ones. And finally, use of the Spanish versions of the subtests would be accessible only to competent and qualified evaluators with sufficient proficiency in Spanish for administration and scoring. Nevertheless, the conceptual structure of the BESA and its development clearly demonstrate that test publishers can produce instruments with the necessary degree of validity required to support fair and equitable interpretation. This success comes directly from attention paid to differences in language and acculturative knowledge acquisition as the Spanish subtests are not mere translations of the English versions. According to the authors, variations in the Spanish language were taken into consideration, including the norm sample, where 17 different Spanish dialects and 7 regional English dialects were represented. Moreover, items were developed for each language based on the markers, structure, and culture of that language.

Ortiz Picture Vocabulary Acquisition Test

The Ortiz Picture Vocabulary Acquisition Test (Ortiz PVAT; Ortiz, 2018) represents another standardized, norm-referenced test that considers differences in language development among ELs and incorporates such considerations into the very design and structure of the test. The Ortiz PVAT introduces several innovative features, many of which stem from pragmatic as well as empirical issues. For example, one of the design goals of the test was to make it applicable to all individuals learning English, regardless of whether the examinee is a native speaker of English or not. Thus, it contains two separate and distinct sets of norms, one for monolingual, native-English speakers, and one specifically for everyone else (i.e., ELs). Due to the availability of the dual norms, the test may be administered to any individual learning English, in whatever manner (i.e., from birth, while they are learning a heritage language simultaneously, or at a later stage in life). Moreover, the test can also be given to any EL irrespective of their first language spoken. The test does not attempt to measure receptive vocabulary development in any language other than English. Although this may somewhat limit information regarding broad-based language ability because an EL's ability in L1 is not assessed, the test does provide essential, baseline assessment of general English language growth and acquisition relative to their amount of exposure to English.

The amount of exposure to English, which directly impacts an EL's English language acquisition, is incorporated into the EL norms. Through information conveyed by the examiner and secured via records and interviews with the examinee's parents and teachers regarding the examinee's age at first exposure, active learning experiences, formal education, parental SES and proficiency, and other factors, a percentage value is calculated to represent the amount of lifetime English exposure possessed by the examinee. Upon completion of the test, the examinee is then compared only to other same-aged ELs with exactly the same percentage of lifetime exposure to English, which can range from 1% to 99%. The test is normed on a broad age range, from 2:6 to 22:11, thus providing complete coverage of the entire school-age range. This feature makes this test ideal for preschool assessment. The fact that the test is receptive in nature also means that very young children, those still in the beginning stage of language acquisition (preproduction or silent period) with very little expressive English language capability, or even those with very limited English exposure, can still be evaluated. Their performance can be fairly and validly compared to that of other individuals of the same age with the same percentage of lifetime exposure to English.

The Ortiz PVAT is not intended to be a comprehensive measurement of language, even for preschool children whose language skills are at beginning stages of development, since it assesses receptive vocabulary only. However, the test does provide a unique ability to work with all children who are learning English regardless of what language they first spoke, how young they may be, or how long they have been learning English. Moreover, because the test is given in English, the examiner need not be bilingual. Practitioners working in school settings can also use the test to monitor progress and evaluate growth, beyond addressing diagnostic questions related to language development and literacy.

Despite there being over a century's worth of study and data regarding the test performance of ELs relative to monolingual, native-English speakers, it is only now that research is being applied in ways that are beginning to greatly benefit practitioners working with young CLD children, providing them with tools that meet the standards of fairness and equity (AERA, APA, & NCME, 2014; Ortiz, 2019). Tests like the BESA and Ortiz PVAT demonstrate the advancement of test development for clinicians to use without concerns regarding potential test score invalidity or lack of fairness. Until these tools and techniques, as well as others that may come after, make their way into the mainstream for practitioners, efforts to evaluate diverse preschool children fairly will remain rather complicated and problematic. When combined with defensible and systematic frameworks for comprehensive assessment, integration of these tools and techniques holds the promise of transforming clinicians' practice, allowing preschool children from diverse backgrounds to receive the type of nondiscriminatory and valid evaluation they so rightly deserve.

A Framework for Assessment of Diverse Preschool Children

As stated at the outset of this chapter, the assessment of CLD preschool children is essentially a unique case of preschool assessment, and it is also a special case of assessment conducted at the broadest level. Although there are many similarities between the assessment of preschool CLD children and the assessment of all diverse individuals, there are also some differences that require special attention to the unique characteristics possessed by very young children that can affect any number of steps during the evaluation process. The following framework represents a recommendation for the evaluation of CLD preschool children. In addition, suggestions for establishing test score validity in cases where standardized tests are used in the evaluation process are also provided.

Document Developmental Experiences

Not surprisingly, the first step in any attempt to evaluate the abilities, skills, or knowledge of CLD preschool children is generating a detailed documentation of the child's developmental background and experiences. The purpose of this step is to establish the degree of development the child actually has relative to monolingual speakers of each language. This is of particular importance for children who grow up in bilingual homes and who do not possess the same degree of linguistic development in either L1 or L2 as that possessed by children in homes where only one language is spoken (Bialystok, 2001). Nevertheless, this does not mean that learning two languages necessarily hinders a child's development. However, differences in vocabulary at a very early age are common and can be easily detected (Bialystok, Luk, Peets, & Yang, 2010). Therefore, possessing the knowledge of a child's language experiences helps provide the context in which to understand and interpret other data and information, including test scores.

In general, practitioners should focus on assessing and evaluating factors that may have affected the child's opportunity to learn. Such factors might have altered the CLD preschool children's age-/grade-expected level of development. It is also important to evaluate, as much as is feasible, current levels of functioning so as to establish a baseline upon which any progress can be evaluated. Areas that would be of particular interest at this point include the examination of first and second language acquisition, type and length of formal preschool experiences, opportunities for learning, amount as well as type of exposure to linguistic and acculturative experiences (in both English and the heritage language), parental level of education as well as literacy in all languages, and the family's socio-economic status. Generally speaking, the more limited a child's experiences in any of the above capacities, the more likely such factors would have an impact on the child's linguistic development and learning. Hence, the greater the likelihood that any measured performance will be low. However, a low performance does not necessarily indicate that the child has a disorder.

Monitor Progress and Evaluate Growth

If an assessment is being conducted in response to a referral that has already been made, then it may not be possible to conduct this monitoring as the timelines dictating the completion of evaluation would preclude it. Nevertheless, proper assessment of CLD children requires progress monitoring and the evaluation of growth while the child is still in the process of learning English (L2) through appropriate instruction, and only after a careful consideration of progress monitoring data can one determine whether further comprehensive evaluation is necessary. Before a preschooler can be considered as having a learning problem, whether it is based on language or preacademic skills, there should be evidence that suggests that despite the provision of developmentally appropriate instruction and sufficient time for its learning, the child does not demonstrate progress relative to their true peers. However, this can be difficult because developmentally matched peers in terms of language (i.e., other ELs with the same amount of exposure in both L1 and L2) may not be available. This would be a situation in which tools such as the BESA or the Ortiz PVAT can be useful in addressing this issue.

Regardless of the method of assessment the practitioner chooses to use, the aim is to evaluate progress systematically in academic skills in English (or the heritage language) using true peer comparison. The latter may be more important in cases where native language instruction is being provided in the preschool environment. Regardless of the language of instruction, it is important to examine directly the effectiveness of any interventions that have been attempted as well as to document the actual degree of growth, or lack thereof. Typical methods that may be used for this purpose include authentic and informal data (e.g., work samples, portfolios) or more formal data collected within an MTSS/RTI framework (e.g., CBM; progress monitoring charts; data from standardized, norm-referenced tests such as the BESA and the Ortiz PVAT). The goal of this step is to evaluate progress and growth only, rather than to determine disability. Only when progress and growth are found to be less than what one would be reasonably expected of other children with the same degree of development in the target language would there be grounds to move to further evaluation and comprehensive assessment.

Evaluate and Establish Test Score Validity

It is likely that many assessments of CLD students will begin at this step. The nature of the educational and referral process often expects practitioners to conduct a comprehensive assessment regardless of whether the criteria specified in the first two steps have been met or not. Whatever the circumstances that brought a practitioner to this point, assuming that standardized, norm-referenced tests were determined to be appropriate and were to be included in the assessment, the next step is to evaluate and establish test score validity. If the child and the practitioner speak Spanish and the child is between 4 and 6 years of age, the BESA can be utilized for evaluating the linguistic abilities of CLD children in English and/or Spanish. Alternatively, if the target language is English only, and the child or the examiner do not speak Spanish, or if the purpose of assessment is to establish the child's general language functioning in English vocabulary, then the Ortiz PVAT can be used. These tests provide estimates of language development that are defensible and valid.

For all other assessments, or when the above conditions are not met, the only remaining option would be to employ the C-LIM to interpret and evaluate the validity of the test data. It is important to note that the C-LIM requires that any subtest scores that are being entered and evaluated be derived from the administration of tests in accordance with the publisher's standardized protocol. The C-LIM relies on empirical investigations of ELs without disabilities who were assessed in English without any modification in test procedures. Any use of scores from tests that are administered in a modified or altered manner would have lost their psychometric properties and cannot be properly examined within the C-LIM. Similarly, because native-language tests (i.e., ones that are given in Spanish) lack sufficient empirical evidence, it is therefore difficult to determine the expected performance of ELs relative to other ELs with varying levels of Spanish language development. Moreover, norms of Spanish tests tend to be developed from monolingual speakers of Spanish. Their use in the C-LIM is questionable, albeit permissible for the sake of qualitative analysis. Valid use of the C-LIM can only be accomplished via initial administration of tests in English and with full compliance with and adherence to the publisher's standardized protocol.

This limitation of C-LIM regarding the strict use of test results obtained from non-modified procedures raises an important aside. Previously, it was pointed out that there are practical concerns that make assessment difficult in cases where the expectation is to proceed in the heritage language, which included the need for the practitioner to be bilingual in the child's language. Additional practical concern involves whether many assessment tools are available in different heritage language, especially for cases where L1 is not Spanish. Combined with the fact that a vast majority of practitioners are not bilingual and/or sufficiently competent to assess in a child's heritage language, there appears to be good reasons to begin all assessments in English first, even for CLD preschool children who are well-versed in their heritage language. Consider also that the usual purpose of testing at this point is to help identify the presence of disability, which, by definition, is predicated upon scores that reflect lower levels of ability, skill, or knowledge as compared to true peers. This is also why low scores require an examination of the influence of cultural and linguistic factors, whereas average or higher scores may not. Due to the type of testing conducted in this step, which tends not to be multiple choice items in terms of test format, an average or higher score is unlikely to be indicative of a deficit. Rather, even if the high test score obtained was not considered as a valid representation of the true ability of the CLD child, the lack of validity extends only insofar as the child's level of true ability may be higher than what is represented by the score. Thus, an average or higher score is highly unlikely to suggest the presence of a deficit, whereas a low score can be brought about by an infinite number of reasons, many of which have nothing to do with the child having a disability (e.g., lack of motivation, enthusiasm, fatigue, sleeplessness, selective inattention, irritability, moodiness, boredom, hunger, inadequate understanding of the task requirement). Given that the C-LIM is based largely on studies where ELs have been assessed in English, it appears to make the most sense in a vast majority of cases to *begin* the assessment in English rather than in the heritage language. Not only does this practice permit every practitioner to engage in and initiate the process of assessment, it also allows for the use of the various methods described herein to establish test score validity.

It is recommended that, for the most part, assessment via the use of standardized tests should start in English *first* whenever possible and appropriate. There are some circumstances in which a bilingual practitioner may well deem that beginning or completing an assessment in the heritage language is preferable, and clinicians who come to such decisions may very well have valid reasons for doing so. The only problem is that such practice provides no real mechanism for the systematic evaluation of the validity of the obtained test scores because neither the C-LIM nor the Ortiz PVAT or English versions of the BESA can be utilized. Practitioners who choose to evaluate in L1 first must recognize that it will be their responsibility to demonstrate the manner in which they determined the validity of their obtained results as well as how such a determination supports their diagnostic impressions and conclusions. For other cases where conducting the assessment in English first is a viable and appropriate option, the use of research findings to gauge performance relative to true peers (i.e., the foundations upon which the C-LIM was built) represents the only option available to practitioners that meets the definition of evidence-based assessment.

Interpretation of test scores can be confusing and sometime counterintuitive, and a full discussion of this topic is well beyond the scope of this chapter. The reader is referred to other, better sources for detailed information (e.g., Ortiz, 2019; Ortiz et al., 2017). In general, if test score data as viewed within the C-LIM are determined to be primarily the result of the systematic and overall influence of cultural and linguistic factors, then the results cannot be further interpreted in terms of their meaning relative to the child's true level of ability. However, this determination is only made when the child's pattern of performance matches and is comparable to the performance set by their true peers in various empirical studies. Because children in the studies that were included in the analysis during the development of C-LIM are ELs without disability and are of average ability, the implication is that any CLD child with a similar pattern of performance is equally likely to be of average ability. This means that their pattern of performance (one that matches the patterns of performance seen in other typically developing EL children in the literature) belies the presence of a disability and effectively precludes the need for any further testing. Only when the pattern of scores as viewed within the C-LIM suggests that performance cannot be accounted for entirely by cultural and linguistic factors can the results be deemed to be possible indicators of deficit. It may be difficult to attributable performance to factors above and beyond what can be reasonably accounted for by linguistic and cultural differences. As such, there is a solid basis on which to continue to the next step.

Re-assess and Re-evaluate in the Heritage Language (L1)

Usually when the assessment process advances to this step, it has been determined that the preschool child does have deficits (in English) that are not due primarily to cultural or linguistic factors, and therefore scores obtained from testing may well be seen as possible indications of actual or true ability. However, a CLD child cannot be presumed to have a disability unless there is evidence of the identified deficits existing in both languages (Rhodes et al., 2005). Thus, when scores generated from testing in English have been determined not to be affected by cultural or linguistic difference, there must still be further support bolstered by data that indicates similar problems and also in the same cognitive areas in the heritage language. In many ways, this step is akin to what is generally thought of as "bilingual assessment," for which there is little consensus regarding its actual definition or the procedures it encompasses. As such, the procedures that may be employed at this step are widely disparate and are predicated upon the very same problems and limitations that led to crafting the present framework.

In simplest terms, the purpose of this step is to re-assess and re-evaluate in the heritage language the same domains of ability, skill, or knowledge that were found to be possible areas of deficit when tested in English so as to provide cross-linguistic evidence that further supports the validity of the original scores. Engaging in this process at this point in the assessment and evaluation process has several advantages and avoids many of the difficulties that are inherent in beginning an assessment in the heritage language. For example, given that the scores obtained from testing in English have already been subjected to an analysis of their validity, there is no need to repeat the entire process to obtain scores from testing in the heritage language. Rather, because the purpose at this point in the process is to provide additional cross-linguistic confirmation of domain-specific problems, there is considerably more flexibility regarding how that evidence is collected. This means that procedures such as modified/altered testing, use of a translator/interpreter, and use of native language tests all become viable options for generating the necessary evidence. Combined with the issues related to practitioner bilingual competency and lack of available tests in the heritage language (which also raises the need and increases the rationale for a translator/interpreter), a wide range of options suddenly become appropriate.

Consider, for example, that although it may be helpful, it is not strictly necessary to generate new test scores for the purposes of this step. Qualitative information and data (e.g., process or error analysis, use of dynamic assessment, task observations) can be valuable and useful with respect to providing convergent evidence that a given area of functioning appears to be a true weakness. Even when test scores are generated, there is less of a concern with establishing their validity as their purpose is to yield ancillary supporting evidence of validity. This means that tests need not be administered or scored in strict and standardized fashion. Moreover, it would also be reasonable to use the exact same tests for follow-up assessment in the heritage. This is because under this circumstance, any observable practice effects that might occur would be extremely helpful in diagnostic terms, especially where concerns regarding learning are central to the evaluation and where an attempt is being made to discern "learning ability" from "learning disability."

How the evidence to support presumed areas of deficit would be collected would also vary considerably. For instance, if the practitioner is bilingual, speaks the language of the child, and has a version of the English test that is available in the child's language, then administering the test in the child's heritage language would represent one method, or perhaps the best method, for accomplishing this particular step in the evaluation process. On the other hand, if the practitioner is not bilingual, but there is a native-language version of the test that was previously administered in English, then employing a translator/interpreter to administer the test in the child's native language becomes yet another viable option. These options become less defensible as the limitations increase, but, depending upon the circumstance, they may be unavoidable and still represent the "best" that can be accomplished. For example, in the absence of a parallel or similar native-language test with which to assess the necessary domains, follow-up assessment could proceed via direct translation and administration by a bilingual examiner who speaks the same language as the child. Similarly, and while not ideal in any sense, the same could be accomplished by a monolingual examiner who administers a translated version of an English test (for which there is no official alternate language version) via the use of a translator/interpreter. At the very minimum, in cases where the child's heritage language is exceptionally rare or where there are simply no individuals with the necessary linguistic competency to provide any form of translation, the gathering of evidence of deficit in the same domains as ones found to be poor in English may boil down to the use of play-based assessment, dynamic assessment, administration of informal tasks accompanied by careful observation, and other types of probing for qualitative data and information.

It is important to recognize that simply having data in two languages that suggests poor performance in each is insufficient to conclude that an individual has some type of true disorder or disability. In cases where the child's development is limited in both languages, such findings would be typical and reflective of limitations in bilingual development, not a language-based problem. Similarly, as children exit preschool and enter a more formal academic environment, the language in which that instruction takes place can have profound effects on the growth and development in both languages. For these reasons, no assessment that has come this far can be considered complete without also attending to the final step.

Examine All Data Within the Context of Developmental Experiences

The most significant obstacle in assessing CLD preschool children revolves around the concept of validity. Although the concept of validity is somewhat binary (i.e., test scores are either valid or they are not), the determination is made on the basis of an accumulation of evidence. The assessment and evaluation framework that encompasses the steps described herein is designed to assist in generating test scores that may be interpreted as valid indicators of an individual's abilities. Embedded in steps 3 and 4 of this framework are two basic forms of evidence that bolster the validity of obtained test scores through various methodologies. They are all bound in common by the use of expectations of test performance that are grounded in either research or actual normative samples comprised of individuals with comparable cultural and linguistic backgrounds. Within the framework, validity has thus been inferred by: 1) test scores from evaluations in English that have been subjected to systematic analysis of the influence of cultural and linguistic variables, where such factors have been found to be either minimal or contributory but not primary factors in test performance; and 2) test scores or qualitative data from testing in the heritage language for the re-examination of suspected weak areas found in English. Testing in the heritage language either confirms or disconfirms the suspected deficits. If average or higher performance was found in testing using the heritage language, it provides evidence that disability is unlikely.

In addition, a third piece of evidence should be added to support conclusions and interpretation of the obtained test scores. This third piece of evidence involves the use of ecological and contextual evidence to support obtained test scores. Known developmental patterns and experiences (e.g., amount of exposure to L1 and L2, preschool and other types of formal or informal instruction, socio-economic status of the family, parental education and literacy level) can provide ecological evidence in this respect. When a careful scrutiny of the available test score data provides and reveals a logical and reasonable explanation that fits the context of the child's experiences, where a notable convergence of patterns of performance uncovered in the evaluation meld well with other case data (e.g., progress monitoring data, pre-referral concerns, work samples, observations, school records, teacher/parent reports, grades, interviews, observations), additional evidence of validity is obtained. Only when all three forms of evidence are met and only when they fit collectively into a rational picture regarding the child's development can there be sufficient confidence in the use and inter-pretation of test scores obtained in an evaluation of CLD preschool children.

Given the advancements that have been made in test development with respect to the validity of test use with CLD populations, there is a strong possibility that the future may bring some type of consensus on what con-stitutes best practices in the assessment of CLD individuals. At the very least, greater attention to and awareness of the issue of differences in lan-guage and acculturative knowledge acquisition as compared to monolingual, native-English speakers as well as other ELs will serve to improve practice and address the problem that is centered around a lack of validity to sup-port fair and equitable interpretation of test scores based on measures devel-oped for native English speakers. Unfortunately, at present, the various procedures commonly employed to address validity concerns have mostly failed in this regard, thus preventing any degree of accountability. Despite the absence of professional standards that specify actual procedures for the evaluation of ELs to which practitioners could be expected to adhere, there are consensus aspects of the assessment that should be documented in a report and which may be used in the interim to ascertain whether a given assessment has been conducted in compliance with standards necessary to demonstrate and establish fairness. A brief description of these aspects is proposed here in an effort to begin discussions that may lead to the devel-opment of standards to which practitioners may abide and be held fully accountable. Assessments that provide the following elements in a documented report would likely meet the standards of fairness which are implicit in the framework presented in this chapter and may be seen as a de facto checklist for those who may wish to assess their own work.

Tools and Procedures

A report should contain a section detailing the deliberate selection of tools, methods, and procedures with respect to the cultural and linguistic factors in the examinee's background—simply listing tests, even native-language ones, is not sufficient. Explanations are provided for any modification or alteration to the administration and/or scoring of any standardized instrument, including the use of a translator or translated tests.

Developmental Language Experiences

The report should contain a specific and distinct section on language development that includes a detailed history as well as sufficient information with which to formulate appropriate expectations of current proficiency. Information should include, at a minimum, age of first exposure to all languages, parental/home language use, parental levels of proficiency in all languages, parental education and socio-economic status, the child's experiences with all languages, current proficiency in all languages, amount of formal education in all languages, and type of preschool or educational programming.

Validity

The report should contain a section that provides a discussion regarding the validity of the obtained assessment data and test scores including specification in relation to how the impact of cultural/linguistic differences were considered and excluded as factors that might have compromised validity of the information—simply stating that scores or data are valid is insufficient.

Results

The report should contain not merely a discussion of results but also an analysis regarding the extent to which cultural or linguistic factors may have compromised cognitive, linguistic, or academic performance (particularly when a child's abilities are estimated based on test scores) and how those factors may have affected interpretive validity. Furthermore, some discussion regarding the extent to which the test scores and converging data are or are not consistent with what would be reasonably expected of the examinee, given their unique cultural and linguistic background and experiences, should be included.

Diagnostic Impressions

The report should contain conclusions and interpretations that are supported by the integration of data. It should also include discussion regarding how cultural or linguistic factors are not the primary reasons for any claimed deficits and that such deficits are above and beyond what would be expected given the examinee's unique cultural and linguistic background.

Conclusion

Assessment of CLD preschool students presents the very same central difficulty as that which characterizes evaluation of all CLD individuals—how to distinguish "difference from disorder." The ability to make this distinction fairly rests primarily on the concept of validity and whether data and information of any type, including standardized test scores, indicate the influence of developmental differences in language and acculturative knowledge acquisition, as opposed to an actual lack of ability, knowledge, or skill. The assessment and evaluation framework outlined in this chapter permits any practitioner, regardless of bilingual proficiency or competency, to be able to engage in and even complete evaluations that support defensible conclusions in this regard. Used in conjunction with other information relevant to appropriate nondiscriminatory assessment, including the consideration of factors such as language proficiency, socio-economic status, opportunity to learn, academic history, familial history, developmental data, work samples, curriculum-based data, and intervention and progress monitoring results, the framework presented herein (along with the applicable tools and instruments) represents an evidence-based method for evaluating CLD preschool children. The presented framework also directly addresses the issue of test score validity. This process in evaluation is accessible to all practitioners and can assist in decreasing the potential for biased and discriminatory interpretation. It also offers a sound and defensible basis by which to determine whether the preschool CLD child's observed development and learning problems are due primarily to the presence of a true disorder or whether they are mere reflections of the powerful influence of cultural or linguistic differences.

Note

1 By definition, "monolingual" means only one primary and significant language. If another language is present, its impact must be negligible, rendering it of little relevance to the child's development in the primary language. If it is not negligible, then the individual can no longer be considered monolingual. Instead, they should be considered as belonging on the bilingual spectrum.

References

American Educational Research Association (AERA), American Psychological Association (APA), & National Council on Measurement in Education (NCME). (2014). *Standards for educational and psychological testing.* Washington, D.C.: AERA.

Bialystok, E. (2001). *Bilingualism in development: Language, literacy and cognition.* Cambridge: Cambridge University Press.

Bialystok, E., Luk, G., Peets, K., & Yang, S. (2010). Receptive vocabulary differences in monolingual and bilingual children. *Bilingualism: Language and Cognition, 13,* 525–531. doi:10.1017/S1366728909990423

Cormier, D. C., McGrew, K. S., & Ysseldyke, J. E. (2014). The influences of linguistic demand and cultural loading on cognitive test scores. *Journal of Psychoeducational Assessment, 32,* 610–623. doi:10.1177/0734282914536012

Dynda, A. M. (2008). *The relation between language proficiency and IQ test performance.* Unpublished manuscript. St. John's University, NY.

Fisher, D., & Frey, N. (2012). *The school leader's guide to English learners.* Bloomington, IN: Solution Tree.

Flanagan, D. P., McGrew, K. S., & Ortiz, S. O. (2000). *The Wechsler Intelligence Scales and Gf-Gc theory: A contemporary approach to interpretation.* Boston: Allyn & Bacon.

Flanagan, D. P., & Ortiz, S. O. (2001). *Essentials of cross-battery assessment.* New York: John Wiley.

Flanagan, D. P., Ortiz, S. O., & Alfonso, V. C. (2007). *Essentials of cross-battery assessment* (2nd ed.). New York: John Wiley.

Flanagan, D. P., Ortiz, S. O., & Alfonso, V. C. (2013). *Essentials of cross-battery assessment* (3rd ed.). Hoboken, NJ: John Wiley & Sons, Inc.

Grosjean, F. (1989). Neurolinguists beware! The bilingual is not two monolinguals in one person. *Brain and Language, 36,* 3–15.

Grosjean, F., & Li, P. (2013). *The psycholinguistics of bilingualism.* West Sussex, United Kingdom: Wiley-Blackwell.

Ortiz, S. O. (2018). *Ortiz Picture Vocabulary Test (Ortiz PVAT).* Toronto, Canada: Multi-Health Systems.

Ortiz, S. O. (2019). On the measurement of cognitive abilities in English learners. *Contemporary School Psychology, 23,* 68–86. doi:10.1007/s40688-018-0208-8

Ortiz, S. O. (2020). The C-LIM Basic v4.0. Retrieved from http://facpub.stjohns.edu/~ortizs/CLIM/

Ortiz, S. O., McGrew, K. S., & Flanagan, D. P. (1998). Gf-Gc cross-battery interpretation and selective cross-battery assessment: Referral concerns and the needs of culturally and linguistically diverse populations. In K. S. McGrew & D. P. Flanagan (Eds.), *The intelligence test desk reference (ITDR): Gf-Gc Cross-Battery Assessment* (pp. 401–444). Boston: Allyn & Bacon.

Ortiz, S. O., Melo, K. E., & Terzulli, M. (2017). Assessment of English learners with the WISC-V. In D. P. Flanagan & V. C. Alfonso (Eds.), *Essentials of WISC-V assessment* (pp. 539–590). Hoboken, NJ: John Wiley & Sons, Inc.

Peña, E. D., Gutiérrez-Clellen, V. F., Iglesias, A., Goldstein, B. A., & Bedore, L. M. (2018). *Bilingual English-Spanish Assessment (BESA) Manual.* Baltimore, MD: Brookes Publishing.

Rhodes, R., Ochoa, S. H., & Ortiz, S. O. (2005). *Assessment of culturally and linguistically diverse students: A practical guide.* New York: Guilford Press.

Ryan, C. (2013). Language use in the United States: 2011. *American Community Survey Reports.* Suitland, MD: U.S. Census Bureau. Retrieved from www.census.gov/library/publications/2013/acs/acs-22.html

Salvia, J., & Ysseldyke, J. (1991). *Assessment in special and remedial education* (5th ed.). Boston: Houghton-Mifflin.

Schipolowski, S., Wilhelm, O., & Schroeders, U. (2014). On the nature of crystallized intelligence: The relationship between verbal ability and factual knowledge. *Intelligence, 46,* 156–168.

Schneider, J., & McGrew, K. S. (2018). The Cattell-Horn-Carroll Theory of Cognitive Abilities. In D. P. Flanagan & E. M. McDonough (Eds.), *Contemporary intellectual assessment, fourth edition* (pp. 73–163). NY: Guilford Press.

Sotelo-Dynega, M., Ortiz, S. O., Flanagan, D. P., & Chaplin, W. (2013). English language proficiency and test performance: Evaluation of bilinguals with the

Woodcock-Johnson III tests of cognitive ability. *Psychology in the Schools, 50,* 781–797. doi:10.1002/pits.21706

Styck, K. M., & Watkins, M. W. (2013). Diagnostic utility of the Culture-Language Interpretive Matrix for the Wechsler intelligence scales for children–forth edition among referred students. *School Psychology Review, 42,* 367–382.

Styck, K. M., & Watkins, M. W. (2014). Discriminant validity of the WISC-IV Culture-Language Interpretive Matrix. *Contemporary School Psychology, 18,* 168–177. doi:10.1007/s40688-014-0021-y

U.S. Census Bureau. (2014). U.S. poverty report. Retrieved from https://www.census.gov/population/projections/data/national/2014.html

Valdés, G., & Figueroa, R. A. (1994). *Bilingualism and testing: A special case of bias.* Norwood, NJ: Ablex.

Wolfram, W., Adger, C. T., & Christian, D. (1999). *Dialects in schools and communities.* Mahwah, NJ: Lawrence Erlbaum Associates, Inc.

Chapter 15

Neuropsychological Assessment of Preschool-Aged Children

George McCloskey, Bradley Petry, Leslie McIntosh, Jeff Kelly, and Joseph Filachek

Definition and Purpose

The neuropsychological assessment of preschool-aged children (NPA-C) has been discussed in the professional literature for several decades (Aylward, 1997; Deysach, 1986; Hartlage & Telzrow, 1986; Hooper, 1991; Hooper, Molnar, Beswick, & Jacobi-Vessels, 2007; Hooper et al., 2007; Korkman, Kirk, & Kemp, 1998; Molfese & Price, 2002; Rey-Casserly, 1999; Tramontana & Hooper, 1988; Wilson, 1992). The application of these techniques, however, remains on the periphery of the assessment mainstream (Baron & Anderson, 2012) despite the fact that numerous neurological and medical disorders and some psychiatric disorders that occur in the early years of life often have associated neuropsychological difficulties that need to be assessed (Heffelfinger & Koop, 2009; Hooper et al., 2007). Additionally, improvements in prenatal and neonatal care have contributed to reduced mortality among sick and injured infants and toddlers. These survivors are at-risk of developmental delays and other complications, and many of these children are now included in preschool education programs and are in need of specialized educational services (Hooper et al., 2007).

NPA-C makes use of well-developed theoretical models of brain development and brain function as well as empirically supported findings that have established connections between observable behaviors, cognitive functioning, and the neuroanatomical systems of young developing brains. Ideally, clinicians engaging in NPA-C possess adequate knowledge of the medical disorders, diseases, and traumatic injuries that may be afflicting the preschool children that they are assessing. Clinicians also should have an understanding of how damage in early childhood could alter the typical course of development of emerging domains of function that become more specialized in later years (Baron, 2018; Dennis, Fletcher, Rogers, Hetherington, & Francis, 2002; Fletcher et al., 2004; Heffelfinger & Koop, 2009; Hooper et al., 2007; Wozniak, 2015).

NPA-C is different from the more typical developmental assessments of preschoolers. Developmental assessments during the preschool years are used to identify more generalized delays in the broad domains of language, cognitive, motor, and social skill development. Although NPA-C may include some of the same types of assessments in the same domains as typical developmental assessments, NPA-C are intended to assess these same domains in more detail and to assess neuropsychological domains that usually are not included in typical broad-based developmental assessments.

Although the prevailing trend is to delay neuropsychological assessments until school age, there are good reasons to conduct these assessments during preschool years. Research on neural recovery from injuries indicates that such recovery is optimal within the first few months following the injury (Berlin, Brooks-Gunn, McCarton, & McCormick, 1998; Butler & Copeland, 2002; Anderson, Damasio, Tranel, & Damasio, 2000; Baron, Litman, Ahronovich, & Baker, 2012; Eslinger, Flaherty, & Benton, 2004; Brown & Jernigan, 2012). Additionally, interventions are more effective and can be accomplished with less time when children are younger. (Bates & Roe, 2001; Diamond, 1991; Espy, Kaufmann, McDiarmid, & Glisky, 1999; Fenson et al., 1994; Gathercole, 1998; Heffelfinger & Koop, 2009; Mrakotsky & Heffelfinger, 2006; Johnson, 2001; Johnson, Posner, & Rothbart, 1991; Ruff & Capozzoli, 2003; Ruff & Capozzoli, 2003; Freitag & Tuxhorn, 2005; Posner & Rothbart, 2006). When performed expertly, NPA-C can play an important role in determining patterns of neuropsychological strengths and weaknesses that can assist in identifying appropriate interventions, educating other professionals about brain-behavior relationships, and monitoring response to interventions. To maximize the effectiveness of an NPA-C, the assessment findings must accurately characterize the child's current levels of functioning in multiple domains and how functioning in these domains may be affected later.

Historical Perspective

Although the neuropsychological assessment of preschool children has a history dating back to the early 1970s, the methodology of these assessments was based on a downward extension of the methods used with adults (Reitan & Davison, 1974). In Finland in the 1980s, Marit Korkman developed a battery of tests specifically designed to assess the functioning of preschool and school-age children in multiple neuropsychological domains (Korkman, 1980, 1988). The revised 1988 edition of the NEPSY was the first battery specifically designed for children that provided tasks that could be used with preschoolers aged 3–6. NPA-C began to gain some traction in the United States in the late 1990s with the national standardization and publication of the first U.S. edition of the NEPSY (Korkman et al., 1998). Drawing on the neurodevelopmental theoretical perspective of Luria (1973, 1980), the original NEPSY provided tasks assessing neurodevelopmental functioning in five domains: Attention/Executive Functions, Language, Sensorimotor Functions, Visuospatial Processing, and Memory and Learning.

The second edition of the NEPSY (NEPSY-II; Korkman, Kirk, & Kemp, 2007) updated the national standardization sample revised, added and deleted tasks in the original five domains, and added tasks in the domain of social perception. To date, the NEPSY-II is the only neuropsychological test battery available in the U.S. that includes tasks from six domains, all of which are standardized on the same stratified, national sample of preschool children. Although it does enable assessment within six separate domains, coverage of these domains is very uneven. The NEPSY-II offers the broadest coverage in the language domain, with six subtests available for use with preschool-aged children. The Memory and Learning, Visuospatial Processing, and Sensorimotor domains offer three subtests each and the Social Perception domain includes two subtests. The Attention/Executive Function domain is the most restricted, with only one subtest available for use with children in the preschool age range.

Prior to the introduction of the NEPSY, clinicians engaged in neuropsychological assessments relied on the selection of various tests or subtests from existing norm-referenced measures in order to assess across multiple domains. Selection of tests for inclusion in these flexible batteries was guided by models that specified the neuropsychological domains to be addressed. Hooper et al. (2007) listed the assessment domains included in several of these models, noting the considerable overlap among them. Additional models also have been proposed since the last edition of this text (Baron, 2018; Baron & Anderson, 2012; Heffelfinger & Koop, 2009). Flexible batteries can be tailored to fit a specific referral question or to construct a comprehensive, broad-based assessment (Deysach, 1986; Hooper, 2004; Wilson, 1986, 1992). The hallmark of a neuropsychological approach to assessment, however, is to include the assessment of domains typically not addressed in traditional developmental assessments and to expand on the coverage of the domains that are addressed by traditional developmental assessments (Baron, 2018; Baron & Anderson, 2012; Heffelfinger & Koop, 2009; Hooper et al., 2007).

Neuropsychological Assessments by Domain

Coverage of multiple domains within a flexible battery approach is achieved by selecting a variety of domain-specific tests or subtests from multiple tests that address the domains included in the neuropsychological model of choice. Based on a synthesis of the most common domains addressed in the various assessment models cited earlier, the following domains are discussed in this section: Language, Visual Spatial, Sensorimotor, Memory, Attention, and Executive Functions.

Language

The development and acquisition of language is critical for overall cognitive functioning. Developmental assessments frequently assess the language abilities of preschool children in a relatively cursory manner with measures of receptive and expressive vocabulary (Heffelfinger & Koop, 2009). NPA-C usually goes beyond the basic receptive/expressive dichotomy to assess multiple aspects of language development. Included among these are oromotor control and articulation, phonological processing, naming, and word generation (Basso, 2003; Conti-Ramsden & Durkin, 2012; Dalal & Loeb, 2005; Korkman et al., 1998; Leonard, 1998). Consistent with the literature on language development in early childhood and the language disorders that may affect preschool children, the NEPSY-II offers six language subtests: Body Part Naming and Identification, Comprehension of Instructions, Oromotor Sequences, Phonological Processing, Repetition of Nonsense Words, Speeded Naming, and Word Generation. Additional facets of language development, including vocabulary, semantics, and grammar within the receptive and expressive broad categories, can be assessed with specific language tests such as the Clinical Evaluation of Language Fundamentals – Preschool, 2nd Edition (CELF – Preschool – 2; Semel, Wiig, & Secord, 2006) and the Preschool Language Scale, 4th Edition (PLS-4; Zimmerman, Steiner, & Pond, 2002). Specific assessments of grammar and morphology can be obtained with the Rice/Wexler Test of Early Grammar Impairment (TEGI; Rice & Wexler, 2001). Tests that can be used to assess various facets of the language development of preschool-aged children are listed in Table 15.1.

Visual Spatial

Along with the development of language, the development of visual spatial processing capacities is critical for overall cognitive functioning as well as later academic success in mathematics. Visual spatial deficits have been associated with at-risk conditions such as low birth weight in pre-term infants (Vicari, Caravale, Carlesimo, Casadei, & Allemand, 2004; Molloy, Doyle, Makrides, & Anderson, 2012). Assessment within this domain typically includes measures of visual perception, spatial processing, and visuoconstructional skill and often examines local and global visual integration and processing. Visual spatial processing can be affected by various medical conditions, diseases, and mental disorders (Bellinger et al., 2003; Dakin & Frith, 2005; Dennis et al., 2002; Fedrizzi et al., 1998; Lorenzo, Barton, Arnold, & North, 2013; O'Riordan, Plaisted, Driver, & Baron-Cohen, 2001; Stiers et al., 2002; van den Hout et al., 2004) and may play a central role in the development of quantitative skills (Barnes & Raghubar, 2014; Raghubar et al., 2015; Verdine, Irwin, Golinkoff, & Hirsh-Pasek, 2014). The NEPSY-II offers three subtests that can be used to assess various aspects of visual spatial processing of preschool-aged children: Block Construction, Design Copying, and Geometric Puzzles. The most recently revised version of the Beery-Buktenika Developmental Test of Visual-Motor Integration (Beery, Buktenica & Beery, 2010) can be used to assess visual-motor functioning. Tests that can be used

Table 15.1 Assessments Available for Use in NPA-C, by Domain

Domain	Test
Language	NEPSY-II. Korkman, Kirk & Kemp (2007). Pearson. Clinical evaluation of language fundamentals – preschool-2 (CELF-Preschool-2). Semel, Wiig & Secord (2006). Pearson. Preschool Language Scale – Fourth Edition (PLS-4). Zimmerman, et al. (2002). Pearson. Preschool Language Assessment Instrument – Second Edition (PLAI-2). Blank, Rose & Berlin (2003). WPS. Rice-Wexler Test of Early Grammar Impairment (TEGI). Rice and Wexler (2001). Pearson. Expressive One-Word Picture Vocabulary Test – Fourth Edition (EOWPT-IV). Martin & Brownell. (2011). Pro-Ed. Receptive One-Word Picture Vocabulary Test – Fourth Edition (ROWPT-IV). Martin & Brownell. (2011). Pro-Ed. Peabody Picture Vocabulary Test, 4th Edition (PPVT-IV). Dunn & Dunn (2007). Pearson. Structured Photographic Expressive Language Test – Third Edition (SPELT-3). Dawson, Stout & Eyer (2003). Pro-Ed.
Visual Spatial	NEPSY-II. Korkman et al. (2007). Pearson. Beery-Buktenika Developmental Test of Visual-Motor Integration – 6th Edition (Beery VMI). Beery, Buktenica, & Beery. (2010). Pearson.
Sensorimotor	NEPSY-II. Korkman et al. (2007). Pearson. Dean-Woodcock Sensory-Motor Battery. Dean and Woodcock (2003). Riverside.
Motor	Peabody Developmental Motor Scales – (2nd Edition) – (PDMS-2). Folio and Fewell (2000). Pro-Ed. Movement Assessment Battery for Children (2nd Edition) – (MABC-2). Henderson, Sugden & Barnett (2007). Pearson. Bruininks-Oseretsky Test of Motor Proficiency (2nd Edition) – (BOT-2). Bruininks (2005). Pearson.
Sensory	Sensory Processing Measure (SPM). Miller-Kuhanek, Henry, Glennon, Parham, & Ecker. (2008). WPS. Sensory Profile 2. Dunn (2014). Pearson.
Memory	NEPSY-II. Korkman et al. (2007). Pearson.
Attention	NEPSY-II. Korkman et al. (2007). Pearson. Conners Kiddie Continuous Performance Test. Conners & MHS Staff. (2001). MHS. Auditory Continuous Performance Test for Preschoolers. (ACPT-P). Mahone, Pillion & Hiemenz (2001). Pearson. Behavior Assessment System for Children – 3rd Edition (BASC-3). Reynolds and Kamphaus (2015). Pearson. Conners Early Childhood Scale. Conners & Goldstein (2009). MHS. Achenbach System of Empirically-Based Assessment – Preschool Form. Achenbach & Rescorla (2000). University of Vermont.
Executive Functions	Leiter International Performance Scale – Third Edition (LIPS-3). Roid, Miller, Pomplun, & Koch. (2013). Stoelting Co. Behavior Rating Inventory of Executive Function – Preschool Version (BRIEF-P). Gioia, Espy, & Isquith (1996). PAR.

to assess various aspects of the visual-spatial development of preschool-aged children are listed in Table 15.1.

Sensorimotor

Sensory assessments are based on a model of perception of sensation using the five basic senses as well as vestibular and proprioceptive systems. Difficulties with sensory processing can have an impact on all other areas of development (Jorquera-Cabrera, Romero-Ayuso, Rodriguez-Gil, & Triviño-Juárez, 2017). Motor functioning is a very broad domain and assessments typically focus on only a few specific aspects of this domain (Korkman et al., 2007; Piek, Hands, & Licari, 2012). Acknowledging the fact that motor control requires sensory input, the NEPSY-II includes the hybrid domain of Sensorimotor functioning. Within the Sensorimotor domain, the NEPSY-II provides three subtests that can be used with preschool children: Imitating Hand Positions, Manual Motor Sequences, and Visuomotor Precision. The Dean-Woodcock Neuropsychological Battery (Dean & Woodcock, 2003) was developed to assess sensory and motor functions but the test age range does not include 3-year-olds. Several tests of motor functioning can be used across the full preschool age range. These include the Peabody Developmental Motor Scales – Second Edition (Folio & Fewell, 2000) and the Movement Assessment Battery for Children – 2 (Henderson et al., 2007). Tests that can be used to assess various aspects of sensory and motor development of preschool-aged children are listed in Table 15.1.

Memory

The relatively slow growth in the development of tests specifically devoted to the assessment of memory has been noted frequently in the literature (Bauer, Leventon, & Varga, 2012; Hooper et al., 2007) despite the fact that the important role of the development of memory in early childhood has been well-established (Cowan & Alloway, 1997; Gathercole, 2002; Temple, 1997). Approaches to the assessment of memory with preschool-aged children have predominately relied on the use of cognitive assessments that feature subtests of memory among the tests of other cognitive functions and domains. These include the Differential Ability Scales (DAS-II; Elliott, 2007), the Wechsler Preschool and Primary Scale of Intelligence – Fourth Edition (WPPSI-IV; Wechsler, 2012), the Kaufman Assessment Battery for Children (KABC-II; Kaufman, 2015), and the Leiter International Performance Scale – Third Edition (Roid et al., 2013). The exception in this area has been the NEPSY, which has offered subtests for the assessment of memory since its first edition. The NEPSY-II assesses multiple facets of memory, including learning and memory, immediate and delayed memory, encoding, retrieval, working memory, memory span, repetition, rote memory, supraspan learning, and material-specific memory. The NEPSY-II assesses these constructs in the form of three subtests that can be used with preschool-aged children: Memory for Designs and Memory for Designs Delayed, Narrative Memory, and Sentence Repetition. Additional specific subtests from cognitive assessment batteries that can be used to assess various aspects of memory processing in preschool-aged children are listed in Table 15.1.

Attention

Attention problems are relatively common in preschool children (Mahone, 2005; Mahone & Schneider, 2012), and ADHD is one of the most commonly diagnosed psychiatric conditions in this age group (Armstrong & Nettleton, 2004; Wichstrøm et al., 2012). Additionally, attention problems often are observed in children diagnosed with other psychiatric conditions and/or with medical conditions (Chang, Shih, & Kasari, 2016; Niemczyk, Equit, Braun-Bither, Klein, & von Gontard, 2015; Nygaard, Slinning, Moe, & Walhovd, 2016; Overgaard, Aase, Torgersen, & Zeiner, 2016: Tondon & Pergjika, 2017). Despite the prevalence of attention problems, the development of norm-referenced tests to directly assess attention in preschool-aged children has been very limited (Mahone & Schneider, 2012; Tondon & Pergjika, 2017). Although the original NEPSY included a Visual Attention Subtest, the NEPSY-II does not include any subtests for use in this domain.

There are three measures currently available to assess attention of preschool children. The Conners Kiddie Continuous Performance Test (Conners & MHS Staff, 2001) assesses the visual attention of children ages 4–5. The Auditory Continuous Performance Test for Preschoolers (Mahone et al., 2001) assesses auditory attention in preschoolers ages 3–6. Despite the limited selection of tests available for assessing attention, the NEPSY-II Statue Subtest and the K-CPT have been very effective in identifying at ages 3 and 4 those children who will be diagnosed with ADHD at age 6 (Breaux, Griffith, & Harvey, 2016). The Leiter International Performance Scale – Third Edition (LIPS-3; Roid et al., 2013) includes two subtests that assess the attention capacities of children in the preschool age range: Attention Sustained and Attention Divided.

Considering the difficulties inherent in assessing the attentional capacities of preschool children, clinicians are advised to use a multi-method approach to assessment (Baron, 2018; Mahone & Schneider, 2012). Attempts to directly assess the attention of a preschool child therefore should be supplemented with information from parents and teachers. Although clinical interviews can be helpful in this regard, teacher and parent perceptions of the frequency of attention problems should also be assessed using objective, standardized, norm-referenced rating scales. The Behavior Assessment System for Children – 3rd Edition (BASC-3; Reynolds & Kamphaus, 2015) provides norm-referenced scores for parent and teacher ratings for an Attention Subscale for ages 2–5. The Conners Early Childhood Scale

(Conners, & Goldstein, 2009) provides norm-referenced scores for parent and teacher ratings for an Inattention/Hyperactivity Subscale. The Achenbach System of Empirically-Based Assessment – Preschool Form (Achenbach & Rescorla, 2000) provides norm-referenced scores for parent and teacher ratings for an Attention Subscale. Tests that can be used to assess attention in preschool-aged children are listed in Table 15.1.

Executive Functions

As recently as the early 1980s, many researchers and clinicians believed executive functions did not emerge until early adolescence due to a slower rate of maturity of regions of the frontal lobes (Anderson & Reidy, 2012; Golden, 1981). This thinking changed shortly afterward, however, as researchers began to document the emergence of many self-regulation capacities in infancy (Diamond, 1985, 1988; Diamond & Doar, 1989; Diamond & Goldman-Rakic, 1989). Since Diamond's seminal studies on the topic in the late 1980s, thousands of research studies on the development of executive functions in children during school age and preschool have been published.

The growth of interest in the development of executive functions across the childhood years was fueled by the publication of the Children's Category Test in 1993 (CCT; Boll, 1993), the NEPSY in 1998 (Korkman et al., 1998), and the Behavior Rating Inventory of Executive Functions in 1996 (Gioia, Espy, & Isquith, 1996). Research has established the importance of the development of executive functions in early childhood for effective self-regulation (Anderson & Reidy, 2012; Blair, 2016; 2016; Carlson, 2005; Diamond, 2016; Diamond, Carlson, & Beck, 2005; Espy & Bull, 2005; Griffin, McArdle, & Freund, 2016; Rueda, Posner, & Rothbart, 2005). Additionally, the experimental research on methods that can be used to assess the executive functions of preschool children is expanding rapidly (Anderson & Reidy, 2012; Akshoomoff, Brown, Bakeman, & Hagler, 2018; Howard, Vasseleu, Neilsen-Hewett, & Cliff, 2018; Isquith, Crawford, Espy, & Gioia, 2005; Lin, Liew, & Perez, 2019; Morra, Panesi, Traverso, & Usai, 2018; Willoughby & Blair, 2016; Willoughby, Blair, Wirth, & Greenberg, 2010, 2012a; Willoughby, Wirth, & Blair, 2012b; Hongwanishkul, Happaney, Lee, & Zelazo, 2005; Blair, Zelazo, & Greenberg, 2016). Despite these advances, the Leiter International Performance Scale – Third Edition (LIPS-3; Roid et al., 2013) is the only individually administered standardized test that includes a subtest – the Nonverbal Stroop – that assesses some facets of the executive functions of children in the preschool age range.

Executive functions of children in the preschool age range also can be assessed using the parent and teacher forms of the Behavior Rating Inventory of Executive Function – Preschool Version (Gioia et al., 1996). The BRIEF can be used to assess parent and teacher perceptions of the frequency of behaviors indicative of executive function difficulties within five specific domains: Inhibit, Shift, Emotional Control, Working Memory, and Plan/Organize.

Intelligence Testing and Neuropsychological Assessments

The inclusion of a major (widely used and well-researched) intellectual assessment battery often is recommended as part of an NPA-C (Baron, 2018; Baron & Leonberger, 2012; Heffelfinger & Koop, 2009; Hooper et al., 2007). Although the use of a battery that assesses general intellectual functioning overlaps greatly with traditional developmental assessments, the purpose for its inclusion in an NPA-C is quite different. Beyond providing a global estimate of cognitive functioning, the subtests of these general batteries offer well-developed and well-standardized measures of specific neuropsychological constructs (Baron, 2018; Baron & Leonberger; Heffelfinger & Koop, 2009; Hooper et al., 2007). In fact, some neuropsychological constructs, such as reasoning with language and reasoning with nonverbal visual stimuli, can only be assessed in a norm-referenced manner by using subtests of general intelligence tests. For other neuropsychological constructs, such as memory, the subtests from these general intelligence batteries often represent the best of the measures that are available. Some of the most widely used general intellectual batteries (for example, the WPPSI-IV) have been criticized for their approach to test development, wherein a test originally developed for adults or school-age children is extended downward with similar subtest formats to assess preschool-aged children (Baron, 2018).

Other tests, such as the Differential Ability Scales – Second Edition (DAS-II; Elliott, 2007) and the Leiter International Performance Scale – Second Edition (LIPS-2; Roid et al., 2013), have been lauded for their developmental perspective and ease of use with preschool children exhibiting delays or challenging behaviors (Hooper et al., 2007). Clinicians assessing younger preschool children with significant delays may find the Bayley Scales of Infant Development – Third Edition (BSID-3) to be helpful in characterizing a child's level of functioning within the language, cognitive, and motor domains, but norm-referenced levels of performance must be interpreted with caution as research has indicated that the BSID-3 norms may underestimate developmental delays (Anderson & Burnett, 2017; Anderson, De Luca, Hutchinson, Roberts, & Doyle, 2010; Baron, 2018; Moore, Johnson, Haider, Hennessy, & Marlow, 2012). The BDID-3 also assesses adaptive behavior and social/emotional functioning. The major intellectual assessment batteries and the specific subtests of each test that are available for use with preschool children are listed in Table 15.2 based on the neuropsychological constructs that they assess.

Clinician Perspective and Process

Most of the tests that can be used in an NPA-C were developed from test blueprints that existed prior to the introduction of the neuropsychological models that are now being applied to guide assessment procedures. Additionally, many of the tests used in an NPA-C may be identical to tests used

Table 15.2 Subtests from Intellectual Batteries that Can Be Used in NPA-C, by Domain

Domain		
Test	Age Range	Subtest(s)

Language/Reasoning with Language/Auditory Processing

WPPSI-IV	2:6–3:11	Receptive Vocabulary Picture Naming Information
	4:0–5:11	Vocabulary Similarities Comprehension Information
DAS-II	2:6–3:4	Verbal Comprehension Naming Vocabulary
	4:0–5:11	Verbal Comprehension Naming Vocabulary Rapid Naming
KABC-II	3:0–5:11	Riddles Expressive Vocabulary Verbal Knowledge
WJ-IV Cog	2:0–5:11	Oral Vocabulary General Information Phonological Processing Nonword Repetition
WJ-IV OL	2:0–5:11	Picture Vocabulary Oral Comprehension Segmentation Rapid Picture Naming Understanding Directions Retrieval Fluency Sound Awareness

Reasoning with Visual Stimuli

WPPSI-IV	4:0–5:11	Matrix Reasoning Picture Concepts
DAS-II	2-6–3:5	Picture Similarities
	4:0–5:11	Matrices
KABC-II	3:0–4:11	Conceptual Thinking
	5:0–5:11	Conceptual Thinking Pattern Reasoning
WJ-IV Cog	2:0–5:11	Concept Formation Analysis-Synthesis
LIPS-3	3:0–5:11	Classification & Analogies Sequential Order

Visual Perception/Visual-Spatial/Visuomotor/Visuomotor Construction/ Visual Processing Speed

WPPSI-IV	2:6–3:11	Block Design Object Assembly
	4:0–5:11	Bug Search Cancellation Animal Coding
DAS-II	2:6–3:5	Pattern Construction
	4:0–5:11	Pattern Construction Copying
K-ABC-II	3:0–3:4	Triangles Gestalt Closure
	4:0–5:11	Triangles Gestalt Closure Block Counting
WJ-IV Cog	2:0–5:11	Visualization Picture Recognition Letter-Pattern Matching Number-Pattern Matching Pair Cancellation
LIPS-3	3:0–5:11	Figure-Ground Form Completion Visual Patterns

Memory

WPPSI-IV	2:6–5:11	Picture Memory Zoo Locations
DAS-II	2:6–3:4	Recall of Digits Forward Recall of Pictures
	4:0–5:11	Recall of Digits Forward Recall of Pictures Recall of Digits Backward Recall of Objects

(Continued)

Table 15.2 (Cont.)

Domain		
Test	Age Range	Subtest(s)
KABC-II	3:0–3:11	Atlantis Word Order
	4:0–5:11	Atlantis Rebus Word Order Number Recall
WJ-IV Cog	2:0–5:11	Verbal Attention Story Recall Numbers Reversed Memory for Words Visual-Auditory Learning Object-Number Sequencing
WJ-IV OL	2:0–5:11	Sentence Repetition
LIPS-3	3:0–5:11	Forward Memory Reverse Memory
Attention/Executive Function		
LIPS-3	3:0–5:11	Attention Sustained Attention Divided Nonverbal Stroop

in traditional developmental assessments. Therefore, it is the perspective that the clinician brings to the administration and interpretation of the tests being used that identifies the assessment as neuropsychological in nature rather than the specific tests that are being used.

It is important to keep in mind that preschool-aged neuropsychological assessment instruments emerged from the gap between the broad-based assessment of infant development and the more varied approaches to the assessment of the intellectual and cognitive abilities of school-age children. Many of the tests that are used in an NPA-C are downward extensions of tests that were originally developed to assess adults and then school-age children rather than upward extensions of tests originally developed to assess infants. Additionally, clinicians that use standardized assessments with preschool children are much more likely to have experience with assessing school-age children than experience with assessing infants. There are important implications for assessment practice here. As discussed in the first section of this chapter, children that are referred for a preschool NPA-C are likely to be suffering from medical conditions, diseases, or injuries that have impacted their daily functioning in some way. Ideally, assessing across several neuropsychological domains may enable the identification of a specific pattern of strengths and weaknesses that can be used to guide intervention efforts. In other cases, assessment may reveal a flat profile of pervasive developmental delays, even when more specific tests are used.

Norm-referenced testing is important because it provides objective methods for identifying levels of functioning, but there are major limitations to test score interpretation when one or more severe weaknesses are identified in a child's neuropsychological profile. Although norm-referenced scores indicating functioning at or below the 1st percentile relative to same-age peers may be objective appraisals of performance that clearly support the need for intervention, they do not offer parents and intervention specialists much insight into exactly where the child is functioning on a developmental continuum. With the downward extension context in mind, clinicians often are trying to apply an assessment framework that connects a preschool child's current level of functioning with functioning that will be expected by school age. The more appropriate framework for interpretation, however, would be to view the child's current functioning in the context of infant development. The neuropsychological profile of a 3-year-old scoring at the 1st percentile reflects functioning that is likely to be comparable to a child age 2 or younger. Clinicians familiar with child development from birth to age 3, and familiar with the assessment techniques used to assess development from birth to age 3, will have a more appropriate context for understanding the performance of a preschool-aged child that is exhibiting severe developmental delays in one or more areas. The context of birth-to-3 development and assessment enables clinicians to provide more effective interpretations and offer appropriate recommendations for intervention efforts that extend far beyond the information offered by noting the presence of an extremely low norm-referenced score.

Although norm-referenced tests are critical for providing objective comparisons of a child's development relative to typically developing similar-age children, clinicians must remain wary of the allure of strict psychometric approaches to test validation and test interpretation. A strict psychometric approach advocates for the use of scores that are identified through analyses as the most reliable. This often leads to the interpretation of composite scores rather than subtest scores due the higher reliability estimates obtained when combining several subtests to form a composite. In reality, despite the mathematical fact that the larger sampling of behavior reflected in a composite score will always yield a quantitative estimate of reliability that is greater than the estimate obtained with a single subtest, the higher reliability estimates may very well be illusory in nature. The idea that error variance is distributed randomly and will even out across multiple subtests, thereby increasing the reliability of a composite score, is a questionable assumption for school-age children and a very untenable one for preschool-age children. From a conceptual perspective, combining the performance from two or more subtests that have poor reliability estimates and may not be representing the actual performance levels of a child cannot produce a composite score that can be considered a much more reliable representation of actual performance simply by the application of a mathematical formula to estimate reliability.

Clinicians must keep in mind that no matter what statistics are reported regarding the reliability of a standardized test, preschool children are inherently unreliable sources of information (Heffelfinger & Koop, 2009; McCloskey, 1990). Variations in performance on well-standardized tests that may be observed from one test session to another, one day to another, or one week to another do not represent flaws in the reliability of the tests that are being used – they represent the reality of early child development. Young children are not very reliable sources of information about their cognitive, academic, social/emotional, or adaptive development. Preschool children generally are lacking in stamina for tasks that require a great deal of listening, attending, and thinking. Taxing a child beyond their capability for meaningful engagement may result in a host of negative emotional and behavioral reactions, all of which may be reactions that are atypical for the child. Clinicians must walk a very fine line between getting the best possible performance and pushing a child too hard or too far.

When the line is crossed, clinicians face the very real possibility of having instigated symptom-like behaviors in a child that is generally symptom-free. A child's sensitivity to failure also must be assessed frequently throughout each test session. If a child senses that they are not doing well, they may begin to withdraw and limit their responding to examiner requests or shut down completely and refuse to continue with the assessment. It may be necessary to alternate administration of individual subtests with play sessions or down time to ensure that valid estimates of what the child can and cannot do are obtained. Clinicians must be making judgments about every task administered in terms of the extent to which performance is a valid reflection of the child's understanding of the task and their ability to offer a response. For preschool-aged children, and perhaps for all children, reliability and validity are constructs that are manifested primarily from the nature of the relationship formed, and maintained, between the clinician and the child.

The validity of assessment results will depend greatly on the application of a process-oriented approach to interpretation; observations about how a child performs a task are crucial in the preschool years and may be much more important than the scores that are produced by the observed behaviors (Baron, 2018; Baron & Leonberger, 2012; Heffelfinger & Koop, 2009; Hooper et al., 2007). This is especially the case when errors or inefficiencies are observed. In many instances, process-oriented observations and interpretation can help to identify specific cognitive deficits that may be at the root of problems when performing complex, multifactorial tasks. Clinicians also need to know how scoring rules affect performance estimates. Although criteria for earning a score on an item may not be met, there may be a large, clinically relevant difference between a near miss due to lack of attention to detail and a response that reflects little or no grasp of the task or its demands (McCloskey & Perkins, 2012).

Clinicians must always keep in mind that the purpose of the assessment is to characterize as accurately as possible the cognitive, preacademic, social/emotional, and adaptive functioning of the child. In some cases, the structure and standardized administration and scoring procedures of norm-referenced tests may limit the amount of useful information that can be obtained during an assessment. It may be necessary to make adaptations to standardized assessment tasks and procedures as a means of identifying ways that enable a child to engage with a task and attain success (Heffelfinger & Koop, 2009; McCloskey & Perkins, 2012). Such adaptation should occur after the use of the standardized assessment procedures. Reporting of norm-referenced test scores should always be based on performance that was obtained using the standardized administration procedures. When adaptations are made, the specifics of the adaptation should be described in detail along with the results of their application so that other clinicians can replicate the procedures and results. In many instances, the adapted procedures may lead to a blueprint for intervention efforts (Heffelfinger & Koop, 2009; McCloskey & Perkins, 2012).

Maintaining a child's attention and effort for the duration of an assessment session can be very challenging. Productive assessment sessions often hinge on the effective use of behavior management techniques to maintain engagement and ensure optimal responding during testing sessions. In some instances, the first author of this chapter has allowed a child the freedom to shape their interactions with the clinician during the first session to see how they behave when no specific techniques are used to communicate expectations and manage behaviors and outcomes. If the child is unable to self-regulate in a productive manner (which is the case more often than not), behavior management techniques are then used in the remaining sessions to observe how the child responds to their use.

Clinical Procedures

An NPA-C should start with an interview of the parents or caregiver to establish the referral question and to obtain a detailed developmental history as well as a detailed description of the parents' perceptions of the child's current levels of functioning across multiple domains. It is recommended that the initial interview be conducted with the parents alone without the child. Brief interview updates can be conducted with the parents while the child is present prior to and after assessment sessions. Interviews also should be conducted with any teachers or other professionals that have had multiple opportunities to interact with the child. Parents and teachers or other professionals should complete ratings scales that assess general behavior, adaptive functioning, attention, and executive functions.

Although an NPA-C is intended to be more comprehensive in nature than a traditional developmental assessment, clinicians must keep in mind the challenges inherent in attempting to assess preschool children, especially those being referred for a neuropsychological evaluation. As noted in the previous section, preschool children generally are lacking in stamina for tasks that require a great deal of listening, attending, thinking, and responding. Taxing a child beyond their capability for meaningful engagement is likely to compromise the assessment process and reduce the accuracy and validity of test results. These circumstances necessitate an approach to assessment that attempts to answer the referral questions in a comprehensive but concise manner. Clinicians seeking a comprehensive picture of the child's current levels of functioning in multiple domains must accept that fact that obtaining such information will require several short assessment sessions, often completed across several weeks, rather than a single-day marathon encounter. Ideally, individual assessment sessions should not last longer than 90 minutes, and in many cases clinicians would be well-served by planning sessions that involve no more than 45 minutes of direct assessment activities. The latter portion of one or more assessment sessions should involve observation of the parent playing with the child and then separating from the child (Heffelfinger & Koop, 2009).

Rather than being viewed as an inconvenience, the necessity of multiple short assessment sessions can be recognized as an opportunity to increase the validity of the assessment. Multiple sessions enable the clinician to see variations in the child's ability to regulate their perceptions, emotions, thoughts, and actions and how their demeanor does or does not change with increased familiarity with the clinician. Scheduling each session for a different start time increases the clinician's ability to gain an understanding of how the child's functioning may vary based on time of day. Clinicians also should be prepared to deal with the fact that a child who initially presents as very shy or withdrawn may become over-active and test the limits of acceptable behavior in later sessions.

To ensure that the child is as engaged in the assessment process as possible, it may be necessary to conduct some (or all) of the direct testing while a parent is in the room, as this may initially be the only way to get the child to engage with the clinician. If a parent's presence is necessary to initiate the assessment, it should be explained to the parent that the most valid assessment results are obtained when parents are not in the room, and that the clinician will signal the parents with a nonverbal gesture when it appears that the child has acclimated and their presence is no longer needed. Parents also should be instructed to remain in the waiting area during the entire assessment session in case their presence is needed again to calm and reassure the child. Clinicians need to be prepared for the fact that separation from a parent may take one or more session to accomplish and in some extreme cases may never be accomplished.

Assessments should involve a full range of input/output channels, using auditory, visual, and tactile stimuli, individually and in various combinations, and require oral, fine motor, and gross motor responses. Assessment tasks also should address pre-academic skills. Pre-academic skill assessment tasks are not different from those used in traditional developmental assessments. What can differ greatly, however, is the perspective and knowledge base brought to bear in the interpretation of the child's performance of these tasks.

Interpretation and Reporting of Results

Interpretation of test results requires the clinician to make judgments about the validity of the assessment process and the assessment results to ensure that the child's current levels of functioning across multiple domains are characterized as accurately as possible. Even when the assessment is judged to be a valid representation of the child's capabilities, the temporary and tentative nature of the obtained results must be kept in mind. During preschool years, developmental changes may occur very quickly; developmental spurts and lags are typical for all children. The possibilities of rapid changes in development should be kept in mind when comparing the child's performance with the performance of peers in a standardization sample. Note carefully the age range bands used in norming test performance. Narrow age bands with two- to three-month increments are much better at characterizing developmental changes than broader age bands in increments of six months or more.

The focus of interpretation should be on addressing the initial referral question through a summary of strengths and weaknesses and a detailed characterization of the child's performance in each domain that was assessed. In summary, the report should describe what the child does well (strengths), what the child has difficulty doing (weaknesses/deficits/challenges), what needs to be done to address difficulties, and who can do what needs to be done (e.g., parents, teachers, specialists). It is in the best interest of the child to avoid diagnostic labeling except in cases where it is necessary to obtain support for interventions or when the assessment results are strongly indicative of a syndrome with known early onset in preschool years. Parents should be provided feedback about the results of the assessment. It is recommended that the parent feedback session be conducted without the child present so that parents can focus on understanding the results and their implications. Over the years, the first author of this chapter has found it beneficial to provide recommendations in three separate sections: 1) what parents can do to help the child, 2) what professionals can do to help the child, and 3) what the child can do to help themselves. Regarding the final section, except in cases of extreme deficit, it is always possible to find one specific action that the child would be able to perform at the request of parents that would help the child improve their functioning in some way. Including one or more recommendations for the child provides the opportunity to instill in the child a sense of personal agency that can lead to increased awareness of the need for, and benefits of, improved self-regulation.

Challenges to Validity and Limitations

Completing a valid NPA-C requires a great deal of patience, sensitivity, and clinical acumen. Even when the clinician performs in an expert manner, the nature of the child's condition is the most significant factor in determining the validity of the assessment's findings. As noted in earlier sections, preschool-aged children are inherently unreliable sources of information. Preschool children's more frequent needs for sleep, eating, and toileting create narrow windows for optimal engagement with assessment tasks. Even when available for engagement, performance on direct assessment measures can be negatively influenced by the relative lack of self-regulation that is typical in this age range. These self-regulation shortcomings include a limited capacity for focusing and sustaining attention and effort – even for tasks that the child may find very interesting, a limited capacity for timely initiation and completion of a response to the clinician's external demands for immediate performance, a limited or greatly fluctuating capacity for regulating emotions, and a limited capacity for separating from parents. Many or all of these self-regulation limitations are likely to be exacerbated in children that have medical conditions, mental disorders, or traumatic injury.

Challenges to completion of a valid NPA-C also stem from limitations of instrumentation and knowledge available to clinicians. The number and type of tests that can be used with preschool-aged children is very limited, typically necessitating the use of tasks from multiple tests that were not normed on the same standardization sample. As a result, the cost of test materials required to assemble a flexible battery can be prohibitive for those who do not intend to make preschool assessment the exclusive focus of their clinical work. For those who do want to make preschool assessment their primary focus, there is a general lack of availability of training opportunities for supervised learning and implementation of best practices in NPA-C (Baron & Anderson, 2012).

Conclusion

The need for more specialized assessment of children in the preschool age range continues to increase. Concurrently, research on the brain development of preschool-aged children continues to grow along with research on new methods that can be used to assess functioning in various domains. These trends are likely to spur greater interest in NPA-C as a specialized form of psychoeducational assessment. Specialized training programs for clinicians who want to specialize in NPA-C, however, is an important growth milestone that has yet to be reached.

References

Achenbach, T.M., & Rescorla, L.A. (2000). *Manual for the ASEBA Preschool Forms and Profiles: An integrated system of multi-informant assessment.* Burlington, VT: University of Vermont Department of Psychiatry.

Akshoomoff, N., Brown, T. T., Bakeman, R., & Hagler, D. J. Jr. (2018). Developmental differentiation of executive functions on the NIH Toolbox Cognition Battery. *Neuropsychology, 32*(7), 777–783. doi:10.1037/new0000476

Anderson, P. J., & Burnett, A. (2017). Assessing developmental delay in early childhood—concerns with the Bayley-III scales. *The Clinical Neuropsychologist, 31*(2), 371–381. doi:10.1080/13854046.2016.1216518

Anderson, P. J., De Luca, C. R., Hutchinson, E., Roberts, G., & Doyle, L. W. (2010). Underestimation of developmental delay by the new Bayley-III Scale. *Archives of Pediatrics & Adolescent Medicine, 164*(4), 352–356. doi:10.1001/archpediatrics.2010.20

Anderson, P. J., & Reidy, N. (2012). Assessing executive function in preschoolers. *Neuropsychology Review, 22*(4), 345–360. doi:10.1007/s11065-012-9220-3

Anderson, S. W., Damasio, H., Tranel, D., & Damasio, A. R. (2000). Long-term seque-lae of prefrontal cortex damage acquired in early childhood. *Developmental Neuro-psychology, 18*(3), 281–296. doi:10.1207/s1532694202anderson

Armstrong, M. B., & Nettleton, S. K. (2004). Attention deficit hyperactivity disorder and preschool children. *Seminars in Speech and Language., 25*(03), 225–232. doi:10.1055/s-2004-833670

Aylward, G. P. (1997). What is infant and early childhood neuropsychology? In G. P. Aylward, *Infant and early childhood neuropsychology* (pp. 1–12). Springer. doi:10.1007/978-1-4615-5927-6_1

Ayres, J. (1989). *Sensory Integration And Praxis Tests (SIPT)*. Western Psychological Services.

Barnes, M. A., & Raghubar, K. P. (2014). Mathematics development and difficulties: The role of visual–spatial perception and other cognitive skills. *Pediatric Blood & Cancer, 61*(10), 1729–1733. doi:10.1002/pbc.24909

Baron, I. S. (2018). *Neuropsychological evaluation of the child: Domains, methods, and case studies.* Oxford University Press. doi:10.1017/s0012162204220837

Baron, I. S., & Anderson, P. J. (2012). Neuropsychological assessment of preschoolers. *Neuropsychology Review, 22*(4), 211–212. doi:10.1007/s11065-012-9221-2

Baron, I. S., & Leonberger, K. A. (2012). Assessment of intelligence in the preschoolperiod. *Neuropsychology Review, 22*(4), 334–344. doi:10.1007/s11065-0129215-0

Baron, I. S., Litman, F. R., Ahronovich, M. D., & Baker, R. (2012). Late preterm birth: A review of medical and neuropsychological childhood outcomes. *Neuropsychology Review, 22*(4), 438–450. doi:10.1007/s11065-012-9210-5

Basso, A. (2003). *Aphasia and its therapy.* Oxford University Press.

Bates, E., & Roe, K. (2001). Language development in children with unilateral brain injury. In C. A. Nelson & M. Luciana (Eds.), *Handbook of developmental cognitive neuroscience* (pp. 281). MIT Press.

Bauer, P. J., Leventon, J. S., & Varga, N. L. (2012). Neuropsychological assessment of memory in preschoolers. *Neuropsychology Review, 22*(4), 414–424. doi:10.1007/s11065-012-9219-9

Beery, K. E., Buktenica, N. A., & Beery, N. A. (2010). *Beery-buktenica test of visual-motor integration.* The Psychological Corporation.

Bellinger, D. C., Wypij, D., Rappaport, L. A., Jonas, R. A., Wernovsky, G., & Newburger, J. W. (2003). Neurodevelopmental status at eight years in children with dextro-transposition of The great arteries: The Boston Circulatory Arrest Trial. *The Journal of Thoracic and Cardiovascular Surgery, 126*(5), 1385–1396. doi:10.1016/s00225223(03)00711-6

Berlin, L. J., Brooks-Gunn, J., McCarton, C., & McCormick, M. C. (1998). The effect-iveness of early intervention: Examining risk factors and pathways to enhanced development. *Preventive Medicine, 27*(2), 238–245. doi:10.1006/pmed.1998.0282

Blair, C. (2016). Developmental science and executive function. *Current Directions in Psychological Science, 25*(1), 3–7. doi:10.1177/0963721415622634

Blair, C., Zelazo, P. D., & Greenberg, M. T. (2016). Measurement of executive function in early childhood. *Developmental Neuropsychology., 28*(2), 561–567. doi:10.1207/s15326942dn2802_1

Blank, M., Rose, S. A., & Berlin, L. J. (2003). *PLAI 2: Preschool language assessment instrument.* Pro-ed..

Boll, T. J. (1993).*Children's category test: Slides for young children.* Psychological Corporation.

Breaux, R. P., Griffith, S. F., & Harvey, E. A. (2016). Preschool neuropsychological measures aspredictors of later attention deficit hyperactivity disorder. *Journal of Abnormal Child Psychology*, 44(8), 1455–1471. doi:10.1007/s10802-016-0140-1

Brown, T. T., & Jernigan, T. L. (2012). Brain development during the preschool years. *Neuropsychology Review*, 22(4), 313–333. doi:10.1007/s11065-012-9214-1

Bruininks, B. D. (2005). *Bruininks-oseretsky test of motor proficiency: BOT-2*. NCS Pearson/AGS.

Butler, R. W., & Copeland, D. R. (2002). Attentional processes and their remediation in children treated for cancer: A literature review and the development of a therapeutic approach. *Journal of the International Neuropsychological Society*, 8(1), 115–124. doi:10.1017/s1355617702811110

Carlson, S. M. (2005). Developmentally sensitive measures of executive function in preschool children. *Developmental Neuropsychology*, 28(2), 595–616. doi:10.1207/s15326942dn2802_3

Chang, Y. C., Shih, W., & Kasari, C. (2016). Friendships in preschool children with autism spectrum disorder: What holds them back, child characteristics or teacher behavior? *Autism*, 20(1), 65–74. doi:10.1177/1362361314567761

Conners, C. K., & Staff, M. H. S. (2001). *Conners' kiddie continuous performance test (K-CPT V. 5)*. MHS.

Conners, C. K., & Goldstein, S. (2009). *Conners early childhood: Manual*. Multi-Health Systems Incorporated.

Conti-Ramsden, G., & Durkin, K. (2012). Language development and assessment in the preschool period. *Neuropsychology Review*, 22(4), 384–401. doi:10.1007/s11065-012-9208-z

Cowan, N., & Alloway, T. P. (1997). The development of working memory. In N. Cowan (Ed.), *The development of memory in childhood* (pp. 163–199). Psychology Press.

Dakin, S., & Frith, U. (2005). Vagaries of visual perception in autism. *Neuron*, 48(3), 497–507. doi:10.1016/j.neuron.2005.10.018

Dalal, R. H., & Loeb, D. F. (2005). Imitative production of regular past tensed by English-speaking children with specific language impairment. *International Journal of Language & Communication Disorders*, 40(1), 67–82. doi:10.1080/13682820410001734163

Dawson, J. I., Stout, C. E., & Eyer, J. A. (2003). spelt-3: structured photographic expressive language test–Third edition. ProEd.

Dean, R. S., & Woodcock, R. W. (2003). *Dean-woodcock sensory-motor battery*. Riverside Publ.

Dennis, M., Fletcher, J. M., Rogers, T., Hetherington, R., & Francis, D. J. (2002). Object-based and action-based visual perception in children with spina bifida and hydrocephalus. *Journal of the International Neuropsychological Society*, 8(1), 95–106. doi:10.1017/S135561771020094

Deysach, R. E. (1986). The role of neuropsychological assessment in the comprehensive evaluation of preschool-age children. *School Psychology Review.*, 15(2), 233–244.

Diamond, A. (1985). Development of the ability to use recall to guide action, as indicated by infants' performance on $A\bar{B}$. *Child Development*, 56(4), 868–883. doi:10.2307/1130099

Diamond, A. (1988). Abilities and neural mechanisms underlying $A\bar{B}$ performance. *Child Development*, 59(2), 523–527. doi:10.2307/1130330

Diamond, A. (1991). Neuropsychological insights into the meaning of object concept development. In S. Carey & R. Gelman (Eds.), *The Jean Piaget Symposium series.*

The epigenesis of mind: Essays on biology and cognition (pp. 67–110). Lawrence Erlbaum Associates, Inc.

Diamond, A. (2016). Why improving and assessing executive functions early in life is critical. In J. A. Griffin, P. McCardle, & L. S. Freund (Eds.), *Executive function in preschool-age children: Integrating measurement, neurodevelopment, and translational research* (pp. 11–43). American Psychological Association. doi:10.1037/14797-002

Diamond, A., Carlson, S. M., & Beck, D. M. (2005). Preschool children's performance in task switching on the dimensional change card sort task: Separating the dimensions aids the ability to switch. *Developmental Neuropsychology, 28*(2), 689–729. doi:10.1207/s15326942dn2802_7

Diamond, A., & Doar, B. (1989). The performance of human infants on a measure of frontal cortex function, the delayed response task. *Developmental Psychobiology: The Journal of the International Society for Developmental Psychobiology, 22*(3), 271–294. doi:10.1002/dev.420220307

Diamond, A., & Goldman-Rakic, P. S. (1989). Comparison of human infants and rhesus monkeys on Piaget's AB task: Evidence for dependence on dorsolateral prefrontal cortex. *Experimental Brain Research, 74*(1), 24–40. doi:10.1007/BF00248277

Dunn, L. M., & Dunn, D. M. (2007). *PPVT-IV: Peabody picture vocabulary test (PPVT-IV).* Pearson.

Dunn, W. (2014). *Sensory profile 2.* Pearson.

Elliott, C. D. (2007). *Differential ability scales—second edition: Administration and scoring manual* (2nd ed.). Harcourt Assessment.

Eslinger, P., Flaherty, C., & Benton, A. L. (2004). Developmental outcomes after early prefrontal cortex damage. *Brain and Cognition, 55*(1), 84–103. doi:10.1016/S0278-2626(03)00281-1

Espy, K. A., & Bull, R. (2005). Inhibitory processes in young children and individual variation in short-term memory. *Developmental Neuropsychology, 28*(2), 669–688. doi:10.1207/s15326942dn2802_6

Espy, K. A., Kaufmann, P. M., McDiarmid, M. D., & Glisky, M. L. (1999). Executive functioning in preschool children: Performance on A-not-B and other delayed response format tasks. *Brain and Cognition, 41*(2), 178–199. doi:10.1006/brcg.1999.1117

Fedrizzi, E., Anderloni, A., Bono, R., Bova, S., Farinotti, M., Inverno, M., & Savoiardo, S. (1998). Eye-movement disorders and visual-perceptual impairment in diplegia children born preterm: A clinical evaluation. *Developmental Medicine & Child Neurology, 40*(10), 682–688.

Fenson, L., Dale, P. S., Reznick, J. S., Bates, E., Thal, D. J., Pethick, S. J., … Stiles, J. (1994). Variability in early communicative development. *Monographs of the Society for Research in Child Development, 59*(5), v–173. doi:10.2307/1166093

Fletcher, J. M., Dennis, M., Northrup, H., Barnes, M. A., Hannay, H. J., Landry, S. H., … Francis, D. J. (2004). Spina bifida, genes, brain, and development. In L. M. Gidden (Ed.), *International review of research in mental retardation* (Vol. 29, pp. 63–117). Elsevier Academic Press.

Folio, M. R., & Fewell, R. R. (2000). *Peabody developmental motor scales. Examiner's manual* (2nd ed.). Pro-Ed.

Freitag, H., & Tuxhorn, I. (2005). Cognitive function in preschool children after epilepsy surgery: Rationale for early intervention. *Epilepsia, 46*(4), 561–567. doi:10.1111/j.0013-9580.2005.03504.x

Gathercole, S. E. (1998). The development of memory. *The Journal of Child Psychology and Psychiatry and Allied Disciplines*, 39(1), 3–27. doi:10.1017/S0021963097001753

Gathercole, S. E. (2002). Memory development during the childhood years. In A. D. Baddely, M. D. Kopelman, & B. A. Wilson (Eds.), *Handbook of memory disorders* (2nd ed.). 475–500.Wiley.

Gioia, G. A., Espy, K. A., & Isquith, P. K. (1996). *Behavior rating inventory of executive function-preschool version (BRIEF-P)*. Psychological Assessment Resources.

Golden, C. J. (1981). The Luria-Nebraska children's battery: Theory and formulation. In G. W. Hynd & J. Obrzut (Eds.), *Neuropsychological assessment and the school-age child: Issues and procedures* (pp. 277–302). Allyn & Bacon is th epublisher.

Griffin, J. A., McArdle, P., & Freund, L. S. (Eds). (2016). *Executive function in preschool-age children: Integrating measurement, neurodevelopmental and translational research*. American Psyxchological Association.

Hartlage, L. C., & Telzrow, C. F. (1986). *Neuropsychological assessment and intervention with children and adolescents*. Professional Resource Exchange, Inc.

Heffelfinger, A. K., & Koop, J. I. (2009). A description of preschool neuropsychological assessment in the PINT Clinic after the first 5 years. *The Clinical Neuropsychologist*, 23(1), 51–76. doi:10.1080/13854040801945052

Henderson, S., Sugden, D., & Barnett, A. (2007). *Movement assessment battery for children-2* (2nd ed.). Pearson Assessment.

Hongwanishkul, D., Happaney, K. R., Lee, W. S., & Zelazo, P. D. (2005). Assessment of hot and cool executive function in young children: Age-related changes and individual differences. *Developmental Neuropsychology*, 28(2), 617–644. doi:10.1207/s15326942dn2802_4

Hooper, S. R. (1991). Neuropsychological assessment of the preschool child: Issues and procedures. In B. A. Bracken (Ed.), *The psychoeducational assessment of preschool children* (2nd ed., pp. 465–485). Allyn and Bacon.

Hooper, S. R. (2004). Neuropsychological assessment of the preschool child. In B. A. Bracken (Ed.), *The psychoeducational assessment of preschool children* (pp. 383–398). Lawrence Erlbaum Associates Publishers.

Hooper, S. R., Molnar, A., Beswick, J., & Jacobi-Vessels, J. (2007). Neuropsychological assessment of the preschool child: Expansion of the field. In B. A. Bracken & R. Nagle (Eds.), *Psychoeducational assessment of preschool children* (4th ed., pp. 435–464). Routledge.

Howard, S. J., Vasseleu, E., Neilsen-Hewett, C., & Cliff, K. (2018). Evaluation of the Preschool Situational Self-Regulation Toolkit (PRSIST) Program for supporting children's early self-regulation development: Study protocol for a cluster randomized controlled trial. *Trials*, 19(1), 64. doi:10.1186/s13063-018-2455-4

Isquith, P. K., Crawford, J. S., Espy, K. A., & Gioia, G. A. (2005). Assessment of executive function in preschool-aged children. *Mental Retardation and Developmental Disabilities Research Reviews*, 11(3), 209–215. doi:10.1002/mrdd.20075

Johnson, M. H. (2001). Functional brain development in humans. *Nature Reviews Neuroscience*, 2(7), 475.

Johnson, M. H., Posner, M. I., & Rothbart, M. K. (1991). Components of visual orienting in early infancy: Contingency learning, anticipatory looking, and disengaging. *Journal of Cognitive Neuroscience*, 3(4), 335–344.

Jorquera-Cabrera, S., Romero-Ayuso, D., Rodriguez-Gil, G., & Triviño-Juárez, J. M. (2017). Assessment of sensory processing characteristics in children between 3 and 11 years old: a systematic review. *Frontiers in pediatrics*, 5, 57.

Kaufman, A. S. (2015). *Kaufman assessment battery for children-II: KABC-II.* Pearson.

Korkman, M. (1980). *NEPS. Lasten neuropsykologinen tutkimus. Käsikirja (NEPS. Neuropsychological Assessment of Children. Manual).* Psykologien kustannus.

Korkman, M. (1988). NEPSY-An adaptation of Luria's investigation for young children. *The Clinical Neuropsychologist, 2*(4), 375–392.

Korkman, M., Kirk, U., & Kemp, S. (1998). *NEPSY: A developmental neuropsychological assessment.* The Psychological Corporation.

Korkman, M., Kirk, U., & Kemp, S. L. (2007). *NEPSY II.* Administrative manual. Psychological Corporation.

Leonard, L. B. (1998). *Children with specific language impairment.* MIT Press.

Lin, B., Liew, J., & Perez, M. (2019). Measurement of self-regulation in early childhood: Relations between laboratory and performance-based measures of effortful control and executive functioning. *Early Childhood Research Quarterly, 47,* 1–8.

Lorenzo, J., Barton, B., Arnold, S. S., & North, K. N. (2013). Cognitive features that distinguish preschool-age children with neurofibromatosis type 1 from their peers: A matched case- control study. *The Journal of Pediatrics, 163*(5), 1479–1483.

Luria, A. R. (1973). *The working brain: An introduction to neuropsychology* (B. Haigh, Trans.). Penguin.

Luria, A. R. (1980). *Higher cortical functions in man* (2nd ed.). (B. Haigh. Trans.). Basic Books.

Mahone, E. M. (2005). Measurement of attention and related functions in the preschool child. *Mental Retardation and Developmental Disabilities Research Reviews, 11*(3), 216–225.

Mahone, E. M., Pillion, J. P., & Hiemenz, J. R. (2001). Initial development of an auditory continuous performance test for preschoolers. *Journal of Attention Disorders, 5*(2), 93–106.

Mahone, E. M., & Schneider, H. E. (2012). Assessment of attention in preschoolers. *Neuropsychology Review, 22*(4), 361–383.

Martin, N. A., & Brownell, R. (2011a). *Expressive one-word picture vocabulary test-4 (EOWPVT-4).* Academic Therapy Publications.

Martin, N. A., & Brownell, R. (2011b). *Receptive one-word picture vocabulary test.* Academic Therapy Publications.

McCloskey, G. (1990). Selecting and using early childhood rating scales. *Topics in Early Childhood Special Education, 10*(3), 39–64.

McCloskey, G., & Perkins, L. A. (2012). *Essentials of executive functions assessment, volume(68).* John Wiley & Sons.

Miller-Kuhanek, H., Henry, D., Glennon, T., Parham, L. D., & Ecker, C. (2008). *The sensory processing measure.* Western Psychological Services.

Molfese, V. J., & Price, B. (2002). Neuropsychological assessment in infancy. In S. J. Segalowitz & I. Rapin (Eds..), *Handbook of Neuropsychology* (Vol. 8, 2nd ed., pp. 229–249). Elsevier. Part 1.

Molloy, C., Doyle, L. W., Makrides, M., & Anderson, P. J. (2012). Docosahexaenoic acid and visual functioning in preterm infants: A review. *Neuropsychology Review, 22*(4), 425–437.

Moore, T., Johnson, S., Haider, S., Hennessy, E., & Marlow, N. (2012). Relationship between test scores using the second and third editions of the Bayley Scales in extremely preterm children. *The Journal of Pediatrics, 160*(4), 553–558.

Morra, S., Panesi, S., Traverso, L., & Usai, M. C. (2018). Which tasks measure what? Reflections on executive function development and a commentary on Podjarny,

Kamawar, and Andrews (2017). *Journal of Experimental Child Psychology, 167,* 246–258.

Mrakotsky, C., & Heffelfinger, A. K. (2006). Neuropsychological assessment.. In J. L. Luby (Ed.), *Handbook of preschool mental health: Development, disorders and treatment* (pp. 283–310). Guilford Press.

Niemczyk, J., Equit, M., Braun-Bither, K., Klein, A. M., & von Gontard, A. (2015). Prevalence of incontinence, attention deficit/hyperactivity disorder and oppositional defiant disorder in preschool children. *European Child & Adolescent Psychiatry, 24* (7), 837–843.

Nygaard, E., Slinning, K., Moe, V., & Walhovd, K. B. (2016). Behavior and attention problems in eight-year-old children with prenatal opiate and poly-substance exposure: A longitudinal study. *PLoS One, 11*(6), e0158054.

O'Riordan, M. A., Plaisted, K. C., Driver, J., & Baron-Cohen, S. (2001). Superior visual search in autism. *Journal of Experimental Psychology: Human Perception and Performance, 27*(3), 719.

Overgaard, K. R., Aase, H., Torgersen, S., & Zeiner, P. (2016). Co-occurrence of ADHD and anxiety in preschool children. *Journal of Attention Disorders, 20*(7), 573–580.

Piek, J. P., Hands, B., & Licari, M. K. (2012). Assessment of motor functioning in the preschool period. *Neuropsychology Review, 22*(4), 402–413.

Posner, M. I., & Rothbart, M. K. (2006). *Educating the human brain.* American Psychological Association.

Raghubar, K. P., Barnes, M. A., Dennis, M., Cirino, P. T., Taylor, H., & Landry, S. (2015). Neurocognitive predictors of mathematical processing in school-aged children with spinabifida and their typically developing peers: Attention, working memory, and fine motorskills. *Neuropsychology, 29*(6), 861–873. doi:10.1037/neu0000196

Reitan, R. M., & Davison, L. A. (1974). *Neuropsychology: Current status and application.* Winston and Sons.

Rey-Casserly, C. (1999). Neuropsychological assessment of preschool children. In I. Romero & E. V. Nuttall Eds., *Assessing and screening preschoolers: Psychological andeducational dimensions* (2nd ed., pp. 281–295). Pro-Ed..

Reynolds, C. R., & Kamphaus, R. W. (2015). *BASC-3 manual.* Pearson.

Rice, M. L., & Wexler, K. (2001). *Rice/Wexler test of early grammar impairment.* Psychological Corporation.

Roid, G. H., Miller, L. J., Pomplun, M., & Koch, C. (2013). *Leiter international performance scale–third edition.* Stoelting Company.

Rueda, M. R., Posner, M. I., & Rothbart, M. K. (2005). The development of executive attention: Contributions to the emergence of self-regulation. *Developmental Neuropsychology, 28*(2), 573–594.

Ruff, H. A., & Capozzoli, M. C. (2003). Development of attention and distractibility in the first 4 years of life. *Developmental Psychology, 39*(5), 877.

Schrank, F. A., Mather, N., & McGrew, K. S. (2014). *Woodcock-Johnson IV tests of oral language.* Riverside Publisher.

Schrank, F. A., McGrew, K. S., & Mather, N. (2014). *Woodcock-Johnson IV tests of cognitive abilities.* Riverside Publisher.

Semel, E., Wiig, E. H., & Secord, W. (2006). *Clinical evaluation of language fundamentals - preschool 2 UK edition (CELF-Preschool2 UK).* London: Pearson Assessment.

Stiers, P., Vanderkelen, R., Vanneste, G., Coene, S., De Rammelaere, M., & Vandenbussche, E. (2002). Visual–perceptual impairment in a random sample of children with cerebral palsy. *Developmental Medicine and Child Neurology, 44*(6), 370–382.

Tondon, M., & Pergjika, A. (2017). Attention deficit hyperactivity disorder in preschool-age children. *Child and Adolescent Psychiatric Clinics, 26*(3), 523–538.

Temple, C. M. (1997). Cognitive neuropsychology and its application to children. *Journal of Child Psychology and Psychiatry, 38*(1), 27–52.

Tramontana, M. G., & Hooper, S. R. (1988). Child neuropsychological assessment. In *Assessment issues in child neuropsychology* (pp. 3–38). Boston, MA: Springer.

van den Hout, B. M., de Vries, L. S., Meiners, L. C., Stiers, P., van der Schouw, Y. T., Jennekens-Schinkel, A., ... van Nieuwenhuizen, O. (2004). Visual perceptual impairment in children at 5 years of age with perinatal haemorrhagic or ischaemic brain damage in relation to cerebral magnetic resonance imaging. *Brain and Development, 26*(4), 251–261.

Verdine, B. N., Irwin, C. M., Golinkoff, R. M., & Hirsh-Pasek, K. (2014). Contributions of executive function and spatial skills to preschool mathematics achievement. *Journal of Experimental Child Psychology, 126*, 37–51.

Vicari, S., Caravale, B., Carlesimo, G. A., Casadei, A. M., & Allemand, F. (2004). Spatial working memory deficits in children at ages 3-4 who were low birth weight, preterm infants. *Neuropsychology, 18*(4), 673.

Wechsler, D. (2012). *Wechsler preschool and primary scale of intelligence—fourth edition.* San Antonio, TX: The Psychological Corporation.

Wichstrøm, L., Berg-Nielsen, T. S., Angold, A., Egger, H. L., Solheim, E., & Sveen, T. H. (2012). Prevalence of psychiatric disorders in preschoolers. *Journal of Child Psychology and Psychiatry, 53*(6), 695–705.

Willoughby, M. T., & Blair, C. B. (2016). Longitudinal measurement of executive function in preschoolers.

Willoughby, M. T., Blair, C. B., Wirth, R. J., & Greenberg, M. (2010). The measurement of executive function at age 3 years: Psychometric properties and criterion validity of a new battery of tasks. *Psychological Assessment, 22*(2), 306.

Willoughby, M. T., Blair, C. B., Wirth, R. J., & Greenberg, M. (2012a). The measurement of executive function at age 5: Psychometric properties and relationship to academic achievement. *Psychological Assessment, 24*(1), 226.

Willoughby, M. T., Wirth, R. J., & Blair, C. B. (2012b). Executive function in early childhood: Longitudinal measurement invariance and developmental change. *Psychological Assessment, 24*(2), 418.

Wilson, B. C. (1986). An approach to the neuropsychological assessment of the preschool child with developmental deficits. *Handbook of Clinical Neuropsychology, 2*, 121–171.

Wilson B. C. (1992). The neuropsychological assessment of the preschool child: a branching model. In: Boller F., Grafman J., series editors. Rapin I, Segalowitz SJ, volume editors. *Handbook of neuropsychology: Child neuropsychology* (Vol. 6, 377). Amsterdam/New York: Elsevier.

Wozniak, J. R. (2015). Executive functioning deficits in preschool children with fetal alcohol spectrum disorders. *Child Neuropsychology, 21*(6), 716–731.

Zimmerman, I. L., Steiner, V. G., & Pond, R. E. (2002). *Preschool Language Scale, (PLS-4).* San Antonio,TX: The Psychological Corporation.

Chapter 16

Understanding the Impact of Poverty and Implications for Assessment with Young Children from Low-Resource Backgrounds

Julia Mendez and Doré LaForett

Understanding the Impact of Poverty and Implications for Assessment with Children from Low-Resource Backgrounds

Introduction and Goals of the Chapter

At first glance, the impact of poverty on learning and developmental outcomes for young children is straightforward. Poverty creates an environment in which restricted resources constrain the ability of the family to provide for children's basic needs. Unfortunately, decades of research on children growing up in poverty have revealed the far-reaching effects of limited resources on a range of child and family outcomes (Children's Defense Fund, 2018; Mendez, Fantuzzo & Cicchetti, 2002). This chapter seeks to organize the literature on poverty and child development to help the practitioner and researcher be more informed regarding how low-resource environments shape learning and child development. A parallel goal is to highlight important areas for assessment that can reveal learning challenges and opportunities for children from low-resource backgrounds.

What Is "Low-Resource" and How Many Children are Impacted?

"Low-resource" is a term used in this chapter to signify that children from low-income backgrounds are often faced with a range of other environmental challenges that are typically found within the research literature on low-income families and neighborhoods. Other related terms that are found in the literature include "low-income children," "impoverished communities," or "children/families from impoverished backgrounds." While definitions have often focused on ways to define and categorize levels of poverty in various communities, the literature is clear in that variation among the experiences of children from low-income households is the norm (Mendez, et al., 2002). In this chapter, we seek to highlight the importance of assessment of variation in access to learning and developmental experiences (e.g., opportunity gap) in order to explain why some children from low-resource backgrounds are able to thrive despite exposure to adversity, while others show less robust growth.

Historically, estimates of childhood poverty have relied upon national data measuring household income, size, and cost-of-living indicators (Bishaw & Benson, 2018). The American Community Survey, which is used to provide annual estimates of poverty status, reports that overall poverty in the United States declined from a rate of 14 percent in 2016 to a rate of 13.4 percent in 2017, and this marked the fourth consecutive year of decline (Bishaw & Benson, 2018).

In examining national data on children living in poverty, the Children's Defense Fund (2018) reported a decline in child poverty from 18.0 percent in 2016 to 17.5 percent in 2017. Presently about 1 in 5 children under 18 are living in poverty, which is just over 12.8 million children (Children's Defense Fund, 2018).

While these figures account for all families with children in poverty, we know that extreme poverty has even greater impact on the developing child (Cuddy, Venator, & Reeves, 2015). Using estimates from the Children's Defense Fund (2018), we see about 8 percent of children experience extreme poverty, which is defined as annual income of half of the poverty level.

Addressing childhood poverty has been a concern for the federal government since the 1960s and the advent of the sociopolitical movement of the Great Society. During this era, government assistance programs such as Head Start were designed and launched to intervene and interrupt the transmission of poverty to the next generation of children (Zigler & Styfco, 1996). To accomplish this, investments were made in communities to offer dual generation intervention programs for low-income children, where efforts were made to impact families and their children simultaneously. Many of these initial foundational principles can be seen in today's Head Start and Early Head Start programs, which have expanded over 50+ years to serve pregnant mothers and their children 0–5 years, along with children with disabilities.

Eligibility for Means-Tested Government Assistance

In addition to school readiness programs such as Head Start, supports from the federal government for low-income child populations include health insurance programs, food assistance, housing and child care subsidies. These means-tested government assistance programs, such as Temporary Assistance for Needy Families (TANF) or Supplemental Nutrition Assistance Program (SNAP), use eligibility and documentation requirements to determine families' access to benefits. When different criteria for eligibility are implemented, this can introduce challenges and inequity into a system designed to support children from low-resource backgrounds. Efforts to address some of these problems across government assistance programs are being pursued. For example, the Child Care Block Development Grant's (CCBGD) most recent authorization allowed parents to keep their child care subsidy for 12 months prior to needing re-approval; prior law required renewal of subsidies over a three-month period, which was a significant time and resource burden for low-income families. Other research is uncovering variation in the user experience for applying for child care subsidies among low-income Hispanic populations (Hill, Gennetian, & Mendez, 2019). Taken together, while means-tested government assistance is available, constraints and burdens associated with uptake of services result in many families from low-resource backgrounds having unreliable access and unequal uptake of these supportive programs (Alvira-Hammond & Gennetian, 2015).

Racial and Ethnic Variation in Low-Income Populations

The United States has been in a period of rapid diversification in cultural backgrounds of families with young children for a few decades. With respect to child poverty, there is a disproportionate impact of poverty (greater percentage of children impacted) within Native American, Hispanic, and African American populations. While African American children had the highest poverty rate in 2017, Hispanic children represented the group with the greatest number of poor children, followed by White and then African American children (Children's Defense Fund, 2018). Almost 1 in 3 American Indian/Alaska Native children and more than 1 in 4 Black and Hispanic children were poor in 2017, compared with 1 in 9 White children (Children's Defense Fund, 2018). Therefore, the dimensions of poverty that impact children in the United States are aligned with opportunities that are available for children from different racial and ethnic backgrounds.

Influence of Equity Perspectives on Childhood Poverty

Increasingly, researchers and practitioners are using an equity lens (National Association for the Education of Young Children, 2019) to better understand the unique experiences of children growing up with limited resources. One of the important tenants of an equity perspective is to recognize the impact of historical disenfranchisement and oppression of different ethnic and racial groups in the United States as a result of government sanctioned practices on the present. These included past restrictions for accessing a free and public quality education, removal of Native populations from their homelands, indentured servitude and slavery, and post-Civil War Jim Crowe practices and past and ongoing violations of civil liberties, to single out a few. Due to these longstanding injustices, achieving equity for all children requires a careful understanding of the unique circumstance of children and their families within a broader society framework. Moreover, recognition of the deficit lens that has been used to characterize the development of low-income, minority children remains a pressing challenge for the field (Cabrera, Beeghly, & Eisenberg, 2012). Through increased awareness and knowledge regarding sources of inequity and the simultaneous development of cultural competence (see Figure 16.1), educators, researchers, and practitioners can strive to offer learning opportunities that promote greater equity. Meeting the needs of all children requires a deeper examination of equity, bias, and other constraints as well as facilitators of children's growth and development.

Nativity or immigrant origin is another important variable to consider when evaluating the impact of poverty on school achievement. Although beyond the scope of this chapter (see also Chapter 14 on Culturally and Linguistically Diverse Children in this volume), it is critically important to recognize that immigrants to the United States have historically been marginalized initially by the dominant culture, and, over time, diverse ethnic and/or religious groups have been successful at development of a bicultural identity. Bicultural competence where individual identity includes aspects of U.S. dominant culture and one's culture of origin has been linked with optimal psychological functioning and mental health in youth (LaFromboise, Coleman, & Gerton, 1993; Nguyen & Benet-Martinez, 2013).

Presently, being of Latinx and/or perceived immigrant origin in today's climate of heightened attention and divisive public discourse around immigration policy creates a context that impacts child development, families, and communities (Mendez, Crosby, & Siskind, 2018). Garcia Coll and colleagues' (1996) seminal framework helped situate the development of minority children within a society that has stratification and myths regarding outcomes for such children. This model suggests that such environments can be promoting or inhibiting for children's development and will eventually influence how families socialize and share their cultural beliefs and practices to contribute to child outcomes. In promoting community environments, early care and education programs can provide secure and enriching settings for children from immigrant families. In contrast, neighborhoods and communities that feel unsafe or discriminatory may lead families to keep children at home (Bartlett & Ramos-Olazagasti, 2018; Matthews, Ulrich, & Cervantes, 2018), to mistrust government services (Vesely, Ewaida, & Kearney, 2013), and to limit their engagement in employment and enrichment opportunities and social networks (Vesely, Goodman, Ewaida, & Kearney, 2015).

Thus, the negative and far-reaching impacts of the current climate around immigration policy for children and families, particularly those facing traumatic experiences, may prove a significant challenge to fostering healthy development (Bouza et al., 2018; Chaudry, Capps, Pedroza, Castañeda, Santos, & Scott, 2010). Moreover, practitioners are increasingly reporting feeling ill-equipped to meet the needs of immigrant families and to know how best to connect them to community resources (Matthews et al., 2018). For these reasons, community-based organizations often play a critical role in facilitating social networks and access to resources for recently-arriving immigrants (Yoshikawa, Kholoptseva, & Suárez-Orozco, 2013). Practitioners can best prepare to work with a diverse population by pursuing professional development

Table 16.1 Elements of Cultural Competence

To build a more inclusive approach to providing for the education and developmental needs within low-income and culturally diverse child populations, cultural competence has been recommended as an investment in workforce development. While definitions vary, generally three components are emphasized within any organization working with children:

1. Critical Awareness/Knowledge – a self-assessment of one's own knowledge and biases about children from a diversity of backgrounds

2. Skills – how to effectively engage and work with others from an intercultural perspective

3. Organization supports – how the organization, school, or agency provides ongoing professional development to support working across cultural and linguistic variation within your workplace

Excerpt from López et al. (2017).

to increase their cultural competence through their organizations or within their local networks (see Table 16.1). For example, experts recommend that early care and education (ECE) professionals examine their own knowledge about diverse populations and seek out training as needed, while organizations should offer continuing education about how to work effectively with culturally and linguistically diverse families (López, Hofer, Bumgarner, & Taylor, 2017).

In sum, while definitions of "poverty" and "low-resource" are varied, implications for access of programs and supports are critical to consider. Additionally, due to the disproportionate impact of poverty on culturally and linguistically diverse groups of children and families, addressing equity and cultural competence within the preparation and conduct of assessment is critically important. We shall return to these issues in the implications for assessment section of this chapter. In the next section, we turn our attention to some conceptual models that help us frame the assessment of low-resource child populations within a familial, community, and cultural context.

Theoretical Model for Understanding the Impact of Poverty on Child Development

To guide our review of the components of low-resource environments that are influential for children's growth and development, we draw upon a number of frameworks that examine children's environments (Holahan & Wandersman, 1987; National Research Council Institute of Medicine, 2000). Ecological theory is useful for helping us analyze the systems that impact child development along with determining how proximal processes that are transactional in nature involving children and others in their environments change over time (Garcia Coll et al., 1996; Sameroff, 2000).

Ecological-Transactional Model of Early Childhood Development

An ecological-transactional model (Cicchetti & Lynch, 1993) is often used to explain how resources and stressors influence child development within specific contexts. In this chapter, we use the proximal contexts for children, namely *home/family environment, early care and education (ECE) settings*, and more distal contexts such as *neighborhood*, to analyze the surrounding context as pertaining to a whole-child approach to child psychological assessment with low-income populations.

Figure 16.1 shows a visual representation of the important dimensions of an ecological model that guide our approach to psychoeducational assessment of young children (Mendez, Stillman, LaForett, Wandersman, & Flaspohler, 2004; Paget & Nagle, 1986). Drawing from the framework of ecological theorist Bronfenbrenner (1979), we consider factors at the macrosystem, exosystem, mesosystem, and microsystem.

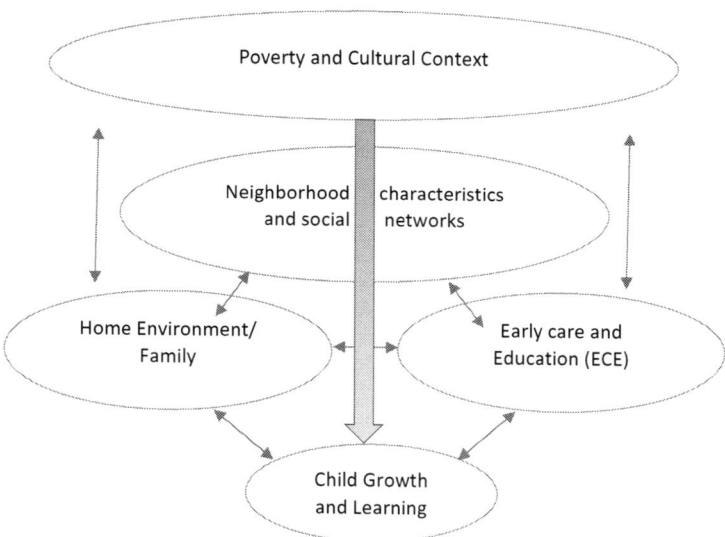

Figure 16.1 Ecological-Transactional Model for Guiding Psychoeducational Assessment for Low-Income Children

Note: This figure provides an overview of areas to consider in conducting a psychoeducational assessment of growth and learning with children from low-income environments. The bidirectional arrows are used to signify the number of transactional and reciprocal interactions between members of the children's microsystem and exosystem contexts. Poverty and cultural context are part of a macrosystem influence that indirectly and directly impacts all the other levels of the ecology.

Macrosystem influences. Poverty and cultural context operate at the macrosystem or broadest level of influence on children's development. As noted earlier in the introduction, some facets of culture, such as race, ethnicity, immigrant status, and other demographic features, are disproportionately associated with living in poverty. However, this does not mean these factors are causal for particular child outcomes; rather, the surrounding broad milieu for the child is established within the macrosystem level, including the myths and beliefs that society holds about low-income children from different community contexts or countries of origin (Snell-Johns, Mendez, & Smith, 2004). For example, we may hold a bias or assumption that an immigrant family from El Salvador has limited opportunities in the United States due to poor English-speaking abilities, when in fact this may not be the case if the parent has access to better employment opportunities and safe housing and the child is exposed to English from an early age at home and is enrolled in an affordable ECE program. Social policies designed to assist families in poverty, such as a federal tax system or child care policy, would also be examples of macrosystem influences (Durlak, 2005; Hill et al., 2019).

Exosystem influences. The exosystem or community level typically encompasses broader community characteristics, such as availability of educational, health, and recreational resources, that affect individual and family life (Levine & Perkins, 1997). In considering children's well-being, neighborhood characteristics, social networks involving the interactions among residents or neighbors, and the information and support found between residents are important (Mendez et al., 2004). In general, members of low-resource communities often face challenges in obtaining knowledge and resources within their own neighborhoods and must develop connections. As an example, researchers in New York City found that among low-income immigrant families, child care centers often serve as a hub for organizing access to other community resources and helping parents develop social networks (Small, Jacobs, & Massengill, 2008). When community-based organizations provide information directly, and as connections form, low-income and immigrant families build social, financial, and navigational capital to be used in future situations (Yosso, 2005).

Mesosystem and microsystem influences. The home environment and the family are a critical, proximal influence on the child's growth and development. For assessment and case conceptualization purposes, including family members within the immediate household, as well as those family and family-like kin who are significant influences on the child, is critical to an accurate and valid portrayal of the children's home/family microsystem. A second key microsystem for young children is ECE programs. In this chapter, we define "ECE" as inclusive of the range and type of setting that provides any non-parental child care for the developing child, such as family, friend, or neighbor care, as well as more formal center-based care such as Head Start or public pre-K programs for 4-year-old children. In considering these key microsystems, which have a direct influence on the child, we must also consider how the child is shaping the individuals within these environments (Crosnoe, Augustine, & Huston, 2012) and how the microsystems shape the attitudes, values, and learning activities of the developing child. For example, low-income African American mothers with strong beliefs about the importance of play were found to have children who were better skilled at playing with peers in Head Start classrooms (Fogle & Mendez, 2006). The ways in which the microsystems reinforce and support one another is captured by the mesosystem, defined as the interconnections among the microsystems (Bronfenbrenner, 1979, 1999). With a strong mesosystem between home and ECE microsystems, children with multiple, interactive, and supportive connections will likely experience less stress and more continuity in their developmental experiences (Mendez, 2010). Research examining home–school connection among low-income children has found abundant evidence that children benefit when adults in these settings have positive and congruent relationships (Waanders, Mendez, & Downer, 2007). Therefore, the establishment of a strong home–school connection may be an underused approach for buffering children from the stress and broad impacts of poverty (Brooks-Gunn, Berlin, & Fuligni, 2000; Mendez, 2010).

Examining Resilience in the Face of Adverse Childhood Experiences

A theoretical model that examines contexts is necessary, but not sufficient, to fully capture how the reciprocal influences across the levels of the ecology for the child produce a given outcome. We need to examine risk and resilience processes during early childhood to provide an assessment of how the child's development is progressing. Almost 20 years ago, Masten (2001) offered a comprehensive framework for examining resilience; she keenly observed that the factors that offset risk associated with growing up in poverty are primarily "ordinary" variables found in any good developmental context. These include optimal levels of warm, sensitive parenting, stimulating home and ECE environments, and access to safe neighborhoods with resources.

Around this time, emerging research on adverse child experiences (ACES) was showing that adults with exposure to significant numbers of family or environmental risk factors were significantly more likely to have psychopathology and/or health-related problems as adults and experience early death (Felitti et al., 1998). Factors measured in the ACES original study, such as exposure to child abuse or having a parent experience psychopathology, have now been used in numerous studies to show similar impacts. Following on from this study, others have noted the related but important concepts of toxic stress (Shonkoff & Phillips, 2000), which refers to the process of how negative impacts of adverse and stressful environments may be mitigated by the presence of nurturing, supportive, and stable relationships during early childhood (Morris, Treat, Hays-Grudo, Chesher, Williamson, & Mendez, 2018). In sum, there are constraints and facilitators of developmental processes and, despite exposure to poverty, low-income children who have access to intrapersonal and interpersonal supports can and do demonstrate resilience (Mendez et al., 2002; Morris et al., 2018).

Research on Developmental and Contextual Considerations with Children Living in Low-Resource Environments

We now turn to a brief review of some of the critical components of the microsystem and exosystem influences on child development within the context of low resources. This illustrative review is meant to highlight factors that can be uncovered within a psychoeducational assessment process. We provide a balanced review of strengths and needs that would be important to consider for low-income children, with an explicit inclusion of literature drawn from culturally diverse racial/ethnic populations.

Family/Home Environment

Low-income children are heterogeneous in their family composition and, therefore, participation in caregiving will vary across households. For example, low-income Latinx children are more likely to be raised in two-parent households compared to their African American low-income peers (Turner, Wildsmith, Guzman, & Alvira-Hammond, 2016). For low-income African American and Latinx households, research has documented the critical role that nonresidential and residential fathers play in child development (Cabrera, Ryan, Mitchell, Shannon, & Tamis-LeMonda, 2008; Downer & Mendez, 2005). Extended family members such as grandparents, cousins, and aunts/uncles are critical supports for diverse groups of children and their parents (Stevens, 1988). Moreover, African American children are the largest racial or ethnic group of children to experience kinship care, defined as care by relatives when a biological parent is unable or unwilling to provide care (Washington, Gleeson, & Rulison, 2013), which shows how family members offer supports when children face threats to their stability of caregiving. Unfortunately, high rates of separation, divorce, and inter-partner conflict (Margolin & Vickerman, 2011) place increased demands on parents raising young children, and chronic levels of trauma exposure for children including child maltreatment, are highest for children under the age of 5 years (Lieberman, Chu, Van Horn, & Harris, 2011; Margolin & Vickerman, 2011).

Research with immigrant households has identified a number of strengths and needs. For example, recently arriving immigrant families may have lower social capital and less reliable access to vibrant social networks (Matthews et al., 2018; Mendez et al., 2018), as well as stress if parents are undocumented immigrants with children who are citizens (Yoshikawa, 2011). Estimates suggest that 1 in 4 Hispanic children have a parent who is an unauthorized immigrant (Clarke, Turner, & Guzman, 2017), and data from the Center for Migration Studies shows that Asians represent the largest growth in undocumented immigrants (AAPI Data, 2017). Low-income households more generally struggle with affording learning materials for the home, enrichment opportunities such as high-quality child care, and time and information to support early child development. Strong work ethic and labor market participation with somewhat stable but low earnings has been identified as a possible strength for Latinx households (Gennetian, Rodrigues, Hill, & Morris, 2015); however, some households may struggle to find reliable and stable employment opportunities with high wages.

Research has also documented variation in parental beliefs about child development that are important to assess during early childhood. For example, in a series of measurement development and predictive studies with low-income children enrolled in Head Start programs, studies found that parents who endorsed high levels of supportive play beliefs were reportedly more engaged in responsive caregiving, and, in turn, their children had stronger peer competence at home and school (Fogle & Mendez, 2006; LaForett & Mendez, 2016a, 2016b). These parents tended to have favorable views of play that were consistent with existing definitions of guided play and playful learning, which emphasize the idea that play serves as a learning context for young children. In contrast, parents were less inclined to endorse statements depicting play as exclusively an activity to be done for fun and entertainment, which is somewhat aligned with definitions of "free play." These studies confirm that many low-income parents do endorse beliefs involving the importance of play for fostering optimal child development.

In sum, we see strengths and needs across components of family structure and composition, involvement by a range of family members in a variety of circumstances, and responsive caregiving accompanied by positive parental beliefs about play and learning. These are many of the attributes and behaviors of the family that we can capture during an assessment.

Early Care and Education (ECE)

Research on ECE has been robust since the founding and resulting national expansion of Head Start over 50 years ago, which today serves just about 1 million low-income children. Generally, low-income children have had lower access to ECE (Tang, Coley, & Votruba-Drzal, 2012); however, new data are suggesting that prior gaps observed in utilization of child care and early education programs by low-income racial and ethnic minorities relative to their White peers may be narrowing (Mendez et al., 2018). For example, data from the National Study of Early Care and Education (2012), a nationally representative sample of children and their families and ECE programs, provides a snapshot of the care patterns in the United States. Across all program types (any form of non-parental care), low-income African American children have the highest rates of utilization relative to low-income White and Hispanic children, while native-born Hispanic children have rates slightly higher than Hispanic children with at least one immigrant parent (Crosby, Mendez, Guzman, & López, 2016). With increasing participation in an ECE program of high quality, this exposure to learning opportunities can help low-income children increase a range of emotional, behavioral, cognitive, and linguistic skills prior to kindergarten. Also, involvement with an ECE setting increases the likelihood that children will gain access to developmental and health screenings that will detect potential developmental problems and potentially facilitate early intervention.

On the challenging side of ECE, we find that many young children are experiencing long hours in care, sometimes greater than 30 hours per week, and long hours in low-quality care can be stressful on children. Research has documented that families with non-standard work hours (defined as work outside of the Monday–Friday 9–5 hours that occurs early mornings, nights, and weekends) often have children in multiple child care arrangements (Crosby & Mendez, 2017), which can create logistical challenges and instability of arrangements if some fall through. We have seen evidence that supply of ECE is unequally distributed, referring to places where such limited care is available that it is called a "child care desert" (Milk, Hamm, Schochet, Novoa, Workman, & Jessen-Howard, 2018). Finally, our knowledge of aspects of quality of ECE programs and important features of classroom and home supports for dual language learner children, defined as young children with exposure to two or more languages, is growing but remains understudied by researchers (Goldenberg, Nemeth, Hicks, Zepeda, & Cardona, 2013).

In sum, access to caring, responsive adults within the home and ECE environments is a critical means of buffering young children from toxic stress (Mendez, 2010; Morris et al., 2018). Unfortunately, resources in these environments are not equally available, and so research must continue to uncover barriers and foster opportunities to achieve equity for diverse, low-income children and their families.

Neighborhoods

The research on neighborhoods for young children tends to involve social organization theory and access to resources of the place and of the residents who dwell and interact with children. Generally, we find that structural factors of the neighborhoods, such as residential mobility, family disruption, housing, and population density, and lack of supportive resources weaken community within low-income neighborhoods (Sampson, Raudenbush, & Earls, 1997). Also, parents living in unsafe, lower-resource neighborhoods may focus more on protecting children and ensuring safety rather than placing emphasis on children's skill development (Furstenberg, 1993; O'Neil, Parke, & McDowell, 2001). Research has shown poor neighborhood climate and neighborhood disorder is related to lower involvement in education by low-income parents of preschool and elementary-age children (Smith et al., 1997; Waanders et al., 2007). More contemporary data show that about half of all children who stay in federally-funded emergency and transitional housing programs are age 5 or younger (Perlman & Fantuzzo, 2010), demonstrating that young children experience homelessness at alarming rates. Research has linked homelessness during infancy and toddlerhood to social-emotional delays (Haskett, Armstrong, & Tisdale, 2015), underdeveloped social skills in elementary school (Brumley, Fantuzzo, Perlman, & Zager, 2015), and high rates of maternal depression (Bassuk & Beardslee, 2014).

Because of the need for safety and connection, schools and ECE programs that foster a sense of belonging for their students and families play a significant role in fostering well-being, and these effects also hold for older elementary and adolescent students (Thibeault, Mendez, Nelson-Gray, & Stein, 2017). ECE programs can also connect at-risk families, including those experiencing homelessness, with immediate community resources. Finally, growing up in high SES neighborhoods is associated with higher IQ, stronger achievement, higher reading scores, and more involvement in play with peers at home and in residents' homes (Chase-Landsdale & Gordon, Brooks-Gunn, & Klebanov, 1997; Leventhal & Brooks-Gunn, 2000).

In sum, developing a good understanding of a neighborhood and the stability of children's housing and family life is critical to guiding interpretation of assessment data. Increasingly, children's experience of homelessness and other housing/neighborhood stressors must be a part of screening for children referred for any cognitive, behavioral, or emotional difficulty during early childhood.

Application: Assessment Considerations for Low-Income Children

To provide a framework for conducting assessments for children experiencing poverty, psychologists need to attend to factors at multiple levels. In general, approaches need to consider measurement of strengths and needs of the individual child, the family, and the broader ECE and community context. Given that delays are often resulting in referrals during early childhood, a rigorous assessment will need to go beyond use of standardized tests and include a range of other procedures. Data collection must involve adults in the settings where children spend time, as well as medical and health records, local data on neighborhood and community factors that promote resilience, resources available in communities, and participation in ECE and other learning opportunities, including religious and/or community programs like a YMCA.

We recognize that practitioners will utilize and perhaps prioritize norm-referenced, standardized tests in their assessments of young children from low-resource backgrounds. There may be practical or legal reasons for this, such as requirements based on policies and practices in various assessment settings such as schools, early care and education programs, early intervention, or health care settings. And although these policies may lead to routines or practices resulting in "standard" assessment batteries, we argue that part of standard ethical assessment practice involves examining the technical manual or examiner's manual to determine the extent to which populations representing the child being assessed were included in the norming sample for the test development.

When assessing children from low-resource settings, it is important to consider norming population characteristics such as geographic region (including geographic areas/cities with high concentrations of individuals living in poverty), race and Hispanic status, country of origin, parent's level of educational attainment, and family income. Limited representation in the norming sample may be taken into consideration when evaluating the validity of assessment data for a given test and may result in interpreting assessment results with caution and/or supplementing with other measures normed on a similar population or that capture the child's ecological context. Although these points are typically included in foundational training on assessment, in our experience they are often overlooked in practice.

Implement Contextually Driven Assessment

We recommend in addition to the training on standardized testing that practitioners become familiar with contextually driven and locally based procedures for guiding evaluations. One strategy for employing a contextually responsive assessment approach draws from Response to Intervention (RTI) or Multi-tiered Systems of Support (MTSS) methods. Although more dominant in K-12 settings (Jimerson, Burns, & VanDerHeyden, 2016; O'Connor & Fuchs, 2013), these approaches are increasingly common in in early childhood settings (Buysse & Peisner-Feinberg, 2013). Falling generally under the term "formative assessment," this approach involves periodically assessing or gathering data about children's knowledge and learning and using that information to make data-driven decisions about instructional practice (Peisner-Feinberg & Buysse, 2013).

There are two types of assessment activities in these tiered approaches. The first, universal screening, consists of conducting brief standardized assessments of all children, with the goal of determining which children: 1) are meeting benchmarks or defined learning goals, and 2) need additional instructional supports or interventions (Peisner-Feinberg & Buysse, 2013). Within tiered approaches, universal screening is often characterized as a strategy to determine whether children are learning the skills and content taught to all children in a given setting, such as the core curriculum being taught in a classroom. Children who perform poorly on a universal screening measure, as designated by some defined benchmark (e.g., below the classroom average, some determined cut-point, etc.), are assumed to need more educational or behavioral supports than what the core curriculum is providing.

The second assessment activity used in tiered models is progress monitoring. The purpose of progress monitoring is to measure children's progress as a result of instructional adaptations (e.g., small group interventions, 1:1 instructional support) and subsequently use the assessment data to adjust and individualize instruction for the child (Peisner-Feinberg & Buysse, 2013). As described by Peisner-Feinberg and Buysse, assessment tools used for universal screening or progress monitoring should have the following characteristics: 1) employ standardized administration procedures that involve direct assessment of the child's skills, which may or may not be norm-referenced; 2) measure key skills that are linked to later outcomes in specified developmental domains; 3) have sensitivity to small increments of change in line with the notion of conducting repeated assessments to evaluate growth over time; 4) provide indicators of the level and rate of growth; and 5) be quick and easy to administer.

When working with low-resource populations, these formative assessment approaches may serve as a strategy for considering contextual factors. For universal screening, assessment data on all children in a classroom can provide useful information such as how the child is performing relative to "true" peers who are experiencing similar learning environments and other contextual factors. This approach contrasts with those that exclusively rely on norm-referenced standardized tests whose norming samples may little resemble the target child or the child's proximal environment. Some have argued that this "local norms" approach may be useful for determining areas of strength and need for children by examining the "typical" abilities of students at specific grade levels within a given classroom, school, or district (Peña & Halle, 2011). This argument has been offered as one consideration for assessing certain populations, such as children who are dual language learners (Brown & Doolittle, 2008; LaForett, Peisner-Feinberg, & Buysse, 2013; Peña & Halle, 2011). These approaches also can be helpful when considering whether the child's performance might be due to low-quality instruction or cognitive stimulation rather than the child's ability or learning potential. Indeed, it has been suggested that the failure of schools to provide adequate core instruction, the benchmark against which a child is judged to determine learning levels and growth, may explain why certain groups of children, including dual language learners (DLLs), exhibit poor academic performance (Orosco & Klingner, 2010).

Formative assessment can be a critical strategy for determining which children have significant risk that may compromise learning in a general setting and require additional supports. We would also expect that universal screening could be used to capture children's exposure to toxic stress as well as other barriers families experience in supporting children's growth and learning. For example, in a study on parent engagement within Head Start programs, we developed a tool to assess common barriers to participation in school programs (Mendez, 2010), to generate solutions for families who were seeking to participate. In another study with low-income immigrant parents, we developed a brief communication measure to assess how effective families felt in being able to communicate with their children's Head Start teachers, and this measure positively correlated with parent report of parent-teacher conferencing (Mendez, Westerberg, & Thibeault, 2013). Other important areas of family needs and strengths could and should be included in a comprehensive approach to understanding the children's learning environment, including parental depression (LaForett & Mendez, 2010) or experiencing homelessness (Brumley et al., 2015), father engagement (Downer & Mendez,2005) and parental beliefs about play and school readiness (Fogle & Mendez, 2006; LaForett & Mendez, 2016b).

Family members always play an important role in the assessment process. For example, they should complete a detailed developmental history about family, school, health, social development, and educational experiences, as well as providing medical information. In terms of children's emerging competencies, parents may have insight into new behaviors that children display at home but not at preschool. Understanding children's language exposure at home can be important for assessment of bilingual children. Data should be collected from parents in terms of who is speaking which languages to children, any siblings and their usage of language with the young child, as well as children's ability to read or write letters in different languages. Parent reports of attention or behavior difficulties can be obtained using standardized checklists for attention or developmental delays (e.g. Childhood Autism Rating Scale-2; Schopler, Van Bourgondien, Wellman, & Love, 2010). Finally, parents and extended family members who are engaged in discussions about the behaviors of the children will be able to support learning goals that follow the assessment, as their beliefs and cultural values will be a valued part of the assessment process (Fantuzzo, Mendez, & Tighe, 1998).

In terms of teacher report measures of child competencies, several measures for the toddler and preschool-aged child should be considered, such as measures of children's interactive peer play and learning behaviors (Coolahan, Fantuzzo, Mendez, & McDermott, 2000). Interactive tasks involving tests of executive function and attention may be particularly useful. In the domain of language, children's exposure to diverse languages at home or in preschool should be assessed, as well as whether those languages are written, spoken, or read to the child being assessed. Developing holistic recommendations that focus on children's development and resilience in multiple contexts will be critically important, as synergy across children's environments can more effectively buffer children from toxic stress than systems working in silos or without connection.

As we look forward, we also know there are significant and continued unmet needs for varied populations experiencing childhood poverty. From an equity perspective, there continues to be a lag involving research and measurement development with American Indian/Alaska Native (AI/AN) and other language minority groups, which precludes a firm empirical footing for intervention planning for these children. Other areas of practice that are likely to see increased work by interdisciplinary trained practitioners include early childhood mental health consultation (Zero to Three, 2016) and infant mental health (Morris et al., 2018), especially as more children enter ECE at younger ages. Finally, psychologists and practitioners working in the early childhood field require ongoing professional development to build cultural competence. These challenges are vast; however, the future success of the low-income populations experiencing such vulnerability so early in development demand our best response.

Conclusion

In sum, this chapter has discussed a range of factors that impact child development within the context of poverty. We have described and recommended the use of an ecological and developmental approach to the assessment of children's strengths and needs, in order to inform learning goals and/or intervention planning. Across domains, research shows the negative impact of poverty on children's early cognitive and social-emotional development relative to children living in less impoverished backgrounds; however, impacts on any given child are challenging to determine due to resilience and protective factors (Mendez et al., 2002). Therefore, we need to caution against initial conclusions drawn from assessments when children from low-income backgrounds have no prior school experience. It is critical to conduct frequent re-assessments in order to form the best picture of a child's abilities after they have enrolled for some time in their ECE or preschool setting. Finally, involvement of the family in all phases of assessment and intervention planning is important, especially in situations where children have experienced trauma, ACES, or other disruptions during the preschool years. With increasing attention to the birth-to-5 population and their developmental and learning needs, we can expect that preschool assessment will be a vital tool for practitioners seeking to maximize the potential of vulnerable children via participation in high-quality educational settings.

References

AAPI Data. (2017). One out of every 7 Asian immigrants is undocumented. Retrieved Online at: http://aapidata.com/blog/asian-undoc-1in7/

Alvira-Hammond, M., & Gennetian, L. A. (2015). How Hispanic parents perceive their need and eligibility for public assistance. National Research Center on Hispanic

Children and Families. Retrieved online at www.hispanicresearchcenter.org/wp-con tent/uploads/2018/04/Income-Brief-No.-2-Perceptions-of-Eligibility-V2.pdf

Bartlett, J. D., & Ramos-Olazagasti, M. A. (2018). Supporting children and parents affected by the trauma of separation. Bethesda, MD: National Research Center on Hispanic Children & Families. Retrieved online at https://www.hispanicresearchcen ter.org/research-resources/supporting-children-and-parents-affected-by-the-trauma-of-separation/. Accessed on 2.27.2020.

Bassuk, D., & Beardslee, W. (2014). Depression in homeless mothers: Addressing an unrecognized public health issue. *American Journal of Orthopsychiatry, 84*, 73–81.

Bishaw, A., & Benson, C. (2018). Poverty 2016 and 2017: American community survey briefs. ACSBR/17-02. Retrieved online at https://www.census.gov/content/dam/Census/library/publications/2018/acs/acsbr17-02.pdf. Accessed on 2.27.2020.

Bouza, J., Camacho-Thompson, D., Carlo, G., Franco, X., Garcia Coll, C., Halgunseth, L. Marks, A., Stein, G.L., Suarez-Orozco, C., & White, R. (2018). *The science is clear: Separating families has long-term damaging psychological and health consequences for children, families, and communities.* Washington, DC: Society for Research in Child Development.

Bronfenbrenner, U. (1979). *The ecology of human development.* Cambridge, MA: Harvard University Press.

Bronfenbrenner, U. (1999). Environments in developmental perspective: Theoretical and operational models. In S. L. Friedman & T. D. Wachs (Eds.). *Measuring environments across the life span: Emerging methods and concepts* (pp. 3–28). Washington, DC: American Psychological Association.

Brooks-Gunn, J., Berlin, L. J., & Fuligni, A. S. (2000). Early childhood intervention programs: What about the family? In J. P. Shonkoff & S. J. Meisels (Eds.), *Handbook of early childhood intervention* (2nd ed., pp. 549–588). New York, NY: Cambridge University Press.

Brown, J. E., & Doolittle, J. (2008). A cultural, linguistic, and ecological framework for response to intervention with English language learners. *Exceptional Children, 40*, 66–72.

Brumley, B., Fantuzzo, J., Perlman, S., & Zager, M. L. (2015). The unique relations between early homelessness and educational well-being: An empirical test of the continuum of risk hypothesis. *Children and Youth Services Review, 48*, 31–37.

Buysse, V., & Peisner-Feinberg, E. S. (Eds.). (2013). *Handbook of response to intervention (RTI) in early childhood.* Baltimore, MD: Brookes.

Cabrera, N. J., Beeghly, M., & Eisenberg, E. (2012). Positive development of minority children: Introduction to the special issue. *Child Development Perspectives.* doi:10.1111/j.1750-8606.2012.00253.x

Cabrera, N. J., Ryan, R. M., Mitchell, S. J., Shannon, J. D., & Tamis-LeMonda, C. S. (2008). Low-income nonresident father involvement with their toddlers: Variation by fathers' race and ethnicity. *Journal of Family Psychology, 22*(4), 643–647. doi:10.1037/0893-3200.22.3.643

Chase-Landsdale, P. L., Gordon, R. A., Brooks-Gunn, J., & Klebanov, P. K. (1997). Neighborhood and family influences on the intellectual and behavioral competence of preschool and early school-age children. In J. Brooks-Gunn, G. Duncan, & L. J. Aber (Eds.), *Neighborhood poverty: Context and consequences for children* (pp. 79–118). New York, NY: Sage.

Chaudry, A., Capps, R., Pedroza, J. M., Castañeda, R. M., Santos, R., & Scott, M. M. (2010). *Facing Our Future: Children in the Aftermath of Immigration Enforcement.* The Urban Institute.

Children's Defense Fund (2018). Child Poverty in America 2017: National analysis. Retrieved online at www.childrensdefense.org/wp-content/uploads/2018/09/Child-Poverty-in-America-2017-National-Fact-Sheet.pdf

Cicchetti, D., & Lynch, M. (1993). Toward an ecological/transactional model of community violence and child maltreatment: Consequences for children's development. *Psychiatry, 56,* 96–117.

Clarke, W., Turner, K., & Guzman, L. (2017). *One quarter of Hispanic children in the United States have an unauthorized immigrant parent.* Bethesda, MD: National Research Center on Hispanic Children & Families. Retrieved online at https://www.hispanicresearchcenter.org/wp-content/uploads/2019/08/Hispanic-Center-Undocumented-Brief-FINAL-V21.pdf/. Accessed on 2.27.2020.

Coolahan, K.C., Fantuzzo, J., Mendez, J.L., & McDermott, P. (2000). Preschool peer interactions and readiness to learn: Relationships between classroom peer play and learning behaviors and conduct. *Journal of Educational Psychology, 92,* 458–465.

Crosby, D., & Mendez, J. (2017). How common are nonstandard work schedules among low-income Hispanic parents of young children? Bethesda, MD: National Research Center for Hispanic Children & Families. Retrieved online at https://www.hispanicresearchcenter.org/wp-content/uploads/2017/11/Hispanics-Center-parental-work-hours-Brief-11.1-V21.pdf. Accessed on 2.27.2020.

Crosby, D., Mendez, J., Guzman, L., & López, M. (2016). Hispanic children's participation in early care and education: Type of care by household nativity status, race/ethnicity,and child age. Bethesda, MD: National Research Center on Hispanic Children & Families. Retrieved Online at https://www.childtrends.org/wp-content/uploads/2016/11/2016-58HispECEHoursAmtTiming.pdf. Accessed on 2.27.2020.

Crosnoe, R., Augustine, J. M., & Huston, A. C. (2012). Children's early child care and their mother's later involvement with schools. *Child Development, 83,* 758–772. doi:10.1111/j.1467-8624.2011.01726.x

Cuddy, E., Venator, J., & Reeves, R. V. (2015). *In a land of dollars: Deep poverty and its consequences.* Washington, DC: Brookings. Retrieved online at www.brookings.edu/blogs/social-mobility-memos/posts/2015/05/07-deep-poverty-income-spending-reeves

Downer, J., & Mendez, J. L. (2005). African American father involvement and preschool children's school readiness. *Early Education and Development, 16(3),* 317–339. doi:10.1207/s15566935eed1603_2

Durlak, J. A. (2005). How to help families promote optimal development in young children. In T. Gullota & M. Bloom (Eds.), *A blueprint for the promotion of prosocial behavior in early childhood* (pp. 93–111). New York, NY: Kluwer/Plenum.

Fantuzzo, J., Mendez, J. L., & Tighe, E. (1998). Parental assessment of peer play: Development and validation of the parent version of the Penn Interactive Peer Play Scale. *Early Childhood Research Quarterly, 13,* 659–676.

Felitti, V. J., Anda, R. F., Nordenberg, D., Williamson, D. F., Spitz, A. M., Edwards, V., ... Marks, J. S. (1998). Relationship of childhood abuse and household dysfunction to many of the leading causes of death in adults: The Adverse Childhood Experiences (ACE) study. *American Journal of Preventative Medicine, 14(4),* 245–258.

Fogle, L., & Mendez, J. L. (2006). Assessing the play beliefs of African American mothers with preschool children. *Early Childhood Research Quarterly, 21,* 507–518. doi:10.1016/j.ecresq.2006.08.002

Furstenberg, F. F. (1993). How families manage risk and opportunity in dangerous neighborhoods. In W. J. Wilson (Ed.), *Sociology and the public agenda* (pp. 231–258). Newbury Park, CA: Sage.

Garcia Coll, C., Lamberty, G., Jenkins, R., McAdoo, H. P., Crnic, K., Wasik, B. H., & Vasquez Garcia, H. (1996). An integrative model for the study of developmental competencies in minority children. *Child Development, 67*(5), 1891–1914.

Gennetian, L. A., Rodrigues, C., Hill, H. D., & Morris, P. (2015). Income instability in the lives of Hispanic children. National Research Center on Hispanic Children and Families. Retrieved online at www.childtrends.org/wp-content/uploads/2015/12/2015-47Hisp-Ctr-Income-Instability.pdf

Goldenberg, C., Nemeth, K., Hicks, J., Zepeda, M., & Cardona, L. (2013). Program elements and teaching practices to support young dual language learners. California's best practices for young dual language learners: Research overview papers, pp. 90–118. Retrieved online at www.earlychildhoodwebinars.com/wp-content/uploads/2016/01/California%E2%80%99s-Best-Practices-for-YOUNG-DUAL-LANGUAGE-LEARNERS-Research-Overview-Papers.pdf

Haskett, M. E., Armstrong, J. M., & Tisdale, J. (2015). Developmental status and social-emotional functioning of young children experiencing homelessness. *Early Childhood Education Journal, 44*, 1–7. doi:10.1007/s10643-015-0691-8

Hill, Z., Gennetian, L. A., & Mendez, J. (2019). A descriptive profile of state child care and development fund policies in states with high populations of low-income Hispanic children. *Early Childhood Research Quarterly, 47*, 111–123. doi:10.1016/j.ecresq.2018.10.003

Holahan, C. J., & Wandersman, A. (1987). The community psychology perspective in environmental psychology. In D. Stokols & I. Altman (Eds.), *Handbook of environmental psychology* (pp. 827–861). New York, NY: Wiley.

Jimerson, S. R., Burns, M. K., & VanDerHeyden, A. M. (Eds.). (2016). *Handbook of response to intervention: The science and practice of multi-tiered systems of support* (2nd ed.). New York, NY: Springer and Business Media. 10.1007/978-1-4899-7568-3

LaForett, D. R., & Mendez, J. L. (2010). Parent involvement, parental depression, and program satisfaction among low-income parents participating in a two-generation early childhood education program. *Early Education and Development, 21*(4), 517–535. doi:10.1080/10409280902927767

LaForett, D. R., & Mendez, J. L. (2016a). Children's engagement in play at home: A parent's role in supporting play opportunities during early childhood. *Early Child Development and Care, 187*(5-6), 910–923. doi:10.1080/03004430.2016.1223061

LaForett, D. R., & Mendez, J. L. (2016b). Play beliefs and responsive parenting among low-income mothers of preschoolers in the United States. *Early Child Development and Care, 187*(8), 1359–1371. doi:10.1080/03004430.2016.1169180

LaForett, D. R., Peisner-Feinberg, E. S., & Buysse, V. (2013). Recognition & Response for Dual Language Learners. In V. Buysse & E. S. Peisner-Feinberg (Eds.), *Handbook of response to intervention (RTI) in early childhood* (pp. 355–369). Baltimore, MD: Brookes.

LaFromboise, T., Coleman, H. L. K., & Gerton, J. (1993). Psychological impact of biculturalism: Evidence and theory. *Psychological Bulletin, 114*(3), 395–412.

Leventhal, T., & Brooks-Gunn, J. (2000). The neighborhoods they live in: The effects of neighborhood residence on child and adolescent outcomes. *Psychological Bulletin, 126*(2), 309–337.

Levine, M., & Perkins, D. V. (1997). *Principles of community psychology: Perspectives and applications* (2nd ed.). New York, NY: Oxford University Press.

Lieberman, A. F., Chu, A., Van Horn, P., & Harris, W. (2011). Trauma in early childhood: Empirical evidence and clinical implications. *Development and Psychopathology, 23*, 397–410. doi:10.1017/S0954579411000137

López, M., Hofer, K., Bumgarner, E., & Taylor, D. (2017). Developing culturally responsive approaches to serving diverse populations: A resource guide for community-based organizations. National Research Center on Hispanic Children and Families. Retrieved online at www.hispanicresearchcenter.org/wp-content/uploads/2018/04/Cultural-Competence-Guide-V2.pdf

Margolin, G., & Vickerman, K. A. (2011). Posttraumatic stress in children and adolescents exposed to family violence: I. Overview and issues. *Couple and Family Psychology: Research and Practice, 1*(S), 63–73.

Masten, A. S. (2001). Ordinary magic. Resilience processes in development. *American Psychologist, 56*, 227–238.

Matthews, H., Ulrich, R., & Cervantes, W. (2018). *Immigration policy's harmful impacts on early care and education.* Washington, DC: Center for Law and Social Policy.

Mendez, J., Crosby, D., & Siskind, D. (2018). Access to early care and education for low-income Hispanic children and families: A research synthesis. Bethesda, MD: National Research Center on Hispanic Children and Families. Retrieved online at www.hispanicresearchcenter.org/wp-content/uploads/2018/09/Hispanics-Center-ECE-Synthesis-Brief-9.19.pdf

Mendez, J. L. (2010). How can parents get involved in preschool? Barriers and engagement in education by ethnic minority parents of children attending Head Start programs. *Cultural Diversity and Ethnic Minority Psychology, 16*(1), 26–36. doi:10.1037/a0016258

Mendez, J. L., Fantuzzo, J., & Cicchetti, D. (2002). Profiles of social competence among low-income African American preschool children. *Child Development, 73*(4), 1085–1100.

Mendez, J. L., Stillman, L., LaForett, D., Wandersman, A., & Flaspohler, P. (2004). Neighborhood and community influences favoring the growth and development of young children. In T. Gullota & M. Bloom (Eds.), *A blueprint for the promotion of prosocial behavior in early childhood* (pp. 113–139). New York, NY: Kluwer/Plenum.

Mendez, J. L., Westerberg, D., & Thibeault, M. A. (2013). Examining the role of self-efficacy and communication as related to dimensions of Latino parent involvement in Head Start. *NHSA Dialog: A Research-To-Practice Journal for the Early Childhood Field, 16*(1), Special Issue on Parent Involvement and Engagement in Head Start, 65–80.

Milk, R., Hamm, K., Novoa, S. L., Workman, C., & Jessen-Howard, S. (2018). America's Child Care Deserts in 2018. Center for American Progress. Retrieved online at www.americanprogress.org/issues/early-childhood/reports/2018/12/06/461643/americas-child-care-deserts-2018/

Morris, A. S., Treat, A., Hays-Grudo, J., Chesher, T., Williamson, A. & Mendez, J. (2018). Integrating research and theory on early relationships to guide intervention and prevention. In A. S. Morris (Ed.), *Building Early Relationships in Infants and Toddlers: Integrating Social and Emotional Research and Practice* (pp. 1–25). Springer.

National Association for the Education of Young Children (2019). Leading with equity: Early childhood educators make it personal. Retrieved online at www.naeyc.

org/sites/default/files/globally-shared/downloads/PDFs/our-work/initiatives/equity_summit_final.pdf

National Study of Early Care and Education. (2012). Administration for Children and Families, Department of Health and Human Services. Washington, DC.

Nguyen, A. D., & Benet-Martinez, V. (2013). Biculturalism and adjustment: A meta-analysis. *Journal of Cross-Cultural Psychology*, *44*(1). doi:10.1177/0022022111435097

O'Connor, R. E., & Fuchs, L. S. (2013). Responsiveness to intervention in the elementary grades. In V. Buysse & E. S. Peisner-Feinberg (Eds.), *Handbook of response to intervention (RTI) in early childhood* (pp. 41–55). Baltimore, MD: Brookes.

O'Neil, R., Parke, R. D., & McDowell, D. (2001). Objective and subjective features of children's neighborhoods: Relations to parental regulatory strategies and children's social competence. *Applied Developmental Psychology*, *22*, 135–155.

Orosco, M. J., & Klingner, J. (2010). One school's implementation of RTI with English language learners: "Referring into RTI." *Journal of Learning Disabilities*, *43*, 269–288. doi:10.1177/0022219409355474

Paget, K., & Nagle, R. (1986). A conceptual model of preschool assessment. *School Psychology Review*, *15*, 154–164.

Peisner-Feinberg, E. S., & Buysse, V. (2013). The role of assessment. In V. Buysse & E. S. Peisner-Feinberg (Eds.), *Handbook of response to intervention (RTI) in early childhood* (pp. 121–142). Baltimore, MD: Brookes.

Peña, E. D., & Halle, T. G. (2011). Assessing preschool dual language learners: Traveling a multiforked road. *Child Development Perspectives*, *5*(1), 28–32.

Perlman, S., & Fantuzzo, J. (2010). Timing and influence of early experiences of child maltreatment and homelessness on children's educational well-being. *Children and Youth Services Review*, *32*, 874–883.

Sameroff, A. J. (2000). Dialectical processes in developmental psychopathology. In A. J. Sameroff, M. Lewis, & S. M. Miller (Eds.), *Handbook of developmental Psychopathology* (2nd ed., pp. 23–40). New York, NY: Kluwer.

Sampson, R. J., Raudenbush, S.W., & Earls, F. (1997). Neighborhoods and violent crime: A multilevel study of collective efficacy. *Science*, *277*, 918–944. doi:10.1126/science.277.5328.918

Schopler, E., Van Bourgondien, M. E., Wellman, G. J., & Love, S. R. (2010). *Childhood Autism Rating Scale – 2nd Edition*. Los Angeles, CA: Western Psychological Services.

Shonkoff, J. P., & Phillips, D.A. (2000). From neurons to neighborhoods. The science of early childhood development. Washington, DC: National Academies Press.

Small, M. L., Jacobs, E. M., & Massengill, R. P. (2008). Why organizational ties matter for neighborhood effects: Resource access through childcare centers. *Social Forces*, *87*(1), 387–414.

Smith, E. P., Connell, C., Wright, G., Sizer, M., Norman, J., Hurley, A., & Walker, S. N. (1997). An ecological model of home, school, and community partnerships: Implications for research and practice. *Journal of Educational and Psychological Consultation*, *8*(4), 339–360. doi:10.1207/s1532768xjepc0804_2

Snell-Johns, J., Mendez, J. L., & Smith, B. (2004). Evidence-based solutions for overcoming access barriers, decreasing attrition, and promoting change with underserved families. *Journal of Family Psychology*, *18*(1), 19–35. doi:10.1037/0893-3200.18.1.19

Stevens, J. H. Jr. (1988). Social support, locus of control, and parenting in three low-income groups of mothers: Black teenagers, black adults, and white adults. *Child Development*, *59*, 635–664.

Tang, S., Coley, R. L., & Votruba-Drzal, E. (2012). Low-income families' selection of child care for their young children. *Children and Youth Services Review, 34*, 2002–2011. www.sciencedirect.com/science/article/pii/S0190740912002563

Thibeault, M. A., Mendez, J. L., Nelson-Gray, R., & Stein, G. (2015). Impact of trauma exposure and acculturative stress on internalizing symptoms for recently arrived migrant-origin youth: Results from a community-based partnership. *Journal of Community Psychology, 45*, 1–15. doi:10.1002/jcop.21905

Turner, K., Wildsmith, E., Guzman, L., & Alvira-Hammond, M. (2016). *The changing geography of Hispanic children and families*. Bethesda, MD: National Research Center on Hispanic Children & Families. Retrieved on line at https://www.hispani cresearchcenter.org/wp-content/uploads/2016/01/Emerging-Communities.pdf

Vesely, C. K., Ewaida, M., & Kearney, K. B. (2013). Capitalizing on early childhood education: Low-income immigrant mothers' use of early childhood education to build human, social, and navigational capital. *Early Education & Development, 24* (5), 744–765.

Vesely, C. K., Goodman, R. D., Ewaida, M., & Kearney, K. B. (2015). A better life? Immigrant mothers' experiences building economic security. *Journal of Family and Economic Issues, 36*(4), 514–530.

Waanders, C., Mendez, J. L., & Downer, J. (2007). Parent characteristics, economic stress, and neighborhood context as predictors of parent involvement in preschool children's education. *Journal of School Psychology, 45*, 619–636.

Washington, T., Gleeson, J. P., & Rulison, K. L. (2013). Competence and African American children in informal kinship care: The role of family. *Children and Youth Services Review, 35*(9), 1305–1312.

Yoshikawa, H. (2011). *Immigrants raising citizens: Undocumented parents and their young children*. New York, NY: Russell Sage Foundation.

Yoshikawa, H., Kholoptseva, J., & Suárez-Orozco, C. (2013). The role of public policies and community-based organizations in the developmental consequences of parent undocumented status. *Social Policy Report, 27*(3), 1–17. Retrieved online at: www. srcd.org/sites/default/files/documents/spr_27_3.pdf

Yosso, T. J. (2005). Whose culture has capital? A critical race theory discussion of community cultural wealth. *Race, Ethnicity and Education, 8*(1), 69–91. doi:10.1080/ 1361332052000341006

Zero to Three. (2016). Early childhood mental health consultation policies and prac- tices to foster the social-emotional development of young children. Retrieved online at www.zerotothree.org/resources/1694-early-childhood-mental-health-consult ation-policies-and-practices-to-foster-the-social-emotional-development-of-young- children

Zigler, E. F., & Styfco, S. (1996). Head Start and early childhood intervention: The changing course of social sciences and social policy. In E. F. Zigler, S. L. Kagen, & N. W. Hall (Eds.), *Children, families, and government: Preparing for the 21st century* (pp. 132–155). Cambridge, MA: Cambridge University Press.

Chapter 17

Linking Assessment Results to Evidence-Based Interventions

Best Practices for Preschool Children

Lea Athena Theodore

Overview

It is not too grand an overstatement to suggest that significant advances in the pedagogy and scientific development in the field of preschool education have transformed educational programming. Approximately 4 million children matriculate through kindergarten each year (U.S. Department of Education, 2015), with eager parents brimming with hope that their child has been prepared to meet the academic, cognitive, social, and emotional rigors required for success, and many parents having sought high-quality preschool education for their youngsters. Unfortunately, not all preschool children have had early learning opportunities or access to education, and many parents lack the financial means to provide the foundational skills and experiences provided in preschool or the socialization that would benefit their child's future education.

Students who lack the requisite pre-academic, academic, and interpersonal skills essential to meet the curricular demands and behavioral expectations of formal education often lag behind their classmates. For many children, beginning their educational careers behind their same-age peers may result in a never-ending attempt to catch up. When children do not learn the essential knowledge to build and advance their learning, a progressive decrement known as the cumulative deficit hypothesis emerges. Hence, if a child does not acquire the fundamental building blocks of learning, that student will continuously underperform across grades because they lack the basic skills to build upon previous learning (Jensen, 1974). Thus, educational deficits increase over time, becoming cumulative, resulting in a growing disparity in scholastic achievement that increases with age. As a result of continual failure, many students drop out of school or end up in juvenile detention centers. As perspicaciously articulated by Jensen (1966):

> All learning beyond the first few weeks or months of life depends upon previous learning. Knowledge and ability develop in a hierarchical fashion; the development of each new level is facilitated by transfer from earlier learning. More complex forms of learning build on simpler forms of learning. When the habits, skills, or cognitive structures that

are prerequisite for some "new" learning have not been fully acquired, the capacity for the new learning will be impaired;... inefficient, incomplete, or even impossible, depending upon the degree of inadequacy of prerequisite skills. Since learning builds on previous learning, weakness at any stage creates still greater weakness at later stages. Because subsequent learning depends upon transfer from prior learning, learning deficits are cumulative. Thus, the term *cumulative deficit.*

(pp. 40–41)

Benjamin Franklin fittingly said, "An ounce of prevention is worth a pound of cure." This simple yet profound statement attributes importance, in this context, to the immense benefits of early childhood educational initiatives. For more than half a century, an impressive coalition of leaders in education, psychology, politics, the legislature, and child advocacy groups have advocated to extend the scope and application of federal laws designed for school-age children, vis-à-vis the formative influence of extending high-quality preschool programs to more children. Investing in high-quality preschool education engenders a social milieu that is unequivocally and inextricably linked to the long-term development of productive members of society, with more students graduating from high school, continuing on to college or the military, or procuring skilled labor positions (Sheridan et al., 2019). Certainly, investment in high-quality early education is necessary to close the school readiness gap between economically disadvantaged children and their more advantaged peers.

History of Early Childhood Legislation

The full thrust of the advancement and importance of preschool education is portrayed in the enactment of federal laws codifying services and accountability for early childhood learning. To appreciate current early childhood educational standards, it is important to understand the historic changes that have transformed educational programs for all students, regardless of race, gender, or disability. More than 50 years ago, the Elementary and Secondary Education Act (ESEA, 1966) was signed into law by President Lyndon Johnson. ESEA, established as a national education and civil rights law, was designed to address inequities in the education system. President Johnson proclaimed education a national priority, providing all students with equal access to learning opportunities. Importantly, preschool education was a significant component of the ESEA. President Johnson moved from inertia to action and used the 1965 law to initiate Project Head Start, the first federally funded preschool program. The federal government established a half-day program to enhance the school readiness of preschool children from low-income families. Head Start began as a multi-component pilot program composed of combined educational, nutritional, and health programs and support services for families and their youth (Bracken, 2013). The grassroots program met with overwhelming success as well as many positive outcomes, despite insufficient federal funding. Resulting from its initial successes, several states initiated their own versions of Head Start during the 1980s. With the increased recognition of the benefits of early childhood education, preschool enrollment is steadily increasing.

Public Law 94–142

The inception of Public Law 94–142 in 1975, the Education for All Handicapped Children Act (EAHCA; P.L. 94–142, 1975), was landmark legislation, considered revolutionary because it was the first federal law mandating free appropriate public education (FAPE) for all children with disabilities, birth through grade twelve. This law had an extraordinary positive impact on millions of children with disabilities across the United States, in every state and local community. The law focused on four goals: a) ensuring a free and appropriate education for all children, with services designed to meet the idiosyncratic needs of each child; b) providing procedural safeguards to protect parents and children; c) supporting states' and local educational agencies' delivery of requisite services to children; and d) evaluating the efficacy of these services (P.L. 94–142, 1975). Importantly, this law set the stage for early childhood education. In particular, FAPE was extended downward to provide services to infants and toddlers, and educational services were broadened to better meet the needs of children between the ages of 3 and 21.

Public Law 99–457

In 1986, Public Law 99–457 reauthorized Public Law 94–142 and expanded mandatory special education to include free and appropriate public education to all children ages 3 to 5. These amendments were fueled by the recognition that more progressive services were warranted to meet the needs of preschool children and their families. Perhaps more importantly, there was a growing national acknowledgement of the fundamental significance and impact of early life experiences and benefits of early intervention and preschool services. Notably, this law provided an impetus for the development and validation of infant and early childhood tests, the early identification of disabilities, and the provision of early intervention services for young children at-risk for educational, cognitive, academic, and social, emotional, and behavioral disorders (Yell, 2016).

Individuals with Disabilities Education Act (IDEA)

Amended in 1990 and again in 1997, EAHCA became known as the Individuals with Disabilities Education Act (IDEA), which continued to ensure educational services for preschool children (Part B). This compulsory special education law set the age for educational rights from birth until age 21, and special education became a federally funded entity. The passage of IDEA provided the driving force for the development of specialized tests designed, normed, and validated for children with specific disabilities. In 2004, IDEA was yet again revised and became known as the Individuals with Disabilities Education Improvement Act (IDEIA), continuing to maintain a focus on the influence that schools play in early childhood development, kindergarten readiness, and the powerful effects that early detection and intervention have for cognitive, academic, and social, emotional, and behavioral functioning in preschool children.

No Child Left Behind Act

In 2002, the ESEA was reauthorized as "No Child Left Behind" (NCLB). Under this new federal law, schools were to be held accountable for closing the achievement gap by holding them responsible for the academic progress of all students. Specifically, the act placed emphasis on ensuring that states and schools boosted the performance of certain groups of students, such as English-language learners, students in special education, and poor and minority children, whose achievement, on average, trailed that of their peers. States were required to bring all students to the "proficient level" on statewide reading and math tests each year, for children in grades 3 through 8. The term "proficiency," however, was idiosyncratic to each school district, but evaluation of districts was conducted annually to assess "adequate yearly progress" or AYP. Schools that failed to meet AYP targets for two years or more were subject to a cascade of increasingly serious sanctions, including the option of students relocating to "better" schools.

Every Student Succeeds Act

In December 2015, President Obama signed the Every Student Succeeds Act (ESSA, P.L. 114–95, 2015) to replace the No Child Left Behind Act of 2001, thereby building on the civil rights legacy of the ESEA. This new federal mandate addressed the most vulnerable students by providing federal funding to help *all* students succeed in school and bridge the achievement gap. Importantly, this new federal law broadened the continuum of services to preschool, emphasizing the importance that early learning plays in the development of high-quality education as well as student success. Such an expansion demonstrates the significance of preschool education as a cornerstone that underpins overall cognitive and social-emotional functioning, ensuring that all students, regardless of geographic location or socioeconomic status, are on track to graduate from high school.

State Standards Movement

In a relatively recent article, Bracken and Crawford (2010) reviewed childhood educational standards for all 50 states, including the socio-political provisions that shaped these benchmarks. The authors found that although the United States is moving in the right direction by employing standards for preschool education, the knowledge, skills, and abilities vary considerably from state to state. Early contributors to the standards movement, such as Scott-Little, Kagan, and Frelow (2003), published an influential report, *Standards for Preschool Children's Learning and Development: Who Has Standards, How Were They Developed, and How Are They Used?*, which called for accountability in early childhood, particularly as it relates to the bifurcation of underprivileged families vis-à-vis those with affluence. In the year 2004, The National Association for the Education of Young Children (NAEYC) jointly published a position paper with the National Association of Early Childhood Specialists in State Departments of Education (NAECS/SDE, 2002), elucidating standards for early childhood education and spearheading canonical curriculum requirements (Bracken, 2013). Although the gravitas of early childhood education attained national recognition in the mid 1960s, the NAEYC has been an active champion and leader in the development of early childhood education standards since 1926 (Bracken, 2007).

Government Influence

Following NCLB, President Bush developed *Good Start, Grow Smart (2002)*, a preschool initiative that emphasized greater accountability, increased qualifications of teachers, and more frequent assessment of 4-year-old children on academic readiness outcomes. Significantly, this initiative promoted the development of early childhood standards across the United States, emphasizing the development of the whole child, including cognitive, academic, social, emotional, linguistic, and healthy growth factors.

In 2009, President Barack Obama invested in *Race to the Top*, the largest federally funded early childhood initiative, increasing funding to ensure that the most disadvantaged children and families benefitted from a high-quality education and comprehensive services. In particular, *Race to the Top* endeavored to meet four goals: implementing standards, assessments and interventions that prepare students to be productive members of society; enhancing the educational data system to measure student growth systematically; recruiting, retaining, and rewarding skilled teachers; and enhancing our nation's lowest-achieving schools (Bracken, 2013). In addition to these goals, *Race to the Top*: highlights science, technology, engineering, and mathematics (STEM); augments school readiness for kindergarten; develops data systems that incorporate special education programs; and refines our educational system so as to develop a seamless transition from preschool through graduate school, for general and special education students (Bracken, 2013).

As evidenced by the history of early childhood educational legislation, significant strides have been made in not only recognizing the influence of early learning on academic and life outcomes but also in the development and expansion of early childhood learning. To continue this momentum, universal school readiness measures and standardized early education practices needed to be cultivated. With respect to school readiness, early childhood educators emphasized cognitive development and building pre-reading, language, vocabulary and math skills, as well as gross and fine motor skills and social and communication skills. It is safe to say that all parents and families want their children to have the best possible start in life, and that step up begins with pre-school education.

Preschools provide rich opportunities for children to learn and develop, yielding long-lasting and powerful results, particularly for disadvantaged children who often begin school in kindergarten, one year behind their more advantaged peers. These enduring effects include scoring higher on intellectual and achievement measures, performing on grade level academically, not needing special education services or being retained in grade, graduating from high school and continuing on to college, securing good jobs, and becoming healthy, productive members of our society. Clearly, a strong connection exists between high-quality preschool education and the level of success that children experience later in life (Newman & Newman, 2012). It is incumbent upon us as a nation, regardless of geography, socioeconomic status, race, ethnicity, religion, or disability, to ensure that *all* young children have equal access to high-quality early childhood education.

Linking Assessment to Intervention

The growing recognition that quality early childhood experiences and programs designed to nurture preschool children's school readiness skills and circumvent challenging behaviors have been influential in the continued expansion of preschool programs, including Project Head Start (Dominguez, Vitiello, Fucciloo, Greenfield, & Bulotsky-Shearer, 2011; Purtell & Ansari, 2018). Current legal mandates (e.g., IDEIA, ESSA) are accountability-oriented federal laws that require schools to provide and demonstrate the efficacy of success through student outcomes. More than a half century of laws, initiatives, research, and subsequent legislation have resulted in the recognition that interventions documented to have empirical support result in more efficacious service provision than programs without such backing. In the social and behavioral sciences, evidence-based interventions (EBIs) are, sine qua non, essential to drawing valid conclusions regarding intervention effectiveness and guiding well-informed decision-making. EBIs are strategies, practices, or programs that demonstrate efficacious results and outcomes when implemented with fidelity. That is, EBIs demonstrate empirical validation of intervention effectiveness and are grounded in research. As intimated previously, myriad proponents have underscored the influence that EBIs play in the amelioration of diagnosed deficits designed to augment preschool children's abilities and skills, placing the child on an ascendant trajectory to healthy lifelong development (Theodore, 2017).

While evaluations are designed to shed more definitive light on the whole child, including personal strengths and weaknesses, it is ultimately the subsequent application of evidence-based treatments that enhance intellectual functioning, information processing, academic achievement, and skill development. Failure to provide evidence-based interventions systematically linked and applied to identified areas of deficit results in cumulative deficits that impede growth over time. Moreover, and equally disconcerting, is that the provision of ineffective treatments does not resolve the underlying issue and may simultaneously exacerbate the problem, while also adversely affecting other academic issues, interpersonal relationships, and social and emotional functioning, culminating in a diminished quality of life (Theodore, 2017). Simply stated, the personal and societal costs of not intervening effectively have lifelong, pernicious ramifications (Bornstein & Bradley, 2003; Dominguez et al., 2011; Sammons, 2010).

The linkage of assessment data to evidence-based interventions may be somewhat confusing and cryptic due to the vast and unwieldy scope in providing precise, practical, and systematic remedial applications for the practitioner. Surface-depth training proffered by professors and other professionals may result in conflicting theories and/or strategies in bridging the performance gap for students. A linear and effective model for bridging the research-to-practice gap is data-based problem-solving, a dynamic process of the collection and analyzation of data, with the desired intent to improve academic and behavioral performance. Data serve as a constant arbitrator regarding intervention and evaluation of student progress. Significantly, data-based problem-solving is the all-important link between assessment findings and intervention selection (Pluymert, 2014).

An important component in this process is the development of hypotheses to identify potential factors contributing to the problem and influencing the acquisition of desired behaviors (Batsche, Castillo, Dixon, & Forde, 2014). Data-based problem-solving is rooted in behavioral consultation (Bergan & Kratochwill, 1990) and is also considered best practice in the field of school psychology. This empirical model encompasses behavioral strategies in developing intervention plans and the evaluation of treatment. In concert with consultation, the problem-solving process involves four essential questions: "What is the problem?" (problem identification); "Why is the problem occurring?" (problem analysis); "What should be done about the problem?" (plan development); and, "Did the intervention work?" (plan evaluation). This process assumes that data accurately reflect changes in the identified behavior(s), can be used to inform intervention development, and are amenable to evaluation (Batsche et al., 2014).

Contextual Factors in Preschool Learning

The increased awareness of the academic, behavioral, social, and emotional benefits of preschool education has underscored the importance that contextual factors play in learning; in particular, classroom or structural quality and process quality (Purtell & Ansari, 2018). High-quality class-rooms are well-designed, safe, and responsive preschool environments that maximize children's participation in activities and foster positive social interactions with others, thereby enhancing opportunities for meaningful learning. Quality classrooms include contextual characteristics such as student-teacher ratio, teacher qualifications, length of the school day, and administrative leadership (Dominguez et al., 2011; Purtell & Ansari, 2018). Process quality refers to the preschool child's experiences in the classroom, such as quality of instruction and teacher support, which include warm and responsive student-teacher interactions. These interactions not only meet the needs of the child but are also associated with language, literacy and social development, increased student motivation, and sense of pride in accomplishments (Purtell & Ansari, 2018).

When problems occur with preschool-aged children, it is critical to consider first the context in which the behavior takes place. The importance of the classroom ecology is instrumental when addressing the specific needs of the child. Assessing the environment to ensure that it is conducive to learning and development means evaluating the physical and social characteristics of the classroom, as the manner in which a classroom is arranged has a significant impact on learning and behavior. As such, the physical structure of the classroom should include a variety of designated areas, such as learning centers, reading areas, a place for naps, art, and play stations, and should include appropriate materials and appropriately sized furnishings (Bracken & Theodore, this volume). Socially, does the child experience difficulty with peer and/or adult interactions? Does the class provide opportunities for activities that promote social interactions? Are these interactions teacher or child initiated? Finally, all children, particularly those in preschool, benefit from clear and predictable routines. As such, it is important to evaluate the structure and consistency in the preschool classroom. Within the learning and social demand-centered contexts, identifying whether the problem occurs during structured learning activities, instructional interactions in general, interactions and/or activities with peers, and teacher-child inter-actions, is integral to understanding the factors influencing the observed behavior. Determining whether the problem behavior is context-specific provides a great deal of information regarding both individual and classroom-based interventions (Lau, Saunders, Beets, Cai, & Pate, 2017).

Problem Identification

The first step in linking assessment to intervention is pinpointing the problem to be solved, which is accomplished via *problem identification* and the development of an operational definition of the problem. In the process of determining the specific problem, multiple deficits may be found. As is often the case, academic and behavioral problems sometimes co-exist, and it is difficult to discern which issue to address first. In such instances, it is recommended that the parent(s) and preschool teacher, along with the school psychologist, prioritize which problem to tackle first. Next is the formulation of an operational definition. A well-defined operational definition describes the target behavior in specific, concrete, and observable terms. Operational definitions are at the forefront of the development of successful interventions and are considered a crucial component to linking assessment findings with interventions (Kampwirth & Powers, 2016). A good operational definition should reflect the concordance of two independent observers that the target behavior has or has not occurred. To accomplish this goal, behaviors must be described in a manner that is understandable to all members of the school-based team (Bracken & Theodore, this volume). In this vein, a heuristic for writing a good definition includes three components: 1) the definition should be *objective* (referring only to observable characteristics of the behavior and/or translating inferential terms into more objective words); 2) *clear* (unambiguous, so it may accurately be repeated and paraphrased by others); and 3) *complete* (delineating the boundaries of what should be included and excluded) (Kampwirth & Powers, 2016).

Once an operational definition has been written and agreed upon, baseline data regarding the frequency, intensity, duration, and latency of the behavior are collected. These data are important because they establish the baseline for determining academic/behavioral change and the efficacy of the intervention selected to ameliorate the problem. Thus, over time, intervention data will be compared to baseline data to establish the efficacy of treatment.

While observing the target student in a classroom, it is important to also gather comparative data on other students in the same classroom to determine whether the target student's behavior is dramatically different than that of the class peer group. Ideally, the peer comparisons should include three students of the same gender, socioeconomic status, and ethnicity as the student being observed. In addition, of the comparative peers, one student should be lower functioning, one student should be a typically performing peer, and one student should be a higher-performing student. When gathering data on the target student and the three controls, a gap analysis should be conducted. Gap analyses determine the discrepancy between observed performance and expected performance, addressing the difference between the actual performance and desired behavior. This analysis is conducted for the target student as well as each of the three peers. Upon completion of data collection, verification of a gap between the target student and/or the performance of their peers is established. This determination provides important information regarding whether the student's performance is idiosyncratic or part of a class-wide problem. Where the gap is found (i.e., student, class) is where the intervention should be targeted (Pluymert, 2014).

With respect to data collection, typically, a minimum of three data-points are recommended, with each of these three data-points collected on three separate days; however, data should be stable with minimal variation, otherwise it would be unclear whether the problem was observed rather than some extraneous variable that skewed the data-points. If the data are not stable, additional baseline observation would be warranted. When reviewing data with the classroom teacher, it is important to determine whether a problem actually exists. If so, what is the magnitude of the discrepancy between the actual and desired behavior? However, if it turns out that the target behavior is not the issue, but rather another problem is identified as a result of the observation(s), then the problem needs to be reconceptualized, re-operationalized, and observed.

Functional Behavioral Analysis

Prior to selecting an effective intervention, it is important to first understand the function of a behavior. School psychologists and other practitioners, in collaboration with the student's preschool teacher, may work together to conduct a functional behavioral assessment (FBA). The goal of the functional behavior assessment is to identify the root cause of the academic, behavioral, social, emotional, or performance deficit. As part of the functional behavior assessment process, it is helpful to collect information about the student by reviewing the student's academic records (i.e., grades, attendance, developmental, medical, and social history), interviewing parents and teachers, and observing the targeted student in various demand-center contexts (Steege & Watson, 2009).

Conducting a functional behavioral analysis involves examining setting events, antecedents, resultant behaviors, and consequences that influence the target behavior(s). FBAs examine the circumstances surrounding the occurrence and nonoccurrence of challenging behavior(s). The goal of such an assessment is to identify events that are reliably or consistently present when the difficult/inappropriate behavior occurs and does not occur. If behavior can be predicted/explained, it can be prevented or corrected. FBAs answer the following questions: a) What event is setting the stage for the behavior to occur?; b) What antecedent is occasioning the behavior?; c) What consequence is maintaining the behavior?; d) What is the function of the behavior?; and e) Can the student be taught an alternative, appropriate behavior to accomplish the same function as the inappropriate behavior? In determining the answers to these questions, it is important to understand the components that comprise an FBA.

Setting events are contextual factors that influence behavior. Setting events are more general and broad conditions that lead to the performance of the target behavior and include characteristics of the situation, task, or demands presented to the child, conditions within or internal to the individual, and/or behaviors of others. Setting events help explain why preschool children respond differentially when presented with the same set of events or triggers. Examples of setting events include: lack of sleep; hunger/unbalanced diet; stress in the household; previous conflict; performance anxiety; loud or busy environments; fear of the unexpected; chaotic or unclear transitions; changes in routines; changes in other environments (e.g., spending the night with one parent versus another); medications (e.g., side effects, the wearing off of the medication); illness/allergies; traumatic events; staffing pattern; time of day (i.e., mornings versus afternoons); day of the week (e.g., Mondays and Fridays); and seasonal changes (e.g., winter months, holidays, rainy/gloomy weather).

Antecedents are conditions that lead to the onset of problem behavior(s) and occur before (and possibly during) the problem behavior. Examples include: being given an assignment that is too difficult or boring; receiving instructions from the teacher; teacher reprimands; parent request(s); toys being taken away by other preschool children; and peer teasing. *Consequences* are events that follow the behavior, and increase, decrease, or have no impact on what the student does. Types of reinforcement and behavioral functions include: positive reinforcement (attention, desired item/activity); negative reinforcement (escape/avoidance); and automatic reinforcement (sensory feedback/self-stimulation, pain attenuation).

The outcome of the FBA should provide a clear description of the problem; events, times, and situations under which the behavior will and will not occur; and the consequences that maintain the target behavior. It is important to determine the function of the deficit, as this will contribute to an intervention designed to help the student be successful. More specifically, the information culled from the FBA provides guidance on new behaviors that may be needed to replace undesirable ones (Steege & Watson, 2009).

Problem Analysis

The next step in data-based problem-solving is *problem analysis*, which involves examining whether the problem is a skill deficit (can't do) or a performance deficit (won't do), and the subsequent development of a hypothesis statement. Decisions regarding a student who has the requisite academic and/or behavioral skills but does not consistently employ them, versus a child who does not know how to perform the desired skill, will result in very different interventions. If a child demonstrates a performance deficit, meaning that the student likely has developed the skill but does not use the skill consistently or at all or does not generalize the skill to other settings, the student may need precision teaching to know when to use the skill appropriately. With respect to skill deficits, or "can't do's," this behavior is likely to be observed across settings, since the child does not possess the requisite skills, either academically, behaviorally, or socially. In such cases, direct instruction of the skill coupled with multiple opportunities to practice, with performance feedback and positive reinforcement, will yield desirable results in acquiring the skill (Gresham, 2014).

While each step of the data-based problem-solving process is vital in the linking of assessment to intervention, perhaps the most critical aspect is hypothesis development, or why the problem is occurring. Addressing this question provides yet one more data point in piecing together a specific and appropriate EBI for the student. As a team, hypotheses are generated using the operational definition of the behavior as well as other relevant data collected to identify the root cause(s) of the problem. Such a procedure is instrumental in selecting an appropriate intervention (Pluymert, 2014).

Intervention Selection

As with all things developmental, there are differences in how students of various ages and developmental levels learn and behave. Thus, interventions must be tailored to fit the idiosyncratic needs of the student and their specific area of deficit. This stage of problem-solving involves selecting an intervention that will close the performance gap identified during the problem identification and problem analysis stages, culminating with an intervention that will specifically address the root cause of the problem (Kampwirth & Powers, 2016). There are several steps involved in identifying an appropriate intervention, which will be discussed in greater detail in the following paragraphs (Mascolo, Alfonso, & Flanagan, 2014).

STEP I: SELECT AN APPROPRIATE EVIDENCE-BASED INTERVENTION: DOCUMENTED EFFECTIVENESS

The selection of an evidence-based intervention is comprised of several key questions that need to be addressed. First, has the intervention demonstrated rigorous evaluation and resulted in meaningful effects on the dependent variable(s)? This information should be well-documented in the literature, with data yielding significant effects in high-quality randomized controlled trials, implemented successfully in more than one setting (school, community centers, clinics, etc.). That is, the intervention is supported by documentation that it has been effectively implemented in the past, multiple times, attending to scientific standards of evidence, with results demonstrating credible, positive effects in multiple outcomes. In making such a decision, it is important to evaluate the internal and external validity of the intervention. When evaluating research studies, the following internal validity components should be documented (Stoiber & DeSmet, 2010):

- Valid, reliable, multi-method/multi-source outcome measures
- A comparable comparison group with the same target population to test outcome differences for group designs
- Statistically significant outcomes
- Equivalent attrition
- Evidence of durability
- Documentation of treatment integrity
- Replicability

To be confident that the intervention will be successful with the student selected for intervention, it is important also to ensure the external validity of the intervention. Intervention efficacy may vary greatly depending on the characteristics of the population (e.g., age, socioeconomic status, percent free/reduced lunch, educational attainment) and setting (e.g., urban, bucolic, white collar, blue collar), which is why it is essential that research employs a rigorous methodological design appropriate for the child receiving the intervention (Stoiber & DeSmet, 2010). For example, if the intervention is needed for a preschool child from a small, suburban town in the Midwest, with primarily Caucasian students, the literature review should focus on randomized controlled trials demonstrating the intervention's effectiveness in a similar setting. Research conducted with a large, inner-city school, primarily serving minority students, would not corroborate nor cross validate the efficacy of the intervention for the particular student in need of support (Sanetti, Kratochwill, Collier-Meek, & Long, 2014). The severity of the problem in conjunction with the developmental level of the child are the most important external validity characteristics to match to the EBI. When evaluating research for the purpose of selecting an appropriate intervention, external validity information should include the following (Stoiber & DeSmet, 2010):

- Descriptive information regarding participant characteristics and the context within which the intervention occurred. Population, conditions, context, and outcomes need to be similar.
- Characteristics such as the preschool child's goals and demographics. The intervention should address the primary concern and at least one of the issues addressed in the *problem analysis* section.
- The selected child should be similar in terms of age, gender, race, and ethnicity to the participants who benefitted from the intervention. If this is not the case, consider whether it would be possible to modify the intervention to meet the unique needs of the child without compromising the core components of the intervention.
- A methodology section that may be replicated.
- Comprehensive description of the resources required to implement the intervention (materials needed, staff training, etc.).
- Treatment acceptability, also known as social validity, assessing whether individuals who employed the intervention liked it. It is important to ensure that teachers and participants enjoyed the intervention. Regardless of how wonderful an intervention is, if it is not liked, the treatment will not be used. Research suggests that teachers prefer interventions that are positive, economically feasible with respect to teacher time, and minimally disruptive to the classroom.
- Consumer satisfaction data.
- Duration of the intervention.
- Cultural relevance.

Contextual factors are also important in determining whether an intervention is a comparable match between the setting in which the intervention was implemented in the literature and the current setting. Factors to be considered include where the intervention was implemented, teacher-student ratio, time of day/year, and resource support. Rigorous evaluations of research should provide well-documented evidence to support efficacious results in school settings similar to that of the school where the intervention will be implemented (Stoiber & DeSmet, 2010).

In addition to the aforementioned validity data and information, a critical review of the literature should also include: whether the intervention was evaluated in a peer-reviewed journal; replication of the intervention across investigators, settings, and participants; other interventions that may be less restrictive, better researched, and/or more efficient; training required for treatment implementation (i.e., do individuals employing the intervention need to be trained or do they have the requisite skills to do so); and the efficacy of the intervention in producing the desired effects. Evidence-based interventions may be found on websites such as What Works Clearinghouse (WWC), Intervention Central, and the National Registry of Evidence-based Programs and Practices, as well as meta-analytic research. For example, an evidence-based intervention from WWC for the development of phonological awareness in preschool children is *Phonological Awareness Training plus Letter Knowledge Training*. This particular intervention is designed to enhance phonological awareness, help learners understand what letters look like in print, and augment early reading skills. The added letter knowledge training involves teaching the individual letters of the alphabet and connecting letters and sounds.

STEP 2: IMPLEMENTATION SUPPORT

Fundamental to employing evidence-based interventions is the need for firm, clear, explicit commitments that all individuals involved in closing the performance gap are on-board with the treatment process. Commitment is critical to initiating and maintaining interventions implemented with fidelity to enhance student performance. Ensuring adequate resources, support, and delineating design logistics are necessary components of a successful intervention. These factors are influential in a support plan and should be identified prior to treatment implementation. Each individual involved in the intervention should be cognizant of his or her respective role(s) and responsibilities. Typically, the preschool classroom teacher carries out the intervention, and it is important to know whether the teacher, or whomever will be implementing the treatment, has the skills to do so. Implementing a treatment without fidelity will likely negate the benefits of the intervention. If intervention and/or staff training are required to ensure fidelity, the school psychologist as consultant should use direct instruction to demonstrate the requisite skills, followed by guided practice, coaching, and performance feedback. This training cycle should be rehearsed and repeated until the intervention is implemented seamlessly during practice sessions. Similarly, the individual responsible for monitoring and collecting data should understand all data collection responsibilities (i.e., how to gather data, the frequency of data collection, how and when to implement progress monitoring measures, and how to record, analyze, and graph intervention data to evaluate progress), and then the individual should determine if modifications in the intervention process are needed (Kampwirth & Powers, 2016; Stoiber, 2014).

Enhancing treatment implementation requires continuous monitoring of child performance. Several methods for evaluating treatment integrity exist, including self-report instrumentation that provides a checklist of discrete treatment steps completed by the preschool teacher, direct observations of intervention implementation, and review of permanent student products that are the result of treatment implementation (Sanetti & Collier-Meek, 2017). Although self-monitoring systems are nonintrusive and relatively easy to use, teachers have a propensity to overestimate rates of fidelity. As such, objective measures, such as external observations, should be used in conjunction with self-monitoring systems. To maximize treatment fidelity, Elliott and Busse (1993) recommend: avoiding psychological parlance; implementing positive interventions, as teachers not only prefer these to negative intervention options, but also find them more acceptable; keeping consultation time to a minimum since teachers have limited time; and increasing the knowledge-base of behavioral principles for teachers, which increases the likelihood that they will employ the intervention as designed.

Finally, it has been well-documented that performance feedback provided to teachers during the implementation of the intervention improves fidelity, and this fidelity is further enhanced when graphic displays of the child's performance are also provided (Noell & Gansle, 2014). Continued data monitoring increases the likelihood that the intervention will be implemented as designed. However, continued communication between parents, preschool teachers, and the school psychologist are also integral to children's success. If managed and articulated in a responsive, sensitive, masterly manner, goal attainment should be readily achievable.

Once an intervention is implemented, it is important for the school psychologist or other school-based practitioners to schedule regular meetings with the team to discuss treatment progress, identify obstacles that may be precluding progress, and troubleshoot issues as necessary. Regularly scheduled meetings allow for data-based decision-making, which is integral to the child's success. Finally, treatment delivery support is yet another way to ensure treatment implementation success, and it includes providing requisite materials, such as data collection sheets, reinforcers, treatment integrity forms, and so on.

Intervention Implementation

Designing interventions is a natural extension of the consultative process whereby school psychologists seek to understand the needs of preschool children, their teachers, and parents (Theodore, DioGuardi, Hughes, Carlo, & Eccles, 2009). Merely implementing an evidence-based intervention does not ensure successful treatment outcomes. Rather, treatment fidelity or treatment integrity is essential for determining whether the child received the intervention as planned, as well as the effectiveness of the treatment under optimal conditions. Many interventions fail due to interventions not being employed in the manner in which they were intended (Kampwirth & Powers, 2016). Monitoring of data, including evaluating child progress and acquisition of the target skill, is contingent upon the integrity of the data. If there is not sufficient improvement in child progress, then the intervention may need to be tweaked or changed to address any idiosyncrasies in its employment. If the intervention is working, treatment should continue until it is time to fade-out the intervention or generalize to other contexts.

Plan Evaluation

During the final data-based problem-solving stage, the goal is to evaluate whether the child met the desired intervention goal and that the performance gap has been diminished. If the preschooler's gain met the goal set during the *problem analysis* phase, then post-implementation planning to ensure that the problem does not re-occur should be implemented, including generalization to other contexts and fading-out of the newly developed skill. However, if sufficient improvement in the child's performance is not evidenced, then the intervention may need to be modified.

One very important issue that should be addressed during the evaluation phase is the extent to which the intervention was employed as planned. Without doing so, it is impossible to discern whether the intervention or some extraneous factor are responsible for the observed performance. If the young child demonstrates limited growth towards goal attainment, careful examination of each intervention component will inform the extent to which the intervention itself is problematic (i.e., not strong enough given the student problem) or if specific aspects of the intervention are efficacious. Alternatively, additional intervention implementation support or resources may be needed to achieve the desired result. Should this be the case, modifications to the treatment should be made. However, if these adjustments do not yield meaningful change in the preschool child's performance, it may be time to go back to the drawing board, by returning to the *problem analysis* stage, or *problem identification,* to redefine the problem behavior. In other words, in the iterations of preschool evidence-based interventions, exploring new ground and mapping that new ground is warranted.

Conclusion

The preschool years are critical for the acquisition of foundational, requisite behaviors and skills for future learning. Everything that a young child sees, does, hears, smells, feels, and interacts with presents a learning opportunity. Preschool serves as the introduction to formal schooling for most children. That is, the preschool setting provides children with their initial exposure to formal learning opportunities that require complex behaviors across a variety of activities. For many children, the developmental tasks associated with each stage of development require the orchestration of many skills, which can be developmentally demanding and require encouragement, targeted instruction, and a great deal of shepherding.

In education, we tend to think that everything is univariate; that is, one problem, one solution. However, in reality, problems are multivariate, with various factors in combination influencing different issues, such as poverty, homelessness, single-parent households, family dynamics, and substance abuse. We need to consider preschool children and their problems from an ecological perspective, taking into account their health, motivation, home life, medical and psychological factors, and peer relationships. High-quality preschool education not only provides greater opportunities for child success but is also associated with improved academic performance, increased social skills, improved attention span, a lifelong appreciation of learning, and an increased likelihood of graduating from high school, continuing on to college or the military or procuring skilled labor positions, and becoming responsible and productive members of society. Certainly, investment in high-quality early education is necessary to help close the school readiness gaps between disadvantaged children and their more advantaged peers as well as play a role in early detection and amelioration of cognitive, academic, social, emotional, behavioral, gross/fine motor, and adaptive functioning (Bracken, 2013; Sheridan et al., 2019).

The intent of this chapter was to provide a practical blueprint for linking assessment findings to evidence-based interventions. For preschool children who evidence academic and/or behavioral difficulties, data-based problem-solving is a logical method in linking assessment to intervention, as it is a sequentially organized method for selecting an appropriate EBI based on the identified problem and evaluating child progress and goal attainment in building foundational knowledge and skills. Dense as the problem-solving decision-making model is, it is replete with wide-ranging academic, behavioral, social, and emotional implications for preschool children identified with a gap in performance.

References

Batsche, G. M., Castillo, J. M., Dixon, D. N., & Forde, S. (2014). Best practices in linking assessment to intervention. Data-Based and Collaborative Decision Making), (pp. 177–193). Best Practices VI P. L. Harrison & A. Thomas (Eds.), *Best practices in school psychology VI* (pp.). Silver Springs, MD: National Association of School Psychologists.

Bergan, J. R., & Kratochwill, T. R. (1990). *Behavioral consultation*. Columbus, OH: Merrill.

Bornstein, M. H., & Bradley, R. H. (2003). *Socioeconomic status, parenting, and child development*. Mahwah, NJ: Erlbaum.

Bracken, B. A. (2007). Nontraditional strategies for identifying nontraditional gifted and talented students. In J. VanTassel-Bask (Ed.), *Alternative assessment of gifted learners* (pp. 1–23). Washington, DC: National Association of Gifted Children.

Bracken, B. A. (2013). *Riverside early assessments of learning.* Rolling Meadows, IL: Riverside.

Bracken, B. A., & Crawford, E. (2010). Basic concepts in early childhood educational standards: A 50-state review. *Early Childhood Education Journal, 37,* 421–430.

Bracken, B. A., & Theodore, L. A. (in press). Creating the optimal preschool testing situation. In V. C. Alfonso, B. A. Bracken, & R. J. Nagle (Eds.), *Psychoeducational assessment of preschool children, fifth edition.* New York, NY: Routledge: Taylor & Francis Group.

Dominguez, X., Vitiello, V. E., Fucciloo, J. M., Greenfield, D. B., & Bulotsky-Shearer, R. J. (2011). The role of context in preschool learning: A multilevel examination of the contribution of context-specific problem behaviors and classroom process quality to low-income children's approaches to learning. *Journal of School Psychology, 49,* 175–195.

Education for All Handicapped Children Act of (1975). §6, 94 U.S.C. 142 §.

Elliott, S. N., & Busse, R. T. (1993). Effective treatments with behavioral consultation. In J. E. Zins, T. R. Kratochwill, & S. N. Elliott (Eds.), *Handbook of consultation services for children* (pp. 179–203). San Francisco, CA: Jossey-Bass.

Every Student Succeeds Act of (2015). Pub. L. No. 114-95 § 114 Stat. 1177 (2015-2016).

Gresham, F. M. (2014). Best practices in diagnosis of mental health and academic difficulties in a multitier problem-solving approach. In P. L. Harrison & A. Thomas (Eds.), *Best practices in school psychology VI* (Data-Based and Collaborative Decision Making) (pp. 147–158). Silver Springs, MD: National Association of School Psychologists.

Individuals with Disabilities Education Improvement Act, H.R. 1350, 108th Congress (2004).

Jensen, A. R. (1966). Cumulative in compensatory deficit. *Journal of School Psychology, 4,* 37–47.

Jensen, A. R. (1974). Cumulative deficit: A testable hypothesis? *Developmental Psychology, 10,* 996–1019.

Kampwirth, T. J., & Powers, K. M. (2016). *Collaborative consultation in the achools: Effective practices for students with learning and behavior problems* (5th ed.). New York, NY: Pearson.

Lau, E. Y., Saunders, R. P., Beets, M. W., Cai, B., & Pate, R. P. (2017). Factors influencing implementation of a preschool-based physical activity intervention. *Health Education Research, 32,* 69–80.

Mascolo, J. T., Alfonso, V. C., & Flanagan, D. P. (Eds.). (2014). *Essentials of planning, selecting, and tailoring interventions for unique learners.* Hoboken, NJ: John Wiley & Sons.

Newman, B. M., & Newman, P. R. (2012). *Development through life: A psychosocial approach.* New York, NY: Cengage Learning.

No Child Left Behind Act of 2001, 20 U.S.C. 70 Section 6301 et seq.

Noell, G. H., & Gansle, K. A. (2014). Research examining the relationships between consultation procedures, treatment integrity, and outcomes. In W. P. Erchul & S. M. Sheridan (Eds.), *Handbook of research in school consultation* (2nd ed., pp. 386–408). New York, NY: Routledge.

Pluymert, K. (2014). Problem-solving foundations for school psychological services. In P. L. Harrison & A. Thomas (Eds.), *Best practices in school psychology VI* (Data-

Based and Collaborative Decision Making) (pp. 25–39). Silver Springs, MD: National Association of School Psychologists.

Purtell, K. M., & Ansari, A. (2018). Classroom age composition and preschooler's school readiness: The implications of classroom quality and teacher qualifications. *AERA Open, 4,* 1–13. doi:10.1177/2332858418758300

Sammons, P. (2010). Does pre-school make a difference? Identifying the impact of pre-school on children's cognitive and social behavioral development at different ages. In K. Sylva, E. Melhuish, P. Sammons, I. Siraj-Blatchford, & B. Taggart (Eds.), *Evidence from the effective pre-school and primary education project* (pp. 92–113). New York, NY: Routledge.

Sanetti, L. M. H., & Collier-Meek, M. (2017). Treatment integrity: Evidence-based interventions in applied settings. In L. A. Theodore (Ed.), *Handbook of evidence-based interventions for children and adolescents* (pp. 3–14). New York, NY: Springer Publishing Company.

Sanetti, L. M. H., Kratochwill, T. R., Collier-Meek, M. A., & Long, A. C. J. (2014). *PRIME manual.* Storrs, CT: University of Connecticut.

Scott-Little, S., Kagan, S. L., & Frelow, V. S. (2003). *Standards for preschool children's learning and development: Who has standards, how were they developed, and how are they used?* Greensboro, NC: SERVE.

Sheridan, S. M., Witte, A. L., Wheeler, L. A., Eastberg, S. R. A., Dizona, P. J., & Gormley, M. J. (2019). Conjoint behavioral consultation in rural schools: Do student effects maintain after 1 year? *School Psychology, 34*(4), 410–420. doi:10.1037/spq0000279

Steege, M. W., & Watson, T. S. (2009). *Conducting school-based functional behavioral assessments: A practitioner's guide* (2nd ed.). New York, NY: Guilford Press.

Stoiber, K. C. (2014). A comprehensive framework for multitiered systems of support in school Psychology. In P. L. Harrison & A. Thomas (Eds.), *Best practices in school psychology VI* (Data-Based and Collaborative Decision Making), (pp. 41–70). Silver Springs, MD: National Association of School Psychologists.

Stoiber, K. C., & DeSmet, J. L. (2010). Guidelines for evidence-based practice in selecting interventions. In G. G. Peacock, R. A. Ervin, E. J. Daly, & K. W. Merrell (Eds.), *Practical handbook of school psychology: Effective practices for the 21st century* (pp. 213–234). New York, NY: The Guilford Press.

Theodore, L. A. (2017). Preface: Introduction to the handbook for applied interventions for children and adolescents. In L. A. Theodore (Ed.), *Handbook of evidence-based interventions for children and adolescents (xi–xxiii).* New York, NY: Springer Publishing Company.

Theodore, L. A., DioGuardi, R. J., Hughes, T. L., Carlo, M., & Eccles, D. (2009). A class-wide intervention for improving homework performance. *Journal of Educational and Psychological Consultation, 19,* 275–299. doi:10.1080/10474410902888657

The Education of the Handicapped Act Amendments, October 8, 1986, P.L. 99–457.

U.S. Department of Education. (April, 2015). A matter of equity: Preschool in America. www2.ed.gov/documents/early-learning/matter-equity-preschool-america. pdf. Retrieved May 31, 2019.

United States. (1966). *Profile of ESEA: The elementary and secondary education act of 1965. Titles I, II, III, IV and V.* Washington, DC: U.S. Dept. of Health, Education and Welfare.

Yell, M. L. (2016). *Law and special education* (4th ed.). New York, NY: Pearson.

Index

Locators in **bold** refer to tables and those in *italics* to figures.